BEING AND THE BETWEEN

SUNY Series in Philosophy
George R. Lucas, Jr., Editor

BEING AND THE BETWEEN

William Desmond

State University of New York Press

Published by
State University of New York Press, Albany

For information, address State University of New York
Press, State University Plaza, Albany, NY, 12246

Production by Diane Ganeles
Marketing by Theresa Abad Swierzowski

Library of Congress Cataloging-in-Publication Data
Desmond, William, 1951–
    Being and the between/William
Desmond.
        p. cm.
    Includes bibliographical references and index.
    ISBN 0-7914-2271-2 (CH : alk. paper).—ISBN 0-7914-2272-0 (PB :
alk. paper)
    1. Metaphysics. 2. Transcendence (Philosophy) I. Title.
BD111.D43   1995
110—dc20   94-8840
                                                                CIP

10 9 8 7 6 5 4 3 2

For Paul Weiss

For, after all, what is man in nature? A nothing compared to the infinite, a whole compared to the nothing, a middle point between all and nothing, infinitely remote from an understanding of the extremes; the end of things and their principles are unattainably hidden from him in impenetrable secrecy.

Equally incapable of seeing the nothing from which he emerges and the infinity in which he is engulfed.

What else can he do, then, but perceive some semblance of the middle of things, eternally hopeless of knowing either their principles or their end? All things come out of nothingness and are carried onwards to infinity. Who can follow these astonishing processes? The author of these wonders understands them: no one else can.

—Blaise Pascal, *Pensées*

CONTENTS

PREFACE

Long, long ago, Plato told us that the human being is neither a god nor a beast, but someone in between. Philosophy too is in between, neither completely wise nor entirely ignorant. What then would it mean to philosophize in between? What is the being of the between? This book seeks to answer the question in terms that are as comprehensive as possible.

This is a book on metaphysics and in metaphysics. It is *on* metaphysics: It seeks to offer an understanding of the nature of metaphysical thinking, and of the fundamental senses of being consonant with that thinking. It is a book *in* metaphysics: It tries to rethink the basic metaphysical questions, in light of these fundamental senses of being. Obviously, these two tasks cannot be entirely separated from each other. Nor indeed can they be separated from the metaphysical possibilities we have inherited from the philosophical tradition. Indeed, this last point relates to another desire of this work, namely, to think metaphysically in such a fashion as to allow sufficient hermeneutical discernment with respect to the tradition of philosophy.

The first chapter addresses the nature of metaphysical thinking, and hence may serve to launch our exploration. The philosopher impatient with prefaces may want to turn immediately to this. My title speaks of being and the between, and in due course I will set out what I mean by the between. I cannot do so in advance, for the very unfolding of our investigation will serve to express more and more adequately what is meant by the between. I must, however, offer some prefatory remarks—remarks perhaps hard to understand fully, since they are written after the fact. Nevertheless, we must begin.

In the first chapter I focus on the question of being and the thinking for which it calls. In the chapters to follow in Part I, I focus on the further articulation of the meaning of being in terms of four fundamental senses of being. Thus Part I can be said to think on metaphysics. By contrast, Part II will seek to think in metaphysics. There I aim to develop a metaphysics in light of these fundamental senses of being. The fourfold understanding of being, articulated overall in Part I, will form the conceptual backbone in Part II to the unfolding of our comprehension of being as between, relative to its extremities of origin and the good. I will address the basic themes of metaphysics:

origin, creation, things, intelligibilities, selves, communities, being true, being good.

What is this fourfold understanding of being? I have given some account of the view in previous books,[1] but the present work is an independent effort to state it in the most comprehensive terms possible. I must state the matter crudely now, but since the crudity will be multiply finessed in the course of the whole work, I ask for forbearance.

The fourfold is defined by the univocal, the equivocal, the dialectical and the metaxological understandings of being. What are these? The univocal sense of being stresses the notion of sameness, or unity, indeed sometimes immediate sameness, of mind and being. The equivocal sense accentuates diversity, the unmediated difference of being and mind, sometimes to the point of setting them into oppositional otherness. The dialectical sense emphasizes the mediation of the different, the reintegration of the diverse, the mediated conjunction of mind and being. Its mediation is primarily self-mediation, hence the side of the same is privileged in this conjunction. By contrast, the metaxological sense gives a *logos* of the *metaxu*, the middle. It puts stress on the mediated community of mind and being, but not in terms of the self-mediation of the same. It calls attention to a pluralized mediation, beyond closed self-mediation from the side of the same, and hospitable to the mediation of the other, or transcendent, out of its own otherness. It suggests an intermediation, not a self-mediation. Moreover, the *inter* is shaped plurally by different mediations of mind and being, same and other, mediations not subsumable into one total self-mediation. The metaxological sense keeps open the spaces of otherness in the between, including the jagged edges of rupture that we never entirely smooth out.

There is an immediacy of this metaxological community. It is at work, before we articulate it reflectively in our categories. It is at work in the univocal, the equivocal, the dialectical, but not known explicitly as such, and when stated exclusively in their terms it is distorted, because truncated. The metaxological is the truth of the univocal, the equivocal, the dialectical. They help define the truth of the metaxological, but we risk error when they are absolutized and claimed to cover the entire milieu of being. The point of this work is to try to address the question—What does it mean to be?—in terms of the significance of this between that marks the metaxological community.

---

1. See *Desire, Dialectic and Otherness: An Essay on Origins* (New Haven: Yale University Press, 1987); *Philosophy and its Others: Ways of Being and Mind* (Albany: State University of New York Press, 1990); *Beyond Hegel and Dialectic: Speculation, Cult and Comedy* (Albany: State University of New York Press, 1992). A succinct statement of the view is offered in my essay "Being Between" (*CLIO*, 20:4, 1991, pp. 305–331) which introduced discussion of my work in that edition of *CLIO*. This essay will also appear in a volume complementary to the present work, *Perplexity and Ultimacy: Metaphysical Thoughts from the Middle* (Albany: State University of New York Press, 1995).

Our sense of metaphysical thinking must take its truth from, must try to be true to, the being of the between.

The fourfold understanding of being does not mean that we must conceive of metaphysics simply as a science of categories. We require systematic thinking, but also thinking that allows a dynamic hermeneutics of being. Moreover, there are perplexities that strike us into troubled rumination at the edge of system. Metaphysics must find room for the thought for such limit perplexities. We might say that the fourfold offers an interlocking set of articulations of transcendence—both the transcending of mind, and the transcendence of being. It gives expression to the essential promise of mind and being, without the closure of either to transcendence.

Hence metaphysics will not be the deduction of a system of categories from an irrefrangible logical principle. As both systematic and hermeneutic, it offers itself as an unfolding interpretation of the many sides of the plenitude of the happening of being, as manifest to mindfulness in the between. To be absolutely true to the plenitude of this happening is all but impossible for us, and indeed failure of some sort is inevitable. But this impossible truthfulness is asked of us, even if inevitable failure brings us back to the truth of our finitude. This failure may itself be a success of sorts, in renewing metaphysical astonishment before the enigma of being that was, and is, and always will be too much for us, in excess of our groping efforts.

I do not subscribe to the view, fashionable in some quarters, that philosophy does not deal with truth, or that it must give up this, its ancient and noble calling. I want to state some considerations that bear on the truth of the following. These remarks make most sense after the fact, that is, subsequent to the effort to understand the meaning of this work as a whole. First, since we are in the middle, the truth of metaphysics is not deductive from some abstract first principle, *more geometrico*. Nor is it a matter of inductive generalization. Inductive generalization takes its sights from the particularities of determinate beings and processes; but our consideration is not only on the level of determinations, but also on the happening of determinate being, the coming to be of determination. Being is manifesting itself; we require an interpretive fidelity to this happening of manifestation in the middle. The meaning of that manifestness is not itself initially manifest. We have to become mindful of its full riches, of its overt concretions, its secret latencies, its potential for deformation and dissimulation.

Second, if we cannot renege on the systematic side of philosophy, we can rightly ask: What are the essential relations between mind and being, between self and other, same and different, identity and difference? What do we make of the perennial perplexities about origin, creation, things, intelligibilities, selves, communities, truth and the good? My claim is that the fourfold sense of being offers a flexible systematic framework that allows us complexly and very comprehensively to interpret the variety of possible relations, and the very ontological richness of what is at stake in each of the perplexities.

Third, does this mean that we could calculate all the possibilities? I reject this way of putting the issue, since some of the essential possibilities are open. They are defined relative to the creative coming to be of beings, out of an overdetermined source of origination; or they define the very opening of freedom in the beings in relation. Our understanding of being in the between calls for the acknowledgment of indeterminacy—and this not in the sense of the merely indefinite. The point about systematic categories is not to impose a skeletal structure on being, and so to bind it up in conceptual domestication. It is to think through the happening of being to the utmost extent of its intelligibility, but not in this to claim to have mastered conceptually its still overdetermined otherness. We might say that categorial understanding is most genuine when it opens beyond categorial immanence, participating in the very transcending of mindfulness towards the dynamic happening of being in the between.

Fourth, this means that the truth of what is at stake has a certain openness to it. If we seek to be true to the concrete manifestness of the happening of being, and if there is a certain latent promise in this happening, the very openness of our "being true" is implied. I will more fully address the notion of "being true" in a later chapter. But I am here saying that there is no absolute certitude, no master category, no absolute knowing in the Hegelian manner. Why? Because all these sacrifice the otherness of the happening of being to the immanence of categorial rationality at home in its own conceptual immanence.

If there is no Hegelian master category, I do not deny that the metaxological seeks the best understanding possible. How is this measured? There are notions of truth consonant with univocity, equivocity and dialectic, and this too will occupy us more fully. I now call notice to a double unfolding that causes us to move from one sense to the next, as a more adequate effort to think through the truth of the happening of being. The double unfolding has to do, first with the *self-coherence* of the specific mode of being and mind, and second with its *truthfulness to what is other* to thought. Let me say something on this.

Thus univocity tries to fix the truth determinately. But the more it is consistent with itself, the more the appearance of something other to univocity makes its demand. The thinking of this other causes us to think in terms of the equivocity of being. In turn, the coherent thinking of this equivocity drives us beyond equivocity to dialectic. Equivocity absolutized subverts itself, and calls for a more positive mediating mindfulness, in order to be true, not only to the transcending of thinking, but also to the truth of being as other to thinking. Further again, dialectic itself, while dealing with the limitations of univocity and equivocity, is tempted to absolutize itself and its characteristic forms of mediation, especially self-mediation. And yet this seeming completion of dialectic is actually its undoing. Dialectic absolutized reveals its failure to take seriously enough the other that is other to thought thinking itself. It absolutizes the self-coherence of thought at home with itself. And yet the end result is a new homelessness of thinking.

It is this new homelessness that impels thinking to the metaxological level. Dialectic cannot be fully accounted for dialectically. We require a thinking that is less willing to domesticate the ruptures of the immanence of thinking by the transcendent other. This is a thinking more open to what transcends thinking, a thinking more patient to transcendence, just in the highest exceeding of its self-transcending towards the other as other. But this last possibility is not a master category. The language of master categories is simply not appropriate, for this mode of thinking demands a divestment of mind's will to master the otherness of the happening of being. There is a transformation of the energy of self-transcending thinking to which the language of appropriating and overcoming the other is not at all appropriate. What is "overcome" is the will to overcome the other. There arises a new willingness to let the happening of being offer the truth of itself to mindfulness.

Fifth, a necessary requirement of philosophical understanding is its capacity to illuminate the matter itself, what the Germans call *die Sache selbst*. There are contemporary philosophers who scoff at the notion, but that is their problem, generated by a threadbare understanding of *die Sache selbst*. We philosophers ask for bread, and what stones are we handed? Commentaries on commentaries on commentaries. . . . What is the matter itself? If one could answer this question in a preface, there would be no need for the book. The book as a whole answers this question: the matter itself is the meaning of being between. As it will turn out, this meaning in the end cannot be completely confined to the between we inhabit, but must extend to the originary ground of that between, and this is not the finite between once again. In our passage through the between, philosophy demands a kind of phenomenological fidelity to the matter itself. Along the way, the fourfold understanding of being will illuminate many key constituents of our habitation of the between—creation, things, intelligibilities, selves, communities.

Sixth, an important consideration is the ability of a philosophy to illuminate the essential metaphysical positions. I give counsel to myself: Do not smash the wheel and proclaim the glorious liberation of human creativity; you, or someone else, years hence, will find it necessary to reinvent the same despised wheel—decked out perhaps with a new name to assuage the pretense to glorious creativity. I think we have to be able to interpret the rationale, the strengths and the limits of the basic philosophical possibilities, as diversely expressed in the history of philosophy. This requires a thinking about them that refuses to stay on the surface of the packaged positions that easily get regurgitated in standard histories of philosophy. We must go deeper, approach the originary sources of perplexity and astonishment, out of which the surfaces of the positions have grown. This means we must already be mindful of the matter itself that has occupied philosophers for millennia.

Much more than being a historian of ideas is asked of us. One must be a philosopher to understand *as philosophy* the history of philosophy.

One's attitude to past philosophers cannot be defined by simple rejection. One learns from them, even when one disagrees with them. And even in disagreeing with them, one ought to have a hermeneutic generous enough to allow one to make strong intelligible sense of their essential contributions. Every previous philosopher worth his salt harbors latent reserves that challenge continued rethinking. I believe that the fourfold sense of being is extremely fruitful for casting light on, as well as helping us recast in a new light, many of the basic philosophical positions. I reject what has followed from the alleged completion of metaphysics by a Hegel, or a Nietzsche, or a Heidegger. I do not simply reject, but hold that the fourfold offers us some basis to rethink the tradition of metaphysics. We must move beyond the paralysis and stultification generated by this rhetoric of the end of metaphysics. Once again the promise will have to be redeemed in the work itself. I add that I have kept scholarly apparatus to a minimum, which is not to say that extensive study does not inform what I say. But this work is not a piece of scholarship.

Seventh, I think that a philosopher is a seeker, and that any genuine philosophy is an adventure of thought. As an adventure, it cannot be judged before the search has begun. There will be many who scoff on the dockside as the ship heaves off. They will congratulate themselves on their prudence in valuing the security of safe harbor, and the solid land. They will even feel superior to those who launch out into the unknown, those who risk their thinking. They feel sure in advance it will come to shipwreck. But perhaps these wise homebodies are the already defeated. How dare you do metaphysics? I am asked. I do dare. But you must also dare, if you want an answer to your question.

And if we philosophers took to heart these prudent discouragements, we might never stir from the spot. Alas, we too seek for home, but we must seek for home to be at home. We are fools, no doubt, to dream of something more. But since the world is so wise, and since the standing army of its sages is always swelled with new recruits, the stray folly of metaphysical adventuring will perhaps be excused in us. We have been told not even to try, so we will not blame the fashionable commentators for the outcome—be it what it may.

Let the wise read as the philosopher writes. I do not ask for uncritical readers, but I do ask for disciplined readers—readers who have studied hard and long, who can take their time to think; readers who have not shunned solitude; readers suspicious of themselves before being suspicious of others; readers patient when demands are made on them; readers themselves adventurers; readers who ask for more that the rhetorics fashionable in academic philosophy, and who hate the substitution of "relevant" ideology for the seriousness of truth; readers with souls full of an intellectual, indeed spiritual generosity, beyond the hermeneutics of suspicion; readers who desire to hear fundamental questions addressed with a genuine intellectual, not to say, spiritual seriousness; readers philosophically rich enough in themselves as to be able to laugh at the pretensions of what sometimes passes for "philosophy"; readers who long for a simple human voice to speak again about the essential issues that perennially perplex us. I do not ask for the impossible. I do ask for what now is rare.

To all appearances I may seem to offer a "grand system," but one should not be deceived. One should not forget the astonishment and perplexity of the singular thinker that nourishes any "system," and that percolates into even its most abstract corners. The philosopher is marked by patience to the truth, even in the very vehemence of his impatient search. Do not mistake what I write for abstract system. But I grant this point: systematic thinking can have a flattening effect, relative to some nuances of singularity, indeed to dimensions of depth. The flow of systematic thinking tends to take on a life of its own, and the sharp edges of the uncomprehended can be worn a little too smooth by that flow. There is also the non-systematic that lies, not only at the horizon of system, but at its source, and that continues to nest in the categorial structures themselves.

There is a strong notion of singularity defended in this work. And I agree: I think the philosopher also has to speak in a non-systematic voice. I have tried to do that elsewhere, and in parts of the present work that other voice will surface unexpectedly. And if the language of systematic philosophy seems often at a remove from ordinary language, this is not an objection *per se,* as long as the thinker always keeps alive in his categorial reflections the memory of concrete happening. Lest anyone think I monger in abstractions, let him do me the justice of acknowledging that I can speak, should I so choose, in more voices than one.[2]

Finally some words of thanks: My sense of gratitude for my first family grows, my father Eugene, my mother Hannah, my brothers and sisters, Mary, Anthony, Colette, Eugene, Gerard. They have shown me, and continue to show me, what the agape of being is. My own family now keeps me alive in, and keeps alive in me, the same agape. Moreover my wife Maria, and children William, Hugh and Oisín always keep me in steadfast and ever new contact with the riches of concrete happening. I want to thank William Eastman, Director of SUNY Press, for the unfailing support and encouragement he has given me. In the academic year 1992–1993, I worked on the revision of this book while a Fulbright Research Fellow, as well as visiting professor, at the Higher Institute of Philosophy, Katholieke Universiteit Leuven. I want to thank the Fulbright Commission in Belgium, especially Mrs. Margaret Nicholson and Mrs. Alice Allington for their hospitality and help. I want to thank the

---

2. In *Perplexity and Ultimacy* I take up some themes continuous with the present work, but in a somewhat different voice, and in a manner less constrained by the systematic requirements of the present work.

students who attended my seminar on metaphysics, and in particular Professor Ignace Verhack. I thank the faculty, Professor Urbain Dhondt, and most especially Professor Carlos Steel, President of the Institute, for making memorable my stay at Leuven. With sadness I remember my generous friend and colleague, the late Bernard Nachbahr, without whom our stay in Leuven would not have been possible. I dedicate the book to Paul Weiss whose friendship I have been privileged to enjoy in recent years, and whose indefatigable work for metaphysics and in philosophy I deeply admire.

PART I

METAPHYSICAL THINKING AND THE SENSES OF BEING

CHAPTER ONE

WHAT IS METAPHYSICAL THINKING?
MIND, BEING, AND THE BETWEEN

The Question of Being

Beginning, we ask the question: What is being? What does it mean to be? This is the question of metaphysics. It is old beyond age, newer than the most novel thought. It calls to us from the dawn of human mindfulness; it calls for its renewal again, even when we seem to have passed the high meridian of science. It is the dark question of philosophy, and the light without which other questions would be dark. Ageless and ever-fresh, it has been asked again and again, and yet in all the answers, the asking once again stands before us, one more time. The asking will stand before us still, even when our utmost response has been tried.

Asking it again, I know that for millennia it has been variously posed and answered. I ask it again, not to downgrade past efforts as misguided and superseded, but because the question bespeaks an elemental perplexity that perennially calls for renewal. Even where it has been answered, often the meaning of the proferred answer grows faint and needs refreshing. Again and again mindful human beings are troubled, perhaps shaken by this perplexity. To ask the question properly demands that we be on its level, and this requires a tireless mindfulness. For even were a true answer given, this still would not be heard, if the hearer did not have the ears to hear.

This defines our present concern—namely, the nature of metaphysical thinking relative to the question of being. We might say that metaphysical thinking articulates the milieu of mindfulness within which this question can be heard. But there is a respect in which simply to be as human is to be constituted in and by this milieu of mindfulness, and this apart from any concerted and concentrated effort of philosophical mindfulness. For we are what we are by virtue of our abiding in the milieu of being in a more or less mindful way. Hence, the question of being is not first one for philosophers, understood as an elite of thinkers. It transcends the difference of the few and the many, for it strikes our humanity simply in virtue of its being, as mindful of itself and what

3

is other to itself. Of course, this matter may degenerate into platitude. Then being will be said to be the emptiest of abstractions—a vacuous generality, indifferently applicable to everything and anything, and hence not applicable with illuminating power to anything in particular. Against this degrading of being we must fight strenuously. There may be a sense of the universal, and the community of being that transcends any abstract universal.

There is, of course, a certain initial indeterminacy in all of this. We are indeterminately given over to mindfulness about being, given over immediately and from the start, even though what is given thus presents its face to us as astonishing and perplexing. We might say that this question rouses itself in us, struggles to shape itself into saying. It emerges like a diver rising to the surface from a deep sea, as if an emissary were being sent to the airy surface and the light. For this surfacing of the question is not first generated by some self-sufficient act of autonomous thought. It comes to us from a depth of otherness, the otherness of being itself, that we cannot claim to control, or completely to encapsulate in our subsequent concepts.

The question is gratuitous in an important, positive sense that will become clearer as we proceed. For it asks the ultimate why of being, but it has no why that we initially can give to it. It is given to us in the power to ask why of all and everything. It is the ground of all whys that we give, but the why of it comes to us from a source that we cannot master. The question of being happens. The happening is in and through us, as the mindful being on whom a call is made, a call we cannot shut out.

I am not saying that being is an object over against us, the knowledge of which we gain by crossing a dualism between us and it. The situation is more subtle. It might be put this way: there is an *ontological intimacy* to our mindfulness of being, which is immediate, and which is not constructed from two fixed poles (say, subject and object) that are then joined together. I am speaking of an indeterminate opening to being that is prior to any determinate question regarding this or that being, or this or that specific aspect of things. This indeterminate opening is not first determinately known as such; it is lived; it is simply our very being, as given to be mindful of being as given. All determinate questions are further specifications of this first indeterminate opening, as we shall see.

We might be inclined to say we are "englobed" by being. But if so, we are not "englobed" in the way a drop of water is engulfed by the ocean. The situation rather is such as to *release* this singular being, the human being, into mindfulness, not just of its own being, but of being *simpliciter*. "Englobed" is perhaps too ambiguous a word, since it recalls, for instance, the homogeneous circle of Parmenidean being. This is not what I intend. Rather it is the release of *difference and transcendence* as other to any such homogeneous whole. The mindful human being is within a community of being that "englobes" it, in the sense of being more encompassing than its singular being; but this is not such as to swallow the singular being within an absorbing totality. Quite to the contrary, the astonishing diversity and differentiation of beings, and precisely within a community of being as common, emerges for mindfulness. Metaphysical mindfulness is aware of difference in itself, as other in thought to being—being with which mind is also intimate.

There is here articulated what I will call the vector of transcendence. "Vector" is not the best word for what I mean, but the truly right word is hard, perhaps impossible, to find. I must note the following ambiguity. "Vector" carries some connotation of "activity"; but I want to call attention to an opening of transcending that is prior to active transcending. There is a *patience* to this opening; yet it is not inertly passive either. It is beyond capture in the standard opposition of "active/passive." Thus by "vector of transcendence" I do not mean a self-conscious intentionality. I mean the advent of original being, as a dynamic process of coming to be, as also a process of becoming mindful. Transcendence comes to us as an *advent*; this is the patience of an original opening. But, one must add, what comes to us in this advent makes us, in turn, *adventuring* beings, beings ventured towards (*ad*) something of which we are not sure, though we are with it, or it is elusively with us from the outset—with us, though in no sense mastered. This adventuring is closer to the more normal meaning of vector. Yet the vector is enigmatic in its origin. There is a going towards being, but this adventuring emerges out of a community with being that already grants the self its opening to being. That is, in us the vector of self-transcendence is both our relativity to being, and our difference from it. It is our being in community with being, and our otherness to being in this community.

The vector of transcendence, I want so suggest, is already a relation to transcendence, and in a sense not reducible to human self-transcendence. Transcendence as other to us works along with human self-transcendence. I know this is an enigmatic suggestion at this point, but I propose to give concrete articulation to the suggestion in terms of the four senses of being: the univocal, the equivocal, the dialectical and the metaxological. My focus in the present chapter is on the nature of metaphysical thinking, but in subsequent chapters I will discuss more fully each of these senses of being. In the second part of this work the fourfold sense of being will form the categorial structure of a metaphysics that traces a path from *origin* to *creation*, from creation to *things*, to *intelligibilities*, and *selves*, from selves to *communities*, to *truth*, and the *good*. Again I need hardly caution the reader that the matter is still to be determined fully.

The Doubling of Metaphysical Perplexity

Metaphysical thinking is precipitated in the between. We find ourselves in the midst of beings. At first, we do not know our beginning; for we have already begun, before we begin to know that we are, and that there are beings, and that we are in the middle of things. Nor do we know at first what it means to be in this middle, or what makes it be a middle at all. Being between troubles us. It troubles us, not in any mode of neutral objectivism, but with regard to the ground of intelligibility, indeed the very worth of being. A cloak of disquiet is spread wide. There is perplexity about the origin, perplexity about the given milieu of beings, perplexity about the essential thrust of self-transcendence. In the adventure of transcending, we wake to the mystery of being, impelled towards an end we know not, from a beginning we comprehend not, in a milieu whose lords we are not.

Our mindfulness here is *doubly* mediated. On the one hand, our perplexity shows us to be *distanced* from the truth we seek. We undergo a kind of indigence at the heart of our being; in that respect, perplexity reveals our *being-other* to the truth of being. Yet this being-other is not absolute vacancy; rather it is a paradoxical indigency of transcending power. Our lack, it might be said, generates the drive beyond itself. However, what drives the lack beyond lack cannot be itself mere lack. The lack points backwards to an inward otherness in perplexity itself that is the promise of a *relativity* to being that is beyond mere indigence.

Thus, on the other hand, we would not be perplexed at all, were we not in some *communication* with being in its truth. This prior communication, I want to suggest, is anterior to the beginning of mindfulness in lacking perplexity itself. It is the original power of being in us, waking up to itself as mindful, and driven beyond itself to mindfulness of being other than itself. This anterior original power is an excess to lack; indeed this excess articulates lack itself as the mode of a finite mind's self-transcendence. This latter transcending faces outside itself towards what is other to itself; then, it may take itself for a beginning, though, in fact, it has already begun; and so, in fact, it comprehends itself as the indigence of lack only because it has *already* been precipitated out of the excess of the original power of being, as anterior to the finite beginning that already finds itself, as having begun.

This double mediation of our perplexity makes it *metaxological*. By this I mean that perplexity is itself a condition of mindfulness that is between: between nonknowing and knowing, between ignorance so complete it knows not its own ignorance, and a knowing so complete that is it not human at all but that of a god. Metaphysical perplexity is a *tense togetherness* of being at a loss *and* finding oneself at home with being. We must not fail to keep in mind both these sides. This doubleness is both our plenitude and poverty, our grandeur and frailty, our highest call to nobility and perennial reminder of infirmity.

At either of these extremes the demands of intermediacy are inescapable. That is, metaphysical perplexity is not a monolinear epistemic drive from a question to an answer, which then lets us put aside the question. Rather it is the probing for an answer, which renews the question again, and in certain respects may indeed *deepen* perplexity, rather than dispel it. And so, in the poverty of our *nonknowing*, we are impelled to something more and beyond, indeed impelled by something more than lack, already at work behind our back, as it were, in the thrust of our transcending. Likewise, in our *knowing*, our plenty, we do not drop finally into sleep, satiated with some feast of gnosis. Metaphysical perplexity is a desire that in being satiated is renewed as a hunger. There is a restless search for the truth that in coming to be known incites the seeker into further unremitting search. It allows no sleep, though no doubt we repeatedly drowse.

This doubleness corresponds to what I will call the *eros* and the *agape* of metaphysics. There is an eros to perplexity; there is also the promise of agapeic mind. The eros of perplexity is driven to transcendence, troubled initially by a sense of lack. The thrust of mind's transcending seeks to overcome that lack, make determinate what is vague and indefinite, complete what is partial and unintegral. In other words, the eros of perplexity is impelled towards as complete a comprehension of the whole as is possible. It is a movement of transcendence wherein mind mediates progessively with being's otherness to make its enigmatic face available to determinate intelligibility. It is driven to the ideal of comprehensive intelligibility and knowing: knowing of the whole. Sometimes, too, it may define metaphysics as an absolutely autonomous thinking. The metaphysician then seeks approximation to the god of the philosophers: thought thinking itself.

Agapeic perplexity is other. It is not driven to transcendence from an initial lack, but from the effective work of a plenitude that is prior to erotic lack. The agape of perplexity is prior to the eros of perplexity, because the lack of eros could not drive beyond itself at all in the first place, were it not energized by an anterior power of being that cannot be described in purely indigent terms. Put differently, agapeic perplexity is not driven by the will to comprehend completely in a mode that subordinates being's otherness to the metaphysician's categories. It seeks to be genuinely self-transcending in going towards the otherness of being as other, and not simply with the view to appropriating it to the self, or the same, or to mind itself. One could say that *mind others itself* because it is about the *otherness of being* and not just about itself. I am noting here an intermediation with being-other that goes beyond the self-mediation of mind, elevated into primacy by the god of self-thinking thought.

In a word, agapeic perplexity points towards the metaphysical thought of the other as other. Its going towards the other as other is not with the view to subsuming being as a thematic intelligibility simply, but to acknowledge its excess as other, the excess of transcendence itself that gives the world of the between. Agapeic perplexity manifests the heteronomy of metaphysics. As I understand it, metaphysical thinking is not autonomous mindfulness. For in agapeic perplexity there is a giving of mind over to the otherness of being that transcends mind, transcends it as a plenitude that could never be exhausted. And if there is any fulfilling of mindfulness here it is not just in a completely determinate knowing, or a complete autonomous science, but in the endless renewal of astonishment and perplexity.

Once again what I have just said may seem enigmatic, but I hope to make its meaning more manifest. What I have just designated as erotic perplexity and agapeic mind correspond roughly to the dialectical and the metaxological senses of being. What of the other senses? I now propose to go back to the beginning again, and with the aid of the fourfold sense, to indicate more fully some of the plural possibilities of metaphysical thinking. This fourfold sense will also help us to rethink different conceptions of metaphysics, such as we find in Aristotle or Kant, or Heidegger, to name but a few.

Agapeic Astonishment

But first, I must call attention to an ambiguity in the above discussion of agapeic perplexity. We must distinguish *astonishent* and *perplexity* more clearly. I want to note an astonishment that opens mind to being-other but that is *prior* to all perplexity. Perplexity is bound up with the self-transcending eros of mind, but what I will call agapeic astonishment is prior to this.

I mean something like this. The advent of metaphysical thinking is in a primal astonishment. Astonishment itself is primal. It is elemental and irreducible. Plato speaks of *thaumazein* as the *pathos* of the philosopher. This is sometimes translated as *wonder* and this is not inappropriate. Astonishment, however, captures the sense of being rocked back on one's heels, as it were, by the otherness of being in its givenness. Plato says *pathos*: there is a pathology in metaphysics. There is a suffering, an undergoing; there is a patience of being; there is a receiving that is not the production of the metaphysician or mind. This pathology of metaphysics, this patience of astonishment suggests being as primally given in its otherness. In astonishment one does not take possession of, or grasp anything. One finds oneself illuminated by a sudden surge of light: something—exactly what is hard to fix—is being revealed. One does not take hold of an object, one is taken hold of by this surge of light, taken out of oneself. One is impelled to self-transcendence by an initially unchosen illumination that is not objectified.

This transcendence is prior to determinate objectification but it is not a luxuriating in indefinite subjectivity. There is a *shock* in astonishment before otherness, a shock easily forgotten in contemporary, sometimes subjectified, usage of the word *wonder*. For in astonishment there is a rupture that takes one's breath away, and yet this rupture by the given otherness of being is the initiation of a going towards the other. This going towards the other has been wrenched out of its sleep, so to say, wrenched out of its habitual familiarity with the things of the world. Astonishment is both a rupture and a renewal, at once a refreshed distancing and a drawing close of mind and being.

Astonishment is therefore an overdetermined beginning. It is not mind in the mode of posing a problem or seeking to produce a calculation. I hesitate to call it simply a mode of mind, since it is a rupturing of mind, a breaking into mind of the enigmatic givenness of being. And if this breaking in comes from the otherness of being as given, it also impels mind into self-transcendence towards being as other, impels it to think otherwise of being. In a word, astonishment awakens us to the happening of being in the between.

We might call astonishment the innocence of the mind as agapeic. That is, it articulates a spontaneous transcendence of mind towards the otherness of being as other. I think this innocence of agapeic mind always stays with every subsequent perplexity, though it can be so covered over and encrusted with later conceptual accretions as to become all but deadened. Notice that the beginning is not in pure thought purely determining itself, so beloved of the idealists. Nor is the beginning in the sense impressions so beloved of the empiricists. The beginning is a giving of being that is not first the product of thought, nor capable of being contained in more standard notions of sense experience.

It is no accident that in opening his *Metaphysics* Aristotle says: a sign (*sēmeion*) of our desire to know is our love of the senses. His words are significant: *hē tōn aisthēseōn agapēsis* (*Meta*, 980a23). There is an agape of the aesthetic. Sensing is not the intake of the empiricist's sense impression. I would say: it is an astonished openness to givenness as the aesthetic show of being. We behold what is other: *Ecce!* Something comes before us; as coming before us, it is prior; it rises before us out of its priority and gives our seeing the jolt of otherness that awakens mindfulness. But this prior mindfulness is anterior to our normal understanding of seeing—namely, as our self-directed perception of what is there. Rather it is an ontological receptivity prior to the usual senses of passivity and activity. For the latter imply that we are perceptually active, while being-other is just there passively, docile to our self-directed mediations. This prior receptivity of which I speak cannot be rendered in terms of an interplay of an active subject and a passive object. Such an interplay both occludes and presupposes it.

To behold: What is beholding? We think of beholding as going from us to other-being. This is an especially dominant modern meaning, where beholding seems to put the perceiver in a position of active superiority to being-other. But consider the notion of *beholding from* being-other. I think of these lines of Wordsworth (*Tintern Abbey*, 102–6):

> Therefore am I still
> A lover of the meadows and the woods
> And mountains; and of all that we behold
> From this green earth; of all of the mighty world
> Of eye and ear.

I ask you to consider the words "behold from." This is my suggestion: agapeic astonishment is like "beholding from"—the other-being comes towards us, and we are called beyond ourselves. There is a *reversal* of directionality relative to the usual understanding of perceptual intentionality, which is said to be "consciousness of. . . ." To the contrary, *beholding from* reverses this intentionality from self to other. It is "consciousness from. . . ." The very word consciousness as a *con-scientia* indicates the "with" (*cum*) and the forgotten gift of the other, the beholding from the other that opens up our perceptual going towards the other.

We might say that there is a two-way mediation in beholding: both a "beholding of" and a "beholding from." Perhaps this "beholding from" is intimated by the classical notion of *theōria* or contemplation—understood as a noninterfering vigilance towards being-other. Not incidentally, *theōria* and contemplation (*cum, templum*) are religious in origin.[1] In "beholding from," the otherness of being opens itself from itself in its otherness; it offers itself to us for our mindfulness, which is only a "beholding of" because it is first a "beholding from."

Beholding seems to imply a certain holding, and we might again think in terms of our *taking hold* of something—as in the German *begreifen*, where "conceiving" suggests a taking hold of, a grasping, seizing. This would be a simplification. Rather "beholding from" is first of all a *being taken hold of*. Hence the connection with agapeic astonishment. The other as other seizes us, and offers itself to our minding, but we then go towards it out of our seizure. This seizure puts us in the hold of the other-being; it puts us in its thrall, enthralling us. This is a receptivity that is both ruptured and enrapt. One is captivated, as if something in the sight of the other falls upon us, showers itself upon us, and we fall in love with it.

This is what agapeic astonishment implies primally: love of other-being as other, which is not first chosen by self-conscious will but given, a gift to self-being. Aptly did Wordsworth say that he was still a *lover*. "Beholding from" calls on the self, enthralls its mindfulness, and makes us beholden to the other. One might say that beholding is a *being beholden* to the other for the marvel of its givenness. *Being beholden* is being held in a community of attachment: one is bound to the favor of the other; one is in the debt of the other. And yet this *being beholden*, though felt as the call of a certain demand or obligation, is not at all imprisoning, but *releasing*. It releases free mindfulness towards being-other as offered to the self. This *being beholden* in "beholding from" is the call of truth. We answer for our *being beholden* when we seek to be true to being.[2]

It would be a mistake to think that an "object" as other simply seizes us, making us passive while it is actively dominating. Rather what is received in "beholding from" cannot be thus objectified, and what seizes us is not the

---

1. See *Philosopy and its Others*, 103–4, 235–36; *Beyond Hegel and Dialectic*, 92, 136–37.

2. The full import of this will emerge in chapter 12.

object as dominating, but the offer of being beyond all objectification, and the call of truthfulness to being that is neither subjective nor objective, but transsubjective and transobjective. The *trans*, or crossing, is at play in the interplay of the subject and object, but is not completely determinable as either subjective or objective. When we behold being from, the happening of the between beyond subjectification and objectification comes towards us, and indeed as making us beholden to it, making us answerable for its truth. The truth of being makes us beholden to it, in the happening of the between. We are metaphysically obliged to be mindful in the between.

An excess of other-being overflows towards one. This is astonishing, not because initially we can make no sense of it, but simply because mind opens up agapeically before it. It is there, and in a sense, it is too much. The first astonishment is simply a mindful joy in this overflow. In other words, there is a primordial *being pleased* with being, prior to all cognitive thematization and objective determination. We are carried along by this overflow, this excess in the middle; we sense even *ourselves* to be overflows of this excess. Our pleasure with simply being greets, and is greeted by, the elemental agape of being itself. There is a primal joy in being that is made to draw its breath in astonishment and that is a sign of the originary advent of metaphysical thinking.

We discover something *childlike* about such beginnings. I do not say childish, though this has been said. The childlike opening is our finding ourselves astonished already in the openness of being. The fact is we do not chose or produce astonishment; astonishment *opens us* in the first instance because the givenness of being has made its way into our sleep, so to say, and opened our eyes to simply see and enjoy the light. Astonishment is not a production of the self, but a gift from as-yet-unnamed transcendence, in and through the otherness of being. The child *lives* this primal and elemental opening. Hence undoubtedly, wonder is more characteristic of earlier stages of human life. Hence also, as has often been noted, children have a spontaneous tendency to ask the "big questions." Do not misunderstand me. I am not offering nice thoughts about the innocence of childhood. And to speak either sentimentally or sarcastically about wonder would miss the point. The human being is metaphysically opened from the outset; this opening is constitutive of its being; and its first primal emergence is in astonishment. All of this is itself astonishing.

In sum, then, astonishment is an indeterminate opening of transcendence in a double sense. Since astonishment is not a mediated production of the self, it comes to the self from the advent of what is other to it; it comes from *transcendence as other*; this is the first sense. Yet in opening the self, it initiates the vector of *transcendence in the self* and its going towards being-other with express mindfulness; this is the second sense. As double, astonishment is in metaxological intermediation with being, though we cannot say this when it first strikes, because of the initial indeterminacy of the opening.

I hear your objection now: Where is the argument, there is no univocal argument here? This is true, but such argument comes *later*. Though the objection touches something true, it does not touch the truth at issue here. For we start with a happening of being in the between. Or rather, we do not start, but *find ourselves* in astonishment as having already started. *Then* we think about what is at play in this beginning, and perhaps "argue" as to the appropriate understanding. This is part of meeting the obligation of truth. But were there no *happening* of astonishment, metaphysics would be a mere scholastic juggling of empty abstractions, perhaps with great virtuosity in the formal mastery of argumentation, but ontologically barren nonetheless.

Another way to put the point would be this. There is a certain *idiocy* to astonishment, which is disconcerting. I use *idiocy* with some reference to the Greek sense of the *idios*, the intimate, private.[3] Astonishment is idiotic, not in a subjectivistic sense, but because it happens to the I as singular. It does not happen to consciousness in general; or to pure thought thinking thought; nor indeed to the sense-registering mind of the empiricist. It is also idiotic because it is a *happening* that initially is without a why. Perhaps *later* we will seek to say why. But in the beginning it is without a why. And so it is *outside system*, though afterwards we may construct a system of categories that will try to render it more or less intelligible.

Yet as idiotic, astonishment is not private, in the bad sense of being locked within solipsistic immanence. As I have indicated, the rupture of the other is already there in it, and in the opening of double transcendence. And it is "general," in that it is constitutive of the human being as metaphysically mindful. It is idiotic in that it strikes to the elemental depths of the human being, depths that elude complete objectification, intimacies that become idiotic in a bad sense, when the self as singular fails to keep alive in itself the promise of the opening to being, first given here.

We then must say that there is an ineluctable dimension of *singularity* to metaphysical thinking. I know this seems to contradict the usual belief that metaphysics must be scientific and hence a public and universal cognition of being. I will come back to this, but for now I want to say that the sources of metaphysics are indeed universal, but universal as idiotic, relative to the astonishment that strikes into the self with the enigma of being. The sources of explicated categorial generality are at a deep level also idiotic: every system is generated out of a source that is not itself a system, but an idiotic happening of astonishment in the singular thinker. The call of metaphysical thinking is singular in its idiotic origins. These idiotic origins are universally given to human beings as mindful. These origins may generate more or less ordered and systematic ways of think-

---

3. This sense of *idiocy* will recur throughout the work. See chapter 3, "The Idiocy of Being" in *Perplexity and Ultimacy*.

ing that have a derived universality. But if these latter universals are not continually watered by the originary astonishment, they quickly atrophy into empty concepts, and metaphysics as such a system of categories itself dies.

Metaphysics is initiated, carried, renewed by *singular thinkers*, not just by anonymous systems. These singulars have tirelessly worked to think better, and their work may issue in systematic articulations that are publicly available for other thinkers, contemporary, antagonistic, and descendent. To speak of *tirelessness* is misleading if we forget that, in the intimacy of being, such singulars have fought weariness and bafflement, despondency and bewilderment. Yet the very freshness of their work comes from a different source that is not itself work, or the production of a work, or a system. This source is manifested in the gift of fertile astonishment. Needless to say, redeeming the promise of this gift is not common. The more mature a singular metaphysician becomes, the more there is a refinement of childlike astonishment. It is never dead. It may simplify itself to an elemental power of mindfulness, a simplicity not of defect, but of a perfection of attention that defies all determinate objectification.

Erotic Perplexity and the Completion of Metaphysics

It would be a false impression if the reader thinks I deny the importance of determination and objectification. I do not. But I must stress that astonishment is not merely *indefinite*, but an *overdetermined* beginning. It is an illumination of the marvel of being in excess of all determination. A sense of the surplus of being, prior to the determination of beings in the middle, is offered to this mode of mind, a mode that itself is surplus to objectified determination. The excess of agapeic mind is the beginning of metaphysical thinking *for us*, called forth in astonishment by a preobjective rapport with being in the overdetermined excess of its otherness. Excess of being in its otherness, excess of mind in us, these two transcendences converge in the middle. Mindfulness originates in us from their communication, metaphysical mindfulness as the perplexed thinking of the rich happening of being in the middle.

It is subsequent to this that the need arises to think *more determinately* on this happening. Now perplexity in a more familiar sense arises. I called it erotic perplexity above. That is, the illumination of astonishment does not so much fade as it draws us beyond ourselves and closer to *beings* in their otherness. The very elusiveness of the illumination is such as to make us keenly aware that we do not determinately know what has been given to us then. This makes us *urgent to determine* what first is given in the mode of overdetermined excess. The primal giving of being fades from focus, for in one respect there can be no focus here. It fades and the givenness of *beings* assumes the focus.

Again remember that the illumination I am seeking to name is first like the air we breathe, in some ways so all-surrounding that it is the least noticed of things. Or it is like the light that makes everything visible, and that itself is overlooked in its very enabling of us to look at things at all. When we first come into the light of being, the light strikes us in its strangeness and marvel and joy. But we live in the light and grasp it not. It enables vision and visibility, but its marvel fades from notice.

Beings demand our attention, not being. The determinate grasp of their being issues its requirement in the awareness that we are *lacking* in definite knowledge. The sense of lack, of ignorance, makes itself felt, after the first astonishment. We must say that erotic perplexity is born from agapeic astonishment. It is necessarily born from astonishment, to the extent that there are beings and not just being; and beings too are initially marvels of thereness. But its birth is ambiguous: its pursuit of the knowing of beings, its will to overcome the lack of determinate comprehension, may be overtaken by the increasing *amnesia* of its own birth. Then it may think of itself as *born from itself*, and not as derivative of a more originary communication with being in its otherness. When this occurs, erotic perplexity forgets its prior origin in an agape of mind wherein being as plenitude offers itself as other to thought, offers its otherness to mind *before* thought tries to think itself, or *before* mind develops its own will to self-determination and the determination of the intelligibility of entities.

In a word, we are tempted to claim that erotic perplexity is *the* originary source. We then conceive of the knower as a kind of empty subjectivity that must determine itself as completely as possible, determine itself to overcome its initial perplexity, determine itself completely in its unrelenting categorial determination of the intelligibility of beings. Erotic perplexity, in this guise, may seek to overcome its own lack by its determination of the intelligibility of beings, through the categories it *determines through itself*. In truth, this putative self-completion of erotic perplexity risks a *loss* of metaphysical thinking; the perplexing question of being is domesticated in a system of categories, putatively emergent in the process of self-determining thought. In my view, this putative completion is less the consummation of metaphysics than the amnesia of agapeic astonishment; its very power to determine thinking is the outcome of a loss of metaphysical thinking. This completion actually completes a loss of metaphysical thinking that is rooted in the more originary sense of agapeic astonishment. We need to return to this origin again.

The above remarks trace a dissident parallel to Heidegger's influential view of the development of Western metaphysics as proceeding from the oblivion of being to its completion, either in Hegelian idealism, or Nietzsche's inversion of Platonism. I stress the dissidence of the parallel. I recognize the force of the claim that there is a forgetfulness of being. I deny that there is a monolinear development in which the origin is obliterated in the progressive realization of metaphysics. Relative to the view I am developing, what has supposedly been completed in the so-called realization of metaphysics is not metaphysical thinking at all. It is really a *turning from* the kind of metaphysical thinking that originates in agapeic astonishment; it is the abstraction of erotic perplexity from its source in the agape of being, and the absolutization of the energy of transcendence at work in erotic perplexity. But this absolutization, and this energy of transcendence turned towards complete determination, is never, in fact, absolute, but is always parasitical on what it comes to deny. This is the energy of transcendence as an excess rather than a lack, an overdetermined plenitude rather than an indefinite nothing, as agapeic rather than erotic.

My view is a dissident parallel, not in protest, but in defense of a truth more complex than is captured in the notion of a monolinear fall from the origin. I believe that the nature of metaphysical thinking is even *inverted*, if identified with what happens within that putative fall, an inversion that becomes perverse, when what putatively happens within that fall is *totalized* as the history of metaphysics. Then, as seems to happen with Heidegger, *one possible history of erotic perplexity* is identified wrongly with the *total happening* of metaphysics. The truth is much more complex. There is a doubleness in the middle all along. That is, agapeic astonishment and erotic perplexity always mingle. Metaphysics tries to keep itself alive in the former, even in the determination of the latter. It is not always successful; "success" may be extremely rare; for "success" may look like a kind of "failure" from the point of view of mastering cognition. "Success" may take the form of properly saying "I do not know." This "failure" of mastering cognition may be the opening of a radical metaphysical honesty beyond determinate knowing.

Agapeic astonishment is always there as initiating the promise of thinking, even in mastering cognition. There is no such thing as the completion of metaphysics. To claim such a completion indicates a complete lack of understanding of what is at play in agapeic astonishment. The very opening of astonishment is the beginning of metaphysics; articulated metaphysical thought keeps this alive even in determinate concepts and categories. The true consummating of metaphysics is not the overcoming of astonishment, but the infinite renewal of the opening to transcendence that comes first to us in it. And there is no completion of this renewal.

The sophisticated reader will have suspected many ghosts from the history of metaphysics hovering around the above account. The suspicion is not misplaced. Let me now try to articulate the development of metaphysical thinking beyond the first origin, and do so in terms of the fourfold sense of being mentioned already: the univocal, the equivocal, the dialectical, the metaxological. In the process the major options for metaphysics in the tradition will be addressed.

Metaphysical Thinking and Univocity

Beyond the primal beginning of agapeic astonishment, and always draw-ing on it, even unknowingly, the energy of transcending expressed in mind's spirit of questioning gets specified into *particular questions* about this, that, and the other thing. The latter are emergent in the between, defined in their distinctiveness and connectedness against the background of an unstated sense of the limiting conditions that bound the between. There is a self-develop-ment of perplexity in this development of specific questions. This is to the point, this is necessary.

Again I recall the familar dictum of Aristotle that all human beings de-sire to know. This desire is here at issue. It is the *determinacy* of questioning that is at stake. Let us not forget the crucial ambiguity in the transition from agapeic astonishment to erotic perplexity—namely, the birth of the latter out of the former, but the possible forgetting of the former in the latter's sense of lack or ignorance. This ambiguity can now be *doubled*, in that the determinacy of questioning turns the direction of mindfulness resolutely *against* ambigu-ity. A deeper ambiguity is forgotten in the will to overcome ambiguity. This is where the intimate connection between metaphysics and univocity emerges.

The invocation of Aristotle is appropriate here. Aristotle is famous for his saying *to on legetai pollachōs*. I concur with this deeply, and the present work is a distinctive working out of a plurivocal metaphysics according to the fourfold sense of being. That said, Aristotle exhibits a strong drift in thought to conceive of being as univocally as possible. Being is not univocal, not equivocal, it is analogical, and the controversies of the millennia are sunk in these statements. I know that. My concern is not now the nature of analogy, but the almost irresistible urge to make being as *determinately intelligible* as possible.

Aristotle offers a threefold division of metaphysics: metaphysics is *first philosophy*, treating the first causes, *aitiai*, principles, *archai*; metaphysics is the *science of being qua being*; metaphysics is *theology*, as the study of the highest being, God. Whether the term metaphysics springs from a librarian's convenience or a divine chance, the etymological resonances of *meta ta phusika* are frequently invoked in relation to the third division, as pointing us to transcendent being beyond physical being. I do not think there is any-thing immediately to be rejected in this inventory of possible roles for meta-physics. Nevertheless, each role remains to be determined in its meaning relative to the nature of metaphysical thinking itself.

There is in Aristotle the view, and it is widespread throughout the tradi-tion, that *to be is to be intelligible*; and to be intelligible is to be *determinate*. Hence being is identified with determinate intelligibility. Hence pure per-plexity is always essentially a lack; for in being open to all, pure perplexity is open specifically to nothing in particular; it is merely the vestibule of meta-physics as science, whether of highest *aitiai* and *archai*, or being qua being, or *ho theos*. Metaphysics comes into its own when the initial indeterminacy of perplexity is specified in terms of determinate questions like: What is it? Why is it? What is substance or essence? And so on. The more determinate a question is, the closer it comes to being answered. For an answer to be an answer it must be determinately intelligible. Lacking this, an answer is no real answer, and may, in fact, reflect a question that is no question—that is, a question not properly determined.

There is a direct line leading from Aristotle to logical positivism with respect to this ideal of determinate intelligibility. With the positivist, the ideal itself is turned against the mother of the ideal—namely, traditional metaphysics. The questions of traditional metaphysics are dismissed as pseudoquestions because, it is claimed, they cannot be intelligibly formulated in terms of an ideal of determinate intelligibility, itself modeled on a certain ideal of empirical verification. It goes without saying that agapeic astonishment is dead and buried in positivism; but the traditional child of that astonishment is also buried as meaningless. In one sense, the positivist is perfectly consistent, but it is a consistency erected on a radical contraction, hence misunderstanding, of the energy of transcendence of mind. It is the perfection of a barren consistency, into which Aristotle had the greatness not to fall.

Of course, the univocal ideal of intelligibility was traditionally linked with the metaphysical *quest of unity*. Any good Aristotelian will remind you that the determination of unity is amenable to a more comprehensive articulation than we find in the anorexic self-starvation of the positivistic mind and some of its analytic descendents. But it is interesting to note a peculiar affinity between positivism and post-Heideggerian deconstructions that assault the ideals of univocity and unity for being totalistic. Such deconstructions might seem the antipodes of positivism. In fact, positivism is one form of the deconstruction of metaphysics. In the words of one of its patriarchs, Hume, metaphysics "must be consigned to the flames." One offers a *scientistic* deconstruction, the other offers a *textual* deconstruction of metaphysics. The question is: Must the ideal of unity always determine *reductionistically* the nature of metaphysics? I do not think so. I suggest that such deconstructions of metaphysics as totalizing univocity themselves univocally totalize the nature of metaphysics. In claiming to free from totalizing thinking, they exhibit totalizing thinking relative to traditional metaphysics. As they seem to take the speck out of the metaphysician's eye, they overlook any beam in their own. They do not do justice to the *plurivocal nature* of metaphysical thinking.

Consider, for instance, the way Aquinas follows Aristotle's claim that whenever a many is ordered to a one, then the one must be the ruler; the many are subordinated to this sovereign one. Must such oneness and sovereignty necessitate violent totality or reductionistic contraction? Surely not. Why not say they may communicate wise order in the whole? Thus Aquinas thinks of metaphysics as the highest study in dealing with the wisdom that is the perfection of all other human arts and knowings. Following Aristotle, he offers a threefold stress. The *first* stress is on intelligibility relative to the intellect. Metaphysics will deal with the highest intelligibilities. The more intelligible realities will offer a knowledge of causes, all the way to the first cause. The *second* stress is on the power of the universal, in contrast to the particulars of sense. Being is the most universal, and from it flow other themes like the one and the many, potency and act. This universal cannot be treated by one of the particular sciences, precisely because of the universality of its universality, which is not confined to one kind of being. Being is more universal than any kind of being, and hence more than the universal of the genus and kind. The *third* stress is on the power of intellect itself. The highest intellectual powers and intelligible beings will be those most free from matter, and hence we must go beyond the universals treated in natural science, as well as those notions treated in mathematical science. God will be the being beyond which thought cannot go. This science will be the mistress or ruler of all.[4]

I ask you: How helpful is it immediately to categorize Aristotle or Aquinas as "metaphysicians of presence" and so, whether they know it or not, as "totalizing thinkers"? Surely must not even a plurivocal metaphysics address many of the above themes, even if perhaps not exactly in the above form? Nevertheless, given our understanding of the origin of metaphysical thinking, the following caution about the ideal of determinate intelligibility is in order.

To be is to be intelligible, and to be intelligible is to be determinate. This view cannot stand as the last word. To the extent that it is a guiding presupposition of traditional metaphysics, it calls for significant transformation. I do not say rejection. For determinate intelligibility comes to be; to be determinate is to be the issue of a process of coming to be, which process itself is not completely determinate. For were it so, there would be no coming to be; there would be no energy of transcendence; there would be no between as the dynamic coming together of the plurality of beings in their coming to be themselves as determinate. Determinate intelligibility points back to its own origin in a source that is not intelligible in the same determinate way. Reference must be made to the origin of coming to be that is prior to determination, and not merely in the negative sense of the indefinite that is only real when it has been made determinate or definite.[5]

---

4. On the above, see Aquinas's *Commentary on the Metaphysics*, Prologue.

5. The univocal ideal of determinate intelligibility can be correlated with the notion of primary *ousia*, and the primary sense of being tends to be determined in terms of beings. I am not denying beings or determinate intelligibility, but am calling notice to the coming to be of beings, a coming into being, and not only a coming to be this or that determinate being. There is an overdetermination to this first origination that is matched by the overdetermination of the first agapeic astonishment. This is not an *underdetermination*, like an indefinite *prima materia* whose abstraction is to be determinately concretized in terms of the form and matter of this substance. If one were to correlate the origin with *to apeiron*, the latter would have to be more than indefinite possibility; it would have to be original in the sense of originative, to get us closer to the coming to be of the determinate.

We have to recall the overdetermined excess of original being. This *agape* of being is manifested in the determinations of beings, but it is not a determinate being simply, not even the highest being in the sense with which God is often identified—namely, the *ens realissimum*. Metaphysical thinking first comes out of a primal source that makes possible, but is not completely rendered by, the will to determinate intelligibility. If we keep alive the memory of that beginning, there is more to metaphysics than the science of being qua being, understood as a doctrine of categories or principles, formulated under the sway of determinate intelligibility.

Aristotle's "all human beings desire to know" recalls the Platonic *thaumazein* (*Meta*, 982b11ff.). And indeed Aristotle sees the connection of marveling and astonishment when he reminds us of the affiliation of myth and metaphysics, and also the delight in the senses. This is to the point. But the point is seriously attenuated, even misunderstood, when the desire to know is understood essentially as a drive to determinate intelligibility, which on being achieved dissolves or kills the initial perplexity that launches the quest. The end of Aristotle's wonder is a determinate *logos* of a determinate somewhat, a *tode ti*. But this end is the death of wonder, not its refreshening at a level of mindfulness marked by deeper or higher metaphysical sophistication. Not surprisingly, Aristotle invokes *geometry* to illustrate the teleological thrust of the desire to know (*Meta*, 983a13ff.). What is geometry but a figure for determinate knowing in which all the ambiguity of perplexity is overcome or dissolved in the solution. The *eureka* that solves the problem is the dissolution of wonder and astonishment. The end of geometrical metaphysics is the death of metaphysics.

Such a geometry of the eros of perplexity satisfies itself, or wills to satisfy itself, in a completely determinate *logos* of the solution. The eros may renew itself on another determinate problem with another determinate solution. But it does not either renew or deepen perplexity about the original coming to be of determinacy, which is beyond determinacy, exceeding it as preceding it, exceeding it as outliving and transcending every determinate solution to determinate problems. This geometry of erotic perplexity betrays its own origin in agapeic astonishment.

Metaphysical Thinking and Equivocity

Mind in its native self-transcendence goes spontaneously towards the beings that are given in the between. It does not first think about *how* the between is given, nor about *how* mind itself does or can go towards beings as other. It has a native metaphysical trust that there is a rapport between itself and being that is other. This spontaneous transcendence is the overflow of agapeic astonishment, but this can be checked. Just in its going beyond itself, it meets with other beings that in their otherness spontaneously check the native metaphysical trust.

Then we find the displacement of agapeic astonishment towards erotic perplexity. For perplexity already is *not* the native joy in being. To be is primally to take joy in being; but in the determinate otherness of the between, this affirmation is sometimes stalled, or stopped, or blocked. The word *perplexity* carries this doubleness: impetus towards being as other, frustration of that going beyond and towards.

It is here, I think, that we face the possible equivocity of being. We might say that perplexity is astonishment astonished; astonished as having its breath taken away and, in that pause of being disconcerted, made self-mindful of its own transcendence as a questioning one, perhaps even a questionable one. The determination of thinking towards univocally intelligible being is checked in its questioning of beings and made to question itself. Frustrated by differences rather than attracted to unities, arrested by disjunctions rather than pleased by conjunctions, metaphysical perplexity mixes marvel and doubt. Let us say that the advent of erotic perplexity brings to mind the rupture of the negative, and a different pathos to the first affirmation of being.

There are a number of points here. An immediate sense of the community of mind and being is not so much done away with as made the theme of questioning. It is made questionable, and hence there is a certain loss of this immediate community. This loss is reflected in mind's own sense of its own self-discord; its spontaneous faith that beings are given to it to know truly is put into question. Similarly, the native faith that being in its otherness is marked by its own inherent integrity and intelligibility may be called into question.[6]

---

6. Consider, for instance, how in modernity the premodern marveling at being as a cosmos, a beauty of order and aesthetic wholeness, comes to be troubled. This appreciation of being as an harmonious, well-ordered, beautiful whole is cousin to agapeic astonishment. Now consider the deadening of nature into a lifeless *res extensa*, metallically regulated by mechanical motions. This testifies to an atrophy, even death of the first astonishment. The latter is replaced by the will to mathematical science, with its practical corollary of technological mastery of nature. Erotic perplexity becomes a will to know that appropriates the indifferent thereness of the lifeless world, and subjects it to technological will to power.

Heidegger is plain wrong to see the technological will to power as the completion of metaphysics. Quite to the contrary, it is the withering away of metaphysical thinking, which cannot be completely subsumed into any determinate science. The earlier Heidegger ambiguously recognized the otherness of metaphysical thinking; the later Heidegger assimilates all metaphysics to the science or sciences of beings, which in the modern era both "complete" and "replace" "metaphysics," so contracted. This may have partial justification with respect to instrumental mind; but metaphysics as *theōria*, understood in a premodern way, was always other to instrumental mind. For strategic reasons—namely, to totalize the whole tradition of the West— the later Heidegger fudges this difference. For discussion of this point in Heidegger, see *Beyond Hegel and Dialectic*, 43–55.

Inevitably skeptical thinking arises. In invoking doubt above, I did not only mean Cartesian or post-Cartesian doubt. Doubt implies a reference to a double, a doubleness of mind: to be of two minds about things, as we say. This doubling of mindfulness is not to be rejected at all.[7] As already indicated, there is always a doubleness in our metaphysical situation. Here the doubleness testifies to a diversification of mindfulness that cannot bring itself back to a unity of intelligibility. The doubling is understood in terms of the failure of univocity, rather than as prelude to a more plurivocal sense of mind and being. Being is said in many senses, but the manyness here frustrates univocity. The double of this doubting is seen as essentially a negative difference, rather than a positive plurality.

Consider the problem of equipollence in ancient skepticism: to every *logos* an equal and opposite *logos* can be put, Sextus Empiricus says. The equivocal sense takes note of the diversity of determinate beings: there is this, that, and the other. But this diversity seems to be a sheer plurality, a differentiation with no clear unity, since the integrity of univocity has been put into question. Metaphysical skepticism is one formation of erotic perplexity, subsequent to the native metaphysical faith of agapeic astonishment. The stress of mind is on the pathos of the negative: we cannot say what beings are or what being is. There seems to be no positive knowing of being.

How do we respond to this? Metaphysical thinking cannot be authentic, if it does not face the negative in the above sense. Beyond the first agapeic astonishment, being has to be as intelligibly determined as possible, but in the process of making it thus intelligible, obstacles arise that cannot be blinked. Mind has to struggle to keep its openness to being alive. It has to struggle against its own temptation to take its already achieved categories as transparent mirrors of the whole. It has to learn the humility needed for a more radical opening of self-transcendence. Skepticism provides the ordeal that puts mindfulness to the test.

Let me cite a crucial case—namely, the way Kant and post-Kantian philosophers dismiss previous philosophers as dogmatic metaphysicians. I think this is seriously to misrepresent the matter. Properly speaking, there is no such thing as a dogmatic metaphysician. The so-called dogmatic metaphysicians are really the professors of a packaged scholasticism whence perplexity has been banished. Any metaphysician worthy of the name is intimate with the searing ordeal of skepticism. He may not make that ordeal a subject of explicit thematization. But what God has decreed to metaphysics that everything has to be made thus explicit? The philosopher may have lived the ordeal in thought, and may have come to the considered conclusion that to turn skepticism into a "method" seriously distorts what is at play in the ordeal itself.

---

7. Consider the German word for doubt, *Zweifel*, with its reference to a double, *Zwei*; see also the word for despair, *Verzweiflung*. The "wound" of this doubling is not only negative; it is also an opening of self-transcending.

The point can be made that the ordeal is itself an expression of the basic perplexity, and that there is something about this perplexity, as over-determined, that resists contraction to any determinate method. We have to read metaphysicians, not only in their explicit avowals, but in the signs or traces of the ordeal of skepticism that may hide in the explicit avowals. There may be a certain decorousness in hiding the wounds of mind—a dignity, I say, not dishonesty, as the hermeneutics of suspicion will charge. The hermeneutics of suspicion is vulgar. It has great difficulty in understanding the nobility of metaphysical thinking. It shows traces of a *ressentiment* that would expose as questionable every hiddenness of greatness. But there is a philosophical etiquette relative to which this attitude is singularly clumsy and coarse.

Metaphysical thinking, in fact, has more than one significant response available to it in respect of this ordeal. The major one taken in the tradition is to renew the desideratum of metaphysics as science. The other response is to purify and renew the sources of perplexity, and to think more deeply the meaning of the agapeic astonishment, and the marvel of the givenness of being in the between. This latter points to metaxological metaphysics.

But to the first: skepticism about knowing being is a negative form of perplexity, but it is seen here as something to be overcome. How overcome? By deepening the perplexity, by radicalizing the negative. This is clearly the strategy of Cartesian doubt. To defeat doubt, radicalize doubt, even to the extreme where it either goes under in complete loss of being and mind, or else reaches a limit that cannot be doubted. Radical doubt defeats itself because doubt has *to be*, even in all its negations. The negativity of doubt then serves to determine something positive. Descartes will think of this in terms of the *cogito*. The question of being as other will be reversed from the other to the being asking about being: the human knower.

Descartes will derive the "I am" from the "I think." But the case can be made that the "I am" is a particularization of the primal affirmation of being, first made manifest to us in agapeic astonishment. The "I think" is derived from the *sum*, itself a gift of the happening of being. When the "I am" is said to be derivative of the "I think," the ontological situation is seen in reverse: instead of the agapeic astonishment before being's otherness soliciting thought, it is now thinking that defines, as derivative from its own priority, any affirmation of being, including the being of self. Thinking takes itself to be absolutely prior. The *cogito me cogitare*, thought thinking itself, lays claim to be the absolute origin. Metaphysical astonishment is flattened, not only into determinate but *self-determining thinking*.

I will not deny the importance of proper mindfulness of the self. But here the power to negate, and hence to determine, passes entirely over to the self. In effect, the between is determined by the self as the power of negation and determination. The middle as other to the self is made nothing in itself prior to this determination by the self; the other as other equally is nothing for itself prior to its determination by the self. The self becomes *the* power to mediate the equivocity of the between. In Descartes, the double of doubt is reduced to the single meaning of a quasi-mathematical univocity, modeled on the clarity and distinctness of ideas to the unitary *cogito*. In addition, a way is prepared for the absolutization of self-mediation by idealism.

This is the tale of almost all post-Cartesian metaphysics. As in premodern metaphysics, we still find a logic of determinacy. In premodern metaphysics, however, the process of being itself gives rise to determinate beings; and the pathos of the metaphysician, indeed the self-transcendence of all mindful-ness, involves some acknowledgment of the ontological marvel of that giving. Whatever way we describe the other or the ultimate other, or origin, the giv-ing of being in the between is *not* the doing of the human self. We go into, transcend in the middle, but the otherness of beings is given to the between from an origin that is other to the self, indeed other to the between itself as the milieu of finite beings. We might say that with modern doubt the between becomes the empty stage of human mediation; it becomes an indifferent mi-lieu serving the self-mediation of the human being.

The logic of determinacy, coupled with the power of negation, fits with the belief that philosophy must be a science. This science will formulate its problems with the exact determinacy of quasi-mathematical formulations. It will attack these problems with the exact directives of a universal and homo-geneous method. It will devise the proper technical language to allow prob-lems and solutions to be expressed with a univocal determinacy that escapes all the ambiguities and equivocities of commonsense usage. It will formulate certain and conceptually transparent solutions that will be binding on every rational agent. Erotic perplexity, passing through the negativity of skeptical doubt, will conquer perplexity completely. In principle the result should be an absolutely rational system, which, in making all being determinately in-telligible, will rationalize all being absolutely.

It did not work. It will not work. Why? Not only because the passage of the question of being solely to the side of the self is itself massively question-able, but because this passage stifles the self of agapeic astonishment, and hence ultimately stifles the source of metaphysical mindfulness. This source cannot be stifled, nor can the giving of being be indefinitely disregarded. The excess of the beginning, and the excess of being that remains after all our rational determinations are complete, bring to mind again the incomplete-ness of the complete system.

I will illustrate briefly with reference to Kant. Why must metaphysics be scientific? Kant's obsession is to make it so. Some of the main considerations include: Hitherto reason has been in discord with itself, revealed by the im-passe in previous metaphysics between dogmatism and skepticism, and also between rationalism and empiricism. Empiricism itself offers another varia-tion on skepticism, in that Hume seemed to deconstruct the traditional no-tion of rational necessity, most famously with respect to causality. Kant accepts the deconstruction of traditional metaphysics, but aims to *reconstruct* metaphysics in terms of a new transcendental philosophy. The categories that make being intelligible are not like Aristotelian categories, which open to forms of intelligibility inherent in the nature of things themselves. These categories are on the side of the knowing self. The sense of origin also passes to the side of the self in terms of synthetic a priori truths, and most radically in terms of the transcendental unity of apperception.

In all of this we find an insatiable quest for completeness, and this most especially with respect to Kant's architectonic ambitions. This insatiable will to completeness was to become even more feverish in the idealisms following Kant. Think of the revealing fact that Kant repeatedly contrasts the "random groping" of all previous metaphysics with his own claim to put philosophy successfully on "the secure path of science" (e.g., *Critique of Pure Reason*, Bvii, xiv). The results are said to be marked by completeness, unity, absolute necessity, and apodictic certainty (see ibid., Axvii-xix). Not incidentally, *geometry* again proves an exemplar. Kant claims his main purpose as the "complete revolutionizing" of metaphysics "in accordance with the example set by the geometers and physicists" (ibid., Bxxii).

Why quarrel with this? Who would not gladly forsake "random groping" for secure scientific enlightenment? Who indeed. And yet, perhaps after all, this contrast of "random groping" and "the secure path of science" can be seen in a very different light. Suppose we ask: Is this "groping" always only a condition of mere indigence? Can we see something more there? Can we not see something of the indeterminate perplexity that lies before and beyond all systems, and that itself is the issue of the first agapeic astonishment? There is a random groping of the lost.[8] But perhaps there is a condition of "being lost" that is closer to finding itself at home with being than is the secure path of science. That is to say, this groping of "being lost" may be more honest about this indeterminate perplexity. Not always perhaps, but it may be.[9]

For there may be a "blindness" in metaphysical thinking that is blind because of excess rather than defect. It has come close to something excessive, and finds itself stunned and disoriented. It does not know for sure where it is, because it has been divested of its conceptual securities. It is blinded in the thought that tries to think beyond the categories that make being determinate. The excess of the indeterminate harasses and makes insomniac its thinking. I suggest that this may be a more radical activation of metaphysical thinking than the architectonic system that emerges at the end of the secure path of science. The enigma was there but covered with majestic con-

---

8. Recall Kant's dismissal of the skeptics (ibid., Aix) as "a species of nomads" of which, happily for Kant, there are few.

9. See "Being at a Loss: On Philosophy and the Tragic," chapter 2, *Perplexity and Ultimacy*.

ceptualization, and now it returns when the self is stripped of the grandeur of the architectonic system. The mind is unhoused again, evicted from the artificial palace of its concepts, and made to wander, be on the way. It finds its way in blindness by a new groping, in a light that is dark in its excess.

Am I imposing on Kant a consideration extrinsic to his scheme? Not necessarily. For this sense of thinking, on the other side of systematic science, can be suggested by Kant's three postulates of God, immortality, and freedom. These ideas, I think, induce metaphysical perplexity as beyond determinate curiosity and secure univocal answers. Our thinking about them is empty if not continually nourished by astonishment.

Thus, once having entered into the ordeal of skepticism, no longer can we naively think of *God* as the *ens realissimum*. Think here of Descartes' evil genius as the negative antipode to the postulate of God as good. This, I know, is the hyperbole of skepticism. It is not a mad thought, but a raising of the question if all thought is mad, unknown to itself. What can science do to put to rest the sinister possibility of the evil genius? What if rational science is a metaphysical swindle? How to deal with this perplexity? Will any science help us? What if the same agonizing perplexity must be brought to bear on the thought of God, the agapeic other, not the malign other that is the evil genius? Is not metaphysical thinking incited by this, but into a mindfulness that is also beyond the competence of every system of scientific concepts? Who has a geometry of God? Is not philosophy as science helpless? But is metaphysical thinking exhausted?

Consider the soul's *immortality*. Suppose that, instead of analyzing the classical arguments, we rethink the meaning of astonishment before being, in light of the marvelous singularity of a life. Think now of Dostoevski on the morning of his first death. He was sentenced to death for political conspiracy. He was halfway into death, on the verge of execution, tilted over the brink of nothing. There was no geometry of death to help. But he was suddenly reprieved, brought back from death, resurrected to life again. The sweetness of the morning air struck him, the song of morning birds, the sky. He was stunned into marveling at the sheer fact of being. This is the resurrection of agapeic astonishment. But it is experienced in a blinding and a groping. Will systematic science ever do justice to what is communicated in this stunning and resurrection? Where is the geometry of life? And yet metaphysical thinking is not finished. It has barely begun. Perhaps thought may even sing being's otherness.

Turn to *freedom*. Can we completely subject freedom to rational necessity? Is there not something strange about the idea of a system of freedom (such as Schelling sought, for instance)? Does not Kant's own categorical imperative show a will to identify freedom with rational necessity, as if he hankered for a geometry of freedom too? But freedom is grounded in an indeterminate original power of self-articulation. And is this original power as indeterminate within the autonomous control of the self? Is it not given to the self from the outset, even before it is a determinate self at all? What source gives this indeterminate opening in selfhood itself? The self does not first give it to itself, for it is a self in virtue of being given that power. The source of autonomy is other than autonomy. Is this source subjected to system? Is the very indeterminacy of freedom itself not outside all system, as in excess of all science? For if rule, law, regulation are determinations of the indeterminate, the indeterminacy of free power is itself *outside* all determinate systems. Original freedom is beyond the law. This, by the way, is also true of evil: a negative otherness that resists complete incorporation into any rational system.[10] In a word, original freedom suggests an enigmatic indeterminacy of being that provokes our metaphysical perplexity.

God, freedom, death and deathlessness, all incite a perplexity that points beyond science, system. And yet that perplexity energizes mindfulness in a genuinely metaphysical mode: thought trying to think being's otherness in excess of univocal categories. One might claim that metaphysics is nourished by such an excess of thought beyond science, contested in its security by the excess of being itself as beyond determinate thought. This is metaphysics that wanders from the secure path of science because it is beckoned along another pathless way. This is metaphysics without method, and without guarantees.

One might also say—with a bow to Shestov—that Dostoevski's underground man is, in certain respects, a more radical metaphysician than Kant. He takes the critique of pure reason to an extreme of skepticism that makes Kant look tame. Kant, we suspect, was too secure on the path of science to expose himself too long to such extremities of perplexity. The underground man has a sour honesty about this otherness to rational science. Admittedly, his exposure to science has also stripped him of agapeic astonishment; this has degenerated into a bitter, spoiling skepticism. There is no help for this bitterness of being, outside of the renewal of agapeic astonishment. But there is also no secure path to this renewal, no method and no system.

Metaphysics and Transcendental Thought

The happening of transcendence is shaped in the between, where mind's self-transcending and the transcendence of being in its otherness meet. The meaning of this community of transcendence exceeds complete determination in terms of a univocal problem and its solution. The Kantian view, as we saw, grows out of a skepticism regarding being-other as transcendent, a skepticism that is one possible development of erotic perplexity. Responding to this perplexity, it turns back to mind's self-transcendence in the belief that

---

10. See *Beyond Hegel and Dialectic*, chapter 4, for detailed discussion.

what falls within the horizon of mind's determination is amenable to methodical, rational guarantee. We must dwell further with this.

In this line of thinking there is a continuation of the Cartesian turn from being-other to self-being as providing the Ariadne's thread through the labyrinth of equivocal being. In more technical terminology, the questions of being-other as transcendent and of transcendence (in a sense previously held to be irreducible to self-being) become redefined in terms of human mindfulness as self-transcendence. Kant's response to metaphysical skepticism is to develop what he calls a transcendental philosophy.

Transcendental here does not mean what it means in medieval metaphysics—namely, a rational treatment of being, one, truth, good, perhaps beauty. These latter were held to be distinctive universals that apply to all that is, not generals/universals that apply to definite kinds of beings. With Kant the *transcendental* passes to the side of self-being, which provides the foundation for the categories of intelligibility. This foundation also claims to provide for correlates to the ertstwhile transcendentals, like being, truth, one, good. The equivocity of being becomes defined in terms of the mediating power of mind itself as transcendental—namely, as providing the basic condition of the possibility of being coming to manifestation as intelligible. Put concisely: being is intelligible because mind makes it intelligible. The sense of being-other as intelligible for itself and through itself, pervasive in ancient and medieval metaphysics, is made subordinate to this transcendental hegemony of mediating mind.

And yet for all this, the question of being-other as transcendence is not definitively laid to rest, nor indeed is the question of mind's own self-transcendence. Kant offers a critical philosophy concerned with the question of knowing. Can the question of being be suspended? How could it be? For knowing is a *being* mindful; it is a becoming mindful of what is, of being as intelligible. There is no way to talk about knowing apart from being. What of the claim that knowing makes itself possible—mindfulness provides the conditions of its own possibility? In this vein Kant will talk about knowing as understanding only what is constructed after its *own* plan; about reason as finally dealing with nothing but *itself*; about mind as making nature answer questions of mind's *own* devising; about the order of appearances we entitle nature being impossible to be thus, or to be known thus, did not *we*, or mind, not first put this order there.

I agree that it is tautologously true that knowledge of being is not possible without knowing; hence obviously a certain mindfulness is a condition of the possibility of knowing being. How, in Heaven's name, could one know being outside of *knowing* being? Idealism saw this platitudinous truth as a great revolutionary breakthrough, but it tells us almost nothing. The complexity of what is involved in this mindfulness calls for further interpretation. And undoubtedly idealism does provide us with significant interpretations, not all of which are to be entirely jettisoned. But one crucial presupposition is present throughout, a result of this epistemological platitude—namely, that *mind* occupies *the privileged position* in the mediated cognition of being. The self-transcendence of mind comes to dominate the mediation, hence determination, of being in the between, to the subordination of being-other in its transcendence. Not only will knowing here claim to make itself possible, but it essays to conceptualize being and the between completely, and indeed its own self-transcendence.

I deny that knowing does make itself possible in this unsurpassable sense. It is rather made possible by the *being* we are. It is made possible by the original power of being that makes us to be the beings we are. This original power does not belong to us, as ours. We are not only possibilized, but actualized as beings of self-transcendence, by a more originary process of coming to be that gives the between in its irreducible plurality. That process first communicates a sense of this giving of coming to be in the agapeic astonishment that marks our mindfulness as metaphysical. This means that we do not first make ourselves possible; we are made possible by a source of being other than ourselves. There is, if you like, a heteronomy prior to autonomy. We are made possible as coming to be, and as coming to be mindful, by an origin prior to the original self or the transcendental ego.

I am not saying that philosophy's critical side is to be neglected, but this side does not always have to be formalized. Nor does it answer for the fulness of what is at stake in the question of being; nor indeed in the question as to what makes possible the self-transcending of mindfulness itself. Kant himself entirely prescinds from this latter question.[11] Transcendental critique, in its elevating into primacy of self-mediation, is finally self-defeating if it fails to go into the question of deeper origin. It becomes an easy step to begin to define transcendence in terms of the circle of cognitive immanence. And though we seem to gain in self-knowing, really we renege on the challenge coming from the transcendence of being-other. Even the gain can turn into a contraction: self-knowing becomes a self-circling self-transcendence in the closure of immanence, not a free openness in the between, opening to being-other as giving itself there.

Admittedly, Kant's critical impulse can be said to be marked by its own equivocity. In a word, the vector of transcendence works on, after all the epistemological strictures and qualifications. Kant is explicit in his honesty that the impulse to metaphysics will never be silenced. In all the scholastic architectonic there is still, in my view, a tortured thinker of transcendence, trying to find a way out of the prison house of immanence that idealistic categories finally create. The intermediate character of the impulse to metaphysics is equivocally appropriated by Kant. This impulse seems inevitably to lead to

---

11. *Critique of Pure Reason*, Axvii: "For the chief question is always simply this:— what and how much can the understanding and reason know apart from all experience? not:—how is the faculty of thought itself possible."

failure, and yet despite the failure, it cannot be obliterated. In his unique way Kant tries to turn this failure into a different success, and to find *other, noncognitive* ways to transcendence. This is an equivocal attitude to *"metaphysics"* that he bequeathed to thinkers like Jaspers and Heidegger.

Metaphysical Thinking and Hegelian Idealism

There is another important response to this equivocity that, far from conceding the paradoxical failure/success of "metaphysics," proceeds to claim a different "success." This is historically most evident in Hegel's response to Kant's antinomies. The antinomies are formulated in the context of an expectation of univocal intelligibility. That is, the "big questions" regarding the world's origin, the simplicity of substance, freedom, and necessity, God as the absolute necessary being—all are treated as determinate problems with determinately formulable solutions. What Kant claims to show is that *two* contradictory solutions can be justified. The one determinate problem leads to two opposite determinate solutions, each of which has as much reason on its side as the other. Put otherwise, we reach a new critical formulation of the ancient skeptical problem of equipollence. There is an impasse relative to opposite determinate solutions. There is a situation of undecideablility, hence an aporia with respect to a single triumphant answer to the metaphysical problem, say, of origin.

What has happened here is the following. There is first a reduction of metaphysical questions such as they appear to agapeic astonishment; they have become problems, determinate difficulties, such as should be amenable to any univocal scientific treatment. As problems, they feed the expectation that there is one determinate, univocal solution. Instead *two* equally justifiable determinate solutions seem to result. This reveals that something is not quite right. Either the problems are meaningless, or the attempted solutions spurious, or perhaps there is inherent equivocity in metaphysics itself, against which henceforth we must inoculate ourselves with the critical *pharmakon*.

All these responses, I think, degrade the nature of a metaphysical perplexity into a determinate problem. In fact, the skeptical side of this perplexity has a deeper meaning than a mere negative, to be obliterated with the production of a secure univocal answer. The antinomies show an equivocity appearing with respect to determinate mind and intelligibility. And this equivocity may serve to renew the opening of perplexity beyond determinacy, and hence indirectly to mediate a way to renew the agapeic perplexity that opens mind to being in its transcendent excess. In all fairness to Kant, I believe his thinking contained something of this indeterminate opening, but he had a bad conscience about it, since it could not yield the determinate scientific cognition he so craved. He was caught between a determinate science of categories and an indeterminate transcendence that could not be stilled. The archaic "groping" could not be defeated. In fact, Kant's movement from critique to critique indicates that his anticipation of completeness always proved premature. Kant was honest enough to allow the indeterminate perplexity to surface again, as he "groped" further.

Hegel understood the degrading of self-transcendence that follows, if we simply remain frozen before the antinomies. Mind becomes the stiff *Verstand*, the analytical understanding that fixes into clear-cut and rigid oppositions. We forget the energy of transcendence that, in the first instance, shapes the differentiation and identification as active dynamic processes. Hegel saw the energy of self-surpassing mind at work even in the Kantian breakdown of metaphysical thought. This breakdown was prelude to a more inclusive breakthrough. That is, dialectical thinking deals *negatively* with the fixity of concepts of the *Verstand*. It deals *affirmatively* in mediating their differences and opposition. It deals *speculatively* with an affirmative breakthrough that thinks the togetherness of the opposites. Take, for instance, Hegel's dialectic of finite and infinite. Applied to the self-transcending of mindfulness, this shows that it is impossible to fix a final and unsurpassable univocal limit. There is always more. We are already in the space of this more: an infinitude of self-surpassing comes to emergence in the finite itself. This is a rebirth of a sense of the openness of transcendence in minding itself, a renewal of the restless perplexity that initiates, fertilizes, and sustains the metaphysical quest.

With Hegel, however, what we find, I believe, is a *rebirth of erotic perplexity*, and moreover, rebirth in the context of the primacy of transcendence understood as *self*-surpassing. This is the legacy of the Kantian internalization of the *transcendental* in mindfulness itself. That is, the perplexity is appropriated in the light of a confidence in the power of thought to *determine itself*. The self-surpassing of thought is not seen as, in part, shaped by a gift from being-other. It is purely within the power of thought's own immanent resources to determine itself as transparently and comprehensively as possible. The purest form of the erotic perplexity in Hegel becomes the pure energy of absolutely self-determining thinking. This is said to overcome the indefiniteness of its own beginning by progressively articulating itself to the point of complete self-determination, wherein all transcendence has been made entirely immanent.[12]

---

12. Kant stood against traditional metaphysics, which he understood as an a priori knowing of substance and transcendent beings. We could say that the dogmatic metaphysicians were *univocalists of transcendence* who produced the death of metaphysical perplexity. But Kant sought a new *critical univocity* through the transcendental unity of apperception. Hegel and the idealists give us a new *dialectical univocity* in pure self-determining thinking. I credit Kant with ending in a fertile equivocity, but Hegel sees this as a mere dualism to be dialectically *aufgehoben*; the doubleness is to be overcome in a totalizing unity. And yet both privilege thought thinking itself, Hegel less ambiguously, Kant more equivocally. (After all Kant says: "reason is occupied with nothing but itself," *Critique of Pure Reason*, A680, B708; see also Axx where he explicitly says: "In the field [of pure reason] nothing can escape us. What reason

Instead of Kant's enigmatic, equivocal, yet deep failure/success, we find here a renewed confidence in speculative philosophy, carried on a critically recharged surge of erotic perplexity that has faith in its own power to mediate every skeptical impasse, and to overcome, in a higher dialectical coincidence of opposites, all the equivocities of being and mind. In addition, this rebirth of erotic perplexity retains a faith in the logic of determinacy. Our lack of an answer at the beginning of erotic perplexity will be progressively overcome by a process of dialectical articulation. This will be said to culminate in a system of logical categories in which the essential intelligibility of all being will be made manifest.

There is a logic of *determinate negation* at work here, and so also the legacy of the univocal sense of being. This is what I mean. To be is to be determinate; but to be is to come to be; hence to be is to come to be determinate. The coming to determinacy is a process of transcendence, not emergent out of an excess of plenitude, but out of an initial lack of determinacy. Negation provides the power to pass from indefiniteness to determinacy. The eros of perplexity appears as the energy of a process of determinate negation, which, through negation of what is now, constitutes a more fully intelligible determination. The process passes all the way to complete self-determining intelligibility. It completes itself in the overcoming of the negative, which is the complete internalizing of otherness and transcendence.

Put otherwise, self-transcendence, in dialectical interplay with what is other, ultimately circles around itself on the way to absolute wholeness. Or, put otherwise again, the whole becomes an absolutely self-mediating circle of transcendence within which all otherness is sublated. Then the real result is that there is no between; there is no transcendence finally; there is the absolute as thought thinking itself in its other; but the other is thought again thinking itself, hence in the end there is no real otherness either. The excess of plenitude that gives the beginning, that sustains the between, and that outlives every completion in the middle and every closed circle of concepts, is occluded.

As I interpret it, Hegelian idealism makes a dynamic circle of erotic perplexity that surpasses its own initial perplexity into a completely determinate science of logical categories. One should not underestimate the rich complexity of Hegel's science of logic. These categories are not mere abstractions, but the issue and the carriers of the energy of mindfulness itself as a process of articulation and transcending. Hegel's logic is not intended as a static system, but as inherently mediated through and through. Nevertheless, the form

---

produces entirely out of itself cannot be concealed, but is brought to light by reason itself immediately the common principle has been discovered.") In both thinkers, and because of this privilege, there is the danger of the closure of transcendence, the closing off of thinking from transcendence.

of the system as a whole is that of self-mediation. Thought is absolutely autonomous, purely self-mediating—self-mediating, even in interplay with transcendence as other. This otherness is never the final position; it is always internalized into the circle of immanence at the end.

In that sense Hegel too is an heir of the Cartesian notion of doubt as a negativity that will negate itself. He is not an heir of the ancient *thaumazein* that is deepened but never finally dispelled. His system evidences the modern obsession to turn philosophy into a science. This science, it will be claimed, is one of purely immanent categories. It will be produced by perplexity become doubt, by doubt become determinate negation, which will overcome itself by negating itself, and so positively determining itself. The process of surpassing partial determinations will fall to the self-determination of thought, which contains within itself all previous determinations. Hence Hegel will claim in the *Phenomenology* to have finally surpassed philosophy as the search of wisdom and made philosophy into actual science or *Wissenschaft*.

The seeming hubris of the claim ought not primarily to worry us now. The hubris itself is based upon a degrading of agapeic astonishment into erotic perplexity, which is then said to be completed through a certain dialectical logic, whereby what is other to thought is always made a subordinate or penultimate moment to thought returning to itself, to thought being completely at home with itself in its own self-produced categorial determinations. I stress there is no degrading per se in erotic perplexity. Rather the degrading occurs when perplexity forgets or distorts its origin, when henceforth mind claims complete autonomy, hence feeds the questionable faith in mind itself as inherently self-completing and as itself true to the whole, indeed faith in itself as simply the truth of the whole.

The completeness claimed by Hegel's system was taken to heart by almost all of his successors, including those most vehement in their wish to destroy Hegelianism. This acceptance of the claim that Hegel's system represents the completion and culmination of Western metaphysics is pernicious. It is pernicious because it is false to metaphysical thinking as nurtured by agapeic astonishment beyond all systems of science and categories. It is pernicious because it simply acquiesces in the untruth that Hegelian system covers all the ground, preempting any other possibility for metaphysics. It is then doubly pernicious, because this acquiescence seems to legitimate a full frontal onslaught on the task of authentic metaphysics and mediately on the whole history of Western thought. Hegel's speculative philosophy is uncritically accepted as the *ne plus ultra* of Western metaphysics, whether transcendental in the pre-Kantian or Kantian sense.

Note I am not now accusing Hegel of being pernicious, but his uncritical critics who invoke Hegel to reprieve themselves from the authentic task of metaphysical thinking. Not only is all of this untrue to the tradition of metaphysics; but there is a different obliviousness of the truth of the metaphysical questions themselves, fostered in the element of agapeic astonishment, and not in any system or history. These questions are never finished, because of the ever-old and ever-new elemental astonishment, and because being-other as transcendent may always rupture any closed circle of categories. These critics of the Hegelian speculation do not renew metaphysical thinking. Too often they continue the degradation of perplexity, without either the greatness of Hegel's thought, or the astonishment that would genuinely renew thinking about transcendence. We must renew thought about transcendence rather than run away from metaphysics. Nor must we run away from dialectic.

Metaxological Metaphysics and Born-Again Perplexity

To what do we turn now? We cannot just determine the overdetermined excess of being as plenitude, for this would be to objectify its nonobjectifiable transcendence. It would be to forget the festive agape of being and to betray the between. To struggle against this amnesia, we need metaxological metaphysics.

What do I mean? Once again I call notice to a twofold exigency here. *First*, thought must remain true to the call of truth that emerges in its own self-transcendence. It must be consistent and coherent with this self-transcendence. Thinking mediates with itself in its mediation with what is given to be in the between. This self-mediating power partly answers to the self-determination of the erotic perplexity, discussed above. But then, and *second*, thought must always, and just in its self-transcendence, think what is other to itself, think it as other. If necessary, it must abrogate its own forms of thought, if the truth of transcendence as other makes such a demand on it. This is especially relevant to what is manifest in agapeic astonishment.

I would argue that Hegelian dialectic privileges the first exigency of thought mediating with itself, and offers only a subordinate role to the second exigency of thinking of what is other to thought. Hegelian thought seeks to overreach what is other, and in this dialectical transcendence make the other part of the process of thought thinking itself. By contrast, metaxological metaphysics renews the thought of the other as not dialectically subsumable in that sense. We reach out to what is other in self-transcendence, but there is in agapeic mind a transcendence different to that of erotic perplexity that wills finally and always to return to self.[13]

Metaxological metaphysics is plurivocal, and not just univocal. I tend to agree with Peirce's praise for what he sees as the "multiform argument" of

---

13. See "Agapeic Mind," chapter 4 in *Perplexity and Ultimacy*. Here I might say I do not completely agree with Levinas's strong contrast between what he calls *ontology* as a philosophy of power and what he calls *metaphysics* as open to transcendence. See my essay on Levinas in *Routledge History of Philosophy*, vol. 8, *Continental Philosophy in the 20th Century*, ed. Richard Kearney (London and New York: Routledge, 1994), 156–68.

the medieval thinkers.[14] He contrasts this with the desire for *one* argument of post-Cartesian philosophers. The current term for the latter approach is *foundationalism,* which tries to deduce all the categories of being from one principle. I agree with the antifoundationalist criticism of the univocalization of being, but do not think that this precludes an other thinking of ground, origin, foundation. "Multiform argument" is demanded by our place in the between, where we must be true both to the self-transcendence of mindfulness and the otherness of being in its own pluralized forms.

This plurivocity is not mere equivocity. Quite to the contrary, equivocity and skepticism are spurs to the further thinking of being and intelligibility. They do not justify us at all in relativistically falling asleep before a perplexity that eludes us. Instead they incite thought to a renewed restlessness. For there can be an equivocal nonanswer—and it is not uncommon in current philosophy—that *exploits* perplexity, even as it betrays it. Such equivocal thinking uses the indeterminate as an *excuse* to slip and slither and slide away from the hardest questions.

By contrast, I think that while we may founder on those questions, nevertheless there may be a greatness in the honesty that faces them in all their intractability. This plurivocity of metaphysical thinking is dialectical, but not in Hegel's sense. Hegelian dialectic is initially open to many ways of saying being, but *in the end* the many ways are included in the one overarching way of the logic of self-mediation. Against this, the plurivocity of metaxological metaphysics takes up Aristotle's *to on legetai pollachōs,* but the manyness is not the dialectical prelude to the reinstatement of total oneness. We must open dialectic to the doubleness implied by its own *dia.* This is the doubleness of metaphysical thinking as born in agapeic astonishment, carried by erotic perplexity, made determinate in terms of its specification in determinate thoughts and categories of being, mind, and intelligibility, but never reduced to the self-determination of that erotic perplexity. The excess given in the beginning sustains the passage through the between and points beyond the between to nonobjectifiable transcendence. This otherness of the *dia* remains in the end, and we cannot close this *dia* into the circle of a *monas,* thought thinking itself.

None of this implies any repudiation of determinate cognition. The latter is absolutely essential. To refuse to be as determinate as possible is to betray the self-transcending power of mind. The world as a between is inhabited by a plurality of determinate entities that deserve the greatest attention, just in their astonishing determinate particularity. Mind would not be agapeic did it not go towards the particularity of beings. This is part of the great power of science.

---

14. "On Some Consequences of Four Incapacities," in *Philosophical Writings of Peirce,* selected and edited with an introduction by Justus Buchler (New York: Dover, 1955), 228–29.

Yet granting this great power, there are questions that still exceed its proper competence. I am not talking about academic textbook puzzles but about the human being as struck into questioning at the edge of all scientific rationalizing. There can be nothing anonymous or neutral about being thus struck. This is why the very selfhood of the philosopher is at stake in a way that is never quite the case in science. The stakes of perplexity are different in philosophy, for its mode of questioning cannot be completely objectified.

We might say that in scientific questioning we seek to be detached from the idiosyncrasy of selfhood, and to pose as determinate a question as possible. The singular I of living mindfulness becomes the anonymous one of univocal mind, scientific consciousness in general. One represents univocal mind, anonymously the same for every rational consciousness, in search of a univocal answer to a univocal curiosity. Philosophy, by contrast, calls for a transformation of selfhood, energized in a new mode of perplexity, which is not just a univocal curiosity about this thing or that thing. It is a kind of indeterminate wondering that may extend to the whole of what is, and indeed to the possibility of nothing. It may extend to the good of being itself, facing the specter of nihilism whereby being is rendered worthless. In other words, the "objects" of philosophical perplexity are not univocal, determinate, objectifiable themes. Nor can the "results" of philosophical thinking be treated thus, be packaged thus. This indeterminate perplexity is the very self-transcending energy of human thinking. It was the ceaselessness of this that tortured Kant, even when he believed he had finally laid it to rest in the system and its categories.

Hence metaxological metaphysics calls for what I call a *second perplexity*, beyond all determinate knowing. Astonishment before being-other is renewed, but thinking also finds itself perplexing to itself. Thought may try to think itself in this perplexity but, contra Kant and especially Hegel, it finds itself *escaping itself* again and again, escaping its own comprehensive grasp in this effort to think itself. When it thinks itself, its thinking of itself again escapes its just accomplished thought of itself. Something other to itself is at work in itself. Its own inward otherness is nonobjectifiable, and hence escapes its own determinate thoughts, even its self-determining thinking.

In this second perplexity, thought thinks itself as other to itself. Thus, in one respect, this second perplexity can regard the enigmatic power of self-reflexivity. Thought floats on a mystery, and on itself as its own inward enigma. *Floats* is not quite right: it is in the mystery; it is mysterious. Thought is not now seen as a problem, univocally or dialectically determinable. It is a mystery, as inexhaustible indetermination.[15] The second indeterminate perplexity tries to articulate this. I am in this enigma, involved in it, participant in it.

---

[15] On Gabriel Marcel's sense of problem and mystery, see my essay on Marcel in *Routledge History of Philosophy,* vol. 8, 131–43.

Thinking exceeds thought, exceeds every determinate thought. There is no thought adequate to thinking. There is always something more, transcendent to the latter.

But it is not just perplexity about thought itself that is here at stake. What is other to thought also induces the second perplexity, often more insistently. Thus the second perplexity is especially called forth when we confront what Jaspers calls "boundary situations" (*Grenzsituationen*).[16] Questions at the boundary are not just questions about the limits of science, though they are that too. They are questions on the limit of determinate cognition, on the edge, *simpliciter*. For instance, death is most obviously a boundary situation. But there is no answer to death, because there is no determinate univocal concept that would put this event within an objective rational whole. Rather this event puts all objective rational wholes into question, and yet the genuine philosopher has to continue to think, despite the severe strain put on the ideal of rational completeness. If we burst out of the system of scientific rationality, philosophy does not end at this. A more authentic philosophizing can then begin. Metaphysics is not exhausted by the rationalistic scholasticism of the Wolffian school or any rationalistic science of being, such as Kant attacked. Rather it feeds on the indeterminate perplexity that takes us to the boundary and that is more radically energized in encounter with the boundary. In a sense metaphysics really only begins at the limits of science.[17]

A different kind of thinking has to take place at the boundary. The boundary is not just spatially "out there"; it is encountered by being in the between; the limit is a liminal place of crossing and crisscrossing. You might object that in dwelling on death, I have deserted life. But that is not my point at all. Quite the opposite, death is thought here with some view to renew the marvel of being. Beyond scientific determination we need what elsewhere I have called *posthumous mind*.[18] Posthumous mind implies a rebirth of astonishment before being, beyond life and death. Let me try to explain.

I need to call upon metaphysical imagination in this following thought-experiment. Imagine I am dead—as I will be, if this is read some years into

---

16. See my essay on Jaspers in *Routledge History of Philosophy*, vol. 8, 143–155.

17. I believe Kant had an intimation of this second perplexity in his restless movement beyond each critique, each time thinking that he was finished. Hegel had some sense of it, but tried to determine it completely. Nietzsche was aware of it, though he expressed it episodically and unsytematically and in the equivocities of aesthetic rhapsody. Husserl had a sense of it, but not directly with respect to being, but with respect to knowing, of which, however, he wanted a new science of science. See also Lev Shestov in the last part of *Athens and Jerusalem*, translated and introduced by Bernard Martin (Athens: Ohio University Press, 1966), with respect to what Shestov calls the second dimension of thought.

18. *Philosophy and its Others*, e.g., 278ff.

the future. But I suppose I am dead, and can look at being from beyond the fret and fever. I would have nothing to gain, nothing to lose. I would look at being without ulterior motivation. I would not look on it for myself. I would want to see its otherness as other. I would want to be truthful, for no other reason than the willingness to be truthful. Such would be entailed by posthumous honesty: a willingness to let the truth of other-being emerge for itself. Now imagine further that I come back from the dead, let us say after a hundred years. I would be beyond being as first lived in the happening of the between. Suppose I look upon being from beyond life, beyond death. Since I look on being from beyond death, and look on it for the truth of its otherness, might not my mind be agapeic? For I am imagining that I behold being from its otherness; I go towards its otherness as other, and I have no reason to interfere with it.

Would this mindfulness be objective mind, in the sense of just being neutral and indifferent? If it is agapeic, the answer must be no. I am imagining that I have come back after death, looking a *second* time, free from the urge to impose my will on being, yet released to see what is good in being for itself, and not just for me. As thus posthumous, agapeic mind would be love of being in its intrinsic good. And if being does not so appear, would not life be metaphysically valueless, ontologically worthless?

What is the point? I hear your impatient interjection. My point is really now to ask the question: If being would so appear from beyond, is it not *now* so from within, as we live it, though now we cannot see it so? And if we cannot now see it so, are we living a condition of metaphysical nihilism, though we do not know it? But you object: Does not this metaphysical imagination of posthumous mind mean that the eye from beyond death will look on life, as now lived, as worthless? I do not think this will be the case, if posthumous mind is agapeic. Quite to the contrary—as we saw with Dostoevski when he was called back to life—the very marvel of being as elementally good will strike us, strike home to us. Instead of vengeance against time, we will seek to be able to love time, affirm and celebrate it as good.

For when we come back from the dead thus, we would do so to find again the things we loved for their intrinsic, indeed unfathomable, goodness. This here was loved for itself; what was beloved in it escapes beyond all categorial determination; we come back to life when we seek the unfathomable goodness of the elemental "to be." I am suggesting that the metaphysician has to be jolted into this displaced mindfulness of being, displaced in the between to be able to think about the enigma of the happening of the between, the beings in it, the mindful human being, displaced into thought about the fact that being is given at all, when there might be nothing at all. And, of course, metaphysical mind is not *now*, in fact, beyond death, but it can be the thinking that faces into death, and tries to think beyond death, not to escape life, but to refresh astonishment at the enigma of being at all, and the possibilty that simply to be is the ultimate metaphysical good.

Thus Socrates' description of philosophy as the practice of death need not be read nihilistically. Nietzsche's interpretation, seemingly insightful, misses. It is an oversight of death as the way of truth that may renew agapeic mindfulness of being as good. The practice of death might be posthumous mindfulness, which tries sleeplessly to be alert to the good of being, beyond my good, beyond the good as reduced to the good for-me. Such would be a ceaseless vigilance, or a listening to a call that says in praise of being: "It is good." The thought of nothing becomes the portal of the thought of being as "It is good."

If the practice of death can release agapeic mindfulness towards being, it also produces displaced mindfulness: dislocated, put off balance, wounded irremediably by suffering the rupturing otherness, made sick for the truth of being, homesick, not at-home even in being-at-home. This displacement is again indicated in Dostoevski's resurrection after being halfway over into death. He was never again at-home, and yet there was a deeper being-at-home in this not being-at-home. Perplexity before being is intensified, even at times to the point of torment, yet there slowly grows the mysterious consent of agapeic mind. The rupture of the between in impending death opens an abyss into possible nothingness; it also opens into a source of being that is beyond nothingness, renews the elemental joy in the plenitude of given being, or being as given, as a gift beyond all human measure.

The Others of Metaphysics—Art, Religion, and Science

I now want to remark on the significance of a certain affiliation, even in their difference, of metaphysics, art, and religion. For the idea of metaphysical thinking I propose is impossible to fit into any *progressivist* model of mind. Such models are pervasive in modernity, and perhaps exemplified by Comte's triadic unfolding of theology, metaphysics, positive science. On this view, religion and metaphysics are the fumbling precursors of positive science, necessary relative to the childhood and adolescent of the race, but now thankfully outgrown. We may study them as interesting relics, but we have no living stake in them. In some measure we are all heirs of Comte. We blanch at the accusation of *regression*. Thus we find such notions in thinkers as radically opposed as Marx and Nietzsche. Even critics of modern Enlightenment have not entirely escaped the progressivist model. Heidegger privileged the originary rather than the later, but even he subscribes to a *destined unfolding* from metaphysics to cybernetics *within* the epoch of Western reason—even though beyond the epoch's boundary, both before and after, a different possibility was given and might be rethought again.

Such progress away from metaphysics to science is tangential to the present view. Such progress only makes sense if mind's unfolding and deepening is determined by a telos of univocally determined cognition. History is not so determined, nor is mindfulness, nor is human life. Nor are agapeic astonishment and the second indeterminate perplexity about transcendence. These are over and above. They are *meta* in the double Greek sense of "above," and "within": beyond determinacy and yet at work in the midst of it. Thus, at the beginning, the truth of religious myth is not flubbed science. Mythic imagination and metaphysical perplexity are indeed not strangers. Myth offers images of transcendence, but is not univocally reducible to determinate science. The point is not determinate explanation, but the articulation and perhaps alleviation of metaphysical perplexity, perhaps the celebration of transcendence in its enigma. Of course, the univocal mind will reduce myth, not see the point. But the point is that there is no *the* point.

Nor need metaphysics be, again as Comte has it, a set of transitional abstractions on the way towards positive science. It is thinking in a different dimension to determinate science. There is no replacement of metaphysics in the alleged maturity of the last act, which inaugurates the glorious reign of positive science. There is a metaphysical thinking more mature than positive science. As suggested, the "big questions" of metaphysics are sometimes very like the surprising global questions children ask. We are often told to give up asking them.[19] What is required rather is a *rebirth* of mind *beyond* determinate science. The genuine metaphysian is a *born-again thinker*, born again in a different dimension of perplexity. What I mean is hinted at, for instance, in Socrates' nescience: I know nothing, he says; but this is a lie; Socrates knew an awful lot of determinate things; rather the nescience is in *another dimension*, beyond determinate knowing.

I cite a very revealing statement of Comte,[20] for it allows me to state a number of important points:

---

19. Arthur Fine tells we must give up asking these big questions, in those terms. He speaks of what he calls the natural ontological attitude. But there is nothing natural about this *natural attitude*. It expresses a kind of platitudinous, academic tolerance: live and let live, but please no metaphysics here. The condescension to metaphysics may not be as pervasive as in the heyday of positivism, but it still survives too widely, unless you identify *metaphysics* with its analytically emasculated version.

20. *Introduction to Positive Philosophy*, edited, with introduction and revised translation, by Frederick Ferré (Indianapolis: Hackett, 1988), 38–39. See Paul Oppenheim and Hilary Putnam, "Unity of Science as a Working Hypothesis," reprinted in *The Philosophy of Science*, edited by R. Boyd, P. Gasper, and J.D. Trout (Cambridge, Mass.: MIT, 1991), 424n45, which praises Comte's ordering of the sciences as "amazingly modern in many respects, as several contemporary authors recognize." It is interesting to compare Descartes' reductionistic view of astonishment to Comte's. In *The Passions of the Soul*, Part Two, section 73, Descartes says, and entirely in terms of the mechanics of movement of the "animal spirits": "Astonishment is an excess of wonder and it can never be other than bad."

Immense as are the services rendered to industry by science, and although according to the striking aphorism of Bacon—knowledge is power—we must never forget that the sciences have a yet higher and more direct destination, that of satisfying the craving of our minds to know the laws of phenomena. To feel how deep and urgent this craving is, it is sufficient to reflect for a moment upon the physiological effect of astonishment, and to recollect that the most terrible sensation we can experience is that which occurs whenever any phenomenon appears to take place in violation of the natural order that is familiar to us. This need of arranging facts in an easily comprehended order—which is the proper object of all scientific theories—is so inherent in our organization that, if we could not succeed in satisfying it by positive conceptions, we should have to return inevitably to those theological and metaphysical explanations that, as I explained in the last chapter, had their origin in this need.

Comte's reference to the identification of knowledge and power is important, for astonishment takes knowing or mindfulness outside our power. It strikes us out of an otherness, which Comte sees only as a violation, not as an opening. What he calls the "urgent craving" is the eros of perplexity trying to overcome its lack through determinate knowing. He suggests the terrible pain and violence of something that astonishes out of the natural order. Why should this be the most terrible sensation we can experience? Is it worse than physical violence, or death? Why should astonishment not spell the death of one mode of mind and the birth of another? Because for Comte there is to be none other than positive science, it is sheer death here. Comte does not become a metaphysician as a born-again thinker. There is satisfaction with the familiar order, and fear of the thought of the other. One thinks of Lucretius in the ancient world when he asserted: *non est mirabile*.

I detect an anxiety that we *backslide* to theology and metaphysics. I sense irritation, not to say alarm, with transcendence, as a threat to autonomy and the familiar sense of the natural order. How does this reflect the so-called rational openness of positive science? There is a fear of an *other dimension to thinking*. This fear leads to a stifling and loss of metaphysics. It is more widespread now than ever. This is why what I say about astonishment and perplexity will be hard to understand for many. They will have forgotten their first birth to being as mindfulness. But they will not have been reawakened from the sleep of determinate knowing. They will not have been reborn. They will not have the mindfulness that is *posthumous* to science. This posthumous mind will look like a ghost, something dead from the past. In fact, it is no dead ghost but the living spirit that, even though deathless, must be perennially resurrected and reborn.

Agapeic astonishment may come from anywhere, from any direction, at any time, to anyone, for any or no reason. There is no doctoral requirement that must be met before it offers its gift. We are all primally metaphysical in that sense. And, of course, it is also obvious that metaphysicians cannot turn their backs on determinate cognition, since part of their task is to make sense of this astonishment, the meaning of being as thus appearing, as well as the plurality of different responses possible in the middle of being. To think the extremities is not to forget the middle that must be traversed to think the extremes.

The second perplexity, the refreshed astonishment, mixes the eros and the agape of mind. To the extent that there has to be an exploration of the determinate articulations of mind and being, metaphysics must respect the determinate cognitions of science and common sense. To the extent that it opens itself to the extremities, it has an affiliation with other modes of naming transcendence, beyond reduction to any determinate cognition, such as religion and art. Determinacy without transcendence forgets the extremes; transcendence without determinacy forgets the finite middle. As a thinker of the between, the metaphysician must be mindful of both. To do justice to both determinate being in the middle and transcendence at the limit, a plurality of ways of saying may be needed.

Certainly there is no one way or specific method by which the rebirth of agapeic astonishment is given to the philosopher. There is something beyond mastery about it. Yet it has been given and humans have struggled to name it and say what it might mean. Religion and art can be two essential articulations of this astonishment. They are carriers of its promise. They can keep it alive in the sleep of quotidian familiarity. Astonishment dies in us when we seem to have interpreted being to our satisfaction and put it in its place. Being falls into invisibility just in its being made manageably intelligible. By comparison, religion and art can concretize the memory of the being-there of being, that is before and over and above this manageable intelligibility. They can resurrect thinking beyond determinate science, in the second dimension of perplexity, beyond the geometry of the intellect.

In illustration of my meaning, consider how the *appreciation* we bring to art shows an attentiveness to the work as other, and as good for itself. Appreciation, we might say, is a movement of self-transcendence that goes beyond self towards the goodness of the other as other. It is the death of the circle of immanence, and the birth of a vigilance in the space between self and other, beyond the self. Thus appreciation is akin to agapeic astonishment. Likewise, the transcendence of self involved in religious *worship* or *adoration* is a placing of oneself before the ultimate, a *praise* of the other without demand, a joy in the glory of the divine. Again the closed circle of immanent selfhood and thinking dies; one is reborn to a different mindfulness in the space beyond self, the space of the middle between humanity and the divine. Again I think the kinship with agapeic astonishment is evident. Appreciation, admiration, adoration, praise are kin of the posthumous mindfulness of the second perplexity beyond determinate cognition.

I recall Aristotle once more when he singles out myth with respect to metaphysics, and both with respect to marveling. It is clear that pre-Socratic philosophy, while raising the question of being and seeking to give a *logos* of *to on*, did not shun the power of *muthos* in so doing. Nor is it incidental that the father of *logos*, Parmenides, spoke in a philosophical poem, which could equally be called the naming of a religious disclosure. *Muthos, logos, poiēsis* were not bureaucratically functionalized and separated. This is because the indeterminate perplexity, nurtured by the astonishment, can never be articulated in a totally determinate way; yet it has to be spoken and hence determined in some sense. It is also significant that the moments when Plato often resorts to myth are at the *extremities* of the *metaxu*, where *logos*, with its drift to fixed determination, might falsify the truth of what is appearing at the limit of the between. *Muthos* gives us a story of origins. Metaphysics too is a plurivocal saying of the origin, the *archē*; and yet the *archē* is not a thing, nor is it objectifiable. The second perplexity resurrects archaic astonishment before being. Hence its affiliation with religious celebration. There may even be a consent to being in this, a certain amen to the gift of being.

Ancient and medieval metaphysics understood the point by thinking of metaphysics as *theōria*. This notion is much misunderstood, when viewed in terms of the contracted concept of "theory," such as we find in post-Cartesian methodology. In the latter, "theory" is associated with the drive for determinate, univocal cognition. A "theory" offers a general hypothesis or model, that itself is as mathematically precise as possible, and that is to be determined as true, verified, in terms of evidence from sense experience or experimental data. A "theory" is merely a possible way of looking at things, until some more or less univocal evidence from objective reality is forthcoming to confer on the "theory" some probability of being true. "Theory" is an abstraction of mind from being as given, with the view to ordering the given, and perhaps to gain control over it. It implies a spectatorial viewpoint, letting us stand over being-other, intent on mastering it through the power of abstract concepts. "Theory" dominates the world through its "fruitful" abstractions.

Not necessarily so with *theōria*: the memory of its origins with the religious festival is essential. The *theōroi* were religious delegates sent by the city states to the games, which were themselves religious festivals, celebrations of the largess of being, largess evident in the great performances and deeds of outstanding humans. *Theōroi* were sent to enjoy the agape of being as ritualized in the religious festivals. There is a watching here, a being spectatorial, but it is a joyful vigilance; it is an entirely active mindfulness that represents the divine powers of consent and celebration. Festive being is an amen to being in its gift and largess. There is nothing abstract or alienated about it at all. To the extent that a metaphysician is a *theōros*, he too is called to this essentially joyful vigilance, this celebrating mindfulness of the ultimate powers, at play in the between.

Hegel understood the affiliation of art, religion, and philosophy, though his sense of the dialectical *Aufhebung* of the first two into philosophy is ambiguous. To the extent that the arresting enigma of beauty and God's transcendent mystery are subordinated to the determinate cognition of Hegel's logic, there is not the resurrection of the agapeic astonishment. Rather there is the claimed fulfillment of the erotic perplexity in a complete self-determining *logos*—Hegel's own science of logic. And yet, in that the energy of transcendence in art and religion continues to live on in philosophy's thinking, philosophy too expresses the second indeterminate perplexity. This is never completely determined, despite all explicit claims to the contrary. Hegel officially may make this claim, but the pathos and profundity of his best thought rises from the deathless astonishment before being, for this is impossible to entomb in the categories.

Heidegger's understanding of the matter is evident in his recalling us from calculative to meditative thinking. He invokes the kinship of the thinker and poet. He broke with Husserl's desire for a new science of science: philosophy *als strenge Wissenschaft*. This latter is not metaphysics, though Husserl, like Kant, saw it as the necessary prolegomenon to any authentic scientific metaphysics. But thinking is not science, not science of science. Nor is the poet a post-Kantian aesthete, a specialist of the aesthetic. The poet is sacerdotal. If the thinker thinks being, the poet names the holy. The poet serves to mediate the blessing of being, the thinker remains attentive to the communication of being.

While Heidegger sees himself as freeing thought from the prisonhouse of "theory," his invocation of the poet as the namer of the holy puts him back in the neighborhood of the religious festival, hence closer to the meaning resonating in the ancient word *theōria*. Heidegger is right to recall us to this different sense of thinking; he is wrong to imply that the history of metaphysics is the stifling of this thinking. There is an unmistakable rupture between the premodern and the modern sense of "theory," such as I have above indicated. The rupture is explicable first in terms of the dulling of the origin in agapeic astonishment; then its further dulling in terms of an erotic perplexity, taken over completely by doubting, doubt that defines thinking as a process of negation and determination; then in terms of a redefinition of erotic perplexity itself as the unstoppable drive to complete categorial cognition that would be master of being. Here, finally, erotic perplexity becomes will to power, not merely indifferent to, but hostile to the truth of agapeic astonishment.[21]

---

21. Heidegger is more ambiguous in his 1929 lecture "What is Metaphysics." But, say, in "The End of Philosophy and the Task of Thinking," written in 1964, metaphysics completes itself in the different sciences that deal with the different beings, and in cybernetics. Thus metaphysics shares in the same forgetfulness of the opening of truth and becomes immersed in the things given in the opening; metaphyics as "metaphysics of presence," so to say, prepares the opening for the sciences by making it the ground of completely determinate cognition. The opening remains unthought. I deny the historicist thesis about the essence of metaphysics necessarily leading to cybernetic science: agapeic astonishment and the second indeterminate perplexity are

Metaphysical Thinking and Being Between

If metaphysical thinking, as I claim, takes shape in the milieu of being, the question of transcendence has nothing to do with a leap out of being into the void, but with the deepest mindfulness of what is emergent in the middle itself. Again the double meaning of *meta* is relevant. "*Meta*" is being in the midst; "*meta*" is also reference to what is beyond, what is transcendent. Metaxological metaphysics must think the doubleness of this tension between being in the midst *and* being referred by self-transcendence to the transcendence of what is other, what is over and above.

I stress that vigilance to the signs of transcendence does not imply the reduction of transcendence to the between. There is a thinking about the beyond in the between itself. What gives the between surpasses the between, though we face towards it, in and through the between. Thus, what I called posthumous mind suggests a rebirth of thinking with respect to the meaning of being in its height and depth, in its spread over the middle, in our implication with being as a community of plurality. The rebirth of agapeic mind demands the articulate thinking of this community.

This is no easy matter. It means a rejection of the idealistic strategy whereby autonomous thought is tempted to impose its categories on appearing and hence only to see what it puts there itself. But the coherence of idealism is also its unraveling: for when thought only thinks itself, the emptiness is evident in its reduction of thought's other to the construction of a category. I think we need a complex realistic fidelity that does not dictate to being, but that puts itself honestly before it. This realistic fidelity makes us attentive to the between as the matrix of thought. We must not let the later conceptualizations cover over what comes to concrete nascence there.

In the middle we are on the way, to where we do not exactly know, from where we are unsure. Mindfulness comes in the middle, out of an enigmatic origin, in expectation of an uncertain end. Existential contingency cannot

---

beyond science at the beginning, and remain so at the end. It is the agapeic origin that is the giver of the opening, and what is given in the opening is the metaxological community of being. This is the between as the milieu of beings, the milieu that is also the milieu of human self-transcendence. For that matter, Heidegger's primary stress on *Angst* strikes me as privileging something closer to erotic perplexity than agapeic astonishment. Hence his focus on nothingness rather than being as plenitude. Hence what follows with respect to posthumous mind and born-again thinking differs significantly from what follows from Heidegger's anguished encounter with nothing. Perhaps the later Heidegger comes closer to agapeic astonishment, but if so I find his articulation of the matter to be riddled with equivocation, indeed sometimes to be unnecessarily evasive of the splendid simplicity of the agape of being. On Heidegger's historicist totalizing, also on *theōria*, see again *Beyond Hegel and Dialectic*, 43–55.

find its substitute in any purely objective system. Nor do we have an Archimedean point to survey the middle as a whole, or to overlook our wavering passage in it. We are amongst, and the density of being touches us; we are participants and intimate with being. As such we live from within what we try to think. But to think from within is hard; some reflective distance is needed; but absolute distance is impossible for us in the within of the middle. To remain true to our intimacy with being, and yet to gain reflective distance that does not distort, is a great struggle. We need an equilibrium beyond objectifying science and idiosyncratic individuality. We need a certain doubling of existential and systematic thinking.

Metaphysical thinking, thus conceived, cannot entirely escape a metaphorical dimension. This is especially evident with respect to the metaxological, and the reborn thinking of the second perplexity. Metaphor itself refers to the double of the *meta*. Metaphor is a carrier in the between; it ferries (*pherein*: to carry) us across a gap; or it is the carrier of transcendence; it is in the midst as *meta*, and yet an image of the *meta* as beyond, as transcendent. It is both determinate and indeterminate at once. It is neither one nor the other, but both in a manner that transcends univocal unity, sheer equivocity, and indeed a dialectic that reduces difference to mediated identity. There is a rich sense of indeterminacy at play in metaphor that functions as articulating a pluralized mediation, and a certain opening of transcending. Metaphysical metaphor is the carrier of agapeic astonishment and perplexed mindfulness in the middle. In Chapter 5 I will have more to say about metaphysics in relation to metaphor, analogy, symbol, and hyperbole.

I conclude this chapter with the following remarks. Metaphysics *does* often put a strain on language, seeming to make it other to so-called "ordinary" usage. It sometimes taxes language with an almost intolerable burden. If mindfulness has not been reborn to the second perplexity, bearing this burden will make no sense. For this rebirth makes restless the transcending of mind, with a questioning that will not stop short of the extreme, even though it must weary itself in search. In fact, it may turn out that there is nothing "ordinary" in the ordinary. The "ordinary" as a manipulable aggregate of determinate entities or happenings may be granted as a pragmatic abstraction, indispensable to our muddling through the twilight of the domesticated middle. But to mindfulness reborn in the second dimension of perplexity, there is the promise of a truth more ultimate. Across the middle a light has flashed, and now the "ordinary" looks dark; thinking reborn into second perplexity turns to the "ordinary" with a new astonishment, with a new groping unfamiliarity. Briefly, being was other, and is perhaps still other, despite the clouding over of transcendence.

And so born-again perplexity contests any taken for granted attitude to being. It puts us on trial; it provokes and challenges. The perplexities of being never yield a univocal answer, indeed resist being formulated as univocal problems. There is a constitutive ambiguity that remains. There is a constitutive openness that persists. To these perplexities we must return again and again. We never master or completly dissolve them. Yet if agapeic astonishment is not allowed to die, the perplexities are buoyed by the confidence that something *more* than insomnia, or threat, or despair may be offered.

We might say that there is both a wager and a promise in metaphysical thinking. In a way this whole work is a kind of wager. One ventures a thought, not quite sure of it, whence it comes, whither it will take one. One has to venture with a certain boldness or audacity. Even then, transcendence harasses us out of every hiding hole, every threadbare or superficial thought, every smug conceptual satisfaction. Even then, a promise is held out in the hazard of thought. That the world of the between is at all, is the wonder. We might say there is an ontological generosity to metaphysical thinking when it embodies the genuine self-transcending of agapeic mind. We wish to think beyond the mind that instrumentalizes. The middle is not given to us as a mere means; it is the place of a way, a passage. Agapeic mind passes towards what is offered in the middle, not simply for some conceptual return to itself, but because the being of the other offers itself for a celebrating, affirming thought. We think the meaning of being, because being in itself is most worthy to be thought.

Yes, we do think to alleviate our own perplexity, our sense of being at a loss, our sense of not being entirely at home in the middle. But not only that, and if only that, the thrust of self-transcendence is contracted. There is the promise in the hazard, promise that now and then is redeemed. I mean that there is a *being at home with being* beyond erotic perplexity, and that lifts perplexity out of its oppression by the burden of the mystery. The mystery does not burden, but lightens thinking. It is as if perplexity gives us a kind of metaphysical migraine, and nothing seems to lift it; it clouds the mind, maybe even crushes it. Yet we can come to mindfulness at home with being, and the metaphysical migraine is lifted; one's whole being is lightened. There is an agapeic mindfulness that is not just a grasp of something in particular, but an enlarged or deepened participation in being itself. We break through into participation in the community of being. Mindfulness is released to dwell more intensively in it. Being reborn to being, one says yes to our mindful community with being, and to its gift.

CHAPTER TWO

BEING AND UNIVOCITY

Prelapsarian/Postlapsarian Univocity

In this and the next three chapters, I will deal with the univocal, equivocal, dialectical, and metaxological senses of being. To isolate these from each other involves some abstraction, hence the current division of chapters is strategic to exposition. When dealing with one sense, reference to other senses will inevitably intrude. In this regard, these four chapters try to offer fuller and more articulate determinations of the indeterminate metaphysical perplexity just discussed. They form a community of approaches to the question: What does it mean to be?

My present focus is on the univocal sense and its diverse ways of privileging the notion of unity. There is no such thing as absolutely pure univocity, for this would be a unity totally devoid of mediation and exclusive of differentiation. Without the latter there would be no happening of the between, no determination of diversity among beings, no speaking about being, and no articulated knowing of anything. Absolutely pure univocity is a limit concept, only intelligible by abstraction from differences, and only articulable by reference to some sense of the interplay of identity and difference.

That said, there is no doubt that the notion of unity is indispensable to our efforts to make determinate sense of being. We will explore many expressions of this necessity throughout the work. Much of traditional metaphysics, I think, is defined by an *oscillation* between univocity and equivocity. This is coherent with the notion of pure univocity as an ideal abstraction. Nevertheless, this oscillation emerges from what we might call a prior *lived* univocity. That is, there is an immediacy to our initial immersion in being, but this is broken up with the dawning of our distinctive mindfulness, and especially its mode as rational self-consciousness. We are visited with a rupturing of our felt, lived kinship with being in its otherness. This immediacy of the community of being (ultimately in truth not univocal at all, but metaxological) is *aesthetic*. The world as given being is charged sensuous presencing, and we are present to this overdetermined presencing in our own flesh—the self as sensing, embodied being.

This is the metaphysical Eden: we are in the garden of being, at home in this rapturous univocity. This is, so to say, *prelapsarian* univocity. The dawning of mindfulness in the body, the emergence of a distinctive sense of self, brings differentiation and the loss of this metaphysical Eden. A sense of the equivocity of being makes an appearance. The self, as thinking about being, is set over against being as other. We might call this the fall into determinate knowing. The other is also set over against us. Being, beings, the world present themselves as enigmas, as ambiguous. As robbing us of the rapturous univocity of the metaphysical Eden, being as other may even present itself as possibly *hostile*. No longer home, we turn *against* it in knowing. We develop *our own rational univocity* to take away or mitigate the seeming threat of enigmatic being. Then we seek to reconstruct univocal being in rational categories. By such means we try to dispel the equivocity, to dominate the otherness over against us, to construct a rational surrogate for the lost Eden of rapturous equivocity. The result will be, so to say, *postlapsarian* univocity.

I am putting the point metaphorically, but it can be diversely developed. And let not the poststructuralist rush in with the snappish indictment: Metaphysical nostalgia! Let them not be so literalistic, so "logocentric." I plead for at least a show of patience. I still want to say that there is something at play in the between, which requires the idea of univocity. How so? There are beings in the between. There are happenings and occurrences, and these are articulated with some more or less determinate identity. The identity does not have to be frozen; yet things do take determinate form and articulated presence. We are perplexed at what is happening and seek to answer questions like: What is that? Why is that? Is that so?, and so on. And naturally, we seek an answer that is as distinct and illuminating as possible. We need to identify what is happening. We identify happening by noting its internal distinguishing marks, its differences, as well as the distinguishing marks that set it off from other happenings. The happening of being is not an ontological ooze, though there is impermanence. Happenings come to determination. The univocal sense of being is *indispensable* in identifying and distinguishing this coming to determination.

Clearly, then, the univocal sense is inseparable from the solid mindfulness of sound *common sense*. There would be no everyday world were things and occurrences not sorted according to their unities and identities. This is not to say that the universe of common sense is only a world of univocity. It is this and more. But it would not be a complex articulated milieu of meaningful happening were it not shaped according to the determinations of the univocal sense. A spade is a spade, and common sense insists on calling it a spade. Otherwise there is no everyday integrity to speech and doing.

Of course, there is more: there are spades and spades, as we say. Common sense univocity is canonized in Bishop Butler's adage: a thing is itself and not anything other. Common sense will agree. But it will *not* agree univocally to univocity; for there are spades and spades. The implication is: univocal things must not be always taken at face value; they are more, things are other; there is equivocity. In this other respect, common sense univocity can be a virtuoso of the nuance of the equivocal. It does not insist on a rigid choice between univocity and equivocity. "It all depends," it whispers with a sly wink.

This tolerance of common sense brings black despair to thinkers who would radicalize the sense of univocity. They would make it the sense most privileged to confer meaning on being. They would make it strict and rigorous, insist on self-coherence and precise determinacy, so as to dispel thoroughly the equivocities of being. Here metaphysical, mathematical, and scientific univocity make their appearance. And perhaps mathematical knowing is the embodiment par excellence of the univocal sense. Such knowing would be impossible without the notion of an ideal unit, an integer, relative to which complex rational operations of calculation can be performed. The number 1 is the number 1 and nothing but the number 1; there is only 1 number 1. The number 1 is not a little bit more, say, 1.000001, or a little bit less, say, .999. It is 1 and nothing but 1.

Nor is there ambiguity about sums of such univocal integers like 2 and 2 is 4. It is not more or less 4; it is 4 and nothing but 4. It is absolutely determinate in itself, and once mind enters the process of rational calculation, mind is ordered to a certain determined outcome. Mind is mathematically univocalized. It may make mistakes in calculation, but these are the faults of its waywardness. The mind has failed to be mathematically univocal. The matter itself, respected for itself, has no such faults, no such strayings into error. The outcome is without equivocity.

This is an ideal I know, and sheer univocity is evident for simple cases. There can be profound perplexities in the more complex cases, say with transfinite numbers, to say nothing at all about the status of nought. The ideal is still to be as univocal as possible, to overcome and dispel all equivocity as far as possible. Hence the Pythagorean horror at irrational numbers, numbers that resisted complete determination as an integral whole or ratio of such wholes. The ideal of rationality as identified with univocity seemed to have been violated.

The attraction of the ideal is understandable. Whatever is equivocal forces risk and decision and agonizing on us; it is linked with the chancy, the hazardous, indeed with the terror of freedom—that is, with our difference from immersion in the rapture of immediate univocity. The attractions of the univocal mind are those of an ordered, clear, methodical *mathēsis*, which yields well-defined results that are publicly communicable to all rational minds. These desiderata are the love and consolation of what Pascal call the *esprit géométrique*.

Ontological and Logical Univocity

The univocal mind, especially in the form of a calculative *mathēsis*, has been powerfully developed by modern science, and I will return to this. But first I want to consider some philosophical versions where univocal mind takes an ontological and logical form. Philosophers tend to be intolerant of the easy tolerance of common sense as it shifts, without any warning in the categorial lights, between univocity and equivocity. Philosophers too would radicalize univocal mind and in this radicalization conquer and transcend the equivocal in being. I cite some revealing instances.

Consider Parmenides, putative father of logic. He passes on the admonition of the goddess: judge with *logos*, *krinai de logoi*, be discriminate with respect to the *logos*. To be thus critical is to accept and to reject, to judge and to include, and if necessary to exclude. Parmenides is offered by the goddess a vision of pure being, which itself is identical with pure *noein*, pure thinking. This vision is revealed after a passage beyond the equivocations of becoming, which both is and is not. Becoming refuses to conform to univocal being; it is self-contradictory, itself and yet not itself, a spade and not a spade, a double and merely self-discordant happening, not real being at all.

Moreover, Parmenides must transcend the many, who are said to wander double-headed, *dikranoi*. This double-headedness is their easy tolerance that slips and slides between everyday univocity and equivocity. The vision of pure, eternal, univocal being, neither more here nor less there, absolutely homogeneous throughout, like a well-rounded sphere, stands counter to the equivocities of becoming and opinion. It also hints at the reconstitution of the lost Eden of the first immediate univocity. This single-minded reconstitution of the lost whole, absolute unity of being, is promised through philosophy itself.

We must not simplify. Despite all quarantines against the contagion of the equivocal, Parmenides is an equivocal metaphysician, and this too despite his being the father of univocal logic. The vision of the absolute unity is *given* to the philosopher at the end. It is not produced by his thought, or by thought thinking itself. There is a *revelation* made possible by the goddess. This gift is related to agapeic astonishment, and the reborn mind of the metaphysician. This cannot be fitted into any logic of determinate univocity, as we saw. Moreover, any such giving, even out of absolute unity, must be *beyond* univocal unity, for there to be any giving at all. Absolute unity cannot be univocal unity.

Plato is an heir of Parmenides, though he addressed the oscillation between univocity and equivocity in a more complex way. He knew there was no avoidance of difference, otherness, plurality. Moreover, these could not be determined as non-being, even if they could also not be determined in terms of the absolute univocity of the Parmenidean One. The influence of mathematics through Pythagoreanism is well known, again testifying to the lure of univocal *mathēsis*. The famous motto above the entrance to the Academy is said to have read: Let no one who has not studied geometry enter here! Notice it does not say that geometry is the *only* study that is presupposed for entry, nor the *only* study to absorb the philosopher, once having entered. There is more, though in the full range of the philosophical mind, geometry is absolutely indispensable. The Platonic philosopher also requires what to complement the *esprit géométrique* Pascal calls the *esprit de finesse*.

We will have more of that finesse, but it is clear that the univocal sense is at work when Plato asks the question of being, relative to the intelligibility of becoming. Becoming is equivocal, but not only so; it participates in intelligibility; did it not, within time there would not even be an *approach* to *epistēmē*. Becoming is not absolutely intelligible, but it is intelligible. How so? By the participation of the things that become in their ideal forms. These forms are ideal unities of intelligibility. They are many, but they still are completely determinate in themselves, monoeidetic, completely homogeneous throughout, simple and uncompounded by any of the mixings of time. We might call them univocal eternal units, by contrast with which time and the mixed things of becoming are equivocal. In the between we are in the happening of the equivocal. But the eros of transcendence points beyond the mixture of the middle to the univocal purity of these eternal units of intelligibility.

Of course, there is still more in Plato, and so rich a thinker always warns us against simplifying caricatures. Plato is a metaxological philosopher, hence his thought is plurivocal, not univocal. The point now is simply to note the univocal strain that composes one of his many voices. Even this univocal strain is immensely complex. Plato recognized that any simplistic dualism of time and eternity, the pure forms of being against the mixed processes of becoming, will not do. The question is: What does it mean to be? One answer is: To be is to be beyond becoming. But becoming is. What then does it mean to be here? The answer given is that becoming, vis-à-vis its intelligibility, participates in the eternal forms; equivocal time is intelligible because it participates in, is a *mimēsis* of univocal eternity. But if so, we are once more back in the between, where the interplay of univocity and equivocity must be made intelligible. And it cannot be made intelligible in terms of one side alone. To explain the play back and forth between the univocal eternity and the equivocal time, we must appeal to a sense of being *beyond both*. This is a further task that Plato takes up in diverse ways, and which we also will take up.

In both Parmenides and Plato the search for univocal unity is driven by response to the possible equivocity of being. Contrary to Nietzschean caricatures, this search is not merely reactive and defensive. There is an inherent thrust in mind towards determination; it is the very nature of thinking to identify and differentiate. Perhaps we search for unity at one level to replace the lost immediate univocity, but at another level we do so because we *must seek* some unity. These two considerations already show a constitutive doubleness in the quest for univocity—and in a sense against the simplicity of the idea of univocity itself.

On the *one* hand, the search for univocity *may be* a potential regression to a lost immediacy, and hence may hide a turning away from being-other in its complex differences. And in that regard, metaphysics *may* take a form that dissimulates a secret trepidation before transcendence, a kind of narcissistic retreat. Being in the middle, we need not deny that this happens. Being in the middle, we must deny that this is all there is. For on the *other* hand, the search may really be for an articulated sense of the *community* of being. There need be nothing regressive about this, regressive in the sense of a turning away from transcendence. The rapturous univocity may simply be the given immediacy of this community. We cannot simply regress to this immediacy. But it may revisit us, resurrect itself relative to reborn mindfulness, after difference. The metaphysical search for "unity" can be this other quest: in difference, through difference, with difference, to understand how things do hold together, in their being at all, in their being intelligible.

This metaphysical search for unity, understood in the above light, is simply a turning towards, a love of transcendence. Because metaphysics is double, it is mixed—inevitably so, since the soil of the development of mindfulness is the rapturous univocity. There is no growth without the fertility of this soil, yet from it grows differences, diversities, oppositions. Otherness cannot be blinked. Yet alienating difference still calls out to be surpassed. This means we must reject the blank denunciations of the so-called metaphysics of presence. The latter refers us really to the empty abstraction of an empty univocity. This empty abstraction of empty univocity nowhere exists in the between. To couple it with metaphysics is to pervert the very nature of metaphysics as metaxological astonishment/perplexity about being and the between.

Let me now turn to the point about logical univocity. For the development of that perplexity both gives rise to logic and also get overtaken by it. Perplexity precedes logic and exceeds it, but in the middle the univocal sense can erect logic into *the* way to make determinate intelligible sense of being. Here we find the workings of univocity in Aristotle's formalization of logic, which, as we know, was considered for millennia to be complete. The univocal mind expresses itself in response to metaphysical perplexity of which it is an expression, but an expression that is chary of its own source. There would be no logic without this perplexity, but once it determines itself in a certain direction, it may turn against its own source. Logic then becomes an ungrateful child of metaphysical perplexity.

What can happen here? Among other things, the question of being can be reformulated in terms of the principle: to be is to be determinate. Here we have Aristotle. To be is to be a determinate *tode ti*. The same principle of determinate identity is at work in Parmenides and Plato but interfused with metaphysical perplexity that still remains in touch with its other fertile and originating indeterminacy. This indeterminacy is more in touch with the rapturous univocity, the immediacy of the community of being, given in agapeic astonishment. Indeterminate perplexity does threaten mind with equivocity, for we cannot say exactly what it is or reveals; it is *nothing exactly*; it is resistent to all our precisions and so seems nebulous, a vanishing nothing. Equally so, claims about the indeterminable plenitude of being strike the univocal mind as also equivocal, since they suggest an excess to determinate being, which cannot itself be pinned down determinately, and which hence, from the view of univocal mind, is all but nothing. To be is to be a determinate something; to think is to think intelligibly, which for univocal mind is to think something determinate; if we do not think something determinate, we are thinking nothing, and hence not thinking at all.

To think logically is thus always to embody the univocal mind. The idiosyncrasy, even singularity, of the I is sacrificed. The univocity of the logical lifts mind to a set of universal forms of possible thought that are binding for all rational beings. It raises mind to universal common being, in the sense that necessarily holds true for all rational sciences of beings. The highest science would be an onto-logic of the highest universals, or transcendentals like being, unity, truth. In the last chapter, I briefly responded to the claim that such universals are empty.

With logicist univocity there is a sacrifice of all the ambiguities of thereness, as of all the internal strains and oppositions that mar the purity of our speech, and that common sense too blithely accepts. Here the principle of identity is a logical formalization of the basic presupposition of the univocal sense of being and mind. The principle of contradiction or excluded middle, inseparable from the principle of identity, formalizes the demand that we shun the equivocal absolutely—namely, the saying of something about the same but in opposite senses. This latter would be a difference without mediation or reduction into a coherent unity, without any resolution of the contradiction. In other words, the self-coherence of determinate thinking with itself is obligatory on the principles of logical thinking, and unintelligible without the univocal sense of being.[1]

Once again we find the oscillation between equivocity and univocity wherein I suggested much of philosophy is formed. The enigmatic plenitude of being is seen as equivocal; the perplexity of mind as indeterminate is seen as equivocal; both are made determinate through the logic of univocity, through thinking that respects the basic laws of logic, also said to be the basic laws of thought. Outside these basic laws, the implication is that there is no intelligibility to being. And so the question as to what it means to be is answered thus: to be is to be logical. This is already implied in Parmenides' identification of *noein* and *estin*. It is more pluralistically expressed in Aristotle. It is reiterated by Hegel when he said that the real is the rational and the rational is the real. There are further qualifications to be made in all cases, obviously, but these major figures from the tradition of metaphysics, despite

---

1. I will say more about this in a later chapter on intelligibilities. I should point out that I use the term logicism in a wider sense than that of the logicism of the earlier part of this century which sought to reduce mathematics to logic.

their major differences, think out of the same oscillation between the univocal and the equivocal. I add this qualification to which I return: all dialectical philosophy, Hegel's included, thinks out of this oscillation, but it also thinks *beyond* it. But even in this beyond, there is a final privileging of unity, a dialectical transformation of univocity.

It seems to me that what is currently criticized as "logocentrism" can be understood as a configuration of this univocalizing approach to being. "Presence" is here reduced to determinate presence, univocally fixed thereness, hence an objectification of the happening of coming to be. I prefer to use the term logicism, rather than logocentrism, since current use of the latter term is often accompanied by a wrong *totalization* of the tradition. To give into this temptation to totalize, even in the name of the critique of totality, is *not* to have transcended the univocal sense. Nor does use of the term logocentrism leave enough room for modes of *logos* that transcend the univocal sense of being. There are *logoi* beyond univocity, beyond determination in one and only one meaning. There are dialectical and plurivocal *logoi*. Logicism is undoubtedly a major formation of metaphysical mindfulness in the tradition. Yet it lived in ambiguous interplay with other modes of mindfulness, such as art and religion, as we have already hinted with regard to Parmenides and Plato.

What are some of the relevant characteristic of logicism? Logicism devotes itself to a certain notion of conceptual analysis. The point will be to introduce distinction into what was initially confused, to introduce differentiation into what was immediately promiscuous, to separate into class, category, kind. Ambiguity will be conquered, every muddle derided, all waffle and nebulousness excoriated. Analysis itself demands precision in thinking, and precision carries the idea of a cutting: the matter is to be articulated along the jointures, much as a body is articulated along the structural lines of the skeleton. We must divide up the case, as in the technique of *diaeresis*, as used by the Eleatic stranger in Plato's *Sophist* and *Statesman*. Opposing points of view must be set forth without shadow and in their contradiction. Consider the medieval logicism of an Abelardian *sic et non*. The univocal mind never mingles yes and no, thus so and otherwise, *sic et non*. It really says *sic aut non*, yes or no.[2] The expectation is that analysis will yield the one true meaning of the matter under question. There can be one and one only such meaning. The logic is one of *either/or*. Its purpose is to exclude what under analysis cannot stand up as completely self-coherent.

---

2. It is interesting that *aut* does not have to be absolutely exclusive of *et*. For one meaning of *aut* refers to two or more logically exclusive alternatives; however, another meaning emphasizes the necessity of one alternative, but *without* excluding the possibility of the other simultaneously. Again it is hard to insulate univocity completely from possible equivocity.

Of course, there are preconceptions about being in this analytical univocity. These preconceptions tend towards the atomistic. There is the expectation of elemental atoms, unsplittable primitives that will be, as it were, the univocal originals, out of which all being and thinking will be composed. (Examples might include Plato's concern with the alphabet of thought, Leibniz's universal characteristic, which he likens to the Adamic alphabet, the early Wittgenstein's concern with atomic propositions.) The univocal originals will be reached by an analytical decomposition of the initial ambiguous given. These basics will be formulated in terms of publicly articulated concepts that have a generality that also escapes beyond ambiguity. The abstractness of such general concepts is just their power; they are univocal, not at the level of concrete determinations of things, but in terms of concepts so unambiguous that no mind properly disciplined to analytical thinking would see them otherwise than other such minds. They are the abstracts of a univocal formalism, indifferently available to the univocal mind that is disciplined to think concepts in their purely formal determinations.

I will return more fully to the limitation of this view in the next chapter on being and equivocity. For now I want to note a major limitation of logicism—namely, that the will to determinacy and analytical intelligibility can be such as to cut off, just in its precision, what cannot be fixed as univocal. This is the very shifting, sliding, ever-changing dynamism of the universal impermanence. It may also cut off the intimate nuances of particulars, that indeed are determinations, but determinations so subtle that they escape encapsulation in the generalizing categories of univocal mind. Such categories, as the abstract determinations of pure univocal forms, may be such as to void or to thin the plenary excess of concrete being, out of which mindfulness initially rises. They rise above the promiscuity of the immediate rapturous univocity and try to found, as it were, a puritanical regime of the pure forms of abstract thought.

This is why, relative to the demand for univocal determination, empiricism and formal logic can be seen to be in a kind of epistemological collusion.[3] Empiricism, certainly classical empiricism, and some of its contemporary variations, brings to bear on being the presupposition that givenness will yield itself to sensory experience in terms of discrete sensa. These sense data are the univocal atoms of givenness that impress themselves on the functionally discrete powers of sensation in the knower. This is a kind of *aesthetic univocity*, aesthetic in the original meaning of sensible and sensuous being or manifestation.

This epistemological presupposition of aesthetic univocity is the offshoot of a metaphysical expectation that given being is always already there as an

---

3. See *Philosophy and its Others*, 212–29 on logic and being mindful; *Beyond Hegel and Dialectic*, 122–23.

aggregate of univocal atoms of aesthetic thereness—"raw feels" on the part of self-being, primitive "sensa" on the part of being-other. But such units of aesthetic givenness are already abstractions from the immediate flow of rapturous univocity. This flow is itself a promiscuous mingling of qualities and values and feelings, of inner and outer, of self-being and other-being. In the flow of givenness none is rigidly determined in terms of such fixed differences. Rather there is aesthetic passage and dynamic transition, prior to stabilization and fixation into univocal units.

Formal logic both matches and colludes with this aesthetic univocity. It brings to bear on mindfulness (as opposed to concrete externality) the presupposition that true and intelligible thought has to evidence what we might call a *dianoetic univocity*. *Dianoia*, we might recall, is the third mode of mind on Plato's divided line, explicitly in the domain of intelligence and the intelligible, and expressly coupled with mathematical thinking. A discursive, analytical thinking is at issue. The presupposition of this thinking is that in abstraction from the reality of the aesthetic univocity, there are corresponding "objects" at the ideal level. The ideas or concepts or categories will exhibit just this dianoetic univocity. These will be ideal determinations of thinking and intelligibility that are just themselves and nothing but themselves, purely formulated through themselves, identifiable to ideal thought, just because they are dianoetically self-identical. Thus, for instance, Plato's ideas are not to be understood in terms of the subjectivistic ideas of post-Cartesian thinking, yet they exhibit aspects of such dianoetic univocity. They are only one example of the tendency to dianoetic univocity in all thinking drawn to any version of logicism.

It is clear that, on this view, we must take the aesthetic and the dianoetic univocity together. For the first without the second yields us a maelstrom of equivocal givenness; while the second without the first gives us but a barren ideality, a merely empty formalism. To cover the field of being in its givenness and its intelligibility, both levels must be taken together, the univocity of the real and the univocity of the ideal. Kant was to make this same point in a different form and in a different context—namely, that of transcendental philosophy, when he says: thoughts without intuitions are empty, intuitions without concepts are blind. When they are taken together, it will be claimed that the univocal sense of being has done its work: to make being as logically intelligible as possible, to effect the union of true being and logical intelligibility. This will hold even in the context of Kant's transcendental philosophy. As we will see, this introduces another variation on the univocal sense of being, only now turned back into subjectivity in train of the so-called Copernican revolution.

As the apotheosis of the ideality of univocal mind, logicism is open to this criticism: the categories by which it makes the aesthetic univocity intelligible are not absolutely true to being in its givenness and otherness. As

abstractions, as dianoetic univocities of thought, they are *not completely* false
to what is given. For the power of an abstraction is partly its truth—namely,
its being true to that from which it is abstracted. But the abstraction of
dianoetic univocity is also an exclusion of other determinations of the plenitude of concrete appearing. In fact, to be a good and true abstraction, it must
be false to the fullness of appearing. Even the notion of an aesthetic univocity
is an abstraction, and hence a falsification in that sense, apart altogether from
its further exploitation at the formal level of abstract thought. Thus we have
a deeply paradoxical situation: *to be true, the abstraction must be false; its
falsity produces the very power of its truth.* In other words, the truth of this
univocity is implicated in the very equivocity that, we now see, it falsely claims
to have surpassed or conquered.

On this point we can acknowledge some partial truth to the Nietzschean
critique of logic as defined in terms of the abstraction of equality and equivalence: instances are to be equalized, appearances are to be made equivalent
cases; otherwise the principle of identity could not come into play; differences, nuances have to rubbed out, all the more efficiently to fit the identical
categories. There is a determination to sameness in logic, an operation of the
univocal sense of being. When we recall its relation to the equivocal, we can
see how that configuration of mind called logical reason can function as an
instrument, an organon in Aristotle's term, to dominate the ambiguity of the
flux in all its nonequivalent differences. Nietzsche himself rejects univocal
identity for equivocal flux, logical unity for aesthetic multiplicity (not aesthetic univocity). He asks philosophy to rethink being in terms of this aesthetic multiplication.

Nietzsche is right and wrong. Right, in recognizing the limitations of
aesthetic and dianoetic univocity; right too in sensing a deeper truth to the
process of being as a becoming that issues in an aesthetic multiplication of
beings. Wrong, in his reactiveness to this limitation, in his failure to give
the right weight to the very *determination* of being in this multiplication,
and also to the process of the determination of intelligibility in the universal impermanence. These real and ideal determinations are not merely
univocal.

Heraclitus, Nietzsche's hero, saw deeper: the flux of happening is shot
through with *logos*, steered by it. It is not a merely indefinite becoming. Becoming, as I would put is, is intermediate, as the happening of the between: it
is between form and formlessness, indefiniteness and determination. It is an
intermediating process of these, ultimately beyond univocity and equivocity,
because it is the issue of an indeterminate power of coming to be, indeterminate as overdetermined excess, not undetermined chaos or void or lack. To
think the meaning of this overdetermined excess we must have transcended
the oscillation of univocity and equivocity; indeed that very oscillation points
us further.

Cartesian Univocity

Perplexity before the happening of being is not dispelled by ancient and medieval metaphysics. To deal with this persisting perplexity, we find in modern philosophy and science a development and redirection of the univocal sense. I will first speak about the philosophical redirection, then turn to the scientific. In the latter case, significant questions about univocity arise relative to classical mechanics and contemporary physics.

The redirection in modern philosophy arises, in my view, from a decreased tolerance of the equivocal, and an increased exasperation with the epistemological insecurity that goes with metaphysical perplexity before being. We happen to be in the happening of the between; there the origin of mindfulness is in an agapeic astonishment before being in its otherness. The perplexity that grows from that is never completely dissipated; nor is there a complete answer to the determinate questioning of beings, arising in the further specification of mindfulness. In other words, there seems to be *no end* to perplexity and questioning, even though for millennia the effort has persisted to rationalize being in terms of univocal intelligibility. The equivocal resists defeat.

This is exacerbated by the fact that the work of univocalizing produces a situation where our relation to the original charge of the happening of the between becomes *distanced* from the first astonishment. In this distancing, being seems to be just there; its excess to rationalization confronts us as another standing *opposed* to us. Any rapturous univocity of being dies down. This deadening of the between, in turn, generates an equivocal difference, hardened by the univocalizing of being—namely, the unmediated difference of an oppositional *dualism*. Being in its otherness confronts us as opposed to us in its lifeless thereness. Meanwhile, we live an inward mindfulness in thinking that is alienated from, seemingly radically different to, that lifeless otherness. Thus there comes to the fore the idea of mind as a thinking subject, thinking over against, and thinking against, the mindless object.

It is in such a context that Descartes tried to harness the energies of mind for a new and more complete univocalizing of being that was to be decisive for Western modernity. I find something profoundly ironical in the fact that Descartes took up his quest subsequent to a decisive *dream* that caused him to dedicate his project of science to the Mother of God. The irony is this: the scientific product will be such that there will cease to be any place for prophetic or revelatory dreams, not to mention devotion to the divine Mother. The quest for univocity that would conquer equivocity betrays (in more than one sense) its own origin in a *rich* equivocity, without which the quest itself would never have moved from the spot. We are reminded, of course, of Parmenides' revelation from the goddess, and the mixing of *muthos* and *logos*.

Note how Descartes described his mission. He tells the *story* of his youthful education in traditional learning, and his break with childhood thoughts.

This childhood was not a rapturous univocity, nor a dwelling in the marvel of being. It was the childhood of possible error, a childhood of *misplaced trust* in the authority of the elders. Moreover, there is a rupture, an epistemological mistrust of the paradigms of cognitions. The mistrust is articulated in the most extreme form in the hypothesis of the evil genius. This is hyperbolic, but that is the point. There is an extremism intended. Why? In order to overcome, once and for all, the equivocality in the nature of human learning, in the nature of things themselves.

The hyperbolic supposition of the evil genius is the equivocity of being become the possible *malignity* of being. Put otherwise, we are at the opposite extreme to the origin of metaphysical thinking in agapeic astonishment. There is no gift of being or mindfulness. There is a mistrust of the truth and intelligibility of being, a mistrust that cannot even be called erotic perplexity. To overcome this mistrust, the negative must be turned against the negative, and the univocal sense of being reinstated in its assurance of completely determinate intelligibility.

There are a plurality of expressions of the last point. I will note the methodological, metaphysical, and mathematical expressions. My view is that the essentials of these expressions can be formulated in terms of the interplay of univocity and equivocity. First, the *methodological* expression is in the belief that if we regulate the mind properly, then it can dissolve all perplexities, perplexities themselves made determinate as clearly formulated problems. Method will provide the most universal means to complete univocal intelligibility. Left to its own immediate resources, the mind will unpredictably develop, depending on the genius or mediocrity of the thinker. Method will overcome that wayward equivocity of idiosyncratic selfhood. It will give us the dianoetic univocity of a procedure that will lift the individual to a universal level. It will articulate ideal regulations thus to elevate all rational agents, regardless of the fortunate talents of individual genius.

The Cartesian method, as it were, technicalizes the univocal mind. It has an analytical and synthetic side. The rules for the direction of the mind are: reduce the given promiscuous complexity to the most simple elements possible; these simples will then be grasped, as if they were irreducible dianoetic atoms, univocal in their irreducibility; as such dianoetic univocals, they will be perfectly perspicuous to the natural light of reason, the univocal mind of *ratio* in general. This is the analytical movement.

The synthetic movement begins once all equivocal shadow has been extruded. The extrusion will be consolidated by complete enumeration of the simples; complete enumeration is itself only possible on the presupposition that to be intelligible is to be countable, one of the key tenets of mathematical univocity, as we saw; then the complex will be reconstructed out of the dianoetically idealized atoms of univocal intelligibility; the reconstructed complex whole will be a synthetic univocal totality, articulated within itself as a completely determinate intelligibility. The method will be the directedness of mind towards the construction of such univocal scientific totalities. Implicit in the direction is the expectation of complete explanation and intelligibility, and indeed complete control. Not only is this methodological univocity said to be completely within the control of mind; it is also with the view to bringing being as other completely within this control.

This brings us to the second point, the *metaphysical* univocity in Cartesianism. This is most clearly revealed relative to the *cogito*. The "I think" is the one being that escapes doubt and hence perplexing equivocity. It is reached by a passage through doubt and perplexity; but it is an immune foundation that stands firm before their dissolving power and the despair of determinate cognition they generate. I will not deny a unity to the self. But with the Cartesian self the univocal sense of being so works as to produce a *subjectification of the univocity of substance*, such as we find applied to things in nature in premodern metaphysics. On this view, the primary sense of the unity of being and of beings is not substance, as given its being and form in the otherness of *phusis*; it is the very subject as a thinking substance.

This univocity of the subject as thinking substance is said to exclude all equivocality. One cannot be in two minds about the being of the mind that thinks, the thinking substance. We must say: "It is." Parmenides' *esti* becomes a univocal "I think, I am." But there is here a contraction of the affirmation of being to the affirmation of the being of the self as thinking. This affirmation of self-being is not, as it is with metaphysical thinking, in touch with agapeic astonishment, a singularized expression of the affirmation of being itself in its worthiness.

The univocity of method and of the subject coalesce in a different orientation to the being of the between. This now is not acknowledged in the plenitude of its otherness; rather its otherness is a dualistic opposite to be overcome. What is more, the expectation of complete intelligibility colludes with the expectation of complete control, and in Descartes' famous phrase, the new science will allow us to become "the masters and possessors of nature." Before we can launch this project, there are other building blocks needed in this scientific synthesis of univocal totality. But again the univocal mind is at work. Most importantly, it influences the standard of veracity as applied to ideas: true ideas are clear and distinct; clarity and distinctness are different modalities of univocal intelligibility in their ability to determinately illuminate the mind, itself as thinking substance the univocal unit par excellence.

There is, of course, the question of Descartes' appeal to the enigma of God. As the infinite and the absolutely perfect, God, properly speaking, exceeds every univocal idea, since any determinate notion would circumscribe the infinite in its excess to all finite delimitation. As I understand the matter, the presupposition of univocal being is so overriding that Descartes essentially *utilizes* the idea of God as a *means* to give intellectual certification to his own wish to invest the powers of the thinking thing with some epistemic and ontological trustworthiness. God is not the enigma beyond all finite problems but, like the soul, Descartes claims, the most easily known. In an astonishingly blithe way, univocal mind quickly puts in its place the astonishment that the thought of the infinite actually evokes. It too will be made to serve its place within the scientific synthesis of univocal totality. God is facilely invoked as the univocal salvation from the equivocal despair generated by the suspicion of the evil genius. The inward otherness of the self, the transcendent otherness of God, the agonizing otherness of a malign evil perhaps at work in being behind our backs, the agape of astonishment and the despair of perplexity that God and evil call forth, all these are subordinated to an epistemological, metaphysical, and mathematical univocity.

The *mathematical* univocity, founded on the putative epistemological and metaphysical univocity, will shape the development of modern science. Not that Descartes is alone in this, as reference to scientists like Galileo and Newton makes clear. I will come to this more fully below. I reiterate that there is a far greater emphasis on practical domination in modern philosophy and science than we find in premodern metaphysics. Relative to the univocal sense, perhaps there was an ambiguous theoretical domination of being in premodern metaphysics. In that respect, we might say that there is Stoic blood in all metaphysicians: the god of thought thinking itself lures us, the god beyond the uncontrollable equivocal, serene in the self-sufficiency of thought completely at home with itself. (Was Aristotle's god, *noēsis tēs noēseōs*, the first Stoic metaphysician? Or was it Parmenidean Being identical with thinking itself?) But this theoretical domination of equivocity served a self-mastery, which, at a certain limit, let be the uncontrollable otherness of the universal impermanence.

Thus it is worth recalling that Stoicism also enjoined a certain metaphysical *gratitude* to being. This was linked with an attunement to being as a cosmos: a beautiful and well-ordered whole, with its own inherent *logos*, which ordered things along the path of their own integral determination. Mind might jubilate in concert with that cosmos. It was not the dead universe of Cartesian univocity, the lifeless *res extensa*, which can arouse no joy, only terror and disgust, shading from suspicion into indifference and finally into revolt. Descartes and his successors were not just concerned with theoretical self-mastery; they desired practical mastery of the otherness of being; they would not let be the universal impermanence in its uncontrollable otherness. The desire is to totalize the univocal sense of being. Relative to being-other, the necessity of a univocal *mathēsis* of nature is formulated as a major requirement.

Modern science and technology are shaped by the submission of human mindfulness to this necessity. And it is a submission, though it calls itself a mastery. For there is no absolute necessity inherent in the happening of the between that dictates that this is the one and only path of destiny for human mindfulness. Quite to the contrary, this path is the destiny that seizes a very peculiar, univocal abstract of the between. And there is far more than pure mathematical univocity at play here, surface appearances notwithstanding.

Compacted in the project are terror, disgust, suspicion, indifference, and the revolt that refuses the dead abstraction of being—an abstraction itself the product of the project. The revolt and the refusal, to the extent that they project the totalization of the univocal sense of being, partake of the same abstraction. They are expressions of the emptiness they so vehemently want to fill. But the emptiness cannot be filled with its own emptiness. The univocal mind will have to allow the resurrection of agapeic astonishment and erotic perplexity. It will have to consent to its own death as totalizing, and its being humbly reborn as one voice in a more embracing community of being and mind.

Post-Cartesian and Transcendental Univocity

Modern philosophy tells a tale of this totalization, and this struggle between death and resurrection. The totalization of univocity generates new equivocities, as well as dialectical and metaxological responses that seek to midwife the rebirth of other senses of being and mind, truer to being and the happening of the between. Let me now remark on how the tale unfolds, first with respect to the self, and then with respect to nature in its otherness.

In respect of the first point, Spinoza here is Descartes' successor in believing that the geometrical method can be universally applied, even to the human being and the ethical. Geometry is a crucial crystallization of the univocal mind. In this instance, it is metaphysically buttressed by an absolutely univocal sense of the totality of being as the One substance: *Deus sive Natura*. Spinoza's exploitation of the Cartesian definition of substance as that which must be conceived through itself alone, per se, perfectly accords with the univocal sense. Spinoza's phrase is: *quod in se est et per se percipitur*. This offers a definition of substance from *both* the ontological and the logical sides. Spinoza sees more consistently than Descartes that there can be one substance, and only one, if substance is what is defined through itself alone. That One is all there is, and so we have what we might call a geometrical Eleaticism.

The geometry of the One is applied to the ethical unity of the self, who will be treated, as Spinoza says, as one would treat triangles, planes, and solids. What is this but a will to pour the thrust of self-transcending mind into the one mold of geometrical intelligence? The *esprit de finesse* is absorbed by the *esprit géométrique*. Spinoza also describes his philosophical desire as not to laugh or curse or lament but simply to understand (*non ridere, non lugere, neque detestari, sed intelligere*). But the mode of his understanding is such as to overcome geometrically all the ambiguities of human existence, be they dark or joyful, and to treat the fleshed self like a dead mathematical construction or equation.

Of course, the equivocal cannot be entirely extirpated. Consider Spinoza's motto: *Caute!* But how could there be a univocal geometry of this admonition or warning? And is not Spinoza often *two-edged* and esoteric in his writing, the Marrano of reason as he has been called? Even Spinoza's univocity of the One substance carries muted traces of the old Stoic jubilation in the order of the cosmos, and of Parmenides' mystic surrender to well-rounded truth, *eukukleos alētheia*. Despite the fixing of determinate identities relative to geometrical intelligibility, there is a giving over of the philosopher to the all-embracing univocity of what elsewhere I call the absorbing god.[4] This last is a metaphysical metaphor for an absolute totality wherein the suffering of difference of the finite self is assuaged by a surrender to an all-enclosing whole. Here too there is a bow to resurrecting the lost rapturous univocity of the beginning.

If fact, we cannot sustain this renewed rapture in the One substance of Spinoza's absorbing god. On this view, nature is devoid of final causes, and so is a whole without goal; it is determined in its intelligiblity by the order of efficient causes that geometrical mind can formulate. As such it is a mechanism. A mechanism is an ordered functioning structure of interlocking well-defined parts, which may themselves be conditional functions, subordinated to the efficiency of the whole. There is no creative indeterminacy in a mechanism. If the human being is a mechanism in that sense, there is no freedom. Thus the univocal sense of being can produce a world that is a cosmic mechanism, within which the self also functions as one more mechanical function, equally and indifferently explicable by the homogeneous geometry of the whole.

I do not deny that Spinoza might be seen to exhibit Stoic strains, especially relative to theoretical dominion of the world; and we may be attracted to the emphasis on the whole, his putative organicism rather than mechanism. And yes, there may be a sense of more inherent unity to the whole in the One substance. Yet within the One substance the intelligibility of the parts in their relations is determined by efficient causality, and in a sense difficult to distinguish from mechanical determinism. Moreover, Spinoza's whole as *causa sui* is also consistent with the absolutization of univocity relative to substance as defined through itself alone. The circular absolutization of self-mediation will return in dialectical form in Hegel's erotic absolute. In both there is no agapeic origination of finite creation as other.

My interest is not primarily with the exegesis of Spinoza, but the univocal sense in modernity. I ask: in the universal mechanism, how do we explain the self-transcendence of mind? This question has haunted the modern univocal mind. It has not and cannot solve it. It is not possible on the terms of Cartesian *mathēsis*. Simply as self-transcending, mind is an anomaly to the universal mechanism; it is excess, a surplus, ultimately indeed a surd. In a word, scientific univocity reduces being to something that cannot account for scientific mind itself. Thus the scientific product issuing from Descartes' above-

---

4. *Desire, Dialectic and Otherness*, chapter 1.

mentioned "dream" cannot account for the "dream" itself, without which the product would *not be* at all. The originating "dream" of univocity remains a surd that univocity cannot explain.

Put differently, there is a disjunction between univocal intelligibility as a product of mind and the living activity of minding that is enacted by the scientist, a disjunction between valueless "reality" and the value-saturated project of the scientist. The point is this: the genuine scientist is driven by a passion for the truth, which cannot be univocalized, the same passion that is the source of a love of univocity. The scientific love of truth as univocal is a love that is not itself univocal. The mind that produces the univocalizing cannot explain *itself* univocally. It cannot explain its own univocalizing of being on the terms of the univocity of being. And univocal mind cannot explain itself or its own love of univocity, for both are *beyond* mechanistic univocalizing.

This is implicitly acknowledged by the Cartesian admission of the "soul," though in practice the anomaly is forgotten, and the mechanization of selfhood proceeds apace. In the latter case, the univocalizing is then applied to the transcending source that produces the univocalizing, the source that is beyond univocality. But the source remains beyond univocality, even as it tries to impose on itself the same determinate univocity it imposes on nature as a *res extensa*. Expressed otherwise, univocal mind, in applying its sense of being to its own self-transcending, is *self-transcendence trying to stifle self-transcendence*. And so it is mired in the deepest equivocity, its own living self-contradiction. Ironically, this is something that should not be even *possible* on the view. Nevertheless, this possibility the univocal view itself produces, when it insists that equivocity should be extirpated.

This, then, is the truth of the univocal self—namely, its untruth and dissolution into equivocity. In practice, the truth of this untruth is usually avoided by a contraction of self-transcendence, rather than a coherent facing of what follows should we stifle transcendence. What this contraction does is turn the affirmation of being in the "I am" into an "I desire" or "I feel" or "I will"—but all understood univocally again as the affirmation of *the entity as entirely for itself*. This is evident is Hobbes, in Spinoza, in Locke, to name a few. The view has many contemporary variants. The human being ceases to be seen as self-transcending in any genuine sense. Even its eros for being is contracted into a functioning of the self-interested mechanism, sustaining itself in opposition to other things, maintaining its place in exploitation of being-other, in the universal mechanism. There is no agapeic self that transcends *for the other*; instead there is a predatory unit of self-interest.

Even this very self-interest shows the metaphysical contraction. Properly speaking, interest is essentially *inter-esse*; it is being in the between, *esse* in the *inter*. But here the being in the between has been defined exclusively by the self; the *esse* of the *inter* has been contracted totally to the self that still, despite the claimed contraction, is still in the middle, outside of itself despite itself, self-transcendence despite its denial of self-transcendence. The double-ness of the between, in fact, cannot be reduced to the self as such a unit of functioning power.

But this is not the end of the tale of the univocalized self. The tale of dissolution is more complex. I will indicate only a few major points. There is in post-Cartesian philosophy, I suggest, a vacillation between the two versions of univocity, mentioned above—namely, aesthetic and dianoetic univocity. Roughly, empiricism favors the first, rationalism the second. Thus Descartes favors the second with respect to the thinking thing, the *cogito*. This dianoetic univocity, expressed in the quasi-mathematical method, will guarantee that the lifeless, homogeneous externality of the *res extensa* will be reshaped by the dianoetic univocity, product of the univocal *cogito*, into an aesthetic univocity. What I mean is that the aesthetic happening of being will be *made* to be mathematically intelligible, even in cases when it resists such mathematization. Descartes explicitly states that if nature does not offer mind a mathematical order, we may construct such orders of our own devising.

Counterposed to this Cartesian or rationalistic priority of dianoetic univocity, the empiricist gives priority to the aesthetic univocity. At best, dianoetic univocity is a copy or representation of the aesthetic univocity; our contact with being-other in the happening of the between is through bodily sensation, *aisthēsis* in that sense. As we saw, the presupposition of this view is that the happening of the between comes to us already cut up into atoms of aesthetic univocity, sense data, impressions, or whatever. The oscillation be-tween the priority of aesthetic and dianoetic univocity is part of the tale of the tension of rationalism and empiricism. This oscillation is reflected in the tale of the self and the other.

What follows relative to the self from this oscillation? In the empiricist case, the priority of aesthetic univocity breeds the presupposition that the self is also to be approached as if it were an atom of aesthetic univocity. But then the expectation of such a self is confounded, most glaringly in the case of Hume who looked into himself and found no unit of aesthetic univocity; he found a sheer flux of impressions, more like an aesthetic equivocity than univocity, succeeding each other with extraordinary rapidity. In other words, we witness here how the thinking thing dissolves from a univocal substance into a feeling thing that loses the hard determinacy of univocity and becomes an equivocal flux of aesthetic flow. And so empiricism dissolves the aesthetic univocity of the self into an aesthetic equivocity. Nor is there any dianoetic univocity finally possible, since this is derivative from the priority of the aes-thetic univocity, and hence is also confounded along with the latter's con-founding. The consistent conclusion must be a complete aesthetic and dianoetic skepticism.

Hume, of course, forgot that in looking into himself and not finding himself, it was Hume himself who looked and did not find himself. He might have searched differently and come to question the univocalizing of sensation and thinking and selfhood, and through this perhaps found a way beyond univocity and its oscillation with skeptical equivocity. He did not. Kant tried to do this, and here we find the oscillation between dianoetic and aesthetic univocity in a more complex, and suggestive form. What I suggest is that to escape the equivocal dissolution of aesthetic univocity, a *different dianoetic univocity* is proposed as the condition of the possibility of all sensing and thinking. This is the transcendental unity of apperception. This is the pure "I think" beyond all determinate contents of categories and sensations.

There are multiple intricacies in Kant's views, but again these are not the primary concern here. The matter is rather the privileging of the univocal sense of being, as applied to the self. We might say that there is a *higher* dianoetic univocity as applied to the transcendental unity of apperception. Let us call it the *transcendental univocity*. What is now being stressed is the irreducible unity of this absolute self. There is significant ambiguity here, in that this absolute self is sometimes referred to as a pure logical condition, sometimes as a purely formal universal ego, and sometimes again in much more dynamic terms, as the source that generates all the categories, and as the source of all synthesis in experience. These ambiguities are fertile in Kant and still continue to occupy our thought.

Nevertheless, the transformation of dianoetic univocity into transcendental univocity risks a higher universal formalism. This, in turn, paves the way for a dissolution of transcendental univocity into what I will call *historicist equivocity*. But first we need to see what attracted philosophers to Kant's view. The transcendental univocity of Kant serves a function analagous to the transcendent univocity of Platonic ideas; both are final sources of stability for intelligibility in the aesthetic flux of equivocal happening. As is well known, the transcendent univocity of Platonic ideas with respect to the aesthetic flux is often criticized and rejected for its seeming dualism. Now, in the Kantian view, this dualism seems to be obviated by transcendental univocity, since the transcendental unity of apperception is said to be *immanent* in subjectivity and not transcendent. Moreover, it is said to function as the *producer* of dianoetic intelligibility, which mediates the shaping of the flux of happening into more or less aesthetic univocity, or clear-cut determinations of being. The univocal sense of being is served *immanently* by the transcendental unity of apperception as the source of determinate categories of understanding—dianoetic univocals. These, in turn, mediately determine the articulated order we meet with in experience. This determinate order of articulated experience is then the *constructed* aesthetic univocity. On this view, aesthetic happening with its dianoetic intelligibility is not, as with Plato and Aristotle, a given one.

The gain of transcendental philosophy is that it opens up a conception, far more profound than either empiricist or rationalist views, of the energy of being and transcendence at work in the self. It makes possible a transcendence of empiricist univocity, of rationalistic logicism, and an opening up of the power of self as an original mediating source of being in the happening of the between. That said, the happening of the between is still contracted, and that because of the inheritance of *Cartesian dualism*, and in perpetuation of the immanence to self as defined by that dualism. The self becomes *the* mediating source that determines the intelligibility of the between. Indeed, it becomes unclear as to whether there is at all a properly robust between, as the happening of the togetherness of self and other. The between rather becomes the self as the medium of intelligibility, medium in no passive sense, but medium as *the* mediating power, the privileged determiner of the intelligibility of being. The self becomes the ultimate source of the determinate intelligibility of the between; the self is the between. The other tends to be defined derivatively, relative to the constitutive or contructing power of the mediating self. There is a subordination of the other in the determination of being, its meaning and intelligibility.

The transcendental self becomes the source of univocity with respect to the other as a dualistic opposite; any being for itself of other-being is not absolute; it is really *for the self*. The otherness and the between are not there as for themselves and as giving themselves; they are given their determinate place by the constructed intelligibility of the transcendental self. Thus the transcendental univocity runs the risk of *retracting* the between into the total self-mediation of the self, with the other playing at best a subordinated, diminished role. There will be efforts to totalize this transcendental univocity in some idealistic doctrines like Fichte's—the other will be made to accept a definition of its being in terms of the self-creation of the self. Transcendental univocity thus can feed into a hubristic, activist univocalization of the otherness of being. Any recalcitrant otherness proves intolerable to this transcendental univocalizing trying to complete itself entirely through itself. We get a transcendental sense of the ancient thought thinking itself, thought thinking its own absolute unity with absolute being. Meanwhile being-other is univocalized to play a supporting role in this absolute self-univocalizing of thought thinking itself.

The univocal sense of being says: to be is to be intelligible, and to be intelligible is to be determinate. In the present instance, this means that to be and be intelligible is *to be made* absolutely determinate by a process of thinking that is absolutely self-determining. The aesthetics of being as given, the happening of the between, the rich mediation of the other from its otherness, are all swallowed up in this absolute self-determining univocalizing. Once again there will be no agapeic astonishment before being; for this astonishment puts the self in humility before the gift of an other. Nor will there be the happening of the between, for the between will now be redefined in terms of the determinate self-construction of the transcendental unity. I will amplify this point later with reference to dialectic and Hegel.

What is now at issue is how we interpret the logic of a transcendental univocity. This univocity is linked to Kant's own insistence on metaphysics as a completely secure and grounded categorial science. It is related to Husserl's analogy between the secure determinate intelligibility of geometry and transcendental phenomenology as the rigorous science.[5] My claim is that the pursuit of transcendental univocity provides no escape from the equivocal, whether at the aesthetic, the dianoetic, or the transcendental level. Indeed there is an equivocal vacillation evident in the description of the transcendental unity of apperception. This is significant for revealing the failure of transcendental univocity, and failure because the ideal of univocity itself has to be transcended.

In this regard, consider the alternation between descriptions of the transcendental ego as, on the one hand, absolute form, or pure logical possibility or absolute *eidos*, and on the other hand, as source of determination, or synthesizing origin of determinate intelligibility. Here is the transcendental equivocation. The first description is consistent with the univocal sense of being, which elevates dianoetic univocity to a higher transcendental level. But at that higher level, the source that comes to manifestation in determinate dianoetic univocity is not itself either a determinate thing or category. There is an *indeterminate originative activity* to the transcendental ego, which, as the source of determinate intelligibility, is not, and cannot itself be, another determinate intelligibility. Expressed otherwise, the dynamic source of intelligible form is itself beyond form. There is an excess to determinate in-

---

5. In relation to what he calls *the natural attitude*, Husserl suggests that philosophy is in another dimension—namely, the transcendental dimension. Husserl speaks of subjectivity as the "wonder of wonders," yet he calls for a *"Mathesis des Geistes"*! By contrast, we think in the between of being; therein also we find "the natural attitude," but this is transformed by the second perplexity, which regards not only the enigma of mind's transcending (transcendental in a post-Kantian sense), but also being's transcendence (transcendental being in the premodern sense). I think Husserl's move to the "second perplexity" is made under the sway of the modern turn to the self as offering the meaning of being to the subordination of being's otherness. The latter tends to be rendered in terms not free enough of the dualism of modern subjectivism. Cartesianism, the "way of ideas," empiricism all suffer from the same defect; they fail to think the between. In a sense, there is no such thing as subjectivism; it is a misinterpretation of the subject, of the always at-work self-transcendence of the mindful being of the self. Mindful selving is always out there now in the between, always beyond "subjectivity" as supposedly confined to an *inner sphere*. Husserl would not entirely disagree. What is at issue is the mediation that takes place in the between, whether self-mediation can cover the between entirely, as I deny, whether there is a mediation from the otherness of beings and being itself that is irreducible to self-mediation, as I affirm; and affirm not to deny self-mediation, but to place it in a differently understood between, as intermediated from two sides, from a plurality of sources.

telligibility about this source. We must say that it is more like living dynamic intelligence than like static intelligibility. And if we still continue to call it "unity," such a unity must be beyond the univocal sense of being.

For if this original excess generates determinate intelligibility, it is not itself determinately intelligible in the same way as its dianoetic productions. There is an immanent otherness to this source that always escapes beyond every univocal determination. This means that the self-transcendence of selfhood has to be thought deeper than any univocalized version of the transcendental ego, and in terms that go beyond the univocal sense. We must also go beyond the immanent closure of self-determining thinking, since in the inward otherness, the source of this self-determining is not itself self-determined. The original power of being as other in inwardness, and as coming to mindfulness in the self, is the origin of the transcendental unity as itself a source of determinate univocity, dianoetic, and aesthetic. This otherness will demand a rethinking of the circle of immanence defined by pure self-determination, and of self-transcendence as agapeic mind.

I apologize for the density of the above remarks, but if they are understood, they offer us a way beyond transcendental univocity, traces of which we find in most post-Kantian thinkers. As it turns out, it is the *other* side of the transcendental equivocity (the side having to do with the putative nonempirical, absolute form of the transcendental ego) that has exerted the more influence historically, and not simply because it was the most followed, but because it was also the most *rejected*. What I mean is that we find a further oscillation between univocity and equivocity. For the ambiguity in the determination of the transcendental unity of apperception as form or universal *eidos* breeds the suspicion of ontological emptiness. The transcendental univocity is then open to the criticism of being only a higher and more general universal than the dianoetic univocity of abstract concepts. In response to this what we find is a certain *recoil* back to the happening of the between.

For transcendental univocity seems to produce an abstract vanishing of being in its otherness and concreteness. The question is inevitable as to how this transcendental univocity relates to the self as it exists in the happening of the between, where it lives and dies and tries to determine its destiny and relation to others. This is the crucial question relating to transcendental formalism. In the categorial emptiness such formalism seems to produce, there can occur a resurrection of the question of *being*. In the history of posttranscendental philosophy, there occurs a recoil back to the happening of the between as existentially lived and historically shaped. This recoil is not to the aesthetic univocity of empiricism, though there were heirs of modern Enlightenment who did recoil in that direction. Rather, the transcendental unity of apperception, said to be a hyperbolic categorial emptiness, is deconstructed in favor of the lived equivocities of existence, or history, or language.

Do we end there? Yes, in that we are brought to our own time; no, in that the perplexity about being is not laid to rest. For even such existential, or historicist, or linguistic concretizations of the transcendental ego are often infected with the equivocities of the transcendental univocity. There persists significant residues of the idealistic absolutization of some version of *self-mediation* with regard to the determination of the happening of the between. For the between is ambiguous. The human being, existentially as heroic individual, or communally as an historical people or linguistic group, may seek to conquer the equivocal between. Such existential, historicist, and linguistic concretizations of the transcendental ego have shaped major responses of philosophers since the completion and rejection of idealism. Yet they remain tangled in reactiveness to a sense of the univocity of being about which they are not completely clear.

In sum: the self-deconstruction of reason in favor of a variety of irrationalisms, or of univocal rationalism in favor of equivocal nonreason, germinates in this tangled equivocity of the univocal sense of being. The ambiguous legacy of the absolutization of self-mediation, I think, is with us still. It haunts even poeticized or grammatological deconstructions of this absolutization. At the outset, the doubleness of the between is reduced to the self-mediating power of the self as a unity; now, the doubleness is dissolved by that same power, but as turned into an equivocal negating or deconstructing power. The mind of finesse, beyond the univocal mind of geometry or transcendental science, still remains elusive. The finesse of the deconstruction of the transcendental ego into the equivocities of language is itself ambiguous. It is not marked by the requisite metaphysical finesse.

Univocity and the Universal Mechanism

What of nature's otherness? What becomes of this? I promised above to say something about this point. In this and the next section I want to note the further development of the univocal sense in conformity with the mathematical methodologism we saw in Descartes. What I think we find is a coupling of mind's self-mediating power with an essentially instrumentalist notion of reason. Once again, the will to univocity produces a dimming of astonishment before the charged happening of the between; instead the putative threat of its equivocity is countered by the flattening of outerness into the lifeless *res extensa*. This latter provides, as it were, the *prima materia* for the work of instrumental reason. We saw that *theōria* in the Greek sense was affiliated with the festive celebration of the agape of being. Now, however, it is turned into *theory*, which harnasses the mind as an instrument to bring being in its otherness within the purview of our projected hypotheses.

In addition, as the drive to mathematical determination is accentuated, the question of purposes is laid on ice. For this question reveals an essential perplexity that we can never properly turn into a determinate problem. By contrast, the mathematically determining mind focuses primarily on efficient causes and what comes to determination from efficient causes in the universal mechanism. Indeed we find a mirroring between instrumental reason and mechanistic determinism. Just as the instrumental mind treats being as valueless in itself, so the valuelessness of being seems to come to meet this mind in the universal mechanism. The crucial issue should not be fudged. Metaphysically speaking, on this view there is no worth to the universal mechanism; the world is essentially worthless being, hence just the sort of raw material on which instrumental mind can set to work. From the side of mind's self-transcendence, instrumental reason completes the loss of astonishment, now degraded into a cognitive curiosity with technicist pretensions. From the side of the transcendence of being-other, universal mechanism produces the degrading of creation, wherein no justification whatever is found for affirming "It is good."

This last point is very important, and invites a brief elaboration, even if at the risk of anticipating ideas yet to be developed. Traditionally, the good was identified with the *end*. The good is what all *seek*, as Aristotle says, and many after him reiterated. It supposedly lies before us, drawing us. But what happens if now we excise final causes? Then we are drawn by nothing. Perhaps we are *driven* by our own impulses and desires. Moreover, once the good as end is dropped, the *beginning* also becomes a mere valueless effecting—the efficient cause of a worthless mechanism. So too human drive/desire is also an effecting, valueless in itself; it too is an instance of the universal worthlessness. Thus the loss of the end brings an impoverishment of the beginning. The human being then wakes up in the middle, between a valueless beginning and a worthless end that is no end. Worthless being without beginning or end—this becomes the happening of the between. If we are true to this—but why be true, why value truth at all, since all being is valueless, why not lie about this?—then human life and the happening of the between are both inherently worthless. This is nihilism and there seems no way out.

The way out I propose is not just to reaffirm the good as end, but to rethink *the origin as good*: the origin is the good, and from the beginning, being is good. This will be thought in terms of the agapeic origin: the good of creation as for itself is given by this origin. We greet it in the primal agapeic astonishment, which is an echo of the primal "It is good." Metaphysical mind demands the thinking of the origin and givenness. If the origin is good, the creation for itself is constituted in being as a good: to be is to be good. All subsequent goods are in the train of the first good of the "to be": to be is simply good; it is good to be. This is a very elemental thing to say, but it is extraordinarily difficult to understand, and astonishing the more we think of it. It makes us suspect that there is untruth and horror at the heart of the modern devaluation of being: loss of metaphysical respect for creation, indeed revolt against its given goodness.[6]

I anticipate what later I will try to say better. Let me just mention Leibniz as one of the few post-Cartesian thinkers to fight this degradation of the happening of the between. His notion of the preestablished harmony is a doctrine that still remains before us to be thought in terms of its deepest possible meaning, relative to the metaxological community of being. Likewise, his struggle to link efficient and final causes shows him, de facto, to be cognizant of the ontological nihilism that follows an excision of purposiveness. But even with Leibniz the univocal sense proves hard to resist. In essence, his universal characteristic is a universal method for a thoroughgoing univocalizing of being. Its purpose emulates Descartes' rules for the direction of the mind. The universal characteristic would be an organon for *every* subject matter, he claims. If we had this organon, all equivocation and difference could be overcome. As Leibniz puts it: If we disagree, well let us calculate! This will silence the squabblings sects. He speaks about an Adamic alphabet which would amount to "a Cabala of mystical vocables" or the "language of magi." This alphabet would give us the ultimate univocal simples. Couple this with the universal characteristic and we would also have the organon of composition to reconstruct from the univocal simples all complex totalities.[7]

Moreover, at times Leibniz's God looks like the supreme logicist, the supreme technicist mind in which a universal will to univocity is expressed: the computation of the compossibility of possibilities, which maximizes the perfection of actuality. The excess of the creative origin, the mystery of the end, the enigma of the between, are subordinated to the totalizing of a universal univocal mind, who knows every determination of being, for being again is at bottom determination. Even Leibniz's pluralism involves a diversification of monads that are said to be windowless. This is a pluralistic variation on the univocal sense of being, even though the units are dynamized, not static. Even in this dynamized univocity, it is the impermeable unity of the monads that is emphasized.

In fact, in the happening of the between there are no windowless monads, since every integrity of being is marked by some measure of the energy of

---

6. There will be a movement from mechanism to organism, from aggregates to wholes in the dialectical way; dialectic will drive erotic perplexity to the end as good, as whole. But this will still not be enough. The metaxological way seeks recovery of the plenitude of the beginning; it will see the happening of the between otherwise too, not just a medium of self-mediation, instrumental or otherwise.

7. See "On the Universal Characteristic" in *Monadology and Other Philosophical Essays*, trans. P. Schrecker and A.M. Schrecker (Indianapolis: Bobbs Merrill, 1965), 11–21.

self-transcendence. The community of being is not constituted behind closed windows but out in the open of the happening of the between. It is easy to caricature Leibniz's idea of preestablished harmony; it is much more difficult to do justice to the deep source of his insights into the community of being. A technicist god is compatible with the universal mechanism, and the apotheosis of instrumental mind. Leibniz's sense of the good and the community of being demands a different God, a different mindfulness, and a different sense of nature.

The Self-Deconstruction of the Mechanism of Univocity

For almost the last four centuries, under the hegemony of instrumental mind, our habitation of nature has been shaped by a certain oscillation between univocity and equivocity. We still live in this oscillation, though the signs all show the need to surpass it. The universal mechanism was first understood in terms of a combination of the dianoetic univocity of theory and the aesthetic univocity of sense experience and experimental data. But in the development of modern science from classical mechanics to quantum physics, we find the basis for thinking the following: the more consistent and coherent we make our dianoetic univocity with respect to the aesthetic happening of givenness, the more the univocal sense of being runs against limits that put its comprehensive claim to the test. I think it illuminating to focus on the strain between quantum physics and commonsense thinking, the basically Aristotelian logic grounded on it, and the governing presuppositions of classical Newtonian mechanics.

Quantum physics deals with microevents beyond the range of direct observation, detecting behaviors in the ultimate constituents of the physical universe that seem to run counter to the more normal ways of thinking that obtain at the macro, phenomenological level. At the latter level, common sense univocity holds that there are things that are there and independent; they might perhaps be called substances, if the person thinks about things; but the main point is that they have delimitable and definite identity, which is this and not that; a thing is itself and not anything other. To say that a thing is itself is to imply that there is essentially *one basic description* that fits its determinately delimited identity. This one description is the definition of the univocal identity of the thing. This commonsense univocity is refined, while being complexly qualified, in the mathematicized science of post-Cartesian thought. The qualitative substances of common sense are quantitatively redefined in terms of the univocal units of matter, themselves redescribed in terms of the so-called primary qualities—namely, mass, extension, velocity, and so on. The so-called secondary qualities—taste, color, and so on—are at the phenomenal level and are derivative, dependent on a relativity to the perceiving mind.

This doctrine of primary and secondary qualities reflects a presupposition of univocity at the level of the basic units of matter. We can calculate and quantitatively measure these units, their interactions, their motions, regularities, and so on. By contrast, there is no univocal mathematical measure of secondary qualities like taste. There is a measure of mass, but secondary qualities have an unyielding equivocity, since their ontological status is finally uncertain. For this status is distributed between "something" in the thing itself, its powers, and the relativity of that "something" to mind.

Note that the ontological status of secondary qualities is *double*, a doubleness seen in a *negative* light in relation to scientific intelligibility. Secondary qualities sprout from two sources that, in classical modern ontology after Descartes, are two entirely opposite substances—namely, mind and matter. The doubleness, the equivocity of their ontological status is linked with the dualism of mind and matter, as well as to the univocity that insists that mind is just mind, and that matter is just matter, and that never the twain shall meet, intermingle, or intermediate. The complex origin of the equivocity of secondary qualities is in a *philosophical* equivocation between mind and matter, an equivocation arising from a univocal insistence that mind is one substance irreducible to matter, itself another absolutely different substance. And so henceforth, the equivocity of secondary qualities is to be excised from mathematical calculations or measurements of nature. The word is excised. They do not fit the ideal of univocity.

There is an irony in this excision, considered as the *end-product* of a will to mathematicize nature in an entirely univocal way. If what I say is correct, this will to univocity is itself based on a prior ontological equivocity—namely, the totally unmediatable dualism of mind and matter that governs the enterprise from the start. The power of mathematical univocity comes from the cogency of its abstraction from the fulness of the ontological situation, coupled with a convenient neglect of full self-consciousness of what is at play in this situation. From the beginning, the power of this mathematical univocity derives from an equivocation built into the originating presuppositions of the entire enterprise. Of course, the equivocity may be kept at bay, but in fact it has the inconvenient habit of returning at absolutely decisive points. Indeed it invades the enterprise at its very heart in the advent of quantum physics.

But first I need to say a bit more about classical mechanism. Relative to mathematical univocity, our power to count integrities, and to calculate the relations of succession and repetition or alternation in these integrities, is undergirded by a rational trust that *counts on* integrities. Hence the view that there is an *invariance* in the primary qualities; the variation in things comes out of composition of the primary invariants; diversity and heterogeneity is the compound of absolute invariant homogeneity. The variance of the secondary qualities is even more variable, given the vagaries of subjectivity.

Integrity here refers to the primary units of the material world, which in themselves are taken to be hard and impenetrable atoms. Let me cite Newton's very revealing description of these at the creation of the world. This hardness is necessary to sustain the endurance of things, and God provided for this by making these indivisible units such that no power could really break down:

> God in the beginning formed matter in solid, massy, hard, impenetrable moveable particles, of such sizes and figures and with such other properties and in such proportion to space as most conduced to the end to which he form'd them; and that these primitive particles being solids are incomparably harder than any porous bodies compounded of them; even so very hard as never to wear or break in pieces; no ordinary power being able to divide what God himself made one in the first creation. . . . And therefore, that nature may be lasting, the changes of corporeal things are to be placed only in the various separations and new associations and motion of these permanent particles.[8]

Newton's emphasis on lasting hardness is a scientific version of the metaphysical appeal to the everlastingness of static eternity to provide the foundation of intelligibility for the vagaries of becoming as equivocal. Of course, Newton's outlook was not exhausted by a corpuscular view. His concern with the explanation of action at a distance, the attractions of gravity across the seeming emptiness of space, induced many speculations, not only about the ether but about the undulatory nature of motion, subtle motions in the universal ether. There is a proto wave-theory suggested in his writings also. His theory of fits, which allowed for particles of light to travel through the ether in an undulatory motion, facilitated both corpuscular and wave descriptions.

Historically, the power of mathematical univocity exerted such an influence that the two sets of descriptions, the corpuscular and the undulatory, were seen to be essentially opposite and hence incompatible with each other. A thing is itself and not anything other; and this principle of univocity applies in mathematical exactness: 1 is 1 and not 2; 2 is 2 and not 1. The sharp delimitation of integrity and identity by means of difference keeps the space between 1 and 2 absolute stable; 1 will never be 2 and 2 will never be 1; if they ever were each other, there would be no concept of 1 and no concept of 2 and hence no counting, hence no arithmetic, hence no more complex mathematics. The working of common sense univocity, refined and complexified and extended by mathematical univocity, extends into the basic constituents of matter itself. The net result is that there can be but *one absolute description* of the nature of things, or one set of absolutely determinate descriptions to account properly for what is at play at the basis of reality itself. All the related concepts of energy, matter, cause and effect, the very being of nature as an entirely determined whole, were defined relative to this.

A shift takes place with quantum mechanics. The latter, as is well known, has its antecedents in discussion concerning the nature of light. Was this

---

8. Isaac Newton, *Opticks* (4th ed., 1730) (reprinted New York: Dover, 1952), 400.

nature to be described in terms of wave theory, as associated with Huygens, or with the corpuscular theory associated with Newton? The two were felt to be incompatible. The great prestige of Newton initially gave a certain prominence to the corpuscular theory, though in the nineteenth century the wave theory seemed to have gained the advantage. Yet developments in quantum mechanics indicate that the packets of energy emitted in radioactive effects or in the exchange of energy within an atom seem to be discrete quantities. The quanta of energy do not shade off into each other along a continuous line of measure. They occur at definite measures between which and the other definite measures there seems no in-between. Hence an electron (in Bohr's earlier model of the atom) will leap from one "orbit" to another, without, it seems, having passed through any intermediate condition of energy. Einstein's equations relative to the photoelectric effect, Compton's work on the scattering of photons, indicate that light behaves like a stream of particles, traveling in discrete packets.

But yet again the same quanta of energy seemed to behave with characteristics that mimic wave motion, such as interference patterns. This is paradoxical for common sense and mathematical univocity: the corpuscle was a unit that was in one place and at one time, definite and determinate; it was a punctiform mass that is exclusively here and not there, and here with clearly determinable coordinates. But a wave motion dissolves these sharp determinacies, since it involves a process of transition from one determination to another, and it is not always easy to pin down intervening determinations with univocal precision. It is here and then not here, and the precise hereness of the now is moving, and hence not rigidly determinate. When corpuscles interact and relate, they also tend to remain external to each other, if their impenetrability is sufficiently hard. And as we saw with Newton's description above, the original particles were thought to be absolutely impenetrable. But when waves interact, they do not do so in an entirely external fashion; they mingle, they give up any definite identity, they merge, they reinforce each other, they interfere with each other; there ceases to be a clear delimitable border between one wave and another in interaction.

If we commit ourselves to the wave theory, do we then have to give up the ideal of univocity? This was not done, since mathematical formulations were devised to determine the nature of wave function and behavior. Though internally static identity no longer holds, nevertheless a mathematical univocity can be devised to formulate the appropriate properties of wave functions. The philosophical question is whether these mathematical descriptions of wave functions are abstractions from the real dynamism involved in the very process of an undulatory unfolding. Are they idealized abstractions that, for the sake of calculation, allow us to take the concreteness of the motion, as if it were determinable in terms of a highly complex mathematical univocity? I think this is true, which does not mean that such mathematical formalizations are nothing but mere instrumental devices for calculation. An idealized abstraction can have its *realistic* truth, though this is never absolute. An idealized abstraction can be *about* something, with a realistic "aboutness" determined in precisely qualified ways. These qualifications themselves can testify to the realistic intent, critically at work in the entire procedure of abstraction.

But this is not the main point here. It is that the two sets of descriptions, each produced under the aegis of univocity, seem to result in a parting of the ways: either one or the other but not both. We may have a unified mathematical formalism here, but there is no one single theory or unified model that reduces both descriptions to itself. Both descriptions refer to energy tranfers and transmissions. The *trans* of transfer and transmission already indicates a dynamism that goes beyond the punctiform mass of classical mechanics. *Trans* indicates a vector of going beyond, from *a* to *b* to *c* and so on. What is the character of this going beyond, this transcendence? Does the punctiform mass go beyond itself? It cannot, if it is a classically described punctiform mass. It can, if it is a wave. But then the transcending of the wave is at the expense of the stable identity marking the classical punctiform mass. We seem either to have self-identity without self-transcendence, or transcendence without self-identity.

In the first case, the explanation of the transmission of energy has to be purely in terms of external collisions and shocks. Action at a distance becomes entirely suspect; for this seems devoid of a medium wherein the necessary collisions between two systems of mass-energy must occur for the transfer to be effected. This is why the doctrine of the ether was once so attractive—it seemed to provide the requisite medium of the transcendence. In the second case, there is a transfer of energy at the expense of the stable identity of the entity. In fact, a wave is itself simply a process of transfer of energy; we seem to have transcendence of identity without, however, any identity, and hence a strange kind of transfer; for what is transferred is transferred to nothing absolutely definite, from something that is also nothing absolutely definite. We seem to have pure process of transfer and transition without anything being the ultimate source, or the supporting vehicle, or the recipient goal of the transfer. In the first instance, univocity gives us atoms in the void; in the second, transitions in the void.

The conclusion reached by some is that we are forced into a *double* description of phenomena. The wave-particle duality is governed by what Niels Bohr called the complementarity principle.[9] We need both particlelike and wavelike language to describe the microhappenings. Notice the word "like" keeps cropping up. This word "like" is already an opening beyond the inflex-

---

9. It is interesting that the symbol of Yin and Yang was central to Bohr's coat of arms. A chief result of the quantum theory for him was, as he put it, that "even words like "to be" and "to know" lose their unambiguous meaning." N. Bohr, *Atomic Theory and the Description of Nature* (Cambridge: Cambridge University Press, 1937), 19.

ible "is" of univocal identity. If an event is like such and such, we open the "is" to the possibility that the event might also be other; likeness suggests an "identity" that is otherwise than univocal identity.

Have we come full circle, returning to the duplicitous condition of Parmenides' hordes who still wander double-headed? Is this doubleness reducible to a univocal unity? It does not seem so, certainly in terms of the meaning imparted to such a unity by classical mechanics. If there is to be a new unity, it will have to be much more complex. Do we here have equivocity at the heart of microhappenings? If so, it should not be taken simply as an entirely negative thing. There were those who took it thus. (Recall above the negative judgment on the *doubleness* of secondary qualities.) They felt that the plurality of descriptions ought to be reducible to a more powerful unity. This was complicated by the uncertainty principle. In the Copenhagen interpretation, this suggests that with respect to a microevent we can know its position with precision but not its momentum; or alternatively, we might give a determinate value for its momentum, but in the process the value of its position has to take on a certain indeterminacy. Or we may calculate within a certain probability range, yielding a number of possibilities within this range, "a superposition of states"—its position is somewhere, we cannot exactly say where, within this range. Against the univocal sense of classical mechanics, there seems to be no one, absolute determinate description of the total happening. Microhappening, in the terms I use, seems to suggest a certain plurivocity.

The opening of indetermination provokes further question. Is there a constitutive indeterminacy at the base of things? Heisenberg spoke of the restoration of the concept of potentiality.[10] Alternatively, is the indeterminacy such as will be progressively overcome as science develops and surmounts its present ignorance? In the first case, indeterminacy is, at a certain limit, insurmountable. In the second case, it is a temporary condition; and even if the precisions of our present knowing always fall short, the conviction is that *reality in itself* is still marked by a system of absolute determinations; in reality in itself there is finally nothing essentially indeterminate. This is partly what is at stake in Einstein's famous adage that God does not play dice with the world. Ultimately there is nothing fortuitous, and everything in its own way is determined, though we may not now have the power to cognize absolutely this ultimate determination.[11] This is the continued life of the principle of sufficient reason, interpreted in a strong, almost Spinozistic sense.

---

10. See "Development of the Interpretation of Quantum Theory," in *Niels Bohr and the Development of Physics*, ed. W. Paul (New York: McGraw Hill, 1955).

11. Thus the theory of hidden variables and the suggestion that a more complete theoretical description will reinstate a completely determinate account.

But even supposing God does not play dice, suppose that God may still enable freedom. Suppose that God may *play differently*. Moreover, suppose that the indeterminacy of God's playing may be affirmative, in a sense quite *other* to the game of dice. The overall view developed here of univocity points beyond absolutely fixed determinacy. I think the issue can be posed revealingly, by an important displacement from exclusively objectivist considerations. *Our perplexity* about determinacy and indeterminacy is itself a pointer to indeterminacy, and in a sense that resists complete determination; there is an excess relative to perplexity itself that is constitutive, even were it the case that nature in itself were absolutely determinate, though we could not know it. This is a variation on a point made in the last chapter with respect to Kant, freedom, and metaphysical thinking. The further question concerns an *affirmative* sense of indeterminacy, both in the self and being-other, and the community between them.

In contemporary physics itself we seem to be barred, by the very nature of our own cognitive approaches, from reaching a final stage of complete determination with respect to ultimate microhappenings. That is, when we perform experiments to determine the values of events at this microlevel, our very instruments are themselves systems of energy interacting with the systems to be known, and hence their use mingles (intermediates) with the system to be known. The knowing itself involves a transfer of energy and hence effects the energy of the microknown. Hence the system to be known is never known absolutely in itself apart from us. We always know it as in some measure influenced by the system of energy used to approach it. There seems to be no pure "in-itself" at this level that we can determine with absolute precision in itself. Our cognitive act, through the medium of the necessary experimental apparatus, affects the object known.

This suggests that there is no purely external relation between the knower and the known whereby the known could be approached without any mediation by the knower. We are involved as *participants* in *interactive* knowing with being-other. We are beyond voyeur spectating. We are beyond dualism, the presupposition stemming from the metaphysical univocity of classical physics. Instead the process of cognition becomes itself a transition or intermediation between two systems of energy. The system to be known can never be known in abstraction from corrective considerations of the influence of the knowing system. The knowing subject makes a dramatic reentry into the seemingly subjectless objectivity of classical mechanics.

The reentry is dramatic in that the mathematicized univocity of classical mechanics was intended to quarantine scientific knowing from the vagaries of subjectivity—*vide* the attitude to secondary qualities. The mathematical univocity defined knowing with parameters of abstraction which obviated references to subjectivity. What is striking here is not that the reentry of the knower comes as a *deus ex machina* into the situation of the new physics. Rather, the very perfecting of the abstractions of the first mathematical univocity, in being progressively brought into fuller interplay with more and more facets of reality, forces the mechanism of univocity, as it were, to self-deconstruct.

I do not want to overstate the case. Self-deconstruct does not mean self-destruct. It means that the faithful development of a scientific univocity generates tensions internal to the results of this development, tensions that reach a pitch of stress with the duality of descriptions which quantum physics demands. If there is a pitch of breaking here, this is not a loss at all. It is a *breakthrough* into a more complex and rich sense of the real. It is the articulation of an undreamt of world, undreamt within the confines of the older, more narrow univocity. The breakdown of the older univocity is the breakthrough into a world of new possibility, both for scientific cognition and for our vision of the marvel of the world.

The enrichment of vision of microevents is matched by what we might call a *startling rebound effect* when the knower also sees traces of his own visage look back at him from his cognitive involvements with nature as other. I do not think this rebound has to be interpreted subjectivistically. I suggest here a shaping of a metaxological sense of being in that the *between* becomes of primary importance. The between offers the context of the plurality of possible descriptions. The dual descriptions are complementary because both fit with something of the richness of the happening of the between itself and reflect it in their own way. Of course, more descriptions may be needed to do justice to the overdetermined happening of the between. This overdetermination suggests an affirmative sense of indeterminacy. This is not merely the indigent condition of indefiniteness that must yield the complete definiteness of total determination.

The between is at work in the things themselves, in the knowing of which the between returns to mindfulness. The between becomes the place of transition making possible the relativity of the human self and the events of other-being. The implication of the knower, even at the extremity of efforts at its excision by objectivist cognition, raises the question of a community between mind and being. This community will not be subjective or objective; it may be transsubjective and transobjective. In fact, perhaps it is just this promise of community between mind and being that really is at work all along in every effort of the scientific enterprise.[12] This community of transcendence, as we shall see, is ultimately metaxological.

Beyond Univocity

I want to conclude with some final remarks on the above dialectic between univocity and equivocity. *First*, I do not think we should extrapolate to

---

12. On objective knowing and this community, see "Agapeic Mind" in *Perplexity and Ultimacy*.

totalistic conclusions from the subject's involvement at the quantum level. Yet the issue of the community of being and mind can be raised at any level of ontological complexity. And admittedly, this involvement at the microlevel is not without resonating significance for other levels of ontological complexity, closer to the concreteness of macrohappening. If at the microlevel, we find the contours of the middle emerging, we are strengthened in our confidence that a more ontologically complex sense of this middle is not false to the nature and the meaning of being. If no sense of the between emerged there, then the larger sense of the community of being, and the community between mind and being, would be compromised. Some determination of the metaxological, or rather of the fourfold sense of being, must go all the way up and all the way down.

Second, if the quantum theory rubs against the grain of commonsense univocity and also of mathematical univocity, yet it is the latter that generates the rub. The perplexities that emerge, in fact, resurrect perplexities about being that more usually emerge within the horizon of commonsense univocity. Commonsense univocity is never mathematically consistent and precise, and hence, as we saw, is always promiscuous with commonsense equivocity. Mathematical univocity wants to rid scientific reason of the latter, purify commonsense univocity of its logically impure alliances with equivocity. But in the end, even mathematicized scientific univocity makes space for paradoxes and perplexities more startling than common sense itself can cope with.

These include: the return of the question of freedom and necessity, relative to determinism and indeterminism; the question of the nature of matter as convertible with energy, and in a manner not void of strong resonances of mind and mind-relatedness; the strangeness of matter itself when we introduce notions like "dark matter," or "anti-matter"; the question of origin; the question of the marvel of the microevents, a world of dynamism and process, yet of intricate intelligibility in the universal impermanence. Out of mathematicized univocity, scientific theory might turn around again into metaphysical perplexity about the enigma of being. We lose our arrogant self-certainty, we become humble before an astonishing universe. At the height of our knowing, we come to know that we do not know. In a word, this acme of determinate knowing can open up the possibility of the second indeterminate perplexity, where the veil of mystery is spread before the utmost extension of mathematical precision.

Third, regardless of future developments—and we cannot scientifically reject the possibility of major advances that may alter the theory—there are metaphysical lessons to learn. The hegemony of a certain univocal sense of being, long dominant in modern classical physics, must be questioned. We must ask especially about the influences of its presuppositions on our view of other ways of being mindful. Pure univocity will no longer do. That dream is over.

Ironically, it is the fuller unfolding of the univocal sense that leads to results that undermine the univocal sense as absolutized. The abstraction is breached in its own self-deconstruction. In other words, the development of univocal science to the very height of its power reaches an acme of achievement in which the ontological basis of the achievement is called into question. Univocity comes to question itself, oppose itself, reverse itself into a double description, a dual voice. I think we are dealing here with an instantiation of the plurivocity of being, prefiguring the dialectical and metaxological senses. Univocity gains its great power from its abstraction from plurivocity, but these other voices now come back. As a result, the meaning of univocity itself must be interpreted with more finesse. Plurivocity is the way into and out of contradiction. Contradiction drives us beyond univocity towards plurivocity, and a different communivocity.

Fourth, we must cease to be seduced by any form of scientism. Scientism, through instrumental reason, believed it offered the path to an absolute univocal enlightenment that would dispel the equivocities of unscientific common sense, religion, metaphysics, and tradition. But its univocal will to conquer equivocity in the end produces a new equivocity. As we suggested, both rationalistic and empiricistic philosophies offer variations on this univocal will. Just as relative to the Cartesian and rationalistic dianoetic univocity, dualism is never overcome, so relative to the dualism implicit in empiricism's aesthetic univocity, there is finally a dissolution of the intelligibility of dianoetic univocity in, for instance, Hume's critique of causality. And this is apart from the new perplexities about causality raised by quantum physics. There is also continuing perplexity about the ontological and epistemological foundations of induction. Scientism asserted itself as a new religious surrogate of the old religion and metaphysics that it wills to repress, but it itself dissolves back into the equivocity of the lived happening of the between.

In sum: the will to absolute univocity is self-subverting, and cannot evade its own opposite, equivocity. This very insistence on univocity itself proves to be equivocal, for no univocal meaning can be given to the univocal insistence. Let me end with a simple, though striking, indeed amusing, example from philosophy. One sometimes finds analytical philosophers dismissing others, say Continental philosophers, for being "wooly." The analytical philosopher strives for as much precision in the analysis of concepts as possible. "Wooliness" is a name for the failure to produce a univocally transparent analysis. The thought is judged negatively on that score. "Wooliness" signals ambiguity, confusion, nebulousness, murk, incomprehensibility.

But what do all the latter mean? Can we give a completely univocal account of them? No, we cannot. This is especially evident if we ask about "wooliness" relative to comprehensibility. Comprehensible to whom? If you answer, to any rational inquirer, you beg the question as to what constitutes rational inquiry, and whether the univocal, however we specify this, is the standard. The analyst will not say: comprehensible to me, since the vagaries of subjectivity and selfhood immediately peep out, and with them the equivocal also. And perhaps what is incomprehensible to you, is not per se incomprehensible, or incomprehensible to a different mindfulness, no less reasonable, though not univocal? And is there not a similar openendedness with notions like "ambiguity," "confusion," "nebulousness" that cannot be entirely rescued from "wooliness"?

This is the irony: when we seek to make univocally determinate the meaning of the standard of univocity, we immediately run into equivocity. The concept of "wooliness" is itself "wooly"! This standard of univocity, used to denounce equivocity, is itself equivocal. Hence analytical univocity is self-deconstructing. Further still, since the standard of univocity is not itself univocal, to be *consistent* with itself, it must concede its *inconsistence* with itself. Thus, the univocal analysis of univocity shows that univocity is itself equivocity—that is, not susceptible to a completely univocal analysis. The flight from "wooliness" is itself a "wooly" flight.

Overall, we reach the same conclusion with regard to nature's otherness as we did with respect to the self. We cannot stay at this level, and make the sense we want to make. Univocity absolutized breeds equivocity, ultimately breeds nihilism, breeds the death of metaphysics. But metaphysical thinking is plurivocal, and has more lives than the univocal. It is impossible to confine metaphysical thinking to this level. It must be resurrected beyond univocity.

CHAPTER THREE

BEING AND EQUIVOCITY

Univocity, Correctness, and the Milieu of Truth

As a methodological specialization of the univocal sense, science is one of the great works of the human mind. Any philosophizing worth the name must take due cognizance of its pervasive role in the modern world. But the philosopher's task is not simply to be a methodologist of science. In reflecting on the meaning of science, one inevitably inquires about the precise status of scientific truth, the role of science within the full economy of human life, and the sense of being at work in its most intimate epistemic and ontological presuppositions. One must be a philosopher of science in this generous sense. Until quite recently this sense hardly existed in Anglo-American analyses of science—science understood as a human achievement, placed within a larger historical and cultural, indeed spiritual, milieu. To reflect on science is not simply to abstract its methodological essence in a pseudo-ahistorical analysis. It is to meditate on the senses of being and mindfulness constitutive of the milieu of scientific truth.

Such reflection may seek to plot the limits of valid scientific cognition within a precisely delimited sphere. But this need not necessitate a negative judgment about other modes of being mindful. One thinks the limits of science to know its strength, but also its weakness in addressing no less pressing perplexities that transcend science. To affirm there are such perplexities is not at all to depreciate science. Science is not the whole, nor does it cover the ontological plenitude of the happening of the between. The philosopher thinks what is other to science in thinking the achievement of science.

Scientific truth is sought under an ideal of univocal correctness. One might say that current philosophy of science raises questions about this ideal, relative to realism and anti-realism, the precise nature of scientific validation, and the significance of science as historical institution. But the ideal itself is insepa-rable from the presupposition that determinate intelligibility is fundamental. To be correct a theory or hypothesis is said somehow to "correspond" to the determinate state of affairs that it purports to describe. The scientific theory or

85

hypothesis must be stated with as much determinate precision as is possible. The limit of such precision would be a mathematical univocity, without any shade of equivocity or ambiguity or indefiniteness. Moreover, the reality thus propositionally determined is itself taken to be a more or less determinate manifestation of being. To be mindful scientifically is to epitomize an objective mode of thinking, relative to a reality that is objectified in just that sense of being appropriated as completely determinate. Scientific correctness objectively dispels the ambiguities of being. There is no objective *mathēsis* of ambiguity, only a *mathēsis* that dissolves ambiguity.

Within its sphere this is to the point, but we are already outside this sphere when we think reflectively upon this ideal of truth as correctness and the will to objective knowing inherent in it. Hence our philosophizing immediately implies a nonobjectifying thought and an implicit sense of the milieu of being within which the univocal correctness is objectified. Relative to the thinking of this milieu, determinate objects could not appear as determinable, and hence as scientifically intelligible, did they not appear out of, or against a "background" that is not itself an object. Some other "horizon" of being, intelligibility, and mind is presupposed that makes possible the appearance of determinate objects as determinate.

"Background" or "horizon" are less than satisfactory metaphors to express what is here in question. This is the happening of the between as the milieu of being, intelligibility, and mind. This milieu, relative to which scientific truth determinately appears, is not itself a determinate truth or being. There is no absolute truth as univocal correctness possible about this milieu, for it is what makes truth as univocal correctness possible. Hence, it calls for senses of being, truth, and mind that are not univocally determinable or objectifiable. For instance, this is part of what is at stake in Heidegger's analysis of the primordiality of *alētheia* relative to truth as *orthotes* or *adaequatio*. Jaspers's name for this "horizon" of truth is the Encompassing, *das Umgreifende*, one of the major ideas in his philosophy as a whole. Put in the terms I am using: this overdetermined milieu of truth is the nonobjective other that is relative to the indeterminate perplexity, that itself drives the self-transcending thinking of philosophy.[1]

---

1. Perhaps in his own way, Kant was aware of this finally indeterminable sense of truth. I think of his paradoxical phrase in the *Critique of Judgment* (3rd moment, sect. 10): "purposiveness without purpose, *Zweckmässigkeit ohne Zweck*." That Kant applies this notion to the aesthetic is not unimportant, but it also very suggestive for the very self-transcending orientation of the human being towards truth as beyond every determinate truth. This is the truth of being relative to the ultimate milieu of the truths of science and the determinate intelligibilities it discloses. Kant, of course, is tempted to restrict correct cognitive truth to what is scientifically validated, even while in practice extending the notion of truth well beyond scientific correctness, as do Heidegger and Jaspers. I deal with truth in Part II, chapter 12.

The Indispensability of the Equivocal

The equivocal sense is no less important than the univocal for answering the question of being. From the beginning the equivocal sense was associated with a doubling of the meaning of saying or *logos*. Hence this example of the dog: the dog refers to the terrestrial animal that barks, and to the star that is hyperterrestrial; and there is nothing in common between the two. We use the same word, but there is no community of meaning between the earthly and the heavenly dog. The voice is doubled between two meanings that cannot be reduced to a more basic unity.[2] But just as pure univocity is a limit, so it is difficult to find absolutely pure instances of equivocity, which would imply a difference without even the hint of a possible mediation. Absolutely unmediated difference seems to be absolutely unintelligible; for even to state the putative absolute difference is in some way already to transcend it. We transcend a simple univocity with the equivocal sense, but I am not advocating we absolutize this either, but see its necessity, both in itself and in its contribution to a more complex mediation of being.

The war of philosophers against unintelligibility has made them generally hostile to the equivocal. This is manifest in the oscillation with the univocal we examined in the last chapter. It is no less true that this war is never finished, and many victories turn out pyrrhic, indeed brief lulls before the hydra of the equivocal sprouts another head to replace the one just chopped. The equivocal is a hydra that cannot be completely killed by univocity; for to kill its many heads demands many hands, and univocity has only one hand at a time. Indeed, I think equivocity is not to be killed but charmed from being a mythic monster into a fabling of the plurivocity of being. We must come to terms with the beauty of the beast. Logical murder, murder repeated methodically, will not do.

The doubling that takes place with the equivocal must itself be taken in a double sense, which, in the long run, is not merely equivocal. There is, if you like, a negative equivocal and an affirmative equivocal. The first turns the double into a duplicitous process. The second sees the doubling in terms of the pluralization of being that is essential to constitute a community of irreducible others, no less irreducible for the fact that there is an intermediation

---

2. Spinoza uses the image of the dog with reference to the star and the animal; they have nothing in common; Spinoza's use of this equivocity does not sit easily with the overriding univocity of his monism. George Kline has drawn my attention to the fact that Boethius (*Commentary on Aristotle's* De Interp., bk. I, ch. 2) makes reference to the equivocity of the term dog, in relation to the sea monster (i.e. the seal) and the barking animal. In addition to these two senses, Philo (*De Plantatione*, 37, 151) also includes the sense of the heavenly star. Spinoza speaks of *canis, signum coeleste, et canis, animal latrans* (*Ethics*, I, 17n.) Spinoza's *animal latrans* is an exact rendering of Philo's *hulaktikon zōon*. Again I thank George Kline for these references.

between them. Generally, the first negative sense of the equivocal has been emphasized, and philosophers have not pondered deeply enough on the positive work of truth at play in the second. In what is to come, I will think between each of these extremes.

Equivocity is not always simply due to us, or the failure of our minds to reach some foundational univocity of being in itself. It is not that we fail being as absolutely clear-cut, laid out in advance in rigidly distinct units, and merely awaiting the correctness of our atomic propositions. This latter view is implied by a certain substantialist realist metaphysics. Then the point of metaphysical knowing will be to produce the univocal categories to correspond correctly with the univocal substances. If equivocity turns up, it is imputed to *our* failure to produce the correct mirroring categories. Categories are demanded with a one-to-one correspondence to beings. In other words, the presupposition of univocity extends to the *relation* of category and thing, as well as to the *relata*.

There are cases where this is true, and determinate univocal intelligibility must be respected. Sometimes reality is already cut and dried, and we manage with mirroring categories to correspond univocally to the determinately identifiable happening. Quite a lot of commonsense experience may fit this schema. But we have not gone deep or far enough. Equivocity is not always just our failure of univocal logic, but is rooted in the character of being itself. Being is metaxological, hence plurivocal. The process of becoming provides the dynamic ground of univocity. Thus the ideal of the cut and dried is an abstraction from this becoming, with a provisional truth. Being as becoming, as flux, as temporal, as process, as ongoing—in a word, creation in the universal impermanence[3]—undermines every effort completely to stabilize being as an aggregate of univocal substances, or units, or elements, or things. These latter are only provisional stabilizations in that creative process of the universal impermanence.

Deeper still, the process itself throws up contrariety, and in the unitary thing itself. The overdetermined plurivocity of being turns towards us as the enigmatic face of ambiguous happening. The equivocal sense is rooted, I suggest, in this enigmatic ambiguity of the happening of the between. This means that our equivocity may be at times a true presentation, a true mirroring of this enigmatic happening. But deeper again, the equivocal sense is not to be taken as the *last word* with respect to this enigma, and especially so if we are inclined just to assert sheer unmediated difference. The dialectical and metaxological senses of being go further, and do so because the happening of the between is itself ontologically articulated in dialectical and metaxological form.

To justify the claim that we are here dealing with an essential metaphysical possibility, I will look at the equivocity of being with respect to the

---

3. See chapter 7 below, "Creation: The Universal Impermanence."

following considerations: *first*, in this and the next section, the question of the nature of nature; *second*, the manifestness of things; *third*, the tangled ontology of selfhood; *fourth*, the sometimes equivocal relation of philosophers to equivocity; *fifth*, the issue of incommensurability. The equivocal also has significance for the enigma of the originating ground of being, but I will postpone this consideration until the chapter on being and the metaxological.

Equivocity and the Aesthetics of Being

Relative to the first point, recall the movement of the last chapter from a rapturous univocity, through the threat of the equivocal, to a variety of univocities, commonsense, mathematical, ontological, logical, transcendental, scientific. As we saw, none of these entirely escape the equivocal, and indeed are locked into a continuing oscillation with it. This is the direction we now take: not to seek a surrogate logical or dianoetic or transcendental or scientific univocity for the lost rapturous univocity, but to return to the *aesthetic appearing* of being. I want to propose that aesthetic appearing is equivocal in terms that are not merely negative. Equivocity tends to underscore difference, diversity, plurality, often in a promiscuous and unmediated form. But there is a truth to all this, one evident if we consider the aesthetics of being prior to any logicization, be it philosophical, or scientific, or mathematical.

For in the happening of the between, initially being is given to us as an aesthetic show. I mean that it shows itself to us in an efflorescence of sensible manifestation. This aesthetic show is much more intimate with the rapturous univocity of being than any subsequent logical or dianoetic univocity. In the happening of the between, being presents itself as a process of becoming that is never completely captured in the static determinations that comprise the ideal of univocal intelligibility. There is a *doubleness* or pluralization to this becoming that demands of the mind its own dynamic doubling. Mind has to begin to think otherwise than in static and one-dimensional categories. It must do this because of the doubleness of what is coming to appearance.

We are more likely to recognize the aesthetics of being if we think of the nature of nature as a process of becoming. Notice here that the word *nature* contains reference to origin in *natus*: a being born, a coming to light as being, out of a source that in itself is hidden. What is born in becoming, nature, and the things of nature, are not simple identities, even when they are singular unities. The aesthetic show of becoming is equivocal in this regard: being is given as excess, as prodigal profusion of coming to be. And while this coming to be does issue in determinate beings, the energy of coming to be is not itself exhausted by any one determinate being or set of such beings; it exceeds every univocalization that would completely define it in terms of determinate being. Nothing can be congealed absolutely in the universal impermanence.

Becoming is the loosening up of all rigid determinacies. True, it is not absolutely indefinite, for determinate identities do come to stability within the universal impermanence. Yet these provisional stabilities in time give way to a new creative formlessness and the forming of further and different stabilities of being. Nothing absolute is, yet things are, and hence the things that become, both are and yet are not absolutely. There is a constitutive doubleness that, as coming to be and passing away, is inscribed ontologically on their being as becoming.

Both the coming to be and the passing away themselves are beyond complete univocal determination. They each reveal not just a determinacy but a process of coming to determination and of passing beyond determinacy. The process of transition from determinacy to determinacy cannot be itself another determinacy. For becoming to be becoming, there is an indeterminacy at work in the between, in the interstices between fixed determinations. This indeterminacy of passing between determinations is as much constitutive of the process of becoming, as are the articulated determinations that come to be and pass away. To do justice to the ontological fulness of becoming, we must affirm this constitutive doubleness: it is not merely indefinite, not merely determinate, but indeterminate and determinate, and the passage between indeterminacy and determination. And this double takes us beyond the univocal sense of being, without our having to deny the proper place of the univocal with respect to the articulation of the determinate as determinate.

Of course, the role of the indeterminate has been variously interpreted. Some still insist on univocity, assert that the process of determination must be another determination, and perhaps even conclude to the illusory nature of the process as process. Process of becoming would be merely the illusory form of stasis; it would reduce to a set of still snapshots of univocal determination that are the points of immobility underlying the appearance of process. Then we try to think the indeterminate in terms of another kind of determinacy, perhaps by means of the eternal determinations of Platonic *eidē*, or by means of a mathematical determination of time for which the lived process of irreversible time hardly counts, and certainly not as regards ultimate intelligibility.

By contrast, the equivocal sense forces us to resist the temptation to jettison or dilute or explain away the suggestion of indetermination in the process of coming to be. So for the mind attuned to the equivocal, nothing is ever absolutely the same. The ambiguous twofoldness of becoming both is and yet is not. On occasion we might even be tempted to regard this as a kind of metaphysical *duplicity* in which what is not insinuates itself as its opposite—namely, as what is. There is a passage between what is and what is not, such that what is not becomes what is, and what is becomes what is not. This looks like a process of equivocation in which nothing remains what it is, not even what is not. We are reminded of Macbeth's exclamation about the ambiguous nature of time itself: "Nothing is but what is not."

(Indeed Shakespeare's *Macbeth* is *the* play about the equivocal.) Becoming seems deceptive, shifty, a proteus that refuses to yield its one name; it slides out of the grasp without surrendering its secret identity. The transience of becoming is erratic, in the strong sense of giving us over to errancy. Becoming is an equivocal error, not the truth of being. The truth of being as becoming is error.

I suggest that we do not have to think exclusively of the doubleness in such ontologically negative terms. This is not to deny the emergence of error with the equivocal. But there are more affirmative ways to look at the equivocal. Thus, we can see in the indeterminate the promise of creative determination, not just the illusory slipping from ontological stasis to ontological stasis, through gaps of nothing that are merely covered over by the rapidity of the slipping. These seeming gaps are really the spaces of ontological possibility whereby the promise of the original power of being is stabilized. Coming to be is coming to concrete determination of the actuality of the power to be. There is an openness to this process of transition from indetermination to determination, and this openness is not to be closed with a fixing, immobilizing determination. Determinate being itself is to be understood as energized even in its integrity; the integrity of a being is the singular working of the creative power of the indeterminate. Its determinate being is a tense equilibrium of original power, poised briefly on time's wave. This poise of the integral determinate being is entirely energetic, entirely dynamic.

Thus there is no absolute univocal stasis. Nothing stays, nor can be stayed; nothing is settled forever. Yet in the universal impermanence there are the determinate poises of the dynamic. The universe of becoming is hence one of promise, promise that itself is ambiguous, since it contains the future as one of passing out of being, just as this present poise of being came to be from a past, antecedent not-being. The ambiguity of the happening of the between is the way it mingles creation and destruction, life and death, the surge into articulated being, the surcease and ebbing withdrawal of the flood of life.

In addition, we might say that being as becoming is both one and many, held together and diversified, not one or the other, but a differentiation of unities into multiplicities and the gathering of multiplicities back into some togetherness. This is already to state the matter in terms sufficiently articulate as to begin to transcend equivocity. Initially, the constitutive ambiguity is not encountered with this articulated response. As an aesthetic show of being, it is met in an overdetermined way. The happening of becoming takes place in a matrix of ambiguity. And we find an excess to this matrix that marks it as a source of origination, and as a coming towards us of a fulness that can be overpowering, overwhelming. I suggest that this matrix of ambiguity points us towards origination as diversification. Nor is there any separation of "fact" and "value" in this matrix. The response of the equivocal mind is thus closer to the original agapeic astonishment through which the human being finds itself opened to the worthiness of being.

For this reason there is a kind of *promiscuity* to the equivocal that will be dismissed by the logicist mind as "confusion," that is, as mixing things up together. But things are mixed up, things are mixed. They are mingled together, confused, and this, in the etymologically correct sense (*con-fusio*): the promiscuity of the equivocal is the confusion of becoming. Things fuse together; they flow into each other. Becoming is ontological confusion in that sense, fluid, porous, mixing and commingling. Being is confusing. Logically one may not like this, if one insists that being and intelligibility must be determinate. But who gives logic the license to dictate to being to be other than it is? Logic may not like the confusion of being but that may be logic's fault, not being's. Logic may have to think the confusion a little less petulantly, less self-insistent on the putative clarity and distinctness of its categorial schema.

But my point is not to exult in confusion. My point is to call attention to a *poiēsis* of intermediate being, prior to all univocal logicism and every mathematicization of nature. This *poiēsis* is not to be confined to any artistic expression we might devise. The very happening of the between is an ambiguous *poiēsis*, an origination process that articulates sensible and sensuous being, and not in any manner that neutralizes matter into an indifferent *res extensa*, or reduces it analytically to primitive primary qualities. The material world is the maternal aesthetic appearance of being (*materia* and *mater* are cognate, as noted before); it is a mother that natures. This mothering nature gives birth to beings as charged with the power of being that is originally and finally in excess of all finite determination. There is an aesthetic intimacy to the metaxological community of being that appears with equivocal becoming.

I want to illustrate this in terms of the doctrine of primary and secondary qualities. This view is the product of aesthetic and dianoetic univocity, I claimed, but it abstracted from the aesthetic equivocity of being as sensuously appearing. This aesthetic equivocity, I now suggest, is truer to the rapture of univocity, since primary and secondary qualities promiscuously mix in the flow of appearing. Perhaps for us humans the central manifestation of this mixing lies in the way we live nature in the intimacy of our bodies. Our bodies are not possessed by univocal souls in solitary self-possession of some material unit. To the contrary, our bodies are lived as equivocally mingled with the aesthetic body of nature. This mingling is never univocal but is an intimate, inarticulate, immediate mediation that marks us as incarnate inhabitants of the between. There is an immediate equivocity between ourselves and nature, itself felt as the flesh of externality, itself originally experienced in our bond with the mother's body. This immediate equivocity shows us to be surges of being in the between, wherein other-being touches us in the flesh, even as we incarnately touch the flesh of other-being.

The thereness of this flesh of nature is not marked by primary or secondary qualities; it is a charged presence redolent of a meaning we cannot now fix, given its overpowering presence at first. Since its sheer being-there is charged with enigmatic presence, we initially live a complicity with thereness, both in the flesh of our bodies and in the body of the world as present to us like flesh. In this primary aesthetic intimacy a process of interchange, and hence immediate mediation, is always going on from the beginning. This initial equivocal intimacy is prior to any distancing produced by the stabilization of self and world into distinct "units." This primal intimacy with being is *intimated* in agapeic astonishment.

In this primal intimacy we find no sensations such as are described by empiricism. There are givens, yes, but givenness is not an aggregate of discrete univocal sensa, void of value. For the latter, we have to *distance* ourselves from the first intimacy, and *reconstruct* appearing as devoid of the charge of its value as simply being. Primary and secondary qualities are abstractions produced by that distancing. They may prove to be useful abstractions for definite calculative purposes, but when they are posited as the elemental truth concerning the givenness of being, they are instead falsifications of the gift of the primal intimacy. For they are not primitive immediates but mediated results, constructed abstractions of a certain aesthetic and dianoetic univocity.

Their usefulness becomes questionable, especially when they generate a *reflective equivocity*, predicated on dualistic presuppositions. So the Cartesian rationalism that separates the thinking thing into its own spiritual univocity and reduces the happening of givenness to a lifeless *res extensa*; the empiricist view that separates aesthetic givenness into hard, objective, primary qualities and soft, subjective, secondary qualities; both these views are linked to this dualistic opposition of self-being and other-being. As participants of the between, self and other have been congealed into a separation without essential mediation, a separation beyond each singly, or beyond both as merely antithetical. What I mean by the primal aesthetic intimacy is very different to these rationalistic and empiricist equivocations. Rather the latter are the complementary opposites of the aesthetic and dianoetic univocities that turn away from or try to conquer this primal intimacy. It is as if dread of being overwhelmed by, or absorbed back into, the primal equivocity of aesthetic happening forces each, as univocalizing, to erect the self and nature's otherness into dualistic opposites, with the latter thenceforth conceived in terms of a constructed equivocity.

I need hardly say that the mediation of this unbridgeable difference has been the desideratum and despair of all philosophizing flowing from these sources. The desideratum is understandable, for this constructed equivocal dualism is the loss of the happening of the between, as the community of interchange and interaction. The despair is understandable but, in fact, unrelievable on the terms that produce it. The terms that produce it are defined by the very loss of the primal intimacy that later they try to remedy, but remedy in terms of the loss itself. But the despair cannot be redeemed thus, the loss is irreparable. Instead we need a different mindfulness that reminds us of the primal intimacy and ontological rapport with the aesthetic givenness of being in its ambiguous becoming.

If there are mediations of mind that remind us of this rapport and this *poiēsis* of being, the *aesthetic mindfulness of the artist* is an important instance. Art is a determination of mindfulness that is nonobjectifying relative to the happening of the between. Of course, there is determinacy with art, for the artist produces determinate works that have a pitch of singularity that is extraordinary. Yet these singularities remain alive with an excess that cannot be determinately objectified. The creative work of the overdetermined origin continues to shimmer in these singular concretions. Creation shimmers in these concretions.

The artist's mindfulness might be said to display fidelity to phenomenological happening in its originary richness. (Matisse: "exactitude is not truth.") It does not articulate this by dividing so-called primary and secondary qualities, neutral sense data and subjectivistic emotions projected onto the neutral thereness. Rather the values celebrated are intimate to sensuous appearing itself. Sensuous appearing is itself worthy simply to be celebrated for itself, appreciated in the marvel of its coming to manifestation. In other words, we find a recovery of agapeic astonishment before the aesthetic equivocity of becoming: this stuns us into mindfulness of charged and expressive presence. We may even find a renewal of our rapport with the primal "It is good" which celebrates the giving of creation. The neutralization of creation into an indifferent, objective "It" is overcome in terms of its originary abundance. Dualistic opposition is suspended. There is consent and appreciation and admiration at the original excess that comes to flower in the primal intimacy with creation.

Thus the equivocal aesthetic of becoming returns us to a sense of nature wherein the dynamism of *naturing* is preserved. Here the old distinction between *natura naturans* and *natura naturata* is not without its point. If we grant this distinction, nature itself is double; it is equivocal between its overdetermined dynamism as naturing, and its determination as natured into particular beings and objective happening. Nature is equivocal as diversifying the original indetermination into a prodigal plurality of beings. If the determinate being is a finite happening of the original energy of being, the finite happening shimmers with the dynamic naturing, that yet exceeds every one of its own natured finitizations. Nor is it possible to separate absolutely the naturing from the natured. The univocal sense of being does tend to separate these two. But the naturing exceeds every finite objectification and hence retreats beyond univocalization.

There is a difference, a doubling, but not a dualism, between the naturing and the natured. A sense for the equivocal makes us mindful of the doubling as more than a provisional failure of univocity, but as a constitutive ambiguity in the happening of being in the between. When Heraclitus said nature loves to hide, I think he pointed us to this constitutive ambiguity. This ambiguity is intolerable to the heirs of Descartes and modern science who would be the masters and possessors of nature. Such mastery is sovereignty over the determinacy of nature natured, but impotence before the indeterminacy of nature naturing. Such mastery is not the sovereign of the whole, but the *dominus* of what is given in determinate objectivity, and even here the fulness of giving escapes this dominating objectification.

It is the artist, let us say a Cézanne or a Monet, who is the inheritor of nature naturing. The artist is not the master, but the servant of the sensuous appearing of excess in the singular event or thing itself. This appearing retracts into its own reserve before all objectifying univocity. The marvel of a great art work is that the infinite reserve is manifested, intimated in the singular sensuous presence offered in the work. There is no reductive objectification of the reserve, the excess. The beyond is there, and yet not there; or it is there as beyond, beyond as there. Such artistry undergoes the pathos of the equivocal; but in suffering the equivocal, in letting the ambiguity reveal itself, something unsurpassable is shown, shows itself in the ambiguity. This revelation of aesthetic showing cannot be exhausted by any set of finite determinate concepts. The constitutive plurivocity of being is intimated in the sensuous showing of ambiguity itself. It is intimated in the pathos and consent—the appreciation that marvels and admires—that places us close again to the primal intimacy of being.

The *Mathēsis* of Nature, The *Poiēsis* of Naturing

It may be objected that I extraneously bring in the aesthetic, but this is to miss my point. The point is that being is first equivocally given as aesthetic manifestation. Very well, you say, but what happens after this first giving? I now want to explore if it is possible finally to suppress the aesthetics of being, even in the most thoroughgoing *mathēsis* of nature. I want to argue against this possibility.

First, I do think that in classical modern science there develops a diminished appreciation of the aesthetic show of being, a loss of naturing as the *poiēsis* of becoming, an attenuation of the poetry of being. Nature is natured and claimed to be captured in the determinations of mathematical equations. Consider some of Kepler's descriptions of the mathematics of nature. I understand these to be still in between: they are uttered with still living memory of the divine poetry of being, yet are anticipatory of a mathematics of the natured, which makes *poiēsis* redundant. Thus Kepler does not just calculate, he sings:

> Geometry is unique and eternal, a reflection of the mind of God. That men are able to participate in it is one of the reasons why man is an image of God. . . . all Nature and the graceful sky are symbolized in the art of geometry . . . Now as God the maker play'd He taught the game to Nature

whom he created in His image; taught her the self-same game which He played to her.

By contrast, with Galileo we sense that the *poiēsis* of naturing is already dimmed: "the book of nature is written in the mathematical language . . . without its help it is impossible to comprehend a single word of it." We do not sense the play of God. The language of nature "is written in the language of mathematics, and its characters are triangles, circles, and all other geometric figures, without which is it humanly impossible to understand a single word of it; without these, one wanders around in a dark labyrinth." Outside of calculation, there is no singing. Beyond or outside geometry, there is not the poetry of being but only our lostness in a labyrinth.[4]

It will not be long before the lost sense of the *poiēsis* of naturing leads to a contraction and final occlusion of the creative *poiēsis* of God. Then God becomes the universal geometer, the cybernetic fabricator, as in Leibniz's cosmic computer. The absolutization of this mathematical univocity leads eventually to the dissolution of God as the universal geometrical maker: the clock-making divinity of the clock-work world is made *redundant* with respect to the working of the made clock. The original dispenser of intelligibility is made dispensable with respect to determinate intelligibility, now taken as self-sufficient. There may be metallic precision in this universal mechanism, but it is inherently a dead universe. A world that is dead takes the place of the premodern living, animated cosmos.[5] The living God dies into the geometry He supposedly made. The universal geometer dissolves into the universal geometry, and we are left with mathematical structure without ultimate ground or source.

---

4. Kepler: "What else can the human mind hold besides numbers and magnitudes? These alone we apprehend correctly, and if piety permits to say so, our comprehension is in this case of the same kind as God's, at least in so far as we are able to understand it in this mortal life." He also says "geometry provided the Creator with a model for the decoration of the whole world," "quantities are the archetypes of the world." This is the famous passage in Galileo: "Philosophy is written in this grand book of nature, which stands continually open to our gaze. But the book cannot be understood unless one first learns to comprehend the language and to read the alphabet in which it is composed. It is written in the language of mathematics, and its characters are triangles, circles, and all other geometric figures, without which is it humanly impossible to understand a single word of it; without these, one wanders around in a dark labyrinth." "The Assayer," *Discoveries and Opinions of Galileo*, ed. and trans. Stillman Drake (New York: Doubleday, 1957), 237–38.

5. Consider how Galileo uses the image of the hand passing over a marble statue, implying that the statue has the same primary qualities as the body. But does this not mean that there is no difference between stone and flesh, between the dead and the living? Consider also his admiration for what he calls "the rape of the senses" by reason in Aristarchus and Copernicus.

Of course, the stress on geometry is not modern simply. And the real problem is rather the absolutization of the geometrical, the apotheosis of Pascal's *esprit géométrique* into the one and only privileged way to make true intelligible sense of things. One remembers the Pythagorean idea that musical and mathematical structures are analagous, each being a harmony of being. In modernity, though not yet in Kepler, there is a loss of the music in the mathematics. There is a devaluation of being. This follows the excision of the good from being, proximately in the exclusion of the good in terms of final causes, but more deeply in the inability to think any other sense of the good—that is, in the failure to envisage an *archeology* of the good, as well as a teleology.

If the *archē* is the good, then being is good and it is good to be. But modern mathematicized science reduces archeology to efficient causality, itself modeled on mechanism with mathematical structure. I am not endorsing Pythagoreanism without qualification, but I am recommending its plurivocity: we need mathematics and music to understand the intelligibility and to hear the beauty of the cosmos. Aesthetic, ethical, religious, and mathematical voices sound together. In modern science, there is a reduction of these plural voices to a dominating mathematical univocity. By comparison, we have only to think of Plato with respect to the good and geometry. In Plato, certainly in the *Timaeus*, geometry is ingredient in the intelligible structures of matter. The geometrical structures of intelligibility are fashioned in matter itself by the demiurge and his helpers. But the geometry of matter cannot be separated from the good of the cosmos. If we cannot understand being as related to the good, all the geometry is finally pointless. Indeed, the major issue about the being of the cosmos is its relation to the good. Otherwise the whole is purposeless, without point, valueless, as is any explanation that rests with this pointlessness.

This reminds us of Socrates' problem with naturalistic, reductionistic explanation, as recounted in the *Phaedo*: the whole thing, even intelligibly explained in terms of naturalistic mechanisms, is pointless, if there is no point to the whole—that is, if the good and being are not intimately related. The geometry of matter, discussed in the *Timaeus*, is itself an issue of the goodness of the origin. The origin, the father of all things, produces the cosmos as the most beautful and good and perfect possible, because it is good to be. Ingredient in being good is the geometrical intelligibility of matter. This is not just a valueless mechanism in a valueless whole. Even the latter is not really a whole, for we have to stopper our ears, when we hear the word "whole," against the inevitable resonance of "cosmos"—a thing of beauty, to be admired, appreciated, loved in the splendor of its being. "Whole" is ineluctably a word of the good, a carrier of memory of the creative *poiēsis* of being, testifying to the good we would extirpate, not to mechanism or worthless efficient causality.

On the issue of plurivocity, suppose we now turn to the world of post-Newtonian physics. Here we find a significant shaking of mathematical stability, even while the virtuosity of mathematicizing gains in power. When we radicalize the mathematicizing urge, first the seeming univocal stability of phenomenally given things dissolves into a set of mathematical equations and relations. This is supposed to describe the truth of things. But this is a truth that saves a set of abstract phenomena. The full concreteness of things is incredibly diminished. Most of a thing, and most especially its qualitative appearance, its aesthetic show, counts for nothing relative to mathematical structure, dianoetic univocity. If the truth of a thing is the latter, then the thing has all but no truth.

But as we saw at the end of the last chapter, this stabilization of Newtonian univocity has given way to the dynamism of the quantum world. Mathematical univocity, we recall, skirts the equivocal in the quantum universe as a world of doubles. Microevents can be described as waves or particles. The double language indicates a complementarity and an undecidability. We need the two languages to describe the doubles. Even in the use of the two languages there is another undecidable doubleness with respect to the determination of both momentum and position. In this doubleness indeterminacy enters. This indeed is taken up into mathematical formulation in terms of statistical probability, instead of strict classical causation. Nevertheless, we are at the edge of univocal causality and necessity. There is a breakdown of univocity when univocity is pushed towards its limits. This is an immanent breakdown that is by no means negative, since it is the prelude to the breakthrough into another way of trying to do justice to the truth of things.

Classically minded philosophers have criticized the uncertainty relations, yet these relations yield calculations and predictions that have been extraordinarily successful. Those who would reiterate classical views have not yielded comparable successes. The irony here is that what seems to be the subversion of univocal precision itself yields an order of univocal precision generally that is not available on, that is far superior to, the singular model of pure univocal precision itself. The dual descriptions do better relative to the world of univocity than classical singular univocity itself seems able to do. We might say that the very dual descriptions that deconstruct univocity open up the possibilities of univocity, beyond pure univocity itself. There is here a kind of immanent dialectic at work, in which the successor to pure univocity is both the downfall and yet the completion and continuation of univocity itself. For one must remember that there is no reneging on the desire to calculate as precisely and determinately as is possible, and to do it better and better. But this desire now is articulated in a more complex, indeed strange context. The old task is surpassed and yet renewed within the horizon of a transformed set of basic presuppositions about being.

What I want to focus on here is what might be significant for the aesthetics of becoming and the *mathēsis* of nature. For the need for a double description affects how we think about the *two* sides: particles become less compact and hard, in the sense that they must now be thought in terms of a minute electrical field or perhaps electron cloud, which indicates a probability range for the position of the electron. Likewise, the field of energy undergoes pressure from the particle side and becomes a more or less determinate center of energy, a wave packet. But, and this is the point, something that is more or less determinate is not univocally precise. If a field is also a center, and a center is also a field of vibration, the boundaries between determinacy and indeterminacy become porous. There is promiscuity between precise determination and more open indeterminacy. The center of energy, as determined by dynamic vibration in a dynamic field, becomes a kind of *open whole*. I know that this is a paradoxical concept from the standpoint of static univocity. Yet it tries to name the doubleness of determinacy and indeterminacy: openness is defined by the delimitation of the whole, while the delimitation of the whole is made to shimmer, vibrate by the openness that remains yet undetermined, and perhaps always indeterminate.

For classical physics an interplay of indeterminacy and determinacy as describing the nature of the *happening* would be rejected. There is no indetermination in the happening; there may be in our description of happening; but proper description will be the overcoming of the indefiniteness of our ignorance by the exactly definite formulation that matches the exact determinacy of the happening. By contrast, for quantum physics this interplay is a necessity forced on thought about nature by the nature of nature. The interplay of determinacy and indeterminism is not confined to our descriptions.

If the indetermination is not a mere empty indefiniteness, what then is it? A more original sense of creative possibility comes to mind. Microevents lend themselves to dual descriptions, each equally possible and indeed equally necessary. This might be seen as a pointer towards the potential plurivocity of being, as exhibited at the microlevel. It may also signal a rudimentary ontological freedom in the happening of energy at this basic level. I say ontological freedom, and imply no projection of freedom in an anthropomorphic sense. I mean a certain openness of possibility inherent in matter-energy at this basic level of microevents, and not just due to ignorance awaiting remedy with the advance of more powerful tools of univocal calculation. This openness suggests something about the naturing of the microevents themselves.

In addition there are other suggestions for the aesthetic show of becoming. Waves are dynamic formings rather than static forms, but what if particles, normally conceived as enduring stabilities, are washed by waves, so to say? Waves are patterns of becoming. The pattern need not be uniform, but it has to be a dynamic to be a wave in becoming, rather than a snapshot that freezes its measured period. In that respect, a wave is *an aesthetic pattern*, where there is a certain harmony in movement, a coincidence of concord and divergence, order and variation. Nor do we have to choose between extremes of inflexible order and amorphous chaos, frozen univocal being and orderless becoming. Instead we find a pattern in motion, an order in unfolding. The becoming of a center of being is itself a dynamic ordering. Thus a wave gathers itself to a crest, crests to break, breaks to reform, reforms to crest and break and renew itself again. It is an aesthetic union of creation and destruction.

We might suggest that the universal impermanence reveals just this forming and deforming. It shows a mixing of necessity and chance, predictability and freedom, regularity in succession and unpredictable surprise in ongoing formation. We might say that the aesthetic happening is a kind of play of variation and intelligibility. It is not just the game of geometry as fixed on static structure. This is why we spoke of microevents as open wholes. This too introduces the notion of aesthetic value. For an open whole is a forming of original energy that constitutes a more or less determinate framing of being, but one that does not enclose, or close off interchange with other determinate framings. Put otherwise, open wholes are a mixture of order and variation; they are double. If chance is ingredient in the matrix of creation, chance is not mere arbitrariness, but the promise of novel possibility in an open space of interplay. The point is that the opening and the interplay are not completely determinate but double, both determinate and indeterminate, and again not in the negative sense of the indefinite.

Implications for the aesthetics of becoming can also be seen in this fact—namely, that the languages of waves and particles need not be taken as completely *literal* descriptions. These languages are taken initially from macrohappening. We discover a transfer from the everyday observable to what is not immediately given to observation. And yet the aesthetic reappears within the mathematization of being. For these languages are metaphorical descriptions, which does not mean fictions simply. They are descriptions that include theoretical models or imagings of what cannot be immediately imaged in everyday perception. To call them metaphors in no sense implies that they lack a truth function. Rather their truth function shows a surpassing of any simple univocal correspondence to a single, fixed state of affairs.

If microevents are like waves, like particles, it seems we need the metaphorical language of a double likeness to image the truth of what is eventuating at an ontological level that eludes direct observation in immediate perception. There is hence a mingling of univocity and other modes of vocality—for example, metaphorical speech that transcend univocity. Nor do we have to say that the metaphor is absolutely equivocal. The metaphor establishes a mediating relationship. Absolutely equivocal saying seems to be a saying, but it is a mode of saying that hides its possible duplicity; it says and it does not say; it is a nonmediation posing as intermediation. By contrast, a genuine metaphor makes a connection. To speak in the metaphors of waves and particles is to resort to aesthetic speech, just in order to do justice to an ontological state of affairs that can also be articulated with great mathematical exactness. What is interesting here is the conjoining of aesthetical metaphor and mathematical univocity. The latter gives precise determinate specificity *within* a universe of discourse that is ineluctably aesthetic and not absolutely deterministic.[6]

I imply no "aestheticization" of mathematics that would dispense with truth-claims. This is not my aim. I intend no diminution of the seriousness of the claims of truth. I am calling attention to the aesthetic appearance of the events of being. Aesthetic is not a merely idle play with possibilities, but the appearing of being, the interplay between our bodied mind and the bodying forth of the original power of being in the events, micro and macro, that constitute the world of creation. Our mindfulness is called to the complexity of truth, which here suggests a certain communivocity of mathematical univocity and aesthetic metaphoricality, a mixing of geometry and finesse. All saying is aesthetic; it is *logos* made flesh. One might suggest that mathematics, as much as art in the more normal sense, is the flesh of mind, the being bodied forth of thought.

Let me conclude these remarks by noting three consequences of the above. First, to speak of "likeness" is to grant a *fallibility* to knowing. We find no absolute univocal certitude to our scientific claims; there is the "likelihood" of its truth, given the preponderance of the evidence and the coherence of the theoretical hypotheses. Yet such fallibility offers no justification for any privileging of subjectivity; rather being and its truth might be other than we think; therefore, continued openness to the thinking of other-being is needed. I suggest that likeness and likelihood are carriers of the self-transcendence of mind towards what is other. They indicate a humility before the other in thinking itself. In other words, likely thinking is not pure self-mediating thinking, nor does it approach other-being as the production or construction of itself. It exactly wants to transcend the latter. It is reluctant to label any of its thoughts or categories as absolutely necessary. Expressed otherwise, likely thinking always is ready for a thinking that thinks not just itself, but the other of thought. It lets the vector of self-transcendence dismantle any closed structure of concepts. It exposes itself to the interruption of being-other, as otherwise than it thinks.

A second consequence concerns the *realistic* side of relatedness. I suggest that the *meta* of metaphor is to be read as a vector of reference and relatedness to an otherness that saying itself does not simply produce out of itself. The *meta* of metaphor reminds us of the *meta* of the metaxological: *meta* can mean both in the midst and also beyond; being in the middle and being related to what is beyond or other. We could say that the *meta* of metaphor recalls us to the double mediation, the interplay and transcending that eventuates in the middle. The *meta* is a vector of transcendence, a going of mind towards an original that cannot be exhaustively included in one univocal

---

6. Some of the language is highly metaphorical, or has metaphorical roots—for example, terms like *quarks, colors, charms, chaperone molecules, buckminsterfullerenes, wimps, black hole.*

language. And so the metaphorical languages of waves and particles are not absolute; their reference to the otherness of the microevent is heuristic, not absolutely constitutive. The *meta* keeps open the space of a difference; the possible otherness of the microevents remains—otherness both in the sense of irreducibility to the knower, and otherness in the sense of retaining its own reservoir of possibility, a reservoir that may still continue to surprise and astonish us with revelations yet unimagined.

The plurivocity of saying seems to be needed, regardless of the very precise mathematical formulations that are available in both languages. A language may be immanently marked by a very great degree of determinate univocity, but when it functions as a *vector of transcendence*, bespeaking the otherness of being, it does not function, vis-à-vis its relatedness to that otherness, with the same determinate univocity. Indeed it cannot, since the vector of transcendence necessarily implicates a process of mediation; and no process of mediation, precisely as a going between, can ever be rendered completely in entirely determinate and univocal terms.

A third consequence concerns the *worth* of being. For were the univocal *mathēsis* to complete itself by entirely eradicating the aesthetics of being, the scientistic univocalizing of being would be nihilistic. All being would be value-less, a worth-less thereness; there would be no basis for the goodness of being. In universal determinism, efficient causation carries no sense of inherent goodness, nor any sense of the goodness of creation, or coming to be. The universe is a worthless mechanism, worthless in the ultimate metaphysical sense, though humans cannot tolerate this and project their own value on the worthless being. This nihilistic devaluation is implicit in the doctrine of primary and secondary qualities, the latter seen as the projection of values from the subject onto the object as in itself inherently valueless.

As I implied above, the aesthetics of equivocal being call into question this doctrine and its descendent variations. In addition, if metaphors are carriers of transcendence, they are more than mere projections of our will to manipulate. If the latter is the truth, it too leads to nihilism. For if the self too participates in the universal mechanism, hence it too is ontologically valueless, hence ultimately its projections of value have no inherent value. Put succinctly: in a valueless universe, human value is itself ultimately valueless. If there is to be a justified claim made by the human being as the creator of value, there must be some ontological basis for value in being itself. For the human being to be a source of value, creation must not only *be hospitable* to the good, but it must *be good*, be itself a creation of the good.

The meaning of these views, I add, is as yet very ambiguous, hence still in the play of the equivocal. Nevertheless, in this play there is promised a resurrection of the aesthetic show of being that opens onto a universe that is not worthless in the scientistic sense. Aesthetic show is the primal appearance of being as charged with value: being is ambiguously there, admittedly good and yet haunted by shadows, flickering between attractiveness and threat; yet the primal intimacy of being is charged with the equivocal intimation of the good. Equivocal being is the chiaroscuro of the good.

The Equivocal Flower: On the Orchid

What of the equivocity of being relative to *macrohappening*? I will talk about nonhuman and human nature. Before turning to the second in the next section, let me offer the orchid as a revealing example of the first. In both cases the aesthetics of being will be crucial.

To exemplify equivocal being, I might have chosen the chameleon, given its power to disguise itself, to take on the variegated coloration of its environment. This is quite revealing. The chameleon does not have a rigid univocal identity; its identity includes the power to merge with the other, to be other than itself, in its absorption into the aesthetics of the surrounding otherness. This being-other, while still being itself, is a dynamic process of interchange with the surrounding environment, an interchange reflected in a change in the aesthetics of the chameleon's own presented identity. This identity is the same and not the same, at one and the same time. We witness a modulation in the self-mediation of the chameleon, while it intermediates with the plurivocal aesthetics of the external otherness. A chameleon is a chameleon, but it is not a chameleon; it is a twig or a leaf or a spike of grass. This pluralization of appearances that present resistance to a fixed univocalization is just what is meant by equivocity.

The unavoidability of language of the aesthetic is especially manifest with the orchid. Orchids are flowers, and often of surpassing and delicate beauty. The orchid family itself testifies to the prodigal pluralizing power of nature naturing. There are about thirty thousand species of orchid. Nature is not miserly. Flowers are immediately associated with beauty, as when we speak of *the flower of youth, the bloom of beauty.* But the orchid is the artful flower par excellence. Its aesthetic show may include the radiance of exquisite fragrance, or the display of exotic coloration, or extravagant exhibitionism.

But the show is double, or a wily complex doubling of identity. Consider the fact that most orchids are named after what they look like, like the lady's-slipper orchid. Their identity is *taken from the other* they resemble. Their identities are double, their own and that of the other. Their own identity is that of the other, but it is still their own, but as a simulation of the other. There is simulation but for purposes of dissimulation, and dissimulation for the purposes of the propagation of the same, of their own kind. They simulate others to be dissimulating with respect to these others; and these others, in being deceived, help the orchid propagate itself. In other words, there is the play of univocity and equivocity in this alternation of simulation and dissimulation. There is equivocity relative to image and original. Which is the image, which the original? Becoming is a double image. There is a co-implication of image and original: the image is the original, the original is the image; one is reminded of the ancient belief in the all in all.

Orchids are especially artful in stratagems connected with their own re-production. They need to attract insects to act as pollinators, to carry the seed between them and their own kind. They must become seducers. Orchids are the *erotic equivocators* of the flower kingdom. They develop their self-presen-tation to lure the necessary insects, often by putting on the pretense that they are the proper erotic double for the insect itself. Some of the orchids mimic other flowers that attract insects. For instance, there are some orchids that mimic the female bee to lure the male bee towards them through the intoxica-tion of look and smell. The male bees goes for his seeming other, his sexual double; but the double is equivocal and he becomes the unwitting partner in another equivocal game of fertilization—that of the orchid, not his own.

Naturally, this situation can be frustrating, in some cases creating a game of endless deferral. There are orchids that mimic female wasps, and frequently they are so effective that the male wasp will go to it repeatedly, in taking and leaving pollen. There results what has been called pseudocopulation between the male wasp and the flower/female, though the male drains himself for the fecundity of the flower. He is fooled by the seducing orchid. Even the word orchid carries this dissimulation of mimicry. The Greek word for testicle is *orchis*. At the base of the orchid stem there is a testiclelike bulb. But this bulb is not a true bulb; it is a simulacrum of a bulb. By contrast with the tulip, whose bulb contains an embryonic tulip, the simulated testicle of the orchid is for storage of water and nourishment. Suppose truth were a woman, Nietzsche said, and the equivocal sense of being coyly insinuates itself. But these orchids are not men, not even women, but only the fakery of phallo-centrism. These testes are no testes; they are the ruses of the equivocal.

These seducers live long. They are rare flowers. Exotic, they are also patient. They can wait on the equivocalness of being. For naturing is in love and the things of creation are wooing; the excitation of fecundity vibrates in this all in all. Naturing at woo waits. To be themselves orchids are willing to play the waiting game of not being themselves. In its extravagant self-display, the orchid hides in wait. Its self-revelation is its self-concealing; it conceals itself in its self-revelation; and it is *both* these opposites at once. In fact, re-vealing is concealing, concealing is revealing; the opposites promiscuously mingle. Their dissimulating reproductive strategies seem to be geared to-wards infrequent fertilization, and yet when the seduction works, the issue can be enormous. They may be univocally symbiotic with one kind of insect, and, comparatively speaking, may only be rarely successful in inducing the necessary transfer of pollen. There is no univocal guarantee of success and the chances of fertilization are not high. Yet when there is success, there may be many, many thousands of seeds.

We understand the equivocalness of the orchid. So you might rightly object: By understanding the equivocal, do we not thereby make it univocally clear? To a degree, the degree to which we precisely determine what is going on. But do we make the meaning of propagation univocally clear? Propagation is via the equivocal, but what is clear about the fecundity of nature naturing? We may know the precise mechanism, but do we have a univocal account of the meaning of perpetuation: the passing on of the energy of being in the passing away of this being? We may know the mechanism, but may have lost the astonishment, and then we have lost the possibility of mindfulness which sees the point at issue. Fecundity and propagation and perpetuation in the universal impermanence show nature naturing to be a strange excitation of original energy that passes on, even as this determinate being passes away. This excitation, this *energeia*, this being at work of the original power of being is given to work in the determinate being.

Even given a measure of univocal determination of the mechanism, our astonishment here is about the *that it should be so at all*. And this is not just curiosity about the what of the determinate mechanism by which propagation is effected. Relative to this *that it should be so at all*, what is univocally clear about, let us call it, this species-affirmation of being by the orchid? The orchid is there; it presents itself; it presents itself otherwise than as univocal; it shows itself as equivocal, hence also as hiding itself in its self-show. This aesthetic double presentation is the joy of being of the flower. It is the song of its thereness. Its existence is its standing out as there, a floral vector of transcendence that affirms its own being in its thereness, that mediately affirms being *simpliciter* in the singularity of its own self-affirming standing out. Its thereness is the singing of its presence. What it sings is: It is good to be. And all the ruses of pretense and equivocation are with the aim to pass on to its offspring this "It is good to be." The joy of propagation in the equivocal fecundity of the universal impermanence is the species-passage, the passing on, of this "It is good to be."

Suppose again, as Nietzsche suggested, that truth were a woman, and suppose again that Heraclitus was right that nature loves to hide? Would not modern science be marked sometimes by impatience towards, sometimes even hatred of the equivocal? Would not its knowing and its practical offshoot, technology, be a violence to nature because of its equivocality? We distrust the earth; we would put it on the rack, put it to the torture, as Bacon wants it—no wooing or courtship of truth here. Torture is the strategy of truth of the instrumental mind that cannot abide anything hidden; the intimacy of being will be forced to yield its secret; this will be a violation of the equivocal mother, *mater*. Hatred of the equivocal suggests hatred of otherness as hidden in an intimacy of matter that resists objectification. Torture would objectify the intimate, but the very truth of intimacy, thus revealed, would be the falsification of its truth.

Suppose nature were an orchid, suppose scientistic man were a stinging wasp. Would not our knowing be like the pseudocopulation of the wasp buzzing in the orchid? No fly in the bottle this. The wasp has passed on the orchid's "It is good to be," and it does not even know it—does not even know it, for all the insect's vehement will to know univocally. Would not the last laugh then be on the wasp?

The Acme of Equivocity: The Human Being

The human being is the equivocal thing par excellence. I say it is the *being* of the human that is equivocal, not just our speech about the human. Being bespeaks itself equivocally, and this is glaringly evident in the human being, where the power of the indeterminate becomes original and freely creative. In the human being, becoming becomes the promise of mindfully directed self-becoming. The promise of human being is a free aesthetic show which, as free, is also an undetermined power to hide and deceive. In this freedom of being the equivocality reaches deepest.

Hence we find no simple univocal identity to the human being, and it has been the despair of history to arrive conclusively at a single, unsurpassable definition. Humankind has been called the rational animal; or the featherless biped, a good joke of Plato—and the joke itself is more deeply mindful than the stiff seriousness of the Aristotelian *horismos*; by *laughing* Plato witnesses to the equivocality of human being. The human being has been called the animal who is always in heat, or the laughing animal, the naked ape, and many more things. The univocal mind will look for one defining characteristic that provides the conclusive essential definition. And yet we have a pluralization of essentials, all of which seem quite reasonable in their own way.

This pluralization tells us that we ought not to be miserly in our mindfulness of the human. Logic is stingy, art is generous, man is prodigal. He calls for imagination and *poiēsis*, the image and *aisthēsis*, as well as the analytical category. Human being is an aesthetic excess prior to logicization. The excess outlives logic. Ockham's razor is all very well as a methodical tool of logic; but the human thinker wields that razor, and hence already testifies to something in excess of the razor. We multiply beyond necessity with man; man is just a multiplication of being beyond necessity, and hence always over and above Ockham's razor. If man were to be cut to size in accord with Ockham's razor, man would not be man.

For man is excess; man is the animal of flourish, the entity of exaggeration and hyperbole. Here the energy of transcendence becomes mindful of itself in becoming, as an incessant othering of the original power of being. For the self of the human is just its othering, its self-othering. It is this excess of self-transcendence that is coming to manifestation in the equivocalness of being, the constitutive ambiguity of being in the between that cannot be reduced to one essential, univocal definition. We are self-multiplying beyond necessity because we are simply the ambiguity of freedom: the promise of yes to being, and the deformed refusal or revolt against being; called to the truth and smug in our little sinkholes of error; wanting to be loved and blithe about our impotence to love; or loving being-other and blithe about the clamor of self-insistence. With us forked animals, as Lear called us, there is nothing univocal, no one definition, no essential definition. This does not mean we lack many essential characteristics. We do exhibit essential characteristics, but there is no one single univocal one that will tell the full truth. Our definition is beyond definition.

Quite so: a definition is itself the product of a process of defining, and man is more defining than defined. The moment there is a definition, the defining proceeds to something other to the definition. With us there is an excess to the defining that is never completely encapsulated in any one definition. The excess and hyperbole of the human being is such that it will throw itself into more and more self-definitions. There is more of the human being in the defining than in the definition, hence no definition can encapsulate the energy of self-transcendence that comes to show itself in this the forked animal.

Nor is this to sing some hymn to the magnificence of humanity. Not at all. Our constitutive ambiguity ranges all the way from the peak to the pit, from the height to the abyss, from grandeur full beyond measure to the misery beyond every word of irredeemable abjectness. The happening of the between is stretched to the extremes in the human being. Man himself is in the between as the very living embodiment of the ambiguity: at once the extremes and the middle, the middle that is the point of conjunction of the extremities, the majesty and the scum of the world.

Moreover, the equivocality is manifest in our being as *embodied*. For there is no objectification of human flesh that does justice to it as flesh. We might say that human flesh is the intimacy of being incarnate, the intimacy of materiality itself. Incarnation is the coming to presence of self in the intimacy of its being. This coming to presence, presence that is not univocal, is first manifest in the aesthetic body. Indeed the incarnate body itself is an extraordinarily compacted self-affirmation, an "I am." Nor is this incarnate "I am" closed in on itself. Since the flesh is in communication with the body of the world, there is compacted in its affirmation an affirmation of being *simpliciter*. The "I am" of the incarnate body is an affirmation of the joy of elemental being as good to be. And of course, these different affirmations are not at first sorted out into different categories; they are promiscuously equivocal. With further development they will become mediated and more differentiated.

With the aesthetic body we are, it seems, in community with the aesthetic appearance of nature's otherness as charged with presence. This aesthetic body is immediately beyond simple univocity, both in its intimacy with being's otherness, and its own self-intimacy. There is a constitutive ambiguity about this body, as both revealing and concealing, as participant in a community, hence public before others, and as also ineradicably intimate, inward, hence always to some degree hidden, or potentially hidden. The body is hence the intermediacy of a double happening: a self-disclosure to others and a welcome of otherness; a reserve of intimate selfhood and a modesty, perhaps fear and trepidation, in the very vulnerability of intimacy before the other. The aesthetic body is a between through which passes the equivocal play of definition and freedom, objectification and the inwardness of subjectivity, the stone and the heart, violence and hospitality, determinate being-there and the excessive indeterminacy of a self-transcending being that can never be completely determined.

The aesthetic expression of the human being takes place on the narrow equivocal ridge of this between. We walk this narrow ridge, knowing a doubleness that cannot be rendered completely by one side or the other. For we are *determinate*, yet we are not determinate: I am not just this, yet I am just this I, and nothing else. And we are *indeterminate*, yet we are not formless and indefinite: more than every determination, yet not more in an absolutely homogeneous indefinition. We are robustly there in our bodies, yet vulnerably there, because the body reveals and conceals, communicates and betrays, what we are in the intimacy of innerness. We are double from the beginning; we are the between as double; and we remain double all through. The equivocality of our doubleness is that constitutive ambiguity, always caught between the mediation with ourselves that is indispensable, and the intermediation with others that confers membership of the community of being. We are not selves confronting others, but selves who are self-othering, and selves in whom the voices of the others already sound from the origin. And we do not first know whose voice we are; for even our own voice comes to us from an other we do not own at first. Even when we become our own person, we do not own the voice.

I suggest also that free *imagination* is crucial to the equivocal aesthetics of self-being. For with the freedom of imagination comes the power to err and deceive. Self-transcendence brings the promise of truth, but the promise can be deformed or betrayed. Freely deformed, we love the darkness, hate the truth, instrumentalize the ambiguity of being, use the equivocal to colonize further the realm of shadows. Generally philosophers have abjured equivocity precisely because error and deception decisively enter here. For we can deceive others by presenting ourselves as other than we really are. There is an inwardness, an idiocy, that I hide in showing to the other a face at odds with this innerness. I am split between the outer and the inner; the truth of the outer is opposed to the truth of the inner; the shown outer is presented as the truth of the inner. In other words, deception of the other is made possible by a self-pluralization between inwardness and outerness, and within inwardness itself; for in order to deceive, the inward knows that the outward is not the inward.

In *self-deception* there can be an equivocality even more intractable than in deception of another. There is an idiocy to equivocal selfhood: an intimacy so intimate that the inner self may not determinately know what this is, may not know itself in this intimacy that retreats beyond all determinate recovery. Man hides from himself, hides his vileness from himself, hides his destiny from himself. The human being can be hidden beyond any recovery by human searching. I think that self-deception itself is clearly not fully intelligible if being is only univocal. How can a self deceive itself? I must deceive *myself* to *deceive* myself; hence I must know of the deception, hence cannot be deceiving myself; and yet I deceive myself. We split ourselves inwardly, and hide one split from another; and yet not absolutely, since there is the possibility of communication between the split selves. If so, there must be a self that is both the splits, while not being either, not being determinately identified with either. There is no way a logic of univocity can fully account for the twisted dynamics of self-deception.

Let me briefly note some significant expressions of the aesthetic equivocity of the human being. Consider the way we *adorn* ourselves, make ourselves *other* than we are, and sometimes in order to *be ourselves* in a more fulfilling way. Or think of our nature as *actors* when we assume the role of another; we become ourselves in being other to ourselves. Consider human *mimicry*: it is done with a free imaginative mindfulness in the human being, not according to a botanical code as in the orchid. Miming is an act of self-transcendence in which the self becomes other to itself, while yet at the same time remaining itself. Our being is double in the mime, doubled in the mask.[7]

All these instances are connected to free imagination. Free imagination releases us from biological univocity, letting the promise of variation and variability arise in our mindfulness of being. Just this break with univocity was viewed with suspicion by some philosophers. Consider Socrates' seeming hostility to actors, artists: they lacked a univocal identity, and were always multiplying roles beyond necessity, and hence in danger of being nothing rather than something. And yet freedom emerges in this power to be nothing. The power of "being nothing" (itself an equivocal phrase) is also the power of becoming other to univocal identity. It returns us to an indetermination prior to determinacy. We can indeed be lost in a formless indefinition, but we also can determine ourselves anew in the indeterminate, re-create the self and being as other, from out of the nothing.

This "being nothing" is not empty at all. It is the overdetermined excess of transcendence at work in us; it is not a mere lack; it is the generosity of being as original, as originative, a generosity at work in the fecundity of free self-transcendence. This generosity, this overdetermined power of plenitude, is freed into mindfulness with the imagination. Imaginative mindfulness is

---

[7] See *Philosophy and its Others*, 78–79.

an ontological condition beyond the spatial determination of materiality. It soars into the being of the other. I imagine what you are; and in that mindful act I transcend myself towards you as other. This is an act of creative attention: I put myself in your life, your being; I double myself in you, in order to mind your truth. Thus imagination is *mind for the other*, a promise of an agapeic movement of self-transcendence that shapes itself in the equivocality of selfhood, itself defined doubly between its own selfhood and the selving or happening of other-being. There is no univocity of imaginative mindfulness. Imagination is ultimately metaxological, but the constitutive ambiguity of the between does have an equivocal manifestation.[8]

This is one reason why psychoanalysis has held that the law of contradiction does not obtain in the so-called primary processes. The latter are beyond the univocalizing mind, closer to the imaginative dynamism of aesthetic being. Opposites promiscuously mingle there without experienced incongruity, in this prereflective immediacy of the equivocal. This promiscuous equivocality is closer to the origin of creativity. It might be compared to the originative chaos out of which form and determination emerge, but which is not itself simply a form or determination. It is an overdetermined plenitude in which there is an all in all, an immediate implication, co-implication of each in every other, and every other in each.

These are, so to say, the waters before God created. As imaginative mindfulness, we dip back again into the primal waters, seeking baptism in the origin, rising once more into original determination. The maternal ocean or womb of the self flows and ebbs in the self. I recall the view that ontogeny recapitulates phylogeny. I recall also the older microcosmic belief that man resumes, is the resume of, all the modes of being in himself. Human being is the equivocity of the all in all. Man is slime, man is rock, man is flower, man is beast, man is himself between, man is vector to God. Man is between himself and the ultimate as other, an equivocal ecstasis beyond himself.

Given this, it is not surprising to discover that the equivocal is nowhere more evident than in human *desire*. The play of indetermination and determinacy here assumes an almost impossibly tangled character. Note again the bond of equivocity, desire, *aisthēsis*, imagination, origination. The self-transcendence at work in desire, shaped in desire's unfolding, is not primordially a matter of categorial logic. And yet there is no simple formlessness to self-transcendence, even though it is not logically univocal. It is not unintelligible, but the intelligibility is not univocal. Desire shows the work of lack in the human being; we desire what we lack; and in this lack there is a subversion of univocal identity. We are not self-identical in desire, but seek what is other, and seek to fulfil ourselves through the other. We seek ourselves as other in fulfilling ourselves through the mediation of

---

8. On imagination as metaxological, see *Philosophy and its Others*, 83ff.

the other. If we seek ourselves, we are not ourselves; we are other to ourselves, and yet we are ourselves in seeking ourselves. We are and are not ourselves. We are a living double in tension, and this doubleness seem irreducible to one univocal identity, once the energy of desire has erupted in selfhood.

Moreover, there is a *pluralization* of selving when desire shows itself to be self-multiplying. The self may seek to satisfy this determinate desire and that. But in satisfying this and that determinate desire, dissatisfaction erupts once again and a ceaseless restlessness is set in motion that continually transcends every determinate desire and satisfaction. There is a necessary specificity to our desire, and yet also an indeterminacy to desiring as continually activated, an indeterminacy that goes beyond the specification of every finite satisfaction. So we find an infinite restlessness at work in the determinate satisfaction of this and that specific desire. The human being is the play between this finite determination and infinite indeterminacy.

The multiplication of desire can be even more bewilderingly equivocal in act. Unlike the determined routine of biological satisfaction, there seem no clearly preprogramed essence to human desire. Since the openness of freedom is at work, we are capable of desiring exactly opposite objects; and at least initially we are not at all sure as to what will finally confer contentment. Nothing in finite satisfactions seems absolutely to slake the self. Any modicum of mathematical precision seems lacking. There is no geometry of desire. There is no mathematics of the good. Ambiguity is written all over human desire.

This is why equivocality arises also relative to the happening of *communication*, community. Another person gestures or speaks but there is equivocality in the signs of intent. There is no *technē* to read this meaning that is not mathematically transparent. It might mean the opposite of what it seems to mean. It might be a crooked communication, indirect, mediated by zig and zag. There might be no straight speaking. It might be beating around the bush. It might be communication by silence, not-communication; it might be speaking to hide silence, not communicating by communicating. Or it might be a matter of throwing someone off the scent, a decoy line of development, clues that lead nowhere, signs that signify nothing, except the false path the deceived is meant to travel. The truth is elsewhere. It poses the enigma of being other than it seems to be.

This "seeming" of truth can be bound up with the *malignity* of the equivocal. "Seems, madam, I know not seems," so says Hamlet. But "seems" is all Macbeth knows: "So fair and foul a day I have not seen" [I,iii]. It seems fair and it is foul, it seems to augur well, but is destined to doom. Banquo rightly asks: "What can the devil speak true?" "But 'tis strange:/And oftentimes, to win us to our harm,/ The instruments of darkness tell us truths,/Win us with honest trifles, to betray's/In deepest consequence" [I,iii].

Macbeth is saturated with equivocation.[9] One can underestimate its power to destroy, as does Lady Macbeth. "A little water clears us of this deed:/How easy it is then!" [II, iii], she says. But despite her assured univocity about guilt, she will go mad. She will walk in her sleep, she who chided her husband for thinking that he had murdered sleep—presciently, but nesciently, she then said: thinking so, it will make us mad.

Macbeth fitfully anticipates his own strangulation by the equivocal. This is a world of distrust, dark with a malice at the heart of things. "Double, double, toil and trouble;/ Fire burn and cauldron bubble" [IV,i]. We are put in mind of the evil genius of Descartes. "Cruel are the times, when we are traitors/And do not know ourselves" [IV,ii].[10] Despair at, leading to defiance against, the malignity of the equivocal seems to be Macbeth's only way out. "I pull in resolution, and begin/To doubt th' equivocation of the fiend/That lies like truth" [V,vi]. Finally Macbeth comes to say of the wicked sisters: "And be these juggling fiends no more believed,/That palter with us in a double sense; /That keep the word of promise to our ear,/And break it to our hope" [V,viii]. The malignity of the equivocal, as the perilous seeming of truth, leads to defeat by the dark and to death.

But there is a *fecundity* to the equivocal, as well as a possible malignity. On this score, equivocity is intimately connected to erotic desire. An other says "no" to one. Is the rebuff really and truly a "no"? Desire may invest the "no" with an ambiguity it perhaps had, it perhaps had not. Is there a "no" that is too coy to reveal its "yes," on first approach? Are there not "yeas" that are tepid, wishy-washy, even antagonistic, communicating the opposite intent to their semantic content? How do we move with the slippery "maybe"? Where are the clear and distinct signs of what direction to take? Or the other person may have no determinate desire one way or the other, until his or her desire is aroused in a certain direction, by one's own approach. Indeed, if the approach is too univocal or direct, it may entirely kill desire. Suggestion rather than statement, a raised eyebrow, not a con-

---

9. Macbeth: "To beguile the time/Look like the time . . . look like th' innocent flower,/ But be the serpent under it" [I,v]. See above on the orchid. "Away and mock the time with fairest show:/False face must hide what the false heart doth know" [I, vii]. We "make our faces vizards to our hearts,/Disguising what they are" [III,i]. See the knocking at the gate: the porter calls himself Hell's porter who lets in an equivocator "that could swear in both scales against either scale." The porter speaks of drink as an equivocator with lechery that makes him and mars him, sets him on and takes him off, makes him stand to and not stand to . . . [II, iii]. This is a little of the comedy of the equivocal, of the erotic, . . .even though we know the grim scene of murder that awaits revelation.

10. This is an exchange between Lady Macduff and her son about traitors. Macduff himself says later "such welcome and unwelcome things at once/'Tis hard to reconcile." [IV, iii].

tract for mutual use,[11] an intimating silence rather than an unambiguous avowal, all of these first *may* be the proper animators of desire; the second, may be its death. Desire as equivocal loves the twilight. For in the play of light and darkness, imagination takes flight, longing is aroused, longing that knows not what it really longs for, but that is often consumed in its own half-blind ardor. We love what we want to love or be loved by; we do not always love what is to be loved.

This is why erotic equivocality is often tied to the aesthetic self. Thus, adornment can be the language of seduction and appeal. To reveal its equivocal desire, the self must mask itself—that is, conceal its desire. It wants to be more than itself thus, not make a violent cut in possibility, wants to revel in the unresolved play of possibility. For the equivocation of possibility arouses desire. The masking of self is a presenting and dissimulating. The masked self doubles its identity, puts itself just beyond reach and draws fascination towards the ungrasped. That a question mark hangs over the masked identity, all the more rouses the attraction of the enigmatic possibility.

Pretense and presence here go hand in hand. We talk about "putting a face on things." This is presentation. But we already have a face, so why the second face, the double face? This is the ingression of possible pretense into presence. We enter the hazard of the possible. We may put a false face on things, on ourselves. An unexpected vistor knocks, and we are disheveled and we exclaim in woe: I am not presentable! We speak of putting our best face forwards, but this too may be an equivocal falsification of presence. At first blush it might seem that the face is the univocal presence par excellence.[12] We speak of taking things at face value, as if face value were primordial and elemental. But if things can only be taken at face value, there would never be a "best face" to put forward. Hence the face mixes the possibility of the equivocal and the univocal. Even its univocity is potentially equivocal. Thus the face value of an orchid is a deception. There is more complex equivocality of the face in the face-to-face of the human.

Consider how equivocal desire puts the best face on for the seduction of the other, and hence for the use of the other to mediate the seducer's own satisfaction. There's no art to find the mind's construction in the face, says Duncan [I, iv], immediately before Macbeth, his future murderer, enters, to be honored by Duncan for courage in battle. There is no art in the sense of *technē*, as say Aristotle defines this in the *Poetics*. And yet there is no way to read the face, if we do not have art, if we are not attuned to the aesthetics of the face. There is no logic of the face, no algorithm or technical rule to read its multiple meaning.

---

11. Kant on marriage: a contract for the mutual use of the genitals!

12. Levinas seems to think this.

So with the face of the seducer, you may not be able to tell for certain if you are being seduced. If you knew for certain, there would be no seduction. There is no geometry of seduction; instead there is finesse in the services of exploiting the equivocal desire of the other. The approach is equivocal, the response is equivocal. For even the yielding may be with misgivings or enthusiastically; and yet this "yes" may be shadowed by the intimation of deceit or betrayal, may be infiltrated by the barely suggested betrayal, over against the explicitly stated avowals of eternal fidelity. We are never absolutely sure. The hand washes the hand, it is said; but the right hand does not know what the left hand does, when they equivocally touch.

Consider the way the lewd look of another shames me, or arouses shamelessness. Where is the univocity of shame or shamelessness? There is none. Where is the univocity of modesty? There is none. Both shame and modesty are equivocal, and mingle with each other. Shame can be fear before the look of the other; shame can also be the inner intimate realization that one has betrayed the promise of transcendence. Sometimes it is *both* together. Modesty can also be a hesitant trepidation before the possible threat of the other, or a reactive lack of adventuring; or it may be the guarding of the deepdown dignity of selfhood, the intimacy of being as beyond all determinate objectification. In this respect, we shun the objectifying gaze of the other, because that look is violating, not just to one's own intimate innerness, but to the goodness of being there, the very promise of the innocence of being there at all. There is a modesty that is shameless, just as there is a shamelessness that loves lasciviously to breach all modesty. Young children have not yet become aware of this equivocality of being there and looking, hence feel no modesty or shame. When mindfulness becomes attuned to the dawn of desire, a dawn that is paradoxically a twilight of light and dark, an in-between and threshold of clarity and obscuring, then being's equivocity arouses modesty and shame together in desire. And again there is no univocal *mathēsis* of this in-between dawn/twilight.

Overall then, desire retains its constitutive ambiguity; the univocity of monolinear satisfaction is denied it, in the unlimited range of its self-transcending. As a being of determination and indetermination, the human self is a playing with possibilities. Kierkegaard understood this equivocity of the erotic and echoed the fascination of modernity with the play of desire itself, with desire desiring desire itself, apart from the discipline of all genuine teleology. Hence the fascination with Don Juan. I do not think we need deny teleology, but this has to be defined relative to the human being's mindful grappling with its own equivocal transcending. The teleology will not be univocal. It will not be equivocal in desire desiring itself. Nor will it be just dialectical, in the sense of a sublation of desire desiring itself into self-mediation and self-determination. It will be shaped metaxologically. This too means that the doubleness is not reduced, but mediated and thought differently within the community of the plurality. There will be no eradication of doubleness, nor of indeterminacy, though the affirmative meaning of both will have to be interpreted.

For there is a deeper significance to equivocity than that related to erotic desire, as normally understood. Equivocity applies to the *very eros of human self-transcendence*, an indeterminate restlessness of which erotic desire, normally understood, is only one determination. Erotic transcendence here names the self-surpassing movement of the human being beyond its own lack, towards its own possible wholeness. Wholeness here is not narcissistic satisfaction that never really breaks with the univocity of undifferentiated unity, even via the mediation with what is other to self. Erotic transcendence is equivocal with respect to the other; for it goes towards the other, and yet goes towards the self via the other. The crucial question is: What does our transcending finally serve, itself or the other? If itself, then is its self-transcendence really self-surpassing, or merely a self-mediating detour back again to the self, at a more complex level of self-differentiation?

Erotic self-transcendence, I want to suggest, is equivocal about its relativity to the other as other. It is tensed in the double pull of the between, where self-transcendence must go beyond itself to the other, and yet also seek its own proper wholeness. Erotic self-transcendence is equivocal self-transcendence, for it does not fully activate the agapeic promise of self-transcendence that goes beyond the equivocal relativity to self and other. Agapeic self-transcendence does not do away with the double, with the plurality; but it hears, in and through and beyond equivocation, the call of a surpassing towards the other that is not mediately for the self.

Erotic self-surpassing can be an equivocal transcendence not only vis-à-vis the other, but vis-à-vis the doubleness at work in its own energy of going beyond. For as erotic, it sees itself as a movement from a lack to a self-completion through the other. The central perplexity then is: Why does the lack itself generate beyond itself at all? How can it do so, if it is simply a lack? Since it does so, it must be more than a lack. In the lack itself, there must be ambiguously at work something more. In the infinite restlessness of desire, something is at work that cannot be fully accounted for in terms of a lacking that seeks to be filled, fulfilled. The lack seeks beyond itself to be fulfilled, only because already in it more is at work than lack. Its energy of transcendence is double, and hence the ground of an equivocity from the beginning. This "more" is the plenitude of being that originates the self as a self-transcending desire. This "more" is the overdetermined power of original being at work even in desire as erotic equivocality.

We must become mindful of this, if the equivocality of erotic transcendence is to be properly faced. Something other is at work in erotic equivocation. But because of equivocation, this is suggested, not determined; it can never be absolutely determined, this overdetermined plenitude that is more than and prior to all lack and all determination. This is the agapeic plenty that is the origin, prior to the origin of desire as lacking, or as empty. It is this *other origin* that suggests to self-transcendence that it is to be for the other as other, and not merely as a detour of the self back to itself. The equivocality of erotic desire *does not know* that this is the different double already at work, before the self-doubling of desire, before its own playing with possibility in the doubling of self and other. This other is already equivocally at work, prior to the equivocality of erotic self-transcendence. And the other as other remains as a call, ever when erotic self-transcendence short-circuits the dynamism of desire and makes it into a circle of selfhood, rather than a more radical opening to the other. And this is all very ambiguous, not because we philosophers fail to give a univocal *mathēsis*, but because it is in itself ambiguous. Our task as metaxological philosophers is to try to offer, as lucidly as possible (which does not just mean univocally), a hermeneutics of this ontological ambiguity.

There are many other articulations of the fertile equivocality of human being, but to close I will merely mention *comedy*. The excess of transcendence makes the human being the only laughing animal. There is no mathematics or geometry of the comic. When we thus determine the meaning of a joke, we kill it; spell out a joke and there is no laughter. There is a different energy of being at work beyond univocity. The suggestion of a fertile indeterminacy must be kept alive—a space of openness and freedom. Comedy arises from the power of equivocation to generate creative possibility. If all being were merely univocal, there could be no comedy. Comedy emerges in a world of errancy and incongruity; and though the absurdity is articulated, it is not absolutely determined; the play of the possible continues in the articulation itself. An absurdity that were a mere mute surd would arouse no laughter; there has to be an equivocal play between a possible intelligibility and its absurd frustration. Not surprisingly, the erotic and everything to do with the flesh—that is, aesthetic being—are the fertile grounds of the comic. This world is one of discrepancy, of slippage, of the strange tensions and conjunctions of extremities in the middle. But this world is to be *celebrated* with an outburst of joyful, affirming laughter. Laughter is ultimately grounded in the generous agape of being, though most of it takes shape in the equivocal.[13]

Philosophers: Equivocators on the Equivocal

What of the philosophers? The dominant philosophical tradition has looked askance on the equivocal. That there might be a certain indeterminacy to the ground, or the origin, that is constitutive will be rejected by any univocal metaphysics. All indeterminacies will be thought to reside on our side, as the result of our failure to produce the univocal determinate account. What I want to do is touch on a few philosophers for whom this is not entirely true. The issue will be continued with respect to the dialectical and the metaxological senses.

---

13. See *Beyond Hegel and Dialectic*, especially chapters 5 and 6 on comedy; see also *Philosophy and its Others*, 257–58. The equivocal also plays an important part in being religious and being ethical; see *Philosophy and its Others*, chapters 3 and 4.

Heraclitus was perhaps the first to take the equivocal seriously in his efforts to think becoming as becoming. His opponents immediately sensed a threat to intelligibility. I think of Aristotle's at times almost obsessive efforts in the *Metaphysics* to debunk the lovers of flux. I do not deny that Aristotle is very effective in debunking those fluxers entirely devoid of any finesse for intelligibility. Yet Heraclitus himself has finesse, since the *logos* is not denied. Rather the resistance of becoming to static univocal determination demands a more complex sense of *logos* and intelligibility, not a denial of the latter. The *logos* runs through all things; it too is dynamic, hence beyond static univocity, which does not mean entirely beyond a more complex determination. The ways of saying of Heraclitus may be frustrating to anyone who is rigidly insistent on a certain analytical standard of precise univocity. But these sayings have an intelligibility that is just as searching and rigorous, even more demanding in terms of the struggle to find the right words to do justice to the complex dynamism of becoming.[14]

To return to a previously cited instance: to say that nature loves to hide may be no coy paradox, but an expression of tremendous honesty. The hiding of nature may be spoken out of the second indeterminate perplexity, perhaps even agapeic astonishment about the excess of being-there as given, which as excess is too much for the finite determinate mind, no matter how comprehensive its schema of determinate categories. There may be great metaphysical humility before the transcendence of being-there in the words of Heraclitus. There may be absolutely no desire to deny intelligibility or to give up the unremitting struggle to bespeak being as best and as truly as possible.

We might think of Socrates as the antagonist of all this, but I have already suggested that his proclaimed nescience makes no sense at the level of determinate *epistēmē*. He is presented standardly as seeking essential definition, marked by the one and only one defining characteristic, hence as a univocalist. But there is much more in Socrates. His lack of satisfaction is, in part, a failure to get the requisite univocity; but it is also more. It is the very perplexity of philosophical mind, which is never satisfied with determinate cognition, and even then must ask about the good, the good that exceeds mind such as to blind it, that exceeds determinate intelligibility as to being its source, as the sun is the source of light.

The famous Socratic irony is relevant. I said that there is no comedy without the equivocal. Socratic irony is one philosophical expression of this. There can be no philosophical irony without the equivocal, in this case, the equivocation in the *logoi* of his interlocutors, as well as in the ambiguity of his own self-presentation. Socrates is a dissembler, a pretender, a masked thinker; he rarely reveals himself simply and directly; he is always playing games. He is a philosophical liar—all in the interests of truth, undoubtedly,

---

14. Think also of Heraclitus' double description of Zeus: Zeus is satiety and desire, heat and cold . . . .

but the truth cannot be such as to neglect the essential role the equivocal plays in the human search for the truth. There is a hiddenness to Socrates as an idiotic thinker, a thinker who hides himself in his self-presentation, though, as Alcibiades indicates in the *Symposium*, what he hides is a divine interior, not the opposite. He himself equivocates about his own identity. Perplexity at this equivocation, in the form of the following question, drove him to philosophy (*Phaedrus*, 229e-230a): Am I a monster more swollen than Typho, or a creature of a more gentle and divine lot?

Much more might be said, and I have said more elsewhere.[15] Not only is there no avoiding the equivocal, but the equivocal will never be conquered by a complete mathematical univocity. For this reason Plato will resort to myth, articulated with all the finesse of superb philosophical imagination. He will equivocally resort to poetry, "illogically" given his logical "banishment" of poetry. The Platonic dialogue is itself riddled with equivocities that do have to be interpreted deeply but are never absolutely dispelled. Hence many dialogues are explicitly aporetic at the end. With respect to the determination of the philosophical problem in a final and unsurpassable univocity, no one uncontroversial answer is given. A further determination is necessary, a greater struggle with the indeterminate.

Plato has been decried as the metaphysician of presence par excellence. This categorization follows an interpretation of the Ideas as univocal units of eternal immutability. There is this strain in Plato, but there is also much more, and that more extremely elusive to univocal determination. The account of eros, the account of divine mania, the attitudes to poetry and myth, to name a few, cannot be fitted into this so-called metaphysics of presence, understood as univocal being without reserve of ambiguity.

There is no univocal flight to the univocal. The philosopher must pass into and through the equivocal. Thus Plato's distinction between the *eikastikē* and the *phantastikē* in the *Sophist* (see 236aff.) is not unlike my suggestion of an affirmative and negative sense of the equivocal.[16] The sophists are master exploiters of the equivocal. The philosophical struggle is for the truth of the equivocal. In this Plato must be as much an artist of the equivocal as are the sophists. Hence Plato gives us philosophical *images* to name the equivocal. The Cave is the metaphor for the domain of equivocal being in a most negative sense—equivocity as seducing us to error, to illusion, equivocity as prisonhouse of the self and the murk of the sordid, cut off from the light of the good. This is the mocking twilight of the equivocal,

---

15. See *Beyond Hegel and Dialectic*, chapters 5 and 6; also "Being at a Loss" in *Perplexity and Ultimacy*.

16. It is very relevant to our purposes that here Plato implies that the true artist works a necessary distortion of the image to get the proper proportions for perception, for proper perception on our part. "Falsification" is necessary to "truthfulness." And sometimes to be "true" is to be "false."

though the denizens of the prison think otherwise. The Cave is the twilight of the equivocal, the mocking chiaroscuro of unreliable flickers. The soul is dungeoned, shackled to itself as its own dungeon. The twilight is double, for another light flickers in the borrowed light. Hamlet would understand: "Denmark's a prison." So would Pascal, bewildered in the labyrinth of a world fallen into the equivocal.

Any philosopher who feels the sting of skepticism has been jolted by the equivocality of being. Not surprisingly the skeptics are one set of Socrates' sons. The equivocity of being is articulated in ancient skepticism with respect to repeated frustration to determine the nature of being in one noncontroversial univocal logic. Recall again the problem of the ancient skeptics like Pyrrho with equipollence, *isostheneia*. To every *logos* an equal and opposite *logos* can be given, as Sextus Empiricus said. This is logicist univocity generating its own impasse when it thinks its own univocity through to the limit. There is a logical undecidability between two propositions, *logoi*, which cannot be adjudicated in purely logical terms alone. There is an opposition without the possibility of resolution on the terms in which the contradictory propositions are posed. This is the equivocal sense at work in logic itself; there is no reduction to univocity; rather logic seems to demand an *epochē*, an *epochē* of logic itself; we are suspended *between* undecidable opposites.

Kant's doctrine of the antinomies is a modern reformulation of this. Two sets of propositions, with respect to beginning, to freedom, and so on, are determined to be equally tenable as rational deductions; but we could just as easily say that, precisely as tenable opposites, they are equally untenable. We cannot say one way or the other with univocal certitude. Understanding seems to run itself aground in skeptical equipollence when it tries to reduce the metaphysical perplexities to one determinate univocal solution. In seeming to complete itself, it succeeds in subverting itself. For the doubleness, the antinomy that reappears at the end is taken to signify that the entire approach to the problem is somehow flawed. Kant shows that a certain univocalizing of metaphysical perplexity inevitably leads to an equivocality, where bewilderment is increased rather than decreased.

Different responses to this situation are possible. One might say that there have been mistakes in the statements of the opposites, that one is more properly certain and univocal than the other. Thus, the antinomy instances *all along* the equivocality it claims to find at the end. All we have to do is, like the methodical Descartes, retrace our univocal steps with a greater discipline on determinacy and attentiveness to mistakes in the chains of reasoning. The antinomy is a failure of univocal mind to be univocal; it does not call the ideal of univocal determinacy into question. Kant wavered here, I think, between the hold of the univocal ideal on him and the suspicion that there was a deeper indeterminate perplexity at work with respect to metaphysical questions. His wavering is itself equivocal.

Other responses would reject the claims of intelligibility. The result is equivocality, but this result is said to follow always from univocal intelligibility. We must give up intelligibility and perhaps celebrate another response to being. This might be what Kant calls faith, which is a moral faith; it might be what Kierkgaard calls faith which is religious. Dostoevski's underground man might seem the complete opposite of Kant's man of pure reason, but if we understand the equivocity of being, we will understand how the dreams of reason give rise to such monsters. The underground man is *perversely* equivocal, because man is not a mathematical equation. This very perversity of the human being is the sign of an ontological complexity beyond univocity, that cannot be approached or deciphered without express acknowledgment of the ontological power of free indeterminacy, its transcendence of determinate univocity. The revolt against univocal reason has reasons of which univocal reason knows nothing. We might say that the very mindlessness of univocal mind itself incites this revolt against reason.

Think here of Kierkegaard's revolt against idealistic reason in his view of the stages of life's way. This evidences the equivocal sense and not just in relation to the aesthetic, though this is relevant. I mean the experience of the *limits* of one stage, and the struggle to move from one stage to another. The movement from the aesthetic to the ethical to the religious in each case comes to the limit of the present stage; but there is no univocal way forward that can be determined in advance and guaranteed by an objective *ratio*. To move to the limit, and from one stage to the other, entails a leap beyond a guaranteed determinate *ratio*. This is a leap into the indeterminate, a free and terrifying leap into the equivocity of the indeterminate. This leap is a metaphor for the energy of self-transcendence in its orientation beyond itself into the excess of other-being. The most terrifying leap is the leap into the religious, where self-transcendence paradoxically leaps entirely beyond itself towards the absolute other; and this even as the leap in the between allows for the coming towards the human being of the self-transcendence of this other, out of its excessive transcendence. This allowance is the reversal of erotic self-transcendence and the laying of self open to being ruptured by the transcendence of the other. In all cases, the ruptures and interstices that come to definition in the between cannot be crossed by any univocal strategy that will determine and guarantee in advance what the outcome will be.

There can be an attitude here that still insists that the univocal mind is the paradigm of rational intelligibility; when this is shown to inevitably lead to equivocation, as in Kant's antinomies, we are shown the limits of reason. Hence we must either jettison or go beyond reason. I must insist that I have no interest in jettisoning reason. The crucial issue rather is the meaning of this "going beyond." This is the question of transcendence. Metaphysical perplexity about transcendence germinates in the equivocal.

Much of post-Kantian and post-Hegelian "irrationalism" has its origin here. It is no accident that the classical tradition of reason is rejected, almost *in toto,* as indeed is philosophy, understood in the classical sense. Strangely enough, Nietzsche is the heir of the Kantian equivocation here. It is not faith, either Kantian moral or Kierkegaardian religious, that Nietzsche offers as a way beyond univocity. The way beyond is a way that is a return to the aesthetic, the aesthetics of becoming itself. Only as aesthetic, only as a work of art, is the world justified; an aesthetic theodicy would be the only possible one. So Nietzsche says. This is deeply metaphysical in that Nietzsche wanted to overcome the deadening of being produced by the univocal *mathēsis* of modern science.

This is where the return to the equivocality of becoming and the divinization of the aesthetics of being serve to ground the transvaluation of values. As a plurivocal philosopher Nietzsche himself tried to exemplify the equivocal mind in his own modes of writing and speaking. These are impossible to reduce to the one voice of logicist univocity or that of a "mere" poet. Though he hated Plato, he is strangely like him in calling to rebirth the poetical necessities of philosophy. These ways of saying are necessary to be true to the excess of becoming, beyond univocal intelligibility. In my view Nietzsche did not think through the possibility that intelligibility itself, and truth and selfhood and being and all the essential questions, are amenable to an articulation beyond univocity. In many ways he remained captive to an aesthetic oscillation between a univocal intelligibility reaching its limits and an equivocal philosophical/poetical speech about what is more. Becoming in itself is equivocal, and though the self may partially mediate its otherness, there is no inherent intelligibility in becoming as other, nor finally in the self, who also is a construct thrown up by an equivocal process of genesis. The being of becoming, in the self and the other, are irremediably equivocal, finally beyond all mediation.

Deconstructionist philosophy is a variation on the Nietzschean equivocal sense. Here we find the critique of metaphysics of presence, understood as the reduction of all becoming to substantival univocity. We encounter a resurgence of a configuration of mind reminiscent of Socratic irony in its debunking of rational pretension. We find a variation of the skeptical problem of equipollence and the Kantian antinomies, where undecidability leads to the suspension of absolutely final rational adjudication of rival claims; we can never be absolutely certain. Since I have spoken on the equivocal sense of deconstruction elsewhere,[17] I will say nothing more. I will leave for the next chapter a related sense of negative dialectic that opens metaphysical mindfulness up to transcendence. This opening leads to the transcendence of any absolutization of the equivocal, such as the one that tempts the deconstructionist.

In the lists of thinkers who are mindful of the equivocal, Pascal must enjoy a place of very high honor. Pascal is one of the few modern thinkers who sought to preserve, in an incredibly complex tension, the play between

---

[17] *Art and the Absolute,* chapter 5; *Beyond Hegel and Dialectic,* chapter 5.

univocity and equivocity. His distinction between the *esprit géométrique* and the *esprit de finesse* contains *in nuce* the entire discussion. But Pascal was no irrationalist. He was one of the greatest mathematicians ever. He could have been a greater Cartesian than Descartes himself did not the stirrings of the heart tell him of something other to mathematical univocity. This something other could not be answered in terms of the mathematical configuration of mind.

Heart here is a metaphor for the core source of human self-transcendence. Heart is an otherness in inwardness that is prior to the univocity of the Cartesian *cogito*. The power of being is at work in the self, prior to the affirmation of being in the "I am" and prior to the express wakefulness of self to itself and being in the "I think." The heart is the source of self-transcendence, where the infinite in its excessive transcendence erupts into the inwardness of selfhood itself. I am putting the matter in terms Pascal does not use, but there is little doubt he felt the full force of the upsurge of this excessive otherness in inwardness itself, and its shaking of the self-certainty of univocal mind. Pascal lived this upsurge as the equivocality of the heart, split in two, wounded in questioning and ardent in seeking, fallen below itself and yet aspiring in faith above itself, desiring to pray and praise, but sick and invalid and racked by sleeplessness.

Pascal is one of the greatest univocalists of mathematical science, and also one of the greatest probers of the equivocity of the human heart. The enigmas of the latter produce the liquefaction of the clear intelligibilities of the former. Nevertheless, we must cling to the intelligibilities to preserve the finite self against its dissolution in a labyrinth of ambiguity that darkens all sense of direction and light. Pascal lived the tension of the two.

Still, the ultimacy of the heart implies no rejection of intelligibility; it means placing it within proper context. Nor is the heart absurd. There are *reasons* of the heart that point to a sense of intelligibility other than that of the reasons of univocal *ratio*. The baffling equivocality has to be thought through more deeply. It has to be *lived* in its perplexity for this thinking to be effective. Similarly, the heart's perplexity must face up to the death of creation that is effected by Cartesian science. The death of nature means the occlusion of the signs of the ultimate good in nature, with its reduction to the primary units of modern science, whether aesthetic or dianoetic. Mechanistic univocity does not produce a merely neutral universal; it produces a dead universe where life is the anomaly; this is a sinister universe. Fear of this sinisterness, we might say, is the beginning of a wisdom beyond geometry. For the heart is equivocally mindful that, in truth, this universe is a creation. The sinisterness of the dead silence comes home to us most horrifyingly in our inability to hear the primal "It is good" of the original genesis. The equivocal heart has to be plumbed to resurrect the music of creation out of the sinister silence of the degraded nature.

In a word, equivocity is inescapable but it is not the last word. The turn to the heart names a different turn to the self than the one offered by the rationalizing *cogito*. The self in its plenitude, which means also its neediness, must be recovered in the happening of the between, if its equivocality is to be faced, and perhaps mediated. The otherness in the happening of the between will not be mediated in its plenitude, unless we recover the fullness of human self-mediation as unremittingly perplexed in the equivocal between. In some ways, Pascal remained trapped in the equivocality he so well named. His mind was marked more by erotic perplexity than agapeic astonishment. The negativity of Cartesian doubt had infected mind as agapeic; he struggled to get beyond its corrosive power, but with equivocal results.[18]

Equivocity and Incommensurability

The challenge of the equivocal to the hubris of scientistic univocity was understood by Pascal at the beginnings of modernity. There is no absolute geometry of the heart, hence of self-transcendence, nor of the community of the "whole," and its original ground in the prior plenitude of being, and especially so, if there is an ontological dimension to the indeterminate that metaphysical mindfulness must think. Deflating the hubris of univocal mind is not the whole story. But since the story is repeatedly unheeded, it has to be repeatedly reheard. A recent variation concerns incommensurability, on which I offer some concluding reflections. This will return us to our opening concern with the univocal science of nature, as well as pointing us beyond both univocity and equivocity.

In the main, preoccupation with incommensurability initially stems from the work of Kuhn. The discussion with respect to science has generated resonances in almost every other field—for example, ethical and cultural thought. The issue is broached in relation to the nature of scientific development. The standard view had been that scientific knowledge is essentially cumulative. This view might run thus: Kepler provides inclusive laws of motion by mathematically plotting the motions of celestial bodies; Galileo dealt with falling bodies with respect to terrestrial motion; Newton is more inclusive again, for his laws of motion govern both terrestrial and celestial movements; finally Einsteinian views encompass all of these, with the addition of relevance to the microcosm of atomic and subatomic events, as well as cosmic macroevents. We seem to have a steady and linear advance in which we have almost a necessitated incremental progress.

---

18. For fuller discussion of Pascal, see my Presidential Address to the Hegel Society of America, "Between Finitude and Infinity: Hegelian Reason and the Pascalian Heart," in *Hegel on the Modern World*, ed. Ardis Collins (Albany: SUNY Press, 1995), chapter 1.

Note that the advance is with respect to unification, universality, and exactness. Such advances are required by the more and more thorough mathematicization of nature. These supply a more and more complete approximation to the univocal *mathēsis* of nature. Univocity: because there is an unrelenting drive to *unify* diverse phenomena into laws, whose power of integrating a manifold of happenings becomes more and more irresistible. Univocity: because this unification is formulable in terms of *universally valid laws* that are the *same* for all events as distributed throughout the cosmos. Univocity: because the *exactness* of such unifying universal laws are articulated with a precision that excludes ambiguity from its calculations.

This cumulative view of the relentless progress of univocal *mathēsis* was often given a positivist or quasi-positivist interpretation. Again we witness the univocal sense. The entire thrust of valid knowing, for the positivist, is to overcome every possible equivocity. Knowing moves from a problem that perhaps may initially appear equivocal, but which on being solved is forever deprived of its previous ambiguity. This is one reason why positivism took such a negative attitude to traditional metaphysics. The latter dealt with issues, like God, the soul, freedom, each marked by ambiguity, perhaps by an equivocal core that might never be entirely eradicated. Metaphysical enigmas are dissident to linear cognitive progress from equivocality to univocality. The positivist reformulated all questions as problems that yield to a univocal solution. "Problems" that would not so yield were dismissed as pseudoproblems. The attitude was: let us have done once and for all (once and for all—a very totalizing, univocalizing phrase) with any thinking that generates the unsolvable antinomies—that is, the equivocities that Kant is said to have shown to be the outcome of classical metaphysics. Such metaphysical enigmas with constitutive ambiguity were to be consigned either to the junk heap of history, or perhaps treated as emotional needs manifesting the weakness of individual psychology. They have no place in the realm of scientific cognition.

It is important to note that it is in the *interpretation* of scientific development that incommensurability is invoked. We are dealing with a *hermeneutics* of science, not a *mathēsis*. This departs from the picture of seamless progress accumulated by more and more powerful univocal science. Instead scientific change, it is said, involves rupture and decisive breaks between the accepted view and the new, different view coming on the scene. This is a revolutionary rather than cumulative view of development. There are differences of scientific theory that seem to resist mediation. To get from one side of the rupture to the other seems to be not entirely possible in terms of a univocalist ideal.

The problem is this. As a scientific paradigm (itself a debated notion) becomes more developed and consolidated, anomalies begin to appear. These may be due to new experimental evidence that does not fully fit the paradigm as already developed. They may regard certain internal strains or instabilities within the theoretical system or systems that constitute the reigning paradigm. There comes a point when the established paradigm fails to do its work. Its development along the lines of a more and more complete univocity yields a situation where sufficient perplexity is generated that cannot any longer be fully accommodated. There is an interim in which different possibilities vie for dominance. Eventually a new paradigm emerges that is significantly *other* to the previously reigning paradigm, and this new paradigm proceeds to govern the reorganization of science from that point on.

Incommensurability is invoked relative to the decision *between* paradigms. This does not seem to be made on the basis of rules that are entirely univocal. This between is marked by ambiguity. There is no one rationally univocal rule that will allow us to adjudicate without ambiguity between competing paradigms. There are a plurality of scientists, each of whom has all the available evidence for adjudication; and yet the judgment may come down differently. On the standard view of cumulative progress, one would expect that the judgment of the better scientific theory would be straightforwardly univocal. It is not so simple. The situation seems to be riddled with ambiguities that certainly are mediated by scientific knowing, but that prove never to be completely eradicable. There seems to be a constitutive ambiguity about the process of scientific judgment.

For again, if two groups of scientists have exactly the same evidence and understand exactly the issues at stake between two systems, and yet they judge differently, the source of that judgment cannot be found in the first forms of exact evidence (aesthetic univocity) and exact understanding (dianoetic univocity)—the processes that are precisely emphasized by univocal *mathēsis*. Something other comes into play. Incommensurability signals a potential equivocity that seems to elude any clear and distinct mediation. Neither one nor the other paradigms has the univocal standard by which its superiority over the other will be evident to the other.[19]

Some critics understood the claim of incommensurability as a derogation from the scientific task into an equivocity that itself was ambiguous. Consider how Kuhn compared incommensurability to a *Gestalt*-switch; "it must occur all at once (though not necessarily in an instant) or not at all."[20]

---

19. "In applying the term 'incommensurability' to theories, I had intended only to insist that there was no common language within which both could be fully expressed and which could therefore be used in a point-by-point comparison between them." T. Kuhn, "Theory-Change as Structure-Change: Comments on the Sneed Formalism," *Erkenntnis* 10 (1976), 190–91. The claim concerning the absence of a common language obviously looks to the univocal ideal, as the reference to a "point-to point" comparison indicates. The "common" must be thought more deeply—see below on the community of mindfulness.

20. *The Structure of Scientific Revolutions* (Chicago: University of Chicago Press, 1970), 150.

One now sees a rabbit in the *Gestalt*, one now sees a duck, and there is no intervening *Gestalt* that allows one to pass from one to the other in a mediated way. You have two ways of looking at the same organization of perceptual space; the two are irreducible, though they regard the same organization of perceptual space; but they are seen in radically different ways; they are seen *as* (again a marker of the equivocal sense). The movement from one to the other is abrupt—it seems unmediated. As with the equivocal sense, the stress falls on difference to the exclusion of mediation.[21]

Hence Kuhn has been attacked as a relativist, sometimes with a fiercenesss that calls to mind an earlier claim of incommensurability—namely, the Pythagorean discovery of irrational numbers. Granted Kuhn was not assassinated, as supposedly Hippasus was for revealing the irrationals. He has been attacked for using the language of *religious conversion*[22] to describe the shift from one paradigm to another. This is a touchy thing. Unlike the Pythagoreans, the standard picture of religion by not a few scientists, especially those with the residues of positivism in their blood, is that religion is *the* domain of irresolvable equivocity. Its claims are pseudoclaims, since no method will ever conclusively resolve them, nor will any clear and compelling evidence be available to verify their possible truth. The claim of incommensurability seems to deny any univocal foundations to the scientific enterprise, and indeed to undermine the confident claim that scientific reason is somehow exempt from all that murk.

Kuhn does specify other considerations that enter a decision. These standards are the following: accuracy, scope, simplicity, coherence and consistency, fruitfulness. But again none of these "standards" seem to be unequivocal criteria. They will be applied differently by different scientists; and a different mixture of them will be given different weight too. Kuhn calls them norms of *value* rather than univocal criteria. As such they have a constitutive ambiguity or perhaps open-endedness. The scientific enterprise seems to be again infected with all the equivocities it had so valiantly struggled to extrude over the centuries. Not only does the absence of an overriding univocity make scientific judgment inherently problematic, but the standards that supplement the more recognized univocities are themselves caught in their own potential for equivocity.

Kuhn has qualified his language somewhat, such that he seems to fall back on more standard ways of describing the adjudication of scientific systems. Some attacks on him have been extreme. It is as if the loss of univocal foundations inevitably leads to an abyss of nonsense, with science itself being

---

21. Thus: "In a sense that I am unable to explicate further, the proponents of competing paradigms practice their trades in different worlds. . . . Practising in different worlds, the two groups of scientists see different things when they look from the same point in the same direction." ibid.

22. E.g., ibid., 148.

dethroned into foundationless knowing. True, his language has been taken up by some with the aim of glorifying foundationless equivocity. Neither extreme does justice to what the real issue is. The issue is not the loss of univocal foundations, but the search for grounds of intelligibility that may have to be articulated on terms other than the univocal sense of being. The search for grounds must rearticulate the meaning of being in its concreteness, in a manner that preserves the truth of univocity and equivocity, while transcending both.

The quest of rational knowing is not to be given up, but the mindfulness of being makes more demands on us. Likewise, the apotheosis of equivocity is itself an equivocal exploitation of an ambiguity that does not do proper justice to the complex process of rational and empirical justifications that mark scientific knowing. To recognize that we need more than the univocal sense of being does not mean that we deny the need for the univocal sense, nor that it lacks its proper jurisdiction, nor that, once we move beyond it, we immediately fall into an abyss of nihilism. Nor does it mean that, in not fearing the latter, we then exult in this abyss, as if the further task of mediation were not demanded, mediation that will be rational in a more ultimate sense, though it will not be only a matter of rationalization.

Kuhn, of course, has been criticized for giving a one-sided picture of scientific change, and with some justification. A more gradualist interpretation of scientific development is possible, which preserves the potential rationality of the changes, without falling back into the more simplistic univocities of positivist and quasi-positivist interpretations. The time in which Kuhn's rhetoric of revolution was embraced with such alacrity is significant. The *Zeitgeist* was then in love with the rhetoric of revolution, and discontented with science in its older and established self-interpretation.

The point here is: in its history science develops a univocal *mathēsis* of nature; it comes to have a *self-interpretation* in light of this emphasis on methodic univocity; but its very success as science, its fuller development as univocal *mathēsis*, occasions situations where the old univocity begins to break down, and equivocity rears its head again. We have seen it already vis-à-vis its interpretation of the happening of nature; here we see it vis-à-vis the *interpretation of science's own history*. Even if there is a *mathēsis* of nature, there is no *mathēsis* of *mathēsis*. There is a hermeneutics of science, an interpretation of an interpretation of the ambiguous givenness of nature.

Science starts with an equivocity it calls a problem, which it wants to solve; it solves it in terms of a powerful univocity, and seems to leave equivocity behind it. But just in this very success of univocity, there is a return of equivocity, and within the enterprise of science itself and its interpretation. This is signaled by the willingness to talk of ruptures and revolutions and incommensurable paradigms, and so on. The historical development of the univocal *mathēsis* gives rise to anomalies that skirt the equivocal possibilities of science itself; there is an immanent dialectic in the hermeneutics of science somewhat similar to the transition in the *mathēsis* of nature from classical mechanics to the dual language of quantum physics.

I stress: this is not at all the end of the matter. I am not advocating remaining at the point of equivocity's return. Rather here we may find a positive occasion for the emergence of an even more complex mindfulness of being. This means that the equivocity must be mediated. The ambiguities, even if finally ineradicable, cannot be absolutized. This is clear from Kuhn, for his appeal to these other "values" is all in the interest of mediating what otherwise seems to be an absolutely equivocal situation.

Put otherwise, mediating reason is not to be abandoned. The idea of mindfulness undergoes a complexification beyond the first univocity and the return of the equivocal. One does not abandon the univocal *mathēsis*; rather more comprehensive modes of determinate thinking, comprehensive in the sense of more truthful to concrete being, have to be formulated. The emergence of the equivocal is a renewed call to fidelity to concrete being, as well as a demand made on mind that it activate its mediating powers in a manner more faithful to the truth of being. The search for truth is not forsaken, nor is the desire for a more rich mode of mindfulness, both scientific and extra-scientific. But the old self-image of science as a triumphant univocity that puts all other modes of meaning in their subordinate place has to be given up. A new community of mind is asked between science and other modes of mindfulness, a community that itself is respectful and supportive of the difference and justified ways of these other modes of mindfulness. Scientific mind becomes a member of a complex community of ways of being mindful. It ceases to be the imperialistic master, as it has seen itself in scientistic interpretations.

A more gradualist interpretation of scientific change tends to do greater justice to the historical *mediation*, present even in changes that seem complete ruptures. Kuhn tends to telescope historically developments that took a longer time, and which *retrospectively* seem like the abrupt switch of a *Gestalt* shift. The ongoingness of mediation interplays with the advent of rupture. Equivocity need not be mediated simply by a univocal *mathēsis*, though this may be part of its mediation. Absolute equivocity, like absolute univocity, is unintelligible in the end.

The thesis of incommensurability has helped us see science as an *historical enterprise*—a complexly mediated knowing, which is institutionalized in the modern world. It is the work of a community of knowers spread out over many generations. The historical community of knowers entails the communivocity of mind. There is no sacrifice of reason, but a recognition that it is commonly mediated, institutionalized in ways of knowing that are never confined simply to an isolated knowing subject. This emphasis on mediation and community bring us closer to the dialectical and the metaxological senses of being, neither of which gives up on reason, though each offers a self-interpretation of mind that cannot be reduced to univocal *mathēsis*, nor to its dualistic oscillation with the equivocity of being.

The appeal to historical community has led to the generalization of the thesis of incommensurability outside science to all areas of human culture, especially in relation to the hermeneutical understanding of other cultures, historical traditions and epochs. When this generalization is ruled by an equivocal sense, such that otherness becomes the antithesis of the same, and without the possibility of mediation, the thesis is questionable. There are differences, but these are not absolutely closed to mediation. Mediation itself is a task of opening out to the otherness of the other; it is not one of subordinating the other to one's own self-interpretation.

Intermediation, as I would prefer to put it, is the promise of agapeic mindfulness. There may not initially be a common language, but we find ways of making a new "we"; then "we" newly come across the gap, and at least partially mitigate the gulf occasioned by the initial absence of a common language. We are always in the between, never windowless monads confined to one side of a dualistic antithesis. Dialectical mediation may risk subordinating the other to the self-interpretation of the putatively "strong" partner. By contrast, metaxological intermediation sees this strength as possible weakness, as failure to be open to the other in the fullness of its otherness, hence as failure to listen to the other on its own terms, as best as possible.

As best as possible: this is an essential qualification. We live in the effects of the tower of Babel. We are not gods of communication; we transcend turbulently in the aftershock of the fallen Tower. The between states the ethical task after Babel. This is the task of communication and this demands agapeic mind. There is no absolutely neutral univocal language or being. Communication is *trans*lation; being is communicated in being translated into properly mindful articulation. And if there is relativism and perspectivism, these are not always invidious. Relativism is relatedness; perspectivism admits the ineluctable singularity of the self as it opens to the other. There is no substitution of one neutral sort of self for another. Such perspectivism requires the singularity of communicating selfhood as embodying the fidelity to the good of responsible community. It has nothing to do with self-enclosed narcissistic subjectivity.

Dialectical and metaxological mind inhabit the between with a hermeneutical richness beyond both univocity and equivocity. This habitation includes crossing and crisscrossing the between. Communication is across this crossing, is a coming across the between. There is nothing univocally fixed about the between of communication. In fact, as we move in the between we always test the limits of so-called incommensurability. Communicating across the between is not a matter of reductive commensuration. Genuine commensuration is a commingling of mind (*cum* and *mensura*: a measuring with or together). This entails not a mathematical measure, but the measure of mindfulness (*mens*). The highest commensuration is a community of mindfulness. This offers no guarantees. We might fail, we always will fail. There is only the trying, and now and then the elusive sense that something has come across, or that one has gotten across.

We *are* as transcending mindfulness in the between. We are never confined to our "scheme" or our "framework." To be so confined would be the sclerosis of the self-transcending *energeia* of mindfulness. We are the promise of always being out beyond ourselves. Our being, as *ecstasis* in the middle, is the always present possibility of overcoming incommensurability. We can only do the best we can, given the limits of our own tradition and ancestral languages. But we are not prisoners sentenced to univocal life without parole. Mindfulness is the free release from such prisons. Moreover, traditions are not only prisons, they are homes. Modern enlightenment failed to see or admit the doubleness here and simply treats tradition as prison. It produced a new prison of univocal *mathēsis*, incarcerating us in Weber's iron cage. There is no algorithm for the plurivocity of being. This plurivocity is the matrix of metaxological responsibility. It demands a different catholicity.

CHAPTER FOUR

BEING AND DIALECTIC

The Equivocity of the Equivocal—A Pointer Beyond

Philosophers dread the equivocal. They fear that contradiction will be sustained not resolved, glorified not conquered. They walk in trepidation in the tenebrous milieu, careworn lest the irrational will triumph; lest causality's chain will snap, and nothing connect incontrovertibly; lest iron necessity will be melted and the whole become a magma of chaos, liquefying the jointures of intelligibility. Our terror of the equivocal is that the voice of the senseless will ring out the last mockery.

The dread is not altogether misplaced. Equivocal thinking can turn into a skepticism, thence into a dissolution of all determinate intelligibilty, thence into an exultation in the power to negate all mediations, finally hardening into a dogmatism of nihilism that insists there is no sense to be made and that no sense will be made. This hardened nihilism is a dogmatic contraction of the self-transcending of mindfulness. This exulting in debunking actually reneges on the hard task of sifting equivocity, of sorting, of thinking into, of seeing beyond the roil of the ambiguity of being. By contrast, the dialectical and the metaxological senses each call for modes of mindfulness that seek to *think through* the ambiguity without reduction. Each demands a hermeneutics of the equivocal—harder, more subtle than sheer equivocity in its tendency to the deformation of mind's self-transcendence into merely sophistical eristic.

The philosopher need not respond to the equivocal by, as it were, battening down the hatches and insisting on univocity in a reiterated dogmatic way. This retreat to univocity will not do. At most it will effect, in a different metaphor, a temporary beating down of the brush fires of equivocity. These will flare into irritated skepticism again, and this renewal of the equivocal will tempt one to be dogmatic in another way: since univocity will not do, and since intelligibility is identified with univocity, no intelligiblity will do, will ever do. The fires of nihilism feed further on this dogmatism of skepticism.

We do not reject univocity, but total retreat to univocity is out. We do not reject equivocity, but the nihilistic totalization of equivocity is out. We need to go beyond both, which means acknowledging the contributory truth of both. The basis in being for the univocal sense is the coming to determinate identity of beings within the happening of the between. The basis in being for the equivocal sense is the double play of determination and indetermination, in the coming to presence of beings in the between. Coming to be in the between is a revealing and concealing at once. And what is doubly shown in this double showing is not just determinate entities: the very process of coming to be is marked by a constitutive doubleness. The equivocal sense moves us close to this doubleness when it acknowledges being's ambiguity.

Moreover, the equivocal sense itself is double, also capturing and concealing at once. This doubleness, we might say, is the equivocity of the equivocal itself. The recognition of this is the first positive step beyond equivocity. Equivocity, asserted as total, is self-subverting. Like everything else that it debunks, it cannot stand. Should it debunk itself, it goes under, but in this going under, the self-transcending restlessness of metaphysical mind is renewed once again. In this going under, and this renewed restlessness, the ambiguous face of becoming comes before mind again. We are not returned to any rigid univocity, but thought is loosened up for something *more* than both univocity and equivocity. These are the dialectical and metaxological senses of being.

Each of these senses is mindful not only of the beings that come to be in the play of determination and indetermination, but also of the importance of this doubleness, relative to being, and most significantly relative to the *milieu* wherein beings come to be. This milieu wherein the double play is effected is the happening of the between. The dialectical and the metaxological senses are more approximate to the ultimacy of this happening in that they are more complexly mindful of this doubleness of the between: not just mindful of beings, determinate or not; not just mindful of a transition between indeterminacy and determination in beings that become; but more deeply mindful of both these as ontologically articulating the happening of the between. Such mindfulness concerns not only this happening, it also faces into the enigma of the very coming to happening, the very coming to being of the between itself.

I focus on the dialectical sense in this chapter, the metaxological in the next, though again reference will have to be made to all four senses to understand each. I first will look at some major articulations of dialectic, which in many respects is coincident with the tradition of philosophy itself. Then I try to explain what is at stake in dialectic, first relative to beings, second relative to the mindfulness of the human being, third relative to the happening of the between. As with the univocal and equivocal senses, I am concerned to show the rationale for its indispensability, without shirking the questions it leaves open, or distorts in the answering. I will conclude with some relevant remarks on Hegelian dialectic.

Dialectic and the Philosophical Tradition

Dialectic has a plurality of meanings which in some respects define the ensemble of options available in the tradition of philosophy. These meanings range from its identification with specious reasoning, to a method for dissolving specious reasoning. They include its all but identification with logic as in the Middle Ages, to Kant's characterization of it as critical of illusion when reason strays into contradiction in treating of transcendental objects, to the Hegelian notion of dialectic as the articulating process of development in mind and in the real itself. Hegel's successors, Marx notably, apply dialectic to historical process, as does Hegel himself. By contrast, dialectic is viewed with suspicion by analytical philosophers who identify it with specious reasoning, pseudothinking, and by many of Hegel's continental successors who decry its imputed totalistic imperialism, an imperialism also imputed to the entire tradition of metaphysics. There are other senses of dialectic connected to Socratic *maieutic*, to the description of the highest philosophical thinking in Plato's *Republic*, to the diaeretic method of Plato's *Sophist*.

Aristotle sees Zeno as the inventor of dialectic,[1] and Hegel concurs. Here I suggest we see the connection with the equivocal. Zeno was a disciple of Parmenides, and intent on defending the thesis of the One. From the standpoint of the double-headed many of common sense, this thesis was folly—not logic but laughable madness. But rather than defend the thesis head on, Zeno sought to upend its opponents on their own terms. By adopting the hypothesis of the many, he tried logically to deduce contradictory consequences, or consequences at odds with the tenets of solid common sense. The univocity of common sense is self-contradictory, riddled with the equivocal; thinking about what is at play in its sense of being will bring to light its inherent self-opposition. Hence the paradoxical conclusions drawn from the thesis of motion, as with the arrow and with Achilles and the tortoise: from motion is deduced the impossibility of the expected motion.

It is important to note that the deduction of paradox (literally what goes *para* to *doxa*, contrary to received opinion) is only possible on the presupposition of what I called a dianoetic univocity: namely, the division of time or motion into atoms of univocal instantaneity, or selfsame units of stasis. And of course it is impossible even to budge from the spot on this presupposition, which is the thesis of the One pluralized in application to the fluctuating

---

1. Aristotle also criticizes Zeno by rejecting his atomistic assumptions. Kant speaks of Zeno thus: "Zeno of Elea, a subtle dialectician was severely reprimanded by Plato as a mischievous sophist who, to show his skill, would set out to prove a proposition through convincing argument and then immediately overthrow them by other arguments equally strong." *Critique of Pure Reason*, A502, B530; see also A504, B532 for Kant's distinction of dialectical and analytical opposition.

world of givenness and common sense. Zeno can only discount the thesis of the many by means of this hidden presupposition of pluralized univocity. His aim is to open thought for the absolute One by the deduction of the internal self-opposition of the many, or its immanent instability; but his aim is already infected by the thesis of the many in this presupposition of the pluralized univocity. Whether we grant his success or not—I do not, for the presupposition of pluralized univocity can itself be dialectically deconstructed—if the thesis of the absolute One were true, this pluralized univocity would be impossible, as would be Zeno's very philosophical strategy of trying indirectly to establish the One.

This allows me to make the following main points. Dialectic has to do with the nature of the *immanent* development of mind and thought; with the meaning and intelligibility of being as *inherent* in being itself; with the conviction that the immanence of the former development is intimately related to the inherence of the latter intelligibility. That Zeno assumes the standpoint of *the other*, and works indirectly to his own view from the opponent's view, implies a *complex interplay* between sameness and difference, self and other. Thus dialectic is concerned with the articulation in intelligible saying of that interplay, with respect to both mind and being. Moreover, it is intimately linked with the sameness of univocity and the difference of equivocity, and most especially with the oscillation between them. The sameness of univocity is Zeno's goal, transcendental univocity; the route to this is through the doxic equivocity of the many and their differences, which are to be set at nought in the very passage through them; thus the goal of absolute unity is thought to be made possible.

Notice that Zeno is Parmenides' disciple, and hence *other* than the father of absolute transcendental univocity. That he must meet the views of common sense and the many indicates that already he knows he cannot avoid the happening of the between. There is no way *univocally* to affirm the absolute One, short of dwelling in the bosom of the One. It is obvious we do not dwell there, once we fall out of the rapturous univocity. There would be no question about the One were we in the bosom of the One. We are in difference, multiplicity, equivocality, hence in the happening of the between. Dialectic is a way of mediating the happening of the between with respect to the fall from the One, with respect to the self-opposition of the equivocal, and with respect to the rational reaffirmation of the transcendental univocity. All of this putatively is done by taking the view of the other, and showing that the view of the other in its self-opposition *leads back* to the view of the self, the other of the other, in this case the thesis of the One.

Of course Zeno's strategies were formalized in logical terms by Aristotle; *modus tollens* follows. Also much about philosophical dialectics is revealed by the use of indirect proofs containing the *reductio ad absurdum*. The *reductio* turns the putative intelligibility of the opposing view into its opposite, the absurd; and in this turning over, it makes space for the affirmation of one's own view. The insatiable quest for intelligibility often works by the negative detection of unintelligibilities, of absurdities in pretenders to intelligibility. And indeed dialectic is often a stratagem of thought that is essentially *debunking* of the absurd. For example, the Socratic *elenchus* draws on this power of dialectic, as do the deconstructive strategies prevalent today. The power of negativity in thinking vis-à-vis the opponent's view works to take apart and expose. The hermeneutics of suspicion is only a less formalized, less rigorous, more equivocal version, of the same will to expose absurdity. The hermeneutics of suspicion is rabble.

Such uses of dialectic for essentially negative purposes were evident in antiquity with the sophists. The sophists were often virtuosi of a dialectical *technē* that could be put to the services of *any* point of view, making the weaker appear stronger, the stronger weaker. The dialectic could be turned into an instrumentalized strategy of thought that could be directed to contradictory ends, like truth and deceit, justice and the springing of the criminal. This is one of the sources of the ambivalence for some in the word dialectic: specious reasoning, and the very heart of reason itself.

This *double possibility* for dialectic is significant. It tells us of a possible degeneration of dialectical thinking into a will to power to dominate the other or the opponent. This is a charge laid against all dialectic in contemporary continental philosophy, but the charge is too coarsely put. Dialectic was always understood in its own potential for equivocal employment. Philosophers like Plato and Aristotle took pains to dissociate a free dialectical mind from dialectic in the service of will to power. The presence of strife in dialectic, and the possible use of strife for purposes of conquering the other, rather than pursuing the truth, is evident in Plato's dubbing of the abuse of dialectic as eristic (*eris*: strife). The desire to win and triumph over the other as opponent yokes philosophy to the will to power; it instrumentalizes mind as another means to domination over other-being. Platonic dialectic was vehement in its efforts to free philosophy from this instrumentalization of mind and truth. This tells against Nietzsche who will see in dialectic only another form of the will to power, masking itself as pure and free of power. Aristotle took pains to attack the sophists in *De sophisticis elenchis*, again trying to free the use of dialectic from the abuse.

One must take note of the doubling of propositions into *dissoi logoi*. Protagoras is said to have written a book, not extant, in which opposed *logoi* to different subjects are proposed. We are reminded of Sextus Empiricus again, as also of the medieval dialectic of Aberlard's *sic et non*. The great perplexity evoked by this doubling is: How then distinguish the true from the false, since reason seems to let itself be marshaled equally on exactly opposite sides of the question? In a more mature form, dialectic tries to mediate a way beyond this seeming self-opposition of reason itself.

Here some light can be thrown on Socratic dialectic, which takes the doubleness to apply, not only to propositions as opposed, but to human beings as other interlocutors, as participants in a conversation. The *participant* is as much tested as are its *propositions*. Again an *immanent* unfolding is followed: Socrates takes what the other says and then tries to see where it leads. Is he guilty of trying to get the other to come to the place that he slyly had appointed beforehand for the meeting of mind and intelligibility? This is a suspicion. In principle, however, such a special pleading and leading is antithetical to what is promised by dialectic: namely, to move from an initial condition of perplexity and disagreement, through both of these as further developed or mediated, towards some condition of rational agreement, where the initial perplexity is alleviated in a more or less determinate answer to the initial question. The interplay of question and answer is pursued with the confidence that there is an immanent logic in question and answer, that the thinking speakers can follow this logic, that indeed they are implicitly contained in a community of reason and truth, a community partially instantiated by the philosophical dialogue itself.

Socratic dialectic here cannot be a merely formal technique since it is the *very selfness* of the thinkers that is tested. Nor is its goal simply a neutral universal definition formulating the *eidos* of the matter at stake. It is also *self-examination* and *self-knowing*. These cannot be merely formal activities. The being of the philosopher in his living truthfulness is at stake. Hence Socratic dialectic as self-examining cannot be exhausted by the method of division and collection of the Eleatic Stranger (*Sophist*). The diaeretic method may define the *what* of the sophist, but never the *who* of the sophist or the philosopher. One notes the final failure of the Eleatic Stranger to catch the sophist in the web of articulated determinations produced by diaeresis: the sophist retreats beyond univocal definition into the intermediate realm of images—that is, into equivocity. The self or "who" of the sophist, and not the "what" of sophistry, is *more* than any determinate, essential definition. We must sift the images to catch sight of the "who" of the sophist. This is why Socratic dialectic turns on the singular selves with whom coversation is in process. At stake is the "who" of the participants, not just the anonymous "what" of a universal characteristic in general.[2]

Diaeresis entails a division into kinds, of genera into species, the differentiation of more general classes into less general, division again and again, until all the articulations are analyzed out. The definition is said to be offered by the complete division, which is in turn balanced by the reverse synthetic order of collection or *sunagōgē*. We are reminded of the modern analytic/synthetic method. This is really on the level of the logic of univocity. But the very *process of passing* from division to division, as well as the synthesizing process that proceeds to gather the multiplied determinations into a new

---

2. See my "Plato's Philosophical Art and the Identification of the Sophist," *Filosofia Oggi*, 11:4, 1979, 393–403.

integration, this dynamic process of analyzing and synthesizing does not figure in the classes divided and collected. This very process is in excess of every class, for again it is not a determination, analytical or synthetic, but is an active *determining* of such determinations. In a word, the determining is not another determination. As the source of the determination, it is positively indeterminate, and as such it outlives all finite determinations, as in excess of these too.

Consider Aristotle's claim (see *Meta*, 1078b) that Socrates' innovation was the *epagōgē* that leads the interlocuter to a generalization through a series of particular propositions. Hence the *epagōgē* dovetails with the emphasis on universal definition. This is true, but it is not all. The living conversation of minds in perplexity cannot be reduced to any formalized technique, nor to completely determinate results, like an absolutely satisfactory, or even a more or less satisfactory universal definition. There is something in excess to definition that concerns the this of the thinker, its idiocy as an I—the living mindfulness of the self. Its perplexity is never completely determined and outlives all determinate answers.

Hence the need of *dialogue* rather than just only the logical treatise. I think Plato here, as the plurivocal philosopher, tried to be true to the between: between the idiocy of the this and the universality of the community, and not just the universal as an immutable unity of univocal intelligibility, but as the community of thinking beings. This will lead on to the metaxological, and the need for images to do justice to where dialectic points us. We might say that dialectic itself is shadowed by an excess when it takes into account the singularity of the thinking and the embrace of a community not reducible to the anonymous universal. In other words, the eros of the philosopher of the between—Plato was such a philosopher—takes us to the limits of dialectic in its logicist forms.

And indeed the meaning of Platonic dialectic is enigmatic. In the *Republic* (see Books 6 and 7) dialectic is said to be the supreme philosophical art. It is noticeable that dialectic is not situated at the level of *dianoia* on the divided line; it occurs at the level of *noēsis*. It has to do with the movement of thinking at the highest level of ultimate intelligibility in which hypotheses are traced back to their ultimate origin (*archē*). But it is beyond mathematical univocity. I do not think it can be identified with diaeretic method, which, as just indicated, operates at the level of dianoetic univocity. There is also the enigmatic movement of thinking beyond hypotheses (*Republic*, 511b). I take seriously Plato's Seventh Letter when it mentions the passage of a spark of illumination between two philosophers. What passes in this spark, what sparks in this passage, cannot be completely articulated in dianoetic terms.

One must also take seriously the discussion of the Good, and the image of the sun, an image reminding us of the purer ether of mindfulness within which the metaphysician tries to move in a community with ultimacy. And if the Good is the *archē* and the ultimate, any logicization of dialectic cannot be the final word. The *archē* and ultimate towards which dialectic moves is excessive, as the source of blinding light that makes possible being and genesis, making also possible both intelligiblity and human mindfulness. This excess of transcendence means that the highest for the philosopher is not logical thought thinking its own categories. It comes to one in a *noēsis* wherein, at the limit of self-transcendence, there is a surpassing of self in patience towards the Good. There the Good gives itself out of its own excessive transcendence, radiates not for itself, but for the other. Highest dialectic is patience, obedience to the ultimate. This is a recognition that to be, beyond determinate being, is to be good.

If the excess of being is the Good, we are in the neighborhood of the "It is good." There is an indeterminacy to this, but in no merely indefinite sense: there is a blinding by the light. We are like bats in sunlight, as Aristotle said, not just like owls of Minerva in the equivocal twilight of falling dusk, as Hegel said. In the present instance dialectic seems to prepare for an opening to transcendence as other, but this is the difficulty: we must not reduce transcendence to our self-transcendence. If dialectic is a method, it is so in the sense of a *hodos*: a way, a way across. It suggests a mediating process that takes place in the give and take of question and answer; and this is inwardized in the inner conversation of the mind, where it takes shape as mind's perplexity about ultimacy.

We find a diminished appreciation of the excess of transcendence when we turn from Plato to Aristotle. We find a tendency to logicism and a will to formalize the movement of mindfulness; its indeterminate self-transcendence is made a form: the soul as the form of forms. Here we have the shadow of univocity again, though to make sense of Aristotle's famous statement—somehow the soul is all—we have to reintroduce the indeterminate self-transcendence of mind, and its power to other itself, and indeed power to be actively patient to the being of the other as other. But this power is not a form; it is beyond form as a forming and an unforming—a becoming other to itself while yet remaining itself. In Aristotle this process of indeterminate determining gets subdued by the determinate as logically univocal. The determinate is the issue of the determining, but the issue as univocal takes the place of the origin, and in the process produces a change of mindfulness, and indeed a certain occlusion of the process of interplay in the happening of the between. This dimming of transcendence is already hinted at by the fading of agapeic astonishment, even erotic perplexity, and its substitution by determinate curiosity about this and that, understood as univocal substance whose being is to be determinate.

Consider the drift to systematization of dialectic in the *Topics*, and generally the drift towards the substitution of formal logic. True, Aristotle does retain a sense of dialectic as dealing with the scrutiny of premises that are generally accepted, or of premises that are probable, or generally accepted as persuasive. Dialectic still has a function in intellectual training. It is not a method of demonstrative knowledge that offers valid deductions from true and self-evident premises. For Aristotle dialectic also has value for arguing with others in terms of their presuppositions and premises. Finally it helps us, Aristotle says, in our approach to the first principles of demonstrative science, principles that are not themselves demonstrated or demonstrable. The ultimate principles of sciences cannot be approached within the terms of the determinate science itself, since these principles are prior to and presupposed by the determinate science. These principles are to be approached through the discussion of the generally held opinions—to do this is a proper function of dialectic.

But quite clearly, this last function opens a can of worms. It opens up the matter of the intelligible beyond determinate, demonstrative intelligibility. Aristotle says that dialectic offers "a process of criticism wherein lies the way [path] to the principles of all inquiries" (*Topics*, 101b3–4). This is an extraodinarily important statement. In effect, it is an acknowledgment of the other to determinate intelligibility without which demonstration could never be demonstrative. For demonstration is made possible by ultimate principles that are not themselves univocally demonstrable. The drift to ordered determinacy is so strong in Aristotle that he does not seize here on something coming into the open that exceeds all determinate systematization, and that hence demands quite another sense of dialectic that eludes fixation in any determinate logic. The drift to systematic determinacy will be furthered by the Stoics and into the Middle Ages. Here the generally underquestioned convertibility of dialectic and logic signals the ingrained nature of the logical ideal of determinate intelligibility.

Hegel grasped the importance of the opening hinted at in Aristotle's point—namely, that there is a *determination process* more ultimate than *determinate products*. The dynamization of self-transcending thinking has to be understood differently to think this process articulately. The systematic determinations of formal logic will not do justice to the process as other to fixed determination. A different logic will be required, a *dialectical logic*.

Hegel was helped on his way by the Kantian sense of the antinomies. Kant himself says that ancient dialectic was always the logic of illusion (*Logik des Scheins*, *Critique of Pure Reason*, A61, B85–86). In fact, he misrepresents the variety of views of the ancients by all but reducing dialectic to its sophistical exploitation. Dialectic now is to be used in an almost opposite sense—namely, in the critique of what Kant calls dialectical illusion. Transcendental dialectic, as he calls it, deals with the illusions that inevitably arise when we try to pass, by means of pure understanding, beyond the limits of experience. And yet transcendental illusions are somehow unavoidable, never to be completely dispelled. It is as if there were something inherent in metaphysical thought that inevitably comes to such an impasse.

Here I see Kant equivocating with respect to what I called the second indeterminate perplexity. This metaphysical perplexity might be called illusory, if by this we mean its transgression of the determinate univocities of validated science. But this is to accept determinate univocity as the standard of what is ultimately valid. And despite the quarantine imposed on mind by Kant's transcendental dialectic, metaphysical mindfulness, by the inherent movement of its own self-transcendence, finds itself still and always perplexed by what lies at the limit of determinate univocity. Kant only sees an equivocity, or an antinomy there; he vacillates between univocity and equivocity, always with a bad conscience, for he could not snap free of the idolatry of the univocal determinacy. And yet he also had a metaphysical bad conscience from the other side, because he knew the self-transcendence of mind as inevitably carrying him beyond. Kant was tortured between the bad conscience of scientific univocity and the bad conscience of a stifled metaphysical mindfulness.

By contrast, I think one can see the vacillation as potentially positive, since it may make us think more intensively of the happening of the between, beyond univocity and equivocity. Kant's antinomies made possible for Hegel this movement to another level, and in relation to the opening suggested by Aristotle with respect to dialectic as a path to the principles of all inquiries. Dialectic, as Hegel understood, is not mired in an oscillation between univocity and equivocity such as Kant displays, but shows a dynamism of thinking at work, even in this vacillating oscillation in the between. This dynamic of dialectic is made possible by another side of Kant that also takes us to the edge of determinate univocal intelligibility, though here from the side of the self, and not, as in Aristotle, from the side of being. This is Kant's sense of the transcendental, understood in terms of *the self as process of synthesizing* that is prior to all determinate analyses and syntheses. This opens up the dynamism of thinking as determining activity within minding itself. In other words, the deduction of the transcendental unity of apperception is beyond a merely formal logical deduction, for it is a regressing movement towards what exceeds determinate form. This is the source of the formal and determinate, the source indeed of the formal intelligibility of the categories and their unification with the manifold of sense that goes into the constitution of ordered, that is, intelligible experience of the world. Dialectic, as Hegel saw, must be newly defined relative to this transcendental self.

This is not to deny that Hegel expands the notion of dialectic immeasurably beyond transcendental subjectivity. But the latter makes possible the transformation of dialectic and its comprehensive renewal. Hegel offers no static formalization of thesis, antithesis, synthesis. The passing of opposites into opposites is more nuanced. Nor is contradiction to be denied; it rather assumes an *enhanced role* as a way to truth. All of being will be said to be dialectical: nature, history, God. Hegel will claim to articulate the logical necessity in all this. He will offer dialectic as articulating the logic of the whole, the *logos* of the whole. The subjectification of being by transcendental idealism will be expanded beyond subjectivism. An interplay between self and other will be granted, and a recognition of the happening of the between. But the happening of the between will be subjected to dialectical self-mediation. Thus there persists the heritage of the univocity of thought thinking itself, and of the privileging of the self in post-Cartesian, and especially post-Kantian transcendentalism. Moreover, Hegel will continue to be an Aristotelian in that determinacy still wins out, though in the form of self-determination. He too will forget the transcendence that Plato fought tirelessly to preserve and affirm.

I will come back to Hegel again at the end of the chapter. But let me summarize for now by comparing Zeno, Kant, and Hegel. Unlike Zeno's use of the *reductio ad absurdum* indirectly to exclude the thesis of motion and the many, Kant's use of the antinomies indicates that *both* of the opposites *might be true*. We might consider the world as beginning or as without beginning, determined by necessity or by freedom, limited or unlimited. The point is that the antinomic nature of reason in itself does not seem to give us a reasonable way to decide between them, hence *both might also be false*. With Zeno the contradiction deduced from the thesis of the many or motion indicates that it cannot be the truth, hence its other is true. For Kant if both might be true, both might be false. This prepares for a dialectical view that sees *both sides as marked by their truth*, even in their opposition to the truth of their other. Even the falsity of either might contribute to the truth of either and vice versa. There is a reciprocal implication between the true and the false.

In sum: Zeno affirms the truth of the other to show its untruth, and hence mediately to lead back to the truth of the One; Kant leaves us undecided; Hegel thinks that the above process of reciprocal implication shows the very process of determining the true in the false itself. Kant affirms the possible truth of one and the other, the possible untruth of one and the other, and leaves the judgment between them cognitively undetermined. Hegel sees the truth of the other leading in itself and out of itself as contradictory and false to the truth of the self; he sees the truth of the self as leading in and out of itself as contradictory and false to the truth of the other. And this process of leading to truth through falsity and to falsity through truth is the very process of determining the truth, the truth that is not the truth or falsity of one or the other, but of *both* in their mutual implication. The process of this mutual implication only reaches *the* truth in the true as whole, when the onesidedness of different antitheses has been transcended in the absolutely self-mediating totality. Dialectic articulates the internal instability of partial truths, false in their truth because partial, yet true in their falsity because the part dynamically points beyond its own internal instability to a more complete determination of truth. This pointing beyond is for Hegel a dialectical *"and so on . . . ,"* all the way to the end of the absolute self-determination of the true as the whole.

Dialectic and Beings

Let me now remark on the meaning of the dialectical relative to beings. These are the main points to be emphasized: first, the reinterpretation of unity and doubleness; second, the notion of becoming as immanent transcendence; third, the stress on immanent development, on organic rather than mechanistic models; fourth, the emphasis on being as mediated, indeed on self-mediation as the dominant mediation; fifth, the teleology of this mediation as leading to the privilege of the whole.

To the *first* point: if the univocal reminds us of one voice, and the equivocal of a doubled voice, the dialectic calls to mind a doubling of voices about being. Thus "dialectic" comes from *dialegein*. The word *legein* is related to the word for *logos*—speaking, saying, giving an account or reason, laying out the intelligibility. The *dia* refers us to a double or dyad. There is a doubling of *logoi* in *dialegein*. Much will turn on how we interpret this double, this doubling of voices. Is it just the self-doubling of one voice, or is it the doubling and redoubling of a plurality of voices, not reducible to one single overriding voice? How we answer this question will determine the difference of the dialectical and the metaxological. Traditionally dialectic has tended to the first answer, while the metaxological offers the second. I want to suggest an understanding of dialectic that *lets open*, that indeed *demands* this second possibility.

A plurality of lines of development are needed to deal with this doubling of the voices of being, the voices about being. The equivocal brings us to the brink of this doubling, but stops short of further mediating its meaning; it takes up residence in the doubling. Two pathways of perplexity are opened up for us, the first relative to the being-there of beings that are other to the self, the second relative to the being-there of the mindful human being. I now address the first, and will deal with the second in the next section.

There are beings; and the univocal sense determines them to be this and that. They have relatively stabilized identities; they are more or less determinate entities. As determinate entities it proves difficult to determine them *completely*. The appeal to univocity would fix such an immutable identity, but it always fails in this. It fails, not because it has not yet reached the goal it so devoutly wishes, but because the very process of univocally fixing being shows the face of *another* side that is unfixing and unsettling of all putative stable identities. It is not that there are no determinate beings; there are; and the determinacies of being extend from the invisibility of microevents to the enveloping immensities of macro, indeed cosmic happenings. But in all of this, large and small, the original energy of being works on, tireless, never spent, to all appearances inexhaustible, despite the alleged work of entropy. The creative power of being does not weary of creating again, though it is old beyond age, and yet it is ageless and more fresh than the earliest morning of youth.

Let time do its work. The process of coming to be and passing out of being is *more* than any determinate entity. To answer the question of being we must think this "more," this "more" that cannot be thought completely in terms of any determinate entity, or all such entities taken as an aggregate. The original energy of being renews itself again and again, reboubles itself over and over. Still beings are there, and when we give mind to this perennial renewal, when we give mind to the ongoing happening of beings as ontological events, we realize that the fixation on stable identities is *relatively true* to the more or less provisional identities that things are, but that it is *not completely true to the ongoing determining of things*, considered as a dynamic process, nor to the repeated renewal of beings again and again.

There are beings, but the determinate beings are such determinations in a process of becoming that cannot be reduced to a set of fixed determinations, any more than a motion can be exhausted by a set of snapshots of immobile instantaneity. The equivocal sense makes us give mind to the othering of determinate identities: things are themselves, but not completely identical with themselves. While themselves, and hence identical, they also become themselves, hence indicating that they are not fully themselves, even while being themselves. Their being-there is to be there in a manner more fully coincident with their ontological promise, a promise that is offered in the present and out of the past, but that looks to the future for its more adequate realization. The equivocal sense emphasizes things as double, identical and nonidentical, same and other, themselves and yet not themselves. This doubleness is itself the promise of a further fuller sense of being, but when the equivocal sense takes itself as the last word, the doubling of beings is seen essentially as the self-dissolution of any claim to immutable self-identity. The stabilization of the energy of being is dissolved into flux without essential form, into diversity without togetherness, into plurality without community.

Dialectic understands the limitation of both these views; but it seeks to recover what the univocal sense offers, and in a form more adequate to the richness of what is coming to be in the happening of beings, and without turning its back on the complexification, indeed pluralization of identity that strikes the equivocal sense. Commonly, the dialectical sense is attacked for its supposed disrespect for the principle of identity and the law of contradiction. This attack evidences a very partial understanding of the issues at stake. It can be said, in fact, that the dialectical sense, in its adequate formulation, tries precisely to do justice to identity, and its ontological complexity, which is contracted too narrowly by the univocal sense. It tries to recover a more complex sense of sameness beyond the threat of dissolution posed by the absolutized equivocal. The above attack on dialectic is really a misidentification of dialectic with an absolutized equivocity in which the principle of identity and contradiction are shown no respect at all.

Let me put it this way. Dialectic is an effort to divine the *going beyond* of this absolutized equivocity in equivocity itself; hence it is the *recovery* of the senses of sameness, identity, and unity that are first specified univocally, but that cannot hold up univocally when the ontological happening of becoming is acknowledged. But the way to this recovery is through the equivocal itself: through the very transgression of the contradiction, the contradictoriness of the merely equivocal will be resolved. We do not retreat to a less complex determination, but advance to a more differentiated and inclusive determination. In the best sense, dialectic is not a disrespect for contradiction at all, but an *interpretation of its significance*, ontological and epistemological, with respect to the happening of beings and the nature of thinking in being mindful. It is not simply mindfulness according to the law of contradiction, but mindfulness of the power of contradiction to drive thinking to the determination of the meaning of being, in a determinacy more richly articulated than univocity, and a wholeness more integrated than the equivocal can offer.

There are determinate beings for dialectic, but their determinacy is not of a self-subsistent character simply there without further mark. To be a determinate being is to *have come to be* a determinate being. Thus dialectic is acutely aware of our being in a world of *genesis*. Determinate beings are there, but not simply there; they are there because they have come to be. Moreover, the process of coming to be there is not reducible to the fact of being-there. The fact of being-there would ultimately be unintelligible were we to abstract it entirely from the process of its coming. There is also the fact that even given the being as already being there, this being is not, nor will it be, always there; it will develop the promise of its own singular being in the process of genesis itself; it will become itself in a more full realization of its own singular ontological power to be. In this directionality of genesis towards the realization of promise, the being that is now, in time will no longer be there. It will come to pass that it will pass out of being. It will be no more.

Dialectic seeks to make intelligible this *full span* of determinate things, determined in the middle between the extremities of a coming to be and a passing out of being. To do justice to the being of a being, it must take both sides into account, the stable side of determinate identity and the open side of the indeterminate. The concrete unity of the being is defined in the interplay of these two sides, between a beginning and an end, and in the span of time between its beginning and end. The unity of a being spans that between, because in the middle it is essentially self-mediating.

The significance of this will become more evident, but now we must reconsider the issue from the side of the equivocal sense. This sense has some appreciation of the dynamized being-there of the determinate thing. It will see the doubling of a being as this pluralized reiteration again and again. It will be attentive to the play of determination and indeterminacy, continuity and discontinuity. But it will sometimes accentuate the *discontinuity* between the repetitions of the thing in genesis; this being is *not* now what it was, it is *not* now what it will be, and in time it will simply *not be* at all. The redoubling of the identity of this being becomes the negating of the determinacy of the identity. The negating consigns things to genesis as *decreation*, rather than creation. Then the equivocal being of becoming will again be said to be barely distinguishable from nonbeing, and in "the long run" to be indistinguishable from it.

We might say here that the dialectic between Platonists and Nietzscheans is determined by this sense of the equivocal, the one taking flight from the equivocity of becoming into the univocity of eternity, the other taking flight from all eternities and univocity into a celebration of the innocence of equivocal becoming. Nietzsche contests the consigning of the equivocal to decreation, and sees in it the fecund matrix of all creative being. The dialectical sense can concur, in recognizing here the creative ground of being as matrix of fecundity. But it will concur, not by consigning univocity to oblivion, nor by showing a reactive disrespect for determinacy, nor by placing sanctions on all philosophers who think about the enigma of eternity. The happening of the between is both determinate and indeterminate, place of creativity, yet creation as a given happening. The beings that come to be in the between are similarly double. The doubleness is not defined by two sides of an opposition—namely, the univocal against the equivocal, the equivocal against the univocal. The double is a togetherness that demands a thinking that is more than these two, and a sense of being that sees their togetherness differently, togetherness because each is ingredient in a more encompassing process of coming to be.

What is this process? This brings us to our *second* point. The process is one of passage and transition. How do we make sense of the transitions? I place emphasis on the word *trans*—a going across, a passing on, a crossing over. We might say: transcendence is working in the process of coming to be. If transcendence is working, we are dealing with transcendence as *immanent* in the happening of being in the between. This immanent transcendence cannot be pinned down to any one determinate form. If it could, then the very *trans* of transcendence would be denied. *Trans* indicates that we are not just here at A or there at B, and nowhere in between; the *trans* is what energizes in the between; only thus is it passage from A to B, taken as determinate points of departure and arrival.

Is this process of passage or transition or transcendence a merely linear succession of A, B, C, to be likened to the series of integers, 1, 2, 3, and so on *ad infinitum*? No. This would be to let the univocal sense again dominantly determine what is at play. The happening of transition is still not thought on this view. The notion of the *ad infinitum* itself shows how this univocity breeds an unacceptable equivocity, for we often substitute *ad nauseam* for this *ad infinitum*. Dialectic transcends this univocity in its giving mind to transcending, as it transcends this nauseous *infinitum*. The transcendence immanent in succession itself cannot be identical or identified with any one item finitely demarcated in such a series itself. It is more than either.

But again the *more* of this *trans* is not outside; it is an immanent transcendence. The process of genesis testifies to this immanent transcendence.

It is at work in all beings to the extent that nothing in the universe is completely static. Everything is dynamized, and the unfolding of the dynamism is neither an inflexible order nor is it completely disordered. There is an ordering that is open, that itself is an emergence out of less articulated orders of relative antecedents. The emergence itself, in turn, becomes the antecedent source out of which further orderings take shape.

This means that the dialectical sense has to be itself *pluralized*, depending on the specific concretion that the play of determination and indeterminacy takes. Some forms of being will less clearly articulate the work of immanent transcendence; some forms will more closely approximate univocal identity in their relatively simple activation of the energy of being; some forms will be more pluralized and hence more ambiguously determined by the equivocal possibilities of being; some forms will more clearly indicate the power to mediate the equivocality and so constitute for themselves a more complex integrity. The work of this immanent transcendence shows the prodigal power of creation, ceaselessly concretizing determinate beings in the universal impermanence, beings with myriad relations to other beings, beings with intricate modes of self-relativity, beings that exemplify the power of immanent transcendence in their species or singular way.

The work of immanent transcendence means that dialectic will be mindful of processes of becoming that go beyond the merely *mechanical*. We touch on our *third* point. The mechanical is an ordering of parts that have an essentially external relation to each other, and to the whole of which they are the functioning parts. As we know, the Newtonian universe was conceived on this model and the mathematical intelligibility it offered. Nothing was essentially implicated with anything else, which is not to deny the relativity of things; the mechanical does not deny relatedness, but specifies it according to a certain model of externality. In mechanical relations terms do not inherently have relations to other terms, nor is there any dynamism inherent in the terms that would drive them into relativity to other terms. The mechanical whole, rather aggregate, is a putting together from the outside of parts that are essentially outside each other. The canonical definition of matter in this view is literally *partes extra partes*. The machine cannot be set to work unless put in motion by an outside source of energy, whether it be the cosmic clockwork set in motion by the clock-making god, or the manmade machine that would not be the functioning order it is, except by virtue of the transcendent hand of man, the machine-maker. Even manmade machines cannot set themselves to work without, say, electricity or petrol, and then they show no immanence of transcendence relative to the power to generate beyond themselves, to generate issue or offspring that perpetuate their identity through the difference of the offspring. In its wily propagation through equivocity, the orchid is a veritable organic god, compared to such infertile aggregates of mechanical univocity, these eunuch idols.

On the dialectical view, absolute mechanism is an abstraction and in a sense, an ontological impossibility. Were not the energy of being as original transcendence at work immanently in some manner, there would be no functioning whole at all. The mechanism is an abstraction from the functioning of being that is, in fact, far more inherent. This is consistent with views already developed that many of the standard pressupositions in classical modern science are subjected to very severe strains, and dialectically so, insofar as they try to bring themselves into conformity with, be true to, the astonishing complexity of concrete happening. Once again a positive understanding of the equivocal is demanded here as the matrix of creative possibility, within which the energy of immanent transcendence sets itself to work, and without which no perpetuation of continuity, nor variable propagation of essential difference, would come to be.

And so not surprisingly, dialectic tends to think of immanent transcendence on a more *organic* model. The reasons for this are clear. An organism implies that this being is a whole unto itself. This is not to deny its relativity to others; but in the web of external relativity, it constitutes its own integrity for itself. The univocal sense of identity is here taken up, but in a context of double complexity: the immanent wholeness of the thing, the external relatedness of the thing to beings other to itself.

So we must say that to be determinate in this dialectical sense is already to *pluralize* the complex of determinations that define the identity of the being. This complex identity involves a *self-pluralization*, for it generates through itself its own characteristics. An organism, so to say, flowers itself out of its own immanent resources, in interplay with its environment of otherness, whence it draws the nutriment and sustenance necessary to the unfolding of itself. Its interplay with the environment of other-being is with the view to furthering the unfolding of its own ontological possibilities. In this unfolding there is evident an *immanent* principle of development. The organism develops itself, is a certain concretion of the energy of being as self-developing. Its self-pluralization is hence not a mere self-doubling as a self-splitting, or negation of univocal identity. Rather it is the process of constituting itself at a more complex level of mediated determinate being.

The self-pluralization that was evident to us in equivocal self-doubling undergoes here a transformation into an essential process of *self-mediation*. This is our *fourth* point. The organic unity mediates with itself, mediates with itself out of its own resources, mediates with itself in interplay with the environment of being-other to which it is related, mediates with itself in its own parts, which have an inherent or immanently implicated involvement with the integrity of the whole. They are not merely parts but *members* of the whole. The parts of the organic whole are not neutral units of univocal aggregation; the sense of the whole is inscribed in the part itself.

Consider this example: the transplanting of parts/organs. When there is a transplant of parts, the body will naturally want to reject the implanted part as foreign matter. The transplanted part is not yet an organ, for it does not yet carry the inherent identity of the whole. Modern medicine will "fool" the whole to accept the foreign, and induce a readjustment in the sense of inherent identity of the whole, wherein the introduced, strange part will finally be made an organically integrated member. Only thus does the transplanted part become an *organ* again. Our very power to "fool" organic integrity itself confirms a functioning of integrity *beyond* mechanism. For the very plasticity of adaptability points to a freedom of being beyond complete mechanical determination, even in determinate mechanisms.

I suggest that the organic whole is a living transcendence of equivocal being in that the pluralization of the determinate organic entity is not necessarily a rupture that undermines all integrity and identity. The pluralization of the self of the organic being is still the self, and the self is reiterated in its variations over a span of becoming or genesis. There is continuity of self in this variation. Hence the variability is not sheerly equivocal. The medication used to suppress the rejection of transplanted parts is a ruse of human medicine that defuses the very rejection of the equivocal that is inscribed in the organic unity of the body. Left to itself it will reject what is not its own, it will reject the foreign; it will be the living refutation of sheer equivocality; it cannot continue to live with the sheerly different. The medication is a ruse that quietens the spontaneous rejection of the equivocal, and buys organic time for the organism as a whole to adjust to the other, to assimilate its foreignness.

Absolute equivocality would be absolute dissimilarity, and the organic whole could not continue to be itself, should it be asked to accept this rupture. There has to be the *double play of similarity and dissimilarity*, for assimilation to be possible. This assimilation is articulated along the lines of a dialectical self-mediation; the integrity of the being is reconstituted, having assimilated the dissimilar and made its otherness a moment of the renewed unity of the whole. Let the deconstructionists say what they like about human texts, but organic nature is no deconstructionist, not even in the ebbing of being that follows when the unity comes to decay and die; for even that too is caught up again in the renewal of genesis and the transitory passage to other forms of life.

This does not mean that the dialectical sense is exhausted by organic being, as we shall see when we shortly come to human self-transcendence as mindful. The stress on self-mediation, already evident with respect to the organic, will be evident in more complicated form in human mindfulness as an immanent self-transcendence. For what dialectic offers is less an affirmation that being is just immediately there, than that being is itself inherently a mediated thereness. This is surely right. The further important issue will not be just to counterpose mediated being to immediate thereness, but to ask

about the precise character of the mediation, whether dialectical or metaxological, and whether the immediate is entirely exhausted by such mediations.

The crucial point now is that dialectic's stress on self-mediation issues
from the *self* of the entity that comes into being, comes to determinacy as
being. To be is to be determinate, but to be determinate is to be determined,
and to be determined is to be the mediated outcome of a process of determining. The being comes into the between, comes out of an initial condition that
is not completely determined, comes forward out of itself into the between,
comes to itself, comes forward towards itself in its passage from initial indeterminacy to mediated determination. The stress is first on the forming rather
than the form, on the structuring rather than on the structure; the latter are
productions of the former; the static is the issue of the dynamic. The dynamism is a vector not towards stasis, but towards the self-realization of the
dynamic. The forming process comes to form, but the form it aims at is *itself*,
as self-forming in an entirely dynamic self. This self-forming is the becoming
whole of the being. To be mediately there as a determinate being is to be and
become whole. That is why coming to be, understood by dialectic, underscores the *teleological* nature of the play between indeterminacy and determination. The sources of this can already be found in Aristotle's account of
being in terms of potency and actuality and the teleology of form, and perhaps consummated in that Swabian Aristotelian, Hegel, who dialectically transformed the teleology of substance into the teleology of subject.

This teleological emphasis, and this is my *fifth* point, has very important.
repercussions. There are ambiguities in dialectical teleology that will only
become fully clear when we turn to the metaxological view of being. It is
evident that the organic metaphor rather than the mechanical orients us much
more clearly to a process of becoming directed towards a fulfillment. In this
regard, dialectic will see the fullness of being in *the end*, defined as the *realized* promise of the determinate being. By contrast, the *beginning* of the process will be described as indeterminate, but this indeterminacy will be *lacking*, as a minimal realization of the power of being. The beginning will be
seen as all but nothing; the process of coming to be will be seen as an overcoming of this initial lack or minimal condition, and the concretization of
the immanent transcendence in the inherent wholeness of the being. The
vector of transcendence in its search for completion will be directed to the
end; but the end will not be a vague and amorphous dream of longing; it will
be the outcome of the process of determination which, in fact, it is claimed
now, is a process of *self-determination*. The absolute goal of the initially
indefinite vector of transcendence will be the whole that is absolutely self-
determining. The teleology of the immanent transcendence will be the
absolutely immanent wholeness of the whole.

This emphasis on self-mediation, on mediated being, on the dynamism
of transcendence as orientation to a *telos*, is not just confined to a being or a

plurality of beings. Dialectic applies it to the whole of being. We must not forget that dialectical thinking is acutely aware of the logic of *relations*, relations again in the active sense of relating. Just as the determinate being is self-relating in its self-becoming and in its interplay with being-other, so relativity on a more encompassing scale is important for dialectic. The coming to be of being in the between is the coming to determination of the co-implication of these beings, of their being together in a community of being. They are unities but they are not absolute unities, for their unity is also defined in this community and in this interplay back and forth between their own dialectical identity and the otherness of beings that are different.

How does this sense of the community of relativity in the universal impermanence affect the emphasis on self-mediation? Does it dissolve it? Does it destroy the teleology of immanent transcendence? I find here a certain return of *univocity,* which is perhaps a mediated variation on a renewal of the rapturous univocity with which we started. Put otherwise, the mediated community of the whole takes the place of this rapturous univocity. This mediated community of the whole is brought to be by the teleology of transcendence. Thus every entity is dialectically defined as double: as both self-relating and as marked by interplay with other beings in the happening of the between. As double, each entity is marked by an internal cleft or split. Each is finite and limited, and its self-relating is never absolute; and yet a vector of transcendence towards absoluteness is at work in each entity, at work even in the cleft within it. Each entity as double is a mingling of internal self-relation and external relations with others. Moreover, these external relations are not merely external, for the self is beyond itself in the between. Relativity is a co-relativity in the community of the between.

One interpretation of dialectic will emphasize that this co-relativity means that nothing is in itself absolute, short of the absolute whole. The very teleology of being is said to be driven dialectically towards this absolute whole. A thing is itself not only through itself but through its relativity to others, which themselves are what they are through their relativity to others. But this process of co-relativity cannot stop short of the whole. Each is what it is as part of the universal whole. And the vector of transcendence at work in each does not stop short at the finite self-being of any determinate entity but implicitly extends to this whole. On this view, the co-relativity of community tends to be defined in terms of a *mutual relativity*, which extends out and out into the web of universal togetherness. The co-implication of the same in the other and the other in the same that we found in the equivocal is here recovered in the sense of the universal interconnectedness of all things, the inseparability of one from the other, of identity from difference, a mediated togetherness beyond univocity. We might put it thus: this togetherness is silent with the univocal, promiscuous with the equivocal, set forth as articulated with the dialectical. In the universal impermanence the process of becoming, as passing from indetermination to determination, defines the happening of the between as the completed realization or fulfillment of transcendence, in the immanent absoluteness of the whole.

In this last view—and I stress that I do *not* think it offers the *last* word—we see the return of the univocal. The idea of the mediated whole recurs to the idea of univocity, but subsequently to the passage through the doubleness of the equivocal. The mediated whole is the reinstated univocity but articulated along the joints of its own immanent or internal articulations. Thus there is a clear line of connection from Parmenides' absolute One as well-rounded truth to Hegel's circle of circles, which is the absolute Idea as self-thinking thought—the latter is logically set forth in its self-development in the encyclopedia of philosophical sciences: the round of self-developing truth. The same image of the circle is to be found even in that equivocal thinker, Nietzsche, not only in his eternal return of the same, but in his description of the universal "monster of energy," as he calls the will to power: this universal monster is the ring of rings, the ring that wills itself and nothing other.[3]

I have already run ahead of myself, for this absolutization of the dialectically self-mediating whole is what I will contest metaxologically. But it is important to appreciate how persuasive the above view is; how it emerges from the limits of univocity and equivocity; how much more complex it is than the usual caricatures and rejections make it to be; how necessary it is, given the proper qualifications following from a metaxological contestation of its absolutization. Without all this no serious rethinking of dialectic is possible. A genuine contestation of this teleology of dialectic demands not only a rethinking of archeology, but also a traveling along the same lines to see where the difference lies.

Dialectic and Human Being

When we turn to the human self as mindful, dialectic becomes even more significant. Being mindful, as transcending thinking, resists reduction to the model of the mechanical. For such thinking is not first an ordered structure of aggregated parts. This is not to deny it structure, but the structures in thinking are not first delimited in their difference and then externally put together. There is a respect in which *thinking as process* has no parts; it is an ongoing mindfulness that does assume a plurality of different forms, but these forms are the product of thinking itself as a self-aware, self-related activity of being. Thinking shapes itself in a plurality of acts of thinking, and different modes of mindfulness. But there is a *self-relativity* at work

---

3. See *Will to Power*, trans. Walter Kaufmann and R. J. Hollingdale (New York: Vintage, 1967), 550, entry dated 1885. Also my "Rethinking the Origin: Hegel and Nietzsche," to appear in *Hegel and Hermeneutics*, ed. Shaun Gallagher (Albany: SUNY Press).

in thinking from the most rudimentary act of mind. This self-relativity also marks the *transcending* of thinking. No mechanical model that aggregates parts can do justice to this prior sense of self-relativity and its self-transcendence, even though it try to explain the thinking of the "machine" as the outcome of the aggregation of the parts. The belief may well be justified that a structure of order comes to inform our thinking as *produced*; but thinking qua activity is informed from the outset by a transcending self-relativity that is not a mere *product* of subsequent parts.

In other words, there is no argument for the being of mind that does not presuppose mind. The real question is: What gives thinking to the human being? Is it simply given to itself? Does thinking give itself to itself? Or is it given to itself as for itself, before it is thinking for itself? The self-relativity is in excess of mechanical and organic structure, because the self-awareness of structure, whether mechanical or organic, is not itself another structure. It is living, concrete, dynamic mindfulness. It is an acting of mind, a minding of structure. But the minding of structure is not itself a structure. And even if it is a *structuring*, there is the astonishing emergence of presence to itself, the intimacy of being emergent into self-awareness that is irreducible to structure. For structure may be intelligible, but also mindless; it may be open to mind, but is not itself mind, minding. The intelligible is not identical with living intelligence.

If thinking goes beyond the external univocity of the mechanical, it also goes beyond the immanent unity of the organic. This latter unity is already manifest in the self-transcendence characteristic of the sensitive organism. Thus the animal is self-transcending in sensing its prey or detecting its enemy; it is in interplay with the environment of otherness, even when retaining a unity for itself. But this self-transcendence never attains the express wakefulness to self of mindful self-mediation. Human self-becoming also begins in what, with proper qualifications, might be called *aesthetic* self-transcendence, in that it is immediately rooted in the interplay between the *embodied* self and the external world. This aesthetic self-transcendence is already informed by an inherent self-relativity. This self-relativity will be dialectically developed.

This aesthetic self-transcendence reminds us of the univocal rapture and the equivocal promiscuity that we mentioned before. To become conscious of what is at play in the univocal and the equivocal is to become aware of a self-relativity immanent in both, but not necessarily working with explicit self-consciousness. The dialectical sense of being is revealed in the mindful human being as a self-relating process that, through the dynamism of its own inherent being, becomes that mindful self-relativity, becomes itself in becoming that mindfulness that is self-relating.

Remember again that this self-relating mindfulness cannot be divorced from its placement in the between. There is a complex process of ongoing interplay with other-being. But dialectic focuses on the immanently self-

mediating aspect of this self-transcendence. Mindfulness is given in a rudimentary way as a self-relativity, even in the rapturous univocity and the promiscuous equivocity.[4] This is not all, of course; it is merely the beginning, but it is
crucial. This mindfulness is not static, but becomes, self-becomes, hence develops, not in terms of merely externally imposed norms but in terms of exigences
inherent to itself. Its development is a self-development; its transcendence is a
self-transcendence; its determination is also a self-determination.

Dialectic discovers a certain rhythm in this process of self-development.
I say rhythm rather than structure, for though there is structure, it is not
static. This rhythmic structure, as we might call it, is related to the prior
sense of being. For the emergence of being mindful is from an initial immediacy that is seemingly univocal. The self senses itself in the primal self-relativity, and there seems to be something absolutely unsurpassable about this
primal self-relation. It is itself in its being related to itself, and this being
related to itself is the unique ground that allows this being to say "I." To be
able to say "I" would be impossible without this elemental self-relativity. Of
course, much more needs to be said, especially with respect to the other, and
to the "I am" as itself supported by a more originary affirmation of being that
comes to singular emergence in the "I."

Dialectic thinks this primal self-relativity in other than static substantialist terms. We are inclined the latter way when we think with Descartes
of the "I" as a thinking thing or substance. But since the self-relativity is
itself an active self-relating, it indicates the self as an original source of the
power of being, not just some sedimented product of this power, misleadingly reified. The self-relativity of the "I" is an activity of self-relating, and
the dynamism itself points to an original source of activity that comes to
self-awareness in this self-relativity. In other words, the self-relativity is immediate, but on closer understanding it is not a merely empty immediacy.
It is an overdetermined beginning; there is more to it and more at work in
it than a bare asserted "I." There is an inward otherness at work even in this
primary self-relativity.

This otherness comes to manifestness in the very hiatus between the self
and itself that is necessary for it to be aware of itself as a self. The original
energy of being uniquely singularizes itself in this "I" that says "I am." This "I
am" immanently within itself points to its own *depths*, as to a ground of active original being that makes possible and supports the relating involved in
the self-relating. Let me put it this way: the primal self-relating is given to
itself; this is its immediacy; but its givenness to itself is not simply its own
giving of itself to itself; it can give itself to itself, because it is first given to
itself; the self-relativity points to an immanent otherness at work in the given
self, before the given self can give itself to itself. This otherness will be very

---

4. In chapter 10 I will discuss this further in terms of what I will call the idiotic self
and aesthetic selving.

important in thinking beyond dialectic as self-mediation and self-determination; this otherness is beyond from the beginning, because it makes a dialectical beginning itself possible. This beginning before the dialectical beginning is an agape of being, a giving by being of the self to itself as for itself, and hence as let free to be itself as for itself, and as other to the source that gives it to be for itself. This origin before the dialectical beginning is overdetermined, not indefinite being. I will return to this.

That the mindful being is given for itself and given as actively self-relating means that the exigence of its own *dunamis* is already transcending the univocity of being. It is itself and not simply itself. It others itself in its self-transcendence. Let the reader here think of the paradoxical power of mindfulness: I can mind this pen that is other to me, and yet the minding of this other is mindful of itself in this minding of the other. Minding transcends to the other, but remains in relation to itself, in its relation to the other. It is at one with the other and at one with itself at one and the same time and in the same act of self-transcendence. There is hence a *double relativity* built into this integrity of self-transcendence: self-relation and relation to what is other. This doubleness provides the spur of self-development itself. Self-relativity finds itself already in the between, in the middle space between its own being able to remain at one with itself, and yet its unavoidable implication with what is other to itself.

In this *doubled between* the human being is tugged in these two directions at once. It is here that we can say that the equivocal supplies a goad to self-transcendence. The equivocal presents the mindful human being with this doubleness in the form of a recalcitrant and inciting ambiguity. Necessarily, mindful being finds itself outside of itself in the between; and while it feels the tug of recovered oneness with itself, it also feels the inescapability of the enigma of otherness and indeed of the ambiguous enigma of its own inwardness. This equivocality of being might be shunned by the univocal mind, but this will not do for dialectical mind. Equivocality provides the matrix for a further development, for it incites the mind to mediate the meaning of emergent being, in a manner more true to the becoming of concreteness, whether inward or outward or transcendent.

There is no retreat from the equivocal; we must pass through it, and perhaps pass beyond it. If we still are fixated on a fixed univocity, however, we will tend to see the equivocal doubleness in purely dualistic terms. Consider Descartes again: the univocity of the *cogito* generates a being-for-self of thinking that is set in opposition to the mindless *res extensa* of externality, and the two are radically opposed domains of different substances. By comparison, dialectical thinking sees the dualism as a *question* rather than an answer, as an incomplete development of mind and being. The terms of this incompleteness need to be transformed for the question to be put in proper context. The dualism is a duality but no absolute opposition for dialectic.

For the very mediating power of mind cannot be fixed in merely dualistic terms. To state the problem of dualism we have to be mindful of both sides of the dualism, and moreover both sides in their opposition. We must think both sides in their opposition—that is, in the putative unthinkability of their togetherness. Thus to think their opposition is already to think both together and hence to think the unthinkable togetherness. The very nature of thinking is to think opposition, hence to think through and beyond opposition. Thinking the other is also thinking, and hence potentially at home with itself again. Thinking can be mindful both of itself and what is other to itself.

Dialectic is merely caricatured in the standard anodyne of "synthesis," "thesis" and "antithesis." Rather the real pain and strife of doubleness cuts through it. This pain is not only external, but is incised in the unfolding of mindfulness itself. Mindfulness falls into perplexity and doubt, beyond the first agapeic astonishment and immediate rapture of being at all. Recalcitrance rises up in innerness, as well as in outer being. The mind is self-relativity but it knows itself as the lack of truth, as cut off in its heart from its heart's desire, mired in error, toiling in ambiguity that mocks rather than welcomes. I underscore that dialectical thinking takes shape *subsequent* to the first agapeic astonishment. It concretizes what I called erotic perplexity.

The pain of the doubleness is felt as the lack of knowing: in one's alienation from the truth, the rupture of the equivocal makes one ill at ease metaphysically. Erotic perplexity is not defeated by this pathos of difference. Quite the opposite: the self-developing transcendence of mind is energized to mediate the indifference, the indefiniteness, even the seeming hostility of the being before it. When perplexity becomes erotic, this doubleness of the equivocal is set forth mindfully with doubting. Doubt itself, as we saw, is related to the sense of the double, as the etymology shows: being in two minds, being between as not-knowing what one knows, or as knowing what one does not know.

This being between in doubt stretches mind between its own lack and the ultimacy of what it seeks. Such a stretching can bring mind to the breaking point of madness wherein we go down into a univocity that is not rapturous, or an equivocity that is lost. Or else the stretching can be the very distention of mind's self-transcendence that reaches ever beyond its present limitations. The urgency of ultimacy can be felt with deeper exurge in the upsurge of lacking doubt. Self-transcendence can be incited more radically towards transcendence.

So we can say that the dialectical view is mindful of thought as a restlessness that is absolute, an absolute restlessness that is a restlessness for the absolute. This is not a conditional and finite restlessness that is here and now determinately aroused, and there and then determinately slaked. There is an infinitude to this restlessness that no finite satisfaction can ever completely quell. This is why the erotic perplexity of dialectic is bound up with the entire transcending exigence of metaphysics. One cannot place a limit on thought and not be nagged by the suspicion that the limit was premature. The limit may involve a univocalization of the final horizon of thinking to quarantine us against the equivocal, or the indeterminate, or the indefinite. But erotic perplexity will renew the restlessness of thinking, just on the limit itself. The limit is drawn, but the drawing is already implicitly beyond what is has drawn— a point well-made by Hegel. To limit thinking thus is already to be on both sides of the limit and hence not really to limit thinking in the sense intended.

I agree with Hegel. The issue between us will concern the kind of thinking that is appropriate on the limit, on the edge between the limit and what is beyond. If we think all metaphysical mindfulness is generated by erotic perplexity, then we will set out to determine further what is beyond, but in a manner that is subordinated to the self-determination of thinking. If we think, as I do, that agapeic astonishment is renewed on the limit, in the reborn metaphysical mindfulness of the *second* perplexity beyond all determinate knowing, then our thinking of transcendence cannot be articulated in terms of thought's self-determination. The overdetermined plenitude reaffirms itself as mystery. What I have just said will make more sense.

In recent philosophy we have been repeatedly reminded about finitude, but for all its correctness this reminder must be finessed. The restlessness of being mindful means that the metaphysician is *witness* to a certain infinitude in thinking. That one cannot univocally substantialize thinking or being; that thinking can wander in the diversification of the equivocal, being itself and being other than itself; that thinking is originally self-related, and can mediate with itself in its passage from thought to thought; all these indicate a power that is impossible to fix finally. The thinking "I" is a singular being, hence finite; but what comes to show in the "I" as thinking is not merely finite; the very self-transcending of the "I" is a vector to what goes beyond the determinate, the limited. The between as equivocal happening is, in part, the lure of the unthought that entices restless desire further and further, beyond mere univocity. The "I" can get lost in this equivocality; it can get lost in itself as a kind of equivocal thinking. For it is finite and infinite at once, and hence seemingly contradictory. It may give itself over to contradiction and equivocation, and justify itself with the belief that this is all it is.

But this is not all that it is. For the sheerly contradictory and equivocal would feel no need to justify itself so. An infinite restlessness of thinking shows itself in the singular "I," but the unfolding of that restlessness has a rhythmic structure. In the process of passage beyond its present limited thought, it is still carried by the energy that is articulated in self-relativity. It *recurs to itself* in that passage from one to the other. Hence its passage is not merely successive, as we would expect with a merely linear series. If the mindful being that passes along recurs to itself in every transition, if its very passage is inherently marked by self-recurrence, then the unfolding of the infinite restlessness is inherently self-relating, immanently self-mediating. This is what the dialectical sense understands.

What is here suggested is an immanent standard in the infinite restlessness that keeps thinking on the way home, or that corrects itself in its possible errancy along the path of transition. Thinking is the bearer of this immanent standard, and hence is not simply defeated by the recalcitrant face of the equivocal. Consider this: if you have a linear series 1, 2, 3, and so on, and if we take its terms with mathematical univocity, it is not completely clear how we get from 1 to 2, from 2 to 3, and so on. But if we remember the recurrence of mind to itself in its transition from 1 to 2 to 3, the problem is seen differently. The transitioning is not another determinate number; the transitioning is living mind that makes the transition, that understands the point of moving from one to the other, whose very understanding of the point is just its passage from one to the other. The words "and so on . . . " indicate that the mind can recur to itself in its own self-understanding at every point along this passage of transition. The infinite of succession that is presented by a univocal series is not enough to explain the movement from one to the other and so on. In a word, mind recurs to itself in succession and so is no longer simply successive; it mediates with itself in successive passage.

Hence the infinite restlessness that moves from one to the other and so on, precisely as self-mediating, cannot be understood in terms of the infinite of succession. It is what elsewhere I called an intentional infinitude.[5] It is intentional to the extent that the restlessness of self-transcendence can be directed through the self-mediating powers of thinking itself. This directing does not imply that the mind knows in a complete determinate manner what the goal is or the last term of the series. Did it know that, it would be an actual infinite, not an intentional infinitude. Rather it is between infinite succession and actual infinitude. What guides it in the between is its power of mediated self-direction, sustained by an immanent standard. The latter is not known with explicit determinacy in advance of all disputed claims; instead it comes to greater and greater determinacy, as mind thinks more and more determinately both about itself and other-being. This immanent standard means not only that the equivocal cannot be completely avoided, nor can error; rather error may itself provide a mediated pathway to truth. We might say that we approach the truth through the exploration of the immanent shortcoming of errors. Dialectic tries to include the truth of error in the truth of being.

Consider the argument in the following way. Let us say we affirm a position A. If all we do is affirm this position, we seek to remain finalized in univocity. Dialectic detects the emergence of internal instabilities in this univocal fixation, instabilities revealed by an upsurge of the equivocal. There

---

5. See *Desire, Dialectic and Otherness*, passim.

will be no univocal A that does not eventually generates its own equivocality. Now let us say we formulate the position B to overcome this internal instability of A and to deal with its equivocation. Dialectic will see that B is not just the sheer opposite of A, for it is generated out of A, and hence it is A's *own* opposite, hence tied to A, even while being opposed to it. There is an implication of the two, not explicable on purely univocal or equivocal terms. If B is really a position that comes to terms with the immanently revealed limits of A, then it will also be a *fuller articulation* of what was at work in A, but not fully captured in A. B will be the truth of A, which would be impossible without the untruth of A. Hence B includes A as a necessary stage of its own development. A is an incomplete version of the truth of B, just as, in turn, B will become an incomplete version of the fuller truth of C, all the way to the full truth.

Why follow this path? Because the process of transition is one of developing thinking itself according to its own immanent exigence. The development is spurred by the self-criticism of error. Thus error is a way to the truth, because dialectical thinking is self-correcting. Being mindful develops under the pressure of its own internal strains, hence error is mediately necessary for truth to come to be. In the language I use, there is no transcendence of equivocality except by passage through it, and that means thinking its truth deeper than the equivocal mind itself does.

Just as previously from the side of other-being we seemed driven to affirm the togetherness of beings, and indeed their interconnectedness in the community of being, so here from the side of being mindful, we are driven to see the interconnectedness of different thoughts that initially seem merely to contradict or oppose one another. The process of thinking, in its infinite restlessness, seems determined to overcome the lacking indefiniteness of its perplexity, and through the immanent standard of its own erotic development becomes more and more inclusive. It seems driven to a comprehensiveness in which the enigmatic becomes more and more determinate, as thinking itself comes more and more to determine its own self-development. The *telos* of its dialectic seems to be confirmed in practice in that thinking, as it develops, does become more and more determinate.

I want to underscore that the dialectic I wish to defend must *keep open the doubleness* that comes into play in the between. This is what I mean. The transcending of being mindful impels the self into the between where, in being beyond itself, it is also in relation to itself; and so in this between, it is tugged in *two directions at once*; and this being doubly tugged is constitutive of its being between. Now dialectic tends to take up the side of self-transcendence as mediating with itself, even in its interplay with what is other to itself. There can be tremendous complexity involved in this. This truth of self-mediation is unavoidable and indispensable. Nevertheless, we must guard against any closed whole, insofar as relativity to other-being is *not* reducible to self-relation.

Do I then argue for an open whole? This idea seems like a contradiction in terms. A whole would seem to be closed on itself, self-sufficient, a completely determined perfection unto itself. How then can a whole be open? Would not the openness undermine the wholeness? The answer I suggest is that wholeness does not have to be understood either in terms of a completely determinate univocal unity, or in terms of a self-mediation that is closed on itself. There is an internal doubleness to some wholes, as both self-mediating and intermediating with what is other to themselves. The whole is open when the work of self-transcendence immanently defines the integrity of that being. Such self-transcendence cannot be contained within the borders of a completely determinate univocal perfection. It is more than that. Self-transcendence is taken beyond those borders, and undermines from within the closure into self-sufficiency. Self-satisfaction is also undermined from without, in the measure that self-transcending meets an other that comes towards it, out of its own self-transcending integrity.

It may help if I mention some examples. Relative to univocity and equivocity, a first example of an open whole might be the *human body* as an aesthetic integrity. It is an organic unity, but also goes beyond this in its expressive form; it is a cosmos, but it is open to the cosmos other to itself. The aesthetic body as adorned is turned into an art work in which the self mediates with itself; but this self-perfecting is never completed; there is always a *more* that is not now determined; beauty draws us as a lure to this more. Beauty is the sensuous presence of being whole, but the openness of the whole carries us beyond the determinate details to an intimation of the *reserve of presence*, even in the manifestation. This incarnate aesthetic whole is more than univocal and yet not merely equivocal. There is a dialectic of wholeness here that also engages the whole person who responds; organic unity becomes the sign of mindful being.[6]

A second example is the open wholeness possible in genuine *work*. Here the human being mediates with its own power and tries to determine its own identity in determining the shape of its material world; in working on the material world it works on itself. Work is open with respect to nature, and with respect to human possibility, even as it tries to perfect both. This is more evident with the free work of art, where the material that is mediated or shaped is the human being itself. The great art work gives to us a concretion of wholeness that is more than any determinate univocal whole; there is a thereness to its manifestness, but also an inexhaustibility that exceeds every determinate analysis we make of it. This excess of the whole, opening to transcendence, renews our astonishment and appreciation of being; and yet the orginative human being mediates with itself in this work too.[7]

---

6. On this more fully, see *Philosophy and its Others*, 69ff.

7. See *Art and the Absolute*, chapter 5; *Desire, Dialectic and Otherness*, chapters 4 and 7; *Philosophy and its Others*, chapter 2.

A third example is the open wholeness at work in *religious inwardness*, where the self is deepened beyond determinate measure and yet in this it becomes more deeply itself. In the abyss of its own inward otherness, it comes before itself and opens to a sense of the infinite that exceeds its own self-mediation. Yet in the tension between its own excess as transcendence and the transcendence of the other, it is being perfected, made whole, never closed even in the radical innerness.[8]

One can say something similar about the open wholeness of *ethical character*. The good is at work in the good person. The good person is the concrete witness of the good, and becomes whole in that service of concretion. But there is no closure to this whole. To close this whole would be the very apostasy from the good. The open wholeness means that the usual opposition between autonomy and heteronomy is not adequate. The witness of the good is not autonomous, for this witness is most true to self-transcendence when it goes towards the other as other, out of agapeic good will, out of the excess of the good already leavening its own self-determination of concrete character.[9]

There is a doubleness in all these wholes, as both finite and infinite at once. They are overdetermined wholes, double but not completely determinate. To be completely determinate would be to exhaust the energy of self-transcendence, and this would be to misunderstand its excess to determination, its inexhaustibility. The open whole as double is both an open determinacy and a concretized indeterminacy, in the excessive sense of a plenitude that cannot be exhausted.

I suggest there is also a certain open wholeness about *philosophy itself*. Thus philosophy may often develop by self-correction, but there is a certain greatness possible in philosophy which for all its flaws is unsurpassable. There is an excess not to be exceeded in the truthfulness of a great thinker, even though that thinker err. The very greatness of the philosopher would be in this honesty before ultimacy, even though this honesty would not give the philosopher absolute knowledge of ultimacy, and would always open the philosopher to the possible controverting by other-being of the claims the philosopher had neglected, or covered over, or forgotten.

These open wholes make us ask about dialectic: Can self-mediation finally be the truth of the whole? Is self-mediation able to do justice to the double interplay that happens in the between? Is there here a tendency to say that, since the self mediates with itself in mediating with what is other, then dialectical self-mediating provides us with the truth of being, truth that does not dispense with the other, not at all, but rather appropriates its truth within the more inclusive context of comprehensive dialectical self-mediation? Is dialectical thinking lured dangerously by a *telos* that is *its own completion* in

---

8. See *Philosophy and its Others*, chapter 3.

9. See *Desire, Dialectic and Otherness*, 163–75; *Philosophy and its Others*, chapter 4.

absolutely determinate knowing? Must the dialectical sense of being and mind end up with an absolute knowing identified with completely self-determining thinking?

This must be denied. It must be denied because we have to think of the play of doubleness in terms different to any equivocal dualism that is to be included in a comprehensive self-mediation. It has to be rejected in terms of the full play of dialectic in the happening of the between, where the transcendence of the other cannot be dialectically included without remainder in any circle of self-mediation. I now address this issue.

Dialectic and the Happening of the Between

Having looked at dialectic relative to beings and to the human being as mindful, we must now look at the *coming together* of these two in the happening of the between. Without question dialectic offers a very important interpretation of this coming together. Traditionally the point may have been put differently, but dialectic's sense of the connectedness of beings in becoming, and its sense of the togetherness of being and mind in the web of relativity, point clearly in this direction.

The dialectical sense, like the univocal, thinks that to be is to be intelligible, and that to be intelligible is to be determinate. But unlike the univocal interpretation, this determinate intelligibility is not a static state of affairs but a coming to determinacy in the very happening of becoming itself. The happening of becoming is itself dialectical as mediating a transition from an initial lack of determinacy towards a more and more realized determinate condition of being. The dialectical happening of becoming is self-mediating; it mediates the concretion of determinate selves who are internally complex in their identity. One might say that dialectical self-identity here is a complex univocity that has appropriated the diversification of equivocity; and by interiorizing the latter, it rescues the differentiation from the fragmentation to which it might otherwise be prone. The matter is explicit with the human self, which is mindful of just this process of establishing its own identity through the interiorization of equivocal plurality. In the process of human mindfulness we come to know the being of beings as also marked by dialectical features. Mind's self-transcendence is not cut off from the being-other of beings. Quite the opposite. No absolute dualism of these two is intelligibly defensible.

Thus dialectic demands a certain *realism* of knowing. I know this goes against the common view. But mind's self-transcendence towards the other reaches the other as self-mediating in its own right. It knows itself as coming to know that being-other. In addition, that being as other emerges out of itself into its own self-determinacy, and so also enters the middle as a complex, pluralized identity. The human being, mindful in its restless self-transcendence, determines itself to enter the middle and there progressively becomes more clear, both about itself and what is other. The two sides, each a different dialectical self-transcendence, meet in the middle; this is the community of their togetherness. Thus, we can say that dialectic can condition the possibility of knowing the other as other: it grants, on the one side, the self-transcending of the mindful human being which, in progressively determining itself, comes to determinate knowledge of what is other to itself; it also grants, on the other side, the inherent being for itself of the other-being, a being for itself that is also self-transcending in progressively determining itself, as it becomes in the between.

It is now that the most difficult point has to be broached. Let us grant two self-transcendences. This is a simplification, of course, in that self-transcendence is multiplied beyond all our computation in the prodigious plurality of the happening of the between. We have a plurality of centers of self-transcendence, all of which are determined in the happening of the between, which is their community or convergence. The issue is how do we determine this *convergence?* It is a mediation. It is the complex interplay of a many. Does this exclude an immediacy? No. But the immediacy is always implicitly mediated. It is mediated before *we* do anything. It is mediated because things as determinate are already defined by a process of determinate mediation whose issue they are. If there is both a mediation and immediacy, there is a givenness to this community. In this section I propose to speak of this community. In the next section I will say something about the givenness.

The community can be described in dialectical terms, but with crucial qualifications that I hold take us to the limit of dialectic. The doubleness of the *dia* has to be preserved. The dialectical being of beings, while establishing a complex self-identity, does not establish them as seamless unities. Their singularity itself is double, shaped by a double mediation—namely, a self-relating and a relating to what is other. This means that a being's identity is never completely contained within itself. What it is within itself is internally defined by what it is in relation to what is other to itself. Its being is hence a *tension* between its own being for self and its being for others; and both these are not themselves without the other. The mediation of the self of a being is *in itself* double, and so cannot be reduced to one single mediation alone. Similarly, the self-identity of the mindful human being is not single self-mediation. In its self-transcendence it puts itself in the tension of the between, where its orientation to the other as other always is in strain with its recurrence to itself. Its self-identity for itself is in strain with its relativity to the other. The fuller meaning of the double mediation will be addressed in the metaxological sense.

Here we have to acknowledge a plurality of self-mediating wholes, wholes that are not necessarily set in antagonistic opposition to one another but are determined as themselves in the play of identity and difference that comes to expression in the milieu of the between. It is not that there is no antagonistic opposition, but this too is contributive to the play of identity and difference, and hence a mediating partner in the constitution of the happening of the between. Discord *may* serve the mediated concord of the between. In this mediated concord each entity is the promise of its own being for itself and its being with the others, as also beings for themselves. In all cases, this being for self is itself an integrity of existence that holds itself together but dynamically so, and hence in stress with the possibility of dissolution, whether coming from inward self-destruction or atrophy, or from onslaught by exterior threat. The happening of the between is no univocal concord, but a tense and fragile equilibrium between a plurality of participants, each a dialectical whole unto itself, but none a whole that can take its wholeness for finality or for granted, each a whole that must repeatedly renew its integrity of being in a dynamic mediation relative to itself and to other-being.

Because of the doubling and redoubling of mediation in the integrity of the participants and in the happening of the between, dialectic must always remain open. The participants of the between undercut the possibility of any closure. The wholes in interplay are open wholes, in interplay just because they are open; consequently the happening of the between cannot be totalized as a singular whole that subsumes all these wholes as lacking parts of itself. There is the immanent self-relativity of the wholes; there is their self-transcendence towards the others; there is their convergence in community in and through the passage of opposition and discord. But the convergence does not redescribe the immanent integrity as a mere part of something other; nor redescribe the self-transcendence as a more encompassing movement that subsumes all it traverses within itself. The immanent integrity has depths of inner reserve that feed self-mediation but which are not determinately exhausted by self-mediation; the self-transcendence has a form that is not at all subsumptive of the other.

What I have said will lead on to the metaxological sense, but it is consistent with an open dialectic in which the *dia* is not reduced to a *monas* in which all otherness is placed as a subordinate and subsumed part. Expressed otherwise, as a community of dialectical open originals, the happening of the between is not itself simply another more encompassing dialectical original. Open dialectical originals are themselves pointers to sources of being that cannot be completely determined in terms of dialectic and the self-mediation that is its great strength. Even less so can the community of a plurality of such dialectical originals. There is a mediation that is beyond self-mediation, and that does justice to the openness of dialectical originals. This is metaxological intermediation in which the doubleness of mediation is so affirmed as to obviate any temptation to the reduction of pluralized interplay to a singular play of one power with itself.

To be alert to this temptation we must be vigilant concerning the strong propensity of dialectical thinking to shortchange this pluralized mediation. This propensity flows from powerful currents at work in the philosophical tradition and the continued oscillation between univocity and equivocity in dialectic. The latter, as I said, tends to recur to the univocal, and especially so when the equivocal is understood as a recalcitrant dualism that stands counter to mediated intelligibility or as an ambiguous indefiniteness that must not be let resist the requirement of determinate intelligibility. This recurrence of the univocal in the dialectical is, I believe, a contraction of the energy of self-transcendence and the inner integrity of beings. But it still is evidence of a powerful propensity.

What I mean is this: the insight of dialectic into the pervasive work of self-mediation can cause it to *absolutize* this mediation as marking the community of being, the happening of the between, now called *the whole*. Then it will be said that the two lines of mediation, that of beings and the mindful human being, are both forms of dialectical self-mediation. Hence both will be said to be *the same*. But if both are the same, then both are articulations of dialectical self-mediation. That is, the unity of their difference is said to be the *process* of dialectical self-mediation itself. And what is the happening of the between? It is their convergence. But now it is said that their convergence is the expression of an underlying sameness—namely, the very process of dialectical self-mediation. Thus the happening of the between itself becomes just a process of dialectical self-mediation, either of a more underlying unity or of a more overarching totality. The two sides of the between are said to be merely two expression of this underlying unity, or else transitional passing points on the way to this overarching totality. The happening of the between is itself determined as a more inclusive process of dialectical self-mediation of which the mediation of beings and human beings are different expressions.

The consequence of this line of thinking is the following. The doubleness of the *dia* of dialectic is either *reduced* to or *sublated* into this one process of absolute self-mediation, as is the pluralism of the different centers of dialectical self-mediation. Even the dialectical self-mediation at play in the middle will serve, in its dissolving phase, to undermine the partiality of these different centers and make them into way stations of the absolute process of dialectical self-mediation. The happening of the between is interpreted as the *medium of this absolute process*, which concretizes *itself* in different forms of *itself*—beings and the human being, nature and history, but each as middles, or means to the determinate constitution of the absolute self-mediating whole. The between, its participants, whether beings or human beings, all serve the same role as media of the absolute process in its mediation with itself. And since this its mediation with itself is absolute, *their otherness*, either from each other, or from the absolute itself, is not any final otherness at all. All otherness is merely the *self-othering* of the absolute process, which is in no way transcendent to the process but completely immanent to it. There is no final transcendence at all, nothing but the immanence of all transcendence to the absolute process of the dialectical self-mediation of the whole.

As the perceptive reader will know, I have just described the completion of the essential temptation of dialectic in the Hegelian form of idealism. There is an absolutization of self-mediation, absolutization that does not deny a mediation with the other, but rather complexly subsumes it in a more overarching self-mediation.[10] The pluralism of the double is rendered as two sides of a dualism that is to be sublated into a more comprehensive unity. What has happened here is that the teleology of self-transcendence has taken complete charge of the determination of the happening of the between and redescribed it in terms of completed self-mediation.

Self-transcendence is on the way, in transition, in passage. I agree. But in the interpretation here considered, it is on the way to the consummation of self-mediation. Dialectic carries it on this way, carries it into and through and beyond even the most recalcitrant otherness of opposition. Moreover, this thrust to the *telos* of complete self-mediation means that the initiation of the process also gets redescribed in terms of a lacking indefiniteness. The beginning of self-transcendence is said to be a lacking indeterminacy; the process of dialectical becoming progressively makes more determinate this initial indefiniteness; the end is the complete determination of this initial indefiniteness. Moreover, this end is not just determinacy as there or as stasis. It is determination that claims itself to be dialectically self-mediating; the complete *telos* of the process is absolute determination, which is to say, *absolute self-determination*. Absolute determination is necessity, the absolute intelligibility; but this is the autonomy of freedom, of absolute self-determination. Where do we find this coincidence of absolute intelligibility, freedom, and necessity? In an idealistic version of *thought thinking itself*. Aristotle's view that to be is to be determinate has been transformed, with aid from Kant's transcendental idealism, into the absolute self-determination of Hegel's thought thinking itself.

What drives this process of progress from the indefinite to the determinate to the self-determined? It is erotic perplexity. Erotic perplexity is an activation of the infinite restlessness of mind before the being-there of beings, in the happening of the between. This activation proceeds from its own lack or indefinition, and through itself progressively overcomes this indefinition, gaining more and more determinacy. It does this by entering the between and interplaying with others. In making these more and more determinate, it

---

10. In Hegelian dialectic there is a going towards the other, no question about this. On occasion the language of self-surrender and renunciation is used. But this is not all the story and the further pages put these occasions in place. If there is any loss of self in going towards the other, this will be penultimate to a mediated return to self. The process will be erotic, finally for the self; it will not be agapeic, or for the other as other. When Hegel, for instance, speaks of self-recognition in absolute otherness, it is quite clear where the final accent falls; it does not fall on absolute otherness, which seems to be at the end; it falls on the self-recognition, which is the real end mediated through otherness.

also makes itself more and more determinate, and finally in knowing the other comes to know itself as the power of self-determination in the process of the whole. Self-mediation is the mediation finally privileged by erotic perplexity, in that the other is known as a means by which the self overcomes its own lack and attains its completion.

In my view this process of erotic self-determination is the *metaphysical metaphor* that basically informs the absolutization of dialectical self-mediation in the totalism of idealism. Thus the Hegelian absolute as original is a merely indefinite, abstract emptiness. It must other itself to be itself. It does not merely enter the middle; it produces it as finite "creation," what we call the happening of the between. But this happening is *itself as other*. It is not agapeically loosed for itself as other; it is produced for the return of the lacking absolute to itself; it is the medium in which the absolute mediates with itself and so returns to itself. In this return the Hegelian absolute completes itself, makes itself really absolute, as the whole that is absolute self-mediation, the Idea, *Geist*, as thought thinking itself.

The logic of all this is very complex, and when understood, very powerful and persuasive. But it is *not* the truth of the happening of the between, nor is it adequate to the openness of transcendence that the dialectical sense itself demands. It is a contraction of the idea of beginning. It makes the beginning an indigent indefinite, an abstraction for itself. It forgets the agapeic astonishment that is the source of the self-transcendence of metaphysical mind. This agapeic astonishment becomes merely something to be determined further, for all intelligibility is still determinate. The sense of the excess of transcendence at work in the beginning is quickly set aside in the forward rush of dialectical determination.

Why is the excess of the origin not dwelt with? Because to dwell with it demands a mediation of mind that is at the border of the determinate intelligibility so beloved of the philosopher. As we shall see, the metaxological sense tries to dwell with this plenitude of the origin and thinks its excess in terms of the metaphor of an agapeic origin rather than an erotic absolute. As we shall also see, the metaphorical nature of this is tied up with our efforts to do justice to the indeterminate, in a more or less determinate articulation that is not contractive. The purely determinate will always seek as univocal a concept as possible which overcomes all the ambiguity of the metaphor. This is impossible if we think the origin as excess.

Moreover, the excess also marks the happening of the between and the partners at play therein. The agapeic astonishment at the beginning means that we look at the happening of the between differently. There is a constitutive enigma to this happening—why it should be so at all. The erotic dialectic immediately sets to work to determine what is it, what happens there. The marvel of the *that it is so at all* is given scant attention. This *it is so* is itself seen as a mere contingency with which the philosopher hardly bothers; or perhaps so-called "contingency" it itself redefined as simply the dialectical necessity of the lacking origin to make itself determinate. To make contingency dialectically necessary may take some of the terror out of its lack of absolute necessity, but it also robs it of its signs of marvel: that it is so at all, that there is no iron necessity that it be so, that it might not be, that it might be otherwise—and yet it is.

This dialectical determination of the necessity of the contingent happening of the between orients mind's self-transcending towards the determination of the *categories* of being, not to the very happening of the between itself. The *very giving* of the between is occluded in terms of the determination of intelligiblity with respect to different kinds of beings within the between, including the human being. Inevitably, there is a loss of metaphysical astonishment in the relentless determination of the dialectical categories necessary to fix the logical intelligibility of determinate beings and process.

What is lost here is something unspoken that shadows the whole system of dialectical categories, but that the absolutization of self-mediation within the system, this absolutization as the system, cannot speak. What is lost is the sense of the *archē* as agapeic; of the happening of the between as the giving of creation by the agapeic origin, giving it being for itself as other and as for itself. What is also lost is the transcendence between the origin and the creation. And in the happening of the between, the marvel of the sheer being-there of beings is trellised over by a network of dialectical categories which substitute their determinate intelligibilities for the elemental being-there of beings. Likewise, the self-transcendence of the mindful human being is redefined in terms of the privileging of absolute self-determination, and the passion of human self-transcending for transcendence itself is bent back into the circle of immanence. All transcendence becomes immanent transcendence.

This result might be taken in two major ways: either as elevating human self-transcendence into identity with the self-mediation of the absolute dialectical process, or as denying any other dialectical self-transcendence except human self-transcendence. In one case we have the religious attenuation of the otherness of transcendence to human self-transcendence; in the other, the atheistic reduction of the otherness of transcendence to human self-transcendence; in both cases there is a significant recasting of the happening of being. Its being-there is no longer situated between the excess of the origin and the uncertain end, a between where the existence of being is in excess of complete determinate intelligibility, where also the excess of human self-transcendence is more than determinate intelligibility. In fact, there is no real between in the robust metaphysical sense, for there is no otherness, whether of the origin, the end, the middle itself, or of man the intermediate transcendence.

Hegelian Dialectic, Being and the Between

What about the issue of *givenness*, as above mentioned? A brief excursus on Hegel will illuminate the issue, as well as round off the chapter.

Hegelian dialectic can be reconstructed in terms of an interplay of univocity and equivocity, and their transcendence. Thus, corresponding to the univocal, we find Hegel speaking of beginnings as inarticulated immediacy, about which all one can say is a bare *that it is*. This is reflected in the beginning of the *Phenomenology* and the *Logic*. In the former we begin with sense-certainty that seems immediately to affirm the expansive plenitude of sensuous thereness, what I call aesthetic being. Hegel holds that this reveals itself to be the opposite of what is claimed: instead of an expanse of plenitude, it is an indigent thereness. All we seem able to say of it at the level of aesthetic immediacy is *that it is*: it is there; it is all but nothing. To speak its meaning we must advance beyond its immediacy.

Hegel holds, of course, that this indigent beginning will *develop itself*. We do not advance it; it advances itself. There is an immanent unfolding into articulated plurality. This diversification is not a mere pluralization, since it is gathered by mediating universals, like space and time, which are the conceptual counterparts, the dianoetic intelligibilities, which match the sense concreteness, the aesthetic show of being. The indigent particularity of the this-here-now unfolds into a network of relations and universals. The effort to affirm the plenitude of the given shows it to be an indigent beginning, which, however, turns itself into a mediation of its own immediacy, such that the determining of the truth of the aesthetic show through thinking is truer than the aesthetic affirmation of givenness. The unity of immediacy breaks itself up into diversity, but this break up and diversification are held together in a new integration.

This rhythm of immediacy (corresponding to the rapture of univocity), rupture, and development into dualistic opposition (corresponding to equivocal diversification), and return to integrated unity having passed through opposition, constitutes the dynamic structure of dialectic for Hegel. Dialectic is shown in the negating power that unfolds from the immediate unity itself, and that sunders the unity into oppositions that are self-oppositions. The return to mediated unity is also the issue of dialectic, now in its affirmative finale. Hegel distinguishes speculative and dialectical reason, but the two are finally inseparable: without the negativity of dialectic the speculative unity is impossible. The speculative unity of opposites is the affirmative truth of dialectic.

This process of the positing of immediate unity, its immanent breakup and self-articulation, its mediated reintegration, is repeated again and again throughout the *Phenomenology* and only culminates when what is implicit in the immediate beginning is *completely mediated*. There is a *telos* in this repetition in that the dialectical process is driven forwards at each point by the failure of consciousness, or self-consciousness, or reason, or spirit to achieve complete mediated identity with itself. The *telos* is the goal of absolutely self-mediating thought. This goal is reached in absolute knowing when the otherness of the immediate is completely mediated, in its being dialectically subsumed in a self-knowing that is absolutely self-mediating.

This absolute knowing as completely self-mediating thought is, for Hegel, the truth of the first "indigence" that sense-certainty misunderstands as the affirmative plenitude of the *that it is*. This "It is" becomes entirely encapsulated by pure self-determining thinking. Being self-mindful completely overcomes any thinking that thinks the otherness of being as other to mind. Being self-mindful completes being as the pure self-mediating dialectical process of thought determining itself. Being is the pure self-determination of thought thinking itself.

This is the second beginning taken up in Hegel's *Logic*. The beginning here is not the expanse of the aesthetic show of being; it is said to be pure being. What is this pure being? Is it the prodigal excess of the plenitude of being as overdetermined inexhaustibility, the origin coming towards the between that strikes us into agapeic astonishment? Not at all. It is being considered as a pure determination of thought thinking its own *categories*. Being is the first category, but as such it is also the most indigent again. The sense of the lack of the beginning that we find with erotic perplexity is again evident here, but mixed with a forgetfulness of the overdetermined plenitude of the agapeic origin in astonishment. Being is a *thought category*, and it is as a thought category that it interests Hegel; it is not being in its excess of ontological otherness.[11]

As a thought category, it is the most universal thought, but for Hegel also the most impoverished. Why? Because it seems to lack all determinations. We think it, and all we seem to think is "It is." What more can we say? All but nothing. Thought struggles to find more determinations there, but finds all but nothing. Again notice how, relative to erotic perplexity, there is a drive to determinacy as intelligibility, all the more insistent in the measure that the excessive overdetermined origin has been shortchanged. The latter is reduced to a mere indefiniteness, and all indefinites must be dialectically determined. The recalcitrance of the origin as excess to complete determination is occluded by this drive to determination. Hegel's interpretation of dialectic follows the articulation of this drive, which again is shaped by the oscillation of univocity and equivocity, and their transcendence through immanent development. Transcendence, relative to his sense of erotic perplexity and the indigent beginning, whether of being or sense-certainty, is formulated in a dialectical logic of determinate negation.

---

11. Consider the critique of Hegel as an "essentialist"—being becomes a thought-determination, a logical essence, as do all other categories; being as ontological in a deeper sense than essence is not broached, much less reached; without this deeper sense, the essence easily decays into logical abstraction, as does being. I think that perhaps this critique is often too easily put to Hegel, but the unease with Hegel underlying it is to the point.

Hegel himself speaks of the portentous power of the negative (*die ungeheure Macht des Negativen*). As I said, Hegel distinguishes negative and positive reason, the dialectical and speculative. These two are inextricable since the negating work of the first looks forwards to the full reintegrative work of the second. The double of equivocity is articulated further in negative dialectic; but the negative is also, as Hegel says, the magic power that converts it into being, and in this negation of negation there is the reiterated mediated unity. We try to think being intelligibly. This means to think it determinately. We fail because of the indigence of being as a thought. In thinking the indigence of being, we think the thought of indigence or lack of determination. Thus the thinking of being is the thinking of what lacks determinations. So the empty indefiniteness of the thought of being seems impossible to distinguish from its opposite, namely, nothing, as another name for the lack of determinations. Being and nothing are opposites but the thinking of each turns into the thinking of the other.

Hegel claims that here in thought thinking being and nothing as *thought determinations*, we have the *passage* from being to nothing and from nothing to being and back again. There is a process of the disappearance of one into the other and the other into the other. This is a reciprocal vanishing of one in the other and the other in the one. *It is a reciprocal self-othering of being into nothing and nothing into being*. Becoming is this passage of both into each other. Notice that the empty univocity of being has now given way to its opposite and this opposite has turned back into its opposite. This process of the radical opposition and promiscuity of opposites, of course, is the equivocal. But becoming is both—that is, the mediated reintegration of univocity and equivocity, the conjoining of the sameness and otherness of being and nothing, conjoining in an entirely active sense as process.

Hegel is often seen as contemptuous of formal logic, but this is a very crude caricature. Quite to the contrary, Hegel is an interpreter of what makes formal logic itself possible. He is as respectful as any logician of the requirement that to be is to be determinate, to be intelligible is to be determinate. His point is that formal logic alone cannot account for this intelligibility, cannot account for itself and its own intelligibility. Hegel is a *more uncompromising logicist* in that regard than Aristotle, for whom he had the highest respect. As we already put it, he radicalizes Aristotle's claim that dialectic provides "a process of criticism wherein lies the way [path] to the principles of all inquiries" (*Topics*, 101b3–4). Dialectic is an interpretation of the logic of logic, the *logos* of formal logic itself. Hegel's view is: this *logos* cannot itself be formal.

Where Aristotle claims that the first principles of demonstration cannot themselves be demonstrated, Hegel is a more uncompromising logician in holding that if the ground of determinate intelligibility could not be made determinate, then intelligibility itself would fall to the ground. In formal logic the univocal stasis of the proposition dominates the ideal of determinate intelligibility. The living *logos* of proposing or positing intelligibility is not minded. The determinations of intelligibility make us forgetful of the process of determining itself. Dialectical logic claims to articulate this process of determining, the *logos* in its determining of determinate intelligibilities.

For Hegel, however, this process of determining is itself made determinate in terms of a logic of *self-determination*. Thus what he calls the speculative proposition is not to be made static in terms of an external connection between a subject and a predicate: S is P. Rather the subject is determined by the predicate; to that extent the predicate is the subject as determined; thus also the subject determines itself to be such and such in the predicate; hence the predicate determines the very self of the subject; it is the self-determination of the subject. So there is a reciprocal passage back and forth between subject and predicate, a passage of reciprocal determination. In truth, for Hegel, the reciprocal determination of subject and predicate is the self-determination of the intelligibility of the whole proposition, or positing, or determination.

What I have just outlined as the passage from *determination* to *reciprocal determination* to *self-determination* is very evident in Hegel's dialectic of being and nothing. To say that being is nothing and that nothing is being seems like an absolute equivocation. Each is absolutely opposite. This will bother the formal logician whose emphasis on fixed univocity makes it impossible to affirm the passage from one to the other. Hegel sees that even ordinary language has greater metaphysical depth than this fixed univocity. He points out in the *Logic* how the word *Aufhebung*, itself a crucial technical term in defining his sense of dialectical logic, has a double meaning in the one word: it means both to cancel, to transcend, and yet to preserve. This double meaning in one is the delightful speculative genius of language itself. The double in the one, the unity of opposites, or the opposites in the unity, makes dialectic truer to this speculative genius than univocal formal logic, or any equivocation that reneges on *logos*.

Moreover, Hegel sees the opposition dialectically as a *self-opposition*, or process of *self-othering*. When being is itself, it is its opposite, nothing; when nothing is itself, it is its opposite, being. But both of them, in being their own opposites, are also themselves again, Hegel will say. There is a return to identity with itself, even in what looks like a process of absolute equivocation. The crucial point will concern the very process of passage, what I call the happening of the between. Hegel, through the eyes of dialectic, will see a univocal immediacy turn into an equivocal process, which is a passing into opposition, into self-opposition, and thence back again. Through the eyes of Hegelian dialectic the happening of the between and the being of passage will be seen as a process of self-determination in self-othering, and self-othering in self-determination. The equivocation of opposites in such a process is identical with one of reciprocal determination, which is really self-determination in the other; and again since the other here is the self's *own other*, it is hence the self itself once again. The happening of the between becomes a passage from the immediacy of univocal determination through the indetermination of equivocation, towards a more and more self-mediated self-determination. The *telos* of passage will be absolute self-mediating self-determining. This will be the whole that absolutely mediates with itself and includes all others and otherness as subordinate phases of its own self-mediation.

Hegel will say that being *has already passed over* into nothing and nothing into being. We are always beyond the immediate beginning; the beginning has already always occurred; the beginning is always already mediated. This corresponds in Hegel's account to what I call the *coming to happening* of the between. I agree we are always beyond the pure origin. I disagree that the origin is the happening of the between as just a process of dialectical transition. The origin is what gives the happening of the between. I see the origin, prior to both determinate negation and erotic perplexity, and groped for through agapeic astonishment, as what gives the happening of the between, but that is not itself self-mediated by the happening of the between. If all mediation is self-mediation, there is no origin other than the happening of the between; the origin would be the latter itself, interpreted in terms of a total process of self-mediation. The metaxological sense denies this view as adequate to the between, as it dissents from the occlusion of the origin that follows in its train.

If we can turn the excess of aesthetic being entirely into a thought-determination, *if* we can make being entirely into a thought-category, *if* we can just resolve to drive relentlessly beyond the forgotten origin, and beyond agapeic astonishment—and I deny all these conditions—erotic perplexity might indeed be harnassed by a logic of determinate negation in which the partial determines itself and at the same time dialectically undermines itself. And this dialectical undermining is not the loss of determination, for negation is determination; rather it is the move to a more express determination, a more inclusive determination that encompasses the partial determinations and contradictions it immanently generates. This process of determination through dialectical negation will proceed by the logic of the *Aufhebung*: this is the *inclusive* self-transcendence of thought itself, which appropriates the self-development of being-other. It will proceed, Hegel holds, to the all-inclusive thought, which is the absolute Idea, the inclusive whole of thought absolutely determining itself. Hence Hegel's *Logic*, like the *Phenomenology*, completes itself in a *telos* answering to the total self-determination of thought thinking itself. The same thing happens in the philosophy of nature, history, the philosophy of spirit, culminating in absolute spirit. At this coronation of absolute spirit, Hegel places the crown on its head, and the hymn he sings is Aristotle's *Te Deum* to *noēsis tēs noēseōs*. This is Hegel's highest amen to being.

Since we deny the conditions stated above, we cannot sing the amen to being in the Hegelian tune. Our *Te Deum* must be different. We might suggest that Hegel's logic of being is not concerned with that "Being is" but that thought is. The stress is on thought from the outset: not the thought of *being*, but the *thought* of being. He thinks the thought of being with stress on the being of thought. The thought of being as thought is seen as thought in its emptiest, most abstract, nugatory, and indefinite form. *Thought is*, not *Being is*. "Being is" looks like a tautology, and Hegel will see it as such. But if we stress the thinking of being, rather than the being of thinking, "Being is" can be seen as other than empty tautology, as rather an articulation of the *redoubling of being* that is given in the happening of the between. Being reappears twice over, redoubles itself, comes out of itself, gives itself as other. Excess is shown in "Being is."

Let me put it slightly differently. The excess at the origin of the redoubling, I suggested, is not comprehended in the reduction to a tautological thought. "Thought is": this might seem to be the thought of *nothing*, because it is not the thought of something determinate. But the original excess at the redoubling of being is really the origin of the fact that there is something determinate at all, and something at all to be thought. With Hegel this original excess is inverted into its opposite. For Hegel absence of determinacy amounts to the being of nothing. The minimal thought is that thinking *is*. By contrast, for us the exorbitant thought, the hyperbolic idea is that "Being is." For Hegel the first thought is not the plenitude of excess in agapeic astonishment; it is the emptiness of the indefinite. The final thought is that there is no final other to thought; there is nothing finally other to thought. Thought is being, being is thought.

As I said above, it is true that there is no argument for mind that does not in some sense presuppose mind. But does this justify the claim that mind or thought is entirely self-justifying, and that hence thinking that is purely self-determining is abolute? I do not believe so. That thinking is at all; that being is mindful, that it is given to being to be mindful—this is perplexing, astonishing. That there should be thinking at all, the being of thinking, and not its nonbeing: this is the mystery of being become mindful of being. Being as originating mind is presupposed by mind thinking being at all, or mind thinking itself.

Even Hegel will say that all we need is the *resolve* to think to get the beginning of the process of his logic under way. We resolve simply to think. Is this resolve presuppositionless, taking nothing for granted? How could it possibly be? I do not just mean that it presupposes some specific thought-determination; *in concreto* it always does, but that is not my point. Let us say it presupposes resolve, and indeed resolve as already in mindfulness. Why is resolve already in mindfulness? Because thought is *already given to itself*. In other words, resolve is responsive to something prior—let us say perplexity about being. In turn, perplexity is also responsive to something prior, let us say, being as given, or even mind as given. But does not perplexed responsiveness to being presuppose something prior—namely the giving of thinking or mindful being to the thinker in perplexity? And is not this giving of thinking about being itself responsive to something prior—namely, *the giving of being itself?* This giving of being is given for thinking, thinking that itself is given to the mindful being. And so the seeming bare resolve to think has layers and layers of ontological presuppositions, prior to thought thinking its own thought-determinations.

If in resolve thought is already given to itself thus richly, then the being of thought as thus given to itself can never be the same as thought giving itself to itself. Put differently, thinking is first *heteroarchic* before any possibility at all of its being auto-generating. By heteroarchic I mean that its origin *(archē)* is in an other *(heteros)*, or other to its own self *(autos)*. This heteroarchic giving ruptures the circle of self-mediating, self-determining thinking. The primary giving of thinking to be at all as thinking points to something more primordial than the circle of thought thinking itself. Simply put: thinking is first a gift. Mindfulness is given in the excess of agapeic astonishment that is prior to erotic perplexity and to all specific curiosities. Specific curiosity determines itself in univocity and equivocity, erotic perplexity determines itself dialectically, but agapeic astonishment finds itself "determined" and released metaxologically. Thence thought may proceed to determine itself in the other three modes, all of which it exceeds, even as original being in its excess transcends all.

We can now see more clearly why Hegel's claim—for a logic of presuppositionless thinking, a self-thinking that takes nothing for granted—is completely *equivocal*, indeed impossible. There is no thinking that can take nothing for granted, for thinking itself is a granting. For thinking does not first *grant itself*; it is *granted to itself*, even in trying to think itself presuppositionlessly. In other words, thinking is only a self-determining because *it is given to itself* to be self-determining; it is granted to itself to *be* thinking. Self-determining thinking is given to itself first out of a heteroarchic origin, hence there is no absolutely presuppositionless thought. Even the latter thought must first be, be given to itself, in order to try to think itself presuppositionlessly.

The idea of taking nothing for granted might seem to be the absolute paradigm of free thought, but it is not. The very giving of free thinking to itself is thus, in fact, *taken for granted, as already having been granted—and not by thinking itself either*. There is something ironic about the situation. For to claim to take nothing for granted, self-determining thinking *must take itself for granted*. It must already be, and be given to itself to be mindful, must already have taken itself for granted, before it can claim to take nothing for granted. Even if it then proceeds to criticize *itself*, it must still be taken as first granted, even if this granting is subsequently dialectically negated or reinterpreted. If we are not careful, we end up obliviating that most enigmatic of questions here: Why is thought granted to itself, given to itself, to think? What is the origin that gives this metaphysical freedom of mindfulness?

To claim that it is thought thinking itself is forgetfully to take for granted the astonishing original giving of thinking to be thinking at all. The very possibility of being thought thinking itself is rooted in a source *other* to the self-determining thinking. For thought is given to itself, before it is the thought of itself. And this giving, this granting is not thought thinking itself—which is always *later* than the origin. Thought thinking itself may claim to start absolutely and without presuppositions but it is already too late: it is a second beginning, not a first source. And when the second beginning claims to be the first origin, it tries to close the circle of beginning and end, but it turns away from the very granting by the other origin, it forgets itself as granted, as a grant of the other origin. There is a paradox here. Thinking takes itself for granted, but really fails to take itself for granted, for it absolutely fails to think itself as granted. It claims to be absolute thinking, but it is thinking that is in fugue from the original granting.

In sum: Hegel's view of being sees a passage from immediacy to self-mediation; being as immediate is completely self-mediated by dialectical self-determination. Autonomous thought, the Idea, is autonomous being, the absolute whole. There is a passage to complete categorial determination of any equivocity of being. There is a return to univocity on the speculative level in the thought that thinks itself in thinking being in its otherness. Being in its otherness is the self-othering of thought thinking itself; this otherness is dialectically overreached by the process of thought completely determining itself. Transcendence is the self-transcendence of the Idea and also its self-return when it knows itself as self-transcendence in otherness. Parmenides' ghost rises at the end of Hegelian dialectic: Being and Thinking are one. The *dia* of *dialegein* is encompassed in a *mono-logos*, the *auto-nomos* of thought thinking itself, and thinking being in its pure immanent self-determination. In this logic that goes from the indefinite to the determinate to the self-determining, there is a loss of the excess plenitude of overdetermined being, a collapse of the double in its fecundity into the singular self-mediation, a loss of the *nomos* of the *heteros*, a *nomos* that is no *nomos* for this *archē* is heteroarchic.

CHAPTER FIVE

BEING AND THE METAXOLOGICAL

The Plurivocity of Being and the Metaxological

We have come some distance, and still we have some distance yet to go. Who travels with me? If I sometimes sound too abstract, or too assertive or solemn, or overly ambitious, or too hard to understand, would I had a lighter touch. Sometimes I have to speak in a way which, were I to justify it, would entail intolerable prolixity. There is a frail human being searching. I am not a thinking machine. I hope the voice of a human being will be heard, not the output of a faceless instrument that generates categories and conceptual connections. The dead ends of the searching may not show up in the discourse, but this does not mean there has been no casting about for direction. My discourse is the distillation of a search. It is the passage through, such as I have found it, that inevitably gets bespoken. So to conclude the first part of our exploration, I now turn to the metaxological sense of being.

Being is given. Its givenness reappears over and over, redoubled in excess of any dialectical reduction to a monism of self-mediation. The excess redoubles itself in the origin, in the middle, and in the end. It is to the pluralization of the mediations of givenness that the metaxological sense speaks. It is not reductive of the pluralization, either univocally or dialectically; nor is it dissipative of it into only an equivocal many. If being is spoken in many senses, these must include a proper understanding of unity, of difference, and of mediated community. These requirements are addressed by univocity, equivocity, and dialectic, in each case with strengths and limitations. The metaxological addresses the same requirements but always keeps in mind the excess of being's plenitude that is never exhaustively mediated by us.

If univocity stresses sameness, equivocity difference, dialectic the appropriation of difference within a mediated sameness, the metaxological reiterates, first a sense of otherness not to be included in dialectical self-mediation, second a sense of togetherness not reached by the equivocal, third a sense of rich ontological integrity not answered for by the univocal, and fourth a rich sense of ontological ambiguity not answered for either by the univocal, the equivocal, the dialectical.

177

I suggest that as dialectic tries to redeem the promise of univocity beyond equivocity, so the metaxological tries to redeem the promise of equivocity beyond univocity and dialectic. It keeps the space of the between open to mediations from the other irreducible to any mediation from the self. The *dia* of dialectic it to be genuinely preserved in its doubleness, and dialectic's promise thus fulfilled. The mediation from the other converges on the middle out of its own excess of being and integrity for itself. And though the other may meet the self in the middle, the intermediation between them cannot be totally characterized in terms of the mediation of any one of them.

There is a convergence of self and other, and a communication from one to the other. This community and convergence is exhausted by none, just as none is exhausted in its express mediation with the others. There is a reserve of excess in the beings in intermediation, a reserve not itself exhausted by their complex, nonreductive community of togetherness. If rather than self-mediation there is intermediation, this is double and redoubled; so even in its being communicated, the excess of transcendence remains reserved as excess. This is so, in the giving of the beginning of the between, in the supporting of its continued coming to be, and in the offering of its fulfilled ontological promise in the good.

If being is given, it is given both for itself and for mindfulness. Mindfulness is itself given to itself to be mindful of being, both in itself and in its otherness as given. Being is given as the happening of the between; but this between is *immediately given as mediated* between a plurality of centers of existence, each marked by its own energy of self-transcendence. In the human being this self-transcendence becomes mindful of itself and transcendence as other. Therefore, the meaning of the "to be" demands that we do justice to the following: first to the givenness of being-there in the between; second to the concretization there of integrities of being; third to the complexity of mediation between beings among themselves; fourth to the complexity of mediation between the human being as mindful and the rest of being in its difference.

This then is our purpose in this chapter: to outline a *logos* of the *metaxu*, the happening of the between. This account will try to do justice to the transcendence of beings in relation to their being; to the excess of the singularity of beings, especially relative to the mindful human being; to the excess relative to the community of beings, and the happening of the between; to the transcendence relative to the original ground of being of this happening. Finally, we must address how all this influences the task of metaphysics. This will bring us to Part II where I offer a metaphysics of creation, in light of the fourfold sense of being.

The Metaxological and the Play of Indeterminacy and Determination

Since the start of this work, we have been reflecting more and more adequately on the traditional belief that to be, and to be intelligibly, is to be determinate. I do not simply reject this view, but its limitations have been made evident, resulting in our thinking of other senses of being that are not intelligible in terms of some set of determinations, whether predicable features, or forms of things, or thought-categories. As we found, the indeterminate reappears, and not as the merely indefinite that must then be made determinate. It reappears as an overdetermination of being, of an original dynamism of being that cannot be finalized or fixed. It reappears also as an overdetermination of mindfulness in which the thought of being as given in agapeic astonishment cannot be exhausted in any finite set of thought-determinations. This overdetermination is the manifest transcendence of being as original plenitude, as itself the festive agape of being.

Let us begin by asking: How does the fourfold sense relate to this plenitude? My answer to follow will serve both to recapitulate and move us forward.

First, with the *univocal* sense we find a drive to reduce this overdetermination to the indefinite, on which fixed determinations of being and thought are imposed. In fact, this putative indefiniteness proves dynamic in itself as a process of becoming. But the category of the indefinite is by no means adequate to name what is at work in being prior to fixed determinacy. Likewise, any fixation of the indefinite by imposed category always proves less than final. Both the process of becoming and the process of thinking continually pass beyond that fixation, even while exploiting that fixation and gaining from it some intelligible lucidity.

Second, with the *equivocal* sense there emerges a sensitivity for the indeterminate beyond univocal determinacy. For the process of becoming itself generates this emergence; it is not a merely arbitrary stipulation by an abstract intellect expressing its dissatisfaction with the thought-determinations of univocity. The self-transcending of becoming and mind themselves recur to the indeterminate, because the indeterminate continues again and again to renew itself in both. Moreover, this repetition is not the reiteration of the univocal same, since the repetition of the indeterminate is the emergence of variability and diversity. Because the indeterminate is overdetermined it can throw up differences again and again, such that, while the differences are differences redoubled, they are reiterated as difference *for themselves*, and hence as other to each other, and not as multiplied univocal variations on an underlying univocal sameness. And so there is here recognized an *interplay* of the determinate and indeterminate. Yet, all too often, the tendency to think in terms of the indefinite still persists; then this interplay is itself characterized as indefinite. Instead of a univocal determination of the indefinite, the equivocal sense then offers us an *indefinite play between the determinate and the indeterminate*.

In fact, the play is not simply indefinite; it is an interplay, and hence a mediated play; it is intelligibly mediated, hence complexly determined too. The play itself is not the articulation of the indefinite but of the overdetermined power of being. The *dialectical* sense, and *third*, offers us a way to think the play between the indeterminate and the determinate in more than indefinite terms. This play is mediated, and the rhythm of the interplay shows itself as a passage back and forth between the terms in interplay. The determinate and the indeterminate are said to define each other. Each would not be what it is without the other, and hence each is necessary for the other. Hence the determinate is the indeterminate, but in the form of its being concretely determined. The indeterminate is also the determinate, but in the prior form of yet-to-be determined being; it is the lack of definition that later will be made definite in the concrete mediated process of determination. Both the determinate and the indeterminate as other are finally alike, both defined as different stages of a process that mediates with itself in the interplay between them.

Thus the dialectical definition of the interplay between determinacy and indeterminacy tends to give the primary emphasis to self-mediation. This is why in the interplay it sees the basis for a transformation of determination into a process of *self-determination* that works through a logic of determinate negation: the negation of the indefinite will not produce another indefinite, but an affirmative determination. Thus the indefinite is increasingly transformed into the determinate by means of an increasingly autonomous self-determination. Through a negativity that is self-relating, the play of indeterminacy and determinacy is interpreted as the self-negation of the indefinite, and its transformation into something definite through self-negation. The transformation of self-negation into determinate self-negation makes the process one of self-determination. In sum, the dialectical interplay of the determinate and indeterminate mediates a move from the *overdetermined* to the *indefinite* to the *determinate* to the *self-determining*.

What can be questionable about this? Answer: the overdetermined as *other* can be occluded, in the beginning and in the end. For if the logic of self-mediation is claimed to cover *completely* the entire interplay, the indefinite *must displace* the overdetermined as other. But this is a diminution or contraction of the overdetermined excess. It is now, and *fourth*, that the *metaxological* sense enters, for it serves to remind us of the excess that is prior to the contraction, an excess that also remains *after* a logic of self-mediation claims to determine itself absolutely. This also means we are *returned to the interplay*, where we begin to see *beyond* the work of self-mediation to the overdetermined as other. This latter, we begin to suspect, makes possible the process of self-determination, even though it is not a process of self-determination only, nor entirely intelligible in terms of such a process. In other words, the metaxological sense reminds us of the resurgence of excess beyond complete determination. The transcendence of being as other resurrects itself again and again. And there remains excess in the origin, in the between, and in the end.

There is excess in the beginning. What I mean is that the overdetermined power of being is prior to and beyond any beginning considered as indefinite. For to be a beginning the indefinite somehow has to be, and to be it must be already given to be; it does not give itself to be; it is a derivative, not an absolute beginning; it is derivative of the overdetermined plenitude to which it is unequal. The metaxological seeks to restore mindfulness of the *that it is given to be at all*. Moreover, this restoration is shaped in a recall of the agapeic astonishment that is prior to all perplexity and determinate thinking about being. The origin suggested in agapeic astonishment is beyond all determination, and yet it is what gives the possibility of all determinacy, and hence too of the delimited intelligibility of beings. As intimated on previous occasions, the origin is given indeterminately in agapeic astonishment. This is why "what" is given in astonishment proves to be so extraordinarily elusive, exorbitantly enigmatic. Hence also its resistant ambiguity is easily turned into equivocal terms; or its ever-renewed dynamism is shunned in favor of fixed univocity; or its enigma is occluded in favor of the self-satisfaction of autonomous thinking, and determined exclusively in terms of dialectical intelligibility.

None of these latter responses are enough. None dwells deeply enough with the happening of the between relative to the excess of the origin. It is the call of metaxological mindfulness to dwell thus. This is not easy. It may be necessary to wait in an indeterminate darkness, endure lack of self-certainty, grope for what one cannot exactly say, speak as intelligibly as possible of what eludes every final why, or how, or whence, or whither. One suffers the resurgence of the second indeterminate perplexity that has been touched by transcendence in the middle, briefly illuminated and blinded by this touch, made to suffer metaphysical migraine in incessant thought of what might have been given in that communication.

There is excess at the end. Granted the prior more of transcendence at the origin, agapeic astonishment is not quelled by being reminded of being's givenness. Quite the opposite: it tends to deepen the more deeply we think the otherness of what is given to be. The excess of the origin is never rendered completely determinate in the middle. And even though the more determinate our mindfulness becomes, the more the middle is rendered determinate, the excess still escapes beyond all this. We face, so to say, the *too muchness* of being that still at the end is beyond all determination. The restlessness driving our mindfulness to more and more determinate thinking finds, even in its greatest success, that there is still more, still an other side to the most exhaustive determination of being, an other side transcendent to determinacy. We find ourselves turned around, as in Plato's *periagōgē* of the soul. The height of determinate knowing turns into a humble consent to the mystery of being, as passing beyond all determinate knowing.

There is excess in the middle. This is evident in the play of the determinate and the indeterminate in *beings*. No being can be rendered so absolutely fixed that any reserve of indeterminacy or promise of being other is completely brought to finalized thereness. Ontological freshness lives on, burns still in finite determinate beings. This freshness is their being renewed in being, again and again. Even when they are passing out of being, the freshness of renewal, passing beyond the dying being of this thing, is never smothered. It still burns on. The metaxological sense serves as a reminder of this inward otherness of things in their ontological freshness.

And suppose we consider the play of determination and indeterminacy relative to the *plurality* of beings. We discover a relativity between beings, one being contributing to the determination of another, another being bringing about the opening of yet another being, in the continuing of a dynamic process of becoming. So not only do beings in their *singular play* resist exhaustion in terms of determination and self-determination; beings in their *communal interplay* escape beyond singular dialectical determination. The community of beings in interplay is not a dialectical self-mediating whole; it reveals a metaxological intermediation between beings who are open wholes unto themselves, without being completely determined in themselves. Their relativity to others and of others to them shows multiple mediations that cannot be finalized, for the ontological freshness still flares there too.

Overall, then, the metaxological sense is mindful of *openings in* the happening of the between. It is also mindful of *the opening of* the between itself, beyond all boundaries of finite determination. Transcendence transcends the happening of the between, even while the between, metaxologically understood, marks an opening beyond itself towards the most ultimate other, whose integrity for itself can never be determinately mastered. The immanent middle opens beyond itself to unconditional transcendence. The relativity of beings in the between do not form a closed circle of mutual self-definition. The very interruptions in immanent relativity remind us that the vector of self-transcending is an infinitely restless seeking of unconditional transcendence. The happening of the between is not completely self-determining, but its unmastered indeterminacy points beyond the middle to the overdetermined excess of the origin as other. This excess is also the excess of the good, which is the excess of the end.

Beings and the Show of Excess—Singularity and the "That It Is"

In this section I will remark on the being-there of beings as showings of excess. In the next section I will remark on the showing of excess relative to the human being as mindful. Then I turn (following section) to the show of excess relative to the community of beings. All together are necessary to specify what is at stake in the metaxological sense. This will then be developed with respect to the happening of the between (following section), and the difficult task of thinking transcendence (final section).

What can it mean to say that beings are showings of excess? It means they are concretions of the transcending power of being that is not closed off in its concretion but radiates beyond even its singular contractions. But why not just say that there are determinate things that serve as objects of definite cognition? Why not say just that there are determinate objects about which we can predicate this, that, and the other, and in this process progressively accumulate knowledge of a very specific sort? I am not denying this kind of knowledge. What is being denied is any totalism of univocity that might claim to subsume completely the ontological enigma of the singular being as given to be. Such a totalism would claim to reduce all the ambiguities of things to completely determinate and unequivocal cognition. Indeed it might enlist the dialectical sense as its ally in such a complete cognition—this would not then be a simple designation only, but an entire systematic network of interrelating conceptual determinations, each as univocal as possible.

But are we then lost in equivocity if we affirm the singular being as ontological enigma? Do we seem to affirm the singular *simpliciter*, thus excluding relations to any others? Such a pure for-itself would exclude relations only to make void all possibility of conceptual determination. The singular might be an enigma, but would it not be one that was completely *empty*? But this is not the point or the result I intend. Such a result only follows if our sense of intelligibility is tied to univocity and a certain sense of dialectical determinacy. An empty enigma would fall outside this intelligibility and we could say nothing determinate about it. But we have already said something about it, hence it must have some determinacy, hence it cannot be simply enigmatic.

But do we then vacillate, equivocate, between emptiness and determinacy? I do not think so. Why? Not only because the senses of intelligibility are not exhausted by the univocal, but because the more we advance into ontological perplexity before the givenness of being, the more there arises the need to rethink the intelligibility of being. But why not think of this advance into perplexity in the standard way? Then one progresses from a vague inchoate wonder before things, through a more specified curiosity and questioning, and into a more determinate inquiry into singular things. Enigma is then acknowledged as a beginning, necessary indeed, but progressively surpassed by more and more determinate inquiry. Ontological enigma would be the *privative* acknowledgment of being that sophisticated science would replace with true, determinate knowing.

There is indeed, on this view, a dialectic between enigma and determination, but the ontological enigma of the singular is no abiding enigma at all. All we have to do is to start to think about it and this enigma of singularity is caught up in a specifying network of universals and concepts. Again we can recall Hegel's treatment of the this-here-now of sense certainty. This dialectical way is akin to the univocal in claiming that determinate knowing replaces all ambiguity and equivocity, if we merely let the dynamism of mind run its course.

The end result here—that the mystery of the singular is dissolved—will not do. There is shown something in the singular that is not reducible to univocal predicates nor dialectical universals or concepts, that is not a mere equivocation in relation to determination, that is not exhausted by being an instance of a universal nor dissoluble into a system of universals. This is so because the singular exhibits a *thatness* that is the show of excess. There is a *that it is* whose givenness of being exceeds its determination as a kind of being. This *that it is* does not make it to be that kind of being; it is that it should be so at all, not that it is thus and thus. Its very being there as singular is given, a gift; this *that it is* is gratuitous from the standpoint of univocal predicates and dialectical universals; these do not supply either the *how* or the *why* as to the *that is it* of the singular. This *that it is* comes from a different height of being, comes from a determining source that is not itself determinate. Such a source as determining is beyond determinacy, and this beyondness of the overdetermined is there as given in the *that it is* of the singular being.

In my view we fail entirely to comprehend what is at issue if we insist that it must be a univocal or dialectical determination, or otherwise an illicit equivocation. It is just the very otherness or transcendence of the *that it is* to determination that is the point at issue. If we are to acknowledge it, we must have a thinking that is patiently open to the giving of that other transcendence.

Let me try to reinforce the point in regard to the *unrepeatability* of the singular. There is a certain irreplaceability to each singular thing; at the deepest ontological level they cannot be replaced by any other, not even another of their own kind. Of course, there are rough equivalences between beings, and obviously so to the extent that their determinations are likenesses, kindred characteristics that repeat themselves as recurrent features across different members of the same kind. This last point is not being denied; the denial is that this is all. The singularity of the thing in its unique *that it is* is its nonequivalence to anything other. It is itself and no other is it, in just that singular sense. There are no univocal or dialectical equivalences for the singular sense of the *that it is* that exceeds every equivalence. It is thus disproportionate to every univocal and dialectical determination, each of which finally and in different ways thrives in terms of proportional equivalence, sustained by a logic of identity.

As exceeding determination, this *that it is* is not subsumable into either a univocal or dialectical logic of identity. Put otherwise, each entity lives its own irreplaceable *that it is at all* from within the intimacy of its own ontological uniqueness. The singular entity in that sense opens into its own intimacy of being, which cannot be completely determinated. This is related to the ontological freshness, as I called it, that continues to renew the being from within its own being.

The pathos of this irreplaceability also lies in the intimation that the singular is a radical *once*. It is given to be once and only once. It will live being from within the intimacy of its own singularity for its temporal span. It will pass out of being into a *never* that seems as irrevocable as the irreplaceability of the "once" that once marked its present gift of being. This once and once only has the pathos of finitude and limitation ingrained in it. But the "once" of irreplaceable singularity comes to shimmer differently when we grow mindful of just this fragility of the finite. There is always a shimmer of transcendence about it, though the shimmer is not named or known.

Metaphysical mindfulness is reminded of it. There it is as given, once it is given, and only once. But once it is given, and for its given time, it floats above its own potential nothingness. It is in being above nothing, it is in excess of not-being; it is there as being, given into the excess of being. It is given into being as uniquely itself, as the excess that for now rides over nothingness, intoxicated with the elemental joy of simply being at all, indeed with the elemental good of the simple *to be* that cannot be reduced to anything other. During its span it is full with the "once" of its *to be*, and this fullness is given out of the fullness or plenitude of the overdetermined source. It is full with being, packed tightly into its own integral ontological compactness, floating on nothing, because the overdetermined fullness gives it to be as full.

It is, and it is not nothing. That it is not nothing, will itself seem to be merely nothing, if we insist that all intelligibility must say something determinate. But the very saying of the determinate already presupposes the giving of being as determinate, and this prior giving of being is just the enigma that is at issue in saying: *it is and it is not nothing*. The ontological enigma of the singular in its irreplaceable "once" speaks to us of this prior enigma, beyond determination; for all determination presupposes it, as what is subsequently to be determined; and what is presupposed is just that incontrovertibility of being there at all; it is not completely convertible into a set of derivative determinations.

This irreplaceability and unrepeatability of the singular as a "once," as a *that it is*, is not, however, a being that is a *closed for-itself*. It is for-itself, but it is *given* to itself as for-itself; its integrity of being as a this is itself the gift of the *that it is at all*. The intimacy of being that each integrity of being lives from within makes it, just in its singularity, intimate with what is not itself but that gives it to itself as for-itself. This is not known as such, since such knowing is a determination of mindfulness. This intimacy of being *is existed* by the singular being. It may be known by the human singular, as we shall see, but this knowing is not completely determinate knowing. The intimacy of being is not closed for-itself, for the givenness of beings as for-themselves exceeds every closure of the "for-itself." The original giving of the "for-itself," the gift of its *that it is,* is not a "for-itself"; it is a gift from the other, an agapeic letting be of the finite being in its singularity.

The giving of being is in excess of any closed "for-self," for if there were only such closed "for-selves," there would be no giving of otherness as other; there would only be a circle of self-giving, which is no real giving. The metaxological sense of an agapeic giving of being for the other as other is here clearly different to the dialectical sense that would finally privilege the closure of the erotic circle of the absolute "for-self." In the singular *that it is*, understood metaxologically, this sense of otherness strikes home in the acknowledging of a radiance beyond all monadic closure. This radiance is the radiance of the singular thing too, but it is not its radiance as a determination it simply owns. It is the excess of transcendence that plays around its singular being, the halo of its being as gift.

If the *that it is* is excessive to determination, it is not merely indefinite, for the singular is a robust concretion of ontological presence. The singular's determination as being is not reducible to any specific determination. Its presence is in excess of determinacy, not defective determination. The being-there of a singular being is beyond every determining because the determinate thing itself is the concretion of an energy of being that surpasses every stasis. Determinate being is itself a dynamic radiance of this energy that communicates beyond itself. The singular exceeds itself.

We might say that the appearing of a thing is not exhausted by its determinate appearances. There is a surplus to determinate appearance. The exceeding of the singular by itself points to this exit: this coming out into being of the thing. There is the energy of appearing, appearing as dynamic process, surplus to determinate appearance. This appearing is the coming forward, the coming out of itself and its ontological intimacy, the coming towards other things of this thing. It comes towards others out of its own inherent plenitude of being. The singular comes into the middle. There is a surplus to determinate presence that is not a determinate presence.

The being of the thing, the *that it is,* comes into the middle—that is, towards the others and out of itself—in what we might call this *reserved manifestation of surplus.* What is such a reserved manifestation? It is a manifestation that maintains its otherness to us, even as it is given to us, gives itself to us. It may be given for us—though this is not necessary—but it is not for us simply. It is given for us because it is first for itself, and in the radiance beyond every self-closure; it is for itself in radiance, and hence never closed in itself. The reserve of manifestation is shown in the thing as coming into the middle and mediately towards us, out of a surplus that is not exhausted by the middle, and that we do not determinately appropriate. The deeper origin of the appearing of things relates to this reserved excess that yet, reserved in its transcendence, radiates.

In all this I do not deny the community of implication with others that marks every entity. The question is rather the character of this community. I situate it at the metaxological level. This implies the need to think a nonreductive sense of community in which the irreplaceable is not sidestepped, nor a proper understanding of the intrinsic value of being neglected. This demands a metaphysics of creation relative to which we can speak of what I call an idiot wisdom.

An idiot wisdom is a mindfulness that respects the intimacy of being, its idiotic being, in all the gift of its thereness, and indeed its transcendence to every determinate science we construct to remake it in the services of our

categorial structures. It demands an agapeic metaphysics in which the beyond of the *meta* is also in the *meta* of the middle. In every irreplaceable
entity this doubleness of reference is at work: its coming into the middle and
towards the others in the middle; its relativity to the *meta* as transcendence
beyond the middle. The excess of the *that it is,* immanent in every singularity,
given by the absolute origin, out of nothing, is an agapeic gift. There is no
final reason for it, for its being-there, beyond its value as being, beyond the
good of the *to be,* beyond its being valued for itself.

Jesus said there was not a hair on our head that was not numbered by
the Father. This numbering is not the arithmetic of univocity; it is agapeic
love of the singular as singular. Only God is on the level of this absolute enigma
of singularity: singularity as being at all by virtue of its being valued for itself
in its singularity. Every sense we have of the determinate this is already and
always a fall away from such a divine sense of singularity. Even as we gain
cognitive determinacy, we are always risking the loss of this metaphysical
appreciation. In the middle we always in some measure objectify this appreciation, sometimes to the point of degrading the singularity. Metaphysical
mindfulness as agapeic thinking demands a reminding of the *more* in the
determinate. This is in some ways comparable to the appreciation of the great
work of art, which is a unique singular, which is yet big with an inexhaustibility that no set of finite determinations can deplete. The singular being is the
great art of God.

Excess, Mindfulness, and the Human Being

We often tend to think of singularity in either atomistic or nominalistic
terms. These latter are different expressions of the univocal sense. Both end
up excluding mediation from the singular, such that the singular comes to
lack its own complex interiority. The categories we use to make the singular
intelligible, like the names we use to designate it or fix our reference, then
become essentially impositions from the outside on the indifferent being of
the thing. Both nominalism and atomism, thus conceived, offer impoverished
versions of the being of singularity as it is for itself.

The dialectical sense sees clearly that mediation must be at work within
the singular, for it to be intelligibly spoken. Its immediacy is also mediated,
and hence a complex *interiority* is possible. The metaxological sense grants
this also, but the question turns on the nature of the mediation. The singular
is a whole, indeed an entire world unto itself. The metaxological sense differs
from the dialectical in denying that the innerness of the singular is entirely
determinable in terms of self-mediation. This innerness is what I called the
intimacy of being of the singular. And while it is self-mediating, it is not a
closed self-sufficiency, but opens inwardly into its own idiocy, where idiocy
here points to the power of being, intimate to the singular, yet at the edge of

or beyond encapsulation in general concepts. This inward idiocy opens into the enigma of the *that it is,* the sense of the reserved excess of overdetermined being that is falsified if it is said to be the same as being that is determined or determinable.

There is self-mediation in the intimacy of being, but the latter also exceeds self-mediation. The self-mediation of the singular points to the otherness of being as beyond self-mediation; and yet this otherness is in mediation with the being of the singular. We here have a pluralized mediation, properly an intermediation. If the singular is an open whole, its opening is both with respect to the community of otherness outside itself, and with respect to the original energy of being which, out of its otherness to the self, gives the self to be for itself. So within the singular there is a double opening: on one hand to an abyss of transcendence within itself; on the other hand, to the community of being and to being beyond itself.

With the mindful human being this is most evident. For no other finite being is mindful in the sense intended. All other beings live the intimacy of being, are themselves supported by the excess of transcendence that gives them to be, and not be nothing. They are immediately at home in the "it is good" of the elemental *to be.* They are, but they are not neutrally, since their very integrity of being calls out of itself into the middle as a speechless "here I am." The speechless "here I am" is also a speechless "it is good," a singularization of being as a value ontologically justified for itself.

The mindful human being emerges into wakefulness of this *to be.* And it can become more and more mindful of the enigma of this *to be at all,* and not only with respect to the being of external things, but with respect to its own singular being. This waking up answers to the call that speaks to us in agapeic astonishment. In other words, agapeic astonishment is from the outset an inarticulate coming towards us of the intimacy of being, and a going towards it, on our part, in an opening of mind towards its otherness. This intimacy of being rouses to itself in the mindful singularity of the thinker struck into astonishment.

There is a respect in which we would not be human beings at all, were not the gift of metaphysical mindfulness given to our singular being. This also suggests that metaphysical thinking cannot be reduced to the disembodied reason of mind in general. It implies the deficiency of any metaphysics that claims to supersede completely the being mindful of the singular thinker in some anonymous thinking in general or universal mind. Metaxological mindfulness is always double: a thinking about the enigma of self-being and that of being other than itself. Any primacy of thought thinking itself, or pure self-determining mind such as idealism recommends, must be rejected as the last word. It is rejected, not because the self-mediating of mind is rejected, but because the deeper self-mediation becomes, the more the self knows itself to be given to itself from a source that is other than and not itself. Its being given to itself is not the production of any dialectical self-mediation; its own self-mediation is made possible by a more originary communication from the otherness of the original energy of being itself.

So when the singular is a mindful human being, the *that it is* takes the form of a speaking "I am." If we stress the "I," we find the basis for saying that here the intimacy of being rouses to itself. The "I" is the minding/minded innerness of singular being, an integrity of being that is self-minding, self-thinking in that respect. The intimacy of this interiority of being becomes the power to think itself; but if we stress only this, we risk truncating the affirmation "I am." There is here an affirmation of being, not just an affirmation of the "I." One might suggest that the affirmation of the "I" would not be possible were it not the singular expression of an affirmation of being. This latter affirmation, emerging into mindfulness in the singular "I," is not the production of the "I" simply; the "I" already is, in order to affirm itself; its self-affirmation is secondary to this "being already," the prior affirmation of being that is given to the "I" before it affirms itself. The singular "I" as affirming its own being is made possible because it is the singularization of the affirmation of being that is *not* its own.

We might say that in the "self-thinking" that is given in the mindful "I am," there is already at work being's givenness, and with this the promise of the thought of being as other to self-thinking thought. The doubleness is, from the outset, built into the singular self-affirmation of the "I am." Since this other, more originary other to self-thinking, cannot be included in dialectical self-mediation, the latter points beyond itself, and within its own intricate immanence, to the otherness of the giving power of being. In the rich immanence of self-mediation an inward otherness is at work that is prior to inwardness as dialectically trying to take possession of itself. This inward otherness breaks down and breaks open all claims to complete self-possession. The self is not itself in virtue of self-possession; it is, and is itself, as primally given to itself, by the power of being as other; it takes possession of itself in virtue of this prior gift.

Another way to say this is that, while the singular self opens inwardly into its own depths, there is a certain *infinitude* to this intimacy of being. Only because of this, does our characteristic desire exhibit an infinite restlessness. We transcend ourselves again and again in desire; we are satisfied with this determinate thing, only to find dissatisfaction resurrected on satisfaction, and another search initiated; and there seems to be no determinate limit to this restless self-transcendence. We transcend ourselves infinitely. But such transcendence beyond self is possible only because the self already opens into the promise of infinitude within the intimacy of its own being. Erotic perplexity is a mindful articulation of this infinite restlessness, and there is no determinate limit to the perplexity or restlessness. Nor is there any one determinate univocal answer that will give peace to one, or an answer

to the other. The erotic perplexity testifies to the work of the infinite immanent within the intimacy of being of the self. Because of the inward otherness, there is neither complete determination nor self-determination of the
power of being of this mindful singular, precisely because that power is given
to the self; it is not first self-produced.

But erotic perplexity is not all, and we must explore the opening in the
intimacy of being even further. In infinite restlessness and the erotic perplexity—each a profound marker of metaphysical mindfulness—we find a sense
of lack and absence also. One is driven to infinite self-transcendence because
an abyss of emptiness opens within self. In one sense the intimacy of the
singular self is just such an abyss, so we often rightly use the language of
negation and *nothingness* to name what is at stake. Notice that when we do
so, we are already on the *other side* of determinate being. If the singular self
as mindful knows itself as a vacancy or nothingness, something about it cannot be rendered in the language of univocal determinate things. The power of
being at play is no thing. The intimate self is a nothing. Clearly many philosophers, like Hegel, Heidegger, Sartre, are explorers of this evanescent being
that is a nothing. The crucial question is whether and how we can avoid the
lapse into nihilism. Nihilism is not inevitable, yet an unnuanced understanding of our infinite restlessness and erotic perplexity might easily see these as
outreachings of human excess that only transcends itself into the void, exceeds itself into nothing.

I do not think that the nothingness evident in infinite restlessness and
erotic perplexity is just an immanent negativity that drives a process of self-
determination. It is rather the *rupture of immanence*, especially in its proclivity to closure into the falsity of complete self-determination. The nothing
cuts into the circle of self-mediation, enters its midst, and disrupts from within
all claims to completeness. Again the human being has an intimate sense of
this nothing as marking its own singular being. Indeed this is the other side
to the intimate sense of its being in the "I am."

Consider. I am but I am also as nothing. I was nothing, I will be nothing.
I am now, existing rather than not being, but existing as something coming
to be outside of nonbeing. Thus the intimacy of the nothing internally stripes
the "I am," and at every moment of its self-affirmation haunts its hold on
being. I am, I am but once, and since the "once" is singular and unrepeatable,
it also is haunted by its "never": once I was not; and there will be a time when
the word "once" becomes the word "never"; once but never more, never again.

I said that singular beings as unrepeatable and irreplaceable also live
this "once" and this "never," and that both are intimate to the being of the
singular. But with the human singular this intimacy of the "once" and the
"never" becomes *mindful* of itself. The nothing, the haunting of the "never,"
never again, shakes to the foundations the self-affirmation of the I, produces
a liquefaction of its hold on being. And when this mindfulness is interiorized,

it undermines all claims to self-completion. It chastens, when it does not mock, every claim to absolute self-determination.

At certain limits the human self, marvel of singularity, can be *crushed* by mindfulness of the nothing and the "never." Its very threat to our being can drive us away from full exposure to what is shown. It can drive us away from the proper liquefaction of false absolutes, and into an absolutization of the energy of erotic perplexity, which wills to overcome completely its own perplexity, but by pushing to the side any enigma of otherness that would again threaten us with reopening an entrance for the nothing. But there is no escape, there can be no escape. We might even will to construct an absolute science to shield us from the enigmas of otherness and their disrupting power. We will refuse to be at a loss before anything and claim that all being is within our power, if we but determine it scientifically. We put a geometry of being in place of the tragedy we cannot finally evade. We run from perplexity's lesson, which may be just the absolute inescapability of being at a loss at a certain threshold of ultimacy.[1] Instead of mindfully dwelling with our perplexity on that threshold, we retreat into the manipulability of the middle, now reconfigured in accord with our univocal or dialectical determinations.

The intimacy of singular mindful being opens up a desert in inwardness, an abyss that is profoundly ambiguous. The ambiguity cannot be evaded, it has to be lived through, thought through. We may get lost in this inward desert as an equivocal labyrinth; we may mediate this labyrinth; but we will never mediate it completely in terms of self-mediation. The metaxological sense passes into this abyss of inwardness and its resistance to dialectical mediation. It is laid open before the nothing; it is exposed to being crushed by the negative; it enters the emptiness of the desert.[2] It insists on mindfulness of the nothing beyond determinate negation. It opens itself to the breakdown of self-mediation in the face of the nothing. The nothing that ruptures is beyond our power. For this reason we have the most intimate sense of death; our very being is a lived intimacy with our own death. The "I am" that is "I am as nothing" is the intimate mindfulness of its own finitude and death. Metaphysical mind demands honesty about death in its singularity.

The opening into inward transcendence does not end here. Nor is our infinite promise exhausted in terms of the restlessness of erotic perplexity. The lack of erotic perplexity, its inhabitation by nothingness, would not be driven beyond itself at all were there not effective in that lack some positive power of being. The lack could not drive beyond itself, the negativity could

---

1. See "Being at a Loss: On Philosophy and the Tragic," chapter 2 of *Perplexity and Ultimacy*.

2. See *Philosophy and its Others*, chapter 5, on the desert and solitude; also on failure and "counting for nothing."

not be self-transcending, were not transcendence in another affirmative sense prior to this lack and nothing. This is where, in the passage through breakdown and the void of nothing, there may occur a breakthrough beyond lack.

For our horror before the nothing in our shrinking from death is the obverse side of an elemental *love of being as good*. The erotic perplexity is, as it were, a troubled son of agapeic astonishment. Astonishment celebrates the being there of being as good. We lose this, though never completely, except in absolute despair, which surrenders itself to nothing. And yet still the world is enigmatic, and in the loss, erotic perplexity takes over. But erotic perplexity is the dimming of the first astonishment, never absolutely lost. Horror before the nothing is a manifestation of metaphysical mindfulness, but it is the meonic version of the affirmation of being that still is at play in the recoil from nonbeing. We would not know the horror of nothing, live intimately the pathos of the "never," be honest about being at a loss, did we not elementally love being, surge on the joy of the "once," know the gift of being at all.

The relation between being and nothing here is not just a dialectical self-determination of becoming, as Hegel would have it. The breakdown of self-mediation opens up an intermediation or communication beyond self-mediation, and a breakthrough into metaphysical astonishment before being in which the *asymmetry* between being and nothing is granted. Being is prior to nothing; being haunts the horror, but in a far more enigmatic and elusive way than the way the nothing haunts our sense of being. Being guards the good of being, even in the horror. The passage into nothing, passage into breakdown, breaks though into a renewal of the agape of being, which guards the goodness of being as good for itself. In this reawakening of agapeic astonishment, mindfulness as metaphysical is made humble. There is no hubris of absolute knowing. We find here the patience of what before I called posthumous mind.

Let me briefly remind you of what I mean. Metaphysical mind is posthumous in trying to think the worth of being, beyond our present immersion in the process of being lived. The speculative imagination is this: one thinks of oneself, having died, as come back to life, as if from beyond death; one is resurrected to the "once," from beyond the "once," from one's passage into and through the "never." Suppose one were dead and came back to one's time, looking for the things of time, the beings and companions and happenings of the middle that shaped one's being here with a sense of intrinsic worth or value. Posthumous mind is this speculation of agapeic mind looking on the happening of the between, beyond the lies of life and beyond the negativity of death. It is as if one were beyond life and death, but not at all to depreciate life, but to renew astonishment at the elemental fact of being at all.

The affirmation of being in the "I am" is already an arousal of this astonishment, an arousal soon dampened down. Posthumous mind would renew this, renew it in the intimacy of being. It is idiotic, both in its intimacy and in its being beyond an exhaustive systematic determination. But the metaphysical imagination of posthumous mind is not just concerned with the "I am," but with renewed astonishment of the *this is, things are, beings are, being is.* Mind returns to this marvel of being, appearing as out of nothing, being born as something again and again, poised in a brief equilibrium over the possibility of its own being nothing. And yet it is there, has come to birth there, and every instant of its thereness is its repeated resurrection to its being there: something, not nothing, given, not self-produced, issue of an origin that gives it its being as for itself, an agapeic origin. The "I am" is itself nothing subjectivistic, but a happening of this issuing into being in the singularity of this mindful self. But all being, being other to the self, is an issuing in that sense too: a creation. And it is good: for the thereness is not neutral or valueless, but worthy to be joyed in, worthy to be affirmed for itself, for the goodness of elemental being.

Still It issues. Still It is. Still It is good. The resurrection of astonishment brings us into the neighborhood of original genesis and the primal "It is good." Posthumous mind brings us back to being in that sense. But this is no sentimental nostalgia. Remember: we are as dead; we are as nothing and have lost everything; we think ourselves as beyond the ultimate loss of death; and yet we would say "good," echoing the primal "It is good." This love of the mortal in its singularity for itself evidences our striving to live agapeic mind for the beloved singular. The anonymous generality of consciousness in general is not enough. For being is not a genus in the logical sense, though it is generational in the ontological sense: issuing, creating. And, of course, we live loss all the time; with time itself, we live loss. Being is given, it is gone, it is gone and lost forever. And yet the gift of issuing continues; it is given again, a regeneration, a new creation.

It might seem that posthumous mind is an impossibility, for we exist in the between. Yet posthumous mind tries to think the beyond in the midst of the between, to become awake to what is at issue in the being of the between. Metaphysical memory is beyond and in the midst, twofold, horizontal and vertical. It passes back and forth, crossing and crisscrossing the between, from time to the thinking of eternity, from that thinking back to love of the mortal.[3] It seeks to be agapeic mind, a likening to divine love of the singular. And indeed a song of festive being may break through in the interstices of the between. Though broken at the limit, by the limit, festive mind surges again on joy, consents to the largess of being, itself a largess, a thanks.

And yet the very worthiness of being *troubles* us. It makes us wonder if we ourselves are worthy of what has been given—both in our own being and in being-other. It is not we who *confer* on being—our own or being-other— its worthiness. Rather we feel compelled to make ourselves worthy of it: in

---

3. See *Philosophy and its Others*, 278–81, where I try to communicate what I mean by interpreting the story of Oisín in Irish saga. I also talk about festive being in chapter 6 of that book.

gratitude and in creating again beyond ourselves, and by being ourselves agapeic to the best extent possible. The height of transcendence calls us to this: to be worthy of worthy being. We begin to make ourselves worthy by thanking: saying yes to being: it is good. We make thanks (*gratias agimus*). Thanking is a doing of being, a being agapeic, a saying yes to the other for its otherness. Making thanks is a making beyond self-mediation, a release towards the good of the other. As a doing of the whole self in the promise of its whole life, it implicates the entire unfolding of our self-transcendence. This is a thought of the other, a mindfulness towards its other-being as good, that takes no thought for the self.

The Metaxological and the Community of Beings

What now of the *community* of beings? As there is a resistance to self-mediation in both the singularity of beings and the mindful being, just so *between* beings there is also otherness beyond self-mediation. The very word "community" points beyond the unity of the univocal, for it is the "unity" of a plurality of integrities, and we must emphasize the word *cum*, "with," as much as the word "unity." There is a pluralized "unity" of "being with," a togetherness of beings in community. And while difference is needed to make plurality possible, this togetherness cannot be any merely unmediated equivocity.

Beings hold together as integrities; the plurality of integrities holds together, even in the incalculable diversity and stunning prodigality of the many. This "holding together" is not a superimposition on plural terms already finished in their self-definition, such that all that remains to do is to cast a net of relations over them in their diversity. Rather the community is constituted by a coming to be; there is something essentially dynamic about community. The active differentiation we find with equivocity is here retained in the articulations of integrities of being, dynamically interinvolved with each other through a network of relatings. "Relating" itself implies an active interinvolving, beyond all established stases and, as we shall see, beyond all determinate objectifications.

The community of being is a coming into the between. "Coming" here signals the work of transcending in each singular entity. Beings come to be in the middle, but coming to be is being in community, for there is no absolutely solitary coming to be. Coming to be is a relation of community, a social relation. If B comes to be, it comes to be from A, and there is a community of relation between the issue and the source. If the source A gives B to be, then the source itself is the promise of community between itself and what has issued from it. Coming to be, even when what comes to be is given its otherness and freedom, is still a social relation; for the free being that is the issue is still defined in its being by its "being with" the source that gives it to be freely.

Of course, since the beings that come to be are for themselves also, concretions of self-transcending power in themselves, the complexities of that "being with" are multiple, often multiplied beyond any clear and distinct disentangling. This is the intimation of the equivocal sense, when it feels the promiscuous co-implication of each in all and all in each.

There is a misunderstanding to be avoided. The coming into community does not mean beings first come to be themselves and then enter community. This is not so. There is from the beginning a "being with," relative to which the coming to singular being reaches any determination. Nor is there simply a coming to community before a coming to singularity. Rather there is no coming to singularity that is not also a coming to relativity with the other. Hence there is no coming to be that is not also a coming to be in community. There is a priority to community in this regard, that no singular is self-generated. Its generation as self is the issue from an other; its very being itself is a generational relation to an other or others.

This understanding of the coming to be in community is related to the idea of creation. Creation is an issuing into otherness and an articulation of a relativity to an other, even in the singular determination of an integral being as for itself. We might say that since the community of being is at all, it is creation that provides the embracing context of coming to be, wherein the plurality of singulars comes to self-definition. We sense this prior inherence of community in creation when we are struck into agapeic astonishment. We may not be able thus to articulate it; all we may do is stammer the "It is" or perhaps the "It is good." But these are not negligible, are indeed momentous. In the "It is" and the "It is good," what is implicated is a more universal sense of the community of being, as coming to be in the givenness of creation. I know many will think of this as vague and indefinite. No doubt much of this is and remains so for us. But when we try to think it through, however, the meaning is not at all indefinite, but rather concerns our initial intimacy with the coming to be of the community of being in creation. There is a prior community of being, which is the immediacy of an overdetermined plenitude of being. This is what is given indeterminately to mindfulness in agapeic astonishment, though when we find the right words for what is given, we see something momentously affirmative in this excess of determination.

Within the given community, determinate beings and the mindful human being live their own participation in the energy of transcendence. They come into the coming into the middle which is the community of being. So what we find in the middle, then, is the coming together, with a variety of different determinations, or different interplays between indeterminacy and determination, of a plurality of centers of self-transcendence. The community of being is the conjunction of this plurality of integrities of self-transcendence. Moreover, this conjunction is less the obviation of difference as the concretion of relativity in difference and across difference. It is not the obliteration of difference in a homogeneous sameness, but rather a going beyond homogeneous sameness and the sustaining of a relativity in the very determination of heterogeneity itself.

I said that the coming to be of the singular is itself communal from the outset. We must now advert to the double mediation at work: each being is a center of self-mediation and hence is for itself; each being is defined in a network of intermediating relations with what is other to itself. Its self-transcending energy, as coming into the middle, is defined by this doubleness, with all the tensions therein, as well as the opportunities for creative origination beyond itself. In itself the being is marked by community; hence its being cannot be exhausted by self-mediation; nor can its relatedness to what is other and beyond.

This is what is at issue in the metaxological sense: a pluralization of the event of mediation such that it is impossible to reduce the plurality to one form—namely, that of an encompassing self-mediation. Something escapes this reduction in the immanence of the between. Mediation is so pluralized that there is no singular mediation that will include all others within its own encompassing hold. The enigma of pluralized mediation itself escapes beyond complete mediation, for the beings in community are free from mediating in the mediating itself.

The doubleness *within* is complicated by the redoubling of relativity to other beings, each complexified in itself, relative to its own inherent double mediation; mediation is redoubled within and hence is beyond self-mediation. Mediation is redoubled *outside*, redoubled beyond the embrace of one singular self-mediation. The process of intermediation is just this escaping from the closure of any form of complete self-mediating, no matter how absolutized. The community of being has to be thought in terms other than an absolutized self-mediation. Community of being is infinitely complicated, complicated in that there is a co-implication of each being with other beings, a co-implication not exhausted in a logic of dialectical determination. The infinite complication takes us to the limit of this logic.

The reader may find helpful the following summary line of thought, for it leads us to the question we want to pose: Suppose the beings in interplay are each dialectically self-mediating, and suppose that this self-mediation makes them wholes; suppose further than there is a depth of infinitude at work in this self-mediation, such as we termed the intimacy of being, and suppose that this were such as to make each of these beings an open whole, a whole that opens into its own intimacy of being and that opens beyond itself into the between; and suppose that beings as thus complexly defined were multiplied without number; then what would we say about the mediation *between* such beings, such as to constitute the community of being?

This is the answer I suggest: the mediation between a plurality of such open self-mediating beings cannot just be any form of self-mediation. Remember that such beings are pluralized within themselves. Were we to answer that community is simply a more encompassing self-mediating whole, we would have truncated the immanent self-mediation of each being in its opening into its own intimacy of being; we would have glossed over the singularity of self-transcendence that each such being is; we would have also closed off its inexhaustibility, and made it a partial, finite manifestation of a more inclusive mode of dialectical self-mediation. In a word, this absolutization of self-mediation is hence a betrayal of self-mediation. Dialectic thus absolutized betrays dialectic. The doubling within, and the pluralization without, escape beyond this absolutization.

It should be clear that the double here at issue cannot be determined in the standard terms of a dualism. Where there is otherness, of course, we always find the potential for opposition, as well as for equivocities resistant to mediation. But since the present meaning of doubling is defined with reference to the community of relativity, standard dualistic language is inappropriate, for it is a corollary of rigid univocal thinking. Nor is the double a vanishing phase of a more encompassing process, an opposition that in its lack undermines itself, to be superseded by a more inclusive unitary process of dialectical self-mediation. This is to reduce the doubling to an ontological level less complex than dialectic. In fact, the doubling is more rich that dialectic as self-mediation; it is the *dia* beyond self-mediation. And since it is itself beyond self-mediation, it is not in need of being subsumed into a community beyond lack. The community offers a pluralization of freedom beyond all self-mediation, and hence beyond freedom defined as self-determination.

Remember that the dialectic that privileges self-mediation takes its sights from the ability of thought to think what is other, and to bring the other into relativity to itself. The conclusion then drawn is that the thought that thinks the other overreaches the other; hence in thinking the other as a thought, it ends up as the thought that thinks itself, but now inclusive of otherness. And its image of community rides piggyback on this self-transcending power and its purported inclusion of the other. Its conclusion is: the absolute community would be the absolutely inclusive process of dialectical self-mediation.

Metaxological metaphysics contests this way of thinking community. It recurs again to the double mediation operative even when thought thinks itself. It recurs also to the self-transcending of mindfulness as not reducible to an erotic knowing that in knowing the other really completes its own lack as ignorance and returns to itself in self-certain satisfied knowing. By contrast, metaxological metaphysics goes towards the other, out of the double mediation of thought, but lets the thinking of the other be guided by an agapeic mindfulness that goes towards the other as other, and not on a mediating detour that recoils back on itself, once having appropriated the other. Agapeic mind is an exemplification of communicative being; it is a being mindfully there for the other as other, and not for the self itself. It goes towards the other, it delivers itself over to the other; and this making itself available for the other is its communication of itself to the other. It communicates itself not out of lack merely, but out of an excess or surplus, out of a generosity of being that gives to the other for the other.[4]

Agapeic mindfulness, as communicative thinking of the other, is an *in-ter*mediation which, in going towards the other, gives itself to the other as other, and does not think about what it gets from what it gives, if indeed it gets anything at all. Its generosity of transcendence is a giving for nothing, nothing beyond the goodness of the giving itself. Agapeic mind gives its understanding over to the position of the other from its otherness, seeks to see the other from within the intimacy of its own integrity of being. It is eccentric relative to self-mediation. There is compassion in this knowing, an undergoing with the other, not a standing above in the mode of mastery or domination.

Clearly, too, the standard models of *atomism* and *holism* will not do. The atomistic model sees a set of primitive univocals and then knits them together in terms of a set of extrinsic connections. The atoms have nothing to do with each other inherently; they are indifferently external to each other. It should now be clear that such atoms are really the sclerosis of singularity, its hardening into a knot of being, devoid of immanent mediation and the energy of transcendence. Inevitably atomism conceives of community in terms of an impoverished version of merely external relations. Externality is also undersood on a very impoverished univocity. The sense of singularity we have developed opens up the intimacy of the being of beings and also their energy of transcendence, such that there are no merely external relations in this aggregational sense.

That said, there is also a holism to be avoided, one which stresses the *mutual definition* of beings in a manner that dissolves this hardened knot of atomic singularity into a network of relations, outside of which it is nothing. This holism sees the relativity of the singular to the others, but *dissolves the singularity* into this relativity. Moreover, it claims a prior implicit whole at work which defines the singular, and a subsequent whole that subsumes the putative singular. Given our account, such holism is not adequate to what is at play in the singular; nor is its definition of the internal relatedness of things adequate to the immanent doubleness of things and the co-implications of transcendences in the relations between things.

Plurality is not precipitated by the splitting of a prior whole into parts, parts then reintegrated into a more articulated whole. Rather the giving of plurality in its otherness and togetherness is a giving of plurality as for itself; singular integrities are not merely parts of a larger whole, but wholes unto themselves, that are also open beyond themselves. As opening beyond themselves, they do not constitute their inherent relativity to others by being subsumed into a larger whole of which they are subordinated parts. The

---

4. I have developed the notion of agapeic mindfulness much more fully in *Perplexity and Ultimacy*.

community of being they constitute is transcendent to such a dialectical whole. There is no totalism of the whole within which the plurality of integrities are sublated, contributory parts.

So we must say that there is the excess of transcendence at all levels, from the beginning through the middle to the end, and the end closes nothing off but rather renews the promise of freedom. The community of being is not an inclusive totality, but a being together in transcendence of which there is no totalization. For this being together constitutes the happening of the middle as the promise of radical freedom from absorption in all totalities. The community and its metaxological togetherness, and the modes of intermediation that shape the energy of transcendence, are beyond all totality. The spaces between beings upheld by community are not subordinate determinations of an all-inclusive totality, but indeterminacies that welcome the advent and adventure of the freedom of its participants. This community involves a pluralization of the excess of freedom.

Indeed this very excess makes the community possible. There is no final determination of what a community of freedom is, for freedom itself is a determining beyond determination. Nor is it just self-determination, for there is a different sense of freedom into which we are delivered by an agapeic relation to what is other. The freedom beyond self-determination is a gift, first *of* the other, then *for* the other. The community of transcendence beyond all totalization is the pluralization and togetherness of this agapeic giving. Community reveals the mystery of ontological generosity.

Let me offer the following image, as suggesting something of the requisite respect for singularity and otherness. I have in mind the catacombs. This might seem a startling image relative to community, since the catacombs are mass graves. Human beings are mashed into the earth, homogeneous humus again. And yet, in death, beyond death, there is a sign of community that seeks to acknowledge absolute singularity.

Consider. One descends into the catacombs outside Rome. The weight of the earth above one crushes with the inexorable weight of death which no human being can bear.[5] In this company of death one is awakened to thoughts of posthumous mind. One assumes the mind of the dead, thinking of what being looks like from the placeless abode of the dead. One is overcome by the view from nowhere, and looks again on being, more slowly, stunned into silence, made pensive by perishing. Wrenched out of mindless immersion in being, one tries to see and think what it is one is immersed in, given over to, tries to think its unmastered mystery.

One goes down into the bountiful earth itself, home of the living, home of the dead. These chambers of burial are often conceived as hiding places for persecuted Christians, but it appears this is overstated. There is another,

---

5. On being crushed, relative to one of Michelangelo's "unfinished" Pietà, and the weight of inexorable death, see *Beyond Hegel and Dialectic*, 236–37.

perhaps more important sense of hiddenness in the earth and in death. One goes down into a mystery that exceeds all thought, contracting into the darkness. In the ensuing enclosure one is mindful that there are thousands upon thousands dead here. There is the numberless pluralization of the dead. These too were once, but now are no more, never again to walk into the air and the light, to feel the solid earth beneath, the soaring sky above, the bobbing blossoms on the trees, the swaying grass to which the breeze whispers "It is good."

As one goes downward and downward, we enter the graves of the paupers rather than the sepulchers of the rich above ground. One sees the places of individual burial, the singularity even in death itself. There are the places, now empty of all bones, of small children. One cannot but sense the loving of singularity even in death again, beyond death, with the hope of being again, even despite the crushing "never," being again as this singular beloved one. There are the altars where the early Christians celebrated Mass, the eucharistic agape of Jesus.

These are not simply mass graves. Hundreds of thousands are buried, but these are not the mass graves we know from the modern totalitarian evil. In the latter mass graves, there are no singulars, there is no respect, no God. Posthumous mind, so to say, demands a metaphysics of being beyond Auschwitz: a thinking of singularity and community beyond absorbing totality. The catacombs look like a mass grave but the meaning is not mass humanity. Each hole of death, each gap of gaping absence, every empty tomb, is a reminder, a sign of the community of irreducible singulars before God. Everyone can step into that space of singularity, is already in it, and every singular will go under into the space of death. But these holes of the dead, these holes in the earth, are also holes of love, holes of the "I" and the "We" that cared for the dead "I"—beyond death, worthy to be loved for itself, beyond what life and death do to it, beyond even the happening of the between. And all this, because the singular "I" is loved as a singular absolute in a community before God, the absolute original.

The Metaxological and the Happening of the Between

Perhaps it will help if we take our bearings. I want to say that the metaxological sense, relative to the other three senses, thinks through the intensive truth of what they state less profoundly. *First*, its understanding of singularity rethinks the univocal stress on *being something* and the *that it is* of beings. It also rethinks unity in a more complex, less closed sense. This is the intimacy of being, the idiocy of singularity, coming to be out of the excessive plenitude of being as originating. *Second*, it rethinks the ambiguity, rupture, heterogeneity of the equivocal. It is mindful of the recalcitrances and breakdowns and tensions of opposition. It knows the pain and suffering, the negativity and death that are the lot of finitude. It opens to plurality, but knows also the interstices of being that resist any easy assertion of continuity and facile reconciliation. It knows the bitterness of lostness. *Third*, it rethinks the mediated wholeness of the dialectical; but this is infinitely open, given both the excess of the inward otherness, and given the irreducibility of mediation between wholes to just another self-mediation. Mediation is an intermediation where there is an infinitely open doubling of being, redoubling beyond self-closure, both inwardly and outwardly.

In this redoubling, transcendence is acknowledged in an understanding of community as beyond totality. This *being beyond totality* refers to the beyond of innerness to totalization, the abyss of idiocy in the immanence of self-transcendence. It also refers to the beyond of superior otherness, transcendence itself as in excess of every immanent self-transcendence. Transcendence is redoubled in the metaxological: transcendence in innerness, transcendence in the between, transcendence beyond reduction to immanence, and yet at work in the intimacy of immanence.

Granted the above, it is now time to remark on the happening of the between itself. I suggest that we can look at this happening in the following *four* ways: first, the marvel of the middle in first astonishment; second, the familiar middle; third, the perplexing middle; fourth, the renewed mystery of the middle in agapeic mindfulness. I will take each in turn.

First, we behold the astonishing middle. Here we need a metaxological rereading of what before I called the rapturous univocity of being. To mindful astonishment there is the primal marvel that being is given at all. In this mindfulness the gift of being intimates that it is an agape, and to be rejoiced in for its own sake, for the intrinsic worthiness of its sheer being there. The astonishing middle comes before us and stuns by its sheer beauty as the showing to us of its inherent value. There is a sheer elemental pleasure in its irreducible otherness. This elemental pleasure is appreciation, where appreciation marvels in the goodness of the showing of being as good for itself. It is precious; it is prized; it is prized for itself with a value beyond all price. The origin of metaphysical mindfulness in agapeic astonishment is our first and primal sense of the goodness of the happening of the between. In this mindfulness we are in the neighborhood of the primal "It is good" and we hear something of its music. There is given to us ontological joy.

What is this? Again it is something elemental, and idiotic, and hence almost unnoticed, very frequently forgotten by philosophers. To be is sweet; being is good, it is good to be. When the marvel of the happening of the between is given to us in agapeic astonishment, we are open to an elemental intimacy, community with being. We ourselves live this community as an incarnate insistence on being. We recoil from negation and death because we are always already this community with being; the singular self-insistence we exhibit relative to our own being is itself an integrity formed out of this community of being. The sweetness of our own being is given to itself out of a more universal goodness that gives the community of being in its value for itself. We so recoil from death that even to be miserably is lived as a value more prized than not to be at all. There is a sweetness in simply being in the elemental happening of the between, as we wake to its ageless thereness and ever-virgin freshness. The happening of the between, when seen in proximity to the primal "It is good," is enveloped in this ontological sweetness, as if it were in a halo of the good.

We do not stay with the marvel of the astonishing middle; it does not stay with us. Mindfulness and the happening of the between fall into familiarity. We might say that the intimacy of being is its familiarity, its familial kinship; but what is granted is then taken for granted. "Familiarity" and "taking for granted" contain the equivocation. The familiar is the intimate, but it is also the not-noted; it is what we cease to mind; its thereness becomes indifferently there. And so the familiar, in this loss of mindfulness, is also not the intimate; its otherness is indifferently other. Likewise, what is taken for granted can be what is acknowledged as granted; and hence there is the grateful mindfulness that sees what is given just as given, as a gift; to take for granted is to appreciate the gift granted. But it is also the exact opposite: no longer to appreciate what is given, to cease to see that it is a gift; the loss of mindful gratitude makes it taken for granted as just there, indifferently there.

There arises the *second* way. The astonishing middle becomes the familiar, taken for granted middle, and it ceases to be a middle. We lose mindfulness of being as the happening of the between. What is given in the between consumes mind in this mode: we fall upon the things of the world; we hunt them, we prey on them, we catch them, we eat them, we dispose of them. The happening of the middle is familiarized, overseen as an aggregate of determinate objects, over which we try to exercise as much determining power as we can muster.

And with the loss of astonishment, there is the advent of a restless curiosity. There is also lost the intimation that the happening of being is to be appreciated, valued for itself. We grow deaf to the "It is good." The being of beings becomes their value relative to our disposal. They lose their ontological integrity for themselves and the concretion of worth such integrities are; they are reduced to their value in relation to our determining power. All the power of determinate knowing and doing takes shape in this fall from proximity to the primal "It is good." This distancing is the work of objectifying mind, of which univocal thinking is one of the most powerful expressions. It takes the taken-for-granted world as ultimate; it has not only lost, it also shuns metaphysical astonishment, since the latter calls into question the possibility of our completely determining the being and value of things, calls into question the view that being itself is completely determinate, hence intelligible in a manner that relieves the curiosity of determinate thinking.

Further again, the familar middle is defined by curiosity as a *problematic* middle. All *real* questions, it is claimed, are essentially problems, with their associated solution or techniques of solution. There is no problem that is not soluble; those that are not soluble are said to be psuedo problems; perplexities beyond problems are dismissed. Hence the problematic middle is heuristically the familar middle again, in that all "real" questions will have their definite answer and there will be no remainder of enigma. The problematic middle is the familiar middle objectified in terms of a set of univocal or perhaps methodologized queries, each of which is only taken seriously because it already anticipates its own possible solution.

Of course, there is gain in this loss of the astonishing middle: the gain in ever-increasing determinacy, and the articulation of the extraordinary richness of determination that does mark the marvelous intelligibility of creation. To the extent that mind is reminded of the latter, its loss of astonishment is never total. The very otherness of creation always harbors the power to rock mind back into astonishment, indeed into celebration of the enigma of what is given to it to think, even to think determinately. Were that loss of astonishment total, there would be the complete stifling of appreciation of being given, relative to the happening of the between, and all being would be completely determined as a mere valueless and indifferent thereness. The result would be nihilism. We would conquer the creation with our powerful curiosity, but we would lose ourselves and creation in their ontological value, just in that victory. The victory would be the death of our metaphysical mindfulness of the happening of the between. It would be the death of our deepest singularity as mindful being.

But think what we may about it, the happening of being is still given. Determine how we will the middle, so long as mindfulness continues, there is always the promise of something other than this determination of being to a mere valueless thereness. The otherness of its givenness will surprise us. Indeed, the very inward otherness at work in mindfulness itself will surprise us. These surprises will perhaps resurrect a sense of astonishment before the givenness of being that renews itself, resurrects itself even in the blackest night of nihilism. The fertility of equivocity will come to our aid here. It will nag the certainties of univocal determination. It will nibble away at our cherished categories. It will place here and there a sliding surface on the seemingly broad and secure path of science. It will shake the seemingly solid foundations. What then happens? The familiar middle will lose its balance. The taken-for-granted centering of being will find itself made eccentric, as unexpected and recalcitrant otherness flares up in the bastions of univocity. In a word, the familiar middle will be defamiliarized. And this defamiliarizing may again open up the intimacy of being in its proximity to the enigmatic givenness of being.

I would put it more strongly. In a paradoxical way, the night of *nihilism* may come to the aid of metaphysical mindfulness. For this night makes *the light itself* perplexing. It makes us wonder if we really know anything important at all, even as we progressively come to know everything determinate. The very night of nihilism itself escapes fixation in terms of purely determinate knowing. It opens an unknowing, and the thought of an other beyond determinate knowing. The fact of our distance from the primal "It is good" fills us with a strange restive emptiness, and the foreboding that we are more deeply lost than could ever be articulated in purely determinate knowing. The "It is nothing," the horror of the emptying of being of its value, may seem to make the happening of the middle the dark estate of grim death. If mindfulness is not itself dead, all of this shocks us, *shocks us ontologically*. The shock of the "It is nothing" produces the breakdown of the familiar middle. And this may occasion the breakthrough of another sense of the happening of the between in which again we move with trepidation towards resurrected astonishment.

The mockery of the equivocal, the shock of the "It is nothing" disquiets us in the familar middle, and it now becomes the *perplexing* middle. This is the *third* way. Metaphysical astonishment is breaking through again in this perplexity, which does not mean it has yet been delivered to a new freedom. Perplexity is at the edge of determinate curiosity, and hence it too can be developed in different directions. Thus, for example, it may see itself as another form of curiosity, as yet merely indefinite; and in overcoming its own skepticism and doubt and ignorance, it will reinstate the determinacy of being but in a more complex articulated fashion. Then the negative of the "It is nothing" is made a negation that negates itself and in the process reinstates more complete determinations of being. This is essentially Hegel's response to perplexity, though his understanding of dialectic will not end in mere external determination, but in consummate self-determination. But the happening of the between will have been returned to its familiarity through the system of categories he offers; there will be no perplexity in the end, and no final otherness, no excess or enigma, and no astonishment.

Metaxological thinking goes a different way, and the end of this is not the dispelling of perplexity, but its deepening at the edge of all determinate knowing. Perplexity, I said, is at the edge of determinate knowing. Hegel is at this edge but he uses the restless self-transcendence of perplexity to expand itself into a more and more complete determinate knowing, culminating in the end of absolute self-determining knowing. But the deepening of perplexity need not serve thus to refamiliarize the middle. Perplexity finds indeterminacies of being, not only with respect to determinate being, but with respect to self-determining being, indeterminacies always elusive at the edge of determination, or always recessively at work in the immanent depth of all determination.

At the limit, perplexity tends to be erotic, hence it is always tempted to misunderstand itself in terms of a drive to self-determination. But the deeper perplexity knows itself, becomes mindful of itself in self-mediation, the more it knows it does not know itself as self-mediation; the more also it is reminded of its own doubleness, as thought called to think both itself and what is other to itself; reminded also of its own inward otherness in which it comes to realize that its power to think for itself is first given to it, and henceforth is taken for granted.

Erotic perplexity developed in this metaxological direction becomes mindful of the constitutive ambiguity in taking for granted, and in familiarity. It looks anew at the equivocities that have been too quickly surmounted by Hegelian dialectic. It is reminded of a granting in the taking for granted, of a community of intimacy in the familiarity of being, of the more affirmative power of transcending being, at play even in the negative restlessness of erotic perplexity.

Metaxological perplexity is reminded of the happening of the between as a givenness that is not self-produced. Beyond the familiar between, the problematic between and the perplexing between, it rethinks the renewal of the astonishing between. This is the *fourth* way. The between now is a mystery in a sense that is not nugatory. Mystery is too often a category of epistemic indigence. This is not what I mean: it is not the indigence of determinate, even dialectical, knowlege; it is the ackowledgment of an excess to these that is profoundly positive. The strangeness of the middle returns in an otherness beyond the middle as comprehended. The strangeness is not that of a hostile stranger, but rather of an intimate from which one has been estranged, which estrangement now begins to be slowly overcome. We move back closer into proximity to the "It is good." Our ears, long caked with misunderstanding, hear sporadically only a faint echo of song. We have been deaf for too long. This deafness can last centuries, as with Western modernity that has systematically closed its hearing to the "It is good." It finds no place for it in its scientific and technological project. It hears nothing. It congratulates itself on its scientific deafness. The signs that come to it from beyond itself strike it as a mere dumb show.

In the resurrection of ontological astonishment, there is again something elemental as in the first giving of being. There is something beyond complete saying, in that the renewal of mindfulness is a renewal of being, and hence not reducible simply to discursive articulation. There is something more beyond every saying, and yet every determinate saying can come to shine with the play of this more in determinacy itself. Far from being a dumb show, it is an entirely different speaking in which being's plurivocity is allowed to voice itself in its otherness. The self-certainty of univocity and self-mediating dialectic are chastened by these voices. They fall into silence, but this too can be the renewal of the expectancy towards the otherness of creation and its reserved possibility or promise. To remain in this expectancy of promise, to remain true to this renewed strangeness of being in the community of intimacy itself, is no easy task. In an essential sense it is not within the control of our self-mediation. Something is given from beyond ourselves which we do not produce. Patience and humility are required of mindfulness in this renewal of the mystery of the middle.

The thinking now needed is the mediated counterpart to the first astonishment. This is what I call agapeic mind.[6] What do I mean? I mean the self-transcendence of mindfulness as it goes towards the other as other, and not just simply as a mirror of itself, or a means to mediate with its own self. It is genuinely self-transcending, for it is the thinking of the other in its otherness. It can never be thought thinking itself, for it is just the marvel of the being of the other that calls it from itself. In being called out from itself, it takes no thought for itself. It thinks beyond itself, thinks in excess of its own self-mediation. And so such a communicative mindfulness is the living exemplification of a coming into the community of being. Its self-concern is, as it were, suspended, and the very astonishing givenness of the happening of the between solicits it into a thinking without cease.

Mindfulness is here beyond will to power. Not that agapeic mind is an impotence. It does show a certain reticence of power, and yet it is a breaking through beyond self-being that does not compensate for a lack within itself but knows itself to be rooted in the originary power of being transcending itself. Out of this root beyond itself it pours itself out beyond itself. We are beyond the confines of monadic self-being, in a letting be, beyond the shock of being as nothing, of counting for nothing. There is a release of freedom beyond self-determination. And if there is an amen to being, it is unlike Hegel's hymn to *noēsis tēs noēseōs*. It is a consent beyond willfulness, a letting be that might look superficially like indifference, but is really a justice of mind, an unwillingness to force being to conform to its thought determinations. I am speaking of a kind of festive mind. This, I believe, is what ancient *theōria* also implied: a celebrating marveling at the beauty and good of being, an ontological vigilance beyond violence or interference.[7]

This agapeic mindfulness is the metaphysical thinking of transcendence. The happening of the between is a metaxological community of transcendences. Suppose we first think of the *outer immensity* in the becoming of things. This immensity can both appall us and exalt us. We face our own nothingness, and yet we feel ourselves strangely native to the cosmos. We shrink to nothing before the immensity, and yet we sing our thanks out into the openness. And there are breakthroughs beyond the sense of void infinity, such as made Pascal afraid, into an appreciation of infinitude as plenitude. We breathe the glory of the sublime creation, in its disproportion to our power to master it.

Suppose then we think of the *inner infinitude* of the self-transcending human being. Such is the greatness of the human being, even in the abyss of its own innerness, source also of its noble wretchedness. And yet the inner

---

6. See again the chapter "Agapeic Mind" in *Perplexity and Ultimacy*.

7. See *Philosophy and its Others*, 298ff., on festive being; also *Beyond Hegel and Dialectic*, 130 ff., on speculative abandon and release.

restlessness of human self-becoming can strike through to its own depth, and come before itself as more than infinite lack, come to appreciate the gift of its own being as a positive power, given to itself by a more original power of being, radically positive in itself.

My point is this: in the community of the between, there is a convergence of the inner and the outer infinitudes. In the doubled middle, the extremes cross and crisscross: birth and death, the womb and the grave, being and nothing, givenness and freedom, finitude and infinitude, the void and fulfilled being. There is a constitutive ambiguity here but it can be more than a mere equivocal lostness. It can offer the signs of finding, or of being found, even in erring; it can be a reminder of home in homelessness itself.

I do not want to say that we just determine the indefiniteness of the external plenitude. The happening of the middle is more than a dialectical self-mediation between these inner and outer infinitudes, such that their doubleness is two sides of one more encompassing process. Rather there is a metaxological community between inner and outer infinity that is not reductive of the otherness of either into a means for one infinite to mediate with itself. The coming to community of the infinite succession of becoming and the intentional infinite of the mindful self, just in their otherness, suggest a more radical sense of the infinite that is in excess of either, and reducible to none, even as it gives them their being for themselves. The astonishing middle rouses the thinking of radical transcendence as itself an agapeic origin.

This is to depart significantly from Hegel's view. The outer infinite for him is a "bad infinite," an indefinite succession which like a line just goes on and on in indigent endlessness. Hegel's true infinite bends back on itself like a circle and is closed. He thinks of the infinite on the paradigm of self-mediation that fulfills itself in the return of self to itself, via the mediation of its own self-othering. In this view, there is no real otherness that is given for itself as other; otherness is self-otherness, and hence not genuinely for itself. It is not given for the receiver; it is given for the giver, and hence not agapeic at all. What Hegel considers to be the genuine infinite mediates with itself; it mediates with itself in its own finitude; it does not give finitude as radically other to itself, does not give finitude as for itself. Finitude is the means, the middle by which the infinite dialectically mediates with itself. There is only one infinite, a monism of the infinite, the absolute totality that only mediates with itself in mediating with finitude. There is finally no otherness; there is no real pluralization of transcendence.

The Way of Transcendence—From Metaphor to Hyperbole

I now conclude the first part of our exploration with perplexities that carry us forward, and some remarks on metaphysical thinking, in light of the fourfold sense of being.

The between is a happening. As a happening, it is without a determinate why that we can specify. Yet it intimates its source in what is not itself a determinate happening. There seems to be no *determinate* reason for the happening of the determinate. But this need not mean that it is unintelligible—absurd in a nugatory sense. That it is at all is the mystery. This mystery of its givenness calls for a rethinking, beyond determinate intelligibility; it does not commit us to a defect of intelligibility. For it is a striking fact that it is sometimes easier to give an articulation of the empty or defective rather than of the full or the overfull. The overfull is too much for us, often too much with us, for us to be able to think it. And so we take its granting of itself for granted. The light itself is impossible to illumine, since it illumines all else and our minds, and hence exceeds being illumined.

If the happening of the between exceeds every determinate why, can we still think of its why, relative to the ontological character of the plurality of integrities of self-transcendence that form a community there? What is the meaning of this happening of community? Is it just an ultimate contingency? How can we think the passage of transcendence in the middle, think the passage as passage? Does the *trans* points us across and beyond? If so, does not the restless surge of human self-transcendence make it impossible for us to stop at the happening? Are we not driven to think about the origin whence, and the ground wherefrom, and the matrix wherein, and the goal whither of the passage of self-transcendence?

And is the happening of the between self-justifying? Or is its justified good for itself the issue of a giving source, making it good for itself, because it is given? Is it given as good because its original ground is the transcendence that is too much, always more, always beyond, and always giving beyond itself as an agapeic origin? Does the happening of the between reveal itself as not self-produced? Does it intimate itself as a creation? Does it suggest not only an ontological bond between beings in the middle, but a bond between the middle and the origin that gives it the good of being at all? Does it suggest ultimate transcendence as in excess of the immanent transcendences at play in the middle?

In Part II, I will turn to these questions, first concerning origin, then in relation to creation, things, intelligibilities, selves, communities, truth, and the good. Each of these will be interpreted in terms of the fourfold sense of being unfolded in Part I. It remains in this chapter to say something about metaphysical thinking as mindful of transcendence. The metaxological sense of being has implications for the nature of metaphysical thinking as *metaphorical*, as *analogical*, as *symbolical*, and finally as *hyperbolical*.

To the first point. Because of our being in the middle, our language of transcendence and origin involves an inescapable metaphorical dimension. Though we remain in a condition of finitude, the energy of transcendence at work in the middle makes this finitude immensely complex, makes it at once finite and a pointer beyond finitude. But there is no univocal direct speech of ultimate transcendence, for such speech would be untrue to the complex intermediations that define the community of being and the very relativity to the origin here in question. Metaphysical language has to be rooted in the concreteness of being as given in the middle, but not exhausted by that, and thus so, in terms of the more emergent in the given middle itself.

Metaphor is an indispensable articulation that preserves a reference to the beyond, even as it mediates an identification between terms that are normally thought of as incompatible, even opposite. When we speak metaphorically, two or more terms are brought into a conjunction that exceeds the two terms and that may occasion a surprising new mindfulness of what is more or beyond the terms taken alone. A metaphor refreshes the attentiveness of mind, sometimes even renews metaphysical astonishment. I am not talking about dead metaphors, where this surprise and astonishment have been made blandly familiar. Dead metaphors are issues of mindfulness that have passed into mindless use.

In living metaphor there is a certain identification of otherness. Though it may pass unnoticed, this is true even of a dead metaphor like "The king is a lion." The heterogeneity between regality and being a lion is articulated in terms of a community deeper than their obvious separateness in the familiar middle. There is an intermediation at work in metaphorical naming. All language, as issuing into naming, is metaphorical in that sense: there is a communication between mind and being, a certain identification that does not issue in a reductive identity but into language itself as the articulation of this minded community of being.

When we say that the king is a lion, there is a transcendence of univocity. For univocity, a king is a king and nothing else but a king; likewise for the lion. And yet there is an identification: A is B. How do we understand that metaphorical "is"? It is not merely equivocal, as it would be for an insistent univocalist who could see no community of being, or meaning, or mind between the lion and the king. In fact, there is a mediation between differents in the metaphorical naming, hence it cannot be purely equivocal. There is a complex conjunction of what for univocity are equivocal dissimilars; there is a community of the two, named beyond their difference, and that is linguistically expressed in the metaphorical "is."

Can we say that the metaphorical "is" is dialectical? Yes in this regard: the doubleness of the two is spoken, and spoken as a community of togetherness. There is a mediated conjunction of the two as different, and this conjunction might be called dialectical, especially so in reminding us of the dynamic articulating that generates the metaphorical togetherness itself. Both are seen together, the meaning of one is expressed in terms of the other, hence there is a passage back and forth between the two that is beyond univocity and equivocity.

But that said, there is more. The danger now is that the metaphorical "is" may be taken as an external and merely imaginative expression of a deeper and more ultimate identity that is only *exoterically* expressed in the metaphor. I mean that dialectic has always to fight the temptation to reproduce univocity at a higher mediated level, hence fight against its own temptation to underplay the always constitutive work of the *dia* or double. The metaphorical "is" must be preserved from a kind of dialectical monism in which the togetherness of differents is merely the exoteric, or provisional, or surface form of a more ultimate identity of all things. If we are not careful here, even the complex mediations of the between, relative to beings, to mindful human being, and to the community, become mere exoteric figurations of this absolute identity. This way the plurivocity of the middle is betrayed. Then, too, the esoteric meaning of the identity will not lie in the exoteric metaphorical "is," but in its translation into purely logical terms or concepts, wherein the remaining residues of otherness and transcendence are overcome. This happens to the metaphorical "is" with Hegel, and we are left with the conceptualization of the whole as thought thinking itself.

The metaphorical "is," as I understand it, keeps itself open as an identification of otherness, hence is never the encapsulation of transcendence, but instead a vector towards and beyond the circle of self-thinking thought. Because the metaphorical "is" keeps the *dia* open, it defines the community of same and other differently than in terms of an esoteric monism of the whole. In that sense, metaphor is metaphysical and metaxological. It defines a complex mindful intermediation between us and what is ultimately other. It offers no direct possession of the ultimate. Rather its indirection is respect for the enigma of the ultimate, expressed in the openness of the metaphorical "is" itself.

The metaphor is a carrying across which is also a carrying between. As I have remarked before, the word "*meta*" can mean both "beyond", but also "in the midst." The conjunction of the two meanings points to a sense of the beyond that is moving in and through the middle. Metaphor carries us through the middle to a beyond that is not a mere beyond in the sense of a dualistic opposite. It is a more, a plenitude as other to the middle, but with an otherness that marks a community with the middle, not an antithesis with it. And this community is not the exoteric expression of a more ultimate monism that absorbs the heterogeneity of community within a self-mediating totality. Rather there is a community *between* originals that are wholes for themselves, yet open and self-transcending. Metaphysical metaphor speaks in the interstices of this community about the excess of transcendence. It also goes to its limit, where it is a periphrasis: it speaks around the border, the perimeter. Its periphrasis is also respect for the other to be acknowledged as other.

So I suggest that if we are to image the ultimate, we need to find metaphors of ultimacy in the middle. Such metaphors would be concretions of the power of being at its ontologically richest. A metaphysical metaphor would be an ontological image, in the sense of an immanent manifestness of transcendence. Ontological richness refers to the double requirement of metaxological being: a certain immanent self-mediation and wholeness; a self-transcending power of openness that may even be open to the other in an unlimited way. In later discussion, erotic and agapeic being will serve as central metaphysical metaphors. They will help us image the ultimate in terms of the richest mani-festations of the original communicative power of being, such as we find in the happening of the between. But this is already to anticipate.

We need now to acknowledge our *limitation* with respect to any dis-course about what exceeds finite categories. We are not the more, nor is our saying. Thus *metapherein* also carries meanings of "to alter" or "to change," perhaps even "to pervert." This is a salutary caution that warns us of erring equivocation. All saying risks a deformation; the ambiguity of the metaphor as a communication risks the perversion of communication into a dissimula-tion. We lose or miss or distort the communication in the deliverance of the communication. The doubleness then can cease to be a rich ambiguity and become a deceptive equivocity. Nor is this a mere transgression of the truth of univocity; it may be a blocking of the truth of community as metaxological. The metaphor enables intermediation; but devoid of mindfulness, we may be tempted to disseminate thought on endless equivocation. Then metaphor dis-ables communication.

The danger of dissimulation, and the desire to defend ultimate transcen-dence from reduction to immanent self-transcendence, means that metaphysi-cal metaphor has something in common with the traditional notion of *analogy*. This is my *second* point. Metaphysical metaphor may say "A is B" (e.g., the ultimate is an agapeic origin), but we have to qualify the metaphorical "is" as metaxological, in order to obviate just the above danger. More explicitly, an analogy will say "A is like B" and have inscribed in it a qualification of the "is" against an univocal reduction or equivocal dispersal or indeed a dialectical monism. We could say that the analogical "is like" is uttered with mindful-ness of the message of the equivocal: namely, with a feeling for the slippery ambiguities when we speak of one thing in terms of another, or when we speak seemingly in one voice of what seems to be more than one reality. In other words, analogical likeness, like metaxological metaphor, reminds us that any monism of the "is" risks being false to the process of seeing one term as the other, or in terms of the other term. In the analogical likeness, the co-implication of the two is a conjunction but never a reduction of difference: the "is" is qualified by an "as;" and this, in turn, reminds us of the conceptu-ally unmastered nature of the "is," as well as the qualified nature of the con-junction of differents.

As I understand the traditional analogy of being, it addresses our efforts to speak of ultimate transcendence in such a fashion that no reduction to immanence follows. And yet being as given in immanence must offer us the language whereby to speak of what cannot be directly given in immanence. There is an analogy between the two, between the happening of the between as given and the ground of that giving as ultimate transcendence. This analogy is a play of sameness and difference. Even in likeness itself there is a play of sameness and difference, for there is no absolute likeness. For if there were absolute likeness, there would be complete identification or identity, hence we would be beyond likeness into pure sameness. Every likeness is also an unlikeness. So we always find a doubleness in analogical likeness. This is consistent with the double of open dialectic and the metaxological.

A difficulty I find is the infiltration of a misplaced univocity, insofar as analogical likeness is subjected to a quasi mathematicization. Indeed in its original Greek use, analogy referred to a mathematical relation. Of course, there are many other later uses of analogy which surpass the mathematical, for instance, the relation between the sun and the offspring of the Good is explicitly called an analogy in Plato's *Republic*. Analogy also was used in connection with the relation of the cosmic elements in Plato, as well as the determination of the proper proportions of justice, with both Plato and Aristotle.

The issue here is the trace of mathematization and hence of the univocal. One understanding of analogy speaks in terms of a proportion between ratios between terms: a:b :: c:d.[8] That we have four terms here is relevant to our moving beyond the triplicity of dialectical self-mediation. The question is: Does this quadruplicity freeze too easily into the form of a quasi-mathematical structure? The quadruplicity of terms defines two sides of the relation of "as," two sides as themselves double: each side of the analogy is itself defined relationally, and hence internally mediated and complex. So the analogical "as" is a relationality of relations.

There is nothing incompatible with the metaxological sense here, if we recall the complex mediated character of beings, mindful human being, the community of beings, the happening of the between: each of these is rendered as doubly mediated, internally self-mediated, though as open, and as other-related with respect to an interplay with what is not itself. But all the terms of the metaxological relation are *dynamized* concretions of the energy of transcending being; hence neither the terms nor the relation can be reduced to anything like a quasi-mathematical structure. Analogy in its quasi-mathematical form fails to escape the limitations of univocity as a fixation of terms. It risks freezing into a grid of relations, a kind of static frame, a mathematical abstraction of relations between relating centers of being.

The metaxological metaphor might be seen as a dynamized version of analogy in this respect. It wishes to preserve the openness of the likeness relation, while insisting on the energy of self-transcendence, which dialectic helps us think concerning being. Traditional analogy does not do justice to this dynamic of transcending, even though its best intent is to preserve the ultimacy of transcendence as other, without denying the intermediation be-

---

8. It is not here relevant to enter into the details of the difference between analogy of attribution and proportion.

tween ultimacy and the finite happening of the between. The image is like the original; but the image is not a static likeness; is it like the original because it is original for itself; if the original is ultimate transcendence, finite images are more like the original to the extent that they exhibit the energy of self-transcendence. The creation is like the Creator to the extent that it becomes creative in its own right, for itself. This created creativity may be a gift, but it is given for the creation itself and hence is inherent in the creation and not a mere epiphenomenon to be dissolved, when the finite work is putatively reabsorbed into the original whole.

The finite image is original for itself, hence double, doubling, and especially self-doubling, self-transcending in the case of the mindful human being. Put otherwise, metaxological metaphorics reinterprets the image and likeness as beyond passive mirroring: the image is being for itself, a creation for itself, original for itself.[9] When quasi-mathematical proportion fixes into a grid, it makes analogical likeness into a passive representation, which it is not really. It is not that there is not a passivity, a pathos to creation, nor a power of representation. There is pathos in that the finite between is not self-produced; it is given. There is representation in that the finite can stand for what is beyond finitude, but this *standing for the beyond* is dynamic; it is a standing out, an *ecstasis*. This ecstasis of the finite is the promise of a creative "being true" to the ultimacy of transcendence.

Consider how in the Platonic view analogy primarily refers either to the relation of image and prototype, or to the relation between a source and its offspring. In the first case, the relation of likeness between temporal instances and eternal paradigms is said to be an analogous participation. In the second case, the idea of origination (as in the analogy between the sun and the Good) is one of analogical likeness between a source and what it brings to be; there is an analogical likeness, never an identity, between the source and what it effects. The first case can sometimes be thought in terms of a mimēsis which can be mathematicized in terms of a structure of relations between two levels or modes of being; this kind of mimēsis can freeze into the kind of dualistic grid I mentioned. In the second case, this freezing can be avoided; it can also help us avoid freezing the first sense. Historically, the influence of the univocal sense and of the paradigm of mathematics has meant that the ultimate has been thought of as beyond the changing realm of genesis, hence as static and immobile; hence the danger of freezing into a static dualism.

In the metaxological view the analogy of origination and the creative relation of source and issue is more fundamental than the analogy that fixes on determinate terms and their determinate relations. The truer insight promised by the analogy of origination is, I think, that the energy of transcendence in genesis is itself an analogical likeness of the ultimate unconditional energy

9. See *Philosophy and its Others*, 87–93, on the relation of imitation and creation.

of transcendence. Hence eternity is not a static unit of univocal intelligibility but the creative *energeia* of absolute transcendence, the agapeic origin. For if, as Plato suggests, time is a moving image of eternity, the case may *not* be that the dynamic is an image of the static, but that the dynamism of time is an image of the more ultimate, exceeding dynamism of eternity, as itself the unconditional energy of transcendence. The dynamic image images the dynamism of the original.

The Aristotelian view may seem to reject the putative dualism of the Platonic account. But metaphysical astonishment and the eros of perplexity count less in Aristotelian thinking of the middle than does determinate cognition. This affects its sense of analogical likeness and the tendency to univocal *mathēsis*. In response to perceived problems with respect to knowledge of transcendence, the Aristotelian development of analogy tends to accentuate the stress of the univocal sense, relative to being within the problematic middle. The Aristotelian development, it seems to me, also has a less rich sense of analogical likeness relative to the ultimate as an originative source, such that the offspring of the source are like to the original, just in the ontological richness of their concretion of the energy of transcendence.

Aristotle does not always avoid a logicization of the analogy of being. He is not as profound as Plato, relative to the ontological analogy of being, founded on the imagistic dynamic being of the world of genesis. Aquinas, I think, tends to vacillate between the logicization and the ontologization, the former with respect to the use of the Aristotelian categorial scheme to answer the question of being, the latter with respect to his appropriation of the idea of the universe as a creation that images the Creator of all. It is only in terms similar to the latter that the energy of transcendence can be thought properly, relative to the metaxological meaning of analogical likeness. The latter warns of the dangers of mathematicized analogy for leading metaphysics astray, and about the inappropriateness of the mathematical form to the thinking of transcendence.

Dialectic itself will undo the fixation of the quasi-mathematical frame. It understands that the terms move, move into the middle and move towards its beyond. The danger here is with a dialectical self-mediation whose movement into the middle is self-absolutizing. Then dialectic courts the collapse into immanence of the absolute original in its transcendence. Dialectical thinking powerfully undercuts the stasis of dualistic thinking, undercuts the freezing of metaphysical analogy into the quasi-mathematical structure that has become dualistic. But that dualism does serve to remind us of the double in another sense—the difference of ultimate transcendence. Dualism is a poor way to preserve this transcendence, but this is what its best aim is, on a more generous interpretation. This is why metaxological thinking is beyond dialectic as closed into its own immanence; but it retains both the *dunamis* of transcending and the stronger sense of difference of analogy. Nevertheless, the terms in a metaxological analogy are dynamic integrities of self-transcending; the middle is not exhausted by a grid of quasi-mathematical intelligibility. When analogy drifts back to mathematical univocity, there is not enough justice done to the *poiēsis,* the eros, and the agape of being, each as movements of transcending being in the between.

Creation as an original image is double; beings are double images, selves are double images. This double image or likeness is itself the ontological basis for the constitutive ambiguity on which feeds the equivocal sense of being. Even if we are tempted to talk about the absolute original as the primary analogate, the *ana-logos* must be seen as a *meta-logos*: there will never be a conquering of the mystery of the meta-logical, or the ambiguous enigma of the ana-logical, in utterly transparent concepts. The metaxological rethinks metaphysical analogy by rethinking the eros and agape of transcendence in the dynamic relativity of analogizing origination. If the primary analogate is the absolute original, the origination of the creation as different will be analogous: creation as outcome of the origin's overdetermined agape, but both given for itself, and driven beyond its own closure by the agape and eros of transcending at work in its own given form of being.

Without reference to the eros and agape of transcendence, the analogy as a static structure is easily deconstructed by dialectic. Then we lack the means to avoid determining the middle purely in terms of an *immanent reciprocity* of terms. When this happens, the *asymmetry* of ultimate transcendence, the difference of the primary analogate as the absolute original, cannot be properly acknowledged. I think that an essential asymmetry has to be preserved differently. Even here, I believe, classical doctrines of God as Creator did not escape the consequences of a certain metaphysical univocity. That is, there was an emphasis on creation as a *one-way* relation between the origin and the world, such that the origin was in no way implicated in the creation. The metaphysical fear was that the origin would be stained ontologically by the imperfection of finitude. In all this, perfection of being is still thought on the analogy of absolute being as pure self-thinking thought, which is defined completely in itself to the exclusion of any relatedness to creation.

By contrast, in the view suggested here and to be developed more fully, there is an asymmetry in agapeic creation, but it is not the asymmetry of nonrelatedness. Agapeic creation is asymmetry per se, in that the relation is for the other as other, and not for a return to self-relation. The transcendence of the origin is hence not incompatible with its solidarity with creation. The perfection of the original is not a closed self-sufficiency; it is overwhole, pluperfect; not a self-completion, but an agapeic excess creative of the other as other.

Instead of a static structure of correspondences, we need the dynamism of likening, of corresponding. There is no correspondence as a determinate relation, if there is not first corresponding as a communicative relating, a communication beyond univocal determination or dialectical self-determination. If analogy can be dynamized in this sense, well and good; it will allow for the double image, the doubling in imaging, hence self-transcendence as relating in corresponding. Likening becomes a creative becoming, where mimēsis and creativity are in affiliation, not in opposition. But if analogy cannot be thus dynamized, we end with a static equivocity, a dualism of fixed opposites. This might then be dialectically deconstructed, or perhaps induce a different drift back to univocity, such as perhaps we see in *pros hen* analogy in Aristotle. I will not deny the one, but will rethink it metaxologically, and in such a fashion as will be compatible with the language of originative self-transcendence. If there is a *pros hen* analogate, it must allow imaging as originative self-transcendence; it must allow for images as self-mediating and intermediating; it must allow for internal complexity of terms, not only structurally, but in terms of sources of structuring, that is, originative sources.

For such originative sources carry the *metapherein* of metaphysical transcending towards transcendence as other. The *trans* is a going across, and a conjoining, and it is a cross beyond all finite conjoinings. The *meta*, as carrying, is between and beyond, double. The doubling metaphoring of metaxological metaphysics reaffirms the doubled "is"—being is, as redoubling, as creative pluralization, over and again, beyond itself, again and again; it is not just self-identifying but othering of self towards the other. The excess in one, the excess in the other are exceedings (in the sense of *ex-cedere*);[10] they are goings out. This redoubled exceeding defines a community in excess. There is always more, always an inexhaustibility beyond final determination.

This doubling brings us to our *third* and *fourth* points—namely, the *symbolical* and the *hyperbolic* dimensions of metaphysical saying. *Symbol* originally refers to a way of *reidentification* and *renewed community*, consequent to an interim of separation, or a between-time of difference or estrangement. Example: a lover leaves the beloved and breaks a ring in two, or perhaps they have two identical rings. These will serve as markers of identity, as memorials of love, even in estrangement or exile. The symbols will be hopeful reminders and promises of renewed love. The exchange of rings at a wedding is symbolical in that sense, symbols of undying love, in sickness and in health, unto death.

There is a certain dynamic holism here. The symbol was the broken tally of an original whole that, on being reunited with its other half, reconstituted the original whole. The lover returns after long absence and recognizes or is recognized by the beloved in light of the symbol. *Sumballein* is to *throw together*: we find echoes here of the *sun* of *sunousia*, "being with;" also the *sun* of sympathy, *pathos together*, compassion; also the togetherness of synthesis. There is a conjunction of two after alienation.

---

10. *Ex-cedere*: think also of the word *to cede*, to allow, to cede or let be, to make way; to concede, to make way for the other.

For example, in the *Symposium*, the word symbol is used by Aristophanes in his great myth of the broken original whole of primal selves. Each of us of is symbol, a broken tally of the original whole. The split or differentiated human self, suffering the pathos of difference, is a living symbol of an original condition of wholeness. Its erotic drive beyond its present partiality is with the view to finding the lost other, as its own other half. Symbols are broken wholes that image the original whole; they partake of the original whole, for they are broken off from it. It is this *continuity of community* between the symbol and the symbolized that allows the search for the fulfilling other, for the *sun* of *sunousia*, the conjunction of others as the two fit together in mutual recognition.[11]

In the metaxological sense of the symbol, given being is not simply the brokenness of an original whole; it is being given with its own original wholeness, given its difference; but its difference as transcending is also its relativity to what is beyond itself. There is ingrained in given being the promise of a *sunousia*, a "being with." The symbol partakes of that which it symbolizes, but the fitting together of the two in *sunousia* cannot be reductive of difference. This is the danger with Aristophanes' image, as indeed with Hegel's dialectic, where the twosomeness is but two sides of a more original or inclusive whole.

Aristophanes puts the whole in the beginning, Hegel in the end. The archaic whole for Aristophanes, as he suggests, was a *hubristic plenitude* that challenged the gods. By contrast, the beginning in the metaxological is an *agapeic plenitude*; hence difference is not a fall from the one, but the generous giving of otherness as other to the other; the metaxological symbol is the image of this generous giving, already an image of community even in difference. By contrast again, the teleological whole of Hegel sees the beginning as an *empty archē*, whose fullness is constituted by the mediation of the between, which is then absorbed into the whole. Hegel's logic of part and whole is a dialectical synecdoche, in which the part stands for the whole, but no part can stand on its own but must be reabsorbed into the whole. We might say that Hegel's whole is a self-subverting synecdoche, because just as the *archē* is indigent being, so also the happening of beings is also indigent, to the extent that no being is the whole, the completed *telos*. The Hegelian sense of the *sun* does not do justice to the community of difference in the between, and to a different community between the origin and this community.

This is why we have to say that the symbol is only one side of the movement to coming together and standing apart. The other side is what might be called the metaphysical *hyperbole*. This is my *fourth* point. In important respects, metaphysical saying as metaxological cannot avoid being hyperbolic.

---

11. See *Beyond Hegel and Dialectic*, chapter 6 for fuller discussion of this in Aristophanes, Socrates and Hegel.

This *huper* is not the *huper* of *hubris*; it refers to the *being above* of transcendence. Hyperbole is from *huperballein*, and what does that mean? *Huperballein* means to "throw above," or "be thrown above."

This is the way of the beyond. This way is a throwing, as is the case with the symbol. Throwing here suggests a metaphysical *exigency*. It is not an option. We are thrown towards transcendence by our being. The metaphysical hyperbole tries to name this process of being thrown above, that throws mindfulness into the *huper*, the beyond. The feet of transcending mind are lifted off the ground and, as Kant saw painfully, the hyperbole may risk empty flight into emptiness. He is right in that this is always a danger when we risk speech about transcendence. Nevertheless, we have to risk that speech, since transcendence is not any option. We are already and always thrown beyond; our very being is hyperbolic. The metaphysical hyperbole can express the genuine desire to speak of transcendence in a nonobjectifying manner.

This is the way of excess. Metaphysical mind as agapeic is hyperbolic in that regard. It is symbolical in being tied mindfully to the given community of being; it is hyperbolic in daring to think the beyond by the way of excess: beyond all union, beyond all *sunousia*. Excess is the way to *huperousia*, beyond being, above being, being above being. Being beyond being is a double saying: paradoxical language is unavoidable.

Here we are able to give a more affirmative meaning to the *equivocal*. Is it surprising that metaphors for God will often have a *dipolar* character?[12] For instance, Heraclitus will tell us that Zeus is both craving and satiety, thus invoking together both the fulness of the agapeic and the emptiness of the erotic. God will be absolute being and absolute nonbeing; the one and more than the one; absolutely transcendent and absolutely immanent. God will be dipolar in terms of the wrathful judge who lets dire suffering come down upon the creatures of the day, and the father/mother who loves her/his creatures with a mad recklessness, beyond all finite justice. There is no univocity of the ultimate. The constitutive ambiguity of the between is the double image that reveals and conceals, makes manifest and reserves, gives being and negates, spurs human transcending to the utmost, yet breaks down all hubris in this majestic nobility of self-transcending.

In my view, equivocal language may have to be *risked* if we want to affirm the absolute difference of the transcendent.[13] Here the equivocity is that to speak the transcendent, equivocally or otherwise, is already to bring it out

---

12. The dipolar character of the religious image is central to the view of being religious developed in chapter 3 of *Philosophy and its Others*.

13. This risk of the equivocal is run by thinkers like Kierkegaard and Levinas. It is somewhat cheap simply to insist on a univocal or dialectical self-consistency in their saying. For this is not to understand fully the intent of the saying. It is to misunderstand the daring of metaphysical mindfulness and its saying on the boundary.

of its absolute difference, and so either not to name it, or to imply that there is no absolute difference. I think this equivocity has to be *lived with* dynamically; it cannot be resolved into a univocal or dialectical determination. The equivocal must be lived mindfully in the irreducible tension of the double middle. There is no escape from its constitutive ambiguity. Even a revelation of the transcendent is itself potentially equivocal, in that in revealing itself, it enters immanence and hence communicates a dangerous ambiguity with respect to its absolute transcendence. Manifested transcendence is in immanence and hence not absolutely transcendent; and yet it is absolutely transcendent as revealed in immanence, for what is revealed is ever beyond encapsulation, even in immanence itself. The constitutive ambiguity persists, after the utmost mindfulness has done its best to think it through. Thus understood, the equivocal is the *threshold of enigma*, a subverter of every claim to have encompassed the enigma of transcendence. It has, so to say, the guardianship of this threshold. It is a suitor in love with the ultimate beloved that it does not know.

As the word for being-with, *sunousia* is also the word for sexual intercourse. This is very evident in Plato's *Symposium* where eros is treated in relation to the *metaxu*. We might say that *huperousia* is beyond *sunousia*, in excess of the lacking being that drives erotic self-transcendence. Into *huperousia* agapeic mind throws itself, finds itself thrown, beyond erotic mind. *Huperousia* comes before it, shakes it from beyond, beyond erotic perplexity. *Huperousia* appears in the redoubling, the rebirth, in another dimension of metaphysical astonishment. And so if we correlate the symbolic saying with erotic mind and its driven perplexity, the hyperbolic saying can be correlated with agapeic mind and its reborn astonishment at the beyond, beyond finite determination. Both the symbol and the hyperbole are on the way of excess. Both are self-transcending movements of metaphysical mind, though in the second the excess of transcendence as other to mind breaks through radically.

There are other significant and revealing connections. Thus if coupled with erotic mind, the symbol can also be seen in terms of the *via negativa*. This is the path of self-exceeding by means of negativity. In some respects Hegel is right here to see determinate negation as an operator of transcendence in dialectically specifying a move from lack to wholeness, and from broken to renewed union, as Aristophanes would have it. This *via negativa* is not without equivocation in that, again as Aristophanes notes, the original whole can risk being hubristic: the excess of the original wholes can be *destructive* of the order of the *metaxu* between the gods and mortals. Thus the way of excess in its power of negation opens into a dark ambiguous freedom, even to the extreme of revolt against divine order. This we might call the dark *huper*: mortals try to usurp the divine as beyond and fall into brokenness. Hubris is the destructive hyperbole. We throw ourselves up to the divine, impelled by the powerful vehemence of erotic self-transcending. This same vehemence of self-transcending may will to displace, conquer, dethrone the beyond; there follows a rupture, a suffering, a fall into evil, and a different lack.

The *via negativa* of the symbol is a redress for this hubris. It says: not this, not that, not the other, in the darkness of the equivocal. It refuses to finitize the absolute, in response to the absolutization of the finite and the hubristic refusal of the absolute. It refuses to objectify the transcendent, thereby turning it into an idol, our image, metaphysical or religious. The *via negativa* is a way towards excess, through lack, which stresses that the transcendent is not this, not that . . . always not, ever more, ever beyond. I think Hegel's logic of determinate negation risks a kind of metaphysical idolatry by reformulating the *via negativa* such that the ever more, the always ever beyond, is subordinated to a system of self-determining concepts. The genuine affirmation implicit in the negative way is made into pure self-determination, self-relating negativity; hence there is nothing more or other or beyond the self-mediating whole. This is a reduction of the way of excess involved in negation; the transcendence of the ever-more, the *huperousia* is brought down to a false synthesis of the *sunousia*.[14]

---

14. What I here call the hyperbole is related to what I called the "post-Romantic symbol" in *Desire, Dialectic and Otherness*, 237–38, 246. The different terminology here is to avoid the ambiguity in the *sun* of symbol. I explain. In Hegel symbol indicates disproportion between finitude and infinity because the finite is overwhelmed by the infinite. The symbol makes the infinite itself into the indefinite, and fails to attain Hegel's own sense of infinity as the dialectically self-mediating whole. This is typical of Hegel who sees empty lack of determination in all beginnings. And the symbol is a mere beginning for him. By contrast, he sees a balance or synthesis of finite and infinite, sense and spirit, in classical art. Then in romantic art, there is a new disproportion, a transcendence of finitude, but in inwardness itself. Note that Hegel then proceeds dialectically to conquer this latter transcendence or disproportion via a certain understanding of religion and philosophy. This relates to the view of art and religion as the exoteric, imagistic form of the truth revealed dialectically in philosophy, itself the complete self-mediation in thought, free of the residues of otherness persistent in art and religion. The symbolic beginning is the indefinite, the classical middle is the determinate, the romantic end makes possible the self-determining completion, for Hegel. On this more fully, see my "Art, Origins, Otherness: Hegel and Aesthetic Self-Mediation," in *Philosophy and Art*, ed. Daniel Dahlstrom (Washington: Catholic University of America Press, 1991), 209–34. But where is the overdetermined plenitude of being as other to all self-mediation? Where is the pluralized sense of infinitude that we discussed above? In the present case, to revert to the symbol is to reaffirm the unconquerable nature of transcendence, relative to a different sense of the beginning, the middle, and the end. It is to point to the hyperbole, the *huperousia*, beyond all art, religion, and philosophy. This is *post-romantic* because it goes the way of excess, known in inwardness; the inward otherness, in its mindfulness of being as communicative, is a metaphysical metaphor for the transcendence of the ultimate other. The postromantic symbol is hyperbolic in dealing with the superior other, through the abyss of interiority, expressed in erotic perplexity and agapeic astonishment. This entails a double mediation, between innerness and exteriority, between innerness and the superior other. This is also *postromantic* because the point is not at all a *subjectification* of being.

Hyperbole frees the symbolic *via negativa* from reduction to the logic of determinate negation. For there is a sense of the nothing in excess of determinate negation, just as there is a sense of the indeterminate in excess of the indefinite. The movement of transcending in the symbol is not closed off to transcendence. We might say that the hyperbole offers a *via eminentiae*, in a metaxologically reformulated sense. The hyperbolic is a way of excess that throws beyond finitude. But this *via* is by way of agapeic mind; hence the point is not to proceed from lack to perfection, but from perfection and plenitude, indeed from perfection in the between to pluperfection in transcendence. Agapeic astonishment intimates the pluperfection that is always already more, always is and will be more, eternally more. The hyperbolic way will pile up perfection on perfection, knowing it will always not be enough to do justice to transcendence. This *via eminentiae* would be the hyperbole of praise. It is necessary to counteract the ambiguities of the *via negativa* which might fall into an empty nothing, or an idolatrous totality.

This hyperbolic way seems to take hold of perfection in the happening of the between, and seems to move from immanent to transcendent perfection. However, the claim strangely is that there is a *reversal* in this seeming mediation from immanence towards transcendence. The so-called primary analogate for this movement from immanent perfection is said to be God, not finite perfection. There is thus implied a *reversal, relative to ultimacy itself*. We do not have its measure; the measure is beyond measure. The hyperbole of *huperousia* names the measure beyond measure. The hyperbolic measure beyond our measure instead measures us. We are not going from perfection here to ultimacy there; but there is perfection here, because there is ultimacy. Perfection here is an image of an ultimacy whose perfection always exceeds immanence. There is a reversal into an asymmetry; finite perfection is a created image of ultimacy. There is no "It is good" in the between, but for the ultimate "It is good" that cannot be encompassed or mastered. In the hyperbolic way hubris becomes humility in the face of the superior. Transcendence as ultimate reverses self-transcendence. In the reversal from the absolute good of the ultimate other, transcendence itself is the original ground of self-transcendence.

I would emphasize that these ways of the symbol and the hyperbole are not flights into the void. There is a groping perplexity yes, as there is metaphysical astonishment. But we embark from where we are in the middle and from what we understand about its richest concretions of transcending being. The human being is already on the way, through the transcending of its erotic and agapeic being. These latter must serve as metaphysical metaphors for the ultimate excess of transcendence itself. But we cannot encompass transcendence as ultimate, since our being mindful is already encompassed by it. Even when being is given, and known as given, it is given with one side turned into its own hiddenness. We have to turn these limits to creative use. Despite our partiality, indeed just in our limit, we may find an indirect way to some sense of what is more.

Our singular being in community becomes a determinate concretion of what in itself cannot be absolutely determined. Our mindful, communicative being, in the between, offers a symbol of transcendence. As such it becomes a movement into the *huper*, hence becomes a hyperbole, as a trajectory out of its own excess into the beyond. For this symbol is not a seamless synthesis; it is ruptured and double, and *huper* even in its *sunousia*. If the symbol responds to self-mediation as ruptured, the hyperbole responds to the movement of intermediation throwing itself beyond itself. The latter is really a *being thrown beyond itself*, since the movement into the *huper* could not be effected by self-mediation. The *huper* itself ruptures self-mediation, throws the self back onto itself. Now the communicative self is with itself differently, for it is then thrown beyond itself. This is the movement of agapeic mindfulness into radical humility before transcendence itself. It is also a movement of exaltation into the superior.

PART II

BEING AND THE BETWEEN—A METAPHYSICS

CHAPTER SIX

ORIGIN

The Question of Origin

The first opening of thinking in agapeic astonishment is an indeterminate mindfulness of being in the midst of beings. In turn, this becomes an indeterminate perplexity about the strangeness of the sheer being-there of beings. This perplexity, in turn, will flower later into a series of specific questions about determinate beings. The question of origin, I suggest, must be understood consonantly with this first opening of mind. For this question is not first about determinate beings and their determinate relations to other beings, even to a supposedly highest, most real determinate being, the *ens realissimum*, said to be the first cause of all determinate beings. Rather this question concerns the coming to be of beings in the between: not their coming to be as determinate, relative to their antecedent, determinate causes or sources, but their coming to be at all, simply as being rather than nothing. Not what they are, but that they are at all, is the marvel for metaphysical mindfulness. The question of origin is not about coming to be in the sense of determination, but about coming to be as *that it is at all*—that beings are in being at all rather than nothing.

Of course, this question is meaningless if being is exhausted by determinate beings, and if mind is only concerned with the determinate cognition of definite things. We have already seen variously in Part I that neither being, the between, nor mindfulness can be so defined or confined. The question of the origin of the determinate is in excess of the determinate itself. When the indeterminate astonishment asks about the origin, it seeks some sense of this "more." For that reason the question only makes its proper sense if metaphysical thinking is renewed by agapeic astonishment and incited by the second indeterminate perplexity, beyond all determinate knowing.

Needless to say, I am not advocating that we shun all articulate determinacy in favor of some mute formlessness. The response I propose will be admittedly speculative, in the sense of transcending the determinate given. Inevitably it runs risks in extending mind thus. But mindfulness as transcending is already this extension. Moreover, this speculative extension of mind will have the point of illuminating what it means to be *in the finite middle itself*. We particularly wonder what the original ground must be like, such that it gives rise to *irreducible plurality*. What must the origin be like, given the ontological character of the pluralized middle? What must it be like to make such a middle possible? Thus this speculative extension of mind cannot be *self-produced*, but must take its sights from its sense of the "more," as this is already defined in our account of the metaxological between. My response will not be an "answer" posing as some absolute determinate cognition. It will be in terms of the way of transcendence, relative to the movement of thinking from metaphysical metaphors to the hyperbole of the ultimate. I also add that it will not be indefinite, since the fourfold sense of being will serve to guide determinately our philosophical passage along this way.

Many dismiss metaphysics just because, like a child, it asks the "big questions," the seemingly impossible questions. I cannot concur with this dismissal, insofar as I find mindfulness to be animated by agapeic astonishment and indeterminate perplexity.[1] The opening of metaphysical mindfulness, and its rebirth after determinate knowing, cannot be fixed just to this thing or that; rather it extends to an often vague sense of being as a whole. Our purpose must be to think through that sense. This will not entail, as with someone like Comte, the development of positive science as an advance away from an indefinite beginning towards determinate knowing. The metaphysician listens to the child. The virgin mind is often alert to the world in astonishment, as the strange thereness of being presents itself. Its innocent ontology may be lost later, but the metaphysician never loses it entirely. And it can be reborn. Otherwise the animating source of metaphysical thinking is neglected and atrophies.

I need, however, to state some other preliminary delimitations. The question of the origin does not primarily respect the question: What is X? Or even Why is this X such and such? Or even Why does X come to be thus? It is in *another* dimension to the hypotheses of physical cosmology, all of which remain in the domain of determinate cognition. Nor is the question one concerning a beginning *in* time, where we argue back and forth about the world's eternity, understood as endless time, or its determinate beginning in a defi-

---

1. If readers cannot abide speculative metaphysics, and still want to read on, they should skip this and succeeding chapters. I cannot guarantee they will find the familar middle later, but they will perhaps find aspects of a more familar middle. But, of course, I think that the familiar middle risks loss of mindfulness of the astonishing and perplexing middle, as I indicated in chapter 5. In my view speculative metaphysics at its best fights against this loss. And if the philosophers of difference cannot open themselves to the difference of speculative philosophy, one wonders what this says about such philosophies of difference. How different are they to the totalizing philosophies of the same they like to lash?

nite time. For instance, Kant's treatment of the first antinomy remains entirely at this level, contracting the question of origin to the world's beginning, or endless persistence, in time—time itself understood in terms of a notion of infinity as an endless series or succession. At *this* level, the so-called big bang theory of contemporary cosmology points to a *determinate* beginning in time. And, of course, this theory is perhaps compatible with endless oscillations between expansion and contraction, hence open to a qualified sense of no one beginning in endless time, but rather repeated beginnings and endings.

Why does the question of origin refer the issue to another dimension? Because endless time or a determinate temporal beginning both presuppose the *that it is* of *something* already being there in being. And this is true, even if that *something* is the very extraordinary *something*—namely, the so-called singularity. The question of origin—Why any *that it is* at all?—is prior to the question of beginning in that determinate sense. The origin, we might say, is not in becoming but of becoming—becoming that itself is granted as a source of prodigal proliferation and heterogenization. We are referred to what is traditionally called *eternity*, but not at all in the sense of endless time. The question to be asked is whether becoming as source of pluralization points to this *other origin*. This is why the present chapter will be followed by a chapter on creation, understood in its proximity to becoming as the second source that issues from the first origin.

This question of first origin extends indeterminately to the whole of being as given. Why being at all? Why being in its inescapable press? Why at all this all-pervasive insistence of being that cannot be conjured away into nothing? Why at all this surrounding and infiltrating and invading and erupting presence of beings in their sheer being-there? The pervasive insistence of the being of beings stuns thought first into astonishment, then into the perplexed question: Why being at all, why not nothing? This is an old, never answered, ever renewed question. It will never go away, because the enigma of being will never oblige us with its disappearance. Nor will human beings, as long as we are what we are, be ever anything but an indeterminate question to being. Leibniz, Schelling, Heidegger, to name but a few, are altogether right to insist on the question.

Not surprisingly, this indeterminate astonishment has often been articulated in the myth that, of course, tends predominantly to deal with origins in terms of divine powers. Myths are religious tales of origins. They imaginatively concretize this indeterminate astonishment into the form of a divine story. This does not mean that all myths are on a par. Clearly, we require hermeneutical discernment with respect to myth. This means that our speculation will have to be mediated critically, both in terms of the fourfold understanding of being, and the metaphysical metaphors consonant with it. What this means will be more evident in the sequel. But we cannot just dismiss myth scientifically as the immature, not to say infantile mind that modern

science has at last outgrown. We never outgrow myth, as we will never outgrow metaphysics. Why? Because we will never completely succeed in turning the indeterminate astonishment into completely determinate knowing.
Moreover, if there is an "answer" to the *second* indeterminate perplexity, it
too must be beyond determinate cognition. Myth may be imaginative metaphysics, but properly understood this can be its power, not its poverty. Nor
will the imagination of the origin, whether mythic or metaphysical, ever be
completely translated into its correlative determinate cognition. Metaphysical thinking is a different thinking of the origin as other, which always remains to be thought again, even in being thought.

Mindfulness, Transcendence, and Finitude

I must say something more about the arising of the question, and something preliminary about the way it points us. Mindfulness, in its indeterminate self-transcendence, outstrips the determinacy of finite things, even as it
delves deeply into their inherent intricacy. We meet obstacles at every stage
of this self-transcendence. At each stage, there is a skepticism and a doubt to
be overcome. Relative to cognition of finite things and processes, we have to
surmount our own ignorance. We have to discipline the mind to close attention to the characteristic being of things. Inevitably, this discipline of finite
thought will tend to consume the mind. We will go no further, and indeed
give ourselves good reasons why not to go any further. Reason can become
extremely busy in thinking up reasons why mind ought to rest content with
well-founded knowing about finite determinate beings and processes. Complex skeptical arguments will lay their traps for any renewed surge of mind's
self-transcendence. Thus Hume would trip mind on the slippery slope of concepts without sense-impressions, and consign the tomes of metaphysics and
theology to the flames—an empiricist auto-da-fé. Kant too will be troubled,
but yet be unable to deny the surge of self-transcending mind. He will insist
that this surge be suspicious of itself; and yet the surge will not cease.

The empiricist auto-da-fé, or the testing fires of critique, may seem to
burn to ash the bird of metaphysics, but this bird is a phoenix and rises again
from its immolation. For finite being proves to be not self-explanatory. It is
there, a contingency. It is, but it might not be. There is no inherent necessity
for its being-there. How then think its coming to be at all? How interpret this
contingency?

If we follow the empiricist hermeneutics of contingency, we dissolve the
question into matters of habit and custom. In my view this is to displace the
question, not to face either it, or the full implication of the skepticism that
should follow. Or suppose we think contingency along the lines of an absurdist
existentialism: contingent being is a surd, beyond which thinking cannot pass.
And yet the existential self either is nauseated by this contingency (Sartre), or

revolts against it. Why nausea or revolt at all, if being just is? What has been sought and not found, what expectation disappointed? Or perhaps the nausea might just be the sickness of spirit contacted by the blocking of transcendence as other, and by the dungeoning of self-transcendence in meaningless immanence. In any case, the revolt against the absurd is mere whistling in the dark, if the dark itself is the ultimate. For then we too, and our bold songs, are the senseless issue of the dark.

Metaxological mindfulness offers a different hermeneutics of contingency as a vector towards transcendence as other. In this view, contingency is not self-produced or self-explaining; it is given to be, and as given in being, points to its being given from an origin that is other to it. Its givenness is not a surd before which we come to full stop; its being is presented as gift, in the marvel of its created singularity. Just that marvel of singularity will have to be taken into account in any account of origin. For it is not abstract being in general that serves as a pointer towards transcendence as other. The proliferation of singularity in coming to be, the prodigious pluralization of rich particularity in the between, show forth the ontological foison of finitude. That very foison throws into relief the metaphysically threadbare perspective of empiricist contingency and existential absurdism.

I admit that there is a kind of *leap* of mind beyond this foison towards the origin as grounding. Does this concede the game to irrationalism? This would be too simple. For the self-transcending of mind is not just self-mediating; rather its intermediation with what is other *always communicates across a gap* between self and other. Such communication across a gap obtains even more in relation to ultimate transcendence, especially if the latter is in excess to all determinate being. Discontinuity, disproportion, rupture, heterogeneity are now of the essence. If there is a leap then, the standard charge of irrationalism does not quite come to grips with the issue. I would go further and say that mind as self-transcending and communicating is *always* leaping. But it can look when it leaps; it can behold as it leaps. Mindfulness is not always a snail crawling slowly on ground; it is sometimes a dancer launching into the air, now here, now there, briefly uplifted with a glorious liberty.

And, of course, if I leap, I may have to run up to a point of launching beyond. The leap then can be carried by the momentum of our self-transcending. What would such a "run up" be? It cannot be, in my view, any syllogism to capture transcendence in concepts, such as we might find in a lightweight, even if logically impeccable, interpretation of the traditional "proofs" of God. On the contrary, it may be a thinking that concentrates the *struggle of a lifetime* of disciplined reflection on the being of what presents itself to us in the between. There need be no merely absurd leap, even though the most thoughtful leap is perilous and fraught with uncertainty.

The very *suspiciousness* of mind about *itself* can prove to be agent of mind's own kindling and self-surpassing. For mind as self-transcending knows itself as discontent with finite limits; its discontent with itself, its radical inquietude can be the spur that pricks it to leap at such limits. And even in self-transcending, one may find it hard to shake the suspicion that we are secretly sustained in leaping by that towards which we leap. The indeterminate perplexity returns in its skepticism of all limited forms of knowing and being. None of these finally answer to its indeterminate quest. We would go further. Then comes our greatest skepticism: Do we overreach ourselves, but only into nothing?

And in a very important sense, nothing seems to be there. Pressed to the edge of nothing, why then do we torture ourselves with perplexities about something "more"? Is this adolescent extravagance again, immature penchant for the imponderable questions? It may be; it need not be. For even on this dangerous edge, the marvel of being haunts us, despite our amnesia when we rest content with the familiar middle. There are ghosts that haunt and that cannot be laid to rest. This haunting is at stake in what before I spoke of as posthumous mind. Nor is ghost the right word, since the marvel is a thereness with the solid substance of the living, ineluctability of being. This we behold in its astonishing diversity, variety beyond mastery. The world teems with things, throngs with beings, great, small, ugly, sweet, on and beneath the earth, things soaring above, things exuberant or menacing in the unknown seas. The world as given is an excess. It is much, too much, too much for us. And *this* excess conspires to make mind wonder again about the origin.

And so we have excess twice, excess redoubled. There is the human being as excess—we are self-transcendence that will not rest, intentionally infinite even in being actually finite, an opening, not just to this being or that, but to being *simpliciter*, and the community of being. Then there is the world as an excess. Creation is prodigal, a lavish spendthrift, nothing miserly; it gives and gives; it renews even when it takes into death; it is a fire that burns and is rekindled in its burning. Metaphysical mind stands at the midpoint of juncture where these two exceeding realities meet. At the midpoint the second indeterminate perplexity is precipitated: What gives this plural excess? Out of what origin comes this "too much"? What other excess do these two excesses betoken? As dynamic processes, are not both excesses already vectors of transcendence, already pointers beyond themselves to the beyond in an ultimate respect, the absolute origin?

In the light of such perplexity, I underscore that the question of the origin is not posed simply out of lack, whether in us or in the world. It is not compensation for the tears of finitude. I do not deny lack and lamentation, nor their metaphysical import, but there is a deeper impetus to the perplexity. Metaphysics need not be a running away from humankind and world; it may be a running towards what is other, carried by a dynamic surplus of being that looks for the origin of all superfluity. It is not, as Nietzsche claims, revenge that asks the question. It may be gratitude for the gratuity of being, its givenness as surplus. Metaphysics can give words to a mode of thanks. Lack and lamentation themselves raise for us the possibility that gratitude is a more ultimate response.

What is implicit in the foregoing can be put more explicitly in the following preliminary statement of three different senses of transcendence. The reader may find it helpful to keep their differences in mind. It is the third that is primarily at stake in this chapter.

T1: The transcendence of *beings* as other in exteriority. Among the important ways of defining these beings, we find the distinction between possibility and actuality. These entities are real as realized possibilities of being. They are contingent since they might possibly not be at all. Their realization as beings is not only due to their determination of possibility, but to their being made possible at all. Especially relative to the latter, they provoke the question: What makes possible both their possibility, as well as their actuality? For it is not just that they actualize possibility, but as contingent they possibly might not be at all. Hence one asks: What makes possible the possibility of their being at all?

T2: The transcendence of *self-being*, self-transcendence. The meaning of possibility is here realized in interiority rather than determined externally. There is possibility as freedom, as self-determination, as the promise of free creativity. In addition to the above question, there is here the further question: Is this self-transcendence merely an anomalous overreaching into emptiness, or a genuine self-surpassing towards transcendence as other?

T3: The transcendence of the *origin*—this would be *transcendence itself*, not as the exterior, not as the interior, but as the superior. This would be the *huper*, the above. The way of transcendence as hyperbolic throws us towards it. Since it is in excess of determinate being, as its original ground, it would be beyond the above doublet of possibility and reality. It would be what we might call the *possibilizing source* of both possibility and realization; but it could not be just a possibility, nor indeed a determinate realization of possibility. It would have to be real possibilizing power, in a manner more original and other than possibility and realization. It would have to be "possibilizing" beyond determinate possibility, and "realizing" beyond all determinate realization.

The question it provokes is: Is there no possibility that it not be? Is it to be? If it is not under any finite category of the possible, if it is above, *huper*, *über*, is it yet the original power to be, or the original power of being at its most ultimate? What must this real possibilizing power be, if it is such as to give rise to finite being as *other* to itself, and hence as making possible the realizing of the other two kinds of transcendence.

For the third sense of transcendence is not to be identified with any projection onto the ultimate other of the first two senses. If we are to speak of third transcendence as other, it will be *through* the finitude/infinitude of the first two. It will not be through self-projection onto the other, but by agapeic transcendence towards the ultimate other. I think this can be done less misleadingly relative to the second sense, self-transcendence, and in a manner that calls into question any objectification of third transcendence. But to obviate what is misleading in self-projection onto the other, self-transcendence will have to be thought agapeically, not just erotically, metaxologically, not just dialectically. Nor does this imply any neglect of the first sense of transcendence. There is no objectification (T1) or subjectification (T2) of third transcendence (T3). But second transcendence (T2), in its ineradicable recalcitrance to complete objectification, is pointed beyond objectness and subjectness to transobjective and transsubjective transcendence (T3). It is also pointed beyond this by the recalcitrance to complete objectification of the *that it is at all* of first transcendence (T1).

Univocity, Origin, and the One

Let us now make our best effort to think of origin, guided by the fourfold sense of being. So we commence with univocity. But immediately we seem to run into great difficulty. Simply put: there seems no way we can speak *directly* of the origin. The paradox is: were we able to speak directly, we could not speak at all. Absolutely univocal speech seem indistinguishable from absolute silence. For if we were one with the origin, we would not *be as other*, and hence could not speak as ourselves, nor of the origin itself as other.

How get beyond this? If direct univocity is impossible, we must try *indirection*. Is this a defect? Not necessarily. It may be a necessary expression of our intermediate condition. We are not, nor can we ever be, identical with the origin. The origin itself is other. If it gives beings their being by way of excess of creative power, it is in some sense *always other* to the beings given being. The difficulties we face are extraordinary. Plato says: it is hard to find the father of all, and once found, impossible to tell. As usual, Plato is wise. We have to speak out of the middle, and in terms of its richest sense of being.

Despite the above difficulty, and because being and oneness seem inextricable, it seems understandable enough that the most immediate thought of the origin would name it as absolute unity. The origin is the One. Why is this understandable? Beings are, and are as multiple; moreover, our being in their midst often strikes us as the confusion of a welter. Inevitably we ask: Does this welter hold together? It seems to, but how? In answer, mindfulness seeks to transcend the middle to think an aboriginal source that precedes, underlies, and embraces plurality. We think the origin in univocal terms. In addition, there is the striking fact that the "is" of beings is incontrovertible. It is everywhere and in all. This inescapable universality of the "is" suggests a sameness to all things that is the *principium* holding them together.

I do not want to say that this train of thought is simply false. I do want to say that the thought of the origin as univocal cannot be the final word. There are hits on the truth here, but the hits also produce inevitable misses. Of course, the view at issue can be found throughout the metaphysical tradition. Thus the question of being frequently concerns what meaning can be given to the being of the multiplicity of beings. *Hen to pan*, one the all, is one of the ancient answers.

Consider Parmenides' answer as one of the first and most radical. There are a number of points here, logical as well as ontological. I suggest that univocal mind is forcefully operative in the Parmenidean approach in its strong insistence on the principle of excluded middle. Either A is, or A is not. Between being and nonbeing there is a gulf of necessary exclusion. I attribute this to univocal mind because the insistence is that being is being and nothing but being. Outside of being there is nothing. There is nothing but being. There is no "outside."

And so the logical point shades into the ontological point: apart from being there is nothing. However, the saying of the latter puts pure univocity in jeopardy; in *even mentioning* the nothing, we risk insulting absolute univocity. Why? In naming the nothing we give it spurious being; we speak as if it were something, as if it somehow were being. Since this is contradictory, we must dismiss such talk; we must be silent about the nothing. Instead we must affirm original being to be an absolutely homogeneous principle. Nothing is outside; nor are there any gaps within it that might negate its pure continuity with itself. Parmenidean being is the origin as radically univocal. There is nothing but this all-embracing unity of being. Beings hold together as beings because there is nothing but original being.

I agree about the incontrovertability of being, and its peculiar inescapable universality. But we must seek a more articulated understanding of these. No philosopher has been satisfied with the extreme nature of Parmenides' answer. The fact is that Parmenidean monism can be seen as the truly logical conclusion of a totally univocal thinking. All is one, all is sameness, and this is said at such an extreme that logically we should *fall silent*. We should not even explain our silence. Aristotle makes this last point against the extreme Heracliteans, like Cratylus. But one can make the same point against those philosophers at the opposite pole. The absolute univocity of Parmenidean being, in its apotheosis of logic, should lead to the death of logos in a metaphysical silence that logically should not even explain itself. For to explain itself, even in accord with the most strict logical principles, is already to reinstate plurality, hence heterogeneity, and hence to fall outside the pure self-continuity of the absolute unity.

Plotinus is here more consistent in saying that to get to the One we have to go beyond, *epekeina nous* and *epistēmē*. We do not get to the origin by any mode of delimited thought, either dianoetic or noetic, because such modes are marked by internal multiplicity, and hence not at the One. A different movement of mind is necessary, an ecstasis that carries the soul outside of itself. This perhaps is one variation on what I call *thought thinking what is other to thought*. The soul is no longer itself; it is other, it is at the One. Of course, Plotinus in his very philosophizing places himself outside of the One. For he speaks, he writes, he tries to understand for himself and to communicate with his fellows. If so, properly put, philosophy is a fall or degeneration. Perhaps it is even an evil. The middle out of which we speak is removed from the One. Were we truly to think the origin, there would be no more thought, no more philosophy. The attained origin would be the end of philosophy.

The neophyte metaphysicians may not find it hard to detect logical difficulties in this appeal to the unity of the origin. Despite this—and the neophyte—there is a real truth at stake here. The major question concerns the *unity* of the origin, and how to speak it. I suggest that, in fact, our very removal from the origin may be the most important point we need to interpret, and interpret not as a defect of being, but as positively constitutive of the being of finite entities. Our removal from the origin, our otherness and being outside, must be consistent with the origin itself, as giving rise to finite beings other than itself. Put concisely: Given our otherness, what must its otherness, as other to us, be like? The view I propose will more fully unfold as we move towards the metaxological sense of being.

I do not think we should disguise the fact that our efforts to speak the origin lead to a kind of *inevitable failure* in our saying. Yet we can think of this failure as something glorious. The very beyondness of the origin may solicit our consent and celebration. Just so, something important may be manifest in the very *strains* appearing when we try to speak univocally about the origin. Univocal mind seeks the seamless consistency of a completely self-coherent *logos*. In fact, its insistence on logical univocity either produces the silence of *logos*, and hence of its own univocal mind; or else it produces an equivocity in which the ambiguities of being reassert themselves. We have already noted the first point, but the second is evident in the inescapability of saying itself: Plotinus speaks, and knows that his speaking of the One beyond all saying is necessarily equivocal. All his reminders and qualifications are efforts to inoculate the reader, and perhaps himself, from the infections of this necessary equivocity. Even Parmenides cannot help but say the "not," and thereby he invariably subverts the pure homogeneous unity he wants to communicate. He is reduced to *commanding* us not to think the "not." But this command—and here is the unwanted sting—is a "no-saying," and hence is itself a form of the "not." There seems no escape from ambiguity into the pure univocity of the origin.

It is true that there are other appeals to original being, both metaphysical and scientific, ancient and modern, which try to alleviate this equivocal condition, and yet they remain enmeshed in it. For example, Plato's recourse to the *eidē* is an appeal to original being; the *eidē* are the originals, the images of which are the particular things in becoming. The being of the *eidos* is original, uniform, *auto kath auto*, simply itself and nothing but itself, beyond the equivocity of the particulars in becoming. Here the univocal sense of original being departs from Parmenides' extreme form, in giving qualified being to otherness, becoming, and the many. One recalls also the proposed "parricide" of Parmenides in the *Sophist*. Plato is standardly presented as entoiled in dualism, yet his sense of the doubleness of time and eternity may augur a nonreductive approach to the transcendence of the origin—namely, the impossibility of reducing to a univocal unity the different orders of the origin itself and finite being.

Similarly, in the modern scientific enterprise (as we saw especially in chapters 2 and 3 in Part I), univocal mind takes the form of a mathematization of nature. This mathematization will strip all ambiguity from being and reconstruct the given as a structure of calculative mind. The equivocity of the qualitative world is reduced to its "originals" in the primary qualities of mass, velocity, figure. . . . The glory of creation, in the flesh of its sensuous beauty, is made the shadow of a powerful, projective subjectivity, a shadow hovering over the neutral skelton of mathematical structure. These originals, the primary qualities, are not Platonic *eidē*, but they are still abstractions of univocal mind, constructs of calculative mind.

Yet consider the fact that Newton was troubled by the question of the ultimate explanation of beings, and made appeal to God. Whether his particular recourse is satisfactory is not now the issue, but that his mind was *significantly troubled* in its search for explanation, so as to be driven to make the appeal. His successors will declare that there is no calculation of the origin, and that the origin ought not to enter the reckoning of any calculation. God will be dismissed from science. They are right in one sense: there is no calculation of the origin. But this is because the origin is not univocal in any sense amenable to mathematization. Nor need we take it a sign of intellectual superiority *not* to be troubled by the question. Quite the contrary. Disregarding both agapeic astonishment and the second indeterminate perplexity, the declaration here is that scientific explanation must content itself, can content itself with the mathematical conceptualization of the regularities of given being. Why being is given at all, how being is given being, such questions will unjustly suffer the auto-da-fé of all metaphysical speculation.

Then the univocal mind will congratulate itself with having made an advance towards positive science and philosophy. In fact, the vector of mind's self-transcendence will have been bent back from its spontaneous upsurge towards the absolute original. Metaphysically speaking, the scientistic advance is a *crooked reversion* to finite being. In its polite moods, scientism may enjoin metaphysical silence. But no polite silence will hide from metaphysical mind the mindlessness here at work relative to the astonishing and perplexing being-there of beings. One might claim instead that, say, the metaphysical myth of Plato's *Timaeus* is truer to mind's perplexity about the origin. It is also metaphysically honest in its posing of the question of the *goodness* of the source. But we still have a long way to go before we can speak of the good.

In brief, the univocalizing of the origin can lead to a kind of metaphysical idolatry: the image we exploit to make transcendence determinate risks, without properly knowing it, an objectification of what cannot be objectified. Hence there is a loss of what escapes objectification. And this very loss influences a turning away from transcendence as other towards the middle, except this has now been reconceptualized as a dedivinized aggregate of finite entities. To fix thus univocally the origin, is thus to unfix the origin. There is an occlusion of transcendence in the very effort to pin it down. In addition, respect for its otherness as other evaporates, as does humility before what remains unmastered. When astonishment has grown feeble, and searching perplexity become tired, or irritated with itself, the enigma of the origin becomes brusquely disregarded, as if it were the least mysterious. And so it goes: metaphysical and scientistic univocity collude in the domestication of ultimate transcendence.

Antinomy, Origin, and the One

It should be evident that, if we are to continue to think the origin, we must go beyond its univocalization. Moreover, this going beyond is drawn further by certain *antinomies* emergent relative to the univocal One. I now propose to explore this, in light of the equivocal sense of being.

Appeals to the unity of the origin suggest that there is more to being than simply the universal impermanence of becoming. This appeal is not wrong. The universal impermanence does suggest a source as itself beyond the sheer impermanence of passing away. The impermanence of coming to be suggests its source as an origin of coming to be, an origin that is not itself a thing that comes to be, nor a being within the process of the universal coming to be.

Here is the antinomy: even if we want to say that the origin of coming to be possesses some kind of "unity" with itself, this "unity" cannot be univocal. Why so? Because, such a univocal unity would be hard to distinguish from inert self-sameness. And were the latter the "unity" of the origin, the origin could *not* be an origin at all. For an origin is *that out of which something comes to be*. But if something comes to be *out* of an origin, that origin must necessarily have the power to originate *beyond* itself; hence it cannot be an inert self-sameness. In a word: a univocal origin could not originate anything beyond itself. Hence if there is a "unity" to the origin, if the origin is one, this "one" must be more than univocal, it must be more than unity with itself. Paradoxically, the origin must be an originative One that is more than one.

To speak of *the One that is more than one* seems to be a contradiction in logic. I call it an antinomy, for it is from the thought of the original One itself that something other arises: it seems that if we think of an original One, we must think the original One as more than one. How can a One be one, and *more* than one? Surely one is one, and nothing but one, nothing more, nothing less? I will anticipate the answer and respectfully suggest: the origin as One is the *indeterminate* one. The One that is more than the One is other than the one.

A howl of derision will arise that this is execrable verbiage. To say nothing else, surely the idea of an indeterminate one is unintelligible? I ask for patience. What is said is not meaningless, though it does strain some normal presuppositions of meaning. Fuller elaboration, demanding concentrated mindfulness, is required. I want to suggest now that, paradoxically, it is the equivocal sense of being that begins more adequately to help us think of the One beyond univocal unity.

Why so? Because the equivocal sense of being puts the emphasis on difference rather than sameness. One cannot univocally bespeak pure univocal unity, for every identity is the marker of difference. To be is to be different, in the active sense of to be differentiated. The identity of a being is marked internally by its own self-differentiation, as well as externally by its distinction from other beings. Unities and identities hence are provisional formations of being in a network of differential relations. Nothing is purely in itself; beings are, but they are as differentiated in and by a process of becoming. Difference is not a static marker that univocal mind can tag with its categorial stickers; difference is inherently dynamic. Differences are themselves the effect or production of a differentiating process. This process is a dynamic origination that is irreducible to any univocal unity.

The question then is: Is this dynamic differentiation the same as the origin? Here I think we must distinguish this differentiating process from a more primordial sense of origin. That is, the differentiation process is a generating source of coming to be *this* and *that*; but the ultimate origin is the origin of this source, referring to the coming to be at all of beings, that they are in being at all rather than nothing, not that they are such and such. Let me elaborate.

Beings are, beings are given, beings are given in a process of differentiating. We might call this process *becoming*. I will have more to say on becoming later, relative to finite creation. For now let us grant provisionally that the *dunamis* of this processive becoming indicates the dynamic nature of being. In becoming being reveals itself as original power. Power here implies no dialectic of dominance and submission; power implies ability to be or do. Becoming as process concretizes, in its differentiated articulation of things, this original power to be. I admit a certain circularity here with respect to the definition of being in terms of the original power to be. But this need not be a vicious circularity. I relate it to the incontrovertibility of being.[2] That is to say, being cannot be defined without invoking being itself. The crucial question concerns the nature of the invocation. I do not think the invocation has to be a mere univocal tautology; rather the equivocal doubling may point towards the *dunamis*, the originative power of being in becoming. And this is the crucial point: it is with respect to this *dunamis* that we are driven to think of the origin, in more original terms as *radically originative*. In drawing our attention to the differentiating process or to the determining of beings in terms of a network of differential relations, the equivocal sense also draws attention to the need to understand the origin as genuinely *originative*, something the univocal emphasis on self-sameness does not get into proper view.

How can we make less scandalous the equivocation implied by the phrase: *the One that is more than the one*. For to repeat: univocally and mathematically, one is one is one; how can one be more than one? The equivocation, however, can be made less opprobrious if the One is a one that can originate beyond itself, or originate something other than itself. Such a One would have to be itself and yet more than itself, in itself and yet beyond itself. Again I suggest that we must take our bearings from the nonunivocal sense of being at play in any process of becoming. Consider. When a being becomes, it becomes other than its present identity; it is itself and yet other; yet in becoming other it also is becoming itself, in a manner that more fully realizes its power to be; hence in its being more than itself, it is itself again, in the sense of being more truly itself.

From the standpoint of a univocal logic, this dynamic process of becoming can only seem like an equivocation. This is true: it cannot be completely grasped in terms of a univocal logic. Process cannot be encompassed by the swift flipping of still snapshots of static instantaneity. We need a logos that itself is dynamic, in order to think alongside, and in rapport with the process of becoming. A mindfulness awakened to the finesse of equivocity can be truer to this truth of becoming. The differential nuances of equivocity draw us closer to genuine origination. There is no calculation of the origin, I said, and I repeat. But a mind finessed to the equivocations of being has a better chance of divining the origin in the differences of becoming.

---

2. The above "circle" is also related to the doubling suggested by the affirmation "Being is"—being appears twice over, suggesting the creative redoubling of being in becoming. Beings are; we are; that beings are is incontrovertible; we close our eyes and try to conjure being away, but we *are* in this meontological conjuration; the press of thereness crowds in on us, even when thought shuts out the press; we cannot shutter ourselves from being, for its press is as much within thought, as without; moreover, we do not first thematize this impress, but live it, live in it.

We need metaphysical finesse here, precisely because there are multiple ambiguities to be navigated, and there is no certain rule or criterion to guide us through these turbulent seas. How can one divine the origin in and through the equivocations of becoming? The major rock we have to circumnavigate is a certain wrong reversion to univocity, in our recoil from all unsettling indeterminacy.

This is a major temptation in the tradition of metaphysics, and amounts to the following. The univocal mind is rightly determined to make intelligible sense of things. In addition, its standard of intelligibility is that being be determinate, that mind and saying be also determinate. To be is to be determinate; to think and speak intelligibly is to be determinate. How then does a process of becoming look in light of this standard? It looks unintelligible, or at least lacking in full intelligibility. A thing in a process of becoming is not fully determinate; it is not itself in a fully determinate way; becoming happens because an unfinished process has to be further determined; and hence there is always a constitutive indeterminacy in any process of becoming, or in any being marked by process. This indeterminacy can be taken to imply that any being in becoming is defective of full intelligibility. And this, regardless of an *orientation* to intelligibility; for after all, the process reaches for a completion wherein the indeterminate is fully determined. Perfect or perfected being must be completely determined. Perfect original being must be beyond all becoming.

This line of thinking leads to the return of the univocal origin, but now interpreted as *the end* suggested by the lack of equivocal becoming. It is not hard to find examples. Parmenides has only to be mentioned again. The many who are caught in becoming wander *double-headed*, he says; those who have passed beyond the portals of night and day see the changeless being, beyond all doubleness, all ontological duplicity, in a total unity of spherical completeness. Likewise, traditional turnings from time to static eternity often embody a similar return of the univocal origin. Eternity is everything that time is not: simple, at one with itself, changeless, resting in itself; time is multiform and discordant with itself, ever mutating, ever restless. We are tempted by a metaphysical flight from time into a static and entirely determinate eternity.

What are some of the important arguments against this view? First transcendence is defined in purely oppositional terms. That is, univocal mind produces a dualism of time and eternity to buffer itself against the terrors of time. These terrors are the visitation of all finite being with death. And indeed becoming *is* double: through its process things come to be; through the same process things pass out of being. Passing out is filled with terror, for beings cling to the sweetness of being, simply being, the gift. Metaphysically we cannot suppress terror at this doubleness. But an oppositional dualism of time and eternity does not mediate this doubleness, but creates a new dyad, with new terrors of its own. If flight to the origin beyond time negates time, then time itself becomes negative, and the becoming we had hoped to ground in the beyond now becomes even more radically ungrounded. If between time and eternity there is no relation beyond an oppositional dualism, then we entrench a *deeper sense of opposition* to time and the equivocations of being.

Moreover, this dualistic thinking of the "beyond" has the paradoxical result of making the transcendent *unavailable* for divination in the world of given being. The dualism sunders time and eternity, becoming and the origin. But the whole matter concerns the *interplay* of these two, not their mutual repulsion. This interplay requires a notion of each that goes beyond a reductive sense of their togetherness and an antagonistic sense of their difference. One must say that eternity as origin is here asserted purely in the mode of negation: eternity is what time is not; the "not" speaks the gulf of difference and transcendence; but since there is to be no "not," why then this inordinate appeal to the negation of given being? The grounding of given being cannot be effected by the negation of given being.

There is also the difficulty that a completely determinate origin could not effect the origination of finite being. There would be no reason for it to do so. It could not be the One that is more than one. There could be no creative self-othering, or creation of the different, in absolutely selfsame eternity. Univocal flight beyond the equivocations of becoming does not divine the origin of becoming. It negates becoming as a defective condition of being, but in this negation it cuts the ground from under the finessed approach to an origin that is not static, determinate eternity. The negation produces, in fact, the *nonrelatedness* of origin and creation. For if the eternal origin is purely in and for itself, then its power to originate what is other, and its relativity to what is so originated as other, is undermined. But it is just this interplay in the middle, this relatedness even in irreducible otherness, that we have to think, not think away.

Notice I am not enjoining, as it were, a Nietzschean rejection of Platonic eternity. The Nietzschean rejection reverses the terms of the traditional dualism, but the reversal is still not released from dualistic thinking. For this rejection derides metaphysical perplexity as only the ontological cowardice of the so-called metaphysicians of presence. It instead exults in the equivocations of being. The dualism of time and eternity is reversed, with lack attributed to eternity, and plenitude to the process of becoming. This reversal of the dualism also produces a negation of transcendence: one side of the double is chopped. It displaces transcendence as other, and replaces it with transcendence in immanence.

Will to power is Nietzsche's name for transcendence in immanence. We can call it the Dionysian origin. The Dionysian origin is concretized in the process of becoming and the self-becoming of things. Nietzsche's name for the origin demands serious thought, but that is not the present point.[3] The point is to interpret the origin without falsifying the ontological richness of becoming as differentiating process. Such an interpretation must seek the origin of this richness in a *richer*, not more indigent, source, and must stay true to the middle between these two, the milieu wherein ontological perplexity is precipitated. For it is there that the perplexity must be addressed. We need to think through the antinomic tension of time and eternity. This desideratum cannot be met by either the Nietzschean or Platonic options in their current standard conception.

In fact, to think the origin as plenitude we will have to go beyond univocity and equivocity, and the dualistic opposition between them. Univocity too easily suppresses difference; equivocity too quickly exults in difference. The first can try to overcome doubleness and multiplicity by stifling it; the second can accentuate difference in a manner that reinstates dualistic opposition in another mode of antithetical, or antinomic thinking. Neither has a rich enough sense of the mediation of differences. Absolute unity tries to bind plurality as sheer opposition, but sheer opposition can return with the vengeance of an unbound equivocity. Metaphysical finesse is needed to mediate the equivocations of being, as well as to hold on to the proper modes of unity, interplay, and community.

We advance along this latter line if we begin to see becoming as a process in which beings both are and also are not. No being is fully coincident with itself, and hence none is fully itself; and yet each is itself, and is itself not as a defective condition of being. That is, beings in becoming are not mere potentialities, understood as the absence of actuality. We might say that beings are *promises*. Their present being promises more than it currently delivers. But to be a promising being is to be in an essentially affirmative condition. A promising being is the promise of more, but the more is there now, already at work, in redeeming itself as promise—or betraying itself, or being betrayed.

Here is the inescapable equivocity. Becoming is the promise of the origin, a promise that makes us ponder the possibility of a two-way interplay of origin and becoming. The promise of being is inscribed in becoming as a process of positive othering. The metaphysicians in flight feel that becoming betrays the promise of being. And they are right up to a point, but in a sense that they do not properly articulate. For since becoming is a promise, it is not the absolute origin or end. It is the mistaken demand of absoluteness from it that engenders their ontological disappointment, and their turning against what "betrays" them. The promise is read too univocally—that is, it is not properly read at all. In truth, every promise is double: it may be redeemed, it may be betrayed. A promise that

---

3. See my paper "Rethinking the Origin: Hegel and Nietzsche," in *Hegel and Hermeneutics*, ed. Shaun Gallagher (Albany: SUNY Press, to appear).

could only be redeemed is not a promise but a determined necessity. A promise that could only be betrayed is no promise but a malicious fatality or a fated straying.

The major point, however, is that the promise of becoming reinserts a *creative indeterminacy* at the heart of being. The doubleness of the "is" and "is not" may be like the strife of Heraclitus that he says is the father of all things. But Heraclitus is wrong if he thinks that strife is the father of all fathers. What he calls the father is an offspring of the origin. The origin is, so to say, a father/mother beyond this father. Put otherwise: the constitutive indeterminacy of becoming is the promise of an indeterminate originative source out of which becoming is generated. And so the affirmative ambiguity of being as becoming points to the indeterminacy of the origin. We now must consider why this is not an indefiniteness, less than the determinacy of univocal being, but a *creative excess of plenitude*, beyond all univocal selfsameness.

But let me summarize: the origin is not the univocal one, but the One that is more than the one. The One that is more than the one is an indeterminate one. The indeterminate One, as we glean from divining the promise of becoming, is other with an otherness beyond all finite identification and othering. It is this never-to-be-completely-determined excess of creative plenitude.

The Dialectical One, The Erotic Origin

A din of commotion arises within. I hear voices of protest coming towards me, rising in me. Where have you been lately? Did you come down in the last shower? Do you not know that this is the end of the twentieth century? Do you not know, as everyone else has known for centuries, that you are not allowed to do metaphysics like *that*? Who do you think you are—the son of Plotinus or Aquinas or Hegel, or one of those? Assailed by a chorus of critics, I am stalled.

To philosophize like a Plotinus or an Aquinas or one of those—Is that a criticism? Or are we only allowed safely to write *on* them, with the scholarly authorization of historians of ideas, not write on the *same perplexities* they addressed? You will snort: *that* sort of thing is not done any more! But surely, I retort, *that* sort of posture is the death of philosophy? Who is dictating what the philosopher should or should not think? Nietzsche, or Heidegger, or one of those? Would that I were able to await my orders from the *Zeitgeist*, or its fashionable commentators. But alas, the "order" comes from nothing but one's ineluctable perplexity. And even if I do not do what I am told, I offer my critics a gift. Let them make me a whipping boy. I give the antimetaphysical police one more chance to exercise their inquisition.

I apologize. I am fighting back. Honest perplexity must be less pugnacious, even when irritated to impatience by stock obstacles. I confess I approach the matter with great trepidation. Do I know what I am talking about?

In a sense, no; in another sense, yes, so far as is humanly possible. I confess I can but try. Why? My understanding of being demands I do. Am I trying to escape being? I do not think so. I am seeking to come back to being, to see it otherwise, and hence perhaps as it truly is. Do I expose myself to the derision of analytical philosophers and deconstructionists? Very well. But I can do no other. The perplexity cannot be refused. The memory of original astonishment cannot be erased.

Are my voices of protest quietened? Not entirely, indeed perhaps never entirely. What then? But is not dialectic a way to deal with disquiet, without denying disquet? Let us see where this way leads.

The equivocal way can be said to generate ambiguities in our thinking of the origin, issuing in directly opposite results: first, the flight from time into static univocal eternity,[4] said to be the fixed beginning and end of time; second, the deconstruction of eternity in favor of time as a differentiating process, without beginning or end. I see dialectic as interpreting this ambiguity, by mediating the simplicity of univocal sameness and the diversity of equivocal difference. Equivocations must be mediated, not merely asserted, and mediated in a way more finessed than can be offered by any return of univocal mind. Dialectic takes us beyond univocity and equivocity into the middle between time and eternity, becoming and its origin. It opens up a thinking of the *interplay* of these two, with a concomitant redefinition of both time and eternity.

This opening takes place on more fronts than one. First, it occurs relative to the range of metaphysical mindfulness. The thinking self comes more into its own as restless self-transcendence. It comes to know its discontent with respect to the finite knowledge of determinate knowing. Mindfulness cannot be confined to this, that, or the other, which is not at all to disparage determinate knowing. Limit is equivocal, in that every limit as plotted is such as to place the plotter on *both* sides, and hence the limit in some manner is already transcended. This equivocation in limit is not negative. It opens up self-transcending mind as the divining power through which we seek to glean a better sense of the origin. It also hints at the possible ingression into time of the origin out of its otherness; or indeed the creation of the middle as the happening of being, creation from beyond the finite limit, as we live it after the origin.

Second, the opening also expands our understanding of the ontological richness of the given process of being. The inherent energy of being is at work in becoming, so in asking about the origin we are not seeking elsewhere. We are trying to think being at its deepest, to the ground down, where the deep down ground is not necessarily a being in any sense assimilable to finite

---

4. On the problems of time and eternity, see *Desire, Dialectic and Otherness*, chapter 4; also *Beyond Hegel and Dialectic*, chapter 1.

beings. Ground can be itself ungrounded, hence an abyss, as much as a source. It can be a foundation in the sense of a fund: a fund is a *fons*, a spring, a creative funding. What absolutely funds may not itself be funded. Finite being as process is a founding, itself the becoming of a transcending energy. Given being is not self-enclosed in some spatial limit that we could draw around it or that it draws around itself. The transcending of becoming images a more originary transcendence (T3 above), in becoming's own dynamic being-there.

Relative to the first opening, we find an increasing self-mediating. Thinkers mediate with the perplexing thereness, and the more articulate they become, the more they mediate some sense of their own being. Self-transcendence is also self-mediation. Relative to the second opening, becoming is not a formless indefinite continuing; it is a definite forming of the determinate; determinate beings are crystalized in their particularity in just this universal forming process. And this is not to deny the provisionality of the forming, since every formation will also be undone and dissolved. But in the happening of the between, within the extremes of coming to be and passing out of being, things are formed with their peculiar identities. Perhaps we should even say they are selved.

Self-mediation in becoming is to be found in the inner and the outer. A plurality of mediating beings converge on a middle and mingle there. The human being inhabits this middle mindfully. The upshot is that dialectic helps us see that every univocal unity is driven out beyond itself: there is no absolute selfsameness, either in things or in more fully self-mediating selves. To be dialectically is to be driven by, caught up in, driven beyond self in an ecstasis in the milieu of being. I suggest that this offers an image of dynamical being as ontologically rich, and in a form that can now be stated with some mindfulness of complex mediation. We do not now mutely gesture towards the marvel of thereness; we recognize that the marvel also includes extraordinary inner complexity and relatedness.

We might say that being as given in this milieu is in a state of dialectical ecstasy. I mean this in the sense that beings exist in standing out beyond themselves, and in so standing out, they enter into a relativity with what is beyond themselves, perhaps also coming to a self-relativity in an even more ultimate sense.[5] This dialectical ecstasy is not of this or of that; it is here, there, and everywhere; it is extraordinarily pluralized. Every entity, as coming to be and as passing away, is dynamized and caught up in an ecstasy of being wherein it becomes doubled: not univocal, not equivocal, but doubly defined—namely, as self-mediating *and* as intermediating with what is other

---

5. As has often been pointed out, the root of existence is in *ex-sistere*, meaning to stand out; *ekstasis* also means to stand out. Existentialism has stressed this ecstasy of existing, particularly with respect to human being.

to itself; as marked by its own self-relativity *and* as participant in a universal relativity. The network of differential relations is mediated into a community of being; the unity of beings is preserved in their self-mediating being for themselves. This mediated nature of unity and difference impels us to think of their source as beyond univocity and equivocity.

How then does this dialectically mediated mindfulness of being help us advance beyond the previous options? This is the advance I suggest: any anti-thetical opposition of finite being and its origin is insufficient, because any such dualism oscillates between univocal eternity and equivocal time, and neither of the latter notions captures either the truth of time or of its origin, a truth now to be interpreted in light of the ecstasy of the middle. The dual-ism is to be mediated; indeed oppositional determinations of the origin are to be transcended. Dialectic suggests that the origin must be both *self-mediating* in itself, and also be capable of *originating* what is other to itself and entering into *relativity* with it. Why should this double requirement be so important? One can argue that, on the one hand, if the origin is radical, it must be *abso-lute* in itself; and yet, on the other hand, if it is originative, it must be capable of some *community* with being as finitely determined. Dialectic claims that these two requirements are mistakenly opposed by the univocal and equivo-cal senses, with unacceptable results—namely, either the sclerosis of the origin, or its deconstruction.

What, more positively, would the dialectical origin be like? The dialecti-cal origin would not only be a One that somehow holds together the diversity of beings, not only dynamical power that originates given being in its finite determincy, it would also be an ultimate source of mediation. Mediation here includes both the origination of community between beings as other, as well as the community of the origin with its creations. The self-transcending vec-tor of beings in becoming, a vector that is also self-mediating, suggests that the origin of all this must be both *self-transcending* and *self-mediating* in an even more excessive sense. We touch again the way of excess. The origin must be a unity that is more than univocal unity, an excess unity of ecstasis and composure, transcending power and serene self-relation, an originary *principium* that gives but that in its giving is never depleted or diminished, for its giving is the gift of finite creation.

We see again the importance of the double requirement, above men-tioned. Our thought of the origin has to make way for the absoluteness of the origin in itself. It must also not preclude its originative relativity to being-other than itself, which other-being is given its own constitutive, self-mediating integrity.

It is relative to this double requirement that difficulties arise, difficulties that are the obverse side of dialectic's strength in addressing the problem of dualism. For in facing this problem, the associated problem of the related-ness of origin and finite being is also broached. A major difficulty with tradi-tional dualisms is that the otherness of the origin is stressed in its *antithesis* to finite being. Inevitably, otherness itself gets invested with the *negative* connotations of opposition. Then the promise of relativity and community is underplayed. While mediation serves to reawaken this promise, it can also shortchange the otherness of transcendence. The recovery of mediated relativity will itself relativize this transcendence of the origin. Even the double requirement, above stated, will be taken to be too close to dualism, and hence to an equivocity that must be surpassed. That is to say, the *univocal sense of the One* will exert its influence once more, this time in a potentially more insidious form, because all the more subtle. I will explain more fully.

We must recall that dialectic underscores the active mediation of mind in encountering and overcoming the initial opaqueness of being. Mind interplays with perplexing being and its mediation alleviates the alienness of its otherness. It comprehends, hence allows mind to be again at home with itself, at home with itself having gained an intelligible sense of the other, and an intelligent appropriation of its intelligibility. In the interplay with the other, mind mediates with the other but also mediates with itself, returns to itself in a self-relation more articulated than its initial starting point.

The question we must now ask ourselves is: What happens if we carry this understanding of beginning, mediation, and end into our thinking of the origin? First, we may fail to see the beginning as the plenitude of full moment; instead it will be an indefiniteness that is to be further mediated. Second, this further mediation will be the *exitus* of the beginning into otherness. It is here that we may speak of the *interplay* between the origin and the finite world as its other. This will not be the end, however, since this *exitus* will be seen as a passage or passing moment. Were it taken as the final moment, we would merely return to the equivocal sense of the origin, where the origin disperses itself into a multiplicity that has no more fundamental togetherness. The *exitus* of the origin into otherness will be seen rather as the middle term by which the initial origin, as indefinite, mediates its own indefiniteness, and hence mediates with itself. In this, and finally, the origin will be seen to return to itself in properly articulated self-relation.

To put the matter otherwise: the dialectical *exitus* into finite being is here rendered as the self-production of the origin that in itself is indefinite. What this implies is that, in effect, the origin *in itself* is lacking; it is perhaps a potentiality, perhaps even an abstraction or emptiness. It is an origin that is nothing in itself, and that is held to gain its concrete actuality only by the production of determinate beings. In turn, this production is now understood as the means by which the origin mediates with itself. It provides the means by which the origin reinstates its own self-relativity, but now at the higher level of articulation that overcomes all indefiniteness. The *reditus* of the production to the source is the self-mediation of the source, in which the source, in its reconstituted self-relativity, produces itself as absolute self-mediation, or as the self-mediation of the absolute.

The dialectical origin, as I have just presented it, is most fully found in Hegel's account of the absolute. But one can also point to many thinkers subscribing to the pervasive traditional scheme of *monas, prohodos,* and *epistrophē.* Indeed Hegel's absolute can be seen to link past and present, in as much as it is a post-Kantian heir of Aristotle's thought thinking itself. Throughout the tradition the unity of the origin is emphasized, but the dialectical view offers a very sophisticated understanding that denies plurality to be ultimately "outside" the origin. If there is plurality "outside" the origin, this "outside" is only provisional. Rather the absolute unity embraces, or more accurately put, *comes* to embrace *within itself,* all of this multiplicity.

What this means is that multiplicity is the *self-multiplication* of the origin. And then again, this is really no self-multiplication, since the multiplicity returns to the source, there to be reabsorbed into the unity of the origin with itself. Finally, there is no irreducible otherness. As thought thinking itself, the dialectical origin does not think itself immediately; it thinks itself mediately through the productions of time that are its own self-productions. So, on this view, the otherness of creation and time are not truly other. They are but the *self-othering* of the origin whereby the origin thinks itself again. The thought that thinks itself as the end is really the truth.

My point is not to dismiss dialectic. Instead I repeat the gains: relative to the complex sense of unity; relative to an appreciation of mediation; relative to the critique of dualism; relative to the defense of the interplay and community of immanence and transcendence. What then makes us dissatisfied? The problem is that if we privilege self-mediation and erect this into the absolute, we fail to think the origin as *plenitude.* Then, further, the twofoldness of the origin and finitude is not upheld in proper support of their difference; they are converted into two sides of a total process of absolute self-mediation. Dualism may seem thereby to be overcome, but if so, the price is high—namely, the downgrading of the otherness between the origin and finite creation. What is irreducibly *affirmative* about this otherness is attenuated into a limit to be surmounted dialectically.

This is not all. For, on closer inspection, it seems there is no real unity to the origin *in itself.* Rather the indeterminacy of its unity is said to be a mere indefiniteness—that is, an essentially incomplete condition that must be converted into the putatively more positive condition of determinacy. Thus the process of finite becoming is only provisionally other to the origin; for it really is the self-determination of the origin, the making determinate of what in the origin in itself is a mere indefiniteness. Hence Hegel will say: God is not God without the world. The origin is not an origin without the finite originated product; the origin is nothing without the originated. This amounts to saying that the origin in itself is essentially empty, an abstraction, at best an indefiniteness of being, to be further determined by the determinate being of the world.

There is more. Even the produced world is itself, if taken as in itself, a vanishing condition of being. It is not produced for itself; it is produced because the origin, as empty in itself, needs it to give itself determinate content. The produced world is the means by which the indefinite origin mediates with itself. The finite world does not stand there with an irreducible difference that marks its being for itself. Its being for the origin comes out in the movement of *reditus* or return, when the origin overcomes its initial condition of indefiniteness through the finite production, and hence comes completely to itself at last.

Let me put the point in terms of our previous discussion of the One. We spoke of a One that is other than the one. But in the present case, the One that is other than the one is not *more* than the one, but *less* than the one. As *origin*, it is the *indefinite One*, not an indeterminate plenitude. The indefinite One only becomes determinately one *at the end*, having passed through the determinate being of finitude. The indefinite One becomes the absolute self-determined One, at the end. This absolute self-determined One is the absolute whole, for Hegel, outside of which there is nothing. Otherness, difference, plurality, finitude, negation, equivocation all have been contained therein. Here there is a return, not of a simple reductive unity, but of a kind of glorious, speculative univocity. The monism of the origin is the absolutely self-mediated monism of the all-embracing totality. Hegel always remained true to what for him in youth, along with Schelling and Hölderlin, was the catch-cry of the "Church invisible"—namely, *hen kai pan*.[6]

I hear a voice grumbling about the rarified abstraction of this discussion. I grant the grumble, and try to mollify it by restating the matter in terms of metaphysical metaphor. The metaphysical metaphor to which I will resort is that of an *erotic origin*. Why is this metaphor appropriate? Consider this. Eros is a dynamic movement of desire seeking fulfillment; it concretizes a movement of self-transcendence, and is ecstatic. Also it is a movement out of self towards the other; it drives the self beyond its immmediate unity with itself, makes the self a one beyond univocal unity, a one that stands out of its own identity towards what is other. Thus, the erotic self is a one that is beyond itself. Moreover, there is a necessary indeterminacy in this process of self-becoming, an openness to what is more and other. In sum, erotic being testifies to a dynamism of being that, in being itself, is beyond itself, and a vector of transcending beyond itself.

Notice that the beginning of eros suggests the opening of the sense of *lack*. I desire something here because I lack that something; eros seeks what it lacks in the origin; its vector of transcendence towards the other and beyond

---

6. Thus echoing the *hen to pan*, one the all, of the ancients. Hegel remained an Eleatic, as he himself clearly acknowledges in his *Lectures on the History of Philosophy*, as we see most clearly in his discussion of Spinoza, not Descartes, as the real father of modern philosophy.

itself is with the view to overcoming the lack of the beginning. I need the other because in myself I am a condition of emptiness, lack, hunger, indigence. Self-transcendence into the middle beyond self is the means by which I relate to the other; but the other in the middle serves the purpose of requiting my lack, of answering my need. I become full, fulfilled in myself, to the extent that I possess the other. The other serves the reconstitution of fulfilled self-relativity on the part of the erotic being. The lack and indefiniteness of the beginning is overcome in the end, through the appropriation of the other in the middle, which other serves ultimately for purposes of *self-appropriation*. A circle of self-relation is traversed in which the ruptures of otherness are appropriated as means of mediation for reconstituted unity with self.

It should be clear that the dialectical sense of the origin tends to be articulated in terms strongly suggestive of this metaphorics of erotic being. I find it pervasive in Hegel. In Platonism and Neoplatonism we find it relative to the *ascent* of finite being to the One. However, the movement *down* by the One is usually described in terms of the overflow of an origin that needs nothing. Hegelianism is thus a more thoroughgoing speculative univocalism than standard Platonism and Neoplatonism. I will return shortly to the importance of the second movement down, and its *asymmetry* with respect to erotic ascent. But there is no asymmetry in Hegel. For Hegel the movement up and the movement down are not two different movements, but two expressions of a singular movement of eternally circular motion, the absolute process of singular self-mediation.

In Hegel we see the erotic absolute, perhaps more clearly than in any other philosopher. For him, the origin in itself, if taken for itself alone, is an entirely lacking condition of being, all but indistinguishable from nothing. To be itself, the origin must become itself, and it becomes itself concretely by its self-othering into the world of finiteness. Yet the finite other is *not for itself* irreducibly; as already a self-othering of the origin, it is *for the origin*, for the concrete self-constitution of the origin. As in erotic mediation, relativity to the other serves self-relation. And this is the end of the erotic unfolding, when the fulfillment of striving selfhood is reached in the complete coming to itself of the self. From the standpoint of the Hegelian absolute, which is the *self-completing origin*, there is no movement up or down; there is just the one absolute circular movement.

I will come back to the limitations of this view, but I do want to underscore its importance. I suggested previously that we must think of origin in terms of our deepest sense of being. The metaphorics of erotic being is *genuinely* an effort in this direction: it tries to do justice to the articulated dynamism of being, indeed to self-articulating modes of being that dynamize themselves. Unavoidably we need such metaphors to think of the origin as self-dynamizing, as self-articulating, as not locked within a static substantialist identity, and as involved with what is other to itself, without thereby forfeiting its own being for itself. Erotic being seeks to do justice to all of these possibilities.

I can also put the importance of the erotic metaphorics in historical terms. Thus, in premodern thought, this metaphorics was employed to describe *our* metaphysical movement towards the origin or end; but the origin or end itself was described in terms *beyond* desire and need. By contrast, in modern thought we find a more pervasive ascription of the erotic metaphor to the origin in itself. There are many reasons for this, but some of the most important include the following five.

First, Platonic dualism, and any speculative metaphysics derivative therefrom, was perceived to be at an impasse, an impasse expressed in the sclerosis of transcendence into a static eternity, uninfected with the seemingly negative condition of erotic being. This sclerosis undercuts the relativity of the origin to finite being, making unintelligible the movement of it towards the finite creation, or indeed of the finite towards it, except by finitude's own self-negation. Against these results, the will to dynamize the origin again is made thinkable by the erotic metaphorics, and in a manner that *immanentizes* the work of transcendence. The original *dunamis* of being is at work in the world of becoming; hence we do not have to negate the world to think original transcendence.

Second, the resort to erotic metaphorics, not only with respect to our metaphysical movement, but to the origin itself, is connected with a rejection of the *impassivity* of the eternal, such as is ascribed to Greek metaphysics. Impassive eternity is taken to be a catatonic god that could generate nothing other than itself, even had it reason or desire to do so, given its pure self-sufficiency and self-absorption, unaffected by anything, not even itself.

Third, the attraction of erotic metaphorics is linked to the hidden percolation into mindfulness of aspects of the *Jewish-Christian* conception of a God actively *involved in history*, and not its mere absentee landlord or catatonic voyeur. It is related to the repudiation of "otherwordly" transcendence, such as is ascribed to the Middle Ages, a transcendence thought to stifle the promise of transcendence in the middle itself.

Fourth, the resort to erotic metaphorics recoils from the pitiful contraction of God that is offered by the *deistic divinity*. It arises from the eventual death of this anorexic abstraction of the absolute. It is of a piece with the pantheistic divinization of nature that, after Spinoza, came to exercise strong influence in the wider culture, even when excoriated by mechanistic science for backsliding. For even if transcendence as other is censored, there can be no finally effective stifling of the desire for transcendence in the middle, and the urgency of ultimacy that marks our intermediate being. Surrogates of ultimate transcendence will spring up, including even the religious zealotry of scientistic enlightenment.

Fifth and finally, the resort to erotic metaphorics is connected with the *historically progressive* and *biologically evolutionary* ways of conceiving the world that have been dominant in the last two centuries. The orientation of erotic being towards a future perfection displaces the plenitude of the absolute from the beginning to the consummating end that is said to be coming.

Many names could be adduced in addition to Hegel's, and some of them avowed atheists. Without offering all the requisite qualifications, I name a few: Schelling, Marx, Schopenhauer, Nietzsche, Solovyov, Heidegger, the later Scheler, Alexander, Whitehead, Weiss.[7] Obviously, none of these are simply dialecticians in the Hegelian mode, and in all there are strains in tension with erotic metaphorics. Some are avowedly hostile to Hegelian dialectic, yet the metaphysical metaphor of erotic being is still effective. The erotic origin casts its influence because its ultimate *dunamis* is not frozen into static eternity but is articulated in an interplay with the world of becoming. It not only helps us think beyond traditional dualisms, it helps us circumvent, or become cold to, the ban on metaphysical transcendence decreed by Kant. As transcending in the middle, the human being can think towards the original dynamism of transcending being, at work in the world or history.

The Exceeding One, The Agapeic Origin

I now meet an objection opposite to the one accusing me of abstraction: I am being *too* metaphorical. Yes and no. No: the present discourse seems not at all metaphorical, in a more normal sense; it seems so remote from everyday concreteness. Yes: metaphysical metaphors, the need of which I have already tried to explain (see chapter 5), are indispensable. I am between: torn between the need to speak and to be silent. So I speak in mindfulness of the silence *in* this speech, as always failing before the origin. Nor can I avail myself of the Heideggerian typographical gesture, which cancels its effectiveness once the initial surprise wears off. Enabling metaphysical metaphors are not typographical gestures, nor are they flighty fantasies. Their meaning is regulated, mediated, and directed by the entire discourse of the fourfold sense of being.

(I beg your pardon, but I succumb and cannot resist trying out the gesture, just once: O̶R̶I̶G̶I̶N̶. There now. Done. Pass on. *Nota bene*: all of this crossing out is in parentheses.)

---

7. Elsewhere I have discussed the issue of origin in relation to a number of these thinkers. See my "Art, Origins, Otherness: Hegel and Aesthetic Self-Mediation," in *Philosophy and Art*, ed. Daniel Dahlstrom (Washington: Catholic University of America Press, 1991), 209–34; "Schopenhauer, Art and the Dark Origin," in *Schopenhauer*, ed. Eric von der Luft (Lewistown, NY: Mellen Press, 1988), 101–22; "Rethinking the Origin: Hegel and Nietzsche"; "Creativity and the Dunamis," in *The Philosophy of Paul Weiss: Library of Living Philosophers*, ed. Lewis Hahn (La Salle, Illinois: Open Court, to appear), especially with respect to Paul Weiss and Whitehead. Weiss continues to develop his view; see *Being and Other Realities* (La Salle, Illinois: Open Court, to appear).

I now turn to the metaxological sense, as enabling us further to think the origin. Since the matter is exceedingly difficult—and for the benefit of those still dubious about metaphysical metaphor—I address it as clearly and distinctly as possible in terms of seven major considerations: first, the limits of the dialectical origin; second, the other One beyond thought thinking itself; third, the paradoxical notion of an infinite whole; fourth, the question of radical origination; fifth, the asymmetry in pluralized mediation; sixth, agapeic self-transcendence; seventh, the gratuitousness, goodness, and nothingness of finitude.

First consideration. Hegelian erotics, just in its coherence, provides the foil we need to think the origin more deeply. This is the question we ask of Hegel: if the origin is originally lacking being, and must produce its other that is itself as other, and do so in order to be itself, in what sense is it itself at all in the first place? And if it is not itself at all in the first place, how then can it be an origin of what is other to itself, much less itself? Stated with maximum concision: *an origin that has to produce itself to be itself, must first be itself in order to produce itself.* And this is to say nothing about the production of what is other to itself. How must it *already be itself*, in order to further effect itself and what is other to itself? In a word, is there not an origin prior to the dialectical beginning?

Does dialectic go deep enough into this already effective energy of being, that must be presupposed for something like a dialectical becoming to be effected at all in the first place? Is the One that is *more* than and *other* than the one to be equated with the One that is *less* than the one? And is the world of plurality as the other of this One to be equated with the One as dialectically self-othered?

The metaxological answer to these last questions is no. First, we must go beyond the univocal origin, because the unity of the origin is more than one. Second, we must go beyond the equivocal origin, because sheer difference or differentiation, while more than univocal unity, and hence more a marker of transcendence, cannot account for the internal self-mediation of the origin, cannot acount for the interplay and intermediation of the origin and the others. Hence sheer differentiation cannot account for the community of finitude and transcendence, as well as the community of finite beings, each as constituted by mediations beyond equivocity. Third, we must go beyond the dialectical origin which, while it does help account up to a point for the inner complexity of differentiated unity, the interplay of immanence and transcendence, and the mediated community of being, nevertheless conceives unity, interplay, and community in terms of the logic of self-mediation.

Take Hegel's famous statement: "The true is the whole." Here this implies that the origin in itself is lacking indeterminacy, which needs the production of finite being to mediate with itself; the finite is the origin in its own otherness, and hence the mirror in which the origin completely determines itself and in the end constitutes itself as the true whole. In this dialectical erotics of the whole, the "more" of the One, the origin's transcendence, is made nugatory. The community of origin and creation is rendered such that otherness is seen as a mark of estrangement, hence in the final run a defective condition. Finally, the interplay of immanence and transcendence is reduced from a double to a singular mediation. And there is no interplay between irreducible others, only the self-interplay of the absolute with itself, love disporting with *itself*, as Hegel says.

Love may disport with itself, but this is the erotic love that loves itself in its loving of the other, in which its possession of the other is its mediated return to self-love. The metaxological sense points to a different love of the origin, which does not simply disport with itself. For there is a love wherein a movement of transcendence takes place, which is not for the self that loves but for the other that is being loved. In the present instance, the other that is being loved is the other that is given being, in the act of being loved. This movement from the self to the other that is for the other, I have called agapeic being.

Thus the metaxological sense grants the One that is more than the one; for original being is ecstatic, a dynamism of self-transcendence: to be a one self is to be more than a one. Likewise, the differentiating nature of this movement of transcendence is granted. Moreover, this differentiating is not just a dynamism of dispersal. There is a pluralization of being that is also a holding together of manyness, in and indeed through the network of differential relations. Equivocal differentiation is mediated.

In addition, this mediation points to an original power that is more than any determinate entity or process of happening that is defined in the differentiation process. The metaxological sense emphasizes the "more" of the origin, its excess to determinacy, indeed another sense of difference or otherness that is not reducible to the determinate differences defined in the differential network of a dynamic becoming. I say "more" because there is a transcendence to the origin that will never be reduced to the differentiating process of becoming or to the mediation of this process in terms of an immanent whole. Nor will any projected totality, whether it is Kant's regulative unconditioned or Hegel's constitutive unconditioned, do justice to the "more" of this transcendence.

Second consideration. The issue can be further put in terms of the traditional apotheosis of the absolute self-sufficiency of thought thinking itself, or variations thereof. Consider what is implied in thought thinking itself. If thought thinks itself, it must be different to itself, while being the same as itself. This selfsameness cannot be a univocal unity; for there is differentiating in such thought thinking itself. How to interpret this difference? Is it just the internal self-differentiation of a whole that is itself and nothing more, that circles around itself in absolute self-mediation? But if so, why the internal self-difference at all? Why is not all difference eternally overcome? If it is, why then does this overcoming need to be eternally reenacted?

Hegel would answer all questions by saying that the absolute is simply the eternal process of producing self-differences and overcoming such differences in the whole. I suggest, however: this internal hiatus reveals a cleft or dyad in self-thinking that points elsewhere than self-thinking. The cleft is a hyphen that sets thinking off from what it thinks; and though what it thinks is itself, there is still a space of difference in this that cannot be itself. For if it were itself, it would be the thinking, the hiatus, and the thought. That is, there would be no difference, no cleft, and there would be nothing but undifferentiated thought. There is a cleft but the cleft is not of self-thinking itself. This setting off is a difference *other* than just a differentiating moment of the self-mediating whole. The internal difference between thought and itself points to another difference that is not just self-given, or given by thought to itself.

Or, this other difference is given to thought by a source that is other to the circle of self-thinking thought. The difference internal to self-thinking comes to self-thinking from an otherness that is not just its own self-otherness. In the thought that thinks itself, the thought of what is other to thought points beyond thought to this prior giving source. In sum: *there is a more originary otherness prior to self-thinking thinking.* How name this prior originary otherness that gives the otherness within thought? The metaphysical metaphor I suggest is that of the agapeic origin. This origin is more than thought thinking itself.[8]

Third consideration. How to characterize this originary other? Is it just a nugatory beyond that vanishes into nothing, thence perhaps to reappear as an indefiniteness that the process of finite becoming determines? It seems we need both negative and affirmative characterizations. For yes, there is a sense in which the excessive origin is "nothing." It is no determinate thing, and if we look for it with minds marked by the inflexible expectation of determinate intelligibility, we will be disappointed surely and find nothing. But this "nothing" is the "more," the more than determinacy, more than determinate identities, more than the determining process of the becoming of finite happenings and things, more than the self-determining transcendence of human being.

---

8. Plotinus is the only philosopher I know who sensed the point, when he tried to show that there is something *superior* to thought thinking itself—this he calls the One. See "On the Good or the One," *Ennead* VI. 9. 2. 33ff. My view—that the agapeic origin is more than thought thinking itself—will not be quite the same as Plotinus's, yet his direction of thought is to the point.

This is the reason we have to speak of this excess as a *positive* indeterminacy. I am not talking about an indefinite beginning that has to become itself to be made a definite whole, but a "whole" that already is a surplus of being within itself, and that out of this surplus transcends itself. It might be called an overdetermined "whole." Such a "whole" would not be perfect, if perfection only implies a determinate completion. Its "perfection" would be, so to say, a "pluperfection." It would be pluperfection, not just in the sense of already having been perfected, but pluperfect as now being, and as always being. Such pluperfection would not be reducible to any or all of the tenses of time. It would be beyond time as always already more than any process of becoming. It would be the surplus of eternity. So also it could not be equated with any catatonic eternity that contracts into itself in recoil from the processes of time. It would be a creative principle that does not just create at a momentous once and then deserts creation. The momentous once is now always. The act of creation is an always continuing origination and sustaining of finite being in being.

This notion of overdetermined pluperfection suggests the idea of an infinite whole. But can any sense be made of this? The idea of an infinite whole seems contradictory from the standpoint of formal logic; for a whole is a determinate unity, bounded by definite limits, while infinity goes beyond such determinate limits. Can we then have any idea at all of an indeterminate whole? The response I offer is: only if we interpret indeterminacy as an unconstrained excess of creative power, creative power capable of agapeic origination.

Suppose we try to put the point relative to the fourfold sense of being. With univocity, we can stress the idea of the whole, but we are inclined to *domesticate* infinitude, whose transgression of determinate limits is anathema to univocity. With equivocity, we can put the emphasis on infinitude, but because we neglect unity or reject wholeness, infinity itself is *dissipated* into futile endlessness. With dialectic, there is a return to mediated unity and wholeness, so much so that the infinite is *sublated* within the self-mediating whole; there is said to be but one whole, wherein infinitude and finitude mediate with each other. With the metaxological, the inexhaustibility of original infinity is seen in its *releasing* creative power: the infinite whole is overwhole; as infinite creative excess, it is originative of finitude as both genuinely other and as potentially infinite after its own finite kind. The pluralism between the finite creation and original infinity is not sublated into a monism of one whole. There is a community between original wholes, one absolutely overdetermined, the others the promise of their own perfection.

It should be obvious that we must think of infinity here as other than an infinite succession or series. We must think of *qualitative inexhaustibility* rather than quantitative accumulation and summation. In a sense, such qualitative inexhaustibility is more than humans can think. And yet we can truthfully point to manifestations or images of such inexhaustibility in our human habitation of the middle. We divine it in the greatness of an unsurpassable artist, in the incalculable nobility of ethical heroism, in the measureless profundity of religious holiness. We praise its creative power when we celebrate being itself as an agape.

Moreover, all these manifestations are *communicative* of significance so ultimate that we could never pin it down to any set of finite determinations. Excess of meaning remains in reserve, even in the very communication of the radiance of ultimate meaning. If these manifestations are themselves overdetermined in meaning, hence recalcitrant to complete conceptualization, how more recalcitrant is creative inexhaustibility itself, of which they are but the finite image? And yet it communicates; for all being, the happening of the between, is its communication.

I may seem to speak with assured articulateness, but in truth I barely stutter broken words, relative to the excess of its communication. Though I hear the charge of verbiage from those who hear nothing of this communication, notwithstanding this I still must stutter.

Fourth consideration. Such an inexhaustibility suggests more than the Hegelian whole that is constituted by a dialectical interplay between finiteness and infinity. The agapeic origin as creative excess would be more than any finite being, and constrained by nothing. It would be the original power to bring finite being into *being*. This agapeic bringing into being would be the free gift of being-other; it would not be the self-creation of the original whole. Thus we do not have to see the infinity of the origin as an indefiniteness that necessitates finiteness to make itself determinate. For in creation, it is the finite as such that is made to be, and to be for itself as other. Finite beings are differentiated in a process of becoming that, as open-ended, does have its indefiniteness. Finite beings partake of the originated infinitude of endless succession and the universal impermanence. But that derivative infinity is not the underived infinite.

What such a bringing of finite being into being implies is an act of radical origination, in the most unconditional sense possible. What would this be? Such radical origination would not be the shaping of preexistent matter through the superimposition of form, that also might be preexistent, as in the making of the Platonic demiurge. Such origination need not look to persuade necessity, but would give out of unconditional freedom. It need not create with conditions, but would itself create conditions, for all derivative determination of being.

The point after all is to think the *ultimate* origin. Remember again that the way of transcendence is hyperbolic. Transcending thinking finds itself thrown upwards at an ultimate limit. Any metaphysical arrogance is entirely out of place, for this hyperbolic thinking is marked by a paradoxical humility.

It is thrown into the face of the absolutely superior, a face of excessive dark, as much as a face of excessive light.

At this radical origin there would not be a pluralism of ultimate conditions, such as we find with Plato, and also contemporary thinkers like Whitehead and Weiss.[9] All pluralism of conditions is penultimate, or a beginning after the origin. Conditions come to be out of the unconditioned origination. Potentiality, form, matter, intelligibility . . . all these are originated, not underived. The radical origination would be a bringing of all into being out of nothing. What this means is all but impossible to say, as is the being and act that thus originates. For all our saying, and all our knowing of origination, takes place in the derived middle, the beyond of which, as radical origination, we falter here to say.

Radical origination is bound by nothing. Why then originate at all? In light of the unconditional nature of this origination, and the contingency of being thus given, there would seem to be no externally imposed necessity to originate, nor to originate thus or thus. Origination rather would be the surplus of the origin, its free, releasing generosity. Originating would be an absolute giving of being. If one wants to say that the origin gives being out of an internal necessity, this is true, if we mean by internal necessity that it is its being simply to give. But then, of course, freedom and necessity will mean something other than their more standard significations. This necessity, whose being is simply to give for the good of the giving, would be absolute freedom, indeed absolute *freeing*. For this giving would free, release, absolve the given from the giver.

This absolute giving would be an unconditional *Here it is*! For such absolute giving would have no reason beyond itself. So there is a sense in which there is no justification of origination except the goodness of creating itself. The excess of the origin would not be an indigence but a marvel of infinite generosity that simply gives because it is good to give. Here we meet a metaphysically elemental appeal to the goodness of being as a gift that cannot be reduced to a further ground. In that sense, the gift of being is groundless, and the pluperfect origin is an ungrounded ground.

Fifth consideration. The metaxological sense suggests a *pluralized mediation* between the origin and the originated. Recall again the double requirement concerning our conception of the origin: that it do justice both to the absoluteness of the origin for itself, and to its intermediation with finite otherness. The paradoxical notion of an infinite whole is indicative of these two sides. The *first* requirement is tied to overwholeness of the origin: this is its excessive transcendence that can never be completely captured in our finite

---

9. See the previously cited paper, "Creativity and the Dunamis."

categories, nor reduced to any finite determinate thing or process. The agapeic origin is thus for itself and for itself alone; it always exceeds us and is marked by a constitutive reserve that will always remain an enigma for us. The *second* requirement is met by the idea of infinity as a creative excess. The for-itself of the origin is not a nugatory beyond; out of its creative excess it originates finite being and sets up that middle space of the *metaxu,* wherein intermediations with finite creation are instituted and given their ongoing process.[10]

And yet the fact remains that what the origin is in and for itself continues to be enigmatic. No process of the self-determination of a finite happening, not even the self-determining of a finite being that is *capax infiniti*—namely, the human being—will allow us to be rid of this enigma. This is what Hegel could not accept. And he uses the *capax infiniti* of the self to conceptualize the being of the absolute as it is in itself, attending too little to the fact that the first is an image of the origin, and not the absolute original. He rides over the ultimate *disproportion* of the absolute original to the finite self as *capax infiniti.* The image is not the original, and this "not" brings us back to *our* perplexity before the origin as it is in itself and for itself. Hegel could not accept this enigma, but it is just this lack of consent to the ultimate disproportion that is the final failing, though it sets itself up as the successful knowing of the absolute.

For there is an *asymmetry* between the mediation from the origin and from the originated. That is why we need more than monological dialectic; we need a dialogical dialectic—that is, a metaxological intermediation. Dialectic is just not adequate when it reduces plural to single mediation, making a symmetry between the "way up" and the "way down." Heraclitus is not right when he says that the way up and the way down are one and the same (fr. 108). I can grant that it may be perhaps easier to make intelligible the "way up," just starting from where we are in the middle. For we are carried by the drive of erotic self-transcendence. Mind transcends itself, infinitely transcends itself; and its infinite restlessness is with the end in view of becoming as whole as possible.

The importance of erotic transcendence is not to be denied. But we must be guarded about applying this mode of dynamic being to the "way down"—not our "way down," but the "way down" of the origin, the production of time itself. We mistakenly ascribe a symmetry to our erotic "way up" and the movement of the origin as itself erotic in the same sense. This sameness is the residue of univocity in the dialectical conception. But the great difficulty is to make some sense of the "way down" at all. The erotic way is not enough.

Let me put the point in relation to Plotinus. Though for Plotinus the philosopher there is an erotic movement upwards, the One that is above is beyond need, so it cannot be erotic. Hence *its "way down"* cannot be the same

---

10. Hence the doubleness in our characterization of *the One that is more than the one* mirrors the metaxological sense of the double.

as *our "way up."* Plotinus suggests a lack of samenessness in these movements: "descent" is by way of "overflow." This is not wrong if the origin is
agapeic and the One is the good: the way of lack, or negation, upwards is not
the same as the way of overfullness downwards. I think that in Hegel's monistic circle any difference of directionality is not finally important, and he equal-
izes the two movements as two moments of a total self-mediation. By contrast, Plotinus preserves the absolute otherness of the One as beyond, out of
which enigmatic beyond, it originates downwards. He does not equalize the
two movements.

Nevertheless, perhaps because a sense of absolute "unity" had a hold on
Plotinus, one wonders if he fully thought through the difference between the
two. Specifically, his erotic sense of upward return seems to infect his idea of
the results of the first "overflow," which then becomes a "fall" from the One.
We are reminded of Anaximander for whom any departure from the original
indeterminate (*to apeiron*) into difference and singularity is a crime against
the origin, for which the just order of time will necessarily seek recompense.

Plotinus, I suspect, does not face the following equivocity: if the One is
the good and the good "overflows," the result of the "overflow" will be good.
And yet Plotinus thinks of all being removed from the One as ultimately a
defective condition, hence in a sense not good; and yet his rage against the
gnostics flies in the face of a consistent logical conclusion from plurality as a
"fall" or "degeneration" from the One. Plotinus is not Hegel, who is himself
an heir of Anaximander in understanding evil in terms of particularity.[11] For
Plotinus the enigma of the beyond remains beyond, and yet a logic of univocity
seems to infiltrate his understanding of the origination of plurality in terms
of a "fall" from the One. To do better justice to his notion of the "overflow," he
would have to think the goodness of the One in terms of an agapeic origin, for
whom the origination of the many is not a "fall," but the giving of finitude its
integrity for itself, and its goodness for itself. Hence his "way up" and "way
down" are sometimes at odds with each other, resulting in an equivocalness
of being in the middle. This can wrongly encourage a gnostic reduction of the
middle to an evil, from which, because it alienates us from the origin, we
must ever strive to escape.

This escape is not to be endorsed, for finitude is to be celebrated with its
own incontrovertible "It is good". The "overflow" of the agapeic origin would
love singularity, plurality, otherness for themselves as other. This is the true
father who loves the child, not because he sees himself there, but because the
child stands with a separate being, admirable in its irreducible singularity,
loved even when the child strays prodigally and even betrays the father. This
is unconditioned love of the singular. If we must use the metaphorics of
prohodos and *epistrophē*, the *prohodos* is not for the sake of return, but for

---

11. I have discussed and criticized the dialectical conception of evil in *Beyond Hegel
and Dialectic*, chapter 4.

the goodness of the finite creation itself. And if there is an *epistrophē*, this too is for the good of the finite creation, in the fulfilled promise of its community with the origin.[12]

I surmise that some ancient metaphysicians, like Plato and Plotinus, had a spontaneously deeper appreciation for the *goodness* of being than we moderns. This goodness is what they, and now we, are struggling to say. They are *not* the metaphysical nihilists of today's stock Nietzscheanism. It is we who are the nihilists who fail to see beyond ourselves. Unlike their philosophical amen, we moderns bring such a hermeneutics of suspicion to bear on being that we expect the origin to be some variation on a dark source, like that of Schopenhauer—a blind, ugly, senseless, striving energy, without care or purpose, violent, indifferent. This is the erotic origin stripped of any proper end—that is to say, futile becoming without end. It is hard not to be put in mind of a gnostic disgust with creation as the swindle or malice of an evil demon. Needless to say, this darkness is not that of the mystery of the good. To find our way beyond this suspicion, we must be reborn to metaphysical trust. Born-again metaphysics would be memory of the agape of the good.

Sixth consideration. I offer no simple rejection of erotic transcendence, but I do think we must surpass it. How do we do this? By seeing that dialectic does not offer a penetrating enough interpretation of erotic being. Eros may drive from lack to completion, from indefiniteness to self-determination, but why the drive beyond lack at all in the first place? The answer is that the lack itself cannot be mere lack; rather its erotic movement is always already undergirded by the original power of being as plenitude. The power of being in search of its other and its own completion articulates itself in the initial lack of eros; but the lack of that beginning points to a more original beginning that is actually articulating itself in the second beginning of lack. It is the plenitude of the original power of being that drives this process of self-articulation; lack develops the self-differentiation and self-articulation of this more original power. Lack as a beginning is the manifestation of a surplus that is a more originary beginning. In our metaphors, erotic being is grounded on the energy of agapeic being. Being as lack is a determination of being as excess. The metaxological conception tries to think this more original otherness, both from the side of the self-transcendence of finite being, and the side of the excess of the origin as absolute transcendence.

---

12. Even Aquinas reveals an interesting ambiguity here: "What God wills, He can only will for the sake of *His own* goodness" (*Summa Theologiae*, I, 19, 2, ad 2–3). The ambiguity is in the phrase "for the sake of His own goodness." This might be seen as, to use Hegel's phrase, love disporting with itself. Or "for His goodness" may be just what is *not for Himself alone*, but for the other. The difference of the erotic and agapeic conception is here at stake.

Thus, I believe the metaphor of an agapeic origin helps us image the "way down" more satisfactorily than the erotic origin does. For agapeic being is not a static substance, nor is it empty nothing, nor is it dead immutable eternity; it is dynamic excess of giving being. Agapeic being is a movement of creative origination that goes forth from itself, from its own surplus, but it does not go forth for the sake of itself; it offers the other being, for the sake of the other. Its self-transcendence is truly self-transcending, since there is a kind of *releasing reversal* between self and other: the self is othered such that the other is given a freedom of being from the giving self. It is let be, but in no indifferent sense; it is let be to be an original center of being for itself, in its own right. The self-transcendence that is a reversal of self is a giving of genuine separateness to the other. Freedom is this separation. And while this metaphysical separateness is a differentiation, it is not the self-differentiation of the One. It is the opening up of the ontological space for the integrity of the finite creation as a world unto itself.

There is a rupture here, but not in any negative sense; it is the rupture that institutes metaphysical separation. Metaphysical separation is not dualistic opposition; in fact, this rupture or spacing is instituted out of agape and not out of opposition. The agape of the origin would be the origin prior to the Heraclitean father, *polemos*. *Polemos* may come to be in this rupture, but this is because the goodness of separateness also allows the free finite being to turn against the agapeic source that gives it being in the first instance. War, like erotic being, is only possible because of the metaphysical priority of the agape of being.

If the agapeic origin is ultimate transcendence, we might say that out of its overfulness, the other as other is created, and created for itself, not just for a return to the origin. Such creation would name a radical originative act that issues in the creature as a singular integrity for itself, given its being for itself, and let be in its freedom in the happening of the between. The overflow of the origin is not an indefinite fulguration, but is for the specificity and particularity of the finite other that is brought into being. Moreover, the happening of the between is *other for itself*, and not the self-othering of the origin. For the agapeic origin does not *become itself* via a dialectical detour through finitude, rendered as its self-othering. There is no absorption of finite creation as a part within an engulfing whole.

Put in more theological language: God does not create Himself in creating the world.[13] God's creation would be the giving of what is irreducibly

---

13. A number of the previously mentioned thinkers who espouse a more erotic concept of God take some such view, but see also Scotus Eriugena: "we ought not to understand God and the creature as two things distinct from one another, but as one and the same. For both the creature, by subsisting, is in God; and God, by manifesting Himself in a marvellous and ineffable manner creates Himself in the creature, the

other to God. This "not-being" God is the space of a disproportion between the two, but it is not the denial of their possible community. This "not-being" God also means that the meaning of nothingness is not that of determinate negation. The nothingness between God and creation would not be a negation that would negate itself and so prove dialectically affirmative. It would name a different sense of transcendence and otherness, and a different relativity between the origin and creation, which would not be that of mutual determination in a self-determining absorbing god.[14]

Seventh consideration. Our final consideration has to do with the gratuitousness, goodness, and nothingness of finitude. This seems like a peculiar triad, for often we think of gratuitousness and nothingness as even antithetical to the good. This has to do with a tendency to think of the good in terms of *necessary determination.* By contrast, the nothingness above implied indicates the gratuitousness of creation, in the sense of its excess to logical specification in terms of any univocal or dialectical determination. The gratuitousness is simply the good of creation itself, that it is good to be, over and above nothing. To be above nothing is the good of being, and the good of being is the elemental answer to the question, What does it mean to be?

The good of being is communicative, and hence inseparable from community. Moreover, the above nothingness as other than self-determining negativity means that community is not exhausted by mutual equivalence. We might say that there is a community in excess of mutuality, a communicating to the other without the expectation of a return, a community in abandon. A disproportion shapes the space of finite transcendence in which the freedom of the creature is called forth, called into its promise. The divine agape absolves the creation into its freedom and offers the space of a free community between transcendence and finite happening, without a dialectic of domination and subsumption.

Put otherwise: God creates the world for the world. This is the meaning of the hyperbolic "It is good, it is very good," uttered by God on beholding creation. God does not say: It is good for me; or it is good for humans to use; but it is good; *it* is good, very good for itself. That is, agapeic origination places the stress on the goodness of the created other in its own being for-itself, in its genuine separateness from the origin. The being for-itself of integral creation makes it a world unto itself that is not merely the origin in its own otherness. An irreducible otherness comes into being between the origin and the created world. Again this is not a dualistic opposition, though it

---

invisible making itself visible . . . the infinite finite and the uncircumscribed circumscribed and the supratemporal temporal." *Periphyseon*, Bk III, 678c-d; trans. I.P. Sheldon-Williams, corrected by J.J. O'Meara, J.J. O'Meara, ed. Montreal, 1987, 305.

14. See *Desire, Dialectic and Otherness*, chapter 1, on the absorbing god.

may become an opposition. More originally, it grounds and sustains the happening of the between, the *metaxu*.

What this implies is that in creation pluralism is *glorified* in the world. Plurality is good, it is not a "fall" from the One that mediates with itself through diversity. If plurality is a creation of the origin out of nothing, the nothing names a gap of difference that conditions the possibility of an irreducible being for-self of the finite. So the community of finite plurality is not to be rendered in terms of a dialectical sublation of singularity. Agapeic origin creates the singular for itself, and not as a mere instance of an anonymous universal or class. It is agapeic love that brings into being the singular, and that sustains and conserves the singular in being. That is, the agapeic origin does not think of itself; it "forgets" itself in its love of the singular, which is thereby given being; this is the ontological reversal.

This reversal relates to the asymmetry between any erotic ascent and agapeic descent. The agapeic origin absolves itself from its relativity to the creation in the sense that, while remaining in relation, it allows the creation for itself to absolve itself from the relation, even to the point of turning against the origin, such as we find in human evil. The agapeic origin is absolute by absolving the finite creation it gives. It absolves in freeing from itself. It never functions as an absorbing god, but as a God who releases finite otherness for itself, and as other to its own absolute otherness. So it retains its own otherness, even while in relation to the otherness of the finite creation.

This is why I think we must speak of a *positive double* between origin and creation, not an equivocal dualism. The excess of origin generates the finite excess of plurality. As agapeic the origin creates absolving relations of otherness. Since it lets be the double mediation between immanence and transcendence, it is the ground that sustains the metaxological community of the self and other, as given being in finitude. This metaxological community is not the ultimate, but rather is grounded in the ultimate origin that makes relations of true otherness possible in the middle, communities that absolve and release their members to their own freedom and relativity to others. In this real plurality there is both a community that allows a release of singularity, and a releasing of singularity into the promise of solidarity.

Consider again, in light of a reborn metaphysical astonishment, the redoubling we find in the affirmation "Being is." I now venture the suggestion that the very givenness of being is this redoubling, this prodigious pluralization that occurs in the happening of the between. The doubling of being named by "Being is" is not an empty tautologous reiteration of the same, nor yet a dualistic opposition. In "Being is" being appears over itself, over again, redoubled in its plenitude and pluralization. Rather than an indigent categoriality, why not see in this redoubling a pointer to the mystery of ontological generosity in which the other is given its being for itself? The redoubling of being would then be agapeic creation that goes forth for the other, letting it be as other, freeing it as other, yet in solidarity with it, implicated in the hope of its good. Indeed one might say that only in such a community of being, as would be given by agapeic creation, can we connect the ontological plenitude of "Being is" with the hyperbolic yes of the "It is very good." Resurrected metaphysical mind is made to ponder a primal originary redoubling, which lets the creative pluralization of finite nature be at all.[15]

You might object that this view has a much too inflated sense of the goodness of the origin. But are things so simple? I think we are actually returned to the time of lamentation, more radically than on the dialectical view. For the releasing of creation is with the view to the unconditional gift of free being. To be is to be free, and to be as free is to be given being as good. But the freedom of being other than the origin is hazardous. Free being is given in a between that is in process. The happening of the between is a universal impermanence. The giving of free being is the giving of a promise, a promise that, just as free, may be betrayed as well as fulfilled. The most astonishing and perplexing thing about agapeic giving is that it lets be even this possibility of betrayal, even to the point of radical evil. The time of lamentation comes in creation when the promise of the "It is good" seems to be engulfed by such deforming betrayal that battens on the very gift of good being. The beauty of creation is warped. And still free being is given.

We might say that as dialectic can revert to univocity, metaxology can allow the reversion of the equivocity of being, albeit in a transformed state. The doubleness of being is irreducible: doubleness of self, doubleness of world, doubleness of possible mediation between finitude and origin, redoubling in the origin itself. There is no univocal geometry of this doubleness, as there is no dialectical method. There is a dialectical probing yes, which lets the *dia* of dialectic reassert itself against any monism of the whole. The metaxological view is willing to let this reversion come, when the course of being wills it so. The doubleness will come out, what we will anyway, and this too in line with the nature of the agapeic origin.

For us doubleness comes out very clearly in the constitutive *nothingness* of finite beings. As created, the possibility of their not-being is written into the givenness of their being. The differentiation process they inhabit, coming to be and passing away, reflects this—created beings are double. And so there is a sense in which *we* are *equivocally* in being, compared to the absolute origin. We are not absolute, nor do we live being in all its agapeic plenitude; we are outside this plenitude, though not totally. Finite being is provisional. It is provided for in time; it is a temporary gift, a gift of time. With the middle we inhabit, between birth and death, the gift is given, and

---

15. The doubling is related to posthumous mind as a redoubling affirmation of being beyond death, and so beyond, if only in imagination, the happening of the between, trying to think how the between might be agapeically loved from beyond, how the community and the singulars within it might be loved in their being from beyond.

then seems withdrawn. As we painfully know, this withdrawing sometimes can be so agonizing and violent that we may doubt the agape of the giver, and see ourselves as forlornly thrown into a dying fall. Thus the doubleness of being in the between can bring sharply home to us the final fragility of finitude.

What can we do then? The great task is to unwind the equivocity, to see if, and how, the threads of doubleness are woven, deep down, into a braid of plurivocal being by the generosity of the origin. The threads unwind and we spin now towards death, nothing again. The great question then is: Can we, do we still say yes to the agapeic origin?

What Then?

Well, what is it then? Is it a being? No, it is not a being. Is it the totality of beings? No, it is not the totality of beings. Is it the being of beings? Yes and no. Is it one? Yes and no; it is one and also the One; and yet it is not one but more than one. Is it other? Yes, it is the other; and yet it is not other, as an opposite; it is an intimate other, with us. Is it two? No, it contains no self-discord; yet it is double relative to our approach, for we must distinguish between its being for itself and its being for creation or finite others, between its pluperfect overwholeness and the excess of creative infinitude. Is it infinite? It is the infinite. Is it nothing? Yes and no. Is it mind? Yes and no. Is it beyond mind? Yes and no. Is it transcendent? Yes and no. Is it eternal? Yes and no. Is it involved with history? Yes and no. Is it power? Yes and no. Is it intelligible? Yes and no. Is it the Good? Yes, but we do not know what that means. Do we know the meaning of these yesses and nos? Yes, perhaps, but there is still much of darkness to be dispelled.

CHAPTER SEVEN

CREATION: THE UNIVERSAL IMPERMANENCE

Creation and Beginning Again

I am a little wary of that title "Creation." Is this not "Origin" all over again? And have we not had enough of origin? And you propose to do it once more! That takes the biscuit!

No, I am not about to do the same again, though I understand the wariness. The meaning of creation can seem to coincide with that of origin. But we need to distinguish three related meanings. First, creation can refer to the *activity* of origination, which brings something into being. Second, it can refer to the *outcome* of that act.[1] Third, we can speak of creation with regard to the *relation* between the origin and the originated being. When we call finite being a creation, we refer to the second sense of outcome. This sense is now primarily our concern, but not in any abstraction from the other two senses. Between the origin and the outcome there is a relatedness whose meaning demands thought. And with respect to all three senses, and not only with respect to the first, the importance of dynamic activity must be keep in mind: the creativity of the original activity does not issue in a *static* structural relation, nor in an absolutely finalized outcome. Moreover, because the relativity of outcome to creative act involves a genuine *otherness*, I speak now of creation rather than origin. Our concern is a second beginning after the first origin.

Since we live in the middle of creation, when before we spoke of origin, it was as if we had regressed to a point of beginning, beyond which there was nothing further. Of course, regression to the origin *in itself* is impossible, but our metaxological understanding of being as plenitude suggested to us sig-

---

1. Compare to the difference between *energeia* and *ergon*, the first as activity, originating, being at work, the second as work, product. This is related to the difference of the first two senses, but with qualifications. Origin is a being at work, but not work in the sense of fabrication, imposing form on matter. The German word *Wirklichkeit* points to something related: the working, being at work of being.

267

nificant metaphysical metaphors. We are always at a remove from the ultimate origin, but the plenitude of that remotion can become a springboard to thinking the origin by way of excess: the origin as *huper* is ontologically richer than the richest of the rich in the middle. This is why—and for other reasons that need not be repeated—we spoke in the metaphor of the agapeic origin beyond all finite beginnings.

And now? Now we are, so to say, "regressing" to the penultimate, thinking this as a "progression" from the ultimate origin. Then we move "forward" rather than "backward." This may be dismissed as speculative, but I am not hiding the fact that we deal with a speculative hypothesis in the following respect. The speculative hypothesis is a *thesis* about the *huper*—the "above," the "more" of the absolutely primal—in relation to the *hupo*—the "below" of the derived. The movement of mindfulness in this thesis is not a simple "regress" or "progress"; it is more an interplay of thought back and forth, or rather, up and down, between the origin and the concrete middle wherein we live and think. This is why I so strongly stress the dynamic nature of the energy of being. Our "regression" from the middle to the penultimate, or our "progression" from the ultimate prime to the middle, takes its sights, as best as it can, from the energy of transcendence at work in the middle.

As we proceed, the metaphysical contours of this middle world will come into more determinate focus, mimicing, if you like, the "forward" movement from the origin towards creation. There will also be an interplay back and forth between concreteness and categorial articulation. If we lose sight of the former, the latter may seem empty at times, especially at this early stage, where the determinate contours of the familiar middle are not yet fully set forth. Overall, however, my desire is ontological fidelity to the dynamic being of the between.

Certain preliminary observations are in order. First, it does not seem appropriate to identify creation with efficient causality. This causality may suitably be applied to certain determinate relations of precedence and consequence between finite beings or processes. But the case is different if we want to think about the relation *between* finite being and its ultimate origin. To apply efficient causality to that relation is less to exceed the bounds of legitimate categorial application, less an unwarranted flight into the beyond, as a contraction of the transcendence of the origin to the level of a finite production.

Thus Kant may be right in denying the application of cause to origin. But is he right in the way he critically quarantines our metaphysical thinking from the origin? Does he not fail in thematic clarity about the difference between the determinate knowing of finite cognition and the second perplexity of metaphysical mindfulness? He wants to "save" metaphysics by putting it on the road to secure science; but this is a saving that does not save. But of course, there is no *determinate science* of origin or creation. Hegel also desires to make philosophy a science, but a related failing appears in his reduction of creation to merely a "representational" notion.[2] Creation is a meta-physical metaphor, not a determinate category. As such it has virtues for meta-physical mindfulness; it helps us think of originative excess.

A second observation concerns the hyperbolic notion of *creatio ex nihilo*. Creation is not the origin in itself. Nor is radical origination, as we suggested in the previous chapter, the self-creation of the origin. Agapeic origination is bound by nothing. Beings are brought into being, called into being out of nothing. To say this is hyperbolic. Though we cannot think this origination from nothing in its ultimate radicality, we will see that the production of newness within the originated creation does suggest some finite analogues. The creation from nothing names an enigma in which something absolutely other is at work. We cannot directly think the nothing at stake. Likewise, we cannot directly think the sense of being that overcomes and that is eternally in excess of this unthinkable nothing.

But if so, why not cease being troubled with the matter? Why bother at all, since our trouble is for naught, and we always and necessarily fail? I offer here but two reasons.

First, the self-transcending perplexity of metaphysical mindfulness can-not impose such a limit on itself. It strains to get a glimpse of what it cannot grasp. If one is not made insomniac by the second perplexity, this will seem like a blind person in a pitch black room, groping for a black cat, which may not be there at all. And yet mindfulness continues to grope.

Second, we meet in the middle world a *constitutive nothingness* that marks the peculiar forms of being found in the creation. In regard to this nothingness, finite thinking fails. But this failure may release another think-ing, at the edge of or beyond determinate cognition, a mode of overdetermined mindfulness, not only perplexed by this nothingness, but in strange rapport with the overdetermined origin. For even though radical origination from nothing names an absolute otherness, this naming is not only turned to-wards the enigma of the origin, it is also turned towards the otherness of *creation itself*. I now mean creation in the second sense of *outcome*. Creation comes out of an origin, but that coming out suggests a doubleness: at once a giving of the plenitude of being, for creation is there; and yet a coming out shadowed by nothingness. For creation would be nothing, were it not for the giving of the origin. Neverthless, it is there, and there it pivots on an irreduc-ible otherness, one side of which points back to the enigma of the origin as absolutely other, the other side of which dovetails into the middle world as marked by its own otherness, that is, its own independent being, as given being *for itself*.

---

2. I discuss, criticize, and offer an alternative understanding of Hegel's view of repre-sentation in *Beyond Hegel and Dialectic*, chapter 3.

Thus creation suggests the essential *separateness* of the outcome from the act that gives it separate being. And yet without that act, the separate world would be nothing. And so too this separation is itself inseparable from the giving of being by the origin. The doubleness of creation then would seem to imply a tense coexistence of independence and dependence. *Independence*, in that the outcome of origination is not the self-origination of the orgin: the creation is other. *Dependence*, in that the creation is not absolutely self-supporting; it hovers over the nothingness out of which it was called into being, and to which again many of its forms of being, perhaps all of it, will eventually return. It has its being as separate because of the generosity of the origin; as agapeic the origin renounces any dominating power over the creature; the origin lets it be as other, because the free origin gives finite being, as itself the free gift of freedom.

This means that we will understand creation metaxologically, as a double "unity" of self-integrity and relativity to the other, or a relativity that sustains rather than dissolves the otherness of the terms that enter into it. The absolute origin creates finite being from nothing out of its own excess of infinite generosity, absolves the creation from itself, gives it its free being for itself, out of which free being a free relativity between the creation and the origin is offered as a possibility. In brief, origin freely creates a free creation.

Paradoxically, this *discontinuity* between finite being and the origin puts us in mind of the doctrine of creation as *continuous*. That is, the discontinuity and possible nothingness of the creation, as outcome, suggests the continuing of creation, as activity of agapeic origination. This, in turn, affects the relativity of the creation to the origin: free and bound, independent and dependent, for-itself and for the other as more than itself, separate in itself and always in community, self-mediating and intermediating.

In sum: the origin creates a separate outcome; creation is out of, but also "outside" the origin. Origin creates other-being, for the sake of the other-being in its glorious otherness. This glorious otherness is the integrity of creation in itself. This integrity is not first a completely determinate and ready-made fact; it is not a fact at all, in the sense of something made *(factum)* from prexistent matter; the integrity of a creation is first a promise. What I mean is that creation is a given process of being made, and of making itself. It is not the self-pluralization of the origin, but the origination of genuine plurality. Creation is the glorious gift of the universal impermanence. What this means we must now try to illuminate by means of the fourfold sense of being.

The Elemental and Rapturous Univocity

Perhaps the most primitive question for determinate explanation concerns the basic "stuff" out of which the creation is constituted. What is the "substratum" of nature? The primitive answers tend to be in terms of the univocity of a universal homogeneity. The primitive question relates to the elemental and the elements. Hence Thales' answer of "water"—this is a metaphysical metaphor for the stuff of universal homogeneity that underlies creation. I say there is a univocity to this, not because we can conceptually specify what this "water" is with objective clarity or mathematical precision. Obviously, we cannot. The univocity concerns the assumption that there is an *underlying sameness* to the heterogeneity of things, a sameness that persists even in the universal impermanence.

The elemental here is interpreted as a universal homogeneity, but our reference to Thales is not intended to lock us into pre-Socratic metaphysics. We need only remind ourselves of the search in contemporary physics for a grand unified theory of the weak and the strong nuclear forces, the electromagnetic and gravitational forces. There can be a pluralization of such homogeneity too. For instance, in ancient atomism we find a pluralization of the univocity of Parmenides' One: the universal impermanence is the incessant displacement and rearrangements of the homogeneous atoms in the void that is itself homogeneous emptiness; change is the surface manifestation of homogeneous units in homogeneous emptiness. In modern atomism, by contrast, the ultimate simple units of "stuff" have now become quanta of mass-energy, but even there the search for a universal homogeneity does not stop. It persists beyond the elements, beyond the atoms, beyond the subatomic particles and forces, all the way down to microhappening; and then, it takes off again, all the way up and out to the celestial spaces and the stars. The search now persists with extraordinarily sophisticated instruments of observation and the power of highly complex mathematical univocity on its side.

This search is one of the noble adventures of the human mind. The question is whether there is a final explanation to stop mind in a reduction of plurality to the immediate univocity of some universal homogeneity. The view I venture is that this is inadequate to the plenitude of creation in its full concreteness. I should repeat that my concern here is not with a *cosmological hypothesis*; it is rather a metaphysical interest in the sensuous being-there of creation, in light of the elemental *that it is* of this being-there.

Reference to a universal homogeneity can be seen as an effort at specifying ultimate being, or something ultimate in being at work in finite creation. To help us get our bearings, I name a few historical instances. In addition to Thales' water, Heraclitean fire is a metaphorical naming of the elemental homogeneity. Anaximander's *to apeiron* seeks to name something similar. I think that Plato's introduction of the receptacle in the *Timaeus* tries to speak to the same point. The doctrine of *prōtē hulē*, prime matter, in Aristotle and his successors, also specifies this universal homogeneity. Indeed, the Greek *hulē* just means something like stuff—itself an elemental word, very hard to translate adequately into other terms. Descartes' *res extensa* names the universal homogeneity in relation to materiality. Will is the ultimate homogeneity in Schopenhauer. What Paul Weiss calls the *dunamis* is relevant.[3] We might also think of the space-time continuum of modern science in terms of its being a cosmological matrix of all physical possibility. Matter is a "knot" or "twist" in the primordial continuum. The space-time continuum is a primordial "plasma," open to possibility with respect to finite happenings, plastic to determinate eventuations. There is a ground of potentiality in creation, where coming to being is a more or less determinate formation of energy.

What can we say about any such elemental homogeneity? There is a sense in which it is not real at all. For everything real is differentiated, hence already in the realm of heterogeneity. The real is this rather than that, such and such rather than thus and other. And so the elemental homogeneity seems merely serviceable as an indefinite abstraction, which literally abstracts all the markers of determinacy from heterogeneous things. This abstraction may serve a notional analysis of conceptual determination, but really it refers to nothing concrete. For instance, one might say, and Aristotle would not disagree, that prime matter nowhere exists, since everything material that exists is complex or composite; it is shaped or formed matter, and prime matter is that state of matter in which the "stuff" would have all shape and form taken from it. So also Thales' water cannot exist at all in itself, since of itself it is nothing with identifiable form; its form comes from the shape of, say, the container in which it is placed. Like prime matter, or the water of the world, univocal homogeneity is a formless element. It does not exist per se. The same point might be made of the space-time continuum; it nowhere exists in a pure form, since what exists materially is a more or less determinate "wrinkle" of that continuum.

Why then undertake the notional analysis at all? Because something in our encounter with being in the middle demands that we also think of an elemental homogeneity. Consider, for example, Plato's receptacle. In the *Timaeus* it is clear that he is perplexed about a peculiar "reality" that fits neither the paradigm of pure being or becoming. Pure being would be beyond all change; becoming would be the realm of diversity and heterogeneity. The receptacle is neither. It is compared to the mother, as if it were a womb in which determinate being were engendered by the demiurge as the father of the cosmos. I know this is all metaphorical, but that is not an objection. I take the identification of the receptacle with space (*chora*) to point to the inescapability of given materiality in any account of cosmogenesis. There is an indeterminate sensuous "being" that is the matrix of all further being, and this is not an illusory form that merely must be transcended, but an indispensable condition for the generation of becoming itself. I take this also as a

---

3. See Paul Weiss, *Creative Ventures* (Carbondale: Southern Illinois University Press, 1992), especially the appendix on what he calls the *dunamis*.

gesture towards the ontological worthiness of "space," given sensuous materiality as such. This is not "nothing," but a perplexing condition of being that
is neither eternal being nor becoming.

We do not have to be Platonists, and yet we can take our cue from this
hint of an all-surrounding sensuousness of space, this universal homogeneity of the nurturing, maternal elemental. I now propose trying to think the
elemental as having its own reality, albeit extraordinarily evanescent. The
Voice out of the whirlwind asked of Job: "Where were you when I laid the
foundations of the earth?" Job, of course, had no answer. The Voice answers
for itself, with some of the greatest poetry of the wonders of creation. We have
to listen to this poetry of creation in relation to the elemental.

One stands on the shore before the ocean and the waters surge and ebb,
come in, trace a mark, go back down. The sea is an element unto itself, whose
enigmas still retreat before the complete accounting of human curiosity. The
sea, womb of all life, amorphous yet form-giving, an other element to us, and
yet it calls to us as we stand there. It is as if the sea were in us, as if there were
an inner ear, listening as in a seashell of spirit to the rise and fall of elemental
creation, flowing within us, mostly unnoticed. Or the winds rush around one;
above one the sky in its limitless expanse vaults over all things; one stands on
sand, but there is the earth at the limit of the sea, the grounding and supporting earth that manifests and hides so many different forms of being. One
stands there at the conjunction of a plurality of indeterminacies: elemental
indeterminacy of earth, water, fire, and air. The abstractive mind will try to
univocalize them in terms of some universal homogeneity, like prime matter,
or the primordial "plasma." But in this process the elemental will be quickly
lost, or reduced to a limit-case we think in order to make sense of the domesticated diversity that we accept for purposes of determinate scientific explanation. The univocal mind, whether it be the philosophic or scientific, will
turn the encounter with the elemental into something abstract, or something that is not elemental.

But there is a different univocity of the elemental. This I speak of in
terms of its *rapturous univocity*, in contradistinction to the analytical or abstractive univocity. The rapturous univocity of the elemental corresponds to
the lived immediacy of our being enveloped in the pure "stuff" of being. Being
enveloped: one stands at the conjuncture of a plurality of elemental indeterminacies—earth, fire, air, water. That conjunction is not an atomistic pillar
box that protects one from the flux of these elements. The point of conjunction is being in the middle where the elements pass through one.

I say envelop, and I might say "washed over." But this is put too much in
terms of one of the elementals. One might say "burned by" the elemental, but
this too names the conjunction in terms of one. One might say "grounded,"
but this also designates in terms of one. One might say, "elevated" or "uplifted" or "inspired," and the same point applies. For the rapturous univocity
is a kind of promiscuous envelopment by washing, by flaming, by grounding,

by uplift and inspiration. One is caught up, and one is not caught up, for one hardly distinguishes oneself from the play of the flux. One is played in the play of this multiple flux. One is the fire, one is the earth, one is the sky, one is the sea; and one is none of them. A call comes to us from the air, an impulse reaches us from the earth, a searing touches us from the fire, an ablution of the waters purifies the heart. One hardly knows that this is happening, for in the elemental we are caught up in the pure play of happening. We are all but laid asleep in the play of the elemental. This is the rapturous univocity.

Here we feel the need for language that is very different to that of the abstractive intellect. One needs poetic power to name the aesthetic happening of this interplay of the elements. This is not only linguistically right but ontologically so, if we are here close to the source of the *poiēsis* of naturing, or coming to being.[4] One might suggest that poetic speaking can be more proximate to creation, prior to the sedimentation of things into a more domesticated diversity. If this is true, the rapturous univocity of the homogeneous is subtle: a sense of the pure *dunamis* of being is here at work, *dunamis* prior to any specification into this, that, or the other, a pure *dunamis* aesthetically calling to us from the elemental, which we can never reach while still insisting on being ourselves in a rigid separateness. We have to yield to the pure *dunamis,* surrender as a lover surrenders. Instead of the neutral abstraction of the *prima materia*, an intimacy of caress, like a gentle breeze, comes to us from a source of becoming close to creation itself. The elemental sings in us, and when we sing the elemental comes through us to articulation. We sing the gift of creation. There is a festive affirmation of the sensuous being-there of finite being.[5]

Consider. I walk out into the air, and breathe it deeply, and in that deep draft, there is a depth of satisfying that nothing can match. The elemental "to be" is intoxicating and marvelous. Without it life is insipid and grey. There is an evanescence here more evanescent than all determinate becoming. Appearing itself is disappearing—the pure *dunamis* of sensuous appearing and immediate vanishing of the aesthetic sheen of the world. If is as if the sensuous were thrown up into being out of nothing and were immediately falling back down again, yet this pure rhythm of appearing and disappearing, arising and falling, could never be articulately registered because, on the instant, the disappearing immediately gives way to sensuous appearing again, and there is no determinate instant we could pin down.

It is as if the sensuous sheen of things, though in one sense a pure flux, were really a floating radiance, afloat on the void, the creation from nothing that astonishingly floats on this nothing, floats and drowns, floats and drowns and yet it is there, pure flux in pure persistence, or pure persistence in pure

---

4. See chapter 2, above, on the *poiēsis* of naturing.

5. See *Philosophy and its Others*, chapter 6, on the elemental and song.

flux. This is the marvel of aesthetic appearance, with the impossible-to-name abyss of nothing as a background that is no background, for it is no ground. This is the marvel of the elemental as the ungrounded gift of sensuous happening in its flux and persistence. We are touched by the inarticulate marvel of the sensuous, elemental world. The touch passes, or we pass into the forgetful determinations of everyday habits. We fall asleep in the pure happening of the elemental, even though our sleep of mind is always within the elemental.

To be attuned to this elemental, we must have, in a sense, the poetry of the child. The virgin mind of childlike univocity lives in and savors the elemental. Hence there is a sense in which the metaphysics of the beginning must be virgin poetry.[6] A child is carried into the night and murmurs: Look at the moon! This is not a merely successful act of indexical reference. It is a naming of presence as happening, and not just the determinate presence of the lunar object. The magic of the night, presided over by the queen of heaven, is exclaimed. We leap in the elemental, we exclaim it, we enjoy it. We are in love with the beauty of the night.

This is not to deny that we are also troubled by its marvel, for the hint of vanishing is carried on the sheen of its sensuous surface. And so we might liken the elemental to the time of Halloween: a sacred time, a sinister time, in which the body of the earth yields its dead. Spirits yet persist that the earth exhales back into the air. The air is haunted by presences, absences. The evening is hallowed, holy. But death disturbs the holy. This is a time of intersection, of this world and the other world, of renewal and menace. The vanished are abroad again, out of the earth into the air. The sensuous world as elemental is haunted. We are haunted. This haunting presence of the sensuous, full of absences, like the poetic metaphysics of the child, can be closer to creation at the beginning. In the beginning we live a taste for the elemental, a savor of the sensible, the sensuous. The surplus of the sensuous given is like an agape, a feast, a festivity: we drink it, eat it, breathe it, inhale it, exhale it. Philosophers too must be poets, or become the children they once were.

The elemental is a condition *beyond good and evil*, considered as *determinate opposites*. To be in it is to be in the inarticulate goodness of given sensuous being-there. It is the paradisal moment that is no moment, since moments are not differentiated. It is the immediate saturnalia, wherein differences are immediately subverted, mythically imaged as the golden age. Metaphysics begins with the baby at the breast. There we taste the first drowsy joy of the elemental. We live our inarticulate nativity to the flesh of being as our native home.

---

6. Vico is one of the few thinkers to have a genuine sense of the point. See especially his *New Science* on the poetic metaphysics of the first humans who divined Jupiter in the thunderbolt.

Subsequently eros will seek this joy of the flesh in the death of cold difference. But I am saying that there is first a sleeping agapeic initiation to being in the elemental beginning, out of which beginning the erotic quest will later spring, and to it also return. The elemental feeds not just the lack, but the secret plenitude of eros. This is a homogeneity beyond lack, where flesh seeks the solid thereness of flesh in its elusive evanescence. Eros will seek this again and again. It will articulate the elemental *dunamis,* and the joy of the elemental, most joyful when it is out in the air, and under the sky or stars, or with the solid earth beneath one, with the roar or murmur of the ocean within hearing. The rapture of univocity is always there, the alluring, liquefying, swooning homogeneity of pure sensuousness.

I think that Nietzsche's condition beyond good and evil is related to the elemental. This is what he calls the innocence of becoming. Of course, there is more and there will be more. Even now there is also the hint of the sinister. And this is not the sinisterness of evil; it is the pathos of innocence itself, the troubled trepidation that this too will vanish; that the goodness of primal joy will go and its glory fade, forever. There is no judgment here, just an impossible sorrow in the glory of joy itself. It is as if the shadow of evil, still unseen over the horizon, cast a blank menace in this place of joy, where it is not, nor should be. Nietzsche is here truer to the elemental than is Schopenhauer. Schopenhauer judges these hints of the sinister to be evil, such that deep down the beginning of creation is ugly, issuing out of an ugly erotic origination of Will as origin. Not surprisingly he will say: better not to be at all; or if in being, better to be quickly rid of being. Schopenhauer's judgment expresses disgust at the elemental, not its glorious joy.

Et in Arcadia ego; I too am in Arcadia, I, death. That it should be there at all is as astonishing as the marvel of sensuous being. And yet death intersects with the time of creation. A trembling troubles the rapturous joy of the elemental. The aesthetic univocity is shadowed by the equivocal. This shadow can be turned into the darkness of the elemental. For instance, when Sartre discusses what he calls *the viscous,* he clearly gives utterance to the fear of being swallowed, engulfed. He resists swooning into the elemental, as if thereby the self for-itself would be consumed by an absorbing god, or a sweet, devouring matrix. The sweet honey of the viscous is not much different to the *nausea* produced in him by the revelation of naked, contingent being in-itself. Like Schopenhaer's origin, the beginning is ugly, disgusting, and a threat to determinate being, not only of things but also of human selves.

When this happens, rapturous univocity, troubled by the ambiguity of the aesthetic, becomes dissolving univocity, and the self for-itself recoils from its own flowing away into the elemental. Sartre's viscous is again revealing. The viscous is a kind of liquefaction of being, an engulfing featurelessness of being *en soi*. We are reminded of Descartes' wax when it is heated—it loses all determinate shape; this malleable material extension is like the universal homogeneity underlying all determinate material formations of being. But the melting wax is a neutral homogeneity, a neutered element. Mathematical objectification here has stripped the elemental of its charge of aesthetic value. We might say that Sartre's response to the viscous goes beyond this neutering to the point of nausea.

Or rather, the neutering turns to nausea, just because the draining of value from the universal homogeneity makes the elemental to be irremediably absurd. It is seen as a disgusting absurdity because now its menace threatens the dissolution of the self being *pour soi*. Sartre is quite aware of the liquefaction of self, but he is both fascinated and repulsed. In this repulsive fascination the self has lost all its mathematical Cartesian confidence. In Sartre's being *en soi* we find a more extensive universalization of homogeneity, that not only menaces the determinacies of external things, but also the definite being of the self. The viscous is the purée of cess.

We find a reflection of this metaphysical horror of the elemental in Levinas's *there is*, the sinister anonymity of existence without existents. I stress that this is *not* what I mean by the elemental. In fact, some of the above thinkers, Descartes, Schopenhauer and Sartre most clearly, turn the aesthetic gift of pure sensuousness into a degraded creation, a menaced happening of the materiality of being. But even the threat of suffocation should be seen in light of the glory of our evanescent being here. Being is happening, persisting provisionally, now floating on void, but sweet with the simple honey of "to be." The honey of being may be sticky in that we cannot escape it; we may even feel we are drowning in sweetness. But this sweetness of being, alluring and swooning and menacing, can draw us in, and there is no nausea. Painless in the aesthetic sweetness of being, surfeited with a cloying enjoyment, we are engorged with the elemental. This can happen in eating, drinking, love, in enjoyment of the aesthetic element of the world. We joy in being, moving in the radiance of the sun, like a grain of pollen floating in the golden air. We cannot enjoy thus either Descartes' wax materiality or Sartre's viscous cess.

Real menace comes later, much later than this primal innocence of creation. Is the elemental shadowed? Is nature haunted?[7] Yes. Putting the point religiously, the gods name the presences. Polytheism names the proliferation of the *dunamis* of pure happening. Of course, there is a monotheism of universal univocity that tends to suppress the pagan rapture of the elemental. This is not the monotheism of the absolute original. If the origin is agapeic, then the joy of the sensuous elemental is carried further into the world, in a love of the mortal, the transitory, the singular. In the elemental the trace of the agapeic origin is revealed in *matter as good for itself*. Sensuous being is charged with value. Its very being there is an ontological good. This is far from the neutral *res extensa* of Cartesianism, the valueless thereness of homogeneous space and its successors in modern science and philosophy.

---

7. On the dangers, see the discussion of country silence in *Philosophy and its Others*, chapter 5.

The polytheism of this *other* monotheism also rejects any gnostic horror before materiality. It affirms the goodness of the sensuous, the goodness of the body, of matter. Thus, for instance, when the body swoons towards rapturous univocity in sexuality, it feels matter more deeply than the neutered univocity of the detached mind that is not aroused, or the gnostic mind that is repulsed even when roused. In a word, to be bodied is good. The swoon into the elemental does not reflectively know this, it carnally lives this metaphysics: matter and body are gifts of the origin, not degradations of the One. This good of the elemental, precisely because it is on the border of the inarticulate, is almost beyond all saying. Yet we try to say it. We must listen to the artist to be mindful again of its charged presence.

What then is the elemental? The elemental names the gift of aesthetic being. I mean this ontologically and not just anthropocentrically. The elemental is the primal aesthetic being there of the world. The sensuous world is given to appearance, out of the surplus of the original agape. Materiality, sensible being, sensuous thereness, are creations, and as creations are the outcome of the agapeic origin. There is a certain ontological worth to material being, to the body of things. The agape of the elemental, we feast on it. The aesthetic body of being is an excess that touches us and that we touch. We feast on this excess of the elemental sensuousness. What passes in that touch is not completely objectifiable.

Heterogeneity and Equivocal Process

When I say that material being comes to determination in the elemental matrix[8] of aesthetic givenness, my concern is metaphysical, not scientific, but I am not incognizant of the dynamic view of contemporary science. Thus we might see the space-time continuum in terms of energetic becoming, a dynamic matrix of process, itself in process. There is nothing static about its generation of all that eventuates in nature. In Newtonian physics, space and time are absolute and separable: space is a universal, empty container, wherein every entity has its determinate, exactly specifiable location; time is homogeneous, uniform, universally the same for everyone. By contrast, contemporary physics shows a world of dynamic happening rather than static entities, where there is a convertibility of mass and energy, where space and time are not separate but unified in a space-time continuum. Space and time are determined in terms of relations rather than separable features of external objects. A network of differential relations come to spatial and temporal determination in the universal impermanence. Moreover, space itself is dynamically conceived as expanding; it is temporalized, dynamized in universal

---

8. I pointed out before how matter is related to *mater*.

becoming. Such dynamized space suggests an energy of transcendence in matter itself. It is not that space is swallowed up by process simply, but that it has to be reconceived in new dynamic terms: space is spatializing, just as time is temporalizing; space-time is processive through and through. The continuum is a continuing, itself in a processive sense.

This means, of course, that there is no absolute univocal homogeneity. In one sense, we are always beyond univocity, always in the middle, where any sheer homogeneity is more or less differentiated. We always begin, or have already begun, after the first origin. As I put it above: creation is a beginning after the first origin. Creation as given outcome is inseparable from heterogeneity. This indeed is the ontological meaning of creative activity—the bringing into being of the *heteros*. I did suggest more than a negative meaning to the thought of homogeneity, namely, the elemental as the appearing gift and vanishing evanescence of sheer aesthetic being there. Reflecting further on this, it became clear that the language it needed could not be univocal, but was fraught with ambiguity. This is not just our failure, but emerges from a fidelity to appearing itself. We must now look at this more fully.

In creation beings are not completely constituted from the outset. They are in process of becoming themselves. So they are not completely coincident with themselves. Heraclitus is right in his contradictory saying: we step into and we do not step into the same river; we are and we are not. The anticipation here surprised is not only that of formal logic, but that of common sense, which looks to reality as an essentially determinate realm of ready-made substances. Heraclitus's saying contains nothing of gnomic riddle. There is a sober truthfulness in this self-contradictory speech; its truth mirrors the energy of process as equivocal. Our problem is not to stop with contradiction, but to face into it more deeply, searching its meaning. There are seven major points I want to make.

A *first* point concerns the kind of heterogeneity produced in creation. It seems that the heterogeneous is not a mere product, in the sense of a ready-made substance. It involves process, invokes the very *dunamis* of heterogenizing. For process is an alteration, where alteration carries the meaning of *alter*. The process is one of making other (*alter*). What is made other? Is it nothing? No, it is something in being that is made other. Indeed, what is made other is really the promise of being something, of becoming something. The original "something" that is othered is not a fully made thing, but the energy of being as will be crystallized into the finite center of determinate existence. What is given to be in creation incarnates the promise of an unfolding of itself. A being is its own promise as marked by an ensemble of powers of being. The full integrity of a being is referred to the realization of these powers, but this will come later (see subsequent chapters).

The promise of becoming refers us, not just to creation as given heterogeneity, but as a process of differentiation that pluralizes heterogeneity. Creation differentiates finite being into a diversity of beings. Nor is the process of othering a mere displacement of univocal units that are shifted in location from here to there within a universal homogeneity or void. Given beings are not atoms of eternal univocity that suffer no change within, on their being relocated in some universal homogeneity or emptiness. Nor are they the systems of mass in early modern physics, which essentially remain substantially at one with themselves, such that their change is merely quantitative. The doubleness inherent in the process of becoming is not an extrinsic disturbance to a reality that in itself escapes all ambiguity, being entirely itself and at one with itself. The heterogeneous equivocity of becoming is the way it concretizes a paradoxical conjunction of being and nothing.

A *second* point concerns becoming as a process of *perpetual transformation*. What is transformed is extraordinarily difficult to pin down. Is there a core of being that passes through this perpetual process of transforming? Is it a mere mixing of elements, as when Empedocles says: there is no birth or baneful death, just a mixing and a separation of what has been mingled (fr. 8). Anaxagoras said: we Greeks are wrong to use the expression "to come into being" and "to be destroyed," for nothing comes into being or is destroyed. Rather a thing is mixed with or separated from already existing things (fr. 17). On this view of change, nothing comes into being or passes out of being. There is just a reshuffle of the eternal univocals that are said to be the irreducible elements of being.

By contrast once again, becoming as process points to something different than a reshuffle of eternal univocals: the paradoxical conjunction, contradictory from the standpoint of univocity, of coming into being and passing out of being, the conjunction of creation and nothing, and "nothing" here in the active sense of a process of nihilation. Becoming is a mixing and a separation, but first it is a coming to be of the beings that mingle and are differentiated. Even then differentiation is not added to becoming from outside; it is qualitatively constitutive of process. Process does not deal with mere possibility, but with real dynamic being, full of promise. The realization of this promise is equivocal, because the promise is that of a being that is also from nothing: the *nihil*, the nothing is enigmatically operant in the being of the creation itself. It is and it is not. We have to say both, though one cannot be reduced to the other. The process seems to be just this equivocal conjunction of opposites. In the seeming universal homogeneity of "It is," the operation of the *nihil* defines the character of creation as a *universal impermanence*. We not only need an ontology, we need a meontology.

A *third*, related point concerns the question: How do we account for the *becoming* of finite being? Philosophers have repeatedly said that nothing comes from nothing. If so, then either nothing is, or being simply is. Do we not end then, as it were, with either the absolute void or with a block eternity? But suppose we say that being only comes from being? Do we not again risk a block eternity, such that the universal impermanence becomes unthinkable? How then think coming to being, with respect to given being that *might not be*?

For the latter given being is such that its ontological constitution is inseparable from its own possible nothingness. Do we not need to think the coming to being of finite being, given being defined in the universal impermanence, and not just eternal univocity or empty nothing? Do we not need to think a double conjunction of being and nothing? Moreover, must not this conjunction be seen in the light of the priority of being?

Here philosophers have sometimes distinguished between an absolute and relative sense of nothing. The first nothing would be absolutely outside of being, the altogether not (*to mēdemōs on*) that Parmenides said was unthinkable. The second nothing would not be thus "outside," but ontologically constituent of the being of finite becoming. In present terms, the first would refer to the unthinkable nothing, out of which the origin calls creation into being. The second would refer to the doubleness of finite being which, as being, is defined by reference to its own possible nonbeing. But can we finally keep these two senses absolutely apart? Or does the *nihil absolutum* cast its meontological shadow in the middle of finite relativity? I think it is very hard to give an *unequivocal* answer to such a question. I suspect that the relative nothing is conditional, precisely as a relativization of absolute nothing: that is, in creation the absolute nothing is qualified by the gift of being, even if that being as given is finite; hence too the relative nothingness of finite being.

A *fourth* point concerns the coherence of the above with an understanding of the original power of being as *plenitude*, as excess. It seems we have to say that in finite process this excess is qualified by the operancy of the *nihil*. But it appears that we may have to call this an *equivocal nihil*, since we cannot univocally identify it with either the relative or the absolute nothingness, to the complete exclusion of the other. This equivocity of the *nihil* will come back below in metaxological form when we refer to a sense of the nothing beyond the determinate negative (the latter is central to dialectic).

What do I mean by the equivocal *nihil*? The equivocal nothing is *not outside* the process as a whole that would be, or even held together, as a whole, by virtue of some strange comfort of the embracing void. The equivocal *nihil* is not out there, outside the finite creation. The doubleness of finite being points to a struggle for being internal to the process of becoming: creation originates in nothing and out of nothing, as the excess of the original plenitude pours forth its gift gratuitously; the very thereness of the finite process is, in one sense, an ascendency of the original excess over the nothing; but this ascendency does not leave the nothing outside of what the excess calls into being; nothing is inherent, albeit qualified by the being of the finite called into being. Finite being is beyond universal homogeneity, beyond an ontological opposition that sets being and nothing completely outside each other. Opposition is ingredient in its being-there. There is a tension in conjunction of being's plenitude and the operation of the *nihil*, as they work together, struggle together in finite being, and finally break apart when the process of becoming comes to the point of its own perishing.

And thus out of this paradoxical conjunction, equivocal becoming pre-cipitates the breaking up of all pure homogeneity. We find a process of othering, but an othering that also diversifies opposition. Othering and opposing mix creation and negation, but they are not merely negative. They proliferate the heterogeneous. They also spur a *metabasis eis allo genos* of our thinking, beyond the abstract formalities of univocal mind. The thought of heterogene-ity makes us dwell in the perplexing equivocations of being. And yet as being that is originated with the mark of constitutive nothingness, as a becoming that nevertheless is an affirmative othering, the universal impermanence still shows forth the glory of creation.

A *fifth* point concerns the *irreversible* nature of the process. The move-ment of othering is through life, towards death, and there is no second chance. From the "once" of the process, to the "never" of its perishing, the arrow of time moves from "once" to "never again." This being will never again be as this "once," within the process of becoming. Here we come across the contin-gency of the finite being. What is done cannot be undone, in the process of becoming itself. Might it be undone in eternity? We cannot say now; we must wait and see. Is the process incapable, as it were, of forgiving? I think one can say there is a *conditional absolution* or absolving in time, in this sense. While the process is continuous, it is also discontinuous. The universal imperma-nence is a perpetual perishing, but it is also an ever-youthful beginning afresh. The gift of being is given again and again. But this temporal forgiving, in giving again, does not undo the unrepeatable. It gives afresh another chance, another gift of unrepeatable being. The promise of the "once" is given again and again. But the unrepeatability of *this* "once" always remains unrepeatable.

There is a profound pathos in this irreversibility and unrepeatability. It is relatively equivocal with respect to the present and future as open, both as a promise. It is relatively univocal with respect to the past as a "has been," as done. This is not to deny that this "has been" can have an effect on the equivo-cal promise of the present and future; it can. The present and future can also have an effect on the relative univocity of the past as a "has been," in that when we try to repeat the unrepeatable, we are made to look differently on the "once," as done. We begin to discern something "more" in it than a univocal "has been." Memory of transcendence *then* at work may be awakened, reawakened. This may bestir one's present "once" and future promise. The relative univocity of the past then can perhaps be forgiven, and saved; but any such agapeic absolution does not derealize the "once" as passed, its "never."

A *sixth* point—again related to the nothing as ontologically constitu-tive—suggests that becoming's equivocity is *not merely phenomenal*. Becoming is equivocal not only for us, it is equivocal for itself. It is not an equivocation that simply appears to be so to our limited minds, and which would disappear were we able to assume a different perspective on finite process. The equivocity is not rendered into an unreal condition from the standpoint of a noumenal realm, univocally beyond all change. The work of negating in the finite process is real. This demands a revision of what we mean by real. Realness is not exhausted by determinate beings, nor by homogeneous being. The *nihil* is intimate to the being of what is finitely real. It is no subjective projection of "negation" by us on what in itself is entirely devoid of anything negative.

If the latter were true, we would have the difficulty of acknowledging the operancy of the *nihil* in human being and thinking. But the operancy of the *nihil* is ingredient in all finite process. Pain, disease, agony, ageing, dissolution, death, all point to a *nihil* at work in being. Beings come to be, come to be determinate; beings fall apart, pass out of determinacy and become nothing. Becoming something and becoming nothing flow into each other, and no fixed univocal boundary can be erected between them. The becoming of things is finite, manifesting an inherent limitation on their energy of being. This limitation is the mark of the intimate nothing. No finite being or process can be absolutely for itself. Its being passes beyond it, first relative to the gratuity of its contingent nature, then relative to its final impotence to dictate its own continuing to be. In death its unique "once" is surrendered to nothing and the "never."

A *seventh* point concerns whether we mean to follow a path somewhat like Zeno's. For Zeno claimed to show the self-contradictory nature of motion and change. Did not he also try to demonstrate the equivocity of becoming? But his demonstration is a *reductio ad absurdum*, performed on the assumption of becoming, but under the guiding presupposition of the *absolute univocity* of being. Change is reduced to a set of atomistic units, instants; or the path of motion is divided into univocally determinate points, a division putatively without definite limit; thereby becoming has already been univocally reduced to a set of static snapshots of motion or change; and, of course, there is no real change when you analyze the snapshots.

So unlike Zeno who, in face of equivocal becoming, wants to laugh at its absurdity, and thus indirectly force his antagonists towards the truth of pure univocity, I think that this univocity is an abstraction of stasis from the dynamism of becoming. If the latter is analyzed in terms of the abstraction, of course, it is absurd, in the sense Zeno intends. The real issue is whether we need a different analysis, or another mode of thinking that is truer to the dynamism of becoming as it manifests itself. Analysis separates into determinate univocal units what in the universal impermanence itself is mixed, and perhaps "unitary" or held together in quite a different sense. A different thinking is needed. Properly understood, the sense of becoming as equivocal moves us more truly in that direction, more faithful to the *dunamis* itself.

Let me try to gather our thoughts and conclude this line of thought. Every being in process of becoming surges forth into difference out of the promise of its own, given original energy of being. Death pulls at every being in process of becoming, even when that surge seems most exultant. Death pulls like the line of a kite in flight; the uplifting air will become still; the line of life will slack, and the surge subside and ebb; the kite will shudder and stall, plunge and fall to the ground. While things are and surging, they seem to be forever; once they are, there seems something irrevocable about their being; their "onceness" has an unrepeatability about it. But this "onceness" is always shadowed by "once now," but not forever; and out of the operancy of the *nihil*, the "never" strikes and lays low—once perished, never again.

The pathos of the elemental stirs again in the perishability of the "once," and in the hint of the "never" that awaits all beings in creation. But in that "once" itself, these things now are. Their unrepeatability is their astonishing being given. The beauty of the flower in process of blooming is both its astonishing dynamic thereness, and its pathos as destined to perish. Beings surge in the prodigal excess of creation in the universal impermanence, out of the gift of the original excess. But beings in process are also pathetic in a deep ontological sense. They *suffer* their own passing, and the passage of the excess beyond them. And this suffering, this pathos, is itself a gift, a privilege, inherent in the glory of creation as the universal impermanence.

Compared to the previous pathos of the elemental, there is now a sharpness to suffering in the equivocity of being. We are in the world of difference to the point of opposition; the creative power of finite being is startled by its other it cannot escape—namely, the nothing. Finite being cannot escape this nothing, because this nothing articulates itself within the process of finite being. And yet the nothing stands in stark opposition to the surge of being, the insistence of being that breaks forth in all creation. In this exceedingly complex equivocity of becoming, we have gone beyond the indefiniteness of the inarticulate joy of the elemental and its vague sense of menace. The equivocity of becoming is not something indefinite; it is determined precisely in the process of differentiation. The surge and suffering of being in their mutual coexistence and opposition are laid out much more explicitly. We might even say that the equivocity of being is much more univocally evident! This is true, but there is also more, since this equivocity, even in such univocal explicitness, asks for further consideration.

Mediated Becoming and Dialectic

Becoming is a process in which differences develop even to the point of antithesis; nor is difference merely an external relation binding one fixed univocal entity to another; once unfolded in a process of becoming, a seemingly univocal being can no longer be said to be itself simply: it is not itself and hence has to become itself; it has to become other to itself; and yet it must be itself to become other to what it now is. The passage of becoming shows itself to be complexly mediated. This mediation we must now address. The points I will make concern, first the meaning of succession, second the role of self-mediating dialectic, third the relation of the *nihil* and determinate negation, fourth the shaping in process of singular being. In the next section, I consider the universal impermanence in terms of metaxological intermediation.

First, can a process of becoming be adequately described in terms of succession? We think of succession as determining the relation of precedence, presence, and futurity: beginning now, process will procede to a subsequent phase, which will then be the present of which the previous beginning now becomes the past; and of these two temporal phases, the future will again be their successor, always their successor. Becoming thus seems to be a process of succession, symbolized by a line that procedes from a point of origin, reaching through a traversed present interim, towards a future that may be anticipated or open. Thus we often think of succession in terms of the series: 1, 2, 3, 4, . . . and so on to infinity. Process of succession suggests a certain unfinished infinity to becoming.

My point will be that this idea of succession really shows the questionable influence of univocity, and cannot fully account for becoming. That is, the stages of succession, or the units of the linear series, are conceived on the model of univocities, strung out like beads on a string. The units are themselves and nothing but themselves, punctual instants complete in their own self-sufficient simultaneity; the stage or the instant is thus in complete coincidence with itself. This cannot work, I think. Why? In process we must emphasize that *passage as passing* is more important than allegedly univocal punctiform stages through which passage is putatively effected. Stages are themselves *passing* stages, hence either must be, as it were, thrust beyond punctiform instantaneity, or be thrust into, or at the very least seep into, the next stage of passage. The stage as punctiform unit is an abstraction from the happening of passing.

In terms of the linear series, and against the abstraction of the univocal unit, we might say that in *passing*, the 1 implicates the 2, and the 2 the 3, and so on. The fact that we can say *and so on* indicates that we have some understanding, perhaps completely unthematic, of just this implication of the other by the one, or the one by the other. We understand the dynamism of this passing through and beyond, even when we cannot univocally or mathematically formulate it. Moreover, there is an energy of passing carrying us beyond the 1 to the 2, to the 3, *and so on.* This energy of passing is, just in its continuity, made discontinuous by the differences it introduces: it not only passes from 1 to 2, to 3; it also makes 1 *not* to be 2, and 2 *not* to be 3, and so on. And once again, our immediate grasp of this *and so on* indicates that we understand, albeit unthematically, the continuing work of this "not," the work of the "not" that will continue beyond the actual units it has managed to carve into identifiable integrities. We unthematically grasp it to be at work throughout the process as continuing passage.

In other words, there seems to be some *more inherent implication* between the members of succession. What this implication is may be extremely difficult to say properly, and we have not managed yet. But certainly we cannot adequately understand it on the univocal model, where a being is itself and nothing other. The univocal order helps us make sense of integrities as for themselves, but there is also a set of differential relations between these integrities, which cannot be explained in the same univocal way. For the differential relation relative to process is not a fixed unit or structure, but a passage and a transition. Equivocal becoming points to this passage and transition, but equivocity too does not do full justice to the inherent implication just noted. For the equivocal emphasizes difference such that relativity as a more inherent bond is hard to acknowledge. Pure equivocal difference rather points, as it were, to mutual repulsion. By contrast, the inherent implication implies a relativity beyond univocity and equivocity.

But this brings us to the *second* point. Dialectical relativity is one way to name this inherent implication in the passage of process. For the passage of any process of becoming is not pure differentiation. It is the differentiation of a beginning that sets the process in motion, and as such it entails a certain self-differentiating. What I mean is this: what becomes, differentiates *itself* into what it now is and was, and what it is not, what it will be. What it is, and what it is not, seem to be antithetical; but this is not so, since what it is and what it is not are two modes of what is it, when we see what it is from the more embracing and concrete fullness of the more completely unfolded process. What is in process is both what it is and what it is not. Seen from the fuller unfolding of the process, these two sides do not fall apart into unmediated opposition; they reveal the self-opposition of what is in process, but this self-opposition itself mediates the fuller becoming of what is in process; self-opposition serves the purpose of fuller self-becoming. This is why we have to say that equivocal becoming is mediated. The mode of its mediation here noted is self-mediation. Passage is a process of self-mediation.

I note the intrusion of a certain *teleological* language. The language of univocity is the language of inarticulate beginnings; the language of equivocity is the language of diversification, but without any particular purpose, except perhaps the diversification itself; the language of dialectical self-mediation is a language of teleology. That is, the inarticulate beginning and the purposeless diversity both serve the purpose of process, which is now seen from the standpoint of a more fully developed end. I do not say *any* end. For the point is not dependent on reaching an absolute end. The point can be made if a process has developed to a provisional or relative end, which we designate by the phrase *the fuller unfolding of the process.* From the standpoint of that unfolding, the richness of what was too quiescent in the univocal beginning, and the togetherness of what seemed merely divided in equivocal diversification, are seen to be essential to the fuller self-unfolding of what is in process.

The language of teleology indicates a certain *directional vector* in becoming. Becoming is not mere local change from *a* to *b,* or mere diversification, which really is no different to dissipation. It is qualitative change in the direction of the fuller self-realization of what passes in the process of becoming. What is at stake is not only a certain deconstruction of univocal notions of identity, but a subversion of equivocal notions of difference. In the first place, what is in process could never really *be* itself, if being were only univocal; univocal being is self-subverting. In the second place, what is in process could not *become* itself, did it not so oppose itself, contradict itself, in the sense of seeking what it is not, in antithesis to what it now is, in order to become what it truly is. Self-opposition subverts itself in a fuller process of self-realization. And this fullness is the *telos* of becoming inscribed in it from its inarticulate beginning. We did not know it then, but we do know it now, when the beginning is articulated, or articulates itself more fully.

Thus becoming is dialectical precisely because it articulates the process of passage along the lines of the self-mediation of what is in process. And there is a sense in which, prior to this mediation, there is but the promise of self. Dialectic, so to say, makes explicit the realization of the promise. The process of passage is self-developing. I do not say this is *all* there is to the promise or process. Nor does it fully define the inherent implication stated above; but it does take us into a dynamized world of active relating. How are we now to think of this dynamizing? We have to turn again to the question of the not and the *nihil*, this time with respect to the notion of determinate negation.

This will be my *third* point. Recall that creation as universal impermanence is marked by a certain constitutive nothingness: it is, but it might not be, it might be nothing, and entities within the universal impermanence will be nothing again, in the passage of the process; the gift of their being is temporary, for a time. Creation as universal impermanence is, but might not be. The question again returns as to how we think this doubleness of being and the nothing.

We cannot simply say that the nought is external to creation, for creation as temporary is defined internally by the nought. We do not have eternal atoms externally related in a void that does not reach into their homogeneous interiority. Being in process is not void, but has void within it. It is hollowed out within, in the sense of being as much lacking in full realization, as being there with incontrovertible existence. The nothing is constitutive for finite being in process of becoming. The equivocal sense of becoming serves to point towards this inner hollowing, this constitutive nothing. What dialectic adds is that this constitutive nothing is necessary to any finite process of self-development. Hence the nothing is interpreted in the light of determinate negation. Determination is negation, Spinoza says, and Hegel repeats it. There is also, as we will suggest, a nothing *beyond* determinate negativity, but we must first deal with determinate negation.

Equivocal becoming shows what is in process to be itself and *not* to be itself, but in dialectical mediation, the not within the process is turned towards an essentially positive result. The not testifies to the negative power that thrusts the inarticulate beginning beyond itself. Process is differentiation, but differentiation is mediation, for it defines the self-becoming of what is in process. Note that this view corresponds to the *erotic* conception of the origin. The lack in the beginning is driven beyond itself by a negativity at work within it from the beginning. But since this negation is the negation of itself, the negativity is a self-negativity. The lack at the beginning negates itself in the process of becoming itself. And so this self-negation is, in fact, the opposite to self-annihilation. It is a processual determination of what the self is. The negation is a determination of what is more positively at work in the initially undetermined process. Self-negation is not only determination, it is self-determination.

How then is process rendered? The passage from beginning to what comes later is differentiation through negation, which negation is determination of what is in process, which determination is the self-determination of what is in process. Differentiation, negation, and determination become constitutive moments of a more complete process of self-determination. It is the inherence of this determinate negativity that produces the differentiation of the process, establishes the definition of determinate articulations within it, and thrusts process towards a *telos* of fulfilled self-realization. This latter wholeness is, in fact, the most positive outcome of becoming, conceived as a dialectical process.

This brings us to my *fourth* point: the process is one of *selving*, of the *singularization* of being. What this suggests is that in the passage of process, determinate beings in their singular selves come to be. Becoming mediates the coming to determination of selves, for in the flux of happening, beings are concretized with a certain wholeness that is for itself. This does not mean that such wholeness is *closed* in on itself. Not at all. The wholeness is always *for a time*. It floats fraily on a surge of self-surpassing that defines process as it passes beyond even this determinate whole. In sum: dialectical becoming mediates the emergence of *open wholes*—determinate beings that are for themselves, both in process of self-realization, and in passage to relativity with respect to other wholes, also crystallized in the process of becoming.

This is a kind of univocity raised to a higher power, in the following sense. The threat of dissolution that always menaces the equivocity of becoming is here overcome by the process itself, such that the unity of the open whole stands for itself in its mediated integrity. This is not the end of the matter. Indeed here we touch on the limitations of conceiving creation dialectically. For the predominance of self-mediation, albeit complexly qualified, and the recurrence of univocity, can lead one to think in terms of a universal holism, a *different monism* at odds with the agapeic origin and creation as the universal impermanence.

I want to admit the crystallization of singulars as open wholes within a "whole" that itself is open. There is no denying the relativity of singular ones to all the others within creation as an open whole. The mediation of selving within this open whole is determined by the original power of being at work in the universal impermanence. But monism subordinates this openness, whether of the singular ones, or the universal impermanence, to a completely self-mediating whole. This is most evident in Hegel where the absolute *telos* is understood as the dialectical self-mediation of one absolute whole. In other words, the universal permanence in its open creativity is closed from the standpoint of this absolute *telos*. This is a closing return of the univocal sense of being, in its final, monistic subordination of otherness and plurality. This is a dialectical Spinozism. It does not matter whether the totality is finally identified with the one substance or absolute spirit, whether creation as universal impermanence is named *natura naturata*, or whether the One as such, God, is identified with *natura naturans*. Whatever form the monism takes, it is at odds with the pluralism of creation, consistent with the notion of the origin as agapeic.

For if dialectic is exhausted in terms of a self-completing mediation, the eventuation of genuine pluralism becomes a mere vanishing medium, devoured by the all-absorbing totality. On this view, the origin's own self-mediation is not differentiated from the creative excess that originates the finite creation and intermediates with it as genuinely other for itself: all are reduced to different phases of one totalistic process of self-mediation. The only negativity is the one internal to this all-absorbing whole, and it serves the self-determination of this whole. Because the origin in itself is not essentially distinguished, either from its origination of creation, or from creation itself as universal impermanence, the reference of creation itself to the other origin, as transcendence, is lost in a totality that is immanence, and nothing but immanence.

We then get the infinite self-mediation of one whole, not a metaxological intermediation between the origin's infinitude and the open world of creation as other, itself the promise of its own peculiar infinitude. For, in contrast to any dialectical monism, the agapeic origin implies that the originated world as for itself is marked by an openness, beyond every closed whole. Hence even in the universal impermanence, it is the promise of its own infinitude. And this infinitude of creation is for itself and not a mere means for the self-mediation of the origin. None of this is to deny the finitude of creation. On the contrary, this finitude is defined just in terms of its being for itself. The agapeic being of the origin, the open promise of creation even in its finitude, define a space of otherness, even in their community. One is *not* the other, and this "not" is not defined by any logic of determinate negation or self-determination. There is not just one all-absorbing infinitude that always and ever mediates only with itself, and with itself alone.

But you may still persist: Is this view really different to Hegel's who, after all, also speaks of the union of being and nothing in becoming? On the surface the views seem the same, but it should be clear that the meaning of being and nothing, and hence also of becoming, are given a different modulation in the present account. I have already spoken critically of Hegel's view of being (e.g., chapter 4, above). I now just add a remark on his statement (*Encyclopaedia*, section 88): being and nothing are the same in becoming. This is not so, not true to universal impermanence. Being is, because it is originated as a gift that is given despite nothing, and in interplay with, though in ascendancy over, the constitutive nothing operant in the universal impermanence. There is an asymmetry between being and nothing in creation as universal impermanence. If being were not prior to and more ultimate than nothing, there would be nothing at all. If there were a parity between being and nothing, we would not even get the absolute homogeneity of entirely quiescent being in which the positive and the negative neutralize each other. We still would get nothing. For something to be, even to be in a process of going under or passing into nothing, this asymmetry has to be. Being has to have priority over nothing, else nothing would be at all.

True, Hegel also states that the difference of being and nothing must not also be forgotten. But this reminder is immediately qualified by the identification of this difference with the inherent unrest of the unity. The difference is *within* the embrace of the unity, which unity is ultimately the dialectically self-mediating absolute. But the asymmetry of being and nothing forces us to think a different difference, to think metaxologically of creation as universal impermanence.

The Middle World of Creation/The Universal Impermanence

Has my reader wearied? I hope not. Is there someone listening out there? I hope so. I know these thoughts put us to the test, and I would I could make them as light as heaven. I can assure my reader I am not lost in the bosom of the Lord. I am a thinking reed trying to glean the import of matters extraordinarily difficulty, not to say mysterious. We are on the last lap of this chapter, so let us now not flag.

What the metaxological sense requires includes the following five considerations: First, it suggests an intermediated doubleness with respect to the difference between origin and creation. Second, it implies a difference between the operancy of the *nihil* and determinate negation. Third, it entails a kind of teleology other than any absorbing monism. Fourth, it indicates a double conjunction of continuity and discontinuity in the middle world of creation. Fifth, it asks us to rethink, in light of the gift of time, the metaphysical pathos of the "once" and the "never." These are the points I will discuss.

First consideration. You break in and put the question: Do we not here again have a return of equivocal doubleness, analogous to the recurrence to univocity with dialectic? What rabbit is now to be pulled from the hat? I think we must see the double differently—not ontological duplicity but in light of the doubling of the power of creation. What I mean is that creation redoubles being, gives rise to beings again and again, issues in a generativity that is beyond simple oneness. This redoubling is creation's promise of infinite pluralization. This new double is the pivot of the between on which hinges the very process of *renewal* that constitutes creation as universal impermanence. The between is the universal milieu of conjunction, the conjunction of being and nothing, of life and death, of the singularization of determinate beings and their togetherness in a community that supports rather than stifles their singularity—and this, even though the singular must die.

The metaxological sense suggests both the origin's transcendence and the real otherness of creation itself, as given being for itself. This point turns on the character of agapeic origination. What this implies is that creation is *not* the origin, nor the self-creation of the origin; as the outcome of origin, it is given being for itself, and irreducible to origin in itself. Here is the primal pluralism between the origin and creation, a pluralism that is not sublated by an absorbing totality. Creation as universal impermanence is an immanent process of ontological transcendence that points beyond itself to its metaphysical ground in the origin in itself, but the gap between the two, even in their community, is always kept open.

Second consideration. We do not find a symmetrical relation between being and nothing here. If creation is not an absolute self-mediating totality, still being has priority, even in the temporariness of finiteness. Becoming does show a mutuality between coming into being and passing away, but it does so *within* the gift of the excess of being itself. The power of the negative is not on a par with this excess original power of being, but is parasitical on it for what power of determination it may display. In itself this negative work is nothing; negative work is always a modification of the originative power of creative being itself. Even the passing away we find in becoming is itself a manifestation of the original power of being. Becoming as becoming is itself a manifestation of this original power of being.

We now must reiterate the difference of the *nihil* and determinate negation, even though both senses of the nothing have to be taken into account. Thus determinate negation is ingredient in creation as differentiating beings into determinately other entities. But there is a *nihil* that is not this negativity but is at the limit of finite being, relative to which finite being is sustained in being, in its sheer givenness of being. Though this nothing is at the limit, the limit is also inherent in the very mode of being of the finite. This limit is no limit, if we think of limit in terms of a specific, finitizing determination. This limit/unlimit is an "opening" of finite being onto its own possible nothingness, a "noughting" that does not define the finite being as this determinate entity, but defines the very finiteness of its very being at all. It is a meontological "noughting," not an ontic negation.[9]

I am speaking of a more radical nothing to the determinate negation. The latter cannot be understood as giving finite being its being *simpliciter;* rather it articulates the kind and mode of its being; it determines its definiteness, its definition both in itself and in relation to other beings. And so this other "noughting" is not the *duplex negatio*, Hegel's negation of the negation. Hegel's second negation makes explicit the affirmative determination of the first negativity. But determinate negation, Hegel's negation of the negation, in no way accounts for the sheer givenness of being itself, the astonishing marvel that it is at all, being rather than nothing. The other *nihil* is to be thought at this ontological/meontological level.

This other *nihil* does not give being, rather being is given despite nothing, given out of the excess of the origin. Given being is but might not be, hence its very being is informed with its own possible nothingness; and this is true of all finite being as being. This possible "noughting" is other than all determinate negativity, which takes for granted that finite being is already granted as being. Just as to stay at the level of determinate being is to be asleep to metaphysical astonishment before being in a more ultimate sense, so to rest with determinate negation is to be draw back from a more radical probing of meontological perplexity before a *nihil* beyond complete determination.

I want to suggest that determinate negation itself presupposes both a more affirmative sense of being, and this other *nihil*. Determinate negation would not be possible at all, did it not draw from the original power of being as in excess of not-being; otherwise there would be nothing to determine or to negate. Negation and determination originally presuppose this excess of being as a positive indetermination, the overdetermination of plenitude. Yet the rich *dunamis* of becoming is ontologically fragile, given its contingent character as in being, without any necessity that it be at all. As is the case with the excess of agapeic being, the inherent possible nothingness of contingent being is beyond recuperation in terms of determinate negation.

The singular beings that are crystallized in creation also manifest the following doubleness: between the fact that they are for themselves, and the fact that each is temporary, and none is a closed self-sufficiency of being. It is as if a vector of transcending defines the promise of their being, a transcending carried by the sweep of the universal impermanence. It is as if the pluralism of creation is sustained in the universal impermanence as a community of beings in passage. There is implication of one for the other, and there is

---

9. One might consider the word "nothing" as verb rather than as noun, such as is suggested by "noughting." The "noughting" of "nothing" (setting at nought) is not as suggestively indicated in words like "negate," or "nullify."

movement from one to the other; there is self-mediation of one for itself, and also intermediation of one for the other and of the other for the one. Passage itself is the promise of an exceedingly rich intermediation of being. But the *inter* always remains open, open within itself in its rhythm of coming into being and passing away, open from the other side of its being sustained by transcendence.

In sum: We might say that creation as universal impermanence is an intermediated *metaxu*: a middle world between the origin and the nothingness out of which it has been brought into being; a middle world that lacks absolute being, yet is not nothing; a middle world that is something given, but given full of a promise of its own openness beyond every closed totality, the promise of its own infinitude. Creation is a transition: not only a transit of being into being from nothing, not only of this being into that being, not only of one form of this being into that other form, not only of beings back into nothing. It is transition as vector of transcendence. Creation as universal impermanence, as it were, reaches beyond its open wholeness to its own transcendent ground.

Third consideration. There is a peculiar kind of *teleology* hinted at here. We cannot adequately deal with this teleology outside of an account of the good (see chapter 13), but we can say this much. If the transition of being towards the good indicates a certain teleology, we must be careful to mark a break with any totalizing sense of teleology. *We must detotalize teleology.*[10] For there is no all-absorbing monism of the end, as of the origin. This does not mean that we jettison purposiveness. But relative to the transcendence of the origin, we need to think a sense of *indeterminate purposiveness*, without fixating on any determinate univocal purpose.

I know that this sounds paradoxical, so I offer the reader some comfort of precedence. I invoke Kant's notion of purposiveness without any definite purpose. This is an important and suggestive notion. Not incidental to our purposes, Kant invokes it in relation to nature as teleological, as an organization beyond mechanism. I think that metaxological being insinuates a sense of purposiveness that we cannot univocally fix to any absolute, determinate teleology. The insinuation does not mean equivocally that we have no purpose at all. Nor does it imply the dialectical teleology of all-absorbing totality.

---

10. Consider in relation to the triadic nature of Hegelian totality, the Pythagorean view that whatever is *whole* is determined by the number 3: for 3 is the number that includes beginning, middle, and end. But if we count beyond 3 (3 equal to 1), then we are beyond totality, and a different sense of wholeness is needed. The metaxological view is able to count to a genuine 2, because it can count to a 4, beyond 3 (3 equal to 1). See *Beyond Hegel and Dialectic*, p. 11–12, on the problem of counting to 2 which, as Aristotle says, is "the least number, strictly speaking" (*Physics*, 220a27).

This detotalized teleology of purposiveness without univocal purpose corresponds, on the one hand, to the second indeterminate perplexity in us, our surge of metaphysical self-transcendence, as well as, on the other hand, to the overdetermined excess of being as plenitude that is always too much, much more than we can master. The openness in the middle world insinuates a thread of purpose in the universal impermanence, but it is a thread that for us only glints now and then. Very often our only guide to follow the glint is our fidelity to the indeterminate perplexity that opens us to the plenitude of being in its excess.

But once more we are always in the middle, carried by our self-transcending that can never be completely objectified, haunted by this detotalized purposiveness that can never be pinned down. Momentous singular events may disclose something of this, but always as a brief interrupting flash of glimpse, which eludes us then, almost immediately. This flash of glimpse is not the end. On the contrary, it makes the perplexity more ardent and more exigent, more at home with itself and yet more troubled. Sometimes it even paradoxically consoles us in disquieting us. If we are so blessed, it may re-create agapeic astonishment.

Fourth consideration. Such astonishment reawakens us to creation as continuous. Things appear, not just once, but once, and again and again. This word "again" puts us in mind of creation as the time of perennial renewal. For we find in becoming an ever-renewed beginning: becoming reveals the power of being to begin, again and again. Every "once" is poised over its "never," but behold, it comes to be once again, renewed again. Time is creation and re-creation; it is the duration, the durability of creation in universal impermanence. Every moment is in being, though it might be nothing, a "once" that is a never again, a nothing or a "never" that is once again renewed: again and again, and again. There is disjunction is this continuity of again and again, the disjunction of the "never" that stands between the "once" and its renewal. So the process is a double happening of gain/loss, impermanence/remaining, creation ever-precarious/ever-refreshed.

What this implies is that creation as continuing cannot be separated from *discontinuity.* The continuing process cannot be sheer seamless flux. I am not talking here of something like the pure *durée* of Bergson, which is closer to the universal homogeneity of the elemental. Time is heterogeneous. What I mean is, so to say, a time of double being: of beginning and ceasing, of being exalted and cast down, of festivity and of lamentation. Creation continually gives rise to discontinuity, whence arises newness, and also singularity and uniqueness. Such discontinuity arises again and again, such that the "once" cannot be understood in a univocal sense. The fecundity of creation gives rises to the newness of the "once" that is infinitely pluralized in the marvel of singularity. Such a pluralization is a repetition that never repeats itself, that never reiterates the univocal same. Creation is an ever-fresh, never-diminished origination of singularity. Time is the gift of singular newness. Everything is renewed every moment under the sun. Continuous creation is this radical discontinuity of heterogeneous time: the ever-renewed ongoingness of this ontological otherness and pluralization. Time is good: good time is a gift of the agapeic origin.

As long as creation continues, even in this universal impermanence, time reveals the original power of being, as over and above every negative, whether the *nihil* or determinate negativity. Time is the continuous renewal of being in the discontinuous.[11] We might say that the community of creation is shaped in this endless renewal in universal impermanence. It is not that there is no provisional permanence in the impermanence. Things are remaining; beings are given and remain for a time. Time is a double, cleft process: it redoubles being again and again, and so is the perpetual promise of the renewal of the primal freshness of being. Yet it is also the senescence of freshness, the weathering and the erosion of beings, the withering away of determinate beings. It is ageless and always ageing, a mixture of the "once," the "never," and the "forever." In the cleft of redoubling time, the determinate singularity of beings is shaped. The singularity is given time, briefly poised, as on a wave, now buoyed up in being and exultant, then dashed and downed and dissolved. It surges and ebbs, it is a coming and a going.

This is my *fifth and final consideration*. The pathos of finitude reappears, as we come back to the *nihil* beyond all determinate negativity. The metaxological conception of becoming does not deny determinacy of being, nor the work of negation, nor a sense of self-determining, but it situates each of these in relation to an understanding of being and nothing that cannot be fully contained in any univocal or dialectical framework. As I already suggested, the coming into being out of excess is matched at the other extreme by a sense of the *nihil* that cannot be reduced to a determinate negativity. Not all negation is determination. There is a negation that is a more radical indetermination—more crushing than any dialectical conception can

---

11. The point can be made with reference to the agapeic origin. We might say that the excess of originative infinitude grounds this discontinuity of time in continuous creation; for excessive infinitude overflows every closed whole. This overflow is both a *rupture* and the *generation of community* across rupture. Rupture: since the closed whole cannot contain this excess and hence is broken open. The generation of community across rupture: since the breaking open is not by negation simply, but enacted by the original power of being, as over and above every negative, be it the *nihil* or determinate negativity.

recuperate, an indeterminacy that destroys in a radical sense, snuffing out, and not simply rearranging the indestructible elements of some universal process of transformation, unshakeably serene *sub specie aeternitatis*.

Let me put it thus: Creation comes out of nothing from an overdetermined origin; things in creation will also go into nothing, from out of the temporary being of the universal impermanence, and this nothing will not be simply another determinate transformation. Against this more radical sense of nothing, appearing and disappearing are more sharply outlined. Creation as a metaxological community in process stands out sharply against the nothingness at the origin and at the end. Against this background, which is no ground at all, a creature is sustained in its transit, both in its own identity and its relational involvement through differential relativity with the rest of being. But in this transit there are losses of being beyond finite recuperation in the middle world.

There is a sense in which only the tragic artist really gives utterance to the *nihil* beyond determinate negativity. Here we find a destructuring indeterminacy, a collapse of the energy of being beyond dialectical recuperation. There is a *nihil* that is too much for us—a dark excess of irrevocable revocation of being. I believe this is expressed, for instance, in King Lear's "never, never, never." This is beyond any univocity or dialectic of determination, though it is made felt relative to a determinate being that is beloved in its singularity. You, the best beloved one, will die, have died. Any singular might be that best beloved one. One can be crushed beyond finite recovery by this death.[12]

Yet the strange paradox is that the marvel of creation can be *heightened* in the face of this dark *nihil*. Suppose one were to think of the "in" in "infinite," not so much as the privative, but as the *disturber* of all finitude. That is, in the interruption of the continuity of finitude, one meets a profound disturbance of being by the "more" and the "not" at the heart of finitude. Both the "more" and the "not" are "in" and yet "other." This doubleness is incised in the inward otherness of finite being. The sense of being as gift is heightened in this conjunction in difference of the "more" and the "not." And only now, while one still is, and has the time, may one glimpse the real givenness of the "once," as absolute gift of the "more."

What does one glimpse? That finite being is a gain beyond nothing, and there is no determinate why to it. It is a gift, and to think of it is to thank the origin. Yet at the other end, death rises up as the negative other of the same gratuitous surd. The doubleness of finite being makes it to be both being and void, gift and loss. The universal impermanence is in the slash between being/void. It is a giving that is given and that gives out: it is given out of the

---

12. See my "Being at a Loss: On Philosophy and the Tragic," chapter 2 of *Perplexity and Ultimacy*. Also on the crushing power of evil, see *Beyond Hegel and Dialectic*, chapter 4, "Dialectic and Evil: On the Idiocy of the Monstrous."

excess of the origin; it gives out in its spending itself, in its passing away, in its being spent in giving out.

It should be evident that we do not have a *determinate answer* to these gains and these losses. There is no determinate answer. But just as we can think the gain as gift, perhaps we have to think that loss as an ordeal of withdrawal or absence. Such an absenting would be an absence deeper than all determinate absences, where we have some presence of the absent one. If it were possible to say it, it would be absolute absence, serving as a negative reminder of the transcendent origin, beyond all finite being and the void. In this absenting, ultimacy for us is deferred, or displaced onto another dimension. In this absenting, perhaps we might say, the origin reserves itself.

Overall, then, we can say that the metaxological sense of the universal impermanence defines the *time of being between*: between the excess plenitude of the origin, and given being in creation; between the nothing within finite creation, and the nothing between finite creation and the origin; between the integral goodness of finitude, and the possible nothingness of the finite; between the praise and laughter and festivity of the first, and the tragedy and weeping of the second; between a double good and a double nothing. Creation continues in the cleft of this between.

But this too is the astonishing. Even if the origin reserves itself, creation as universal impermanence is ever rejuvenated, ever restored. It is replenished and always young, though always ageing and ever old. As ageing beyond all mortal age, it is perennially fresh, and has no age. Creatures *within* creation age. They are given to themselves to refresh creation. Age is the dying of *this* creature, death the time when the renewed beginning passes beyond *this* creature. But the universal impermanence is still the time of beginnings. It is the ageless time of generation wherein the generosity of being, always expending itself, is not depleted or spent. For us, to be is to create generously beyond ourselves, regardless of the nothing that is lurking in wait. Our ageing, even our dying, can be a different beginning, a different birth—rebirth of agapeic astonishment before the glory of creation.

CHAPTER EIGHT

THINGS

Things and Mere Things

What is a thing? What are things? We use the word "thing" almost without noticing it, but it names something elemental yet enigmatic. There are things: fish and fowl and beasts, things that crawl, that leap, that think, that weep, artificial things, things of the spirit, things of moment, things beneath contempt. In the most general sense, things are certain determinate happenings of the power of being. In that sense, human beings are things too. This does not mean that all things are one of a kind. To the contrary, the diversity of things, as well as their singularity, is striking. Of course, there is a derogatory use of the word "thing," as when we say: "It is a mere thing." But there is no such thing as a mere thing. This derogatory usage springs from an objectification of thing into a concreteness more contracted than is warranted. A mere thing is the objectified abstraction of a concrete thing.

Things are creations of the original power of being, happenings of this power in the universal impermanence. I do not mean that things are mere *epiphenomena* of a more basic power. For creation gives rise to a more obstinate and resistant thereness: an independence from the origin in itself. Even if we say that things come to be as creations of a more basic creative power, they still come to be as *for themselves*. Creation in the universal impermanence pluralizes the original power of being in a manifold of diverse but singular happenings. We call these singular happenings things.

Required us of now will be a certain phenomenological fidelity to appearing things. Things are for themselves, are in themselves, encountered with a recalcitrant thereness, a thereness not to be reduced to mere things. The stubborness of things, the fact that they are there, that they are something rather than nothing, that as there they stand before us, stand there as themselves—all these things must be thought metaphysically. Our task is not to forget the grounding conditions of origin and creation, but to think the singularization of the creative power of being that marks the happening of things. Since the singularization is also a pluralization, the question of the one and the many will also have to be pursued.

I want to argue for a pluralized interpretation of the thing. Univocity, equivocity, dialectic, and the metaxological each has its place in this interpretation. And so also compared to the last two chapters, we now move closer to *beings in their determinacy*. We are now on more familiar territory: things are determinately available to us in the middle.[1] We are in the midst of things. Things crowd us on all sides; we are ourselves things in the midst of things. In this crowd of things, the press of being takes the form of real and incontrovertible determinacy.

It is not that there is not much vagueness and indefiniteness, but beings as there discipline us, remind us of the course of things. Things have a nature that follows its determinate way, even against our will to determine it otherwise. Things are so and so, whether we will it so or not. This throng of things may induce bewilderment or confusion, and sometimes does to the point of madness or distraction. Then we are so *cast* among things that we drown in diversity. And yet the serious demand of things is the discipline and patience of mind to the nature of what is given in creation. Things call for our attention, and indeed respect. Even if we secretly will to circumvent and change things as given, we can do so successfuly only by first granting them attention and provisional respect. And such respect, provisional or more lasting, is what feeds metaphysical thought about the being of things.

The major points we must discuss include: first, the singularity of things, seen as dynamical through and through; second, the pluralized presencing of things as singulars; third, the overdetermination of this presencing with respect to the unity and properness of things; fourth, the placement of things in community. This placement raises the question of plurality in another sense—namely, the kinds of things and their diverse intelligibilities. This will be the theme of the next chapter.

The Unity and Spread of Things

The univocal sense rightly reminds us that to be is to be a one, in fact, to be a determinate one. We ask: What is a thing? And we answer: a thing is a cow, or a dog, or a flea, or a sparrow in flight, or a snowflake falling. We then ask: What kinds of things are they? And we answer: animals or insects or birds or some kind of such and such. Our questions and answers move towards more and more determinate information, and more and more general classification. Such questions do not quite articulate our primary concern here. Things are; things are this, that, and the other; but what constitutes their

---

1. See chapter 5, above, on the "familiar middle."

being things, their being as things? What makes a thing a thing—a thing there, present, and not a mere possibility, and not nothing? This is a metaphysical question and not a scientific or commonsense one, each of which takes for granted the thingness of a thing.

The metaphysical question does not regard a general concept abstracted from a range of things, for what is primally striking is that a thing is always a *this*. Again the univocal sense comes to our aid. As singular happenings, things are unities. The truth of univocity comes especially into its own when we are dealing with beings under the guise of determinacy. If a thing did not in some sense have a determinate unity, we might hesitate about the intelligibility of calling it a thing. The intelligibility of things is joined to their determinate unity.

So far so good, but we have to elaborate the point. First, one can claim the determinate unity of a thing makes it to be *for itself*. It is defined and determined in itself. Things have a measure of "selfhood," which is for itself. Every thing, so to say, "selves." I am not using "self" here as including reference to *mindful* self-mediation, such as we find with the human self. We will come to this in a later chapter. The identity of a thing is its "self," and this "self" is its own inherent determinate unity. It is not simply imposed on it from the outside, the way a cookie cutter imposes form on an amorphous dough. The determinate identity is inherent; it is the thing itself.

That said, we must immediately avoid too static an interpretation. This is always a temptation with univocal thinking. Univocal mind says that a spade is a spade, and nothing other. It is worth citing Bishop Butler again: a thing is itself and not anything other. This is all true, but the spade as spade or the thing in itself is more than a static congealing of being. It is a determinate concretion of the original power of being, and hence determinacy itself is the crystallization of a creative energy that is not itself just a determinate thing. The determinate identity of a thing springs from its power to be in excess of absolutely static determination. The unity of a thing can never be thus congealed.

When the univocal mind yields to the above temptation, we find interpretations that invoke an underlying static substance or substrate. I demur with respect to the common rejection of Aristotelianism as a static substantialism; Aristotelian substance is dynamized through and through, as indeed substance is in Leibniz. But the interpretation of these figures is not here the issue. I am quite willing to say that the unity of a thing is substantial in this dynamized sense. But to avoid the implication of a stasis that stands under changes, at the level of qualities and determinations, I am willing to prescind from substantialist language. What underlies and endures in the determinate identity is the original energy of being that is singularly specified and concretized in this thing, as both this particular and also as this kind of thing. It is not that we have dynamical being at the overt level and static being at the covert or underlying. We have different modes of dynamical being in the underlying ongoingness and the overt presentation of the thing.

I propose we think of things as emergent into their own thisness. The universal impermanence of becoming is dynamical through and through, but it does not dissolve into a flux without any determinacy. The pure flux would be like a fog so thick that nothing could be made out as definite within it. Properly speaking, there would be no distinct center of perception (the "self") trying to make out things and shapes in the fog; there would be no thing in this pure indefiniteness. In fact, things stand out in the flux of impermanence. They stand out, not because they stand in the static sense, but because both they and the impermanence are determinations of the original power of being.

Things emerge into definiteness, as the trees and the fields and the animals at dawn emerge into a stark morning thereness. And I do not think it right to say that the determinate was simply statically there in the indeterminate, the way supposedly a picture is "suspended" in the photographic negative. Emergence is itself a dynamical appearing in which the constituents that compose the appearing are themselves dynamical. The "this" appears as a "this" by coming into the foreground, and against a background that helps to outline its difference. But neither the "this," nor the foreground nor the background are static. Were we to reduce the process of emergence to the development of a snapshot, there would be no real development at all, merely the application of an extrinsic manipulation to give overtly what was always statically there covertly.

I underline the coherence of the thing with the background conditions out of which it emerges—namely, the nature of the origin as excess plenitude, and creation as universal impermanence. Though unities of finite being are brought to be, they are not absolutely complete as creations, but are marked with the promise of self-completion. The integrity of a thing is a unity in process. The for-self of created things is emergent in the dynamical process of coming to be. Becoming and temporality are essential to it, and its integrity for itself is open. Its promise emerges out of the created indeterminacy of the universal impermanence.

Of course, the univocal stress on determinacy can produce too rigid an objectification of the thing. We must avoid this, since it contracts the concreteness of the thing. The thing is not an object. I think it is more helpful to say that the thing has its place. It is located in space and time, but its location has a more intimate resonance than were it but a mere neutral glob of being dropped on top of a neutral homogeneous space, alloted its time in an indifferent continuum of passing moments.

A thing dwells here or there, now or then. Its place is its *home* in being. There is it. It might perhaps be elsewhere. Perhaps it might not be at all. It may yet be elsewhere. But now it dwells there. It is placed there, emplaced. Its being placed involves the breakup of any purely homogeneous space; it is a rupture in any monism of a pure continuum. Moreover, the place of the thing charges the space with a particular resonance. The thing as placed has a present, is present, has a presence. Such presence is a singular qualification of any neutral homogeneous time. This is why its dwelling there does not completely yield to a mathematical univocity in a system of coordinates in a neutral space and time.

For things are *voluminous*. We tend to say, they fill space, but perhaps it is better to say a thing is a present spatialization of the original power of being. By voluminosity I do not just mean volume such as might be reduced to an aggregate of nonvoluminous points, reached by an analytical process of infinite division. The voluminous unity of a thing is not quite divisible in this sense. Rather atomic points are analytical abstractions from the voluminosity of things. Voluminosity is not a quantity of homogeneous matter merely, but a certain particular stressing of space. It can be subjected to a homogenizing analysis, no doubt, but voluminosity as appearing is marked by the stress of particularity. Admittedly, this can be very nuanced, and needs more of the mind of finesse than the mind of geometry to sense it. A still life by Cézanne— this has the feel of the voluminosity of things.

As placed here rather than there, a thing has its place in the sun, which no other thing can usurp. This singularity is connected with space and time, but we must see the latter as processes of spatialization and temporalization. Consistent with the idea of creation as universal impermanence, I suggest that spatialization and temporalization might be viewed as transcendental conditions of the being there of singular things. I mean this ontologically, and not just in the subjective sense of Kant's transcendental aesthetic. Kant's space and time are a priori forms of sense intuition. But spatialization and temporalization are ontological conditions of the possiblity of the *aesthetic presencing of particulars*. The original power of being spatializes and temporalizes things. Thus, again relative to the voluminosity of things, the thing does not so much fill space and time, as rather it is a fulfilling of space and time, a spacing and a timing of the original power of being in this particular stress of singularity.

So we might suggest that spacing and timing are dynamic processes that articulate the creative power at work in the universal impermanence. Consequently, just as space is not an external frame for things, so also time is not an empty receptacle for the containment of ongoingness. Time is a promise of full timing. But as with all promises, there are betrayals as well as redemptions. There are losses as well as successes. There is sorrow as well as the leap of joy. And there will be death too at the end, to welcome the weathered or eroded existent.

Timing means that things have an *interim* life, a time span in the between. So also their time span is the extension of their singularity beyond any closed monadism. That is to say, the unity of the thing is self-transcending; it is a transitive unity, a unity in transition. Its timing is its transience. The

interim of a thing is its duration in the between. Endurance is an en-dura-
tion, where the "en" means both an "in" (en-during in the between) and a
"one" (being a one in the between). Obviously here duration is not Bergson's
pure *durée*. Rather a duration is a singularly stressed time transit, or process
of self-becoming. What this implies is: *the thing is temporary in itself*. Temporary refers not only to the finitude of its span, but also to the promise of its
creative becoming within the interval of its enduring. It creatively becomes
for itself as a creative issue of the universal impermanence, itself as the ontological matrix of creation, itself grounded in the primal creativity of the absolute origin.

The above view asks us to see "objectivity" in another light. The above
presencing of things reveals that things are not objects simply. Rather things
are turned into objects by an objectifying regard. A thing is first a thing;
objectivity is an imposition on the thing by an other who minds the thing
reductively and abstractly. Objectivity is an abstraction of thinghood. More
strongly put, it is an excision of the resonance of placement, of habitation, of
intimacy with creation. The universal impermanence is the background out
of which the thing presences, comes into the determinate foreground for its
particular duration. Emergence is out of this matrix, but the matrix of creation, and its reference to the agape of the origin, mean that the sign of the
good is presented in the very "this" of a particular presencing. This is the
resonance of intimacy in the thing. The particular has an intimacy of being,
and this deepest intimacy is its value for itself.

The very being of the thing, as something that is a being for itself, is
essentially of value. As the ancient doctrine held, to be is to be a perfection.
Presencing is not pointless. Indeed, on the view I am suggesting, presencing
is the very point of the thing's being for itself. There is an intrinsic worth to
the elemental being of the particular thing as particular. Otherwise stated:
the thing is a concretion of the original power of creation, but this original
power is not to be understood apart from the agape of the good; the excess of
the origin is its goodness, and beings are given because being is good; the
being of creation is good, hence the being of particular things is also a good.
This is ontological value, not anthropocentric value. It puts us in mind of the
worth of being, outside of any relativity to our will or evaluation. All our
subsequent valuing of things is derivative from this primary ontological worth
of things.

When a univocal objectifying mind neuters the thing, it is heedless of
this intimacy of worth in the thing itself. It is guilty of an ontological aggression on the thing in the full presencing of its being. The initial presencing of
things is saturated with value. Remember again the child's wonder when it
beholds a thing for the first time and exclaims with joy: Look at the moon!
The first leap of joy at the being of things is the elemental rapport with the
marvelous particularity of creation in its intimate goodness. The childlike

leap of joy is nearer than any "objectivism" to the presencing of things out of the matrix of creation and the saturation of this matrix with ontological worth.

It should be clear to the reader that presence, as I use the term, cannot be assimilated to the so-called metaphysics of presence. In a way, I am offering a metaphysics of presence, but not in the usual meaning of presence—this entails the reduction of being to a neutralized objectivity, available for an imperialistic mind. Presence, as I mean it, is more primordial than this, and in direct conflict with any reductive univocalizing of being. Even if I grant the need of univocity, I am enlarging its meaning beyond the standard metaphysics of presence. Presence is extraordinarily rich, rich with the resonance of intimacy and goodness. There is no stifling of mystery; quite to the contrary, the presencing of things shows intimately the power to astonish.

It should also be obvious that when I say that a thing is located, I also mean something quite different to what Whitehead helpfully criticizes as the doctrine of *simple location*. Whitehead attributes this view to the scientific materialism of the seventeenth century, and its offshoots up to twentieth-century physics. Briefly it runs: a material thing is there in space and here in time, or here and now in space-time, in a *perfectly definite sense*. This holds true whether we see space-time in an absolute or relative sense. For whether we arrive at a definite location of a material thing in absolute or relative space, the doctrine of simple location states that this definiteness is *all* that has to be said about the thing.[2] The absolute definite spatial coordinates and the punctiform instants of time, or both together in time-space, allow no inherent transition into what is other. In the region of space-time, merely external relations obtain between matters, which in no way inherently implicate each other. Matter also becomes indifferent to divisions of time; lapse of time is accidental rather than essential on this view. Transition has nothing to do with the material, which is always just itself equally at any instant; the instant is itself conceived as without transition in itself; the world is simply a succession of instantaneous configurations of matter.

This doctrine of simple location is, in the terms I use, due to an excessive univocalizing of being. Whitehead even speaks of "one-eyed reason, deficient in its vision of depth," with reference to the rationalism of the eighteenth century that efficiently exploited the doctrine of simple location, the foundation of the seventeenth-century scientific scheme.[3] Locations in space and time are made into univocal points, pinpointed with the calculative exactness and precision demanded by the univocal mind. But this is a fixation of ongoingness, both in the thing itself and in the thing relative to other things and other regions of space-time. The dynamic is recomposed of precisely calculated statics. If you

---

2. See *Science and the Modern World* (New York: Macmillan, 1925), 49.

3. Ibid., 59, 58.

will, this might be called Whitehead's critique of the metaphysics of presence. Still, location and presencing have to be thought further. Whitehead would agree. I take his criticism of the fallacy of misplaced concreteness as connected with his way of going beyond reductive univocity.

I also believe we must rethink concreteness, location, presence, all as going beyond univocity, but we cannot simply eviscerate the determinacy of being emphasized by univocity. We must speak of *location*, in a manner that incorporates dynamism. How so? Suppose we speak of "locale" or "dwelling" or "habitation." Do we not point to determinate places that carry the resonance of intimacy, of presence that is more than univocity? We point to presence as transcending objectification, in the very determinate itself. For a locale is a place of ongoing intimacy of being.[4] A locale is a spread of insistent being that dwells there, making its presence felt. Nor is a dwelling a neutral frame, though it may enframe a being there that is a value for itself. The "promiscuity" of space is evident in locale, for there are no absolutely definitive boundaries in the process of ongoingness. This is true for the locale of the thing. Taken to excess univocity does lead to the doctrine of simple location, but location is not thus simple, nor to be completely calculated according to the precisions of a univocal *mathēsis*.

For a thing does not simply live *in* its locale; it lives its locale. Its locale also lives it, as a *spread of being* that spatially and temporally extends beyond itself, and beyond all punctiform spots and instants. The spread of a thing in its locale is its singularly stressed timing and spacing. In invoking the spread of being, we can underscore singularity as for itself, but we do not have to end up in a punctiform solipsism of entities. For the spread of singularity already contains its implications with those other spreads of being that define the singular spacing and timing of other things. Space-time is spread out. A thing is a spread of being, a being broadcast on the extension of space and the distention of time. A spread is a spreading out. It is transcendence in singularity, beyond centripetal self-absorption in solipsistic identity.

Though our discussion thus far has been pegged to univocity, we already see that the singularity of things suggests an understanding of the "this," which is not a point of existence contracted into itself. The fact that things are for themselves as singular implies a self-definition that is not self-enclosed. In the elemental "this" of the thing, the dynamism of being is at work. The "this" of the thing is itself a singular happening of the original power of being. Moreover, there is a certain intimacy of being characteristic

---

4. The word "local" is used, for instance, in Ireland as refering to one's local public house. The local is a place of intimate community where a good time is promised, where good *craic* and celebration are possible.

of the "this" as "this."[5] This is the charge of the thing's value. That a "this" is at all is a good, a perfection, a realization of the power of being, realization not in any closed way, but in an ongoingness of achievement and promise. The spread of a thing in space-time is just this ongoingness of ontological achievement and promise.

The Plurivocal Presencing of Things

As a singular "this" for itself, the thing is not an undifferentiated monad. It presents itself under the guise of a manifold of appearances. As internally differentiated, the thing is a unity that is more than univocal unity. Its self-presentation is its appearance. The question now is: What is the nature of this appearance?

I want to amplify the idea that things are aesthetic presences. I mean aesthetic with its etymological reference to sensuousness as such. Aesthetic here does not imply a conception of human art; and if it does imply an art, this would refer things to the *poiēsis* of the origin. Things are aesthetic presences, emergences in the universal impermanence of creation. Their aesthetic presence is their sensuous being there in their full concreteness. Aesthetic here has an ontological rather than transcendental meaning, such as we find in Kant's transcendental aesthetic of space and time. Ontological refers to real conditions of possibility that cannot be confined to the knowing subject. Spacing and timing are ontological conditions of the possibility of the aesthetic appearing of a thing. It is the very original power of being as spatialized and temporalized that is the ontological condition of the possibility of beings being there sensuously. In that regard, things might be called poems of creation, sensuous works of art of the original power of being.

I think we need to invoke equivocity relative to aesthetic presencing. Why? Consider the following. The thing is self-articulated, presenting itself in a plurality of different attributes or characteristics. The thing, a unity, is also many, is a self-pluralization, a series of presentations of itself. Here it is often argued that such presentation immediately invokes a *knower* to whom the presentation is made. Therefore, this pluralization of presentation must be *subjectified*. Instead of the univocal contraction of the thing into an object, this view moves in the opposite direction and *subjectifies* this self-presentation. The presencing of things, their aesthetic appearing, is reduced to a set of *perspectives* that are not inherent in the thing itself but mind-dependent.

There is an element of truth in this, but not exhausted by the one intended. The appearance of things may be for mind; but it is for mind to be

---

5. This will emerge in mindfulness with the idiot self; see chapter 10.

true to the appearance of things, to their own self-showing. When mind becomes agapeic, it transcends itself towards this show of the thing in its pluralized otherness. Mind reverses its own for-itself into a mindfulness of the thing as for itself in itself. In a word, the show of the thing is the thing showing itself.

Thus self-presentation does call out to another; this is ingredient in manifested spread. But the self-showing of aesthetic presence arises from the thing itself. It is the presenting of the thing to the otherness of all being. This can be an *unknowing presenting*: the flower that blooms does not bloom because it will be seen; the grass growing on the hillside does not speak itself to the sky, because it knows another will respond to it; nor does the sun shed its warmth because it knows whom it will kindle. Each thing speaks itself outwardly and knows not if there is an ear to hear its particular voice. It knows not that it speaks, but it speaks itself nonetheless. Its destiny is to present itself outwardly under the guise of its manifold of aesthetic appearance. This is the ontological work of the thing itself. Things "selve" of themselves. This "selving" does *not* mean we subjectify the thing.

Here I think it helps to recall again the doctrine of primary and secondary qualities. This offers the classical bifurcation of thinghood into two extremes of objectivism and subjectivism. With this doctrine, and briefly, the thing itself is sheared of all the rich qualities of phenomenal concreteness, and its core reduced to the primary qualities of mass, extension, figure, and so on. The sound, the smell, the taste, the very savor of qualitative concreteness are secondary, outcome of an interplay of the mind with the thing that in itself has none of these qualities. As essentially defined by its primary qualities, the thing has no qualities that cannot be subjected to a measure of mathematical calculation. Hence the aesthetic quality of things becomes redefined in terms of a quantative measure that can be homogeneously applied to all quantities. The numerical unit of quantifiable measure governs this mathematical univocalizing of quality. And so not only do aesthetic qualities become secondary, the very singularity of the thing is dissolved into this numerical measure of homogeneous quantity. This doctrine univocalizes the thing in itself in such an objective way that the concrete qualities of things are made merely equivocal—that is, mainly dependent on subjectivity, though it is sometimes left indeterminate as to whether some "powers" in the thing itself do correspond with the secondary qualities (e.g., Locke).

One can say that this doctrine diminishes the thing on two fronts. On the one hand, objectivity contracts the range of concreteness. On the other hand, subjectivity is placed outside of the thing in a mind that has essentially nothing to do with things in themselves; meanwhile the "selving" of things that presents itself in their aesthetic appearance becomes nothing inherent in the thing itself. *Equivocity* is influential here in the very negative sense that a difference gets erected into a dualism of opposites. On the one extreme we have, for instance, Descartes' *res extensa*, and on the other, the pure thinking thing of the *res cogitans*; and the two have nothing to do with each other. Thinghood has been de-selved, objectified, reified in a homogeneous neutralization of thereness; selfhood has been abstracted from things in their concreteness and hovers mathematically over the quantitative homogeneity of externality, ready to impose the categories of its *mathēsis* on that homogeneity.

This equivocity of a difference turned into a dualistic opposition means that really there are *no things* in Descartes. In different but related senses, there are also no things in Newton and Hume. The thing is decomposed under the gaze of the objectifying, univocalizing mind. Contrary to this, I hold we must restore the subject to a mindfullness beyond univocity, just as we must restore the world of things to themselves as aesthetic presencing. This is what locale and habitation imply. Things presence aesthetically, present themselves, and are seen as such when the mind as other is in proper community with them, in proper rapport with things.

Since this rapport is beyond mathematicizing, it brings us to a more *affirmative equivocity*, relative to presencing. I say equivocity now with the suggestion of a richer notion of ambiguity. If things pluralize themselves, they are plurivocal in themselves. They utter themselves; they outer themselves; they bespeak themselves in more ways than one. I suggest that our plural perspectives on them is in response to this plurivocity of the thing in itself. The differentiation of the thing is just this, its qualitative plurivocalization. This is where the notion of aesthetic presencing links up with the idea of ontological value: the qualitative presence of things is the very charge of aesthetic value in them. What are we to make of this aesthetic value? We come to *appreciate* them for their thereness.

In this regard, one might make the case that only the artist sees things. The rest of us, and even the artist most of the time, see and do not see. But when a thing is appreciated, it is seen in a light that is not merely the excrescence of a fantastic subjectivity. The light is an illumination of the thing itself in the charge of being it invokes. In other words, this appreciation of things is at the opposite extreme to the objectifying mind. The latter lacks appreciation for the qualities of things; it will merely calculate the quantity of mass or energy, energy understood in a quantitative sense, and not the ontological sense of the at-work (*en-ergon*) of the original power of being. Appreciation is a mindfulness for the worth of a thing in its ontological thereness. It calls also for a fine sense of ambiguity, a mind of finesse seeking to find its way in the equivocations of things.

Thus from the point of its perspectival presentation, a thing can present itself under opposite guises. The water is warm to the hand that is cold, cold to the hand that is warm; or it may be cold to the hand that is cold, or warm to the hand already warmed. Things will present themselves differently relative to the other upon which they make a call. The equivocity is inseparable from the thing itself as a reservoir of plural possibilities. Different possibilities will get actualized in the process of interaction constituted in concert with the call on the other. This happens in the between. A thing may be small or big, or may be big and small, depending on perspective, but this seeming contradiction is not something that comes from the outside to the thing itself. The thing presents itself plurivocally.

Recall our previous discussion (chapter 3) of the chameleon and the orchid, for their doubled identities, their being other than their seeming identity, or their inclusion in their very identity of a complex power of seeming other. Undoubtedly, we see things as such and such. But seeing "as" can also be a seeing "is." When we see a thing as other, we may really be seeing it as it is. For instance, the orchid is as it seems to be, though it is also not as it seems to be. The "as" need not be disjoined from the "is," as if the "is" had to be univocally objectified only. The "is" is plurivocal; hence what is can be seen "as" a plurality of manifestations. The "as" may pluralize the "is" but is not thereby divorced from the "is"—as if the "as" had to be equivocally subjectified, while the "is" remained objectively univocal, rocklike and not to be budged.

In a way, the "as" metaphorizes the "is," but the metaphorical "as" may well be truer to the "is" in this metaphorizing. Metaphor may be a revelation of reality. *Metapherein*—the thing carries itself across to revelation, metaphorizes itself; this is its spread beyond univocal identity. In its self-metaphorizing, it reaches out to more, reaches into the *meta*, the middle. The metaphorical "as" thus seeks to identify the plurivocal "is" of the "this" in its otherness. Thus the thing may be, so to say, an *ontological metaphor*, bespeaking the power of being, and not just the human imagination. If the thing is a *poiēsis* of the original power of being, then the metaphorical "as" may well be in rapport with the "is" of the thing, and rapport in an entirely realistic, though not objectivistic, sense.

Again it may be the artist who sees things, insofar as his mindfulness is closer to, more intimate with, the matrix of sensuous appearing, as already charged with value. For there are no things in general. Generalities always lose sight of the singularity of the singular. The singular as singular is to be seen or heard or touched. The qualitative presence of things emerges into definition and unity against the background of a more equivocal matrix of aesthetic value. What is primary is not a valueless neutrality of primary qualities; what is primary in emergence is a promiscuous energizing of being there. This promiscuity is *transition* in the thing. Transition is the coupling, linking, relativity of things with other things. The pluralization of the thing and things is promiscuously charged with an energy of value.

The artist can name this thereness and this emergence, and do so in a nonobectifying way. He can name the dynamic spread of things in their aesthetic presencing. The artist may see things here because he is appreciative of the ambiguity of aesthetic presence. Appreciation, as we suggested, is an ontological opening. When we appreciate something, we value it for itself, and not with the ulterior purpose of turning it into a mere means to an end, or something useful for us. We value it for itself because it is a value in itself. Such appreciation is a vigilance to things that celebrates the value of their ambiguous, plurivocal presence.

Without question we are more familiar with this ontological appreciation when we turn to the *human body* as aesthetic presence. And this is always charged with value, equivocal and more. But there is a community between the aesthetic body and the body of things as aesthetic presencings. We live this when we are younger, when the promiscuity of self and things is still fluid. We forget it when mind settles into an entirely objectifying mode. It is recovered to the extent that mind resurrects its own agapeic mode. Agapeic mind is the origin of ontological appreciation and also the consummation of mindfulness that reaffirms its community with things, the aesthetic joy of this community. But agapeic mind requires the metaxological sense, to which we will come.

We must make a final point with respect to the artist as seeing things. It is this. While we are not here dealing with an objectification of the thing, there is a *severe discipline* involved in openness to the plurivocal presence of things. A hard readiness and awakening to things is needed. An aesthetic tolerance of otherness is required.[6] Tolerance now is not defined as a neutral indifference or disinterest; it is a heightened interest, which nevertheless is noninterfering. It is an *inter-esse*, a being between, that is potentially agapeic. It is a willingness to allow the thing in its otherness manifest itself without interference by our abstract mediations. Aesthetic tolerance is an ontological respect for the thing in the thereness of its otherness.

Such respect and tolerance also involve a love of singularity. Not surprisingly, art is a great celebrator of singularity just in its manysidedness, just in its plurivocity. The "this" of things is appreciated; but the "this" is no pointillistic particular; in its intimacy of singularity, the "this" is the promise of an entire world unto itself. The singular is a certain promise of infinitude. It is a singularization of the plenitude of being as original and dynamic. Its spread carries it outwards in space and time, but its intimacy as singular deepens inwardly into its own ground in an original power of being that is more than any finite determinate thing. This love of the singular mirrors the love that originally gives being to the singular out of the excess agape of the origin. The ontological respect of the singular is here a faint echo of the divine appreciation of the work of creation: It is good, it is very good.

---

6. See *Philosophy and its Others*, 102–9.

Overdetermined Presencing/The Intimacy of the Proper

The question now arises: If a thing is many, and if its manyness is tied to the ambiguity of its aesthetic presencing, what then *is* the thing at all? Does it not dissolve in a welter of appearance? What of its oneness? Does it not decompose into a pandemonium of manifestation? Rather than say *It is manifest*, should we not say instead *There are manifestations*? Is there but a diversity of manifestations, *without* things?

This route has been taken in the history of philosophy. I think most notably of Hume. Hume dissolves things as substances into rapid successions of impressions, marked by contiguity and customary connection. He holds to no inherent unity beyond the flow of impressions; at most there is extrinsic aggregation. *Impressions*, on this view, become *subjectivistic* versions of manifestation. There are manifestations for us—that is, appearances as sense impressions. A similar tendency is to be found in all phenomenalist doctrines that deny a noumenon as the bearer or upholder of the phenomena. Indeed we find a reformulation of the traditional doctrine of substance in which the difference between accidental and essential properties is collapsed: there are impressions, but no inherent essential properties, other than arrangements that the human knower organizes for a particular purpose. If there is a thing, it is a *construction* of the knower for whom there are appearances.

This doctrine leads, I think, to the cul-de-sac of a bad equivocity. For not only does it dissolve the thing, but if it is logically consistent, it must also dissolve the phenomenalism to which it resorts in order to rescue some sense of the identity of the thing. If the identity of the thing is a construction of the knower, what prevents us from applying the same line of argument to the knower? Nothing at all. In fact, Hume does this, and the self for whom there are appearances dissolves in the same way as substance other than the self. Hume draws back from the full dissolution of the self by reconstructing it as a congeries of impressions that are built up over a time through habit and succession, and so on. But there is no inherent self, in fact, and properly speaking no rich organizing center of experience that would construct the welter of impressions into more or less stable phenomena. We end up with the differentiation of the "thing" and the diversification of the "self," but both without any inherent unity. Hume is thus a precursor of the critique of the metaphysics of presence, and there is only a small step from him to the difference of the Derrideans. The equivocal sense of being seems to reign supreme.

This reign of equivocity is itself equivocal. It is self-subverting. We cannot avoid the search for some more inherent sense of unity. I say *search*, rather than *construction*. For the view here defended is that the thing itself is differentiating. It differentiates itself into a plurality of appearances. The traditional doctrine of differentiae is quite apposite here. These differentiae are not phenomenal merely, nor secondary qualities that we project unto what in itself lacks any unity. They are the self-expression of the unity of the thing itself. Differentiae are the self-differentiation of the thing. They are the appearing in which the unity of the thing pluralizes itself, internally differentiates its own inherent unity.

And the problem is not how such differentiae inhere in the thing itself, as if they were categorial constructions that we impose on some undifferentiated matter that does not bear them. This is to ask the question *backwards*. It is to approach the thing from a point *subsequent* to its inherent self-differentiation. It is then to start from differentiae as already *abstracted* from the thing by us, and to ask how we reconnect this abstraction to the thing again. But there is never this dualism to be bridged in the original process of the thing itself. There is no dualism between itself and its differentiae; it is its differentiae; its differentiae are its self-manifestation.

I want to argue that the overdetermined ambiguity we saw previously with the plurivocal presencing of the thing points us beyond equivocity to a more dialectical understanding of the thing, and in the following manner. We do not give up the search for determinate identity in this rich ambiguity of appearing, but we must ask the question differently. Why should we think in terms of a *dualism* of unity and differences, especially if the differences are the self-articulation of the unity, its self-differentiation? Why not think of the thing, if you like, as *doubling itself* between its inherent unity and its external differences? Why not connect this doubling with its active process of spreading itself? Dialectic asks that we think in this other way. This doubling, in fact, may be seen as the vector of the thing's own self-transcendence, which yet remains at one with itself in its impetus outwards. Thus the doubling is not a dualism of opposites but the thrust of creative energy that out of itself produces itself outwards. And what it produces outward is again itself, in externally articulated form.

If there is this doubling of the unity of the thing, as I think there is, equivocity does not have the last word. With equivocity differentiation tends to be asserted without a balancing stress on integration. The thing may then be *rightly* recognized as a plurality of properties, and in principle such differences seem to be without limit. A thing can be said to be this and that, and the other, and so on, ad infinitum. The only limit seems to be the finesse of our discriminating powers, or perhaps the instruments we use to detect minute and infinitesmal differences. The problem, of course, is that this unlimited differentiation seems to dissolve the thing into an infinite succession of differences. The thing that holds the differences together itself dissolves into nothing.

By contrast, a dialectical account allows us to speak of a *prior* and *subsequent* sense of unity. This is what I mean. We may speak of the thing's prior unity as its inherent being for itself. This is what it is; but this first existence is not inert but self-differentiating; it differentiates itself into a plurality of appearings, which again are not anything other than itself. It is here that the sense of second unity or second existence comes to be; the dynamic thing doubles its original identity, and the second identity it gains, subsequent to self-differentiation, is itself again. It is the first unity articulated in the form of a second self-differentiated unity.

On this score the traditional doctrine of potency and act can make a lot of sense. The thing is itself to begin with, but itself as a *dunamis*, a reserve of real power; in itself it is this reserve of the power to be. The *dunamis* dynamizes the thing, energizes it; the work of being works in the thing. The result of the work is the self-actualization of the thing in a manifold of ways corresponding to the pluralized power to be, inherent in it. But this self-actualization is the thing again, the realized energy of the original *dunamis*. It is not a second thing. The energy of the realized thing is the double of the original *dunamis* of the thing, but the double is the thing itself. The doubling of the one is the one again, both necessary and inherent in the one for it to be self-articulated. If we link *dunamis* and act to substance, very clearly the resulting doctrine of substance has to be thoroughly dynamized, as it is in Aristotle.

A dialectical account claims that the thing shows itself as inherently self-mediating—its doubling of identity is just its self-differentiation and self-mediation. Such an account claims to account for the thing's inherent unity at a level of greater complexity and concreteness than offered at the univocal level. In brief, *it tries to make intelligible the dynamic nature of a unity in process.* By comparison, a univocal understanding will assert a unity at this definite point in space-time, and only at this one point. The problem then is to account for the "carry over" of the same unity to the next absolute determinate point in space-time. But, paradoxically, our too fixed sense of identity *dissolves* the thing in the *intervals between* determinate points in space-time. The *continuing* or "carry over" of a thing *over* a duration, or extended process, or from point to point, becomes hard to conceptualize.

One might propose that the equivocal stress on difference allows the "carry over" from point to point, and so seems suitable to account for process. But its limit is the obverse of univocity; for it makes unclear *what it is* that is being carried over from time to time and space to space. There seems only the differentiation process of "carrying over," but nothing determinate is being carried over: sheer process, sheer differentiation, but nothing in process and nothing being differentiated.

From the dialectical standpoint both these views (things but no "carry over"; "carry over" but no things) are abstractions from the process of the concrete thing. A more comprehensive mindfulness of concreteness shows the thing to be *both* these processes. It is a unity inherent in itself, yet one that is self-differentiated; the self-differentiating carries the unity across the flow of becoming; it is a unity in process that mediates with itself in its own differentiation. If we can speak of the dialectical unity of a thing, what would this be? It would be a unity that *spans* time-space. Thus the *spread* of a thing reveals a self-transcending unity that is also self-integrative. Such a unity

transcends every inert identity, broadcasts itself on the universal impermanence, though in this broadcast it is not necessarily fragmented; for it can
gather itself in its own manyness into unity again. The power of its unity is a
power of self-transcending, self-differentiating, but also self-integrating. Moreover, this last is not a closure of the thing, for the thrust and spread of its
vector of self-transcendence is not thereby brought to a dead stop. As long as
the thing is, it is this dynamical process of self-differentiation and self-
unification. Only in its perishing does its power of self-broadcasting and self-
integration begin to fail. Short of death this process goes on.

A thing's dialectical unity is not a closed monad but an open wholeness,
one open to new differentiation and renewed integration. Indeed it continues
to be only to the extent that it performs and reforms this process of differentiation and integration. It is a whole that is also open *beyond itself* in a more
extended sense, since the process of its own self-differentiation and self-
integration takes place within the larger dynamism of the universal impermanence. In that context there is not just one process, but many processes of
many such open wholes. I will come to this next, but for the remainder of this
section, I want to make some remarks on how, in light of the above, we might
rethink the doctrine of *properties*. I will suggest a notion of what I will call
the idiocy, or intimacy of the proper.

Relative to univocity and equivocity, it is easy to see why a doctrine of
the thing and its properties might develop. Properties are those appearances
of the thing, its aesthetic presences, that come to manifestion with the differentiae of a thing—in our terms the movement from univocal to equivocal
concreteness. In fact, the relatively static identity of univocity cannot do full
justice to a property, for there is a charge of intimacy in this word. Nor can
equivocity, since there is no adequate allowance for a center of being that
would be the integrative source of the differentiae, hence again no property
in this more intimate sense.

Nor does the doctrine of primary and secondary qualities offer an adequate substitute for this traditional distinction between accidental and essential properties. Just as I said there are no real things in the Newtonian or
Humean scheme, so one can say that there are no real properties in Newtonian
or post-Newtonian science, even despite its doctrine of primary and secondary qualities. I say this because property suggests what is *owned in a singular
sense*. But this sense of ontological "ownness" is of no real interest to science,
Newtonian or post-Newtonian. At the level of univocity and equivocity, there
is no real accounting for the notion of essential property. So any philosophy,
dominated by the sense of univocity, hence haunted by its correlate equivocity,
that tries to give an account of an essential property is doomed to frustration.
If the "proper" cannot be accounted for at the level of univocity, the
deconstruction of the "proper," which trades off the equivocity of univocity,
also locates the issue of the proper at the wrong level entirely. The

deconstruction of the metaphysics of presence is only the deconstruction of an abstraction or simulacrum of true presence. True presence, true properties must be understood at another level of ontological consideration.

The dialectical idea of the thing as self-mediating implies this more intimate sense of the proper, and hence offers us better resources to think the notion of the essential. The last point I will develop more fully in the next chapter on intelligibilities, but by essence is not meant an *eidos* that subsists in its immutability outside the process of the thing. This would be to place essence in an univocal eternity. Essence is at work in the thing itself; hence the thing as dialectically self-mediating is closer to Aristotle's notion of immanent form. Dialectic makes us think an intimate unity of self-differentiation and self-integration in a process of self-becoming. This sense of the thing as belonging to itself, as being dynamically itself in becoming, points to this intimate sense of the proper. The thing shows itself as proper to itself; it holds itself together appropriately. And this appropriate self-collectedness is the activity of its being; it is not extraneously superimposed. The thing "owns" itself.

This locution of "owning" seems to have a suspiciously economical sound. But of course, the "economical" itself, as a *nomos* of the *oikos*, the home, the dwelling, can have the ring of the intimacy of being.[7] The "economical" sense of which we are suspicious is the *instrumentalized* meaning of property. In that meaning, the property can be detached from the owner or the bearer. Paradoxically, such instrumentalized property is not proper at all, in the most intimate sense of property. For the intimate proper is not thus detachable or instrumentalizable. The dualism of owner and property owned is transcended. The intimate proper is hence not defined by a set of external relations; it is the internal relatedness of the thing to itself. It is *proprius*: the thing is proper to itself, appropriate to itself, is itself its own process of self-appropriation.

One might even suggest that things as dialectically self-mediating have their own singular essence. This is to depart from standard Hegelian dialectic, where particularity is subsumed into universality. There is another sense of the propriety of the "this" that is not completely subsumable into a mediating universal. There is, I am suggesting, an inherent self-relation that is the intimacy of the thing to itself, its idiocy. If things "selve," they have, as it were, their proper names, though we humans do not have the book wherein these names are written down. We are led to the idea that every created thing is proper to itself, appropriate for itself, right after its own self, good for itself. This worth proper to things is not economical value in the instru-

---

7. See chapter 3, "The Idiocy of Being," of *Perplexity and Ultimacy* for a more extensive discussion of this intimacy.

mental sense. It is "economical" in that things are properly "at home" with themselves. We humans are very poorly endowed in the capacity to see the uniqueness of singularity at work in this rightness of the self of things. Perhaps we have to invoke again the divine "It is good." The origin, in agapeic mindfulness, knows the proper names, each thing being numbered in this intimate sense, down to the hairs on our heads and the grains of sand on the seashore.

If properties are plurivocal manifestations of the self-appropriating thing, there are also manifestations that express the *excess* of the thing, or that contrariwise do not diminish the being of the thing, were they excluded from a consideration of its singular essence. Such manifestations have sometimes been called *accidental* properties, though it is very difficult to know finally what is accidental and essential. One is inclined to say that *our* definition of essence and accident always slips from the singular essence, since our minds are more at home with generalizing abstractions that fail to see the essence in the accident, or the proper in the seemingly stray manifestation. A thing is more than itself as a univocal identity, and this flourish of excess is, in one regard, ingredient in its singular essence. In another regard—that is, for our convenience, or for the sake of management—we can pay less attention to some of these flourishes of excess as not really affecting the persisting being of the thing.[8]

Finally, the idea of property calls attention not only to the thing's intimate identity but to the openness of dialectical self-mediation, and so to the spread of the thing *beyond* self-appropriation. The thing's self-appropriation takes place in a middle where the thing reaches out to appropriate from its surrounding world what it deems appropriate to the prospering and perpetuation of its own identity. Self-appropriation breaks the boundaries of self-sufficiency, and the reach of a being touches the dynamic self-appropriations of other entities. Appropriation here has its *centrifugal* energy, not only the centripetal energy of self-appropriation.

And so the unity of the thing is not only dialectically self-doubled, but doubled in a further sense: it is doubled in a way that potentially reverses the centripetal directionality of its own self-appropriation. Its spread spreads beyond itself towards the other, towards all other things. Its proper identity is implicated with the proper identities of other things, and there is no way absolutely to abstract its singular essence from the glorious plurality of creation as a community of all other things. A complex relativity with the other comes into play. The thing's identity is not only self-relational, but relational vis-à-vis other self-relational entities. This is why the thing must be seen metaxologically.

---

8. The idea of essence has its own ambiguity, to which I will return.

Things and Community

I am conscious of the generality of what I am saying, and of the tension between this and my stated aim of doing justice to the concrete singularity of things. Can this tension be eradicated? It seems not. Yet we can remind ourselves of the singularity we risk forgetting.

How could one forget it, I ask myself. It is a glorious summer evening. I walk out of doors and look up. I see swallows dynamically dot the sky. I see them swoop and dive and climb again into the higher air. They are in their element. They are lost in play like children, chasing and squealing, ducking and plunging, wheeling and soaring again. I am mute with admiration. What is a swallow? An integrity of vibrant energy. It flies, a speck of free being, spry against the background of blue heaven. It is like an acrobat over the void, buoyed up in air, the element of almost nothing. It is in itself, quickened. Is it congealed in identity? No. It is lithely at home with itself in flight. What is its flight? Itself—its transcending. What does it reach towards? Almost nothing—and yet the others with which it plays: the fly it catches, the air it breathes, the invisible element supporting it, the elusive other it pursues. Not floating, but as if leaping over nothing, a delightful being delighting in simply being. In itself, outside itself, at home with itself, reaching to what is other and beyond: metaxologically double in the universal impermanence.

In trying to give an account of this metaxological doubleness of things, I will underscore four connected considerations: first, the relational or communal identity of a thing; second, the freeing of this communal identity from an idealistic monism; third, the need to rethink the traditional insistence of being, the *conatus essendi*, in light of the torque of ontological tension created by this double relativity; finally, we must look at the reappearance of the notion of ontological value.

First consideration. If, as I previously claimed, there is a proper oneness to things, have we then subordinated difference to identity? Or does difference also have to be thought further, not only beyond equivocity but also beyond dialectical self-mediation? I think so. Things are not only one, not only many within themselves, not only self-mediating unities; they are also singulars placed within the community of beings. Their habitation and locale is most richly expressed relative to this emplacement. Their self-definition is itself defined relative to this community.

If dialectical self-unity recovers the truth of univocity after equivocity, the metaxological community as entering the thing's self-definition recovers the truth of otherness and equivocity, but after dialectic. The very power that allows self-mediation in process of becoming is not exhausted by any return to self in which the energy of the thing finds complete self-closure. Things are not only striving to be themselves for, in St. Paul's metaphor, all creation groans. Does creation groan only that things may become *themselves*? That yes, but also the vector of transcending in things reaches beyond itself, strives in a relativity to others. Plurivocal transcending is also a turning of self-identity to the full range of otherness in the manyness of beings.

This turning to others is not to be interpreted only in terms of a *lack* that entities exhibit. Consider: the heliotropic flower will turn towards the sun, and will do so in circumstances that are not enabling; place it at the back of a room, with the window to the light at a distance, and in time it will twist itself in the direction of the day. Does it do this because it needs the light, and hence out of its own indigence? Yes it does, but there is more than indigence here. Rather the very *dunamis* of its identity, *dunamis* in an essentially positive sense, is a turning of the self of the flower towards the light. A relativity to the light is *already inscribed* in its being; the other is already at work in its identity, even though altered environmental circumstances are sometimes needed to make this plain. In some form or other, the community of being already calls in the plurivocal identity of the thing, even when the energy of active self-relation dominates the mode in which the thing identifies itself.

What I am saying calls for a qualification of simple external or simple internal relations. First, we must modify the notion of *internal* relations by saying that everything is implicated in every other thing, but implicated out of a self-identity that is dialectically *rich* in itself. It is not the mere lack of a part that drives the thing in search of its engulfing whole. The thing is already a splendor of integral being, and correspondingly its implication with the other is not only defined by lack. The community of beings, wherein self-relativity is conjoined with interrelativity, is not entirely amenable to a dialectical logic of parts and wholes. Rather we require a metaxology of whole and whole, each an integrity unto itself, but none a closure on itself against the others.

Second, we must modify the notion of *external* relations, because the integrities in relation are not mere static points, whose relativity is a superimposed pattern coming unto the things from above, or from the outside. We must conceive of externality as a relation of othering in a dynamic sense, whose promise is always at work in the thing's integrity. Consider my example again. The heliotropic flower has its integrity in itself, but this integrity in itself is also other to itself, and other to itself, not simply in order for it to be itself dialectically. It is other to itself because it is already defined in a dynamic intermediation with other integrities of being that cannot be dialectically appropriated to its own identity. The sun is other and external; yet the sun is in the flower's being, as defining the promise of its integral self-becoming. The flower's othering of itself—its turning to the sun—is already its spread beyond itself, in itself. It is beyond itself by being itself defined by an inherent responsiveness to an other that is an integrity beyond it. Its othering of itself intertwines with a call of the other—the radiance of the sun—that both comes from outside and erupts within it. The sunflower that spreads

itself outwards and upwards is self-othered, but also othered from itself by an
exteriority that is *both* exterior and interior to it, at one and the same time.

Just as dialectic helps us reformulate internal relations, the metaxological
helps us reformulate external relations. But the second is necessary to the
fulness of the first, in that it prevents the dialectical reformulation of internal
relations ending up in the monism of an absorbing whole, wherein every
finite entity is finally seen as a part of a larger whole, and every finite whole a
part of the one all-absorbing totality. If we do speak of the whole, we should
see this as an open whole—that is to say, a community of wholes. The community of such wholes is marked on the internal relatedness of things, but
not as parts of larger wholes simply, but as integrities unto themselves. Likewise, dialectic and metaxology together makes us rethink exteriority, not as
the mere adventitious connection of things essentially extraneous, and the
superimposition of a connection by a dominating third on things, otherwise
opposed or indifferent to each other. Exteriority has to be rethought in terms
of community in irreducible otherness that gives things the space in which
they become themselves.

Things are for themselves but in cooperation with the other things that
constitute their partners and neighbors, even enemies in the surrounding
environment. Relational identity involves cooperating community, as well as
hostile recoil. The deer is relationally defined by the tiger in hostile recoil,
but defined by cooperating community in its own herd. The hostile recoil can
be itself ingredient in a neighborhood, in a positive cooperative sense: the
tiger culls the herd of its old and infirm, and hence the death of one is not
only the sustenance of the other, but also the perishing necessary to keep
vigorous the health of the first.

We might here speak of partnership in a neighborhood of being. Thus
the tree in a forest is a partner in a neighborhood. Within this cooperating
community, different species exist in a mutuality of dependence, which dependence offers the single tree its independence for itself. As independent, a
tree draws its life from the soil below, the sunshine above it, the rain running
down its bark, the wind shaking its branches. But it not only receives from
air, soil, and sky, it also constitutes a neighborhood of being for other entities
whose independence is grounded on their dependency on it: birds nest in it,
insects infest it, mosses grow on it. The others of the tree are both within it
and outside, and we cannot fix the within and the without in any finalized
sense.

Even the more or less enduring shape of the tree is a formation of original energy wherein there is a process of incessant give and take. When the
process of give and take ceases, the tree ceases to be and decomposes. Decomposition is itself a process of communal give and take. Hence the tree exists as
for itself in a community of interaction, which is an incessant process of transition between itself and what is other to itself. The identity of a tree in a

forest is the *neighborhood identity* of a process of give and take. The give and take is continuing in the universal impermanence.

The tree is a neighborhood in the neighborhood of the forest, and the forest is a more inclusive community of beings that mediates the differences of a large number of species. But the forest in itself is an incessant process of interchange within itself, and also between itself and the neighborhoods of being that, as other, are its environment of definition. And this process of transition can be extended further. But the between of neighorhood does not finally reduce to a single monistic neighborhood. There is no engulfing community of being that would be the singular process of complete dialectical self-mediation. Such an engulfing totality would be the denial of the very openness between others that defines the very nature of a genuine community of beings.

Within a neighborhood of being, understood as such a community, there are a plurality of open dialectical integrities. Their transcending self-mediation constitutes a neighborhood of metaxological community in which the otherness between things is not, can never be, eradicated. The loss or the overcoming of this irreducible otherness would, in fact, be the death of the community of being, the congealing of creation in its inexhaustible fecundity.

Relative to such a community in otherness, exteriority concretizes ontological *respect* for differences, and demands such respect of our mindfulness. This is foreshadowed in what I called the aesthetic tolerance of otherness. It is as if the artist of the community, in the aesthetic presencing of things, already offers to things the promise of this ontological respect, and hence the promise of a togetherness of being that is not reductive of real differences. The aesthetic presencing of things reveals their intimacy with creation, with other creatures in creation. This intimacy is their immanent interrelatedness, but it is also a tolerance of plurality as irreducibly plural. The otherness of things as aesthetic presencings is first of all let be for itself by the agapeic generosity of creation.

And so to dwell intensively with a thing is to find unavoidable a communal definition of its being. Suppose we think of a thing as a *poiēsis*, a work of creation. But a creation is double—both a whole unto itself, and also an opening of being that resists complete containment within the boundaries of any framed whole. Thus seen, a thing is a gracefully formed flourish of the creative power of being; in itself it communicates with the whole of creation by the simple elemental being there that it bespeaks; it partakes of the family of being; it can be mother or brother or sister or father or cousin or ancestor or descendent of all other things. As a work of creation the thing images the primordial power of creation. *Image* here means the concretion of original power to be, aesthetic presencing in the most robust realistic sense. As such an image, the thing is also a reality for itself, hence it is an original. Its doubleness is this: an original that images an original beyond itself. It is an original image of an original that finds concretion in all aesthetic presencing but that is never reducible simply to aesthetic presencing. The image even as original for itself is eccentric: centered in itself, it is decentered, centered in an other that is not a mere extrinsic outside but that is radically intimate to the thing, more intimate to the thing than the thing is to itself.

Second consideration. This concerns the need to free the thing's communal definition from the more usual idealistic route of an overarching monism of the whole. My strategy is to reformulate dialectic such as to keep things open to other things, and each in its own integrity. For the intensive self-mediation of a thing reveals its promise as *beyond* complete determinate objectification. Hence the thing's integrity is enigmatic in its own way. Its being can never be quantified completely in terms of a univocal *mathēsis*. It is, as it were, marked by an inward otherness that resists total determination in clear concepts. Even if we say that the thing is just self-determining, and hence determinate in a dynamic sense, still this energy of determining points to the work of active determining that cannot be completely objectified and thus determined completely. So each integrity manifests a "more" or an inner excess, beyond complete determination. This inner excess is not an indefiniteness that awaits later determination. It is the active original power to be that is the core integral act that continually sustains the possibility of the integrity in process.

What is "proper" to this inner otherness of the thing is that its being, as thus indeterminately dynamized, can never be completely appropriated. Inward otherness here means: an unmastered, unappropriated abyss, about which we hesitate to say that it belongs to the thing, since a thing is a thing by virtue of the giving of this generating energy. We cannot say that the thing owns it, because its ownership is a gift. The thing puts its roots down into creation and into the origin, and this deepest root retreats beyond all mastering. There is no appropriation of what is most appropriate and proper and interior to the thing, its relation to the origin as recipient of the gift of being.

Moreover, this unmastered excess is pluralized in singular ways in all other entities that are integrities for themselves. Each is participant in the gift, and at the deepest ontological level the gift is the community of being. If all the other things are self-mediating in a way that resists complete appropriation, there is no absolutely encompassing whole that will subordinate the internal otherness of things, or their external otherness, to one totality. The idea of totality does not capture the complex balance of selfness and otherness, difference and unity, at play. As acknowledging a stronger sense of otherness, beyond equivocity and dialectic, the metaxological way reminds us of the unappropriated nature of otherness, both within the thing in its integrity, and between things as integrities unto themselves. The space of inward otherness and the stressed space of the otherness of the between remain open.

This is the metaxological doubleness of the thing: for itself, but with the suggestion of the excess of inward otherness; for others external to itself, others with their own integrity and excess of inward otherness. The *inter* is complexly qualified by the inner dialectic of the things. The *inter* is no mere contiguity, but an interimplication and interinvolvement. We may usefully isolate things for purposes of abstraction and calculation, but in itself no thing is isolated. It is a spread on the universal impermanence of creation. This spread is its particular involvement in the community of being.

One cannot but recall Leibniz's view that every monad mirrors the whole universe from its own perspective. We modify this to say: as dynamic unities, things are monads, things are originals; things as dialectical integrities mirror—that is, singularly image—the community of being; they are open wholes in community with the open whole of creation, as itself a pluralism of wholes. Leibniz has been criticized for isolating the monads, when he says they are windowless. The locution is unfortunate, probably due to a strain of univocity in Leibniz's view of the individual. But the monads are not windowless. This we capture in the openness of dialectical self-mediation.

I suggest, however, the following more interesting possibility: community not constituted simply by monads looking out their windows, but community effective from the origin, even if it seems that the monad is condemned to solitary confinement. Properly speaking, there are *other* windows in the seemingly windowless monads, if each monad mirrors the universe from its own point of view. For these mirrors are windows—that is, they are not just mirrors that reflect the face of the self of the solitary monad. The seemingly solitary monad may look into the mirror of itself, but the face of the whole of otherness begins to look back at it, and not just simply its own face. The face of the singular monad, conceived as an open whole, sees in the immanence of its own face the face of the open whole, the community of being as an open whole. The mirrors that hang in the cell of solitary identity are not mirrors for self-identity; they are the glass in which the face of the origin returns our searching gaze; the face of the absolutely other looks on, even though the monad only expects itself as its own double. In this mirror the double is not the self in its own self-doubling; it is the startling face of the irreducibly other, the double that looks out with the eyes of the primal one.

Leibniz does invoke the chief monad to provide the overarching viewpoint to synchronize the plurality of created monads, and he has been scoffed at for invoking a deus ex machina. Would that things were as simple as the scoffers contend. His notion of preestablished harmony has also met jeers, but it ought to be rethought more deeply. Preestablished harmony is related to what I refer to as the call of community inscribed in the thing in its excess to determinate appropriation. It is "preestablished," in the sense that communal relativity to other things is ontologically constitutive of the identity of a thing in its own being for-self. It is a "harmony," in that this relativity is the aesthetic value of a community. It is a harmony of a harmonizing of voices. It is univocity become plurivocity become communivocity. In a harmony of harmonies many voices sing together, none loses its integrity for itself, yet each also acts on behalf of, sings for, the beauty of all together. This is the voice of the community of being composed of many singing voices. Aesthetic presencing is heard again: things sing, and creation does not simply groan; creation sings, and the song it sings is "It is good," "It is good to be."

Third consideration. We also need to rethink the *conatus essendi*, the insistence of being, if a metaxological doubleness is inscribed on a thing's own integrity for itself. For the spread of a thing makes its being both centered in itself, and also decentered towards what is other. The decentering is not administered simply by a shock from outside; rather an other *center* is at work in its own center; its own center is not a single center, but rather is in itself defined as openness to the other. This makes for what might be called a *torque of ontological tension* that drives the dynamism of becoming in an intertwining of self-mediation and intermediation with the other. Of course, inevitably we are tempted to *tilt* the balance of this doubling and privilege one side or the other. Thus the nominalist view will accentuate the first, the idealist the second, vis-à-vis the relational definition of a thing in a network of other things. Both these views abstract one side from the complex doubleness. If we emphasize integrity alone, the relational community of beings is either denied or reduced to an aggregate bound together extrinsically. If we emphasize relational identity only, the thing's integrity either vanishes, or is redefined as the epiphenomenon of relationality. In the latter case, there is no real relationality, since there cease to be robustly irreducible centers of being that are to be in relation.

Let me offer a relevant example of the intertwining of these two forms of mediation. Recent studies of dominance of the male fish, the African cichlid, gives an interesting picture of the work on identity of a double relativity, this interplay of self-mediation and intermediation.[9] The dominant males not only have more visible self-presentations—for example, brighter colors—but they are simply bigger and more aggressive; the subordinate males are dull colored and meld with the female fish. Dominance is defined in intermediation, albeit the intermediation of an order of power in which genetic perpetuation is the major exigence. The future of the kind is being perpetuated in the stand-

---

9. See *Journal of Molecular Endocrinology*, as reported in a *New York Times* article, December 11, 1991. Note that in what follows the scientific information there given is susceptible to a metaxological interpretation.

ing out of the aggressive males. So this singular standing out is, even in the power of the singular, always for the community.

Dominance is here the spread of a self that is spatially expressed as range over territoriality. The "myness" of the ascendent fish extends to the territory he dominates; self-identity has its territorial spread. Thus a dominant fish has a different emplacement, a different locale, habitation. But this is not merely extrinsic. An entire biological change has been noted to occur when a fish becomes dominant: the brains cells in the hypothalmus are six to eight times larger than the equivalent cells in their subordinate fellows; their testes also grow bigger and they begin to produce sperm. Their very biological identity at the level of brain and genetic activity is altered in rapport with changes in the sociality of the species. Contrariwise, when a dominant fish loses its ascendency, or is placed in the presence of another more dominant fish, its overt self-display will alter, and its bright colors diminish to the average dullness of the school, diminish to being unnoticeable. This diminution in exterior self-display, in aesthetic presencing, will be matched by a retraction of biological functioning: the hypothalmic cells in the brain will shrink, the testes will shrivel and cease to produce sperm. A new struggle for dominant self-identity will induce previously subordinate fish to seek to spread their influence over the others and the territory. There will be a new struggle for, as it were, the social spatialization of self-identity in interplay with others.

Note the language of enlargement and shrinking. This is metaphorical, but metaphorical of the spread of a being. It is as if the energy of being in an identity can reach out and beyond, or contract and shrink back into itself. The very expansion and contraction of bodily being are expressions of this extension and retraction of the energy of self-identity. And this is not only true of external bodily modification. The modification is much more intimate. Sociality shapes the brain in its cellular and molecular activity, as much as the brain shapes sociality. It would appear that the changes in social relation trigger brain changes, that in turn trigger the production of gonadotropin-releasing harmone, that in turn again triggers the pituitary gland to produce harmones that enlarge the testes and begin the production of sperm. Social dominance, correlated with a mode of intermediation, influences the very identity and hence self-mediation of the particular fish, and does so in the physiological intimacy of the flesh of the fish. The old debate pitting nature against nurture will not do. There is rather a multiply complex interplay between two different mediations: self-mediation in which the thing presents for itself; and intermediation wherein the thing self-presents before and for the others. In the middle, these two mix, in tension and in togetherness.

Of course, the mix and tension will be different with different things. Men are like fish, but the likeness is analogical. In no way ought we to extrapolate univocally from fish to humans, where the ontological deepness of selfhood matches an openness to the other, which promises an ethical self-sacrifice that is in another dimension to biological self-sacrifice for the species. We will come to this in later chapters.

Consider now the insistence of being that is expressed in the singularity of things. This insistence can communicate itself as aggression towards other beings, or as violence, if this insistence is not properly respected. We see this in the interplay of the fish: insistence meets insistence, each in its own spread; and the socializing of the plural insistences yields a new determination (different in the dominant and subordinate fish) of the self-shaping of the original self-insistences. It should be clear, I think, that this insistence of singularity cannot be solipsized, in that the call of the community of others is always and already at work in its singular expression. There is more at work in self-insistence than self.

I do not simply deny the classic doctrine of a being's *conatus essendi*, but I do want to reinterpret it significantly, in terms of the doubling/pluralizing of things at the metaxological level. The solipsizing of this *conatus essendi* springs from an inadequate individualism or nominalism. In fact, the urge to being that is defined by the *conatus* is, in previously used terms, both *erotic* and *agapeic*. It can be erotic: the insistence spreads beyond itself in relation to what is other, but this spread beyond is for the self. It can also be agapeic: the insistence of being in its relation to the other can express itself for the other, and not for a return to the self.

I think that traditional interpretations of the *conatus* have tended to give it a primarily erotic modulation, and have great difficulty with the agapeic opening to the other that we especially meet in human community. Indeed we also meet it in nature and nonhuman community. Thus we might think of biological self-sacrifice as an unconscious agape for the community of the others of the same kind. One thinks of the ecstasy of death for those male spiders who must expire in the embrace of the generating female. Neither knows that their eros, their mixing of life and death, is an agape for the kind, a sacrificial being for the future other. Both the erotic and agapeic interpretation of the *conatus* imply more in this insistence than self-insistence. In the erotic case, the "more" is seen in terms of self-mediation in the other; in the agapeic case, it is seen in terms of an exodus from self towards the other that is not undertaken simply for the self. In this latter case there is a death of insistence of being as self-insistence. The *conatus essendi* reverses this self-insistence into the willingness to sacrifice for the other.

This will be developed in later chapters, but let me try to indicate the mix and torque of ontological tension relative to the pluralism of beings. If entities are doubly mediating, there is a kind of fault line of internal difference running through the thing's unity. This is reflected in a doubleness of necessity and freedom. So we might look on a thing as a *double unity of free and bound dunamis*. What is the bound *dunamis*? It is the source of repetition and identity, the basis of sameness and also the source of given relativity to other things. What is the free *dunamis*? It is the source of the differences of the thing, the source of potential newness, also the source of a free relativity to others. A thing is the unity in tension of free and bound *dunamis* or the original power to be. This tension is comparatively slack in the least complex entities. No thing is without internal complexity, but in entities that approximate more nearly to univocal unity, the complexity of internal difference is at its least intensive level.

Inanimate things, for instance, are more marked by bound *dunamis* than organic and human things. A rock exhibits itself, aesthetically presences, with a relative stability and sameness much greater than a flower; for its original power to be is bound to less complex possibilities of repetition, and less expansive possibilities of breaking out of repetition. The inner tension will become more torqued as free *dunamis* begins to prevail over bound *dunamis*. This prevailing increases with the complexification of inner difference, which is also a deepening of complex integrity for self. Inner difference and inner integrity go hand in hand; but the deepening of inner difference frees a being from the bonds of repetition. Then the call of the other is not only inscribed in the self's integrity, it can begin to be differently heard in a new mode of free responsiveness.

The inner tension between free and bound *dunamis* is most extreme with the human being. Here the freeing of the energy of transcendence has a rebound effect on the bound energies of repetition, such that the self forges its identity in process, in a manner open to the unexpected, the surprising, in the newness of the time of creation. With the human being identity becomes explicitly self-making through the difference of free power to be. We are not only bound to the other, we are called to a free responsiveness that shakes the foundations of all repetitions, a responsiveness that binds us to the other in a bond that cannot be encompassed by any bounding power.

Again we must connect this double tension with the metaxological definition of the thing as doubly mediating. We might say that free *dunamis* increases the hiatus internal to self-relation. The hyphen is a cleft in univocal self-identity, but also a spread of the original power to be of the self. So here too negation and the sense of nothing are unavoidable. Openness and the sense of nothingness are twins—for finite entities, Siamese twins. The cleft of openness is also the opening of the space of transcendence. The spread of a thing opens in this energy of transcendence; through transcending, free *dunamis* breaks up the repetitive sameness of things, implicates its identity in an interplay with others. The thing as double is then both free and repetitive interplay, original and habitual being. The intermediation rebounds back on self-relation and increases its inner tension. Depending on how this tension is mediated, there will be increase or decrease in the the potency of free *dunamis*, as we saw with the fish.

This doubleness unfolds all the way up from inorganic through organic to living and mindful being. Properly speaking, this double in tension is not just a dialectic between free and bound power to be. It is a complex unfolding and concretion of the *fourfold* sense of being at different levels of ontological complexity, determined by the predominance of either free or constrained *dunamis*. Thus things as predominantly *univocal* display a self-relation and interrelativity that is mainly necessitated. Things as *equivocal* show the lack of inhibition of free difference. Things as *dialectical* show the rebound on dynamical self-relation from out of the free energies of difference; they bind themselves in their free unfolding and are more or less self-determining. Things as *metaxological* display another freedom after this dialectical rebound of self-determination; they find themselves called forth into the highest freedom on the basis of the *highest pitch of tension* in the self as for itself, and on the basis of the most demanding struggle of transcendence towards the other. This most demanding struggle promises the highest release of self from the prison house of its own bondage.

It needs to be said that there is *suffering* in all of this pitching of tension. For the complexification of the original power of being in the direction of free *dunamis* is both an increase in the promise of real freedom, but also an increase in the suffering of being. Freedom here again is properly metaxological rather than just dialectical, since dialectic will want to confine this freedom in the autonomy of self-determining being, wherein the negativity of the suffering of being will be appropriated as a vanishing moment. Metaxological being increases the suffering of being, because it raises the call of the other to a new height and unparalleled request for responsiveness.

Moreover, suffering here is not the inactive passivity that a dialectical thing will want to surmount actively. Suffering of being is the trauma of the impact of otherness on the self in its active self-relation. When a thing selves in this explicitly metaxological way, there is a sense in which it is no longer a thing, but a self as person. There is a rupture of, a disruption of, a violence to, even a *death* of bound, unfree *dunamis*. The thing must die for the self as person to be born. This death is the trauma of metaxological being in which the thing dies as *existing* its bond with the other, only to be reborn as a self that can *choose* its bond with the other, as its ethical destiny. This death is also a disruption of the erotics of self-insistence: the *conatus essendi* freely restrains from insisting on itself, and willingly wills to become a being for the other.

Fourth consideration. This concerns the reappearance of the value of things, but this time, given the last consideration, ontological value invokes ethical value. The *dunamis* of the thing points beyond univocal unity and equivocal difference to a forming of the original power of being that is a self-formation, self-becoming. But this self-forming, as the transcending spread of the thing, not only points back to its origin, it also points ahead to its own possible completion. Forming looks forwards to finality, and not in any closed way, but as the open purpose that carries the becoming of the thing to the release of its proper wholeness. There is no finalized finality. Rather, there is at stake a *second* sense of ontological value—namely, the *realization of the promise* of ontological perfection in the first sense. This second ontological value is itself double, invoking both the purpose of self-realization, and also that of the intermediated realization of the community of beings.

Of course, dialectical and metaxological possibilities are more explicitly evident the more complex the ontological constitution of the thing. A thing that is and becomes itself in a process of development is both more explicitly self-shaping, and also shaped in its membership of the community of others that constitutes its environment of development. The promise of ontological value, the becoming of the perfection of being as given, is in the process of being redeemed at this more complex level of metaxological community.

Unexpectedly, we are asked to think again about the singularity of things. The idea of bare indigent particularity, which serves as a mere instance of an abstract universal, will not do in thinking about things. If the "this" is a proper one, it cannot be exhausted in univocal terms. Rather the truth of univocity is to be seen in the light of the "this," now interpreted beyond dialectic. Relative to the metaxological truth of the univocal, I again invoke Leibniz, but this time in relation to his principle of the "identity of indiscernibles." According to this principle, two things exactly alike cannot, in fact, be different, for if there are no discernible differences, the two collapse into one. Leibniz denies such a collapse relative to the unique singular identity of every existent thing. A thing is not itself, if it does not bear a difference that makes it uniquely itself. There is a "thisness," a "myness," that is irreplaceable.

One might be inclined to locate the difference at the level of *differentiae*, but there is a deeper locus in the irreplaceable unity. This is the singular that is for itself absolutely. Does not this seem to contradict completely the metaxological emphasis on relativity to the other? Superficially yes, but on a deeper level, no. It all turns on the depth at which we think the community of being, relative to this irreplaceable singularity. It is not incidental that what I see as Leibniz's doctrine of irreplaceable singularity is tied up with a view of God as Creator and the principle of plenitude. The perfection of the world is demanded by the perfection of the Creator; the first perfection demands that creation exemplify the perfection of the Creator to the maximum possible. If God were simply to repeat God's self without a difference, God's perfection would not be respected.

I prescind from analysis of Leibniz's theology, though it is susceptible of a subtle reading. I just suggest that mere repetition would univocalize God, in the sense of reducing God's work to the finite reiteration of bound *dunamis*. Then, as with Spinoza, there is no creation, only the necessitated determination of God in the necessary determination of the course of things in the world. Thus also Spinoza, and Hegel more dialectically, will redefine the free energy of God as rationally determined *dunamis*, necessitated as self-determined. But beyond univocity and dialectical self-determination, hence beyond Spinozism and Hegelianism, there is a different sense of the freedom of being. In fact, God thought metaxologically would be—with a bow to Cusanus—the maximum, indeed the more than maximum, the over-determined excessive plenitude of the free original power to be. And so the sense of the agapeic origin I have adumbrated is reflected in the creation of unique singularity: the being of the thing is loved unrepeatably for itself, and hence has its being in this ontological generosity that is absolute—uncondi-tionally for the singular thing itself, in the ontological worth of its being. The community of creation is the ontological bond of irreplaceable singulars, freed into their singularity by the excess of the agapeic origin.

This release makes us raise the question of plurality in another sense—namely, the kinds of things and their diverse intelligibilities. Our concern now must be to think the community of creation in terms of its intelligibilities.

CHAPTER NINE

INTELLIGIBILITIES

The Question of Intelligibility

Things come to be in the universal impermanence, but are they just there? If there, how there? Are being and beings intelligible? If so, why? If so, how so? Can we avoid these questions? No. This negation might seem dogmatic, but no, it is a considered no. These considerations will emerge, but they are formulated in an historical context in which intelligibility has been put to severe test.

This is what I mean. In not a few strains of contemporary philosophy, in continental philosophy mainly, we find an unprecedented onslaught on inherent intelligibility. Intelligibility is often construed as a grid of categorial schemas that the human knower imposes on "reality" to further its *own* will to power. Intelligibility, it is implied, is a conceptual or logical mask for will to power. We are to unmask the mask, and expose the absence of a basis in being for intelligibility.

The proximate historical source of the view lies in the dissolution of idealism. First, in Kant and his idealist heirs, the active knower is elevated into the privileged ontological and cognitive position: the knower "constructs" intelligibility, does not find it. But then, in the post-Hegelian heirs of idealism, the "knower" is said to be itself equivocal; its privileges seem to crumble, when the human-all-too-human face of a less noble will to power peeps out from the idealistic disguise. Like "reality" other to the self, the self goes the same way as the intelligibility it previously was supposed to construct. It too becomes an instance of the same will to power, in itself unintelligible.

First, intelligibility is said to be constructed by the self-mediating knower. Then intelligibility is deconstructed by the same knower. Then the self-mediating knower is deconstructed, or deconstructs itself. The upshot is that both self-being and other-being ultimately reduce to nothing but unintelligible and valueless will to power. If the latter does produce intelligibility, the intelligibility so produced is itself ultimately the production of an unintelligible surd. Being is absolutely equivocal: intelligibility is ultimately absurd—that is, unintelligible.

This outlook is pervasive in many strands of post-Kantian thought. The merest mention of intelligibility will be quickly put upon by a hermeneutics of suspicion. In tandem, a paradoxical combination of ontological cowardice and will to power will be imputed to the metaphysical quest, and to the great metaphysicians. Cowardice: in their cowering failure, or lack of nerve, to encounter the unintelligibility of being. Will to power: in their compensatory conceptual aggression on this same unintelligibility, an aggression that would force being to speak in the language of our "intelligibility."

I reject this block totalization of metaphysics and this summary arraignment of intelligibility. Our ultimate sense of intelligibility is not divorced from how ultimately we understand the origin. I think an interpretative aggression is to be attributed more to the hermeneuticists of suspicion than to their victims. In my view, the absolutization of will to power is tied to a deconstructed variation of an erotic absolute, in which the affirmation of being is reversed into aggression towards it, an aggression then imputed to all our cognitive searches of being. This degraded erotic absolute itself follows a deconstruction of the apotheosis of self-mediation, in which the other to the self is always seen as the self itself, in its own projected otherness. We might say that will to power cannot see the other as other because it distorts, in its own energy of being, the promise of agapeic mindfulness that goes towards the other as other. Self-mediation as will to power cannot see the intelligibility of what is other to itself, except as the projection of its own categorial schema. It cannot entertain the possibility of origin as an agapeic source, nor of the givenness of creation and things in their plurivocal, metaxological promise. Far from being a new openness to being's otherness, it solemnizes its inherent unintelligibility—that is, its absurdity. This way represents a severe contraction, not to say suicidal impulse, of the self-surpassing transcending of mindfulness.

Can we avoid the question of intelligibility? In an important sense this question is its own answer. For all questioning is an activation of the dynamism of mind, the precipitation of more or less determinate perplexity. As an energizing of mind, questioning potentially takes mind out of itself towards other-being. Mind may also be perplexed about itself; but here too the movement towards the other is at work, since it is mind itself as other to itself that generates this self-perplexity. Perplexity is in the face of what now makes no sense, or what confounds expectation of sense on the old ways of thinking. But in the face of what is not yet intelligible, questioning transcends itself towards possible intelligibility. Thus the anticipation of possible intelligibility is the presupposition of all questioning.

This is not to deny the plurality of modes of intelligibility, and that our expectations of certain kinds of intelligibility may be confounded. For instance, the expectation of mathematical intelligibility with respect to ethical practices will be confounded, not because ethical practices are unintelligible, but because the mode of intelligibility proper to ethics cannot be contained within mathematical conceptualization. The plurivocity of intelligibility affords a multiplicity of possibilities. Ingredient in the process of determining intelligibility is proper discrimination concerning the appropriate possiblility with respect to this or that particular ordering of being. Nor is this to deny that there are *limits* in the modes of intelligibility that seem available to the human mind.

Our question right now does not regard this or that specific mode of intelligibility, but the more englobing question of the intelligibility of being and beings. It concerns the ground of such intelligibility, if affirmed. It concerns also whether that ground can be said to be intelligible in exactly the same way as are the things whose intelligibility it makes possible. These questions are extraordinarily difficult, and every attempted answer is fraught with risks, if not flawed liabilities. But there is no reason intrinsic to mind or being that forbids our pursuing them. Quite to the contrary, the questions are precipitated spontaneously with the spontaneous activation of mind. They come to the mind as metaphysically perplexed. Their very indeterminacy matches the indeterminacy of the second perplexity of metaphysical mind. Our task as metaphysicians is to be as articulate as possible about the meaning of intelligibility as it emerges in this matrix of indeterminacy, or rather this matrix of betweenness, where we participate in an interplay between indeterminacy and determination. We cannot escape such questions if we are honest, for some unarticulated response to them is effective, even in philosophers who explicitly reject them as illegitimate. Those philosophers do not know themselves.

Those who philosophize in the shadow of will to power may charge the question with hubris. We must reject the accusation, if metaphysical mind is already on the *other* side of will to power. Metaphysical perplexity yields to a troubled astonishment before the marvel of being. And if perplexity is nourished in agapeic mind, then the question of intelligibility is deeply a matter of metaxological openness to the enigmatic *otherness* of being. Hubris is just that egocentric vileness that the metaphysician wants to extirpate. For hubris is just the degraded form of the self-surpassing *dunamis* of mind as agapeic, the form accompanying the degraded erotic absolute that is will to power.

Of course, mind's reach may exceed its grasp. The ultimate ground of intelligibility may not be itself intelligible in a manner that yields completely to our efforts to conceptualize it. Not every intelligibility is determinable in a univocal manner. But equivocal absurdism does not follow. There are modes of intelligibility that take shape in complex interplays between indeterminacy and determinacy. The excess of indeterminacy may itself have to be taken into account to do justice to the intelligibility of the determinate. This does not mean that the excess is the merely unintelligible in itself. This would only be so, if all intelligibility were exhausted by determinacy. What eludes our full comprehension is not the same as the unintelligible in itself. The point is suggested by our discussion of the origin. There is an excess to the agapeic origin that goes beyond every determination we attempt, and this by the very "nature" of the origin. Yet this does *not* imply the judgment that the origin is simply absurd, or devoid of intelligible relation to the intelligibilities available to us in the milieu of finite creation.

Unavoidably our sense of the ultimate ground of intelligibility is related to the intelligibilities we discern in the milieu of finite creation. Hence the degraded erotic absolute of the will to power tells us something significant about what its advocates can see in the being of finiteness, and what they fail to see. Our sense of the origin as agapeic excess relates to what we discern in the milieu of finite creation and its promise. This promise asks us to risk our perplexity in a humble effort to speak about that ground of intelligibility. If we are always in the between, we are also, as self-transcending, *between* creation and its ground, and know it or not, *both* enter into the determination of our metaphysical sense of intelligibility.

As will emerge more fully, there is inherent in the anticipation of questioning an *indeterminate trust* in the availability of proper intelligibility. This is related to our sense of origin. Consider it this way. We ask about the ground of intelligibility and often answer in terms of putative first principles like sufficient reason and the law of contradiction. I think that such determinate principles presuppose a prior indeterminate trust in intelligibility, as well as a prior grounding origin. Thus one might ask: If demonstration depends on principles of demonstration, what demonstrates these principles of demonstration? It cannot be just another determinate principle; for this too is open to the same question. There must be a prior sense of "principle," in the sense of a *principium*, or originary source, relative to which the indeterminate trust in intelligibility is defined. But there is no *determinate demonstration* of this, since this source of trust is presupposed by rational demonstration.

A rational demonstration—for instance, geometric proof—requires prior principles—for instance, axioms. But what establishes the prior principles? There comes a point where we cannot answer in terms of another determinate proof or principle. Thus, the question is connected to Aristotle's view of dialectic as opening a path to the principles of all inquiry (see *Topics*, 101b3–4; discussed in chapter 4, above) beyond determinate demonstration. Overall I propose to offer a metaxological rethinking of this way, passing though the determinate intelligibilities of the between. I do not offer an outside Archimedean point, but speak from the middle and the meaning of the indeterminate trust and the sense of its originary ground as emergent therein.

Thus also the question is connected to contemporary antifoundationalism. This can be seen as reactive to an excessive univocalizing of intelligibility, as, say, in Cartesian notions of indubitability and certainty, leading in turn to an excessive *distrust* in intelligibility. We too will have to face the challenge to intelligibility of the equivocal. Overall, I will try to specify in outline some of the major modes of intelligibility with reference to the fourfold sense of being.

Intelligibility Produced and Inherent: The Possibilizing of Possibility

First, however, in light of the onslaught on intelligibility, I take up the question: Is intelligibility inherent or produced? The answer I suggest is: both inherent and produced, and in a number of senses. Let me elaborate.

Suppose we say that intelligibility is produced. What I mean is that intelligibility is not absolutely intelligible in itself, but requires some reference to the origin. I will suggest below the reason for this, but first I want to say that intelligibility need not here mean some order of lifeless eternity. Without excluding intelligibilities that are transtemporal, I am suggesting that intelligibility is itself a creation. Philosophers have often considered this matter in terms of an *order of possibility* that is the transfinite condition of finite being. For instance, Leibniz's God produces the possibles and creates the world as the optimum concretion of their compossibility. There is an order of eternal possibility, and finite being is the concretion of such possibility that is not itself a finite being. The question is: What can we say about such an order of possibility?

Some have argued here for possibility defined in more *logical* terms. Possibility is what is not inherently contradictory: if A does not entail logical contradiction, A is a possible. Here logical univocity, understood as the source of the law of contradiction, dictates the basis and definition of the possible. Notice also that logic and the law of contradiction are themselves based on the principle of identity: to be is to be determinate. This definition of possibility is tied generally to univocal mind and to logic, and more specifically to the principles of identity and contradiction.

But how then do we answer this harder and prior question: *What makes possibility itself possible*? This question is not about what makes possibility actual, in the sense of determinately actualizing this or that particular possibility, but about the very ground of possibility as such. What makes *possibility* itself possible? What, so to say, *possibilizes* possibility, possibilizes in an active, generative sense? We are asking about the *very opening up* of possibility in an ontological sense. Possibility possibilizes, makes possible certain happenings of being, but what possibilizes possibility itself? To my knowledge not many philosophers have even raised this question, this perplexity at the edge of determinate intelligibility.

The law of contradiction will not do. For it is derivative from the univocal sense of being and the principle of identity; but the full fourfold sense of being indicates not only a sense of possibility, but of concreteness, in excess of what univocity can determine. This is the claim, and I will have more to say about univocity and contradiction. The point here is: we seem to need a more primordial sense of possibilizing, if possibility itself possibilizes. We need to acknowledge the *power of the possible*. Put this way: we need a more primordial sense of the *dunamis* of being—namely, the original power to be. This original power to be is more primordial than possibility as derived from the law of contradiction. We might think of this primordial power as the *first possibilizing*, in contrast to the *second possibilizing*, which refers to the determinate realization of a particular possibility. This first power of the possible is a creative possibilizing.

What does this mean? I suggest we might think of the origin as the primal and ultimate power of creative possibilizing. What this implies is an ontological sense of possibility. Apart from this, I want to argue, logical possibility is all but empty possibility. Almost anything is possible this latter way, depending on the limits of conceivability. With a little ingenuity, of which we humans have little, almost anything might be possible. But if logical possibility is all but empty possibility, nothing is really possible as ontological possibility. Indeed without this further ontological possibility, "everything is possible" can come to mean "everything is impossible, nothing is really possible." For how do we get from logical possibility to being? Possibility is what might be but that is not; hence its proximity to nonbeing. But how does logical possibility, as it were, leap over its own almost nonbeing into being? To make intelligible this coming to be, there must be, I suggest, another sense of the possible, other than logical possibility.

Consider here how the Medievals used the term possible being as all but synonymous with our contingent being.[1] Possible being is being that is, but that might not be. What is noticed is this constitutive nonbeing, as well the *that it is at all* of the being. By contrast, necessary being is said to be beyond possibility in *that* sense, beyond possibility and impossibility—there is no possibility of its possibly not being. In this regard, possibility is deeply related to contingency with respect to ontological status. Contingency does not have the possibility of its own being, nor the actuality of its own being, nor the complete ground of its being, within itself alone—all are grounded in an other, which is not to deny its created being for-itself.

I think this ontological sense of possibility is more metaphysically pertinent to the question than the merely logical use of some moderns who, somewhat impertinently, impute a confusion of the logical and the ontological to the Medievals. Those Medievals were superior who knew that the grounds of logical possibility had to be thought all the way back to the ontological ground. They were not necessarily confused about the difference between the logic of propositions and actuality, but were concerned to push the question all the way to the origin of possibility, actuality, and intelligibility, and hence mediately

---

1. See most famously Aquinas's third way. But Aquinas also relies on the logical definition of possibility. Thus, in speaking of God's power, possibility is defined in terms of logical contradiction: "Something is judged to be possible or impossible from the implication of the terms: possible when the predicate is compatible with the subject, for instance, that Socrates is seated; impossible when it is not compatible, for instance, that a human being is a donkey." *Summa Theologiae*, 1a, 25, 3; see also 1a, 25, 4 and 5.

of the intelligible propositions of logic. Among moderns—and we need not agree with the details of their different views—Leibniz and Hegel had each an understanding of ontological possibility.

Why not describe this ontological power of possibility as *will to power*, as a serious post-Nietzschean philosophy might do? The answer turns on our understanding of the origin. In my view, will to power, indeed any variation on an erotic origin, cannot adequately possibilize concrete being. The indefiniteness of such an initially lacking origin makes nothing possible, without the presupposition of *another* sense of origin, in my terms a more agapeic sense of origin. Nor does an erotic origin make possible the *real other*; the real ground of possibility in this creative sense is the agapeic origin. Moreover, this issue of the ground of possibility extends all the way up and all the way down. And though we might here seem to deal with rarified metaphysical issues, there are momentous consequences for human existence, with respect to our deepest understanding of ethical selfhood and community. Agapeic possibilizing makes possible the other as other. The erotic possibilizing of will to power finally circles around the for-self; real otherness is finally impossible on this ontologic.

In other words, possibility is not a final surd, determined at best by logic and contradiction. Without the further sense of possibility, there might perhaps be eternal possibility, but of such a sort that it would really make nothing possible in a genuinely *creative* sense. In addition, if the creative ground of possibility is not completely defined by logic and the law of contradiction, we may even have to ponder the possibility that, so to say, God's logic is not identical with Aristotle's. We are indeed beyond the logic of thought thinking itself. The creative ground of possibility may harbor what look to us like contradictions, possibilities that are reserved to logic. It is said that for God "All things are possible." What possible meaning can possible here have? Might we not have to think possibilities of being, as other beyond our thought? Our response ought not to be univocal or even dialectical irritation, but metaxological perplexity. Metaphysical pondering may have to mull on the "more," the mystery of absolute transcendence.

Putting this to one side, let us turn to more familiar ground—namely, to the *finite realization* of possibility. But there is also nothing in possibility as defined by logic which explains the concrete realization of possibility: *this and not that*. Consider here, for instance, the way Whitehead resorts to God as a principle of *limitation*, to explain why this rather than that possibility is determined. Whitehead's point is very relevant, and the question to which he directs us is crucial. But the idea of God as such a principle of limitation is a rather thin idea. Again I think we need the more primordial idea of creative possibilizing, to explain both the ground of possibility as such, and finite determinate realizations of created possibility.

In fact, Whitehead's principle of limitation does not explain the possibility of possibility. There are just "eternal objects," seen as other to God;

everything, God, eternal objects as possibilities, concrete occasions, all of these are, as he puts it in one place, individualized modes of the "one underlying substantial activity," which is equated with "Spinoza's infinite substance."[2] But this means that the one underlying activity is really the ground, equally of God (if God is one of *its* attributes), of eternal possibility, of modal differentiation in individual multiplicity, of actual occasions. Very well, we must here push back to the ground of possibility, but then for Whitehead everything is an individualized articulation of the One. We must now take into account the description of the One, but Whitehead's One is an erotic absolute. In the end there is possibility, but only relative to the self-pluralization of the one underlying activity—Spinoza's monism again. By contrast, I want to say: only with the agapeic origin as ground of possibility do we try to make sense of the other as other, and hence genuine plurality, and not just self-pluralization.

Whitehead claims he wants to save God from responsibility for evil; as principle of limitation, God divides good from evil. However, this means finitizing God as one articulation of infinite substance. But if God is one articulation of the One, and if everything derives from the one infinite substance, evil too derives from the One. Hence the possibility of evil must be derivative of the One. Hence if God, as one articulation of the One, fights evil, God fights the One. Hence the ultimate is self-discordant. And is this again not an erotic absolute struggling with itself and its lack—in order to be itself? The One becomes equivocal, and certainly not the agapeic origin.

I know some commentators distinguish Whitehead's God in *Science and the Modern World* and in *Process and Reality*, but the notions of the primordial and consequent natures of God can be seen as variations on the erotic absolute, in which the God of the end is more absolute (if this is a coherent locution) than the God of the origin. The agapeic origin suggests a different approach to evil, preserving both God's absoluteness and relatedness to creation. With respect to the "letting be" of real freedom, there is a sense in which "all is permitted," which does not mean that "all that is done is good." The creative possibility of real freedom is the promise of agapeic being. The creative possibility of original freedom lets the finite other be other for itself, even to the point of the betrayal of the promise of being, to the point of radical evil, the refusal of and revolt against the creative agape of being.[3]

Relative to transtemporal possibilizing, suppose we suggest that intelligibility *comes to be* out of a source more primordial than itself. If so, the origin cannot be a dead order of eternity; it must be likened to a living, mind-

---

2. See *Science and the Modern World*, 70; "Spinoza's one infinite substance" is referred to again on p. 177, in chapter XI on God, where God is identified with the principle of limitation.

3. See the chapter "Agapeic Being" in *Perplexity and Ultimacy*; also the chapter "Perplexity and Ultimacy" with respect to God and possibility.

ful eternity whose possibilizing would be inseparable from creative power to be. If, then, we were to say that intelligibility is the creation of "mind," this would not mean it is the product of our minds. Rather creation reveals itself as ordered and structured because it is the issue of an ordering and structuring source. I here recall the plausible claim that a certain notion of God served as the *ground* for the initial *metaphysical confidence* that nature could be known scientifically. The issue is large, but certainly in early modern science, to say nothing of ancient cosmologies, the interconnections of God and mathematical intelligibility were felt along the pulses by some of the great scientists, Kepler, for instance. Our ontological confidence that nature offers to mind a rational order derives indirectly from the confidence that there is a ground of that order, a source that is *metaphysically trustworthy* in an ultimate sense.

The paradox is that the very *success* that flows from the initial metaphysical confidence can produce an *amnesia* of the original confidence. That nature is rationally ordered initially stuns us into metaphysical astonishment, but when we contrive to give a more and more determinate articulation to that rational order, we become primarily preoccupied with the intricacies of this determinate articulation, and the first metaphysical astonishment inclines to droop. Intelligibility as mechanically explicable will displace the mixture of metaphysical and scientific perplexity. The question of the *grounding source* of the intelligibility will be declined, if not excised.

We metaphysicians, however, cannot capitulate to this wilting of astonishment, and not because we refuse to take the step into determinate intelligibility, but because, having taken this step, it still remains that determinate intelligibility is not self-explanatory. There is an astonishingly complex, yet simple intelligible order in the nature of things, which science more and more brings out into explicit cognition. Granted this order, we are not so engrossed in it as to forget the enigma of that intelligibility as such, as a whole, and why it might be, why it might be thus and thus, and not otherwise. The given intelligibility of things does not explain itself for the metaphysical perplexity that seeks to fathom the ground of intelligibility as such.

If we think the origin as agapeic, what follows for, and how does it cohere with, our understanding of what it means to be intelligible in the between? The major consequence will be the absence of absolutely unconditional necessity inscribed in the given order of intelligibility. It is so, but it might have been otherwise. There is a certain limit to our grasp on intelligibility here, since we touch an extreme where we cannot say further why it is thus so and not otherwise. So it is. And if there is something more we can say, it is not by way of thinking God's thoughts before the creation of nature and finite spirit, as Hegel says about his own logic. We cannot invade the mind of God, but that is not because we do not think what the mind of God might be like, given the character of creation, or how that character is confirmed, given the thought of the agapeic origin. I know this talk of God will irritate some, in the way that Einstein's utterances about God's not playing dice, or God's being sophisticated but not malicious, grated on some of his colleagues. Yet there is something entirely right in such talk, insofar as it tries to keep alive the question of the ground of intelligibility.

What happens if we do succumb to metaphysical amnesia? It seems to me that there is no deliverance from the nihilistic results of modern scientism: the world becomes dead, like the dead order of mathematical intelligibility it supposedly instantiates. It may remain intelligible, but it is an intelligibility without meaning or purpose. The given intelligibility is ultimately unintelligible. This deadening of the world and this purposelessness of intelligibility ultimately makes the world unintelligible for us. And not surprisingly, in reaction to this, the human being feels forced to *produce out of herself or himself* some more purposeful intelligibility in an *otherwise absurd* world. Thus the human being becomes the origin of intelligibility to fill the gap produced by our amnesia of the origin. Moreover, this production of intelligibility is effected *over against* nature, now become a degraded creation. Creation declines into a mere indigence of unintelligible thereness. We have here the silent, empty space that made Pascal afraid, or the neutral homogeneity that is the material for Descartes' will to impose mathematical order, or again the nauseating, undifferentiated viscosity of Sartre's being in itself.

Sartre in particular exploits the contingency of creation, but it is contingency *rendered* absurd, because it falls short of a certain ideal of absolute necessity. It has *become* a contingency without intelligibility. The sense of produced intelligibility I want to suggest takes on a very different modulation because of metaphysical memory. I agree there is a gratuity about intelligibility that is not dissipated by reference to the order of some lifeless, mathematical or logical eternity. But the primordial energy of original being is not that of any dead eternity. The intelligibility of the creation as universal impermanence has a produced contingency relative to the origin, though *within creation* itself intelligibility may present various faces of *conditional necessity*. That is, within the order of creation, there are necessities that follow, once certain conditions are, and are granted as obtaining. Not all finite intelligibility has this character of conditional neccesity. But conditional necessity within creation is compatible with another ontological contingency relative to the *very being of creation as given*. This last is my point: intelligibility as contingent, as gratuitous, is a giving of the source. The contingency of creation does not mean we negate intelligibility, hence give ourselves over to a contingency that, as indigent of absolute necessity, is marked as inherently absurd.

This last view is not uncommon among recent interpretations of nature, but it seems to me our truthful soundings of nature tell against it. And so we come to the point about intelligibility as *inherent*. Philosophers may argue about realistic and antirealist interpretations of science, but the scientist who does not take some more or less qualified realistic view is in the minority. We ought to take this seriously. The scientist sounds nature, and rejoices when the sounding resounds with the intelligibility of what previously seemed mere noise. This intelligent joy in intelligibility is not simply due to the internal coherence of scientific languages, but to the vector of transcendence immanent in scientific concepts themselves, as oriented beyond themselves to nature in its marvelous otherness. Just that otherness of nature's intelligibility draws forth the mind beyond its own self-closure. Scientific thought about nature is not the thought of thought; it is thought about what is other to thought. A certain community comes to be between mind and being when being in its otherness is known. That community of the between occurs when the intelligibility of nature in its otherness comes to be known by the mind in its self-surpassing. It is not just that "we make sense of the other," but that "this other makes sense for us, to us." It is only a contraction of the between into one of its sides—namely, our side—that causes us to absolutize the first formulation, and to forget the second.

For the second side implies that intelligibility, even as produced, is also inherent. We discover that being is intelligible because creation as there is already an outcome of the origin. This is an element of the wisdom ingrained in the ancient way of talking about the *universale ante rem*. I am not advocating a Platonic realism, which divorces the universal from the thing, and I will return to the question of the universal. I merely want to invoke this old locution as a reminder of the priority to our mind of a certain inherent intelligibility, discoverable in creation itself. Intelligibility is inherent because it is produced, in the way that an art work is the concretization of an order that is already there because of the work of its artist. Creation is a *poiēsis*, and shapes a dynamic order on which our soundings of intelligibility are dependent, and to which our soundings must remain faithful, at the risk of mere wishful thinking. The invocation of the art work and the *poiēsis* of creation is intended also to warn against an excessively rigid and static order of intelligibility. There is a dynamic pattern of order and variation, sameness and otherness, consonance and dissonance, a togetherness of meaning and enigma in the intelligibility of a work of art.

I need to add that this inherence of intelligibility leads to a *second sense* of intelligibility as *produced*. The plurality of intelligibilities extends the range of openness in the wholes that are intelligible. Intelligibility is not incompatible with a certain openness in creation. We find a togetherness of structure and free indeterminacy; and as things become more ontologically complex, their intelligibility lets open a greater play of free indeterminacy. Indeed as order and structure themselves become more dynamically complex, the free openness of indeterminacy is more and more activated as a possibility of being.

I anticipate, but the production of intelligibility in the second sense comes into play with the mindful self as producing, producing *beyond* the given inherent intelligibility. This is sometimes treated in terms of culture and nature, but unfortunately, a misleading dualism often seeps into this treatment. As the realm of human self-production, culture is thought to be entirely other to nature. We find a historicist dualism instead of a naturalistic dualism.[4] Against this, a rethinking of nature as creation offers a deeper sense of the community of the creative self with creation as other. The production of intelligibility, the culture of mindfulness of creative human beings, is itself grounded on creation in the first sense as the issue of the origin, though it grows beyond the given, inherent intelligibility. The dynamism of transcendence passes beyond given intelligibility to creative intelligence. This second production of intelligibility is not a will to power asserting itself in the void of cosmic absurdity. It is the production of intelligibility that is in *ontological cooperation* with creation. The intelligibility of being becomes intelligent. With this, intelligibility becomes purposive anew as a creative mindfulness of being and the origin.

Drawing a Line—Intelligibility and Univocity

In turning to intelligibilities in the plural, suppose we start with the alleged condition underlying the view that intelligibility is a production of our will to power—namely, that in itself being is unintelligible—let us say, a pure flux void of any inherent distinguishing marks. This would be a pure flow of being, a kind of viscous energy that in itself is like an amorphous magma. Were being of such a character, it would be difficult to account for intelligibility as inherent.

What do we do with such an alleged condition? Suppose we try to draw a line in the amorphous magma. The drawn line offers us a point of reference and orientation, hence inaugurates some sense of intelligibility. On the supposition that being were amorphous magma, the line itself would immediately begin to decompose. The form of intelligibility we impose would immediately begin to deform. That does not happen, in fact. The line marking our sense of intelligibility remains steady, if only temporarily. A temporary point of orientation is enough for us to obtain an initial sense of direction. That the line remains provisionally steady implies that there is a *hospitality* in the putative amorphous magma to our effort to demarcate an intelligible point of reference. This hospitality is not something we impose on the so-called magma. Hospitality to our productions of intelligibility is inherent in the nature of being itself.

Admittedly in the hypothetical case under consideration, this hospitality is absolutely minimal. But that it *enough*, enough to open up the possibility

---

4. See *Beyond Hegel and Dialectic*, chapter 1, on the varieties of historicism, and especially 24ff.

that there is inherent in the nature of being some opening for intelligibility. Though this is minimal, it is already a refutation of the view we entertained for argument's sake, namely—that being in itself is simply unintelligible. This view itself, we must now say, is unintelligible, because it cannot in any way explain just this minimal hospitality of being to our putative productions of intelligibility.

Suppose the world in itself is said to be radically unintelligible, absurd; and then we humans impose intelligibility on the absurd. But this view, I submit, is itself absurd: the human being just "pops up" out of the primordial unintelligibility, moreover pops up as a complex organism, as a system that is intelligible, an extraordinarily well-articulated system of being, and more to the point, an intelligent system. Thus intelligent system pops up from absurd chaos, and then this "system" imposes system on the chaos. The freakish emergence of the human being becomes the origin of intelligibility within a community of being that putatively offers no inherent hospitality for intelligibility. This human being is a mere deus ex machine, and is not even a god— unless an absurd freak be a god.

This is straining ontological credulity: that an ultimately unintelligible, yet intelligent system, the human being, grounds intelligibility in a universe at bottom unintelligible chaos. The same argument that one can make against Nietzsche's view of "value"[5] can be made of this view of intelligibility. If being in itself in unintelligible, the human being as a being is also unintelligible, and every one of its so-called productions of intelligibility is finally ontologically unintelligible, absurd. Why do I insist on this point? When talking to the deaf, you have to raise your voice. But of course, these Nietzscheans are only *playing* at being deaf. If they were completely deaf, they would hear nothing, understand nothing intelligible, and hence it would be best not to waste one's voice.

I find a similar straining of credulity in Nietzsche's progenitor, Schopenhauer. For Schopenhauer suggests a reversal from the absurd origin, Will, to the Ideas as objectifications of the absurd Will; there is also the unintelligible rupture and reversal of our will into will-lessness in art and religious renunciation.[6] By contrast, I venture that intelligibility can only be the objectification of the origin, if there is a hospitality in the origin itself to intelligibility. If so, the origin cannot be properly described as chaos or as absurd. We must think of the overdetermined intelligibility as the origin of determinate intelligibility. I find it hard to see any hospitality to intelligibility in the origin, as conceived by either Schopenhauer or Nietzsche.

---

5. See my "Rethinking the Origin: Hegel and Nietzsche"; also *Philosophy and its Others*, p. 281–82.

6. See my "Schopenhauer, Art and the Dark Origin."

The sons of Nietzsche standardly accuse metaphysics of a fascism of concepts, of imposing categories on the otherness of becoming, and so on. But if this critique of metaphysics were correct, there would be no basis for critique. I ask that this critique have the intellectual integrity to critique itself. For if true, *all knowing is imposition*, and there is no basis for critique itself, or for privileging any system of will to power. As a system of will to power, "metaphysics" is as good, or as bad, as any critique, as just another system of will to power. It makes no difference, finally. If all is power play, then the deconstruction of metaphysics is disingenuous, if not dishonest. Indeed, it is ungrateful to the intelligibility it must exploit to deny intelligibility—absurdly.

But enough of these manufactured cartoons of "metaphysics." Let us continue the line of thought initiated by the hypothesis of drawing a line in the putatively amorphous magma. One might say that intelligibility begins to be articulated for us when a line is drawn in the indefinite. Let us recall the Greek horror of *to apeiron*. Let us connect *to apeiron* here with the indefinite, rather than the overfull sense of infinitude. This horror suggests a kind of metaphysical recoil from the lack of intelligibility of sheer indefiniteness. Intelligibility comes to appear just in that line demarcated in the indefinite and that marks a boundary between the indefinite and the defined. The upshot: to be intelligible is to be definite and bounded; to be unintelligible is to be indefinite and boundless.

There is much to be said for this view. For we discern the emergence of intelligibility in the determination of the indefinite that draws a boundary line. The boundary line is the marker of a limit, and without such markers of limit, there is no intelligibility for us. Otherwise being remains like an absolute fog, a vaporous homogeneity in which nothing is distinguishable. No definite thing is set off from some other thing, and we are all but lost in this fog. The marking of a line is, as it were, a univocalizing of being that is prior to determinately established univocity.

Drawing a line is like making a *cut*. The connection of this cut with intelligibility is contained in the very word *precision*—it carries in its root (*praecisio*) the same cutting that we find in the word *incision*.[7] In other words, to be precise is to expose intelligibility along the lines of being, in the way that an articulation sets forth the anatomy or inherent structure of a being or happening. To articulate is to be precise about the jointures of a being—that is to say, its own internal articulations. I know that the word *cutting* has a violent ring to it, but violence to other-being is not really my point. This is more a certain congruence *between* lines we draw and lines there, already drawn. Every line we draw is not necessarily there, but some lines are, even if they are very squiggly. The *hospitality* of being to intelligibility is not just a passivity of other-being to our activity. It is a more dynamic welcome.

---

7. One here thinks of the Greek *krinein*, as well *krisis*, and critique; one also thinks of the German *Urteil*.

Not that we are passive either, even while receptive. Lines, distinctions, precisions show us already to be in a world that is not glutinous. This is this and not that. But lines, as more or less precise, are also *negations* that allow the *affirmative presencing* of what is distinguished. Such negations open a space for the articulation of identity and difference. And as identities become articulated, we are pointed to univocal being in a more determinately established sense. Is this articulation of identity just our doing? I want to suggest that being-other as a becoming is a process of self-opening, self-precising. The bounded wholes that come to be and emerge in this self-precising put an end, albeit relatively, to indefinite endlessness. In the opening that takes shape in a becoming, there is a provisional steadying of happenings within the universal impermanence. In the constancy or steadiness within the universal impermanence, delimited wholes are brought to shape, or shape themselves, out of the original matrix of creation. What is delimited is a term, a provisional whole, a terminus. One thinks of the Roman god *Terminus*—essential divinity for the marking of a boundary, of a landmark. Terminus is related to the Greek Hermes, carrier of messages between mortals and gods; indeed, the original Hermes were phallic stones designating burial places, markers of the difference and crossing-zone of life and death, this world and the otherworld. Drawing a line can have the deepest significance for life, and what is beyond life.

So also we might say that in drawing a line we see the emergence of terrestrial measure. Thus geometry is literally a metrics of the earth. The measure is a standard cut or precision. Measure (related to *mensura* and *mens)* is a *metros* that, as a sameness or *the same cut*, can be reiterated. More generally, this line of first intelligibility marks univocal being in terms of the limitation of a finite whole. Indeed, it is here that the classical sense of intelligibility arises. There is no merely indefinite being. To be is to be determinate, a determinate being, a this somewhat. The merely indefinite is chaos, and hence unintelligible. To be minimally intelligible is not unlike a line drawn across a bank page or in sand: there is a reconfiguration, indeed transformation of the ontological space of thereness. Drawing the line sets a boundary against the unintelligibility of indefinite chaos, sets forth the space of being as intelligibly articulated within itself.

I am *not* saying we must tie intelligibility to the idea of the indigent indefinite. To the contrary, our understanding of origin, of creation, directs us to a matrix of intelligibility that is far more ontologically rich than the vacancy of the indefinite. If you like we may think of chaos in a creative sense: as a matrix of indeterminacy that, out of its excess, gives rise to rich determinations of being. Creation intimates an origin prior to the drawing of the line that makes it possible for us to think of the emergence of intelligibility, as always beyond mere indefinite homogeneity. Creation as universal impermanence is not unintelligible in itself, but a generative process of differentiation. Just this *dunamis* of inherent differentiation might be said to constitute the basis of its hospitality to our efforts at articulating determinate intelligibility.

Strangely enough, it is here that we also discover the basis for rethinking the traditional *principle of identity*. Creation as universal impermanence is always more than indefinite homogeneity, yet it allows the emergence of relatively homogeneous determinations of being. Entities come to be as intelligible integrities. These integrities offer the basis for the ontological units that ground the univocal sense of intelligibility, and its precise articulation in the principle of identity: a thing is itself and not anything other. This principle formalizes what is at stake in the drawing of a line in the alleged original indefiniteness. We might say that it arises in the face of the potential equivocity of being, in the following sense. The becoming of flux seems to dissolve all fixed determinations, and in the face of this dissolving, we make something intelligible by determining it univocally as itself and not another thing.

Does this claim reverse equivocity and univocity? It does and it does not. It does not, since for us even to have a sense of equivocity and to feel its threat, we must already have at least a minimal sense of determinate beings. Absolute equivocity without determination would be absolutely unintelligible. So any speaking of equivocity is impossible without some minimum sense of univocal determinacy, and hence of minimal intelligibility. Yet equivocity does precede univocity in a different sense, for we are now trying to frame in more firm form what initially for us is opaquely at work. Spontaneously being is made intelligible in a more or less univocal way; spontaneously we inhabit a world that is not sheer indefiniteness; simply to inhabit the world is to dwell in a world of already shaped determinations. But the enigmatic being at work of intelligibility as determination is prior to any thought, univocal or other, we might subsequently give to the character of intelligibility.

True, a stronger fixing of univocity is often sought when it dawns on us that the spontaneous determinations of intelligibilities are not immune from their own erosions, given creation as universal impermanence. In the face of this erosion, intelligibility is more formally determined in terms of the principle of identity. Nietzsche's invocation of will to power trades off the claim that this formal determination of the principle is an imposition of univocal intelligibility on a putatively equivocal flux. There are elements of truth in this view, but it is a simplification, if taken as the whole story.

For example, Aristotle already has many excellent rejoinders to the extreme Heracliteans. I put it by saying that their repudiation of the principle of identity not only reduces being to formless flux, but reduces their putative *logos* of becoming to what elsewhere I dubbed, perhaps too tartly, *fluxgibberish*.[8] The sheer assertion of indefinite flux is not intelligible. It does not explain the determinate integrities that come to appearance in the uni-

---

8. *Philosophy and its Others*, 225.

versal impermanence. It cannot explain itself as, in its own way, a determinate account of intelligibility. Eventually, the sheer difference it seems to affirm is swallowed up in an absorbing monism of becoming, wherein all differences are finally dissolved. It should be silent, for any speech depends on a determinate saying of a determinate somewhat. And it has no right even to the silence that would gesture to explain itself, for it has forfeited the basis of such explanation.

I underline that I am *defending* the principle of identity as an appropriate formulation of univocal intelligibility. I do not say that univocal intelligibility exhausts the plurivocity of intelligibilities. Nor does this defense deny becoming. Nor again is the principle merely "logical," in the sense of a "master concept" we use to stamp intelligibility on becoming. To the contrary, the principle has ontological weight, which again is not to claim that it exhausts the fullness of being. The ontological sense of identity is tied with the orginal power of being in creation as universal impermanence. The emergence of determinate beings is not imposed on the flux by us; it is the inherent eventuation of finite and bounded happening.

The principle of identity itself finds many different expressions. Our commonsense notions are governed by it. So also are the sophisticated refinements of mathematics and science. The laws governing the successions and regularities of phenomena are thought of as precisely determinable; the sharper our precise determination, the more we believe we have rendered the connections of events intelligible. Mathematical formulation is, and has been considered to be, the ne plus ultra of precise determination; there is no room for waffle and wavering, and we seem to be in the presence of pure intelligibility itself. Not surprisingly, from the Greeks to the present, philosophers have irresistibly felt the seductive spell of mathematical precision. *Anankē* itself seems to sit enthroned in majestic mastery over this mode of univocal intelligibility.

But the majesty of univocal intelligibility will not finally satisfy us. It is not exactly that, as Whitehead said, "the exactness is a fake," but that the exactness is derivative, not primordial. The exactness is only a fake, if we abstract it from the process of coming to determination of intelligibility, and absolutize it in this isolated abstractness. The reader will have some sense of the way univocal being already opens out on two sides, the side of origin and the side of boundary or wholeness. The side of origin opens univocal being to the overdedetermined power of being that makes the determinate be determinate. The side of whole opens beyond any fixated boundaries, into the network of relativity to other-being that constitutes the metaxological community of being. Univocal intelligibility fixes, with more or less determinable precision, the·transcending power of being, but it does not exhaust that overdetermined power.

Much more could be said, but I must confine myself to some relevant remarks about a thing's intelligibility in terms of its identity, its properties, and its alleged essence. If to be intelligible is to be a determinate "this," what then is a "this"? A standard response invokes the thing's particularity. Traditionally, it has also been felt that this response is rather minimal. We have a determinate "this," "this," "this." We seem to have but an aggregate of pointillistic particulars, with minimal intelligibility in themselves, and at best extrinsic connections with other pointillistic particulars. I agree: the reservation about particularity in this form is well placed. If the univocal unit of being is a self-enclosed monad, we can say little more of it. Nevertheless, we can and do say more, hence our account of intelligibility has to be more expansive. We have to search for an intelligibility inherent in the particular that is richer, and an intelligibility between particulars that is less extrinsic.

Often this expansion of the meaning of intelligibility is confined within the horizon of univocity. More is required, I believe. However, the process of ontological amplification standardly is reflected in a move from particular to universal. This too is a correct move, but it is full of ambiguities. I think we must acknowedge a twofold complexity. First, the "this" of particularity is internally intricate; it is intelligible as a particular, because it is not just a bare particular; the particular itself is inherently self-differentiated. Second, this inherent self-differentiation is not just its alone; it shares it specifically with other particulars of its own kind. Thus the internal difference of the particular points to a sameness at a level of being, other to the particular as such—namely, the universal.

It seems to me that the move from the particular to the universal is very frequently effected by an emphasis on the generality of the second aspect that undercuts the complexity of the first. That is, philosophers display an inveterate tendency finally to locate the basis of determinate intelligibility at the level of the universal rather than the particular. I want to rethink this, and do so by means of a reinterpreation of the richness of particularity, which correlates with a sense of the universal, not as an abstract generality, but in terms of the particular's intermediated place within the community of being.

The particular is there as a "this," but we do not simply fix it as there; the process of being settles it in its locale. It is hence a determinate *poiēsis* of an indeterminate original power. Particularity is determination that also bears a kind of surd: it is this rather than that, here rather than there, now rather than then. This surd is not absurd. Rather it is not completely determinable in abstract concepts, for these are geared towards a more general intelligibility. It is just the irreplaceable singularity of the "this" that is here intimated. Perhaps again it is the artist who names the particular in just this irreplaceable sense. The particular is a world unto itself that intimates its own creative origin and emergence into definition. The "this" is unique with a certain intimacy of being that gets passed over when it is made intelligible in terms of general samenesses.

The particular is not indigent of intelligibility but is present in creation out of the origin, present with a presence that is elusive and resistant and, in its own right, mysterious. One sometimes gets an intimation of this if one repeats the name of a thing again and again. What happens? The name seems to fade into meaninglessness, but we can come to be in the presence of the particular thing, sheerly in the particularity of its being there. And this sheer being-there of the particular, in its peculiar "onceness," can take on the aura of the extraordinary. I am talking about the astonishment that waters the spirit of philosophy, and that indeed is the wellspring of *all* mindfulness. We normally inhabit the faded ripples of this astonishment; but for once the name dissolves as a useful label and becomes murmured like a caress of love, turning us towards the thing in its singular otherness.

This revelation of intimate strangeness most often comes to us when the other is a *beloved human being*, yet it is not unknown with respect to any being. There is an activation of agapeic mind with respect to this intimate presence of the particular. The strangeness of the being is intimate to the intimacy of our mindfulness. It is the lover or poet who "names" this intimacy of strange singularity, without reduction to abstract generalities. My point is that this "naming" gestures towards the origin of intelligibility in the particular, since it tries to enter the very original emergence of the particular into its own being for itself. It is as if we come closer to the original creation as the primordial act of love of the origin towards the creature as an irreplaceable singular. Except in rare moments of breakthrough, we do not live in proximity to the origin in that sense.

Hence normally our "naming" of the particular tends to be more remote, less agapeic. We settle for determining univocal intelligibility in terms of specific properties the particular displays. We have already spoken of this in relation to the thing. The thing is intelligible in a pluralized way because its univocal intelligibility is marked by differentiae of which we can give a determinate account. The particular is red and prickly and smells like roses. . . . This is an enrichment of univocal intelligibility, not by a pointer back to the overdetermined origin, but by the further determination of the particular as established in its locale. But even here univocal intelligibility is both useful and under stress.

Useful: because we can say that the thing is more or less red, with discrimination we can even pin down a "precise" shade of red. It is more or less this, that, and the other. We can even go the way of univocal *mathēsis* and try to measure the differentiae, not in terms of the sense qualities given in common sense perception, but in terms of calculable quantities that elude direct observation. The doctrine of primary and secondary qualities is a refinement of the univocal sense of determinate particularity in which the qualitative thereness of the particular is replaced by quantifiable systems of matter in motion. When these are said to be the real fundaments of the differences available in phenomenological givenness, ontological justice is not done to the particularity of the particular. This dissolves into a congeries of generalities, formulated in terms of a system of mathematical abstractions. Despite the ontological injustice, there is no question that this determination of intelligibility can be extremely useful. The main ingredient in its historical influence has been just its usefulness, its "success."

Under stress: the more we try to pin down the properties of a particular, we more we are nagged by the suspicion that there is an unavoidable arbitrariness in how and where we draw the line that demarcates. Where is the line that fixedly differentiates this shade of red from that? The word *shade* gives the game away. There is no rigid line; there is a shading of one red into another, even while being distinguished from it. There is a continuum, even while this is punctuated by differences that emerge in their difference as we move along the continuum. There is no rigid line, not because the continuum is an undifferentiated flux, but because the particular is not made up of a concatenation of fixedly distinguished properties.

The more intimate we become cognitively with the particularity, the more its irreducibility comes home to us. In principle we might even make an infinity of discriminations. We might shade it more and more finely, and yet not be absolutely certain that we have exhausted all its possible properties. This is evident in the microscopic route followed by the reductive work of univocal *mathēsis:* the finer textures and granulations of matter in motion begin to escape beyond our self-certain univocities. The promise of a certain latent infinity emerges in the finite particular itself. Any enumeration of the properties of a particular is always for us a finite abbreviation of the plural shades of discriminations that open before us. Hence beyond a crude univocity, the very consolidation of univocal intelligibility in terms of determinate properties really opens up a promise of inexhaustibility. This opening occurs both in terms of the downward reduction of a particular into its elemental energies, and the onward development of the thing in its own rich unfolding. There is also a certain mingling of our mindful discriminations and the differentiations that emerge in the particular itself.

Intelligibility and the Challenge of Equivocity—on Contradiction, Sufficient Reason, Causality

With this surfacing of potential inexhaustibility, have we sacrificed intelligibility once again? And with this mingling of our mindfulness with the intelligibilities inherent in the particular, have we left the door ajar to the skeptical dismantling of intelligibility as inherent? The answer is a qualified no, because things are both inherently self-mediating and also intermediated in a network of relations defining the community of being. We really require here both the dialectical and metaxological senses of intelligibility, but in this section I want to address the above questions. For they renew the challenge to intelligibility of the equivocities of being. I will focus on three points: first, relative to contradiction; second, relative to sufficient reason; third, relative to causality. Contradiction, sufficient reason, and causality are major considerations in any accounting for the meaning of intelligibility.

First consideration. In fact, the challenge to intelligibility arises from the above determination of univocal intelligibility itself. How so? The enumeration of the properties of a particular "this" is with the intent of making the particular intelligible with respect to a set of univocal predicates or attributes. But the development of this enumeration seems to have no univocal, inherent end. We can refine our predicative discriminations more and more, even to the point that univocal precision seems to vanish. Relative to this one particular, an infinite succession of attributes seems to unfold. Relative to a plurality of particulars, an infinite succession of different entities seems to pass before us. The self-differentiation of the particular seems without end; the self-dissemination of a plurality of particulars seems to be a sheer diversification of different entities. In a word, this seeming dissolution of intelligible unity in the very pursuit of univocal intelligibility seems to entail the vanquishing of determinate intelligibility by a more basic equivocity.

The law of noncontradiction arises here as a rejoinder to the possible deconstruction of intelligibility by an allegedly more basic equivocity. The principle of contradiction is continuous with the principle of identity, only the meaning of univocal intelligibility now becomes the dictate to reason: avoid equivocity! A is A; A is not not-A. To say A is not A would be to undermine the very identity of a being and its univocal intelligibility. Equivocity here implies *double-talk, double think,* where the double in question is a determinately exclusive antithesis. This is not the gradual shading of difference into difference that is compatible with the notion of contrariety. We are now dealing with an inconsistent doubleness, which puts before the mind an *either/or,* around which we cannot, and ought not to slide. Classically the reductio ad absurdum reveals the hidden equivocation that renders questionable a standpoint's intelligibility or truth. Univocal antitheses, implicit in the standpoint, are shown to contradict or cancel each other; they cannot both be right.

More will be said on this in relation to dialectic, but it must be remarked that the law of contradiction is absolutely essential within the realm of univocal intelligibility, and with respect to the imperative of mind to make determinate sense of being. To the best extent possible, mind must remain true to this task. In the present case, equivocity, as seeming to dissolve intelligibility, is actually inseparable from univocity. So there is an instability in the claim concerning a more basic equivocity beyond all univocity. Equivocity is defined in an interplay with univocal intelligibility as the determinate ideal; the equivocal either falls short of this ideal, or else tries to dismantle it. Vice versa, the desire to rise above this equivocity can take many forms. Thus the Platonic resort to transtemporal universals, not only tries to deal with the problem of particular identity, but also to transcend becoming, rendered equivocal. The particular is given its *intelligible identity*, by reference to its participation in an eternal *eidos*, which exhibits the characteristics of determinate univocity, rendered transtemporal. The *eidos* is itself and nothing but itself; it is pure intelligible identity. Likewise the eternal realm of *eidē* as a whole constitutes the kingdom of pure intelligibilities on which the duplicitous equivocity of becoming is ultimately grounded. What becomes is never completely itself; it is always other to what it ought to be; it is in the domain of suspect difference or nonidentity.

Platonic realism suggests a *universale ante rem*, as grounding the intelligibility of the particular in becoming. As I already suggested, this notion is not to be entirely rejected. Recall previous remarks on possibility as possibilizing. As possibilizing, transtemporal possibility would not be a static structure, but would manifest the impetus of creation. To speak of a universal *ante rem* would be to indicate an ontological status as not produced by the human mind. But the dynamism of creation would mean that original possibilizing also concretizes possibility *in re*. This latter suggests the immanence or inherence of intelligibility.

Aristotle is credited with raising the appropriate question: If universal intelligibilities are transcendent, how do they relate to the articulation of intelligibility in the things themselves, here in this world of genesis and *phusis?* In truth, Plato first formulated the problem, as anyone familiar with the *Parmenides* knows.[9] Let me put it thus: intelligibilities are thought because we want to make intelligible sense of being as appearing to us; but if the resort to intelligibility as *explanans* is too divorced from the world of becoming as *explanandum*, then we do not escape equivocity, but introduce a new equivocity, not now *in* becoming, but *between* becoming and intelligible being. In other words, intelligibility must be inherent in becoming as *explanandum*, for intelligibility to be the *explanans* it purports to be. In fact, the doctrine of participation is a response to this equivocity, and it is more complex than normally understood. One is not sure if Aristotle did really get the point when he dismissed it as a mere metaphor. Essential to the point is the following.

Intelligibility must itself be pluralized, in that it must have a universality that is not merely historicized, and yet the intelligibility cannot be completely divorced from the process of becoming. Intelligibility must be both transtemporal and ingredient in time. One might say that participation is a likening relation that tries to speak to this double requirement. Such a relation is between identity and difference, a mingling of sameness and otherness, not one or the other, but both at once. Mimetic likeness is a mode of

---

9. There are still more aspects to the Platonic approach. See my remarks below on the plurivocal approach of the Platonic dialogue to metaxological intelligibility.

intelligibility appropriate to the middle, as between time and eternity. Neither absolute transcendence nor absolute immanence will speak for the intermediation between intelligibility as transtemporal possibility and the happenings of being in becoming. Mimetic intelligibility articulates the middle between time and eternity. Admittedly, we need an idea of metaxological community to make more sense of it.

If there is an order of intelligibility as transtemporal possibility, and if such possibility is creative possibilizing, this latter cannot just be free-floating possibility, but possibilizes the intelligibility inherent in the temporal process of creation itself. Interestingly, the ancient locution of the *logoi spermatikoi*, the seminal reasons, is here suggestive of creative possibilizing. We notice the very inherence of generative power in the reason or the *logos*. Leibniz retains this generative power in his own understanding of the possible. He says: "Every possible is characterized by a striving (*conatus*) towards existence, and may be said to be destined to exist, provided, that is, it is grounded in a necessary being actually existing."[10] I would say: creative possibilizing is grounded in the origin. Of course, this reference to *conatus* can be rethought in agapeic terms, and not just in erotic terms (such as we find in Spinoza). Creative possibilizing participates in the agapeic creation of the origin, hence shares in the agapeic dynamism of self-transcending being, hence concretizes inherent intelligibility in the realized being of the determinate particular. As issue of agapeic possibilizing, this intelligibility is inherent in creation, as for the being in itself.

Like Platonism, the *mathēsis* of modern science also evidences a desire to rise above equivocity. But rather than resort to universal intelligibilities transcendent to the sensuous world, it seeks to articulate laws of inherent intelligibility, in terms of the universal regularities governing all systems of matter in motion, or of energies in their ongoing definition and interplay. Here there can be no question of a dogmatism of univocity that would simply assert intelligibility and insist that we take or leave the assertion. Nor is there any question of simply acquiescing in equivocity qua equivocity. Such an acquiescence is incoherent: it reneges on the quest of intelligibility, while at the same time justifying its own reneging as true to the nature of things.

And yet, despite these different desires to rise above equivocity, something more is augured. Equivocity not only spurs us in quest of intelligibility, it also confronts us with certain recalcitrant perplexities. Univocal intelligibility has a definite boundary, but into what does it shade? Into senselessness, or into nothing? The infinite succession of particular things seems just to go on and on. Is the ongoingness of the universal impermanence riddled with ineradicable ambiguity? In the end, does it come to nothing, since it has no

---

10. Leibniz, *Selections*, Philip P. Wiener, ed. (New York: Charles Scribner's Sons, 1951), 92.

end? Once again, there arises the great question about the ground of intelligibility and mind's quest of it.

Second consideration. This great question is often answered in terms of the principle of *sufficient reason*. As traditionally formulated, this principle is continuous with the principles of identity and contradiction, as well as causality, all articulated within the ambit of the univocal sense of intelligibility. We can state it thus: to every happening of being, a determinate reason, or cause, or ground can be given. The principle formulates the rational conviction that every happening can be accounted for in terms of its proper intelligibility. The hard metaphysical question is: What is the ground of this principle itself, what intelligible basis has this conviction of reason? The principle expresses an expectation of rational grounds, but what is the ground of that expectation of grounds? We are asking the grounds of reason itself, when reason itself claims to be able to supply intelligible grounds to every happening.

Different options have been proposed. One answer says: the principle is self-justifying, because to answer the question of its justification, one has to assume the principle. This is a crucial consideration, for it shows our mindful being as inescapably in the middle of intelligibility. But the issue can still be pressed. Perhaps there is no ground to this principle at all; it is perhaps a pragmatic or hypothetical or heuristic instrument. But these responses do not answer to the sense of ultimacy imputed to the principle; they are, so to say, too middling, in a tepid sort of way. No doubt, often we do use the principle thus. But more radically, we think the very grounds of rational intelligibility, in a genuinely universal sense, are at stake. The pragmatic or heuristic solutions are too wishy-washy, and do not meet the full blow of negation that can come from skepticism.

Another answer simply denies any rational ground. The principle is "grounded" on something entirely *other* to reason, and this in no benign sense either. Schopenhauer is a classic case: sufficient reason is grounded on no rational ground, but derived from the ultimate, which he calls the Will; and there is nothing reasonable about this blind, endless, insatiable striving, or dark energy of being. Even though finally I differ with Schopenhauer, I agree that this is the level at which the question has to be put. It brings us back to how we understand the origin. I elaborate.

One might make the case that the principle of sufficient reason is, in an important respect, *beyond* the law of identity and contradiction. For its meaning is not exhausted by univocity and determinacy; rather it determines certain senses of rational determination and univocity. It is, we might say, their a priori condition. We might say it gives formal expression to a certain *ontological trust* in intelligibility and an *epistemological trust* in reason. But neither of these forms of trust are exhausted by their univocal determination.

The ground of univocal intelligibility is not itself another instance of univocal intelligibility; for this very ground is implicated in the more embracing trust in being's intelligibility, and has a universal sweep built into its self-transcending embrace. This is related to the crucial point I made at the outset of this chapter—namely, that inherent in the anticipation of mindful questioning is an *indeterminate trust* in the availability of proper intelligibility. The meaning of this prior, indeterminate trust, which is both ontological and epistemological, is tied up with our understanding of origin.

I take Schopenhauer's tactic as a retreat to a kind of ontological equivocity about reason, *prior* to univocal intelligibility. Nietzsche and many post-Nietzscheans share this tactic. The tactic itself gives expression to a *distrust* concerning the claim of idealism, especially Hegel's, that reason completely justifies itself in terms of absolute thought thinking itself. By contrast, here the *other* of thought thinking itself comes to the fore. But this otherness is interpreted as outside univocity and intelligibility—namely, as equivocal unintelligibility. I do not think this will do; nor will the idealistic apotheosis of self-thinking thought. Radical metaphysical skepticism is perplexed about the ground of intelligibility, but it seems to be drawn to a basic option: yes, the ground of sufficient reason is other to any determinate exercise of reason, and hence beyond univocity. But is this other ground, the erotic "ground" of Schopenhauer, or his various descendents, or is it more like what I call the agapeic origin?

Remember that Schopenhauer's erotic ground was prepared for by the erotic absolute of idealism, only Schopenhauer (taking much from Schelling—ungratefully) privileges the dark side of that absolute, and all this in the train of the self-deconstruction of idealistic reason. By comparison, I propose we think the ground of sufficient reason in relation to the agapeic origin. What this ground is, is not subsumable into the principle of sufficient reason, since it is the very originating source of the latter. Neverthless, there is community between the two: the agapeic nature of the origin allows it to be open to what is other to itself, precisely as other; its agapeic mindfulness is its "rationality," in a sense that is excessive to our mindfulness. Yet we do touch agapeic mind in our own self-transcending.

For agapeic minding involves a *founding trust*[11] in the inherent worth and significance of the other. My suggestion is that this trust finds a determinate expression in the principle of sufficient reason. We might say that this latter trust and principle are ingrained in our being, as creations of the agapeic origin, ontologically constitutive of us as mindful beings; they are images of the origin in us. In the Schopenhauerian option, there is an unintelligible reversal between the irrational origin and the principle of sufficient reason.

---

11. See the next chapter on what I call agapeic selving, which is marked by an indeterminate willingness to be open to the other as other.

How the blind origin turns its darkness into the latter light is itself hard to make intelligible. The light of reason becomes a duplicitous epiphenomenon of a more basic unreason, the absurd Will in itself.

In a way I am here addressing a variation of Descartes' hyperbolic supposition of the malign genius. This hyperbolic supposition risks the ruin of all intelligibility and truth: putative intelligibility is the swindle of an evil ultimate. By contrast, the notion of the agapeic origin suggests a ground of founding trust beyond this. It "justifies" the trust we have in reason and hence the principle of sufficient reason. The agapeic origin incites thought to conceive the basis of ontological and epistemological trust in intelligibility as going all the way down and up in being. The Schopenhauerian option has at the basis of all being a kind of malign genius, now rebaptized as Will. The principle of sufficent reason is one of its objectifications; hence it is ever haunted by the ugly darkness of its origin. There is no ultimate reason at all for reason, and hence no ultimate basis for intelligibility.

Not surprisingly, a rash of absurdist doctrines has proliferated from the late nineteenth century to the present. The ontological degrading of idealism's self-thinking thought into Schopenhauer's blind, ugly Will follows the degrading of Hegel's erotic absolute. Moreover, lack of mindfulness of the agapeic origin sets in motion a slippage from *erōs uranus* to the *erōs turannos* of self-assertive will to power, which finally reveals itself as full of sound and fury, but signifying nothing. Meanwhile, univocal *mathēsis* continues on its Enlightenment ways, blithely unconcerned with the radical questions of metaphysical skepticism, deaf to the din in the madhouse of metaphysics, though it too is one of the inmates.

Third consideration. Metaphysical madness may ensue if the principle of sufficient reason is not properly understood, but the course of things, despite us, still persists in its intelligible being. I want to return to this. One must note that the criticism of the principle is often connected with a critique of causality, and this, in turn, is associated with a rejection of foundations, identified univocally with a so-called First Cause. In addition, so-called static being is rejected in favor of becoming. I want to reiterate that these criticisms are parasitical on an inadequately explored univocity, that is supposedly overthrown in favor of equivocity, but that still holds the whole way of thinking in thrall. I am not denying the challenge to intelligibility of equivocity, but I think we are pointed positively towards a different metaphysics of becoming, beyond a false either/or between univocity and equivocity.

The self-differentiation of the particular, and the diversification of a plurality of particulars, need not undermine intelligibility. Rather we are called to enlarge our horizon. Becoming may subvert an abstraction of univocity but intelligibility is not thereby dissolved. Quite to the contrary, intelligibility must be inclusive of the dynamism of being; it cannot be a formal static structure. After all, equivocity does remind us that an identity can be other to itself, that particulars can be self-othering, that self-othering identity can be a process of self-becoming. The more inclusive intelligibility has to be a self-activating intelligibility, an intelligibility not just determined, but determining.

So we must introduce the category of *development*. The category of change is less rich, though in many respects development is not unrelated to what traditionally was called substantial change. The idea of development reminds us of a dynamism of becoming inherent in the particular itself, and the flow of particulars. A dynamization of intelligibility has to follow. Indeed, intelligibility comes into a deeper intimacy with creation as universal impermanence and the *dunamis* of the original power of being. As we shall see, we must move towards a more dialectical understanding of intelligibility.

Relevantly, the principle of sufficient reason is often expressed in terms of causality, by Leibniz, for instance: to everything that happens, there is a cause, all the way back to God as the necessary being and First Cause. I have indicated that "cause" should be used with diffidence in relation to the origin; it carries too great a danger of univocalizing the origin, fixating its creative power. I find this contracted meaning of "cause" in Hume's reduction of the relation to one of merely customary connection. For him there is no inherent connection between the prior and the consequent; only habit leads to the formation of expectations of regular connection; hence causality has no purchase on the future, no necessary purchase, since the customary connection involves no inherent necessity on which we can rely. This view has caused agonies for philosophers of science who have felt the threat to the idea of induction, and its central place in scientific prediction. The intelligibility of the scientific enterprise is dependent on some version of causality as epistemologically and ontologically trustworthy. If a rationally justified expectation of future intelligibility is without foundation, the enterprise seems to totter.

Hume's analysis of causality seems to reveal the equivocity of its claims to intelligibility. The result precipitates skepticism, on the one hand, and on the other, an attempted rescue of the idea by means of a subjectifying strategy. However, the causality, supposedly revealed as equivocal, is conceived in too narrow univocal terms that Hume never transcends. From the outset, cause and effect are defined in terms of two determinate units of happening; each is itself, and not anything other; each is itself and not the other; cause is univocally fixed as the prior; effect is univocally fixed as the posterior; and each is univocally itself and not the other. But the metaphysical game is already over, so to say, once the determination of intelligibility is fixed in these terms. Nothing remains but to spell out the implications of the initial fixation. For, of course, this univocal fixation of both cause and effect must necessarily undermine the intelligible connection and interplay of the two. How, in Heaven's name, can they have any other connection, except one that is introduced *ab extra*, if in themselves they are so univocally retracted into their own fallow self-identity? We, the perceivers, are the ones who must supply the connection, out of the drift of our past experience and the customary contiguities that condition us to the expectation of future contiguities.

The fixation, at the outset, of univocal intelligibility must fall apart, precisely because it is an abstraction from the concrete happening of the universal impermanence. Therein what is glaringly manifest is the reality of *dynamic transition*. What is the transitoriness of becoming but this dynamic process of transition, this dynamic process of formation and transformation? Univocal intelligibility may seek to impose a static form of structure or connection on this process of transformation. It is surprised when the universal impermanence frustrates its will to reset the transformation process into a set of abstract forms. Hume does not learn the lesson of his own skepticism, does not profit from the equivocity emergent from the abstract fixation of univocal intelligibility. The lesson should be: let us strain to think of intelligibility more deeply and concretely; let us not remain fixated with a mere abstraction of intelligibility, and of experience, and of particularity, and of being, and of causality.

For there is a sense in which causality is derivative rather than primordial. At the more elemental level, there is the aesthetic presencing of the metaxological community of being in its immediate, sensuous thereness. This aesthetic immediacy of the community of being is the prereflective sensuousness of the given world. We are first in the midst of this, but do not yet know ourselves as distinguishable entities; nor do we set apart one determinate thing from another; nor do we yet objectify the sensuous flow of things, and strip from the thereness the charge of presentness, its ontological value as a gift of being. The aesthetic community of being as elementally given is the immediacy of the metaxological, the milieu of sensuous being-there. This milieu is the place of an incessant interchange between beings, an original flow of same into other and other into same, without as yet clear borders between same and other, or a reflective sense that we are in a milieu at all. In the passages of interchange and interaction in the between, there is interplay that mixes determinate happening and open-ended flow. The aesthetic immediacy of the milieu is a flux and reflux, where we find a porosity of incessant intercommunication.

What we normally call cause and effect are derivative from, and dependent on, this more elemental flow of incessant interchange, this aesthetic and immediate passing of one into the other. Cause and effect are later, more univocal crystalizations of the passage of the prior into the consequent. They are objectified determinations of the immediate overdetermined flowing. Thus causality is an intelligible mediation of the aesthetic immediacy, a fixing of its flow in which relativity is already at work, but not brought to express articulation in all its intelligible connections. And this prior immediacy of relativity in the milieu of aesthetic being holds true as much for post-Newtonian, post-

Cartesian causality, as it does for Aristotelian causality. These are but different interpretations of the intelligibility of the relativity at work there.

What is cause and effect relative to this transformational sense of developmental intelligibility? It is the creative power of possibility that is bequeathed by present events to their future descendents, present events themselves the descendents of prior events that generate effects beyond themselves in the univeral impermanence, and again through the creative power of possibility. What is induction? It is our reasonable anticipation of future intelligibility on the basis of our epistemological trust in the present inheritance of past regularity. There is no problem of connecting an absolutely fixed univocal cause with a similar univocal effect, for no event is thus univocally fixed in the transformational process of becoming. An effect is the present inheritance of the self-othering of another dynamic event we call a cause. Hence transitions are not empty gaps upon which we impose our categorial necessities. Transitions are passages of creative possibility; indeed they are passages of promise, since possibility is intended in the dynamic sense. Such a passage of promise is really what a heritage is.

This passage of promise is deeply tied to our sense of the ground of intelligibility and reason, understood as an agapeic origin; this is the ultimate ground of our epistemological and ontological trust. The passage of ontological promise is not an empty promise. We need the humble vigilance of agapeic mind to open to the promise of creation. Moreover, there is an open-endedness built into the idea of ontological promise. Promises are openings to the future, anticipations of coming to be that may not always be redeemed in the form that present expectation determines. Hence the openness of the future is the promise of the surprising, the unexpected, even the marvel. Promises are open to redemption, or betrayal, or failure. Hume is so far right, that there is no *absolute necessity* in anticipating future happening from present antecedents and past precedents. There is at most a conditional necessity; but this too may be ruptured by the unexpected. The contingency of forms of intelligibility in creation is not at all denied. I interpret the contingency differently to Hume. Hume has a thin understanding of the metaphysical implications of contingency.

This openness of contingency to what is other involves no denial of intelligibility, but rather specifies the mode of its conditional necessity. Conditional necessity seems like a contradiction, again to the univocal mind that just asserts that necessity is necessity and contingency contingency, and the two are exclusively other. To the contrary, contingent necessity means that, given these conditions of being, one has a justified rational expectation of the following consequences. The determinate justification of the rational expectation is just the set of qualifications that the mindful knower formulates as a result of his vigilant openness to the complex happenings of events. But there is a givenness that is not absolutely necessary (it is, but it might be otherwise; it might not be at all), hence contingency infects the entire passage to conditionally necessary consequences. The "mustness" of consequences following from prior events is not absolutely determined. The passage of ontological promise from past, through present events, to future possible events is a complex intelligible determination of a creative overdetermination that we name as the original power of being. Much may happen in the passage through the transformation process that diverts, or converts, or changes the passage from being a univocal linear transition from a delimited cause to a delimited effect.

Creation is so multifarious and its intelligibilities so plural that it is often difficult to find in concrete happenings those clear lines of univocal connection: univocal cause to univocal effect. Very often, we have a cluster or community of antecedent conditions, leading to another cluster of subsequent effects, which also is a happening of events with a kind of family resemblance to the family of conditions. My critique of Hume's univocalizing of causality is not to be misunderstood. We can and do specify more or less univocal conditions, named as causes, and especially so in ideally isolated systems. This is part of the great power of modern physics, for instance. Newtonian mechanics is formulated in terms of an ideally isolated system that in its powerful mathematical univocity throws intelligible light upon the cosmos in its law-governed happening. But there is an unavoidable abstractness about it; it is abstracted from the fullness of concrete happening. Relative to the intelligibility of the latter, the promiscuity of causes is often very difficult to disentangle. While the clarity of univocal lines of connection are most clearly formulated by ideally isolated systems, this clarity begins to become more fuzzy, the more complexly concrete the happening that is under investigation. Fuzzy does not here mean indefinite, or lacking intelligible conditions, but overdetermined relative to a community of causes or conditioning possibilities that enter into the intelligible constitution of the particular happening.

It is not only, as again Whitehead said, that "the exactness is a fake," but that there is *more than exactness in play,* and it too is intelligible, but not exactly in the mode of the fake exactness. One can also see why Hume's sense of the univocity of discrete happening, of succession as mere external contiguity, is consistent with the univocal atomism of Newtonianism. With this univocalizing of the units of a temporal happening, there can be *no ontological promise* in a passage from the prior to the present to the future. We have promiseless happening, sheerly identical, sheerly different. In this promiseless happening there can be no intimacy of relatedness between events. The resulting merely external relations are false to the promise of happening. There is an intimacy of connectedness, even at this level, an ontological community between cause and effect. And again this is not absolute necessity, but a given conditional togetherness. Nor is my point to invoke a vague "for the most part." Just as the intimacy of connectedness is not a hazy togetherness, so the rupture of possibility is different than a mere lazy divergence from the "for the most part." The latter divergence would be a very sleepy-headed otherness.

Intelligibility and Dialectic

Previously (in chapter 4) we saw that dialectic allows of plural interpretation. But with specific regard to the question of intelligibility, dialectic can be directly linked to the above considerations—namely, the principles of identity, contradiction, and sufficient reason, and these seen in the light of the actuality of development and process. Moreover, dialectic is directly a rejoinder to the challenge of equivocity to intelligibility. For the question arises as to the intelligibility of identity and contradiction themselves as principles of intelligibility: Do they ground themselves, hence provide the warrant of sufficient reason? It has been notoriously difficult to offer a justification entirely beyond rational controversy. The view I propose is: dialectical intelligibility emerges in response to the rational justification of the univocal and equivocal senses of being, and the correlative notions of identity, difference, and contradiction.

I will illustrate the point with reference to Zeno who reveals some of the distinctive modes of thinking that condition the formalization of the principles of identity and contradiction. Zeno's famous paradoxes of motion and plurality are gambits in a defense of the One. They serve as shields against the ridicule of the many by turning the laugh back on the common sense and pluralist mockers. The hypothesis of the One is not directly defended, rather indirect argumentation claims to show even more absurd logical consequences to the supposition of plurality. Here we see an oscillation between univocal intelligibility and equivocity in a number of guises. Zeno indirectly defends absolute Parmenidean univocity by logical exploitation of a more relative univocity, namely, the principle of identity that fixes terms in determinate definition, making them to be themselves and not anything other. In regard to this relative univocity, time is proved illusory, because the instants of time are univocally fixed as punctiform and static; likewise, the arrow cannot really move, since every moment of movement is reduced to a frozen snapshot of stasis. Likewise, Achilles will never catch the tortoise, because every interval of distance is univocalized into a static frame, which itself is divisible into another univocal frame, and so on *ad infinitum*.

Indeed Zeno's notion of becoming is as promiseless as Hume's causality. There is no basis for transition in the static frame, no movement takes place within any of the frames. And in a sense, Achilles would not even take the *first step* to overtake the tortoise, which properly could never get ahead of Achilles, since again no motion would be ultimately intelligible. Zeno's point is that the supposition of motion and manyness, coupled with the principle of univocal intelligibility, yields paradox—that is, yields laughable consequences relative to the expectations of the pluralists. Logical madness is made to follow from the supposition of manyness as wedded to a strict ideal of univocal intelligibility. Zeno uses univocity to derive an equivocity, to show as unintelligible, in light of the principle of univocal intelligibility, the hypothesis of the many.

Nevertheless, the seeds of dialectical intelligibility are sown in Zeno's use of the *reductio ad absurdum* and in indirect proof. The *reductio* reveals the hidden equivocations that render questionable a particular claim to intelligibility or truth. It shows two univocal antitheses to contradict or cancel each other; they cannot both be right. The *reductio* only works if we implicitly accept the principles of identity and contradiction. The emergence of absurdity is the manifestation of a failure of intelligibility with respect to these principles. What is the moral of the story for Zeno? Only a more radical logical univocity will rescue us from the paradoxes thereby generated. Is this the only intelligible outcome? Surely not. If the only lesson is an indirect route back to Parmenidean being, we really have reneged on amplifying the notion of intelligibility needed to deal with creation as universal impermanence. And we cannot escape the logical and ontological embarrassments ensuing from any reassertion of the One, which fails to make some sense of the production of plurality, and the intelligibility inherent in the becoming of creation.

Dialectic is a self-conscious effort to deal with tensions inherent in the principles of identity and contradiction, in the light of the ontological complexity revealed in creation as universal impermanence. It tries to come to terms not only with the logical instabilities in an absolutized univocity, but with the ontological texture of becoming, without reneging on its intelligibility. Thus also it speaks to the defenders of pure flux who argue against inherent intelligibility. Far from undermining intelligibility, the return to becoming asks for a more nuanced sense of being than the univocal. It is granted that equivocity reemerges when a thing in becoming seems to be other to itself, and hence to transgress the law of identity. A thing in becoming is itself and not itself. If it were simply itself, it would be absolutely unchanging. Since it does change, it is not coincident with itself, or with the full promise of its own being. A thing in becoming has to be made intelligible with respect to this its lack and promise, which means its inherent possibility to be other to what it presently is. And yet the promise of what it is to be, is again simply itself. It becomes itself, though it cannot be itself to become itself, and yet to become itself it must also be itself; indeed, to become itself is to be itself.

Thus it might seem that this process of self-becoming is contradictory to the law of contradiction. Much ink has been spilled on claims made here. Sometimes the shock to contradiction is softened by saying, "in one respect" it is this, but "in another respect" it is not this; and the two respects are held so apart that any mutual contamination is prevented, and hence any affront to the law of contradiction. This would be all very well, were not this prophylactic against contradiction itself equivocal; it falls into the equivocity it claims to avoid. For the whole point here is that these two "respects" are dynamic unfoldings of the same integrity of being. Even if they are restated as two possibilities of the being in becoming, they are possibilities of the same being, and hence their difference is subtended by their togetherness in the unity of the being in process. However we put the point, self-opposition seems inherent in the becoming of a being, self-opposition that is held together in tension by the integrity of the being in process. There is no imposing of a logicist model on the development of a being. Univocity is far more logicist in that regard. The question is whether the inherent complexity of a process of development forces us beyond univocity, without miring us in complete equivocity. Dialectical intelligibility is one major way of making that development meaningful.

Consider. A happening is the becoming of the energy of being, concretized in determinate integrities of existence. This process, while determinate, implicates a necessary reference to the indeterminate. The fear of the univocalist that we fall into equivocity is misplaced, for the indetermination implies the openness to the future that marks any process of becoming. If there were no indetermination, there would be nothing beyond pure changeless being. The happening of the between is not such a world. The reference to indeterminacy might seem a slap in the face to the classical notion of intelligibility as essentially determinate. But determinacy need not be sacrificed. Indeterminacy need not be a nebulous, unintelligible indefiniteness that will be made intelligible by being made determinate. It can be seen as affirmatively constitutive of a deeper and richer sense of dynamic intelligiblity.

So while indeterminacy may refer a happening to future promise, it also may refer it to origin, that out of which the determinate process of becoming is concretized. Ultimately this is the agapeic origin as excess overdetermination of original creative power. But put that to the side, and consider the more proximate condition of a finite process of becoming. Indeterminacy then refers to the creative power of possibility inherent in creation as universal impermanence. Initially there is an indeterminacy to possibility, precisely as possibility. To the degree that the possibility is realized, then indeterminacy is made determinate: a concrete definition is put upon the possibility. This creative indeterminacy is constitutive of all particular processes of becoming, as the background matrix of possibility out of which a determinate process is crystalized.

Then there is the further, or continuing operation of indeterminacy in the very crystalization of creative possibility. Now our consideration is at a level of a determinate process: A is a determinate process, which becomes A1, which becomes A2, and so on. The important issue here concerns the between: between A and A1, between A1 and A2, and so on. How do we explain the *transition* that is continuing? The transition is a between that is not one or the other, and yes it is one and the other. Thus the transition as transition is not a *univocal* determinate happening. But neither is it indefinite. Rather it is a *determining*, where the accent falls upon a dynamic activity. A transition is a *going over*—the going over of an original indetermination into a determinate formation. One cannot univocalize the process of determining, precisely because the *trans* of transition is a transcendence of the clear-cut

identity of univocity. This going over is a process of self-othering. It is a determining rather than a determination, a determining of the indeterminate, again
suggestive of the creative ground of change.

Moreover, intelligibility is not renounced, for the indeterminacy is oriented towards determination. At this level of consideration, we meet with the
correlation of possibility and actualization. The determination of the indetermination is a process of self-othering in which the possibilities of the original
are realized. But the other so attained is not other to the original; it is the
self-origination of the original in a more complete determinate form. This is
not to say that all its original possibility is exhausted, but certainly its promise as possible being is more completely realized by this process of becoming.
A process of becoming determines the indeterminate, actualizes the possible,
but the realized possibility is not absolutely other to the original in search of
fuller realization. Dialectical intelligibility seeks to give articulate form to
such a process of self-realization.

Hence compared to the more static mode of univocity, dialectic seeks to
be truer to developmental intelligibility. There is an integrity to process that
makes us invoke the intelligibility of the *self-developing*. Any happening that
we make intelligible in more than static terms calls for some version of this
view. For instance, the intelligibility of an *organism* clearly invokes a structure in process of change; the sameness of the process is not a static form; a
static form of intelligibility would make unintelligible what is concretely salient about the whole organism as process. So too any happening to be described in terms of activity or doing must invoke some notion of what we
might call functional intelligibility. Functional here does not mean merely
instrumental. It means the ontological doing of the being in question, its
ergon, the being at work of its original energy of being. Here the structure
across a process of development is a structuring that reiterates a certain pattern of self-formation. And so the mode of dialectical intelligibility can be
called self-mediating intelligibility, in that it renders process articulate as
one of self-realization.

A major point we must not neglect is the *teleological* nature of dialectical intelligibility. If the original indetermination of possibility is a beginning;
if the process of self-formation is a middle, in the sense of a process of self-
mediation; both of these are inseparable from a goal—namely, the fulfilled
self-realization of the process. The original indetermination, passing through
the self-mediation of a process of self-formation, is with the view to the ripe
determination of the promise of the process. Thus dialectical intelligibility
can be seen as oriented to the end of a fulfilled self-determining intelligibility.
Here we have a dialectical answer to the question: What does it mean to be
intelligible? Answer: to be intelligible is to be self-determining.

Notice how if univocity returns here in the emphasis on both determinacy
and self-identity, yet the latter are given a far more complex expression. The
self-determination of dialectical intelligibility incorporates a dynamic notion

of self, and a notion of determination that includes within its intelligible definition the indeterminate origin that initiates the process towards intelligibility in the first instance. Meanwhile, the end of self-determining intelligibility
is the fulfilled self-determination of the indeterminate beginning, via the
mediation of a determinate becoming, which is really the self-mediation of
the entire process.

There are limitations with this view, as we shall see, but also important
advances. For example, we are led to a reinterpretation of the *universal*. Beyond the *flatus vocis* of linguistic nominalism, beyond the empirical generalization, beyond the univocal eternity of the Platonic *eidos*, the universal is
self-actualizing in the process of becoming itself. We might think of Aristotle
and Hegel, both of whom rightly remind us of the immanent universal at
work in being, in a properly dynamic sense. The universal is manifest in the
self-unfolding of the particular, which is no atomistic point, but an individual
concretion of the original energy of being. The universal emerges in a process of self-becoming, reiterating a dynamic sameness within process, across
process. It is not imposed *ab extra* on the flux; it is a mode of ontological
togethernness, wherein the phases of a process are held in the unity of a
dynamic self-unfolding. Nor is structure a static form; it is a structuring that
is developmentally defined through the temporal articulation of complex interlocking functions and doings. On this score, one recalls the old example of
the acorn and the oak. Or one thinks of DNA as a ground of determinate
possibility unfolding in the organism as a dynamic intelligibility.

One might even make the case that, relative to a dialectical sense of
developmental intelligibility, Aristotle's four causes show far greater ontological reserves than modern extrinsic notions of cause. Thus, the four *archai*
might be said to express a plurality of modes of intelligibility of which quantitative measure is not the standard. The vision is of qualitative process, and
this is not a sop to common sense, but metaphysically mindful of, attentive
to, the ontological richness of thereness. One does not have to accept Aristotelian cosmology to discern the superior quality of the metaphysics. Thus the
four causes can be reinterpreted as giving a fourfold articulation of a developing thing, in a middle that is itself a dynamic universe in process: matter
refers us to the aesthetic appearing of the thing; efficient cause refers us to
the antecedent others of generation; form refers us to the self-shaping of
original energy; end refers us to the realized self-mediation of that self-shaping, which is not closed on itself but open to intermediation with others in
the transformational process of the between.

With dialectic it is hard to avoid the language of holism. "We murder to
dissect." So said Wordsworth. But dialectical intelligibility is not homicidal
in that way. It tries to stay true to the self-articulation of self-organizing wholes.
For instance, if we consider the integrity of the organic body, each part is a
member, but as a member it also is its own whole; yet the member functions
in unison with the unity of the whole organism. The holistic language of part

and whole reflects a more *inherent* notion of intelligibility than does the standard language of causality. For a part is defined with necessary relation to the whole, just as a whole is unintelligible without its organization in terms of definite parts. A pure part, a pure whole, neither would make sense; rather intelligibility is determined by a mutual relatedness of part and whole; the part articulates the whole, the whole rescues partiality from mere fragmentation, and confers a mode of complex unity on the inherent differentiation of the actuality.

Indeed the inseparability of dialectical intelligibility from some form of holism means that no entity can be understood in inert and free-standing isolation. *Within* the entity, its integrity is self-articulated into its vital and self-organizing parts. *Between* the integrity and other integrities, there are complex modes of holistic interconnection. That is, the integrity of a being in process of becoming mediates parts into a complex whole, while the mediation between integrities within the universal impermanence is rendered intelligible relative to a hierarchy, or series, of more and more embracing wholes. The more complex the intelligibility, the more embracing the whole; less complex intelligibilities evidence a more restricted range of holistic embrace. Because of the restriction on the embrace of intelligibility, unintelligibility emerges at the limit, and the partial whole undergoes a falling to the ground, or a return of equivocity or self-opposition. This, in turn, points beyond itself to a more embracing intelligibility—namely, a less partial whole to embrace the previous partial whole as its own part. Thus the widening circles of intelligibility evidence an ever-increasing inclusiveness of the complex, mediated whole.

Of course, some philosophers have extrapolated from this to the ultimate intelligibility, defined as the whole of all wholes, or as Hegel puts it, the circle of all circles. I do not think we must subscribe to absolute monism, but we can endorse the break with merely external relations. Univocal intelligibility tends to fix terms in their determinate differences, such that the relations among a plurality of such intelligibilities are entirely extrinsic. The dynamizing of intelligibility, and the processual natural of self-unfolding, undermine such a fixation of univocal terms. Every term, in some measure or other, implicates a relation to what is other to itself. Its very self-othering (which dialectical intelligibility tries to make articulate) is a vector of transcendence towards the other. An integrity of being is not intelligibly determined in free-standing isolation; it is determined in itself, because it is determined in a dynamic process of relativity to what is other to itself. What is more, this relativity to the other is, at least in part, internal to its own self-definition. The other enters the constitution of the essence of the integrity.

I conclude that dialectical intelligibility testifies to a porosity of relativity, in which the opposition between internal and external is all but impossible to fix as an opposition. It is a provisional contrast in a temporal process of self-unfolding. This means that the intelligible identity of an integrity is doubled, doubly mediated: self-relativitity and relativity to what is other. This doubling has to be given a more than dialectical modulation. The issue here will not be a relation of part to whole, but of whole to whole; and not of part to whole, with one whole then being redefined as part relative to a larger whole; it will be one of the community of original, open wholes, the relativity of which cannot be reduced to, or included in, one overarching whole. The language of holism is not entirely adequate to the intelligibility of the metaxological.

Intelligibility and the Metaxological

One could say that the present work in its entirety tries to give an account of metaxological intelligibility. It seeks to make sense of being by thinking it metaxologically. All intelligibility entails, in some measure, a *logos* of the *metaxu*.

For instance, it is possible to reinterpret causality in the following way. Suppose we think of causality in light of creation in the universal impermanence. We say A causes B, which as effect, in turn, may function as cause of C, and so on, *ad infinitum* in the universal impermanence. We find an open unfolding of cause/effect. In creation there is a bond between the original and the derived which, in turn, may be original again. But this bond is in becoming, in the impermanence of passage. The flow of this bond in becoming is first; causality is a flow of origination and derivation, obtaining in the flow of the universal impermanence. Hence causality is not primordially based on external relations between two fixed events or entities in the flow. The first basis of causality is in the impermanence itself. This is the matrix of different modes of mutuality, of passage from A to B to C, and so on, of incessant interchange. The effectiveness of cause stems from the original power of being in creation. This originative power effects and relates to the events that issue from it, issue from it with an otherness that makes the effect also for-itself. The first flow of the creative power of the universal impermanence is the basis of causality as a real relatedness. The common way of stabilizing cause and effect into two delimited events is an abstraction from this first flow. It is a univocalization of events in the flow, that as thus fixed and stabilized seem to lack the connection implied by causality. The inherence of the bond between events, creatively expressed in becoming, is lost from sight.

This account is not intended to do away with external relations, nor yet to reduce to internal relations, such as we find in idealisms. In the latter, causality finally becomes *self-causing*, reflecting the view of ultimate being as *causa sui*. In the metaxological view, such as we saw with origin and creation, there is a movement from a transcending source (in the present instance, called "cause") to the derived as *other for-itself*, and hence as not simply for the source itself. Externality and plurality are articulated in this movement. This externality is not an extrinsic contiguity or succession, but a more intimate relation of source and derived. Nor is this intimacy the internal relativity of the idealistic self-cause, for the issue, or effect, is for-itself, given for-itself. Thus understood, causality shows the face of *community*, and in an agapeic sense—the effect is genuinely other to the cause. Agapeic causality is the issuing into being of something *new* in the effect. Not just contiguous succession of merely external relations, not the self-causing of idealistic internal relations, becoming as creation in the universal impermanence is genuinely an *alter*-ation: not the reiteration of the univocal same, nor the circling of same around itself in *causa sui*, but the new arising of an other as for itself.[12]

Keeping in mind my point about this work as a whole, I will confine my remarks to intelligibility as both inherent and relational. For there exists a tension and co-implication of these two sides. Intelligibility is the setting forth, the articulation of *relations* between things and events, relations that define the *being for-self* of these happenings. So, even the thing's particularity is intelligible as a relation—namely, the self-relation that initially manifests itself as a diversification into a plurality of properties. Properties and predicates are also relations, and not in a sense confined to self-relation. Nor are relational properties the mere convenience of a manipulating knower; relational properties defined the essential locale of the entity. The form of a thing is its essential self-shaping, and this is a dynamic self-forming. But this self-forming is also relational, and in a double sense: self-relational and interrelational. While dialectical intelligibility emphasizes self-relationality in interplay with otherness, metaxological intelligibility underlines the openness of the *inter* of interrelationality, an *inter* not subsumable into one larger self-relating totality. This form of intelligibility might be said to include the other forms, but does not include them in a dialectical totality, but rather as setting forth into articulation the open space wherein the plurality of intelligibilities are emergent and defined.

The point must be put comparatively. The view I am outlining moves towards an understanding of intelligibility that is both more and more complexly inherent, and yet also defined by increasingly rich relatedness: we move from simple identity, through self-differentiating identity, through organic and self-determining being, to mindful being that is freely other-relating. There is an opening up of determinacy towards self-determination, to

---

12. On the self-causing of idealistic internal relations, see Hegel, *Encyclopaedia*, #153. Hegel does use reciprocity to "overcome" the infinite succession, but reciprocity is ultimately defined in terms of self-mediation in mutual symmetry. Metaxologically understood, the universal impermanence is not such idealistic reciprocity—this is more radical other-ing, alteration, as well as perishing, loss, passing away that passes beyond dialectic.

interdetermination, to creative indeterminacy. There is an opening together of innerness, of communication and community, as we move from determinate intelligibility to what I will call the *huperintelligible*.

First, the metaxological view affirms the truth of univocity relative to ineluctable particularity, but with a fuller significance than univocal intelligibility can deliver. In mediating its own identity, a particular puts its root down into the ground of being, and reaches out to its emplacement within the community of beings. With respect to these two sides, metaxological articulation opens up univocal intelligibility. Within the heart of particularity, the origin of its self-articulating identity is in *excess* of its own self-mediation. For there is no way that, completely through itself, it can either cause itself, or explain its own being and its distinctive intelligibility. Within itself it is characterized by relativity to another. There is its relativity to the origin, as the creative plenitude out of which it is generated. Even its relativity to its own inward otherness is marked by an ontological inexhaustibility that no set of univocal predicates will ever completely master. Moreover, the others in the relativity of the community of beings are also marked by relativity to the origin, and to their own distinctive inward otherness. Beings are creations. The trace of the overdetermined infinitude is in the concretion, both immanently relative to its distinctive particularity, and transcendently relative to the web of interconnections that bind things to each other in the universal impermanence.

Second, metaxological intelligibility looks to a kinship with a transformed sense of the equivocal. Because of the irreducibility of the *inter* of interrelations, the space of betweenness can be diversely stressed, plurally modulated. There is no one mode of intelligibility that will do justice to what is at play in the middle, for we cannot articulate that play in a completely determinate way. Why? Not because there is a surd of the absurd, but because the play of determinate intelligibility points to its source in an overdetermined creativity. If this last is intelligible, it is not intelligible in terms of determinate structures, or univocal predicates and forms. But if equivocity cautions us about any claim to determinate intelligibility, this caution can be transformed into an acknowledgment of mystery. The ground of the intelligible in a determinate structure is a determining, overdetermining structuring that is not sheerly unintelligible, but that is, and remains, enigmatic to every determinate structure that we impose. Something always remains unmastered.

Admittedly, equivocity tends to destabilize intelligibility, leading either to dualistic opposition between unmediated terms, or to an absurdist celebration of what escapes beyond the intelligibilities of univocal mind. But this is not enough, either with respect to univocal intelligibility, or with respect to the mystery to be acknowledged. A constitutive ambiguity remains that, even while mediated, is not exhausted by one overarching unity of determinate intelligibility. The excess that remains unappropriated in all our mediation is not the sheerly unintelligible, but rather the huperintelligible. This *huper* is the symbol of the above and beyond, the superfluous radiance of light that is dark to us nocturnal creatures, like Aristotle's bat blinded by the sun. This excessive light is not the absurd, as if the only choice were between determinate intelligibility and nonintelligibility. It is not any determinate intelligibility but the origin of determinate intelligibility, hence a huperintelligible that reserves its constitutive mystery, relative to our determining minds.

A way to put the point would be to compare the huperintelligible to something like living intelligence: a dynamic minding rather than a structured minded. Minding is not absurd or unintelligible, but in its living actuality, it can never be reduced to a determinate structure. There is also a certain intimacy of being about minding; this is the opening of univocal intelligibility into the inward otherness; and yet this inwardness is not a mere privacy, but the milieu of an intelligent, even spiritual commonality. Relative to such community, universality cannot be reduced to a general structure or law or regularity, but rather is activated in the self-transcending intelligence of living mindful beings. In other words, intelligence is living intelligibility that is beyond determinate intelligibility. It is also that without which determinate intelligibility would not itself be fully intelligible. The universality of intelligence, in this communicative sense, reaches towards its fulfilled promise in agapeic mind. For agapeic mind, even in the deepest intimacy of its own inward otherness, is radically open to and transcending towards the other as other.

This transcending power of mindful selfhood becomes evident with dialectical intelligibility. We can say that the self-relativity of all beings reaches its clearest articulation with the self-conscious integrity in which this self-relation wakes up to itself, become mindful of itself. This clearest articulation is also the most perplexing. The identity of all things involves a dynamic self-relation, but not all forms of being are awakened to this dynamic self-relating in a self-knowing or mindful manner. This is why we tend to restrict the appellation "self" to the human being. But all things "selve"; in the intimacy of particularity, they are "selving"; they are themselves—barely articulated "selves" in most cases, more complexly and richly in others. The self-relation wakes up with living intelligence, and begins that leap of transcendence beyond determinate intelligibility to determining intelligence and the huperintelligible. Metaxological intelligibility articulates a community of self-relating centers of being. There is, so to say, a sleeping community at the less complex level, where a web of relativity is ongoing without being mindful of itself as such. But we have an explicit metaxological intelligibility when these centers of self-relating being are mindfully awakened to themselves, coming to themselves in the self-transcending ecstasis that defines their self-surpassing towards the others.

Third, while dialectical intelligibility is primarily nourished on a logic of self-determination, metaxological intelligibility tries to articulate the coming to formation of an interdetermination. Where the first tends to point towards a privileged self-causing, the second faces into what might be called the *heteroarchic*. What do I mean? I mean an origination, an *archē*, that "determines" out of the other, the *heteros*. The interdetermination now in question cannot be described in terms of mutual determination. True, the latter is in play; but the heteroarchic "determination" of even mutual interdetermination modulates the between with a certain asymmetry. Metaxological intelligibility is asymmetrical. Dialectical intelligibility is symmetrical—the same measure, the same *metros* is applied to all and to one, to the self and to the other. The same *metros* is the principle of self-determination, self-relation.

This one measure cannot be applied to the excess of overdetermination that grounds interdetermination. We cannot pour the excess of the transcendent indeterminate into a mold of intelligibility where the mystery empties itself in a logic of pure self-determining thought. Violence to the mystery here breeds indifference, even violence, to the excess of spiritual community at work in the interdetermination. The excess of the *huper* cannot be brought under the umbrella of self-determination. Undoubtedly, we may attempt to do this because of fear that mystery will degenerate into sheer equivocity, hence threaten the loss of intelligibility. The perennial possibility of this loss has to be readily acknowledged. Yet we must live with the excess and the enigma and the ambiguity differently, without reneging on the demand of intelligibility. The disproportion to determinate intelligibility of self-transcending mind as huperintelligible must not be forgotten.

There is no one determinate measure because living mindful beings make up a nonreductive plurality, as we can see from the following threefold consideration. The *first consideration* is this. Each participant in the community is self-mediating, but this mediating directs us to the inward otherness of its self, which articulates itself relative to the original indeterminacy of the energy of being out of which it is created, made a determinate this. And this original indeterminacy, both of the ultimate origin and of its own latent promise of freedom, is never completely self-determined. The particularity of the *for-self* is its singularity in this heteroarchic sense. At lower levels, this commingling of *for-self* and heteroarchic being may be minimal (but even the minimum of numerical difference can be shown to be a commingling of *for-self* and heteroarchic being). As singularity becomes more ontologically complex and rich, the more full becomes the power of self-determination, but equally so does the power to communicate: the promise of heteroarchic being matures with the maturation of singularity. And what is the power to communicate but the power to enter community mindfully? Thus the fuller the self-mediation, the greater the power of self-transcendence, and the greater the openness to the other as other. So the more mindful the participation in the community of being, the more the possibility appears that the mindful being will be agapeic. Singularity is intelligible, but the more intelligible it is, the more huperintelligible it is. Singularity selves into mindful being. This we normally call self, but now we see self otherwise—namely, in the light of the promise of agapeic being.

The *second consideration* regards nonreductive plurality. I have been speaking of the singular, but suppose we now pluralize the above considerations. The others are also like this. I say *like* because of the asymmetry in proportion itself; the measure is never simply the same. Here too there is a side turned away from determinate intelligibility, a side beyond delimited structure. All the others are reservoirs of indeterminacy. The side turned away from determinate intelligibility is a well of creative freedom, a promise of creative possibility. The singular selves in community are new beginnings that begin to fullfill the promise of creative possibility. We confront the limit of intelligibility in the determinate sense, but as measurelessly pluralized. This measureless pluralization takes us into the community of the huperintelligible, that is not, for all that, a community of the unintelligible.

The *third consideration* emerges when we bring together the first two considerations. We then see that the between is determinately intelligible, but is also constituted by the community of the huperintelligible. Take the simplest case of two dialectically self-mediating wholes. What is in question is the mode of intelligibility of the *community* of two such wholes. The view here must be: the intelligibility of the interplay that constitutes this community of open dialectical wholes cannot be exhausted by dialectical intelligibility. Why? First, because the singularity of such wholes is not completely subsumable into another whole; it can be a member of a different community of wholes, but that community cannot be subsumed into one whole that overarches the many wholes. Second, because the inward excess of each open whole in itself resists complete self-mediating determination. As the creation of the excessive infinite, the finite creation is also always unmastered by any categorial mediation we might devise. The new intermediation in the interplay of two open dialectical wholes is open beyond every dialectical whole.

Hence, there is no absolute monistic intelligibility to encompass the community of open wholes. The logic of part and whole, the mainstay of dialectical intelligibility, gives way to a different relativity of whole and whole, not subsumable into a set of nested wholes, themselves nested within evermore encompassing wholes. The community of a heteroarchic plurality of originals, each an open whole, is only intelligible if the spaces of huperintelligible otherness are kept open, never reduced, never turned into a fall from unity, never redefined as mere vanishing moments on the way to determinate intelligibility. These very spaces of huperintelligible otherness are the very sustaining places of creative freedom. The self would not be itself, nor the others be themselves, and all would not be together, were it not for the irreducibility of these openings of otherness that are other, say, to the sublated otherness of Hegelian dialectic.

We might then say that metaxological intelligibility seeks both to acknowledge integral singularities of being, and to formulate the web of relations that articulate their *being between* in the universal impermanence. There is an incessant passing to and fro amongst beings in the between. These passageways are causative, determinative, and creative. Metaxological intelligibility tries to offer a *logos* of passages in the between. The web of relativity that defines the passageways of being between cannot be reduced to the logic of self-determination that we find in dialectical intelligibility. There is something to all beings, selves, and others that is beyond self-determination. This is not to deny freedom, but to rethink it on a heteroarchic basis, as opposed to modernity's dominant sense of autonomy: *auto-nomos*, the law of the same. The heteroachic intelligibility of metaxological being is beyond the law of the same, the *nomos* of *to auton*.

There also follows a transformation of both internal and external relations. Internal relations must be reformulated in terms of the intimacy of being, in a double sense. Remember that the defenders of internal relations are usually thought to deny the resistance of a being's *for-self:* no entity is for-self, but all entities are what they are in relation to other entities; the *for-self* is dissolved in the web of relations, the passages of the between; singularity seems swallowed by holism. We must question this in light of a double interiority: first, the inward otherness of the self of a being; second, the otherness of its origin, beyond its antecedently conditioning determining cause—this is its ontological root in the absolute origin. The first interiority is not that of a precious subjectivity; there is nothing solipsistic here; the *solus* of the *ipse* is a communicative source, a deep in itself, and in its innerness, a pointing to the second interiority of the origin, beyond all determinative causation.

In respect of external relations , we often conceive these as an extrinsicality among beings, or between the knower and known, to the point of denying any community between beings or between mind and being. To the contrary, metaxological intelligibility requires a new sense of external relations that constitute community itself. The latter must be understood on the agapeic model, or its potential for this, in which the other is let be as other. Externality does really sustain otherness, really preserves independence and intimacy, separation and relatedness, both together. Externality is plural relatedness that brings to social shape the promise of an agapeic community of being.

Overall we are placed beyond a dualism of external and internal, beyond a dialectic of *ex* and *in*, beyond the subsumption of either into the other, which yields a sublating idealism on the one hand and a reductive materialism on the other. We might suggest there is a nonreductive community of *ex* and *in*. The relativities involved in the prefixes *ex* and *in* are all-important. For instance, one could see Hegelian dialectic as reducing the *ex* to the *in*; while a variety of realisms, empiricisms, and other modes of objectifying thought, reduce the *in* to the *ex*. In particular these latter views cannot explain the intimacy of being involved in the mindfulness that, as it turns out, here inappropriately objectifies all being-other. On this score idealisms are superior, because their logic is more attuned to the happening of the *in*. But the *ex* of otherness, of what Peirce calls secondness, of transcendence, the *ex* of agapeic mind and origin can be wrongly reduced to the *in* of erotic mind.

With respect to the happening of being as lived from within, there is a certain intimacy of self-relation that is not included in a determinate system, not even a self-determining system, since it is the source of such dynamic system. Nor is externality as objectified to be equated with the heteroarchic dimension of metaxological intelligibility. This latter externality is rather related to the ecstasis of creative excess. Creative excess is heteroarchic. Objectified externality reduces metaxological externality to univocal intelligibility, and tends to put a causal determinism in place of creative origination. The original happening in the passage of the between is approached voyeuristically rather than agapeically. The lived withinness of a becoming is lost, as is that community of innerness that marks the huperintelligible dimension of metaxological togetherness. This approach yields mechanism, not even organism, much less the community of freedom. With respect to the latter, there is also a limit of intelligibility in the possibility of unpredictable surprise, of the unexpected marking freedom beyond determinate intelligibility. Communicative being is both an outcome and a new beginning, a perennially new beginning, though the trace of openness to newness goes all the way down.

Dialectic here passes over to the living communication of dialogue. One philosophical image of this is offered, for example, by the Platonic dialogue. In fact we here find the four modes of intelligibility at work all together, in a plurivocal way. Some words on this will serve to racapitulate this chapter in a new light, conclude the current concerns, and advance our exploration to the next matter.

Thus, for instance, Socrates' conversation often reminds us of Zeno's use of the reductio ad absurdum, and hence not only of dialectic, but also of univocity, equivocity, the principles of identity, contradiction, and sufficient reason. It is concerned to move from the discord of equivocal speakings to an intelligible concordance of intelligent speakers. It unfolds from the seeming equivocity of *doxa* and its seeming univocal examples towards the univocal intelligibilty of *eidē*. But it also moves from the seeming univocity of singular speakers towards a metaxological community of mindfulness, a movement that is mediated by a dialectical development that faces and seeks to surpass a pressing equivocity.

In addition, this dialogical movement often unfolds by an immanent critique of the other, not to return us via Zeno's reductio to Parmenides' One, but to help us articulate the common *eidos* or universal, defined in a self-coherent *logos*. *Logoi* mediate between the particularity of examples and the universality of exemplary *eidē*. Moreover, the mediating universal is revealed through the immanent unfolding of *logoi*, even those that are seemingly at war with each other. Thus the challenge of equivocity and contradiction are turned to affirmative purposes in intelligibilities that pass beyond their discord. There is a continuing search for the basis of intelligible identity through the universal, and beyond self-discordant and contradictory *logoi*.

So also the Socratic admonition against *misology* (*Phaedo*, 89d-91c) is relevant to the skepticism about intelligibility produced by the equivocity of speaking. It relates to the question of basic ontological and epistemological trust. Misology is a kind of reactive skepticism, even hatred of reason, arising in recoil from a previously misplaced and excessive trust in a limited form of reason. In our terms, misology arises from our wrongly absolutizing univocal intelligibility, only to find that this absolute fails—and then the only option left seems absolute equivocity. When I speak throughout about *amplifying* the notion of intelligibility, I am also arguing against misology, in face of the collapse of an absolutized univocity. To amplify not only means "to enlarge," but also "*to make more ample*"—not just in the sense of "more true to," but this in a *generous sense*, as when we speak of an "ample measure" of food. We are generously offered full enough, and indeed again some more.

This intimation of "something more" emerges in dialogue in relation to a notion of the universal or idea that is not exhausted by a formal *eidos*. This other universal as emergent in intelligent communication pertains to a *community of spirit or mindfulness*. This is where a dialogical movement becomes most explicitly metaxological. For the *living speaking* is as important as the determinate *spoken*; and there is no living speaking without a *living speaker*. Metaxological dialogue does not only search the intelligibility of propositions, it also addresses the discernment of persons—the discrimination between their genuine or fake mindfulness. But living, singular speakers are not just eidetic intelligibles; they are huperintelligibles engaged in intelligent communication. In a word, the community of living speakers is the huperintelligible togetherness of mindful beings, intelligent beyond determinate intelligibility. Moreover, such huperintelligible dialogue never loses touch with the intimacy of singularity, the ontological marvel of it, in its suggestion of the agapeic ground.

In sum, there appears before us again the possible intelligibility, huperintelligibility of agapeic being. We are forced to go beyond the self-determination of dialectical intelligibility, beyond the autonomy of dialectical intelligence, beyond even the community of huperintelligibles in their unmeasured asymmetry, to the ground of agape as the absolutely other. This ground is the basis of the always open between. Therein the destiny of particularity is to selve into mindful singularity. Therein we find an opening out at the level of singularity, at the level of community, in the very transformation of the between from just a network of relativity into a new possible community of mindfulness. Intelligibility then demands a further exploration of the meaning of the universal. This cannot be the dualistic or even dialectical opposite of the particular become singular. It cannot be anonymous. It cannot be the dead eternity of the logical abstraction, nor the crushing abstraction of the world historical universal. It must be agapeic. The idea, the ideal, becomes the communicative universe of the *idios*, the intimate. The huperintelligibile community of living mindfulness turns us towards the examination of selves and communities.

CHAPTER TEN

SELVES

Selving

It is appropriate now to turn to selves. For our reflections on origin, creation, things, intelligibilities, all suggest a process of *selving*. First, origin originates the creation with a being for-itself that is other to the origin. Second, creation as universal impermanence articulates the promise of this being-for-self as a double metaxological process of self-becoming and becoming-other. Third, things show themselves as distinct concretions of the original power of being which evidences this double process: entities are complex open wholes, marked by tension between inner self-differentiation *and* relativity to other entities. We might say that things as wholes open themselves to the promise of selving. Finally, intelligibilities point beyond static structure: being is intelligible because it is open to being minded. But to be able to mind being intelligibly is to be *more* than intelligibility—it is to be intelligent. Intelligent being minds being, because being is the promise of being as mindful. We cannot finally make intelligibility intelligible without reference to mindful being. In sum: the promise of singularity, concretized in the being for-itself of creation, selves through things and intelligibilities, and begins to be mindfully realized in the human self.

Consider further how the existence of things is both particular, yet mediated by intelligibility. Thus, *inorganic beings* are complex unities held together, as more or less stable wholes, in connections with other unities in the universal impermanence, connections that to a degree are defined externally. *Organic beings* are more complexly intelligible: the inherence of self-becoming is evident in the way the unity of being holds itself together, yet also developmentally integrates itself in a process of self-becoming. Here in the between there is a tilt towards the promise of internal self-relativity, even in external relations. Further again with *sensitive beings*, the space between internal and external relativity is even more complex. Animals, for instance, complexify this inherence of self-mediation, in that they register and respond to their exchange with things as other. They mediate and monitor their own inherent unity in this dynamic process of interchange. The animal is in itself in such a mediated way that it is also outside of itself, in its responsive sensitivity to the being of others. And these others can be "in" it too, insofar as entities and features of its environment are salient to its own self-maintenance.

With sensitive beings the vector of transcendence is clearly manifest, in that their sensitivity places their being outside of itself. And yet again they are in themselves in this outside; indeed the outside comes to have a sensed being within the sensible entity. But the vector of transcendence is not absent in inorganic and organic beings. No inorganic being is so stable or inert as to be devoid of some reactions to other beings. Organic beings are clearly outside of themselves, in obtaining and appropriating from what is other the wherewithal of their own self-maintenance, like light being photosynthesized by a leaf, or a root ingesting nutriments from the soil.

When we come to properly *mindful beings*, like the human self, the togetherness of internal and external relativity is most complexly qualified and stressed. Mindful being begins to realize the promise of creation for-itself as given by the agapeic origin. This being for-itself qualifies the between with the greatest depth of inwardness, of self-mediation; but at the same time it becomes the greatest possible openness to what is other to itself, the promise of a potentially universal openness to the other. The vector of self-transcendence in the human being opens universally, at least in promise, to all the community of being in its otherness, as the self-mediation of this being deepens beyond measure towards infinity. Put otherwise, infinite inwardness goes hand in hand with a certain promise of inexhaustible transcendence. This self is original in a new way. For its being for self can become being for others, and not just again for-itself alone; it can become an agapeic original. The human self is a one that is more than a one. It is an intermediate original that images the absolute original.

While we normally think of self in relation to the human being, and while there are compelling reasons to mark human distinctiveness, important considerations also ask us to see our continuity with the rest of being. For things selve; they manifest their particularity as uniquely theirs in creation. This selving is not a mindful selving in the way it is for human being; it is an immediate selving in which the mediation is not awakened to itself. But this should not blind us to the fact that things in themselves are intelligibly mediated. Their self-mediation and intermediation is *their* doing, even if that doing is not mindfully given to itself. Their immediate doing is in itself mediated.

Looking now at the human self, we find *both* a continuation of creation and an astonishing new manifestation of the original power of being. In no way do I want to suggest that selves can be abstracted from their communities. Where the present chapter focuses mainly on modes of self-relativity, the next chapter will complete the picture with its emphasis on modes of togetherness. But there is no self-relation that we can detach from relativity to otherness. Overall, we move from intelligibility to mindful being, from particularity to personhood, from aesthetic givenness to the embodied, incarnate self, from being to being mindful, from being mindful to being as a community of original selves and others.

The human self comes into being, emerges, unfolds, becomes, or betrays what it promises. There is an integral being in and across this process of being, emergence, unfolding, realization. Being here is as much verb as noun: the activity of being, as well as the being so acting. This is why I want to speak of selving. But selving, like being, is plurivocal. It is spoken, or speaks itself, in a manifold of ways of being, all of which are yet its own, are yet simply itself. The fourfold sense of being will again throw light on this being one's own. This being oneself as one will be seen as a manifold self-becoming that comes to the limit of self-becoming.

The Idiot Self and Univocity

Throughout the history of reflection on the self, perhaps the most reiterated notion is the soul's simple unity. The soul is undivided, uncompounded. This was a life and death matter, for from this simplicity the soul's very deathlessness was said to follow (see Plato's *Phaedo*). In recent discussion, the single notion most commonly *rejected* is just this undivided unity. There is said to be no soul in the traditional sense. Frequently, selfhood is seen as a result of various processes: neurological circuitry, biological heredity, psychological formation, social conditioning. There is no inherent unity to selfhood, no unity per se; unity is a derivative construction. It will even be said that the unity of the self is a fiction, something made. The constructed self too can be deconstructed in light of the more basic making powers. The origin of self is in these forces as other to it; the self, it is said, is decentered. In addition to neurological, biological, psychological, social conditionings, we find invocations of will to power, or historical epochs, or *différance*, or language itself, to explain the derived constructions of self.

In emphasizing becoming and process, do I ally myself with these tendencies? Does the rejection of soul as spiritual substance follow from such an emphasis? If one speaks of universal impermanence and heteroarchic intelligibility, as I have, how can one speak of something like the soul's simplicity? In speaking of the origin as the *archē* that is *heteros*, without which nothing would be or be intelligible, do I not radically decenter the self? Yes and no. Yes the self is decentered. No: in this decentering, self as transcending has also its center within itself.

I want to defend a unity in process, in incarnate becoming, in ageing. Against the above fictive self, I want to speak for a radical singularity that is consistent with agapeic creation as given for the otherness of the creature. Heteroarchic origination gives the particular its being for itself; this being is its own, irreplaceable, singular in an absolute sense: its for-itself is its own, and no one else's. It cannot be alienated, though it can be given to the other, say, in sacrificial love. But this is a different decentering to the above ones. Strangely the latter, even though they construct the self as the derivative of *other* forces, seem incapable of understanding the self as the promise of agape, and thus as radically for the other. Ironically, they seemed bound to think the self as a mode of either reactive or dominating power, as made in a network of such power relations, as itself trying to be powerful for itself in this network.

The univocal sense offers us a first approach to this singularity of self. A self is itself and nothing but itself. Even when it is other to itself, it is still itself. Even when it reacts to what is other, even when it tries to dominate or sacrifice itself to the other, it is still itself. Almost immediately, of course, we are pressing the limits of univocity, but it seems to me that all the pressure occurs relative to something elemental that is for itself. This elemental self is itself and nothing but itself. Perhaps we may speak of its simplicity and indivisibility, though this will have to be further qualified. We might say that to be a self is to be an original unto oneself.[1]

Admittedly, the language of substance today raises expectations that can get in the way of speaking of this elemental self. The justice of these expectations is another question. I must leave it to the side, beyond saying that the metaphysics of substance is not at all as threadbare as its denigrators claim. I want to say that to be a self is to be a distinctive center of the original power of being. This original power is not a static determination but evidences a process of determining, and hence in itself is more than any determination. In that respect we are not dealing with a *static* substance. But we could call self a thing, if we remember that things are not static unities; they too are concretions of the original power of being; things are determinate wholes that carry the trace of the overdetermined origin, and hence are never closed in on themselves completely. The indeterminacy of the original self is to be understood affirmatively as a source of origination. As a power of determining, we can also call it a source of spontaneity and freedom. This elemental self *is itself* as a determining source of its own free becoming. It cannot be completely objectified, and hence always resists complete encapsulation in concepts. This is not to say that it is beyond all saying. Its very being is an active origination that is also a communication of itself.

The aspect we now consider is its givenness to itself, its self-communication, its awareness of itself at the edge of all determinable concepts. We are impelled to speak of a primal feeling of ourselves as for ourselves.

---

1. See *Desire, Dialectic and Otherness*, chapter 2, where I speak of original selfhood. As I indicated above in Part I, the univocal sense of being is operative in Descartes' notion of the thinking thing or substance. He is not entirely wrong if we recognize that both "thing" and "thinking" are more complex than he thought. Self is a thing that is not a thing, as we will see more clearly with desire's equivocity. On univocity relative the transcendental ego as pure universal formal ego, see Part I also.

The human self—and this is felt singularly by each singular self—has an in-eluctable sense of itself as itself and itself alone. This is I. We have this taste of self, smell of self, this aura of self that each singular lives alone for itself, and lives inwardly. It is the inner taste of itself of inwardness itself.

This is a sense of *mineness* that accompanies everything the self does. Most of the time it is not noticed at all, certainly not made a theme of thought. It is borne by us in our pragmatic dealings. We may notice it, for instance, when we wake in the morning. We wake with a distinctive taste of ourselves. When we get busy, the taste is submerged in the dealing and doings we must carry out. Or we wake in the middle of the night, and all the props of the day are gone, and in the dark there is this source of awareness, positioned in its insomnia on the bed, but in its physical position also positionless. Now the stream of awareness is not given over to engrossment in external determi-nate things, and hence is just the accompanying awareness of itself, here and yet nowhere, in the dark a perplexed presence to itself that tastes the taste of itself in its own perplexity.

This elemental self, as we might call it, is a preobjective self, for it is prior to all objectifications of itself, and prior to its own awareness of objects that will give determinacy to its own initially indeterminate mindfulness of itself. This nonobjective selfhood is a singular mindfulness of the original power of being that senses and feels itself as a unique becoming that is for itself in the vast enigma of the universal impermanence.[2]

While hard to say, there are different ways of suggesting it. Here are some. I eat a meal, and as I eat the meal hungrily, I am engrossed in the food; but there comes a point of satiation in which the elemental satisfac-tion of the body makes itself felt in awareness; my sense of myself as replete comes over me; I am myself and nothing but myself in that repletion, and I cannot communicate completely in discursive terms what the living from within of this repletion is. I sigh and say "Delicious!"; but how thin the word is without that infinitely textured sigh. I drink a draught of beer; I intimately know the taste of the beer; but I also intimately know myself inwardly as enjoying this taste of the beer; in the enjoyment of the beer there is a self-enjoyment that is finally beyond all objectification; for it is a sense of self that can only be lived and enjoyed and not completely captured in concepts. A smack of the lips may be all that communicates this savored enjoyment in innerness.

---

2. The original self is not active or passive, but is active in a sense that is prior to doing, and is passive with a patience beyond passivity; this is its participation in the origin and its continued receptivity in its very being to this gift; original selving is a finite origin after the origin, but this finite origin, patient and energized, is closer to the origin than the self as determinate; the original self is the indeterminate locus of selving. On solitude and the self as the place/noplace of meonic contraction, see *Philosophy and its Others*, 229–42.

Or consider the experience of weariness. One is weary beyond all tired-
ness. One wants to lose consciousness of self, but one cannot. One seeks sleep
but repose evades one. One is gall to oneself, riveted to oneself as this tired
and fashed self. One is insipid to oneself and inescapable, though one seeks
reprieve in sleep. One is fastened to self as the unpalatable staleness of oneself, and this self-fastening is felt as an insupportable burden. But there is no
deliverance. One can get up and try to lose oneself in activity, in objectification and objects. All the advice is to do just that, and hence for a time to forget
oneself. But now the distraction fails, and one is again an infinitely weary
energy, a listlessness of being that is indissolubly bound to itself and will not
sink into the sweet oblivion of sleep. Each singular self is thus indissolubly
bound to itself and know itself as its own self, even though it would escape
itself into sleep or into doing or into distraction, even into violence.

This elemental self is original, and its development will include its passage through the equivocity of being, its own dialectical self-mediation, to its
metaxological intermediation with others. But what now concerns us is selving
as prior to objectification. I am speaking of a kind of indeterminate self-presence. Since it is indeterminate, it is also ambiguous to call it self-presence, if
we identify this latter with a clear and distinct self-determination. This indeterminate self-presence is floating, and indeed much of the time *absent* to
itself. The normal duality of presence and absence does not really apply. For
we could just as easily call this elemental self a nonthing as a thing; it is
nothing at all, if our sense of things is exclusively zoned on fixed determinate
entities.

It is no-thing, however, not because it is a mere emptiness, but because
it is an affirmative promise of a more radical realization of itself. It is more
than determinacy; it is indeterminate as an excess of being over and above
objectified beings, over and above the ego itself considered as an objectified
being. This elemental self is a nonobjective being. Its being might also be
called an original unity of nonbeing, for-itself as beyond beings, and beyond
its own being as determinately objectified. This nonobjective elemental center of original power pervades all the dimensions of the self, considered as a
developed and determinate being, but it is not identical with any dimension
simpliciter, nor is it exhausted by any of these determinations of the self as
objectified. It is more than all of these, and yet it is their source, and also the
pervading self-presence that is in each and every one of them.

This nonobjective sense of self suggests the nonreducibility of the inner
feeling of mineness to physical, biological factors as scientifically objectified.
It may be the case that I may not have this feeling without certain biological
preconditions. But the conditions will never fully comprehend the innerness
of the self-feeling as mine, precisely because the latter is non-objective, while
the former is a congeries of objectifications. This is why to speak of elemental
mineness is not at all to subscribe to a Cartesian or any objectifying dualism.
The fact of this elemental self-relation, known intimately as mine in inward-

ness, cannot be rendered in any objective explanatory scheme, for it is precisely the lived inwardness of "subjectivity" that is at issue. This elemental mineness will never be explained by congeries of non-mines, in the reductive sense intended. It will itself always be presupposed, and conveniently forgotten, in the exploitation of the reductive objectifications for supposedly explanatory purposes. The most astonishing, enigmatic yet salient "reality" to be explained is simply forgotten or explained away, though all the while it is presupposed and used in every act of mindful explanation.[3]

This elemental self is idiotic, again in the Greek sense of the *idiōtēs*: the private, the intimate—what is on the edge of, or outside, or other than—more publicly available generalities or neutral universals. This idiotic singularity points to a rich "univocity" that is not subsumable in any system of categories. Against the normal philosophical predilection for defining the particular as unintelligible without its covering universal, here we must ask about a this, which resists the standard Aristotelian intelligibility. According to the latter, to be intelligible is to be a determinate somewhat, but this particular has an idiocy, an intimacy of being that is on the other side of determinacy, and that to be itself must remain on that other side. If it were not to remain so, there would be no determinate self-presence possible for the self as a delimitable and intelligible this.

This elemental idiocy is suggestive of the mineness of the self as *opening into otherness within itself*. Every self is a this, and the this is lived from within as mine and nothing but mine. Each singular self is an unduplicable point of view on the world; but within the elemental mineness, there is not

---

3. Consider the so-called *double-mind*, split-mind, split-brain associated with experimental data based on surgery to patients. This, I believe, is best thought in relation to equivocal being. But in all these cases, there is still the problem of the unity of the self as *lived from within*. This is intractable to all physicalist reductionisms, even reductions to two minds, identified with two "brains," identified with two "persons." In fact, to be in two minds is part of the paradoxical nature of mind itself; indeed to be in three minds, four minds, in multiple minds. This is self-transcending self-pluralization; and yet this pluralization is "mine." In mindful selving there is a strange unity of unity and manyness—and this without any reference to brains, one or more. The integrity of the for-self of the singular I is lived and minded from within its own interiority—this "withinness" is the unique singular savor of the "myself." Again see *Philosophy and its Others*, 229ff.; also "The Idiocy of Being" in *Perplexity and Ultimacy*.

Even split-brain patients act outside experimental circumstances as integrities of being for themselves; they are this one person, and treated as such. For instance, they are not given two votes in an election; if they make a pledge or promise, it is not one or other side of their brain that is held responsible. Only in experimental circumstances does the disconnection syndrome appear and the divergences in behavior associated with right and left hemispheres of the brain. The "patient" acts and is still treated as an integral person, despite peculiarities revealed relative to experimental circumstances.

the pure self-transparency of either the Cartesian or the transcendental ego. There is an elusive, shifting, floating, nonobjectifiable mineness. This mineness, as thus beyond determinate encapsulation, is also *not* mine, in the sense of a determinate possession that I can simply claim. What is most my own is not my own.

This elemental self is preobjectively most my own, most intimate to me; hence it is idiotically mine and mine alone; it is outside the nonidiotic system of shared objective universals. But as idiotically my own, and as never possessed even while my own, it is never owned by me. It is an inward otherness, more intimate to inwardness that all its own self-possessions. The idiocy of the self in this inwardness is an opening to otherness within itself. Indeed its excess suggests the promise of an inexhaustibility. Its unity in itself is not that of a closed whole, because its own internal wholeness opens out, within its own wholeness. It opens beyond self-possession to the otherness of the original power of being (and mediately to the otherness of the origin) that is given to it for itself in its singularity.

This sense of inward idiocy makes us defend, not only the radical singularity of self beyond all objectification and reduction, but also the opening of the self within itself to its own inexhaustible dimension of depth. The "monad" of self is infinitely rich in itself. The reserves of self cannot be exhausted by any finite possibility; there is a certain infinite promise at work here that transcends all logics of determinacy. For while determinacy is necessary to deal with expressions and determinations of this infinite promise, an exclusive logic of determinacy cannot deal with the promise *as* inexhaustible. To the extent that logics of determinacy privilege a fixed univocity, we have to go beyond logical univocity in this sense to deal with this "univocity" of the elemental self. We have to return behind a logic of determinacy to what we might call the aesthetics of selving.

Aesthetic Selving and Equivocity

The aesthetics of selving relates to the fact that the elemental self in the idiocy of inwardness is first *felt*. We first sense ourselves, taste ourselves, savor ourselves. We are sensitive selves who are sensible of ourselves. Selving is also aesthetic in being bound to sensible appearing. This is important in reminding us of our bodied being.

In certain respects, the idiot self is prior to aesthetic selving, because the latter is already "objectified" in the body, positioned, "posited," "there," hence more determinate than the idiotic I. The latter points to a prepositioned, preaesthetic, prereflective I. In fact, however, it is impossible to fix an absolute distinction between the idiot I and aesthetic selving. The immediate unity of the self is first felt for itself as a bodily immediacy. Mind is still sunk in its body; the sense of the self as inner as opposed to outer is not firmly fixed. This is the immediate unity of the self as aesthetically elemental.

In the happening of the "I" in the promiscuity of the inner and outer, of the conscious and the bodily, there is a sensuous "I am," that is at work. The self affirms itself as a sensuously existent unity of being. I do not mean affirms in the sense of propositionally saying itself. I mean that *its very being there* is the affirmation. The aesthetic affirmation of being is the very existence of the self. Existence here is intended to convey some of its etymological roots: *ex-istere, ex-stare*: the self is *ex*: it is an exit, a "standing out"; its existence is felt in itself as this standing out. The bodied being is this standing out of the singular existent into the community of being of creation.

This aesthetic "I am" relates to a certain primal *self-insistence* that defines the mineness of the self. This self-insistence is notable, for instance, in infants and younger children; the insistence of the energy of being plays in them, cries out in them, immediately, without self-consciousness motivation, without reckoning or ulterior motive.[4] The aesthetic "I am" is this cry of the bodied self, which seems to say: "Here I am." The I here calls out of itself to an indeterminate other, anyone, the mother, the father, the creator. This is an "I am" of being in the body itself. It signals an elemental festivity of existing, a joy in self that is an enjoyment of being. The *ex-* of existence makes the "I am" a "Here I am"; thereby it makes the standing out of the self into the very presence of an incarnation. The focus of that incarnation is that the self has a *face*.[5] The self as facing stands there, comes to a stand. It is not the faceless anonymous "one." The "one" is everyone and no one; it stands nowhere.

The significance of the above is that at the elemental level there is a *community with otherness* even in the most idiotic inwardness. The aesthetic

---

4. Here are other instances that suggest the point. Consider what it means to deal with a particularly obstinate child. What does the stubbornness mean? A resistant particularity that seems absolutely immovable; an elemental "myness," ownness, prior to self-reflection and self-objectification. When people used to speak of "breaking the will," what is being "broken" is the "root" of self-insistence (to "break" this would really be a kind of death). Thus the *torturer* tries to destroy this root of self-insistence, also at the root of our freedom. Less extremely, *sarcasm* is a speaking that tries to get to this root and visit on it a spiritual violence. Think also of the experience of *being shamed* or *being embarrassed*. When one blushes for shame, one may blush to the roots. What are those roots?—the vulnerable, absolutely "touchy" self. Or think of oneself as sore with an illness, one cannot be touched one is so tender; to be in contact is to be in pain; as if the only alleviation were to return to the prepositioned idiocy, self-awareness floating in itself without the press of being. Or consider *two aggressive boxers*, as we say, going "eye-ball to eye-ball"—silent idiotic selves each trying to cow the other, facing down the other with violence out of the idiocy of self-insistence. Think, by contrast, of the first enjoyment of the other: the idiotic amen of the infant to the breast.

5. I have discussed the signifying power of the human body, of eye, ear, nose, voice, and so on, in chapter 2 of *Philosophy and its Others*.

self is the flesh of inwardness.[6] But flesh and incarnation concretize a primordial sensuous bond with being beyond the self. To be incarnate is to be bodied in a place of interchange. Moreover as incarnate, the self is mindful, at least potentially so at this point. It is not in its flesh as neutral. For this reason we have to argue against every dualism that rigidly separates the self from its body, and the bodied self from the body of the world other than itself. Such dualisms, Platonic or Cartesian or empiricist, are abstractions from the emergence of the self in its body in the between, and fixations on the abstractions, that now become alienated versions of both inwardness and exteriority.

The incarnate body is a fleshed "I am" which is also an "I am with." For the "I am" could not otherwise be also a "Here I am," were not the other already implicated in the elemental affirmation of the self. The incarnate "I am" is an immediate certainty of self-presence, a self-certainty before all concepts of itself. To put it this way is already too abstract, since this self-certainty is just the immediate, lived intimacy of the self in relation to itself. Immediate self-relation in the aesthetic body: this hyphen of self-relation is important: it signals a space of otherness from the beginning: self-relation is also self-differing. Both will be more fully developed, pointing to the difference of the other beyond the self. The "Here" of the "Here I am" will become metaxologically stressed.

Another important point about aesthetic selving is this: here we feel both the vulnerability of inwardness and the press of being in its otherness on that inwardness. For at this point the self has no fixed boundaries. This is the nonobjectified indeterminacy of inwardness; it is an indefinite sensitivity. Everything presses in, invades, since there is no fixed distinction of inner and outer. The ocean of otherness can come on us, as in an inundation over a thin dike. The press of being is its very impress. Aesthetic selving is shaped by the impression of being. Beings pass into us, incessantly. Again one thinks of the infant, though this inundation can return at any point: the fixed self is broken and something other breaks through. Death may be the last breakdown, and the last breakthrough, but now the self is not fixed but a being flooded by things. The aesthetic self is a site of flow and passage, in and out. In the element of the flesh it is already a between.

---

6. This aesthetic selving is very hard to capture in discursive language. There is a kind of *communicative silence* at the edge of discursive language. Think of the erotic silence/communication of sexual intercourse: the body at/in pleasure groans, grunts, at the limits of language; this is the intimacy, idiocy of pleasure, outside all general concepts. "An intimate moan"—translate that without remainder into public, discursive concepts! And yet there can be a depth of communication, community in that idiotic moan, that murmur, that purr. Its full meaning cannot be objectified. Or think of the other extreme of pain, and the return of the body to silence/communication. A cry of suffering, a sob: what are the words that capture a sob? None. This too is elemental.

A crucial consequence is that in aesthetic selving we find a kind of *patient self*, a self passive to the press of the world. We are subjected to the suffering of being. The aesthetic self is an elemental passion of being; it undergoes the world; the press of being washes over and in and through it. We have to say that passion, suffering, a patience of being, are at the roots of selfhood. This is highly significant, I think. For the sense of *the value or disvalue of being* is here first registered, known intimately in innerness. This suffering of being is always with us. What we do, will do, is based on what we suffer, what is given to us, what is refused to us, how we consent to or refuse what is given or refused. But such patient suffering of being is not only painful. It is no less true that we *suffer joy*, we suffer happiness. It comes over us. We are given over to joy in being, originally. Joy is a gift of goodness from the other who loves us.

This is why the mother and father as incarnate presences are so important. This is perhaps also why the elemental smile has ontological significance: we respond spontaneously to the welcome of incarnate presence—the agape of being is ingrained ontologically in our flesh.[7] I underscore the fact that this suffering of being betokens something entirely different to the self-positing ego of transcendental philosophy or idealism, or the self-assertive humanity of Marxism, and Nietzsche's self-aggrandizing will to power. Passages into and through the patient self are the transitions of transcendence that pass from without in, as well as from within out. We suffer the press of being from without, and the exigency of transcendence from within. Aesthetic selving reveals the incarnate fluctuation between this press and this exigence in the happening of the between.

With the aesthetic self the mind is in the body such that consciousness and the unconscious mingle. And since the body is itself rooted in sensuous nature, there is an incessant flux and reflux between the flesh and nature. The fleshed self is an integrity for itself but not closed in itself: in itself it is a communication back and forth between itself and nature as aesthetic. So also there is a tremendous process of interchange *within* the body itself. So much is going on that it does not all appear to consciousness.[8]

---

7. On the smile, see *Philosophy and its Others*, 272–73.

8. Think of what happens in hypnosis—a lot is going on that we know and yet do not know. In one current jargon, there is "information processing" going on beyond consciousness. Consider this example of "split consciousness" relative to equivocity. A person is hypnotized with respect to one hand. The hypnotized hand when put in freezing water feels no pain, or little; meanwhile, relative to the other hand, what Ernest Hilgard calls the "hidden observer" complains of the pain as excruciating (see E. Hilgard, *Divided Consciousness* (New York: Wiley, 1986), chapter 9). The self is both "aware" and "not aware" of pain, "aware in not being aware" at one and the same time. This is double and contradictory, but it happens.

Leibniz spoke of this when he distinguished between perception and apperception. The aesthetic self as flesh is perception that is not self-conscious in the more clear and distinct sense of apperception—this will be a later mediation. We might call this the working of *manyness* within the body, and it is the basis of ideas like the unconscious. Selfhood puts its root down into the body as itself rooted in nature.[9] Selfhood is not just a function of self-consciousness, self-mediation. It entails an integrity of being that is a bodied mindfulness. Aesthetic mindfulness is on the threshold of transition between the somatic and the consciously mindful. The aesthetic body is both a radiant self-transcendence and a *memory* in flesh: it retains the traces of its interchanges with externality and the passages of its own internal self-mediation.

It should be clear why I correlate aesthetic selving with the equivocal sense of being. For an indeterminate sense of unity, the I felt as I, floats in a sea of thereness. The I felt as I passes back and forth between innerness and outerness, and still feels itself as I. It erects no fixed boundaries, and the sea of thereness is itself charged with value: thereness is felt as good or repulsive, as threatening or welcoming, as edible or as horror. In a word, the indeterminate univocity of the I floats in a sea of charged equivocal being.[10]

---

9. The elemental unity is not that of a static thing, but there are no static things anyway; unities are integrities in process, of powers, of acts that do the powers of the self. Nor is it the unity confined to the level of consciousness. There is a unity beyond *explicit* mindfulness. This is the inward otherness; not the unity of thought thinking itself. Think here of *sleep* with respect to the root of the aesthetic self in the body. Think of sleep as both a source and grave or death of self; think of waking as like a flashflood of consciousness. The aesthetic self is an immediacy of immersion in the flow of creation, the universal impermanence; there is here no *literal* univocal self; a sense of aesthetic unity reaches down into the idiot self.

10. Consider: the child sees a shadow on the wall and cries out in horror. He recoils at the monster. We adults smile. We soothingly say: there is nothing there. We add to ourselves: he has "projected" his fears onto the blank space. Nothing there. Yes, there is nothing there, but there is a meaning to this "nothing" quite different to the "projective" interpretation. This latter is a Cartesianized stripping of the immediate aesthetic charge of otherness. There is no value/disvalue, beauty/horror "out there." There is nothing out there.

Yes, there is nothing out there, but this "nothing," in a sense, is what the child sees, the horror from which the child recoils. The shadow is not just a blotch on the wall onto which "value" is "projected." The shadow, as a horrifying thereness, is the shadow of a threat. What is the threat? It is the threat of nothing to the being-there of the child—finite being, vulnerable always, always shadowed by its constitutive nothingness. The horror of this shadow—in the threat of this particular shadow/horror—is pre-objectively recognized by the recoil of the child. Indeterminate threat, indeterminate anxiousness, indeterminate negation of being—the shadow on the wall is the charge of nothingness. (Does pain as a discordance of the body with itself, does the

Aesthetic Selving and Mediation: Desire, Imagination, Memory

But there is more, since the aesthetic I is itself equivocal being. This is especially evident when we consider that this floating of the I in its body is disturbed by *the eruption of desire* in this body. This eruption takes our considerations to a further level of complexity. The felt I does not float without resistance. It hits against the jagged edges of otherness outside itself; it is jolted from its daydreaming by the surging insistence of desire that sends the charge of its own vulnerability through the flesh. This eruption of desire in the aesthetic being of the self introduces a break with seamless immediacy. Desire is immediate, a spontaneous eruption in the flesh that is not first the result of choice; but as an immediate emergence, it is also the emergence of a new sense of difference and hence of the possibility of mediation.

Desire reveals the energy of transcendence in the aesthetic self. Desire is a threshold mediation that erupts in the body as the sense of lack. To maintain itself the self needs what is other to itself; it needs to adventure in otherness to find and appropriate the wherewithal necessity to preserve its own integrity of being. The first upsurgence of desire is also testimony to the power of self-differentiation as at work within the self. The self is not a unity that is full of itself to the point of being inert. Rather desire, felt as lack, indicates an absence in human identity, an absence recognized as such. The I feels itself as lack in desire; it senses itself as not what it is, while it is what it is not. In other words, we are clearly beyond any univocal logic, since there seems to be something paradoxical, if not contradictory about this self. We could say the unity of the self is self-contradictory in this regard: it contradicts itself, for in its desire there is precipitated an energy of transcendence that turns against the security of all and any inert identity. This energy of transcendence turns against its own attainments and sets out in search of a fuller activation of the energy of transcending. This it does by turning against itself, negating itself, then to find opening up, in the resulting space of lack, its need for the other beyond itself.

Does this confirm the view of self as a kind of Sartrean negativity? Not quite. Yes there is a negativity. We do evidence the power to say no in radical form. We can refuse given being; we can refuse to be identified with our own present achievement of being; we can even revolt against being as a whole.

---

ugly as a discordance of the body with outerness, equivocally suggest an aesthetic prefigurement of evil which is ethical and spiritual?)

You may say I make too much of this. Well, think of how it would be if we aesthetically lived in a world of shadows: what rapport with being then? What of the aesthetic "I am"? How distorted this would be then, cut off from the glory of creation. We sense the contrast of creation as glory, creation as hostile horror. The child lives more immediately this charge of creation—more fluidly, openly, more receptively, because prior to objective determination.

However, I think that the lack cannot be identified with the self, since it is a determination of the original power of being that marks the self as a "one" that is in excess of determinate univocal unity. There is "more" to the self than the relatively stable identity of a thing; this "more" is expressed in the sense of lack. But this is, so to say, a negative articulation of the affirmative power of being at work in the singular self. For it is not lack that desires; it is the self that desires in its lack. And this self is not just essentially lack, but an affirmative openness to what is other to itself, and to the to-be-achieved realization of its own promise of being.

So we may say then that desire breaks up inert self-identity and hurries the self in search both of what is other and of itself as more fully realized. There is a self-differentiation here, that is also a transcending of the antithesis of inner and outer. For desire clearly sends the self beyond itself as simple innerness; to satisfy itself it has to enter the middle between interiority and exteriority, and seek what as other will requite its own lack. Desire opens up the self to its own middle condition of being, where it also attains a greater differentiated sense of itself and what is other to itself. A further concretion of the process of selving is manifest: the I felt as I becomes the seeking, appetitive I.

In this process, desire and *imagination* are allied. For imagination is also a threshold power of being emergent in the aesthetic body. In line with an old distinction, we may speak of reproductive and productive imagination. The first registers the exterior and the body's interchange with it. The second articulates the power within the self to generate from its own resources the shape of its response to being, whether inner or outer. Desire sends us in search of ourselves and the other, imagination allows us to begin to articulate explicitly the shape of that sought self and that other. Thus too imagination is emergent at a point where fixed distinctions between inner and outer are not yet stabilized. The power of free self-articulation emerges from the aesthetic body as itself a given articulation of being. We might say that imagination energizes the self with free original power.[11]

For imagination is original. It originates in the self the opening to the other as other by opening up the self as the free power of self-articulation. It does this in the aesthetic body, but in the process transcends it. Consider: if we could not imagine in the free sense intended, we could never imagine what it would be like to be different to what one presently is. Only a freely imagining being can put itself in the place of what is other to itself. Imagination is a power that releases our original identification of difference. While remaining myself, I imagine the inner being of the other as other. I may even *become that being as other* by assuming through imitation what I imagine that other to be. Similarly, through that same free power I can imagine *my-*

---

11. See *Philosophy and its Others,* chapter 2, "Being Aesthetic" on imagination and the original identification of difference; also on imitation and creation.

self as other. I dream of as yet unrealized possibility that I vaguely sense is slumbering in the present self. Thus imagination is central to the genesis, the determinate articulation, and the creative formation of any career of self-transcendence.

Again with imagination, as with desire, we come across equivocity.[12] The image is never unambiguous, never univocal. Thus we often discover a promiscuity between the self imagined as other, and the other to the self imagined by the self. The self as desire is self-insistence, lacking what it needs, and yet it is carried by the vector of transcendence beyond itself. The self as imagining is shaped in a middle, now between innerness as other and outerness as other, and now again between outerness as sometimes merely the projected fantasy of innerness and innerness as sometimes hard to separate from the introjected image of the other, like the mother, the father, or even the big bad wolf. Often it is extraordinarily difficult to distinguish. Desire and imagination *begin* the process of self-differentiation and the respect for otherness as other; they do not complete the process. Their aesthetic equivocity is never entirely left behind in all subsequent developments. The promiscuity of inner and outer has yet to be more clearly distinguished, to prepare a different marriage of self and other-being. Desire and imagination evidence the immediacy of the metaxological community, but they do not fully mediate an explicit mindfulness of it.

Once again, the I is not univocally itself in desire and imagination; it is other to itself; it is in search of the other, or in search of itself as other, or it is put in the place of the other by the self itself as self-othering. We cannot fix the boundaries between; for the I is a being-between, as each side and the other too, and their conjunction. I am tempted to speak here of the self as *metaphor*. For metaphor (*metapherein*) implies a "carrying across," a "carrying between." So by metaphor I do not mean a mere fantasy; I mean an original image, original because originative out of itself, an image because ultimately only fully itself in relativity to what is other to itself, in which it participates and to which it is likened. The self is a metaphor in this sense of

---

[12] The aesthetic self can manipulate the equivocity of appearances. The Irish, somewhat bemusedly, somewhat derisively, call the equivocal self, *"Tadhg an dá thaobh,"* "Tim of the two sides." This being "two-faced" was experienced at a fundamental level by Boethius when the Janus character of *Fortuna* was shown to him. Boethius is told by Lady Philosophy that his distress has revealed "the two-faced nature of this blind goddess, *Fortuna*" (*Consolation of Philosophy*, book 1).

   Other equivocal phenomena that might merit further reflection include: divided attention; weak will; self-deception; the fugue state; distraction and dissociation; the self as divided against itself. Or consider self-hatred relative to the idiot self and the elemental self-love. Can one hate self or body, if the very being of both evidences an elemental self-love, self-affirmation? Real self-hatred must be at another level, in contradistinction with this elemental self-love.

a *metaphorizing*. This is not all, we shall see, but it is essential to make some sense of the strange power of self-transcendence that marks the human self.

Let me put it the following way. The self as metaphor differentiates itself into *images of itself*. In fact, it *generates itself* in the images of itself to which it gives rise. For what are these images but its own aesthetic appearances, or incarnate embodiments. In other words, the self as metaphor is a carnal mindfulness. Moreover, in this differing from itself, it also pluralizes itself, multiplies itself. And this is the strange power of the self: it is a one that originatively produces itself as a multiplicity; it is a unity that cannot be inertly retracted into self, but *is* in its self-production as a multiplicity of itself. The self pluralizes itself in its activities, its doings, and in principle we find it hard to say which of these doings is simply the self. All are and none is. The self is itself and nothing but itself in all these acts; but none of these doings are itself, none exhaust its originative power and promise, hence none of them are it.[13]

Put otherwise again: the self as metaphor is the imaginative concretion of this strange "unity" of original power that is also more than a unity, since it exceeds itself in the determinate productions of itself as deed and act. This "unity" is a self-transcending original: an original for itself, a going beyond and out of itself towards what is other; an original of itself to the extent that its doing of itself also makes it to be the kind of being that it is; an original for itself again in taking to itself its *exitus* into otherness and its gaining of itself, its gaining on itself, in its own self-exteriorization.[14]

This is already very complex, but it is not the end of the matter. For there is a deeper equivocality calling for further minding. This is what I mean. The self-transcending of desire differentiates and pluralizes the self. But this self-transcendence reveals in us an *infinite restlessness*. This restlessness is so ambiguous that we often are tempted to think that desire's self-transcending is, in the end, a restlessness *for itself*. In this light, and to overcome its lack, the self may take *the multiplication of itself* as simply the process by which it fulfills itself. Then we take ourselves to be in search primarily for *ourselves as other*. We seek to find ourselves by multiplying ourselves without end. The infinite restlessness then proceeds from this self to that self without end, and each self is a self-formation of the energy of the original self. But the very

---

13. The phenomenon of "multiple personalities" might be seen as an expression of "self-multiplying" in which the many are not integrated in a one. But all selves are plurivocal: there are many voices in the one voice; there are the voices of the others in the voice of the I; this communivocity of the unity of the self is most evident with the metaxological, agapeic self. All speaking is a pluralization, doubling of the self. Even to talk to oneself in soliloquy or monologue, one has to be two—speaker and listener. Monologue is hence dialogue with the self as other. Plurivocity is unavoidable.

14. I speak of original selfhood as a metaphysical metaphor in *Desire, Dialectic and Otherness*, chapter 2.

process of going from self-formation to self-formation without end is now seen as the whole point of transcending.

This is equivocal in an entirely questionable manner, in that while everything is here self, in another sense nothing is here self. For the self does not in the end come to itself at all. It scatters itself abroad on a multiplicity of possibilities, all of which are itself, and yet none of which are genuinely itself. In search of its own self as other, it slides around the shock to self of the real other, and thence also does not come to itself as other out of this shock of the other. For at the best the real other solicits a recoil back on itself of the self in flight, there to take stock of itself.

Every self is multiple, so in some degree equivocal. But some multiplications of self are games of distraction from self in which the excitement of new energy diverts us from that radical taking stock of ourselves—where we are, where we have come from, who we are, where we are going. This taking stock is necessary to the genuinely plurivocal self. Self-transcendence, when equivocal in the above manner, can be in flight from self, and not towards the other either. We dissipate the original energy of our being because we cannot face the selves that we are in promise. We need to remember who we are in our self-transcendence. What this means is that *memory* is needed to balance desire and imagination, and to ballast the quest of self-transcendence. Memory must mediate the metaphors of the equivocal self.

It will be helpful if we step back a second, and see in outline the unfolding so far. Thus, a complex process of self-differentiation comes into play in the aesthetic self. Desire erupts, but its roots are in the equivocities of the originating aesthetic matrix of flesh. Desire becomes more articulate, comes to know and mediate the difference of inner and outer. Imagination emerges in desire's self-transcendence in that it puts the self before itself as other. The original power of imagination comes from depths beyond conscious control. And yet imagination allows us to gain some possession of that depth of inner otherness also. I imagine myself as other and can then perhaps try to become and be that self as other; perhaps this is a better selving that may be closer to what I am in the abyss of inner otherness. At the same time, imagination enters the middle between the self and the outside other, and makes space for a crucial *reversal* in the vector of transcendence: in imagining the innerness of the other, I imaginatively place myself in the other, become the other, and hence begin also to see self from the view of the outside other; I replace myself with the other; hence there begins the process of self-transcendence, which is also the transcendence of self.

Nor is self-transcendence a pure self-differentiation. Transcending thrusts one forward, and in going forward, one lives but one is also lived. The I is not an infinite succession of different I's, without end until the end of death. The elemental self-presence at the primal level also becomes more articulated. Desire and imagination mediate that elemental nonobjective self-awareness in its very passage of transcending. But memory is *absolutely crucial* for this mediation to be effected. What kind of memory is this? My suggestion is that memory here is not primarily the retention of traces from the past; rather it is the perduring of the elemental self-awareness in the passage of transcending or becoming. The transcendence is a *self*-becoming precisely because the center of that self-becoming remembers itself. It nonobjectively gathers itself to itself in the process of its own self-diversification. In other words, memory is not at first the retention of objective information, but the inescapability of the self-mediating center that cannot disown its own selfhood. Memory is the inescapable return of the self to itself in a passage of becoming. This is a nonobjective memory.

Of course, there are theories claiming that selfhood is "constructed" of memories: without the aggregation of memories into a "bundle" or association there would be no self-identity.[15] Memory is obviously crucial, I agree. But this view puts the cart before the horse. We must distinguish a more original, nonobjective memory from a derived memory of such and such subsequent happenings. These cited theories refer to this second sense of memory; but this is already a determination of the I, in this primal, nonobjective sense. If I did not have this primal sense, I could not remember my memories as *my* memories, and hence could never be "constituted" by the "bundle" said to be my identity. The nonobjective, idiotic mineness is elemental. It is from the origin a nonobjective relation to itself, hence memory of itself, return to itself; it is itself as gathered to itself apart from, indeed prior to, all self-dispersal. Memory, as normally understood, is really a more determinate specification of this elemental memory of self. Thus, for instance a man who is amnesiac has lost his hold of these determinate specifications, but does not lose the primal memory, return to himself. Hence there is the possibility that the determinate memory will be jogged again and return to the self as the primal self-relation. Then the nonobjective I is reconnected with a set of its own determinate specifications that have temporarily escaped beyond its self-conscious possession.

We must say that memory, both in the primal and the specified senses, is indispensable in staking out the *space of innerness*. Memory in the determinate sense is ingredient in a self-differentiation that is also a development of

---

15. The theory has its origins in classical empiricism and associationist psychology. David Parfit offers a recent version of the "bundle" theory: there is no individual person, only a grammatical construct, a conventional name given to a bundle of elements. Parfit quotes the Buddha with respect to the doctrine of No-self, but he is much more a Humean with a twentieth-century education. His "bundles" rebaptize Hume's association of impressions into congeries. There is no intrinsic unity. The theory cannot explain the *conatus* of self-insistence, nor the intimacy of mineness, nor the active nature of self of which Hegel's self-relating negativity and Sartre's nothingness give a far better understanding. A view closer to the Buddhist No-self is to be found in the notion of agapeic selving that I develop below.

interiority. The self-relation of the I here gains an enormous expanse of self-transcendence. But self-transcendence is not just into the externality of the material world; it has an *intensive* directionality that opens up interiority as a world unto itself. Memory opens up the self in its inner otherness as all but an inexhaustible abyss. There is no end to the abyss of memory. The press of the world that passes into inwardness, and the slumbering latency of the self's original power, mingle in the abyss of memory, and there is no plumbing this bottomless well, in both its illuminated spaces and its darknesses.

Memory is thus paradoxical: it is indispensable for articulate self-differentiation and self-possession, and yet it is never entirely in our self-possession at all, and what is "in" it can never be completely articulated. It ever recedes beyond our power to repossess it, and yet without it we could never possess ourselves, even in the qualified sense. Memory again is a threshold mediation: between the self-mediated I in its provisional self-possession, and the otherness of selfhood that seems to recede into the original otherness of being in innerness itself—this original otherness that we do not know whether to call self or something other. Memory is a between in innerness itself; it is, we might say, an inner threshold of transcendence. That is perhaps why in antiquity it was called the mother of the Muses. The Muses are the generators of all our creative, originative work. Memory, so to say, mothers these mothers. It is the threshold mediator between our original power and the original power of the agapeic origin—the mother/father of all.

Erotic Selving and Dialectic

The aesthetic self can equivocally diversify itself, but if that were all, in the end there would be no self.[16] The self is desirous being precisely in light of its orientation to an end. Thus imagination may put before the self-in-process an image of itself as other, as more fully realized and true to itself. Imagination may put before one the truth of the self, as a goal to be realized; desire moves the process by which one catches up to oneself in a more satisfying realization of one's own original promise. Desire and imagination thus testify to both one's infinite restlessness and one's orientation to some immanent wholeness. These two sides—namely, our infinite restlessness and orientation to wholeness—are unavoidable.

Yet they seem also to be in unavoidable tension: every whole seems broken up by the renewal of the infinite restlessness; just as the infinite restlessness,

---

16. Consider Socrates' criticism of actors/artists in the *Republic*. The actor produces many other identities in the different roles he plays, hence risks the loss of one, univocal self in all this role-playing. But, of course, this self-multiplication is part of what it means to be a self. Without it one could not have what Socrates wants—namely, justice as good care for the good of the other.

by itself, seems to lead to nothing, and so to rob one of any full, realized concretion of oneself. Here I suggest the self's *internal opposition* takes us beyond univocity and equivocity. The tension of self-opposition, between the infinite restlessness of self-surpassing (equivocity) and the desire to be at one with oneself (univocity), provides the basis for a further articulation of self as dialectical and erotic.

Memory again is crucial. In a passage of self-transcending the self does not simply scatter itself into an unrelated multiplicity. Even the self in flight and in hyperactive distraction still retains the nonobjective memory of itself, though all its diversions are intended to smother this primal memory of itself, quell the call of the idiotic self and what would well up there, were it let. Memory, as developed remembrance, comes later, but it is the fuller return of the self to itself in this very passage of restless transcending. While this returning is always there as a possibility, it is made explicit when the self realizes itself as the power to recollect itself in a process of self-becoming.

Desire, imagination, memory are concretions of the original energy of innerness, idiocy, but they mediate *mindfulness*, and not least in relation to the ideal, whether this be the erotic or agapeic self. What is good about the erotic self is that the I has to decide for itself, decide itself: the will to be oneself is a being true to oneself; and this a form of mindful truthfulness. This is necessary for ethical self-perfecting where we try to become good. So, for instance, commitment is not a *sheer* willing, it is a *mindful* willing. The existential self is an I by more than sheer protestation against the universal or reason. We especially find an existential mindfulness in the erotic will to be oneself in being true to oneself. The idiocy of the existential I is a constitutive innerness, also a hiddenness, that cannot be completely objectified or functionalized.

Here is another way to express the relation of desire, imagination, and memory. Desire reveals an upsurgence of difference in self; imagination articulates the inner spontaneity of self; memory keeps and gathers the harvest. All three, but especially memory, mediate the mindfulness of the self. Hence *memoria* is related to *mens*. Desire, as imaginatively mediated through mindful memory, is transformed from appetitive nisus into the "I will, I can" of erotic selfhood, and this when the self is reminded of itself, or reminds itself of itself. By contrast, when the other is minded, desire is transformed by memory into the "I am willing" of agapeic selving, as we shall see. Desire and imagination are mindfully recollected, beyond playing with possibility, and beyond equivocating about responsibility, indeed beyond the self-mediation of recollection. They are gathered into good will and trust in the other which are available for expenditure in an abandon on self-transcending. Mindfulness is pervasive throughout the self-transformation, and most clearly so in the transition from erotic to agapeic selving, but it is at work from the start, albeit inchoately, in the idiotic self, and the aesthetic self.

We may now be more explicit with reference to a process of self-becoming by distinguishing the following related moments. First, there is a *primal integrity* to the self that is preobjective. Second, the *dynamism of self-transcendence* specifies the promise of this original self. The risk run here is always that of self-distraction, or self-loss, or self-betrayal, or self-deformation; though again the self that loses itself is still the primal integrity for itself; it has, however, betrayed the promise of its own originality. Third, there is a subsequent, *achieved integrity* of selfhood wherein the self tries to realize the full promise of its own originative being. This "second integrity" is impossible without memory as recollective. In the passage of self-becoming, the self makes repeated reference to the integrity it is, and integrates its primal integrity in the achieved self it is bringing into being through the process of restless self-transcendence. This second achieved self, even in the infinite restlessness of self-transcending, may concretize something of the promise of human wholeness. The promise of human wholeness is realized in this complex interplay between the infinite restlessness of self-transcendence and the creative restoration in that restlessness of the achieved, articulate integrity.

There is another important dimension to all this. That is, the bottomless abyss of memory opens into the depth of self as a being of infinite worth. It is inexhaustible in itself, and its value cannot be finitely determined. This infinity in the self is also the source of its infinite restlessness, because no finite endeavor can catch up with, or match, or be finally adequate to the source of the infinite worth, and the promise of being at work there. Every finite endeavor, every determinate expression of desire and imagination, falls short of what wells up from this abyss. And yet this inexhaustibility is the reason why we can speak of the human being as an end in itself.

We may say that the human being is an integrity for itself that is priceless, because it is infinitely prized; it is already whole unto itself in a deep ontological sense, regardless of the determinate finite endeavors it will subsequently undertake to realize its promise. Its being an end unto itself means that it is incomparable. Again we have to recognize the irreplaceable singularity of selfhood. This singularity fits no objective mode of particularity that is the instance of a genus or the exemplification of an abstract universal. The singular as *idios* is beyond such categories as an incomparable integrity for itself, a center of being that in its integrity is inexhaustible. It is this sense of idiotic integrity, incomparable singularity, that is felt by the primal, elemental I.

Desire, imagination, memory can thus be seen as modes of the self-mediation of the I that gives expression to the dialectic of its own being. The dialectic is between primal integrity, infinite restlessness in self-transcending, and achieved integrity that realizes some of the promise of the inner infinity. However, I want to obviate any impression that the process is one merely within innerness itself. This is not so. The self adventures in the universal impermanence, and is put to the test of the otherness of creation. Its self-transcendence puts it outside of itself in the world, relative to whose otherness it seeks to keep a hold on itself, not distract itself even as it opens out to the other. The dialectical self is a self of activity: it acts in the world. The common dualism between the inner and outer does not hold up; we are beyond the usual subject-object distinction, not because the distinction collapses, but because the adventure of the self is *between* innerness and outerness.[17] In one sense, it is always in this between, now tilting towards the inner, now towards what is other and outer. The self as activity goes beyond the felt, aesthetic I, bathed in the equivocities of being. The self is not just the fleshed "I am," but the more developed self-insistence of the "I can" or "I will."

The self is dialectically self-mediating precisely because it actively expresses itself relative to what is other to itself. It externalizes itself into the between; it becomes itself in what it does outside of its own innerness. It goes towards the other in the between, the better to be and become itself in tension with the other that also comes to be in the between from its own integrity. Inevitably, there is tension between the plurality of particular participants in the between. By acting into the between, the self, however, is the anticipation, and sometimes confidence, that its own self, and sense of self, will be confirmed there.

There are many expression of this dialectically self-mediating I. The very idea of *acting* itself has strong dialectical connotations. To act is to place oneself in a public space, but to place oneself there as a center of agency that expresses the expectation that the world can be brought into some closer

---

17. Because there is mindfulness, the processes of mediation, self-mediation, and self-consciousness are related. This is why the idealists spoke of self as "subject-object." It is not confined to one side of the duality. I do not think we have to put it as Hegel does, when he says the self "overreaches" the other. In itself the self is "subject-object" in self-consciousness. It reaches to the other outside, but does not overreach. This will come out more fully below. But this self-mediation is not merely contemplative; there is a praxis, a self-positing as an active self-objectification—self-externalizing is a doing and acting of the self. I believe the claim to "overreach" the other is inseparable from the idealistic deification of "thought thinking itself." But this attenuates the other that thought also thinks without reducing it to itself. The hyphen in self-reflection, self-consciousness, self-thinking points to an other, but an other higher than thought thinking itself. (See my remarks on Plotinus with respect to the origin.) There is an opening in the self. What of the hyphen, the gap, middle? What grounds this gap? Is it just the self? The other of self? The self in its otherness? Or what is radically other to self? The view I suggest is that this opening is originally due to the other beyond the self's own otherness; yet the self in its own inner otherness can become a co-creator of this opening; though again the power to co-create is itself originally given by the more original other. This will make more sense relative to agapeic selving.

conformity with the desires of agents. The process of conforming may involve opposition, but the power of agency acts as a will to overcome opposition, whether by guile, by force, by threats, or by transformation.

I will mention two other examples: *work* and *art*. In work the self transcends itself towards the world of otherness, be it nature or the human community; work is the expression of power, but the power is such as to transform the otherness into a production that putatively expresses the worker's power and desire. The worker is externalized in his production, and at least in nonalienated labor, he comes to recognize himself and mediate with himself in his producing of what is other. The opposition between the self and the other is mitigated in the way the working self recognizes itself again in the production as other. The end result is not simply the production, but the self-mediation of the worker in which the sense of self is confirmed, consolidated. The worker is producing himself in producing his works. The "I can" may be tentative at the start, but it becomes an "I will" that consolidates the "I can" in the acquisition of the requisite productive skills. If successfully employed, they lead to a new active "I am." The sense of self-worth articulates itself at a further level of power in this second "I am."

The example of art is not unrelated to this. Here the material worked on can clearly be selfhood itself, as objectified in the sensuous production that is the artwork. The artist returns into himself to reactivate the sources of originality within. The artist goes into himself to go outside of himself and to concretize the indeterminate original power that comes to expression in the creative will. The artist goes outside of himself and works on the otherness of the sensuous medium, which work provides the discipline, not only of the art, but of the artist in the struggle, not only with the material, but also with what is amorphous in himself. There is tension and opposition within the creative self; there is tension and opposition between the creator and the material on which the artist works; there is struggle between the creative self and the work that is both realizing human power and yet is resistant to that power. But in the passage through this self-opposition, this opposition with otherness, inner and outer, this opposition with the recalcitrant work, the artist comes to himself, in coming to be at home with the work. The work may come to concretize a certain inexhaustible richness in which the artist sees an image of the realized promise of human wholeness.

Nor is the process ever finished in a static sense. The restlessness of infinite desire briefly finds a peace in the wholeness of the great work, but the peace is itself the peace of mindfulness, not sleep. It is an energization of selfhood that refreshes it rather than lets it slumber, an energization so full that the self may feel it as a painful loss of ultimacy when it again returns to the relative sleepwalking of its more quotidian occupations. The excess of ultimacy surges up in the inner otherness of the self when it has retreated into its intimate sources of creation. We call that surge inspiration. The inspiration is not merely inward, for it calls for a concretization and external anchoring in a work that is there in the world. Artists are themselves, there in the world, when they work on their work; but the great work is the memory of the flash of ultimacy, the excess of the origin that is never exhausted in any determinate thing, or property, or account, or concept. This flash of ultimacy leaves its trace in the strange inexhaustiblility of a great work. Artists are the servants of this flash; though in being the midwives of its worldly concretion, they also mediate with the trace of ultimacy that surges forth into expression in their own inspired, creative power. The former calls for metaxological intermediation, the latter allows the side of dialectical self-mediation.

Moreover, there is a wider sense of art than art. What I mean is that, in any process of self-formation, there is a *living art of selving* whereby we both become ourselves, see ourselves as other, and see the other as other to ourselves. Ultimately this art of selving, like all art, is metaxological, and creativity is agapeic, not just erotic. But no work need be produced, whether artistic or not, for this process of dialectical self-mediation to be operative, and for the acting self to come to itself in more articulate shape in its self-externalization in the between and adventure with otherness. The self is a *doing of itself* that is always in *interchange* with what is other. In this interchange it is offered the possibility of coming to itself in a more articulate form than it could have, were it locked within a self-communing interiority. Once again there is no fixed determinate boundary that would wall off interiority and exteriority from each other; there is interchange in the between, and incessant passage to and fro. To act, to do anything, is to be in this between of incessant passage. The human self, nevertheless, can mediate with itself in this passage, and do so in a self-willed and self-knowing way.

Furthermore, our doings in the between go to determine our more established character. As self-mediation becomes habitual, we *do ourselves* in certain characteristic ways, which inevitably congeal, or solidify, into a well-established, determinate person. The habitual character is the second self, the second nature, what above I called the achieved integrity—though sometimes that second integrity is lacking in genuine integrity. I am speaking of the determination of the indeterminate promise of selfhood that this I becomes over a lifetime. Normally we think of this as *the* self, but this is very incomplete.

There is always more, there is always the exigence of more, the infinite restlessness of transcendence that spills over every determinate character we consolidate. There is nothing absolutely set in concrete here. We easily forget the original fluidity of selving as a dynamic transcending. The creative self, like the artist, is one who can dip down into the original indeterminacy. Of course, the risk is of the renewal of formlessness in the overdetermination of the primal elemental I. And yet out of that return to formlessness a new form may creatively come to be. Because of this, one can never say that a human being is finished; there is always promise. Where there is no such promise, one is on the other side of the last judgment, either in hell or heaven. On this side, even the most genuine self-creation is always short of absolute self-perfection, which is not to deny that great humans do touch perfection, or perhaps are touched by it and carry away its glow, wounded by its radiance. We might say that the agapeic self also risks a formlessness—it becomes nothing to let the other be—it may ask nothing for itself. I will come to this below, but here I am concerned more with the connection of erotic selving with dialectical self-mediation. The self forms *itself* in its adventure in the between and towards the otherness. The basis of this is in its capability to other itself; it can produce itself externally, and this externality is itself again in objectified form. We can say that the inner otherness of self produces its innerness in the otherness of externality—the deed, the work, the creation—and the external otherness offers it the mirror in which it comes to recognize itself. It re-cognizes itself in that it remembers its own integrity in the otherness; it re-cognizes itself because it already elementally cognizes itself in the immediacy of the idiotic/aesthetic I. Thus in its external productions it mediates the equivocities of its own innerness, its imaginations, its desires, its fears, hopes; it gains a picture of itself in its productions, gains, so to say, a mediated metaphor of itself, in and through which it is carried towards itself again. It images itself externally, but knows its own originality, knows itself as its own original, in the images it originates; it recurs to itself and so is relatively at home with itself in its self-externalization.

I stress that there is no absolute home given to us, or created by us in the between. There is no absolute wholeness possible for the self, if we mean unsurpassable completion. The wholeness appropriate to human selfhood is between indefinite incompleteness and such total closure. We are between a being-at-home with ourselves and a not being-at-home with ourselves. We are *both* at once, and the *interplay* between them. And there is never a closed resolution that completes the picture in favor of one side or the other. We remain open wholes. The quest for wholeness remains open, for the restless excess of self-transcendence will always return to make us sleepless again.

Why do I speak here of erotic selving? The following remarks will try to answer this, as well as show the need to go beyond erotic to agapeic selving.

The excess of the self, spoken of above, is the source of its infinite restlessness. A pure whole is never restless with itself; it is perfect and needs nothing; or it is perfectly at home with itself. Not so the human self as original. As an open whole, the excess of its original energy is a share of the pluperfection of the true origin; its excess even in the experience of desire as lack is ultimately a giving of the original energy of being, it is a generous overflow of this good. In addition, its need of the other, which it lacks, is in tension with the original giving of its being as affirmatively generous towards the other. This means, however, that the self-insistence that comes to be in its ex-isting and in its self-differentiation can surge up as an energy that smothers memory of the community with the other, and of the origin beyond the self.

In other words, the self in the surge of self-insistence can forget this origin beyond itself as original. It can seek to turn itself as original into a self-contained and self-sufficient power, or at least will to be, try to be so. When this happens the self-insistence forgets or denies the reference of the *ex* of its own existence to the origin beyond itself. It then becomes an "I am" without a "Here I am." The "I am," as thus closed into its own original power, asserts itself in its own self-production. It tries to make its own whole by making itself the goal of its own infinite restlessness. It loves itself and nothing but itself.

Perhaps I move too fast, so let me reformulate the matter. Dialectic is related to erotic selfhood precisely because it tends to sees the beginning of self as a lack; then the lack calls for determination, indeed for self-determination; for without that further self-determination, the beginning seems to be really nothing in itself; it becomes something for itself by reaching out to what is other to itself and coming to possess that other; in possession of that other, it appropriates the other to itself; in this appropriation, it mediates the determination of its own self-appropriation; only now at the end and as the end, is the self said to be a self proper.

I do not deny that this corresponds to an essential possibility of selfhood in the between, to the extent that self-mediation is privileged. Why do I call the result *erotic selving?* Because the erotic self is driven to assert itself in response to its own initial lack; it asserts itself by entering into interplay with what its other to itself; but the other is beloved, precisely because the other serves to overcome the lack with the initial self; hence the beloved is to be possessed to enable *self-possession*. In the interplay between self and other, self is finally given the dominant position.

I repeat: I do not deny something corresponding to this in the self-becoming of the human. For we are insufficient to ourselves and become ourselves in interplay with the other; and we do appropriate the other to ourselves; the love of the other returns to the self, and the other is very often, perhaps most often, sought for this return to the self; we possess ourselves in possessing what is other to ourselves. The self-transcending restlessness of desire here seeks wholeness but it subordinates the other to the goal of its own immanent self-satisfaction. The erotic self finally tries to appropriate the other to itself and make it serve the riches of its own self-appropriation. I think that this is incomplete, and if the completion is claimed here, it produces a deformation or deviation of the dynamism of self-transcendence. The erotic self may be glorious, yet it is always the hazard of a perilous spiritual hubris. It risks puffing itself up on the original surge of self-transcendence, begetting an apotheosis of the for-self, as if it were the absolute.

Not accidentally, images of mastery, whether self-mastery or mastery of the other, are pervasive here. For instance, I consider Socrates' account (in the *Symposium*) to be ambiguously erotic: it is erotic in the classic sense, in speaking of a lack seeking its satisfaction in its possession of the object that it initially needs; it is ambiguously erotic in that the otherness of the Good sought, at the end of the process of self-development, actually *reverses* the directionality of transcendence: the final revelation *comes* to the erotic self, comes from the other, not the self itself. By contrast, I see Hegel's concept of the self, indeed of the absolute and all being, as essentially erotic: the beginning in itself is an empty lack, an indefiniteness that has to be determined in order to be itself; it is itself by becoming itself, by determining its initial indefiniteness; it relates to itself in its self-determination, and returns to itself always having enriched its own internal differentiation by its passage into and through otherness; there is no irreducible other in the end, only the self in its own otherness. We love the other, because in the beloved other we recognize ourselves again, because all there is to recognize is self, and nothing but self, self in itself, self in its own otherness.[18]

Thus what I am calling erotic selving can be related to what Hegel calls self-determining negativity. This is an ancestor of Sartre's self as nothingness: desire is an insatiable lack that wants to devour omnivorously what is other to itself; it even wants to devour the divine and in the process become God. The omnivorous eros sees everything other as a threat to the freedom of the for-self to assert itself in an untrammeled way. Both Hegel and Sartre are right relative to desire, though only partially so. Desire does reveal the self as a no-thing, if by thing we mean an identity inertly full with itself. The latter cannot be what the integrity of self means. Nevertheless, Sartre's assertion of the self as nothingness risks perverting the affirmative excess that is the more original manifestation of the infinitely restless power of self-transcendence. Then the self as lack determines its erotic fulfillment in its opposition to all others who are inherently threatening to its own freedom for itself. It says: either dominate or be dominated. This is cruder than Hegel, for it is the master/slave dialectic turned into the final story of the self in relation to the other. The self wills that there be finally nothing that is not beyond possession, everything will be finally for-itself, only then will the insatiable void of the primal lack be overcome. The desideratum is an illusion because it is based on a mistaken idea of self, a mistaken idea of the other, a mistaken idea of God, of being, of creation, of relatedness. The latter is reduced to the degraded erotic interaction of the sadist and the masochist. This is the master/ slave relation enacted in the flesh of a self that must conquer, and yet who is nothing apart from an other that must be conquered. The absolutization of the erotic self, as hubristically puffing up its own for-self, falls into this degradation of selfhood and otherness, unless it regain both itself and the other in relation to the generous excess of the original transcendence.

---

18. On eros in the *Symposium*, and in relation to Hegel, see *Beyond Hegel and Dialectic*, chapter 6.

What honest philosopher would deny the sly tenacity of human self-insistence, not to mention our mendacity and malice? But that is not the present point. The horrors we can concoct, and in the name of freedom and autonomy, are only too evident. The power to negate is clear with erotic selving. We are this power, and the power to try and assert ourselves in the negation of the other. Deformation takes form, one might say, with the smothering of the plenitude of excess, which is the origin prior to the lack of the erotic self. Consider even Socrates' account of the lack: eros has parentage in divine festivity, divine drunkenness, divine agape, not just in *penia*, poverty.[19] In absolutizing the power to negate, we disregard, even trample on, the prior source.

Perhaps Nietzsche is the modern thinker who most lived these equivocities of erotic selving. The Nietzschean self as asserting itself as will to power, the overcoming of self by itself, the overcoming of its own past, the past of humanity in itself, and its own creative work—all these call to mind the erotic self, concretized in more incarnate form than Hegel's dialectical self. Everything Nietzsche says, however, is ambiguous, in that the will to domination is tempered by the intimation that it is really an original plenitude or excess of energy that forms itself in the creative self. Even here Nietzsche is equivocal, and fails to get beyond erotic selving. For even the overflow of abundance is understood by Nietzsche as the will to power willing *itself*—that is, overflowing for purposes of its own *self-glorification*. The will to power of the "I will" will have to undergo a severe education to do justice to the prior plenitude, and Nietzsche does not himself bring its significance properly into the light of day.[20] The self-insistence of the *conatus essendi* on which the erotic self is carried will have to undergo transformation. The *ex* of existing will have to be remembered to bring us back to a different understanding of the origin, one that cannot be rendered in the language of will to power. The language of will to power will have to be entirely reformed. The "I will" of the will to power will have to become the "I am willing" of the metaxological agape. The erotic self will have to become the agapeic self.[21]

---

19. Ibid., 329ff.

20. I have discussed this more fully in "Rethinking the Origin: Hegel and Nietzsche." There I also explore the surprising kinship of Hegel and Nietzsche in relation to their different versions of an erotic absolute.

21. Consider Schopenhauer's reversal from will to will-lessness, though Schopenhauer cannot fully explain what he rightly sees in the movement from the first to the second. By contrast, Freud found it impossible to conceive of anything but self-love. What else could a hermeneutics of suspicion find but the dark origin, the preobjective I as a sucking center of selfish, egotistical being? Utilitarianism is sightless of this darkness; its fixation on the calculation of self-interest blinds it to the full sweep of human self-transcending.

Let me now recapitulate what I have been saying relative to major options in the philosophical tradition. Thus the aesthetic self has some correspondence with what is called the empirical ego, except classical empiricism
completely overlooked the idiotic self, which is absolutely necessary for there
to be any experience or sense-impression at all. If there were not this primal
center of self-awareness, there would be no sense-experience as experience,
felt as mine, sensed in innerness itself. The empiricist emphasizes the senses,
rightly; but his view of the ego is a descendent of the Cartesian dualism of
inner and outer, hence it has a deracinated understanding of sensuousness.
Its sense impressions are really abstractions from the flow of sensuous
thereness wherein the aesthetic self, the incarnate I, is first rooted. This is
another deficiency following its blindness to the idiotic I. The classical empirical ego inevitably deconstructs itself, in the Humean respect of ending in
skepticism: for appearances to the self that is no self must be merely equivocal appearances. We also get the equivocal self that is hard to distinguish
from a hall of mirrors or a labyrinth. And though classical empiricism recon-
structs the self from congeries of sense impressions, its equivocal use of
memory (equivocal between primal self-recurring and subsequent remembrance), really shows the empiricist as oblivious to the consequences of the
fact that one's constructed self is a complete fabrication and nothing else.

A dialectical understanding of self develops in response to such
equivocities. We see a historical parallel in the response of transcendental
philosophy to empiricist skepticism. Kant rightly saw the equivocity of empiricism as actually being parasitical on a more original, a priori notion of
self. Called the transcendental ego by Kant, it is the condition of the possibility of all ordered experience, and of experience as that of a unitary I. Kant
himself counterposes a formal universal ego to the deconstructed fragments
and associations of empiricism; the universal ego is the formal capacity to
gather the multiplicity, the manifold into an ordered unity. The *transcendental equivocity* here is that this gathering cannot be merely formal. It has to be
an active forming. The transcendental ego must be more than a universal
logical form of experience, it must be an active ego. Kant himself equivocates
between those two poles, but he has momentously placed the primary focus
on the active self as mediating the significance of the between, as the place of
the interplay of self and other.

Idealism runs with this momentous insight, completes it in Hegel, but
also undoes it in its completion. For the dialectical self of idealism brings out
the questionable dominance of self-mediation in this entire process. The dialectical self is essentially an erotic self, the consequences of which will be
seen by Hegel's successors who deconstruct the claim to pure autonomy by
the active idealist subject. Pure reason or Hegelian *Geist* becomes the erotic
self of Nietzsche's will to power. But the erotic self that has lost its proper
relativity to the other beyond self-mediation inevitably degrades eros itself—
voilà Sartre!

But the deconstruction of idealism also deconstructs the erotic self and we get a further twist in the screw of skepticism: a new equivocity, a new hall of mirrors in which the self no longer feels its dignity. The mirror of the self now mocks it; its pretensions to absoluteness are illusory, but there is nothing else, no absolute at all; the labyrinth is not a dark tunnel to the center where the devouring Minotaur of madness or absurdity awaits the shattered ego. The self is nothing again, an absurd nothingness, a desolate void that is suspicious about its own creative claims, suspicious of all being, itself included. Its nothingness should return it to its primal, elemental for-itself, the dark night of its own meonic contraction where it might again perhaps regain contact with its own inner other and the otherness of the origin. We should be returned to the dark night of sleepless perplexity, where mindfulness might perhaps be visited by metaphysical astonishment. But so long as selving is conceived of exclusively in these erotic terms, this will not happen. We fortify our condemnation to the prison house of the vile self. To be released from the prison house the self has to renew its own inner otherness and its bond with the origin, and become an agapeic self. And if at all some Minotaur awaits, alas who now is the Minotaur but only ourselves?

Let us absolutize ourselves. Very well; we end by devouring ourselves. Let us love ourselves. Very well; we end by hating ourselves, scourging ourselves, and with a ferocity that is inexplicable on erotic terms. There is more. Otherwise we are lost.

Agapeic Selving and the Metaxological

Mindfulness involves our return to self in the pluralization of being that constitutes the forward living of our self-becoming. A transcending is inherently a self-becoming, when it is mindful of itself in its passage from itself towards what is beyond, and towards itself as beyond itself. Since our dialectical self-mediation cannot be closed, the eros of selfhood can neither possess the other entirely, nor take complete possession of itself. That there is *always more* is evident in desire's infinite restlessness, and in imagination's power to creatively envisage a way of being that more completely answers the promise of self. This envisagement may agitate us to further self-transcending, even while putting before us an ideal goal towards which we try to reach. The infinite restlessness points us back to the otherness of the indeterminate power of being that finds its mindful upsurgence in the self. And while this indeterminacy may be expressed as lack, it cannot be understood entirely as lack. The meaning of this must now be explored relative to what I call agapeic selving.

I speak here of the agapeic self for a number of reasons. First self can be mindful of itself as shaping its own self-becoming from a well of *affirmative excess* that it cannot completely master in its own self-mediation. Even if it mediates with itself, the excess that wells up in it is never exhausted by any determinate formation of self, any definite self-mediation. Moreover, one is not simply lacking a selfhood that one must seek by the outward thrust of self-transcendence. Rather, this outward thrust is the centrifugal fling of the original plenitude, which is itself in a more elemental way than the lack we also experience. The agapeic self is an overdetermined source of origination; it is not merely indefinite possibility; its power is the very definite power of generosity, the excess of original being, which is also the expression of the primal freedom of the self.

We might speak of creativity as the generosity of being, the free power to give itself to what is other to itself. If the agapeic self is self-transcending, this self-transcendence is a giving of being, its own being, to the other, and for the other. There is no insistence on a return to self. The self goes forth from itself, like Abraham at the command of God, not knowing where the wandering or exile will end up, and not asking where, and not asking for a return to the first home in the end. It goes beyond itself in giving itself; and though there may be a return to the self, this is not the point of the first giving. The giving is not for the self; the giving is for the other; and though it may be the case that the other returns the generosity, that return is not asked or sought; if it never comes, the agapeic self would still give beyond itself.

The closure that tempts the erotic self is perforated. Possession of the other, self-possession, are not the point. Mindfulness here is doubly stressed. With erotic selving, mindfulness as recollective returns the self to itself in self-mediation. This is the thinking that is at home with itself in thinking what is other. This selfhood is erected into a god in the traditional apotheosis of self-thinking thought. The latter is the erotic self that is thought to transcend eros in complete self-possession. But the result is a death of originality; for the source of creativity cannot be a bounded whole; it must be an excess of infinite energy that transcends every bounded whole.

Agapeic selving puts us in mind of this. The self is dispossessed of any self-sufficient monadism, and its self-divestment transforms the energy of being into a new selving that is not intent on possession of the other. The self does not mindfully return to itself simply, but becomes mindful of the other in a manner that pressures a breach in the circle of self-mediation. Mindfulness becomes a thinking of what is other to thought; and though this is a thinking, at the same time it is a release from thinking, a release of thinking from itself towards what is other to thought and that can never be reduced to a thought—namely, the irreducible being there of the other. This is the true self-transcendence of thinking, of mindfulness itself become agapeic. This transcending is the image in human being of the being of the absolute original.

We might say that in erotic self-transcending, the self is more than the transcendence, while in agapeic self-transcending, the transcendence is more than the self. In other words, the agapeic self is not self-mediating but intermediating between self and what is other. It intermediates because its own plenitude is brought to bear on the between, in a willingness to let the promise of plenitude in the other come to manifestation in the between and out of its own resources. Though one brings oneself to the between, one does not impose on it with a will to power that would stamp the between in the image of oneself. The plenitude, so to say, carves out a hollowness in itself, a hollow that is really the shaping of the hospitable space of freedom in which the other is free to be and become itself. The agapeic self is then doubly stressed in the between: between the excess of its own original power, and the willingness to suspend that power in the interests of the other; between its own being there, and its willingness not to be there in a manner that retards the coming to the between of the other. It puts itself there, but in the manner of putting itself aside. It is there as power, but as power there is consent to powerlessness.

Nothing can be forced, for then the freedom that is the gift of being would be deformed. If nothing is to be forced, nothing can be guaranteed. One gives oneself to the between with hope but no insistent expectation, with longing but with no demands, with patience but no imperiousness, with full presence but in waiting for the presence of the other, and hence in the chiaroscuro of enduring and absence.

The agapeic self turns aside the erotic temptation to reduce the plurivocal stress of transcendence to a singular self-mediation claiming total power of being. Its desire, imagination, memory, mindfulness open up in an intermediated way, between the self as power of transcendence and the other as itself in the integrity of its own transcendence. We might suggest that the metaxological space between self and other is a middle between infinitudes. As well as the self's inward infinitude, there is recognized the infinitude of the other. This other infinitude can be the infinite succession of external becoming, the universal impermanence; it can be the self-mediating infinitude of an other self; it can be the actual infinitude of the absolute origin. The agapeic self is not defined by a dialectic between *its own* finitude and infinity. In itself in knows this dialectic, but it is also mindful of the metaxological intermediation between the promise of infinitude of its own being and the promise of infinitude in the other.

It should be clear that the mediation between such a plurality of infinities cannot be a self-mediation in which one subordinates the other to itself. I am not talking about quantitative infinitude, but of spiritual inexhaustibility, if only in promise, and this can never be included in another. We need a different model to that of part and whole. I am talking about "idealities"—centers of mindful being that cannot be objectified into quantifiable things that might be included in a larger whole. Ideality communicates, and may indeed try to possess the other; but the possession is always partial; absolute possession, were it even possible, is a betrayal of the freedom that constitutes the meaning of mindful ideality. Absolute possession of freedom would be the hellish ambition of Lucifer, bearer of the light. It would be the antithesis of the agapeic gift of freedom that marks the generosity of the original light, the light of the origin.

No selving can be thought outside social relations, and communities will be our theme in the next chapter. But the point is especially true of agapeic selving. The agapeic self *as self* is a singularization of communicative being. This does not mean that, in the community of being, it is devoid of deep interiority. Quite the contrary, this, its idiocy, is the basis of its desire to establish relations of solidarity and intimacy with others, and where possible to foster the social conditions that allow the release of the original energy of other selves. The agapeic self is for the other. In this respect its self-transcendence is decentered. It is decentered because its center is outside of itself in the between; this it shapes, not just for itself, but to free the other to be itself as other. But in thus being decentered, being outside of itself, it is also recentered, not in the sense of simply being for itself, but in being-at-home in its not being-at-home with itself, happy in its unhappiness with itself, happy with the other even when this means the extirpation of its own contentment.

It is recentered in the between, the between that as ideal is, so to say, a community of idiots, and no one fully knows the enigma of spiritual community that is there at work. There is no one standing outside the intermediation of the metaxological between that will dispel this enigmatic milieu for the participants who live and have their being there. This is essential to agapeic being for the other; it does not know itself fully; it does not have absolute self-knowledge that offers it a univocal certainty; it knows itself as rather the trust that the good is at work and to be fostered in the middle. I am not the good; I am the servant of the good; and that is why I must be for the other. The good asks that I be there in the mode of agapeic good will. The "Here I am" now answers the summons of the good.

So if the agapeic self gives itself over, it is not the "I will" of decisive self-assertion; it is the "I am willing" that is also willing to be nothing, even in the plenitude of its power and in the excess of its original energy. The "I am willing" is the "Here I am," now ready to be a sacrifice for the other. Sacrifice literally means to make sacred. The agapeic self seeks to sanctify the willingness that gives itself up as an offering for the good of the other. It seems to me that this is entirely at odds with any apotheosis of will to power. The agapeic self is not a self-relating negativity, but is the indeterminate willingness to give up its self-insistence for the good of the other, and even in the face of the negative. We might say the agapeic self, in its rare heroism, is a generosity of being beyond all negativity, and the negation that comes on us in death. Its generosity may even reach beyond death. In ceasing to cling to its own self-preservation, the agapeic self is beyond death. It shows a heedless love of the other that may count its own life as nothing, if this proves necessary. It is the vessel of the outpouring of a great affirmation of being, an original amen to being, even in the face of the terrible, of suffering, of ugliness, of mourning, of loss. The agapeic self lives the agape of being; it lives being as a feast, being as a festive celebration. This festive celebration is the finite echo of the primal festivity in the creation of being by the origin, the primal yes, the unsurpassable pluperfect "It is very good."[22]

I speak of something that is rare among us. Perhaps only God is truly agapeic. And yet it is at work among us, in us. So let me try to situate agapeic selving relative to idiotic, aesthetic, and erotic selving.

First, the agapeic self might be said to realize the promise of the idiotic self. For it is mindful of the abyss of inwardness that constitutes the singularity of self. It knows this abyss as the inexhaustible transcendence of self; it knows this as the infinite worth of the singular; it knows the promise of this infinity and its free release into living for the other. The idiotic self opens inwardly into a bottomless deep, and this is a creative excess that is the gift of being by the absolute original; this wells up as an infinite demand made upon the idiotic self in its deepest inwardness. The idiotic self is prior to self-objectification, but now the agapeic self is mindful that an infinite demand by the original other is at work in the elemental self that is itself, here and yet nowhere, a thing and yet nothing.

The plenitude and the demand of transcendence are the calls to responsibility at work even before the elemental self has objectified itself or been objectified into a determinate self. The infinite excess of the origin is at work prior to the lack felt in desire, as the call of transcendence that does not use the language of lack, except in the ambiguous sense of asking the self to be nothing, if necessary, to let the good of the other come to be freely. But such "being nothing" is really highest power of being. The elementally desiring self does not know it when it experiences lack, but this infinitude of the origin is at work more intimately than the intimacy of its own primal idiocy.

Second, the agapeic self is the realization of the promise of aesthetic selving. As we saw, there is an affirmation at work in the sensuous self, in the flesh of incarnation itself. The aesthetic "I am" is as much an affirmation of being *simpliciter*, in the beauty of its sensuous worth, as of the self that enjoys the sensuous being there of things. The "I am" that exults in its incarnation is exulting in the elemental joy of being in its otherness, that we breathe in and want to breathe in, that we exhale and would that our whole being

---

22. On being as festive, see *Philosophy and its Others*, 298ff. We might also think of thanks. One is given something, but it is received as a genuine gift only in being hospitably welcomed. And it is not the thing or the possession that touches one in the gift, but the generous freedom of the other that has made itself available without care for itself. Real thanks has nothing to do with abjectness before another who has one in debt. Real thanks is simple, elemental appreciation of the transcendence of self-insistence by the goodness of the giver.

were carried completely outside of itself on that exhalation to the otherness of the world. We would breath our festive joy in incarnate being to the farthest stars, the remotest heavens, and beyond.

The aesthetic "I am" is like the flow and ebb of the great ocean itself, mysterious whisper of a great beyond, at the horizon, beyond the horizon. And the I follows the withdrawing waters as they retreat along the shore; and the vector of its longing would say yes to what transpires in the sea's deep murk, monsters and all. The ebb and flow of being that breathes in the incarnate flesh carries into the aesthetic "I am" the inarticulate hint of the agapeic yes, where the self has opened all the doors of self, never to be shut, and gone abroad recklessly into the boundless light of day. The equivocities of being are the ambiguous and enigmatic ciphers that remind selfhood of its community with all being in the between. I am the brother of the monster.

Third, the agapeic self realizes the promise of the erotic self. One discovers that intimate to self-transcending is a pledge to the other. The singular I is owned, is its own self, but as my own I am not a possession of self, not in my own possession. Ownness is not self-possession, for I come to own that I do not own myself. I am called to own up to what I am and do. I commit myself; I give myself to what I do; I am that giving of self. But this, this commitment, in fact, is already a *commission* of self. It is an undertaking in advance of one's responsibility, indeed of one's being, before another. Later I say: yes that was my act; the yes is the owning acknowledging by which I open myself to judgment. I do not disown my act, disown myself. I lay myself open to the judgment of the other, because I am already pledged.

One might say that the committed self is the self as a *promising being*. The "I am" is an "I will" which is an "I will be," that articulates the vector of self-transcendence to the future I, both in its openness and its pledge. I hold myself open to the future, but it is myself that I pledge. I promise myself is an agapeic act, for it is a giving of one's word, which is oneself, to the other. Thus the self is the promise of itself, both itself now and its future anticipated self. The promising of self, the promising self remains itself, and yet always gives itself away, though it vouches for what it gives away. What we normally call disownment is not only a betrayal of the promise of the self, but a disfigurement of the actual self, a disavowing that is a betrayal, a lack of ontological fidelity bound up with the most intimate truthfulness. And yet this commitment as commission is all bound up with one's being pledged to the other. We might venture: the acknowledgment or confession "I did this" means "Before you this is who I am." And maybe we can only make that last confession before God.

The self does not finally seek itself when it seeks itself. It seeks what is other to self and it finds itself in finding what is other. I say finds but also mean loses itself. Its dialectic must be carried beyond the coincidence of opposites to the point of paradox. Loss of self is self-finding, for real self-transcendence is both, but none are possible without the finding of the other as other. The "I will" of the erotic self is expanded by the erotic self to an "I am willing" in which the I is willing to erase itself in favor of pure willing. But this pure willing could equally be called will-lessness, in that the vehemence of self-insistence has been suspended. A more self-transcending willingness than the "I will," than the "I am willing," takes possession of the I and makes it pure willing, pure trust.

We see the face of it in the child who looks up to the parent with the look of faithful adoration. The agapeic self too becomes like a child looking in adoration to the father of all, and this face of the child is the face of idiocy. But the idiot self has gone through the suffering and sacrifice that the universal impermanence bring on us all, and yet we say yes. The child may suffer, but is willing to will beyond the wounds of being, with a new patience of being, a new receptivity, a purified willingness beyond all will to power.

Again there is something idiotic about this, for there is no way to make this willingness completely determinate. What I am talking about is an indeterminate willingness, matching the indeterminate perplexity we find in metaphysical mindfulness, or the indeterminate celebration of the beauty of being we find in aesthetic mindfulness. What is the object of the willingness? There is no object; it has no object; it is the simple and elemental willingness to be open to all, even that which kills me. It is a purified self-transcending that, as it were, elides self in transcending itself, an energy of being that is absolute availability. And because it is indeterminate, it is in excess of every determinate account and hence resists the reduction to determinate intelligibility. An agapeic self cannot univocally tell you what is the object of its willingness; it is a heedless love of the whole. The best word for its love is God.

The agapeic self: an intense space of fullness that listens for what is coming towards it; a space of fullness that goes towards what is coming, but that yet stays stock-still, where it is. Or: a space of emptiness in an open countryside that awaits patiently for the wind to blow through it, as it will, the wind of winter that bites, the breeze of summer that softens. Or: a thereness of availability, a nothing that does not shout itself, a meeting in the middle where the original powers of being communicate and fructify beyond themselves, and where the silent spaces sing.

Let me put it this way. Just as there is an objectless hatred and rancor that can anchor itself on anything,[23] batten on any object that enrages it, because it is good, so one might claim that there can be a kind of objectless

---

23. Nietzsche and Scheler have drawn our attention to this in relation to *ressentiment*. The *negative* is granted, as it were; but to my knowledge no one has recognized, in quite the terms I am urging, the affirmative counterpart of an indeterminate willingness that grounds the determinate "I will" or "I am willing," or definite loves of determinate beings. Perhaps this is not surprising. For the love this indeterminate willingness loves is God.

love that is infinitely available to anything, whether good or evil, fair or foul, alluring or repulsive. Like the light of the sun, it shines on friend and foe, beauty and deformity, nobility and scum. It shines even for the good of those who revile the good. This is what I mean by the pure movement of willingness in which the self hardly knows itself. It has lost itself in giving itself away, but as pure transcending it is itself just this losing, this giving of itself.

In more conventional terms, the agapeic self is *disinterested*, and this is taken to mean that its interest transcends self-interest. It is not lacking in interest; rather its interest is in the other for the other. In fact, its very being is simply interest. Its *esse* is interest, *inter-esse*, where the stress is on the *inter*. In other words, *interesse* puts the self into the *inter*, puts it outside of itself, beyond self-interest, makes it disinterested in that regard. What we normally call self-interest is really a qualification of the *inter-esse*, which can distort the *inter* into only a medium or a means for the self. In one respect self-interest is an oxymoron, for all interest is already outside of the self into the *inter* and the metaxological happening of being there. The true interest of *interesse* is the love of the between, but self-interest is a truncation of this between in which the *inter* is made into the means of reversion back to self. This can happen in the reversion of erotic self-transcendence that smothers the interest of agapeic selving. Hence self-interest is not the primordial movement of self, nor is essence the correlatively defined *conatus essendi*. Essence is the inter-essence, where the reversion to self is itself reversed in the movement of self-transcendence of the agapeic I.

I must stress that the going out of the self introduces a *turbulence*, almost *blindness*, into the teleology of desire. Desire is oriented to an end, a *telos*, to a certain wholeness, but the opening of wholeness that occurs in agapeic transcending goes beyond every determinate end. It is endless transcendence, infinite in this sense; it is beyond every determinate and bounded whole. I do not mean Hegel's "bad infinite," the progression from end to end, endlessly; as Hegel conceives the bad infinite, there is no wholeness at all; but in the present instance it is the wholeness of the self that is opened out. Where erotic selving risks allowing the wholeness of self to subordinate any radical otherness, agapeic selving reinserts the openness into wholeness, for the energy of infinity is at work in all our efforts to be whole. The infinite ruptures the whole, not in the sense of shattering it, but in being the excess that broadcasts itself over the limit, gives itself limitlessly. This is the *exitus* from self that is without end, the relativity to the other that is not for the sake of a *reditus* or return to the self. But this self-divestment—and this is the paradox—is itself the movement of plenitude as it communicates itself; it gives itself in trust of the other.

I find myself forced to resort to plurivocal language to do justice to the matter. The agapeic self is *both* whole and open in its transitions. It is a transmission, it is a between: between passive and active, and not passive or active; between suffering and willing, and not suffering and willing; between imitating and creating, and not imitating and not creating; between patience and doing, and not patience or doing either. Yet there is a kind of return to the first, because agapeic acting, willing, creating, doing are germinated in passion, suffering, imitation, patience. The passion of being that is always already spread out in the elemental I, returns in the end here, in the end that is no determinate end. The final and primal willing returns, or is offered to us, at the end in the face of death, death of the other, death of the self: the amen, the yes when nothing more can be done, and the self becomes nothing. This kenosis of the agapeic self is its golgotha—golgotha of the self-insistence of the erotic I, that suffers the mourning time of loss, yet still cleaves to metaphysical trust. The agapeic self is a sacrifice in which the self surrenders again the gift of its given being for-itself.

Of course, the offer of the final and primal willing is held out to us *in life*, and not just before death. The person who tries to welcome the offer also tries to love the neighbor, even when the neighbor threatens it in its being, perhaps hates it for loving it. To love the enemy is to be beyond the self-insistence of the erotic self. It is to say yes to what may destroy me, like Saint Francis kissing the leper. And so the agapeic self can be for the other to the point of enduring violence to itself, death: forgiving and not demanding acceptance, loving without asking to be loved. This agape of self is idiotic because it is beyond death, a kind of posthumous singularity. The responsibility to the other beyond death is a response to the other that offers no self-justification. Indeed the agapeic self grows in remorse at its failing in responsibility, at loss, at fault. It grows less and less justified. There is the growth of a guilty self. In a way, I am always a failure, always a shame, and there is no escape.

Why are we already committed before we commit ourselves? Why is the agapeic self commissioned? If its mission is a sending to the other, who sends the self? Not another human self, for that self too is commissioned. It is hard to suppress the thought that our mission to the human other is commissioned by a transhuman other. Is this nature as other to us? It seems not, since the willingness at work in agapeic selving transcends nature's being there. The best word for the source of our commission is God.

The name "God" arises in the inward otherness of the deepest intimacy of our being. Our commission is not quite a *demand* of the agapeic origin, for this origin makes no demands; not demand but promise, hospitality, welcome, and solicitude. Then when the welcome is heard, there is no rest in the rest, no rest for the self; no rest in any concept of the self, no rest in any doing of the self, or saying or achievement or enjoying or hoping, no rest even in the name "God," but fear and trembling. The agapeic self is heteroarchic: subject to the other and thus a subject. The "I am" become "I am here" becomes "I am yours." One must heed the appeal of a responsibility that is a hyperresponsibility, a responsibility that is limitless, for all, even those who cannot be named, and those who are beyond all touch. It is true that we cannot discharge this responsibility, nevertheless we do live its restlessness. I know too that this is hyperbole. It is an impossible responsibility, and yet we must endure the sleeplessness of its impossibility.[24]

Being commissioned is being summoned, called. The readiness of the self is its beginning as agapeic origin. I must bear witness, bear testimony. There is a reversal between self and other. I am commissioned by the other, therefore I am committed. I commit myself—like a good deed or a crime—because I am already commissioned. I am myself, I am my doing of self, I am my enacting of responsibility, in my committing of myself. I find myself commisioned because I am, as it were, a being under orders, orders that in no way enforce. I find myself as a free obedience, which is patience to the good of the other. I am called; I must obey. The highest freedom, the least avoidable necessity, coincide. Being commissioned is election. The absolute singularity of self is a commission to agapeic being.

To conclude: the unfolding of self from the elemental I of idiotic inwardness is thus from the aesthetic passion of immediacy, into the self-insistent I of self-will, through the self-mediation of the ethical will, to the religious passion in which the I radically gives itself back to the between and its origin. Agapeic being is itself idiotic, as are its festivity, its grace, its gratitude, its releasing, its compassion, its pardon. Its idiocy points to an intimacy of being beyond all intimacy. I am reminded of Augustine's claim that God is *intimior intimo meo*. Recall my previous remarks about memory as a bottomless abyss of self; it is an abyss even in recollection. Beyond recollection there is our remembering of loss, and, in a sense, of our being lost in God. This we can remember but we cannot recollect it completely to ourselves, since the memory is not our doing. The agapeic self is, as it were, dipped into this intimacy beyond intimacy, or this intimacy floods it, unasked, inundates it with an influx or access of saving light.

How do we get to this intimacy prior to the intimacy of self-relation, the idiocy of the absolute other beyond the idiocy of the self? How do we get to the primordial idiocy? There is no way that we could construct. All our later talk is the memory of a flood that swamps mindfulness, or the memory of a breakdown and a breakthrough. Or it is a failure of self-mediation that opens up a crack through which the origin sings, in the patient, suffering self. The suffering self is brought to the impasse of counting for nothing. I am nothing means I am the willingness that would say: be it done unto me according to your word; here I am, do with me as you will. There is, in the absolute patience, the offered creation of a new agapeic self from the nothing, even from the ruins of the erotic self. There is the meonic contraction of the erotic self to the primal source, and its transfiguration from nothing, and the death of itself, into a new energy of going out.

---

24. Dostoevski and recently Levinas have stressed this. See my discussion of Levinas in *Routledge History of Philosophy*, vol. 8.

CHAPTER ELEVEN

COMMUNITIES

Being Related

The opening to the other of the agapeic self reminds us that selfhood, like the many senses of being, is inseparable from the relatedness of beings. Origin, creation, things, intelligibilities, selves—all are ingredient in the determination of different modes of relatedness. Thus, origin is the *communication* of being to what otherwise would not be. Creation *holds together* the plurality of finite beings in the universal impermanence. Things comes to self-definition in *incessant interplay* with other things. Intelligibilities are modes of *relativity* whereby things are diversely held together in the universal impermanence. Selves, while self-relating, realize their promise through their *community* with other selves, the things of creation and the origin. Community, in its many forms, must be made the theme of reflection.

My present emphasis on modes of togetherness complements, and in some respects completes, my previous emphasis on modes of self-relativity. Self-relativity cannot be sundered from community. The more we become mindful of our self-relativity, entering into the inward otherness, down into the abyssal intimacy where the ontological roots of our being are energized, the more we come to know transcendence as the promise of an agapeic self-surpassing. The self, even in its singular idiocy, selves as a self for the other. Neither above or below, neither within or without, is there escape from community. Community is the very milieu in which self-surpassing and transcendence come to form and fruit.

We thus come closer to the meaning of the metaxological sense of being. Should readers retrace the unfolding of our thinking from origin to now, they will see the promise of community effective all along, even when not made the theme of explicit reflection. The present chapter is a more intensive meditation on the same milieu of being that was always our concern, whether stated or implied.

There are communities, not just community. There are different possible ways of being together. These ways are defined by the ontological

417

complexity and richness of the beings that are together or held together. Thus some modes of togetherness define beings in nature, beings that themselves are intricately variegated, depending on the range of their defining ontological powers and intelligibilities. Other modes of togetherness define human beings: here freedom's open promise is crucial in preventing any closure of community into an absorbing totality. Further, there are modes of togetherness between the origin and creation, including the human creature: here the freedom of the latter and the goodness of creation interplay to allow the possibility of a community in which creation, and especially the human creature, can participate in or defect from the primal generosity of the origin. The given promise of the creature is its becoming agapeic, and so a giving source that not only may renew the creation, but co-create in the renewed creation. This would be a communal yes to the agapeic origin.

Nor does this exclude the strain of tension, of conflict, of differences turned into hostilities, of outright war. The milieu of being offers the promise of plurality, plurality defined by a pluralism of communities, but reneging on this promise is always possible. More extremely, in certain communities a violence of being seems to be constitutive. Between the promise of harmony and its redemption, there is the time of war and the desert of lamentation. Besides the goodness of creation, there is evil—not just senseless suffering, but the enigmatic malice of iniquity. There are the wounds of being, the dead, the desecrated, the lost, the forgotten, the execrated, the tortured, the damned. These too wrench the heart of any mindfulness that would fain think the goodness of creation.

In our account, the univocal and the equivocal senses will have more direct relevance to the modes of togetherness of beings in nature. Here we find a certain immediacy to the community of beings as given. A togetherness is at play that is not necessarily known as such. With human beings, mindfulness, in many different forms, mediates the work of communities. The dialectical and the metaxological senses receive far more prominence, the first as explicitly emphasizing the self-mediation of a community, the second as explicitly underscoring the intermediation that, even in holding together a plurality in incessant interplay, prevents community from closure. Still, all four senses are diversely operative in human communities and nature as other. Their operation keeps open, as we shall see, the communication between the origin and creation. If there is a community of communities, it is this last communication that is also the first.

Nature and Community

In an important respect, community transcends a strict univocity. This strict sense would reduce plurality to an identity without difference, and clearly then the notion of community is impossible. To be thus univocal would be to exclude relativity to the other, to be simply a *this one* and not in any way other than *this one*. As stated on a previous occasion, such a univocal identity is an unreal abstraction of unity. It nowhere exists. The thinking of it is precisely as abstracted from a web of relativity that constitutes some mode of togetherness and hence community.

That said, there are communities with links to the univocal sense of being, insofar as the latter places primary emphasis on the determinacy of things and intelligibility. There are modes of togetherness that are *immediately* at play in the universal impermanence. These modes constitute the communities of beings that do not exhibit explicit mediating mindfulness. That is, there is a mediation at work in the immediacy of these modes of togetherness. They are immediately given mediations of pluralities.

The most elemental of such communities are space and time, or spacetime as contemporary physics has it. This is a minimal sense, in that spacetime constitutes the primal physical basis of the togetherness of all things. Finite creations are in space-time. What exactly this small word *in* means is extremely difficult to say. As a first approximation, it suggests less some super container as the ontological place of finite happenings, where and when things come to be, and come to be in their being together. We might say that spacetime is the *aesthetic spread* of finite creation. But this immediate spread is the home of all bounded, determinate happening. Things are held together in space-time, where *in* again does not refer to a bounded container that encloses things as themselves bounded wholes, but refers to the aesthetic happening of the milieu of finite creation.

By aesthetic spread I mean the material, sensible manifestation of the originative power of being. By milieu I mean a middle that is no bounded middle but that is indeterminate in its extremities of source and goal; a middle that has no absolutely *determinate* source and no absolutely *determinate* end evident to us, and hence an open middle. As this milieu, space-time holds together, not by embracing from such putative extremes, but by being the aesthetic happening of the surge into determinate existence of the original power of being, which in itself is in excess of determinate beings. The holding together, so to say, comes out of the ground; space-time is that incessant, continuous energizing that crystallizes in determinate entities and happenings, each of which would not be held together in being without the upsurge of this original, plastic energy.

There is a deeper ground for this basic togetherness, if we think of it as having reference to its own source of origination. For we can think of the reference to origin as a specification of a mode of togetherness, and hence a specification of some communal relatedness. This is evident in the very word *nature*. *Natura* indicate a birth or process of birthing, a coming into distinct being out of an original source. But birthing, naturing, is a *social relation*— most evident, I suppose, in the relation between a parent and an offspring. We could say that nature includes reference to a social relation—that is, the community of togetherness of the origin and its creation. Think here how the community of a people is sometimes called a *nation*, a word derivative of *nascor*; a people becomes a nation when it shares intimate reference to a common origin. Analogous considerations might be applied to the word *native*. In a word, we and all finite beings are native to nature, members of creation as the community that offers us our material home, matrix of all becoming.

The Greek word *phusis*—implying the process of coming into being, this upsurgence into the light of manifest happening—is also related to *phu*, which contains reference to the process of being born. We get a better sense of the implied activity of relating in the idea of nature naturing, *natura naturans*, rather than nature natured, *natura naturata*. Naturing is a relation of togetherness of the origin and the creation. The communal nature of this is nowhere more evident than in the thought of the origin as agapeic, which itself concretizes metaxological relativity as a giving of being for the other. I will refer again below to the metaphor of mother nature and the materiality of creation.[1]

Space-time is an indeterminate holding together of finite happenings, and hence is not strictly univocal, but it gives rise to entities that are more determinately univocal. This thing, that thing, the other thing come to be within the aesthetic community of the primal energized flow. You might say that space-time, purely as this indeterminate possibility of holding entities within itself, is a kind of promiscuous univocity. Differences are dormant within its perhaps limitless reserves of original energy; they are dormant as undifferentiated, but then come to be in the differentiation process that constitutes the process of becoming. The process of becoming differentiates the promiscuous univocity of the pure flux of space-time. There is then a sense in which the latter flux is an abstraction from the aesthetic happening of concrete being, which is always in some measure differentiated. We think this abstraction, however, to explain why the process of becoming as differentiating is ceaseless. The process includes perishing, as things fall out of their individuated differentiation and back into the promiscuous togetherness of the primal flow. Yet the process in incessantly renewed. It is renewed as happening

---

1. We might relate nature as birthing to the idea of genesis as generation. The genus is a generated community. The kind connects one to others of one's own kind. These are one's kin. One's relations are generated by a family of togethernesses. The passing from generation to generation is produced by time. Natural kinds are communities of kinship—not necessarily mindful kinships. Kinds are families, generated likenesses, images of an indeterminate origin. Time itself becomes generativity in space, that is, as material, aesthetic spread. So it is dangerous to univocalize space-time with respect to notions like contiguity, and external relations. The latter easily become just analytical deconstructions of modes of original relativity, elemental relatedness. Beings are first together in the generational flow of becoming.

because there is an original source of being that is always old and always fresh, forever ageless and new, and yet aged beyond all ageing.

When we turn to the determinate happenings in space-time, we find the specific workings out of this being together. Being together is at work at the most elemental physical level. Thus the current search for a unified theory might suggest the univocal sense, yet it does so equivocally. There is an effort to unify the four basic forces: the weak and strong nuclear forces, gravitation and electromagnetism. What are here called four forces are actually modes of community; they are modes of togetherness. The weak and strong forces point to modes of being together at the subatomic level, modes that go to make the unity of an atom. That is to say, a certain community itself provides the basis for a more complex unity, which, in turn, on the molecular level enters into community with other like or unlike unities, again to be held together into a more complex unity, itself the harmony of a plurality of unities.

The univocal mind tries to state these modes of togetherness with as strict a mathematical determinacy as possible. The four basic forces can be formulated with precise mathematical accuracy; and yet that precision of univocal determination expresses the very being together of the basic material energies of finite happenings. Hence despite the mathematical univocity, there still have to be *other descriptions* of what is at play here, and this all in the language of a certain kind of sociability. Thus, for example, we talk about forces of attraction and repulsion relative to electrons and protons, or with respect to electro-magnetic effects. We speak of nuclear or chemical bonds. *Between* the basic energies and elements there is the happening of a sociability. The word *association* itself repeats that same happening of sociability. That certain elements have greater or less predilection to enter into reaction with, to bond, or pair, or not, with other elements, indicate communities of being at work.

Consider the following examples. Think of talk about *noble gases*. Obviously, this language of social association was forged in an age that had not yet given itself over wholeheartedly to democratic ideals. For the noble gases are those that are the most aloof, those least likely to enter into reactions and bondings with other elements. They are standoffish elements. And yet they are honored with the epithet *noble*—as if the more democratic elements were less than noble, those elements whose range of association were more expansive. These would be the elements that were not snobs, though to the haughty disdain of the noble gases they are merely vulgar. They are plebs, *hoi polloi*. But the vulgar, precisely because of the more universal range of their associations, inherit the earth.

Or consider descriptions of recent experiments that trace the movement of neurons in the formation of the brain. The standard view had been that there is a predetermined genetic code that in advance assigned different neurons to different parts of the brain. Recent experiments indicate that there is far greater variability in the migration of neurons. Neuron cells spawned from the identical "parent cell" will migrate in very diverse ways that do not seem genetically preprogramed. (I note the language of "mother cells" and "daughter cells," "sibling cells," the social language of family.) The final position of the migrating neurons seems determined by their relation to certain "neighboring" neurons. This settling down with certain neighbors is not clearly understood (signals from neighboring neurons seem important). The migrating neurons arrive in a neighborhood of residence, to be greeted by what are called axons, which help the newcomer neuron adjust and settle into its residency. All of this seems to indicate what we might call the happening of a certain sociability. The place of the individual neuron is defined by its relations to its neighbors, and not simply in terms of a predetermined code of which it is the mere agent and carrier. The neuron's social place is settled as much through others as through itself. The neighborhood it settles in becomes its home. Some scientists have even spoken of the "British" versus the "American" plan. In the British plan, destiny is determined by one's ancestors; in the American plan, destiny is determined by one's neighbors. In any case, if we compare all this to the noble gases, we find far greater social flexibility and mobility in these neurons.

Let me now turn from the micro to the macrolevel. Think of Newton's language in speaking of gravitation. Gravitation is a force of attraction, but Newton directly talks about "sociability" in a number of places. As we know, he was nagged by the problem of action at a distance. The force of attraction of gravitation is a mode of togetherness of systems of mass. It can be formulated with the precision of mathematical univocity, and yet what is thus being formulated is the happening of a universal sociability. The problem of action at a distance is, if you like, the physical analogue to telepathic communication, nonphysical action at a distance. The supposition of the ether, and indeed Newton's mixture of corpuscular and undulatory theories of light propagation, evidence, in part, his efforts to make intelligible sense of the universal sociability. It was as if the partners in the association had to touch each other at some point, whether directly or through an unbroken chain of intermediaries. The happening of communication, the propagation of light, or the attraction of gravitation across immense distances, seemed to demand this chain of intermediation.

In worrying about the ether, was Newton touching the fringes of what I call the metaxological milieu of being? If space-time is already the aesthetic happening of this milieu, the problem of action at a distance need not arise in quite the form in which it was classically posed. Communication across difference, if you will, action at a distance, is always taking place. Or there is no action across an empty distance simply, since the so-called distance is itself a mode of the happening of the between, the metaxological milieu. Such communication is never that of univocally fixated poles in interplay across a completely vacuous between—such a between really can never be bridged or traversed or mediated. If you like, the poles already pulsate; the poles are already in the between; the between itself is the supporting medium of the very process of universal communication. The togetherness, the community, is a primary given, an aesthetic happening; the univocal units are abstractions from its primary flowing. The real question is not action at a distance, but the meaning of the milieu in which the happening of communication takes place. The contemporary space-time might be said to be closer to this happening than the empty absolute space of Newtonian mechanics.

But you interject: Is not all this talk about communication, association, sociability, just mere metaphor? I might say yes, and cite the fact that the happenings just mentioned can be stated with more or less mathematical univocity. This is true. But is the truth of happenings just such a mathematical determination? Is the language of sociability only the superimposition of an otherwise dispensable language that does not touch the univocal thing itself? I believe things are not so simple. The mathematical univocity serves the intelligible determination of certain happenings in space-time. It *serves*; it is not the complete master. For these happenings are not simply univocal intelligibilities; they are concrete happenings that are not themselves just mathematical determinations. The mathematical determination is *of* the truth of the happening; but the happening is a mode of togetherness, a community. The language of community serves the truth of the happening, as much as does the mathematical determination.

For the reality of the milieu is not simply the set of structured intelligibilities that a mathematics can formulate. The putatively metaphorical language has its truth, its indispensable truth. This truth cannot be converted without residue into a mathematical univocity, insofar as we must be true to the concreteness of the happening—precisely as a happening of being and not as a mathematical form of intelligibility. In fact, one might say that the univocal *mathēsis* and the metaphorics of sociability are necessary to each other; none swallows the other, and neither is complete without the other. The clear determinacy of one needs the rich indeterminacy of the other, and vice versa. The stability of one needs the openness of the other; the abstraction of one needs the concreteness of the other. Nor should the indispensability of metaphorical saying surprise us, if space-time and the modes of togetherness at work there manifest the *aesthetic* happening of the original energy of being.

An important pointer is found in the language of materialism itself. This language prides itself on its excision of anthropomorphic projections, or ways of treating nature's thereness as like us. But, of course, *matter* derives from *mater*, the word for *mother*. Matter is maternal, it is mothering, it is the matrix of all formations of physical systems. Twist and turn as you will, this mother will pursue you. The discourse of materialism is haunted by a maternal metaphorics. Premodern nature was explicitly a mother. This woman was subjected to the neutering of a univocal *mathēsis*, which included the masculinization of knowledge as power to master and subdue. But, of course, servitude and control are also social relations; subordination and subjugation are modes of togetherness. Subjugated nature is reduced to the being there of a community of neutered materiality. Then there is the sadist knowing that puts her to the torture, as Bacon says, puts the body of the world under a violent interrogation, lest she might be a witch. But nature as a common mother is still a fount of community, and not necessarily in the degraded form of mastery and servitude.[2]

One could also claim that the mechanistic metaphor, held so dear by classical materialists, is a tissue of anthropomorphisms. Machines are entirely manmade; to denommate nature as a machine is to apply the metaphor of an entirely humanized construct to what itself is not human or exclusively human. A mechanistic metaphorics is far more anthropomorphic than organic and maternal metaphorics. The latter at least preserve the otherness of the process of coming to being, which cannot be reduced to the control of a human process, as a machine in principle can. The irony is that classical materialism mothers its own maternal metaphorics, while it claims to rid the world and science of all metaphors—and maybe mothers too. The refusal of the mother and the metaphor is a narrowing of the community of being, for mothering and metaphorizing originate modes of togetherness, are themselves modes of originative togetherness.

Perhaps the unavoidability of metaphors suggests the *inescapability* of some anthropomorphism, and not necessarily in a bad sense. Such inescapability might reflect the unavoidability of some community of kinship between us and nature, even in its otherness to us. Anthropomorphism is metaphorical of community at work between us and nature. Of course, the danger is that the *two-way* character of that communication is reduced to what and how *we* speak about nature's otherness. This reveals an unavoidable ambiguity; we can guard against it, but never entirely eliminate it. Our anthropomorphic language has always to fight any temptation to think that the otherness of being is merely the mirror in which we recognize ourselves. In fact, what we need are metaphors with the power to decenter us towards the otherness of nature, metaphors that truly carry us (*metapherein*) into the community of the between. In truth, as long as the *dunamis* of transcendence is at work, we will be thus carried, willingly or not, and hence forced to resort to some imagistic language that can never completely escape some anthropomorphism. In brief, there can never be an absolute mathematical univocity of being.

Important implications follow if we now turn to the notion of an *environment*. Nature as the aesthetic happening of the space-time plasma consti-

---

2. It is interesting how difficult it is to avoid the image of the body when speaking of communities. We speak of *corporations*, and *incorporation*, of bodies of people, of the *body politic*. We speak of being members of a body or group. The Church is spoken of as the *mystical body* of Christ.

tutes an environment. But environment signifies a more determinate togetherness of things. The particle word "en" reminds us both of the embrace of community and also the reference to unity in that embrace (the Greek *hen* is one). The environment defines the maternal embrace of the natural community. Not unexpectedly, in classical physics, that maternal embrace vanishes; there is no such enfolding environment; there is a mere aggregate of atomistic centers of mass in motion; at best the embrace of the whole is the iron hold of a machine on its parts. And yet despite this, the language of classical physics is still the language of community. To speak of aggregates is to speak of modes of togetherness. A machine is the concretion of a togetherness. Even if, with Hume, we reduce causality to a mere customary contiguity, contiguity is a connection, and a togetherness, albeit very minimal.

The language of classical physics essentially bespeaks a dead community of being. Some have seen this dead community as the result of a murder. The univocal mind of modern *mathēsis*, in Wordsworth's phrase, "murders to dissect." It is as if a voyeurist univocal mind chose the cold, metallic touch of a cosmic machine over the nurturing embrace of the maternal earth. By contrast, the astonishing reserves of renewal in the aesthetic happening of nature, the ageless power of generation deep in the being of becoming, offers a very different sense of natural community, one I think more consonant with post-Newtonian physics.

The unavoidability of the language of togetherness, even in the machine world, is again revealing. It is revealing not of the absoluteness of the machine, but of the derivativeness of the metaphor itself. What is pitiful is the poverty of the metaphor. A machine is a community that has been all but deprived of everything essential to community, most especially the power of inherent togetherness. The community of the machine is a togetherness where external relations obtain such that each part has nothing inherent to do with the other parts; each is atomically for itself, has no intimate connection with any other; the connections are all extrinsic. As they are extrinsic, so also is the mind that surveys them, just as the God who generates the clockwork world is an extrinsic creator.

I use external and extrinsic with connotations entirely removed from what is at stake in terms like transcendence, otherness. The externality and extrinsicality of the clockwork cosmos are ontologically degraded forms of transcendence, otherness, and difference. A proper sense of the latter will preserve the external without sacrificing the togetherness, or the inherence of relativity in the cosmos itself. Why is the clockwork cosmos a degraded community? Because it is an abstraction from the original community of nature, an abstraction that it takes as elemental and absolute, when in fact it is derivative and relative to a certain point of view.

The degrading of the environment follows inexorably. This is one of the major stories of modernity. The degraded environment issues from the disrespect of humans for the community of nature, of which they themselves are members, albeit members who can deny their membership, the easier to lord it over the community without metaphysical misgivings. The degraded environment is the image of our failure to acknowledge the community of which we are members, let us think what we will about our own superiority. We are empowered to be ourselves by the original energy of being that is concretized in the community of nature; but in the gift of our emergent freedom, that very power is turned against its own natural matrix. We have been blithe and invigilant about the violence possible for that free power. It is now clear to any mindful person that the promise of free power cannot be redeemed at the expense of the degradation of the community of nature. Not only does this degradation degrade nature, in the long run it is self-subverting of the power of the human being also. It degrades human freedom by violating its community of being with nature as other to the human.

The ecological crisis is thus the tale not of a loss, but of a deformation of community. The crisis is also a reminder, a call for renewed mindfulness in thought and deed. It is a reminder of the promise of community in creation, of creation itself as a community. No account of it in terms of extrinsic juxtapositions will do justice to the relativity of beings within creation. The word *ecology* itself implies a network of interconnecting things, happenings, processes that finally cannot be separated from each other, wherein the happening of one will affect the happening of all the others, however indirectly and remotely and faintly. Creation is a belonging together of beings where all beings belong. Nothing belongs together in the degraded environment, except pestilence and foul air, and the pollution of noise and invisible cancers. Nothing belongs to anything else with intimacy of inherence and relation. All things merely belong to the squandering human, and here too belonging is the possessing of a victim one has licensed oneself to ransack.

As coming to crisis, the ecological degradation may be at a moment of turning that might be seized to renew the promise of community. The crisis may be a moment of *kairos* where the breakdown of degraded community may offer opportunity for renewal. The postcrisis community will have to be a community of penitence to atone for the false community of still regnant hubris. Hubris will want to keep the blinders on its baleful eyes. Renewal will not come without suffering and penance.

Self-Relating Sociability and Communicative Doubling

Things are integrities that embody a togetherness, and in that respect things are communities in themselves. We might thus speak of a being's *self-relating sociability*. The selfness of a being is its communion with itself; the bonds holding a thing into its own unity involve this self-communication of a thing with itself. But this communication is double, in that it opens beyond self to what is other. And as self-communication becomes more complex, relative to a being's richness of ontological powers, the more it can communicate with beings other than itself, hence participate in more and more complex communities.

A being is a concrete organization of the power to be, but an organization is a communication of such power. Hence the sociability of beings reflects the different organizations of the power to be. We find different sociabilities in subatomic particles/waves, in atoms, in molecules, in cells, organisms, animals, humans. Each subsequent organization is a more complex community holding together into integrity the richer ontological powers of being that come to manifestness. The richer the community, the more it is a community of communities.

Relative to *inorganic nature*, the self-communication of things displays intricate patterns of differentiation and relation. The self-communication becomes more complex at the level of *organic nature*; one begins clearly to see a self-relating integrity communicating with itself as a center of organization in development. Hence the language of community appears far more evidently. With organic nature we think of things as self-developing wholes, and the language we use to describes such wholes is a language of community. I mean that the communication of the thing with itself is its own self-articulation, as we speak of a tree's growth in terms of the articulation out of the roots of the branches and limbs; the parts do not belong to the whole in a merely external way but are the self-externalization of a self-communicating center of organic energy. Note that this self-externalization also puts the self-relating integrity into the space of the between, where a different sociability with the other is also at work, a sociability not reducible to the self-relating sociability.

When we come to *animated, sensitive being*, the self-developing whole is even more evident, for instance, with the communication of the genetic code to the entire animal, let us say from the union of egg and sperm. The self-communication is the propagation of powers of being from an original zygote, a propagation of the original power of animal being itself that is both distributed into and through its articulated parts, and that also refers back to the original center of self-organizing. (This is generally true of homeostatic systems, only here we have an explicit "feed-back loop," as one of the jargons has it.)

Moreover, the power of communication *beyond* self-communication also become evident. The animated being reaches to what is other; in its sensitive interplay with the sensible, it registers the other with which it interplays. This communication with externality is registered in terms of the self-communication of the animated being itself. That is, the relation with the other appears in the self-awareness of the animated being, rudimentary though this may be. It does so because the self-externalization of the thing is not lost in externality; rather the self-communicating center exhibits sufficiently rich powers of being to mediate with itself in its mediation with what is other.

The language of sociability becomes even more pronounced with the animal. For the sensitive being is a self-developing whole that is self-feeling, self-sensitive, in interplay with what is other. The subordinate parts or powers that get integrated in the self-communication of the organic thing are not simply parts, but evidence a certain wholeness peculiar to themselves. Thus we often speak of them as members of the body. For instance, the hand is a well articulated member of the body, but a hand has its own integrity; hence a three-fingered hand is not a whole hand; and yet this well-formed whole, the hand, communicates with the whole of the body of which it is a member. A member is a part that has an integrity to itself, and that yet cannot sustain itself, if cut off from the community of the whole. The self-communication of the animal whole communicates with its members, which, as subordinate integrities, communicate with the center of the being as a whole. And so, for example, a pain in the hand is registered as a pain in the hand, but it is also a pain that affects the entirety of the bodily self, and it is known by the central organizing self-awareness of that body.

As we see, the more complex becomes the integrity's self-communication, or self-relating sociability, the more there comes into play the integrity's communication with what is other to itself. This is most manifest with the *human being*. Here the self-communicating integrity not only feels itself, but minds itself, becomes mindful of itself in its interplay with what is other. The emergence of mindfulness in the aesthetic body signals the appearance of ontological powers more complex and rich than are to be found in inorganic and organic being. The organization of the self-communicating integrity reveals itself as at once more unified, more differentiated, more capable of self-transcendence, and more capable of communication with what is other. Mindful self-communication shows the power of free self-development, the power of free self-transcendence, the promise of free communication with what is other to itself.

This momentous development will expand, in an extraordinary way, the range and indeed the meaning of community. When self-communication becomes mindful, not only does the integrity of being come to know its own difference and selfness, it also knows the irreducibility of differences other than itself, knows the irreducibility of others to itself, and most importantly, knows that there are others that are for-themselves as integrities of mindful self-communication. There emerges mindful communication with the other. Here appears the possibility of community as also shaped by the communication *from* the other, out of itself, as another center of mindful self-communication. Mindful communication with the other goes hand in hand with the mindfulness of self-communication. Here dialectical and metaxological communities receive their clear expression. Self-relating sociability opens beyond itself to the intermediated sociability of the between.

At this juncture we also cannot avoid oppositions, even in modes of togetherness. The equivocal sense of being must be taken into account. No

harmony is possible without differentiation; all harmonization is always beyond tensionless univocity. Being together always involves tension between
exclusion and inclusion, repulsion and attraction. So the power of communication exists in tension with retraction, as well as the power to be in antithesis to other-being. A being's self-communicating integrity is the very
possibility of antithesis, since its self-insistence inevitably enters into compe-
tition, as well as cooperation, with other entities. Their togetherness is always
a mingling of harmony and strife.

We are reminded by the equivocity of being that strife need not always be
conquered. If the togetherness is a site of strife and harmony, the between
can be dominated by one of the participants, one can overcome the power of
the other, reshaping the resultant togetherness via the subordination, perhaps even death, of the other. For example, the lion and the lamb live in the
togetherness of the ecological community, but this togetherness is also a food
chain. Hence their togetherness is not a simple harmony of equilibrium; it is
a harmony that is won in strife itself, and in this case in the destruction of the
lamb. The togetherness of lion and lamb includes the devouring of the lamb
by the lion; but that very strife is the harmony of the lion and the ecological
community.

The equivocal sense also sheds light on the dissolution of a being's integrity and its harmonies of relativity. As a togetherness of energies, a being
holds itself into a unity, but the togetherness is precarious, it is fragile. It is a
coming to a togetherness that is always finite; it is subject to the dissolution
of the harmony attained. Inevitable dissolution accompanies the self-
differentiating of the thing, accompanies its self-relating sociability. It also
accompanies every togetherness of a plurality. A community of plurality is
ever a fragile happening, to be sustained and renewed by the energies of the
members. Since these energies are finite, the togetherness grows old and
tired, reaches a limit of renewal. It falls apart. It goes under. It dies.

Obviously every mode of togetherness is a relation, but relation here has
to be understood in a dynamic manner. A mode of togetherness is a relating;
the accent falls on the dynamic of relating itself. Of course, there are relations that are static structures, for instance, the spatial relations of a triangle
that geometry will univocally determine for us. But such static relations are
themselves the outcome of active relatings—the very activity of articulating
the triangle as a certain determinate configuration of space. The drawn triangle materializes, and this too in an active sense, these relations as already
having been articulated. Insight into the structure of relations relives in a
dynamic way the active relatings that come to determinate configuration in
the articulated triangle. The equivocal sense of being, in stressing differentiation, reminds us, against the temptation to stasis of the univocal mind, that
all relations as stable are the expressions of dynamic relatings. Static structures are the happening of the dynamic energy of being; we have to think into
the structures to the active structuring that births them in the first place.

It follows that if relations are dynamic relatings, every mode of determinate togetherness has the rhythm of finitude ingrained in its flow. This dynamic shows itself as an origination, an unfolding, an achieving, a renewal of the achieving, a limiting of the renewing, and finally the retracting of the *dunamis* of relating. In some cases, there must be death to renew the rhythm of relating once again. Very often, we do not see the rhythm of relating clearly, since death and life overlap, and the renewal of life hides the sad undergoing that is the destiny of all finite relatings. The shadow of death that accompanies modes of togetherness also conditions that struggle between harmony and strife, and adds a deeper tension to the equilibrium between the two. The self-insistence of the members of a togetherness, itself stressed by its own finitude, relates to what is other in terms of its own death, hence too in terms of the death of the other. So as long as death shadows all modes of togetherness, there cannot be absolute harmony—not the harmony that would regress behind difference; not the harmony that would transcend the tense hostility built into difference, and redeem difference as affirmatively sustained beyond all strife.

Thus all differentiation is double-edged. It is the basis of a more complex pluralism, within things and between things; it is also the source of possible violence, in things, between things. While being the bearer of the living identity and togetherness of beings, differentiation is also death bound. What is positive here? The answer I suggest is the pluralization of possibility beyond univocity. This pluralization is the basis for a more expansive range of community. The fact that metaphor was unavoidable with respect to "univocal" communities points to this—namely, that there is the potential for much more, already at play in the primal togetherness of the space-time continuum. This is not unrelated to the operation of chance and indeterminacy. These are the basis of new combinations or new joinings, or departures from relations already formed, not merely in a disruptive but in a creative way.

One might point to a certain anarchy here, but if so, this is an anarchy that dissolves fixities in order to fertilize the possibility of new communities, new modes of togetherness. Such a creative anarchy is really an *archē* of the new. If it is a disordering, it is a disorder of seeking, that may later yield a new ordering of togetherness. And indeed this seems to be ingredient in creation: the renewal of formlessness, the risk of breakdown and loss of order, the struggle for new organization in the indeterminate energy itself. We could suggest that equivocity precipitates community into a return to a kind of orgiastic promiscuity of the energies of creation, where fixed structures and possibilities are dissolved, but also melded into new forms and possibilities. In the promiscuous mingling of one and the other, one is not sure which is which, but out of the uncertain mixing, novel forms can be born.

Communities must take this risk of anarchy if they are to perpetuate, and renew, and transform their given orders of togetherness. The perpetuation of a togetherness can finally never be done by freezing the achieved order of relations into a stasis. It is perpetuated by always being renewed; and renewal is inevitably the introduction of differences that change, transform, and of course possibly deform, the given order of togetherness. This is the very risk, the equivocal hazard of communities. The freezing into stasis is a refusal of that risk and that equivocity, and the will to impose on beings an impossible univocity. This latter will seeks to perpetuate a relating by reducing it to a static structure, but it defeats its own intention, which was actually to preserve the given order of *relatings*.

This equivocal hazard of togetherness is evident from lower to higher levels. We interfere with the togetherness of subatomic energies and we create the nuclear bomb, and in the use of nuclear energy, risk every kind of cancer that the given order of nature did not previously possibilize. Or we perform genetic mutations, reorganize the cellular togetherness of an organism, and behold, there issues forth a monster. Or we make a slight adjustment in a government, and in the space of that alteration, a usurper grows to topple the king. Every difference opens a possibility of something being otherwise. Every difference carries constitutive ambiguity. Every difference is a promise and a hazard, such is the necessary equivocity of communal being.

I will confine myself to two significant expressions of this hazard and promise, first in relation to the natural cosmos, second relative to human community.

Relative to the natural cosmos, recall our production of the degraded community of the environment that now escapes no one, or that no one escapes. This is the equivocity: the degradation is the result of what was anticipated as an unprecedented *release* of human promise, in the form of human mastery over the natural conditions of human life. The difference of the human being shows itself as a great promise and the great hazard. Our difference to the rest of creation is in our free difference. This free difference releases us from dependence on what, paradoxicaly, we continue to be dependent on.

This free difference is double: independent and dependent at once. This doubleness can wreak havoc with the community of creation, and has done so; for it can express itself, and has done so in an unprecedented way in modernity, as the power to oppose the given conditions of the natural community. Indeed our own being shadowed by death; our own loss of trust that being is good, even given death, good beyond death; our own excess of self-insistence; our slippage from the sense of being as agape; our lack of trust that there is a community of creation of which we are members, a lack both expressed in, and deepened by the mechanization of nature; all these and more contribute to the compost wherein breeds a metaphysical rebellion against creation.

What results? Free human power, creation's most noble promise, becomes its dark opposite, in pursuit of the realization of just that promise. Our creative power becomes our metaphysical violence against the world as creation. Why does this happen? It happens because the doubleness is not minded deeply enough. Were it so minded, our ontological community with creation, even in all the equivocal hazard of finite being, would have been kept so to the fore that we could not contemplate the ontological aggression that we now barely see for what it is—a deformation of being and not univocal progress towards the realization of its promise. We destroy our community with creation in the self-assertion of our own power against nature, as if nature were either dead in itself or a hostile opposite to be subjugated and deprived of all its recalcitrant otherness. We make the garden of creation a fetid, toxic dump.

The equivocity of being in community is intimately related to the doubleness that, as we saw above, emerges in modes of togetherness from inorganic being to the human being. This is the doubleness between self-communication and other-communication. This doubling emerges in all things as themselves dual modes of relativity and mediation, and hence too of togetherness. Modes of togetherness are expressed in terms of both self-mediation and intermediation. There is tension and stress and potential opposition in this doubling. This equivocality does not exhaust community, but it is presupposed by dialectical community where the struggle for mastery is notable, as well as by metaxological community where the struggle for mastery is replaced by service for the other.

Shortly I will come to these, but I must first address the second point mentioned above. The power of ontological violence enters into selfhood and community. I find it illuminating to think about the traditional way of speaking of this: the expulsion from paradise. Paradise is the garden of creation (*pairi daēza* from old Persian for an enclosed garden or park). The garden of creation, we might say, is the community of given being. We can see, I suggest, the momentous original ontological violence as arising in relation to what I am calling our self-relating sociability. That is, self-communication is inseparable from communication with all things other, but with the emergence of the evil will, the self-relating sociability ceases to be a society, ceases to be a mode of togetherness; the self is not together with self, or with creation, or with others, or with God. The evil will arises when the self-relating sociability turns itself into a *closed* self-communication. The immediate result is loss of community with creation, figured in the story by the loss of that primordial communication between humankind and the rest of nature that obtained prior to the closure on self. Then creation and other humans become hostile opposites, equivocal in a potentially malicious way: they are threats, we are not entirely sure; we become threatened, and hence aware of our nakedness in shame. With the original self-relating sociability there was a self-love that was entirely void of shame; and it was not narcissistic, for it lived the community of creation. We now can hardly conceive what this shameless community might be; it is a shamelessness beyond good and evil, because it was in the good. Self-relating sociability and other-relating communication did not divide; such a divorce would make no sense.

We shut ourselves into a closed self-communication, and the story says we were driven out of paradise. Properly speaking, we are not driven out, we drive ourselves out, because we shut ourselves in the false self-absolute. The shut-in self shuts out the other, and shuts out nature as creation. Then the community of creation becomes the "state of nature," with its *bellum omnium contra omnes*. Cain killed his brother Abel, and this fratricide expressed in all of its depth the primordial equivocity of human community outside of the goodness of creation. The other as a rival, a threat to my absoluteness, must be possessed. Moreover, Abel was not any other, he was a brother. This contradicts Freud's myth about the first murder; it is not the murder of the father; the first murder is a fratricide. We see together the reality and promise of human community as familial, and the destruction of that reality in death of the brother.

Interestingly, Cain is described as the builder of a city. This is the manmade community outside the community of creation, and the origin of world history with its blood and horror and progress. By contrast, Abel was a sojourner and a stranger on the earth. We might suggest, he was in the between time, between the degraded creation and its re-creation, remembering the first goodness of creation, on the way, and not on the way to the city of world history. Is this why his sacrifice, his service, found favor with God, while Cain's did not? Because it served the between as for God?

Cain is envious of the goodness of Abel; he seems to kill him for no other reason than envy of the good and wanting to possess it for himself. Envy of the good is pure spiritual malice. This is the evil will in radical refusal, or violating recoil from the goodness of being. The shut-in self wants to possess the good without sharing—that is, only in self-communication outside of the community of others and creation. But no one owns goodness. That is why ultimately the good is the ground of all modes of togetherness, of community. The true good is not diminished in being shared; its self-communication is for the other, and the self loses nothing by giving it to the other. Quite the opposite, it gains all by giving it away; the good is augmented in being shared. This is the profound promise of self-communication that is not shut up, but that in its very being is for the other, in communication with the other. Cain hates the community of the good; he kills because he wants to possess the good; but he kills the good in wanting to possess it thus. This killing, possession, is the death of the good, of community.

Cain built a city. What does this say about the city? It says that the shadow of violent equivocity darkens all community and communication. A brother is a murderer. A smile hides a dagger. A seduction is a rape. An ally is a serpent. Deceit, malice, masquerade as honesty and goodwill. Evil pays its compliment to the good in its murderous envy. The power of this murder is its impotence, and its being parasitical on the goodwill of the good.

But since equivocity is double, there is a positive side to it. Communication is more than univocity, and another community is promised in the baffling richness of all ambiguity. The evil exploit this ambiguity to baffle maliciously; the good are perplexed at the face of an enigma. This face of enigma communicates, but it is not univocal; it speaks in many tongues, many of them not understood at all. Community communicates itself in a plurivocity that looks to the redemption of equivocity. This communivocity is the metaxological togetherness of a pluralism of voices, where no one voice shouts down the other voices, or reduces them to itself. Even the voice of evil too is allowed its say, with its smirk and sneer of "Polyanna"—allowed, let be, in the hope that, in time, its freedom will be converted into the redeemed voice of a good.

The Community of Distracted Desire

Communities are convergences of transcendences in the between whose social shaping is hence relative to the character of the transcendences, or the fullness of their activation. I will look now at three increasingly more ultimate activations of human self-transcendence relative to the communities they shape. I will call these the community of *distracted desire*, the community of *erotic sovereignty*, and the community of *agapeic service*.

The community of distracted desire emerges from the frustration of any univocal formation of human self-transcendence. By univocal desire I mean an appetition that is unidirectional, that has one form and one objective. For instance, we might say that animal thirst is unidirectionally oriented to drink. In univocal desire we find a one-to-one correlation between the seeking and the sought, the transcending and its *telos*. Animal appetition is self-transcending, but is so univocally; hence the round of its biological drives and satisfactions is similarly constricted. With such biological community the between is the place of relatively uncomplicated activations of transcending. We have, say, the sameness of the herd, except perhaps for the dominant animal that emerges from the mass, because of the vehemence of his biological urges.

Animal desire is not completely univocal, and this is even more so with human desire. It frees itself in its activation of self-transcendence from the univocal circle of routine biological sameness. Thus human thirst can be expressive of a multitude of desires, of which the thirst for water may be but one. Thirst may bespeak a deficiency, or lack, or longing of the entire self, and have nothing to do with the hydration of the organism. This may include thirst for God—the psalm says: as the deer longs for running water, so does my soul thirst for God. The desire itself and the *telos* sought are not univocal determinate objects. We may not be at all sure what is the aim, if any, of our longings. There is a free indeterminacy about desire that also perplexes desire itself concerning any fulfilling *telos*. Desire excites itself beyond univocal satisfaction, but perplexes itself in this self-activation.

This twisting of desire in its own pluralization is nowhere more evident than with sex. Sexual couplings are incarnate modes of togetherness where bodies are activated relative to an energy of transcendence, a going beyond in the flesh itself, either an opening to the other, or a seeking of the other. The sexual surge of the human being is not univocally confined to the rutting season. There is no rutting season. The activation of transcendence in human desire lacks a single determinate season. Beyond puberty, which releases the equivocity of sexuality, it is potentially all-pervasive; it is all times and no one time. This is the excess of human desire as sexually expressed. In many ways, sexual desire is quintessentially equivocal, in that we never know with mathematical univocity what is at stake or at play. An ambiguous look passes silently between members of the opposite sex, and what does it mean? Does it mean yes or does it mean no, does it mean try but you will not succeed, does it say no but mean yes, or seem to imply yes only to draw on to endless tease? There is no univocity.

The infinite restlessness at play in this renders even more ambiguous desire's equivocity. If we cannot say for sure what the goal of all this is, we might be tempted to revert to desire itself and its own self-activation. The result? An endless excitation of desire, for the sake of desire's own self-excitation. The other to be loved, why this is really only a means by which the self-excitation excites itself. This arousal of self-transcendence is equivocal about the other. What is certainly clear about this surge of restless urge is that there is an arousal of energy, regardless of the other sought. We are tempted to think: the arousal is the point, the other a means of excitation. One cannot confess this, of course. One equivocally plays the game as if the other were the beloved.

What if we pluralize such restless beings? They congress as a community of equivocal desire seeking itself in distraction from itself. What is this? This is a community fostered on, and fostering, the denial of any inherent goal to desire. All things serve desire's satisfaction, but since there is no real satisfaction, they really do not serve satisfaction but the endless arousal of dissatisfaction. Each member of this community is for-itself, but for itself in a manner that does not really take the other as other into account, except insofar as the other is for the self. The for-itself of this self is a distention of univocal desire; self-transcendence is not really seized in its promise beyond univocity; it is mere excessive distention. Hence characteristically, the human being is understood in terms of self-preservation and perpetuation, and a variety of hidden mechanisms by which evolutionary process supposedly works for the survival of the fittest. The selves in community are distended atoms of this desire for-self.

This community is the society of limitless consumption of the other. It is a community of devouring desire. Why devouring? Devouring, because desire's distention knows no univocal end, concludes there is no end to desire, hence moves to consume all things, lest perchance in the plethora of things there might be one or two or more that might conceivably offer some peace to its waste expanse of dissatisfaction. Quantity of possession drowns the quieter thought that selves might be together through the quality of their being. Quality of self, as well as intimacy of communion is lost, since the self in distention is almost entirely extroverted onto this, that, and the other thing. The excess of transcendence thus distended is not self-transcending.

This community promises limitless satisfaction, because it claims that there is no limit to satisfactions. What it delivers is limitless dissatisfaction, precisely because there is nothing that will inherently satisfy such selves. In endless and indifferent consumption, this devouring community produces a nausea of spirit. It empties selfhood into a middle that is really the social dramatization of spiritual distraction. It cheerily welcomes us all into the community of diversions. Diversions divert the self from itself, divert it from having to look the other in the eye. Diversions divert desire from its endlessly renewed misery, divert it into renewed forays into distraction after distraction, all the while brazenly reassuring us that this miserable hunt for distraction after distraction is the good life.

The distension of selves into a middle of distraction empties selves of their intimacy, their inner otherness. This is a community of hollow selves. We have given ourselves away, believing that the next distraction will be the thing itself, but there is nothing around each corner of promised novelty. There is nothing in the other either, since the other has been drawn into the maelstrom of distraction. Life is an entertainment, but it is boring entertainment. Even the entertaining entertainment is boring entertainment. A shadow of sadness, a shaft of horror falls, when the diversion palls, falls into the interstices of quiet.

The selves of distracted desire are the most bored beings, for our diversions reach an empty satiation where we know ourselves simply as disgust with self. Our pleasures become our odium, our self-love our self-hatred. Our relativity to others is also hidden hatred. For an other so used will reflect back our own emptiness, and so redouble disgust with self. Of course, self-disgust, like desire itself, can excite itself to further disgust. Many now will welcome shock or provocation or outrage. The outrageous self has to outrage because there is deadness of spirit in all the entertaining diversions. This deadness cannot be coaxed into renewal without penitence before the emptiness. But this is intolerable. Instead outrage will be heaped on outrage, until outrage become free-floating rage. The coy promise of limitless satisfaction first tendered by the community of distracted desire now consumes itself in an unanchored, indefinable rage, against self, against the other, against the between, against everything and against nothing. This indeterminate rage against being is infernal transcendence.

This must end in the violation of the deepest intimacy of selfhood and community. We end in a community of aestheticized vanity, wherein we are numb to the delicacies of quiet inwardness, coarse to the dignity for which the other appeals, crude with respect to the promise of communication that might occur in the middle, if only the shouting stops, empty of civility, decorum, modesty, shame. The numbing of self, the coarsening of community, makes the between the empty space where selves roar, even if they say nothing. This is the togetherness of hell. And do not say I paint a phantom. It is here and we have seen it.

Even though it be marvelously well-organized in a bureaucratic way, even though managerial experts smoothly shape the efficiency of production and consumption, the community of distracted desire is a heap. One thinks of Plato's Cave. The many will work but satisfy their appetites in a life of extended consumption. In modernity human self-transcendence is loosened from its community with the other as transcendent, whether the divine, or the good, or the other ethical self. Desire excites itself, for itself, just as, with Descartes, thought thinks itself, for itself. Thought also thinks the new mechanistic science so that desire can desire itself, desire its limitless satisfaction by subjection of things other. There is an irony in the fact that this community of equivocal distraction is most let loose in mirror images of mechanism. Mechanism is an epitome of univocal *mathēsis*; but if the human being is analogously thought of as a separate atom, then its desire as distended becomes the predatory foraging of a free-lance individualism. The thinking thing become a desiring thing, becomes an atom of predatory transcendence in which no other will be allowed to curb its assertion of complete autonomy. It is self-law, *auto-nomos*. Where there is a *heteros*, there can only be external relations between one atom of self and another. The space between them is abased into a valueless middle.

Just as the world of aesthetic happening is robbed of its charge of value, the public space of the between is said to be a neutral context. In itself it is worthless; as a middle it is a mere means. The evacuation of inwardness is mirrored in the deterioration of public space; we are atoms in the void, though unlike the systems of material mass, we are predatory atoms, willful atoms that distend themselves through endless appetite into the empty between. This view voids the singular and the communal of their depth of ontological richness. The singular is entirely externalized, and viewed as if from the outside, while the communal is defined as a set of after-the-fact external relations. Modes of togetherness are merely extrinsic, while selves are without the inherent intimacy of inwardness. The selves in community of distracted desire are not even atoms in the void, they are voids in the void. For their transcending is emptied of its inner intimacy.

The mechanization of the world, the univocalization of the self as a free-lance individual, issues in the community of equivocal desire, because the energy of transcending cannot be put to sleep, even in this mechanized univocalization. With its twisted promiscuity this community is a paradoxical outcome of a totalizing univocity. The society that in human history most loudly proclaims autonomy is the most managed society in human history. The self that in human history most loudly shouts its singularity and difference is an atom in the heap of what may be a spiritual conformism more complete than at any time in human history. The society that announces novelty every minute of the day is the society most bored with each new announcement, and bored then again with its own excitement and boredom. The hard clarity of univocal enlightenment produces the murk of dark and roiling equivocity.

The evacuation of the self, then its release out of its own emptiness to emptiness outside, the neutered public between, describes the society of totalized consumption, but it equally applies to the society of totalitarian order. There is a centrally managed production and consumption in the totalitarian state; there is a decentralized production and consumption in the consumer society. If both exhausted the possibilities of community, we would be hard put to escape from spiritual bankruptcy. The mode of togetherness in both are extrinsic connections. In both, the between is the empty space of exploitation. Private and public are, in a real sense, both desecrated. Behind both formations of togetherness is an essential ontological aggression. Work itself is an aggression on creation in which the lording animal wills to reshape all creation's otherness in the image of its own desire. But since the lording animal's desire is equivocal, the end result must still be equivocation, in which no one really knows if there is ever peace or not, joy in being or not, or war following war, and wretchedness the end of all our futile quests.

The Community of Erotic Sovereignty

There is more to eros than equivocal sex. Nor need selves be distracted. We can mediate with ourselves and in some measure can be at home with ourselves in the expanse of our self-transcending. We can be integrated to ourselves, even when in search of the other to answer the lack or need we undergo in our own desiring. The energy of self-transcending is not dissipative without end or outcome. The self comes out of itself, but this coming out has an outcome—namely, that the self comes to itself in coming out of itself. What I call the community of erotic sovereignty answers, as a mode of togetherness, to this gathering of self to itself, in its coming to be with the other.

First I note that equivocity continues here, in that a certain strife does shape the community of erotic sovereignty. There is always strife in the between: the self is strife when not at home with itself; there is strife between self and other, since they face each other ambiguously. In this facing, there may be a welcome to a self coming out of itself; or rejection or violence or rebuff or undermining. One cannot be sure in advance; hence the between is a place of *hazard*. To risk oneself, one may have to fight against oneself, and the trepidation that risking will deprive one of oneself. One may decide that it is better not to adventure in otherness, lest the adventure deprive one of the idiotic feeling of self-worth. In truth, we are already given over into the community of the between. The issue is how we stand together in the between.

The erotic self may mediate the equivocity, both in the public space of togetherness and in the inner tangle of its own desiring being. Such selves together may come to be themselves in going to meet the world of otherness. In meeting with the other, there is more than equivocal desire at play. There is perhaps an appeal for dignity, perhaps the hiddenness of a now turmoiled, now quiet inwardness. Self-transcending comes to rest on the others, and here comes to look at itself from the point of view of the other. Put differently, the other turns the self mindfully back to itself, offers it a way to be at home with itself. The dissipative effects of distraction may themselves be dissipated.

If one adventures in the between, and stays true to the togetherness there, in mindfulness of the other, one finds, as it were, an anchor outside of self, in the steadiness of the other. This steadiness offers the opportunity for our transcending to steady itself, and so to come to itself more truly. In a word, the other offers me back myself. In accepting this offer, I become myself beyond the dissipation of distraction. I am called to myself from the other; the other sends me home to myself from the extroversion of endless, distended discontent. The other says: look at you! I look. I look and do not like what I see. Even if I like what I see, I do look, and I see. I see perhaps for the first time, through the other, but beyond the eyes that the other has given me of myself. I see myself.

Again this all takes place in a dynamic relating. It is happening all the time but we do not attend to it. We are attending to the other, attending to ourselves, though we do not attend to our attention, or become mindful of our doubled mindfulness. I see myself as incarnated in a community of togetherness. I must go out of myself and enter into togetherness with the other; the other arrests desire's dissipation in equivocity; being arrested, I am thrown back on myself. I am seen, I see myself. Through the other I come to recognize myself; through the other's recognition I come to self-recognition. Why is re-cognition important? Because it implies a reference back to a prior knowing of self.[3] One comes to know oneself, though one immediately knew oneself; one comes to remember oneself as an integrity, preceeding and exceeding every dissipation.

I do not say that the other is a means by which I come to myself. This will be a danger, and will remain a danger. The coming of the self to itself, in its outgoing towards the other, is erotic sovereignty. It is erotic, because the self proceeds through its transcending from its own lack to self-fulfillment; it is a sovereign, because its togetherness with others gives the self back to itself, with a confirmation of itself and its powers. The community of erotic sovereignty gives selves to themselves as autonomous. The autonomy is mediated by the togetherness, out of which, nevertheless, it is emergent for itself.

---

3. I previously spoke of this relative to idiotic and aesthetic selving.

This autonomy is not simply the willful self-assertion of free-lance individualism in equivocal community. It is the coming of the self to itself in its inherent richness. This is made possible by its togetherness with others, for just that togetherness allows one to rise above its conditioning circumstances and be for oneself.[4]

The sovereign self has come to mastery of itself in its self-development. It breathes freedom in the companionship of other such sovereigns. Self-assertion is not the point, nor is domination. A sovereign self is at home with itself and at home with other sovereign selves. They do not threaten. For they relate to each other from a certain fulfilled sense of self, not from privative positions. The companionship is full of mindfulness and hence of respect for the other. Yet each member is sovereign for itself; it is its achieved wholeness, and so may not even feel any need to assert itself. The community of erotic sovereignty is the companionship of selves who are together as open wholes. Whole: each is a rich self-mediating integrity for itself; open: the relativity to the other is not slighted, either in terms of its antecedent others that offered the self back to itself, or the present or future companions, to whom the sovereign self will be open, or go to meet, out of its achieved plenitude.

All of this is, of course, a result. It does not happen simply; it does not come easily, or often; it is the rare outcome of an arduous process. Let me refer to Hegel. We can say that for Hegel the process of winning through to erotic sovereignty must pass through the struggle to the death that is a struggle for recognition, the struggle *to be recognized* of the master and slave dialectic. Now sovereign mastery does not belong to the master. For the master is finally nothing in himself, except as parasitical on the work of the slave. The community of erotic sovereignty is beyond that dialectic, though Hegel thinks it can be reached only by passing through it. The dialectic of master and slave is actually, in the terms I use, not fully dialectical. It is an equivocal relation, since the victor is the defeated and the defeated is the victor; or rather, there is no clear positive outcome at all, on the terms of this interplay itself. One cannot be released from this equivocal dialectic, unless another sense of dialectic, beyond master and slavery, comes into play, and such a dialectic must have a metaxological dimension. I will come back to this.

---

4. Consider this example, though there is a certain ambiguity in it relative to my point. I run a race. Why? Is it just to defeat the others? Yes I want to win. But why win? Part of the answer is that I want to triumph, though not simply over the others. Triumph is excellence achieved, being the best possible. One triumphs over self, over the pain of conditions, over opponents too. But the other incites one to the best. To win is not just to crush the other, but to be the achieved excellence. Of course, there is ambiguity also in that runners will speak of *killing* their rivals, or of *dying* in a race—namely, becoming exhausted.

Our self-relating sociability must win through to an achieved integrity of self in the between. There it is together with other selves, also engaged in the adventure of integrity. The community of erotic sovereignty is the community of such achieving wholes. The question now is how further we describe this community. Because of the dialectic of self-mediation, Hegel opts for the language of *the whole*. Even if the members are open wholes, *as together* Hegel sees them as parts of a community that encompasses the interplay of the participating members. The community is a dialectically self-mediating whole within which the selves are together as subordinate wholes, open to the encompassing circle of the larger whole. This is how Hegelian dialectic sees being together: conflicts between wholes are mediated and overcome through a more embracing whole, relative to which the opposing wholes are subordinate parts; the most embracing whole is said to be the comprehensive togetherness.

As I understand Hegel, the absolute whole is said to be *the* sovereign self-mediation. The most embracing community becomes itself a kind of sovereign self: an absolute erotic self, call it absolute *Geist*, since the members of the community are for it. Here the holistic togetherness transcends the extrinsic connections and mechanistic metaphors of univocal and equivocal views of community. There are no merely external relations. The sovereign self, in being itself, is not itself for itself in abstraction from its relativity to others. Its external relativity to the other is internally mediated by itself. So, in some measure, external relations are partially mediated internal relations, insofar as the other has been interiorized as a constituent of the identity of the self, both for itself and in relation. We might say that when the erotic self is thrown back on itself from the other, the other comes back with it, is *brought back home* with the self recollecting itself. The internal sense of the self's achieved wholeness bears this external relatedness within its own mediated self-relation.

I am putting the matter in terms that are not always Hegel's, because what I want to say is not coincident with Hegel. Thus the sovereign self-relation is a complex of internal and external relations. This is more complicated than a dualism of internal and external relations. The internal relations of the self to itself includes its external relations to what is other. The self at home with itself never forgets that home is as much *given* to it by the other, as *won* by itself through its own adventuring endeavors. The erotic sovereign wins its being at home with itself, but it would never win did not the other *offer* it a home outside itself, a resting in the restlessness of its self-transcending. This is a doubling of the self in community beyond dualistic opposition. As Hegel would understand the erotic sovereign, this doubling is subordinated to the primacy of self-relation, wrongly I think. I hold the doubling remains irreducible to self-relation. This will be more evident later with the community of agapeic service. The doubling will offer primacy to an other-relatedness, which is beyond the standard dualism of internal and external relations, beyond in a metaxological rather than dialectical sense.

Not surprisingly, the metaphors describing the togetherness of erotic
sovereigns tends to be *organic* rather than mechanical. Organic metaphors
point to integrities of being that are self-developing, and that yet have a certain completeness for themselves, perhaps even being autotelic. Sometimes
such organic self-development is taken as a metaphor for free self-
determination, autonomy. Erotic sovereignty is actually more complex than
this, yet the organic metaphor readily suggests itself as far richer than any
mechanical model. The community as organic is a self-mediating whole whose
members are subordinate self-mediating wholes. Freedom is autonomous self-
mediation within a community, which is said to be the more absolute organic
togetherness of an autonomous self-mediating whole. The shadow of certain
Hegelianisms again appears.

One must hesitate here in some trepidation. The ambiguity of applying
organic metaphors to freedom turns on the relation of an organism to difference. The organism relates to difference through repulsion or assimilation. Assimilation is a "making like," and every likening also preserves an
unlikeness. But organic assimilation per se accepts within the integrity of
the organism *only what can be made like*. What cannot be thus assimilated
is "alien matter," to be expelled as waste, or overcome with medicine or
therapy. Organic togetherness has a clear limit on its tolerance of otherness, indeed actively works to reduce or expel any difference that will not
change its character to make itself amenable to subsumption within the
whole. Thus the trepidation. The organic metaphorics can foster murderous consequences when the "alien matter" is a people that cannot be assimilated to the dominion of the prevailing whole. The Holocaust clearly
shows the evil danger in this organic metaphorics, and this even more so,
when the killing of the Jewish "bacillus" is accomplished with the efficiency
of mechanical power such as has been mustered through modern technology and techniques of managerial control.

Suppose we couple the organic metaphor with the mechanics of managerial efficiency, and both with the image of the erotic sovereign. The grim
shadow of the totalitarian state looms. We see the majesty of sovereignty degenerate into the power of terror. We see that Stalin was only a dialectical
Hitler, no less an efficient "desk murderer" of the others who cannot or will
not be ingested into the totalitarian Moloch. In other words, the majesty of
erotic sovereignty is turned into the liquefying power of terror, invested in
the figure of the leader. And there can only be one master, a god for whom all
else is. Moloch is invested in his sovereign self. Every other is for this Moloch,
and if it resists, it will be crushed, pulverized into more manageable matter.
Moreover, the despotic power of less totalized communities are steps on the
way to this outcome. What is Hobbes' Leviathan but an erotic sovereign in an
equivocal sense: a center of all but absolute power that has to terrorize the
community of equivocal desire to prevent its degeneration into the degraded
state of nature, the *bellum omnium contra omnes*? Stalin and Hitler did not

win any peace by checking this war, but waged it further to its extreme, exacerbating it to the limit. Nothing is left but terror incarnate, perched on its throne above a heap of grinning bones. This is the sovereignty of the kingdom of death.

In such wise the equivocity of organic holism falls beneath the affirmative achievement of wholeness possible in the community of erotic sovereignty. For there is a dialectical togetherness of autonomous wholeness, beyond the master and slave equivocity, and beyond the deformations of dialectical togetherness that follow when we take this equivocity to be the essence of dialectical togetherness (as do Marx, Sartre, Stalin, Kojève). Human self-mastery is not won out of a master-slave dialectic. It is won in part, in part given, in an interplay that is dialectical and metaxological. The above deformations of erotic sovereignty twist the true meaning of dialectical togetherness, which itself cannot be fully achieved on dialectical terms alone. So let me now state some of the genuine gains of the community of erotic sovereignty. I will then speak of some of the dangers.

A *first, major gain* is the recognition that the participants in a community of erotic sovereignty are marked by an inwardness with an infinite reserve of worth. With us the self-relating sociability comes to explicit mindful self-mediation in its intermediation with other selves, that are also explicitly self-mediating in a mindful way. In the between of togetherness the erotic sovereign is thrown back upon itself, returned to itself, in a return from encounter with an other I, in whose eyes and face an unmeasured depth of inwardness has been sensed. The togetherness returns the self to its own inward otherness. Moreover, this return is a conversion of desire's infinite restlessness; the trajectory of self-transcending recollects itself in this conversion, and comes to mediated mindfulness of itself, not merely as an incessantly extroverted discontent, but as an unmeasured source of self-transcendence within itself.

The community of erotic sovereignty opens up this unmeasured source of transcending for the self as for itself. The source of self-transcendence is not a lack seeking completion elsewhere; the source is already rich in itself, a fount of self-articulation and relation, beyond all determinate measure. The depth of self-relation emerges in mindfulness of the infinite promise within. Of this promise the infinite restlessness is one expression, but not the only expression. The more this depth mediates with itself and understands itself as an originative source, the less can the movement of self-transcending be characterized simply as an infinite restlessness of endless lack. There is another restlessness, a new sleeplessness, but it is a different sleeplessness, a different desire.

Dialectical community opens up the original depths of self-relation, points to selfhood as an end in itself of infinite value, because a source of transcendence beyond finite measure. The hyphen of self-relation is a hiatus of articulation within the integrity of self, but this gap opens because a more original source of articulation makes possible the difference between the self and it-self. This difference allows the self to become mindful of what is at play in itself, become mindful in a recollected way. The source of origination is the self in its inward otherness, which divides the self from itself, yet also allows the mediation that brings the self back to itself in mindful self-relation. This source is the original transcendence, which constitutes self as being beyond finite measure.

We must acknowledge that the community of distracted desire also lives this transcendence beyond finite measure, but it is unmindful of the meaning of its own transcendence. It squanders its restlessness for the infinite in infinite distraction on an unmeasured quantity of finite satisfactions. But nothing finite will either quell the infinite restlessness, nor answer to the unmeasured reserve of promise that surges up in the inward infinity of self. The difference between the communities of distracted desire and erotic sovereignty is this: in the first, the other is a mere means, hence does not count for itself in the endless self-excitation; in the second, the other faces one with an infinite reserve of its own, beyond measure, and this facing arrests the infinite restlessness and send the self back, converts it to a reversion to self, in which it becomes mindful of its own infinite reserve beyond finite measure. Erotic sovereignty is won in this appropriation of self beyond finite measure.

A *second gain* is this: while self-mastery is won, the essential co-implication of the self and the other is not denied. The relation of togetherness is not between two beings fixed in themselves, and defined for themselves within a network of external social ties. Quite to the contrary, the trajectory of self-transcending would dissipate itself endlessly and finally into nothing, were it not arrested, and brought to the task of taking stock of itself, by the face of the other that always stands before it. For in each fugue of transcendence into distraction, the face of the other haunts the flight. The face may be the face of a mother, or a father, or a friend. . . .

The other asks the self in diversion: Who are you? In answer, the diversion may be renewed. But the question cannot be indefinitely deferred. To defer this question indefinitely would be to void our very being as transcending selves. Indefinite deferral would be infinite distraction from the task that haunts us: to be and become the selves we are. The call is voiced in the arrest of the other, but the call comes to us from within the movement of transcendence also. It is both other to us and internal to us; it is not we, and yet it is our most intimate self that calls out, that calls on itself, that calls itself to be itself.

I want to emphasize that this internal relation to the other is not the *obverse* of an external relation, considered as an extrinsic connection. It is not that the erotic sovereign is really nothing in itself and everything only through a web of relativity. This actually would be to dissolve the sovereign self in a tissue of external relativity; community becomes an infinitely spread out web of external relations, and the identity of anything within the web is just its being within this web of relations; internal relations, on this view, constitute this being within the web. But this will not do, since the inward otherness of the sovereign self vanishes.

As we now see, this inward otherness is coextensive with its infinite reserve beyond finite measure. And this cannot be dissolved in the endless web. Being arrested by the facing other, and thrown back upon this infinite reserve, brings the relation to the other within the self-relation of the sovereign self. But that *within* is then, and this is crucial, *inherently pluralized*: we find the self-relating recovery of infinite inwardness, but also a listening to the voice of the other within that recovered inwardness. Put otherwise, the inwardness is a *community of voices*, not all of them that of the self, and some of them capable of breaking down and subverting every claim made by the self to be a completely self-sufficient whole. Internal relations here mean that the innerness of the self is a family of voices. If this is dialectical, it is because it is essentially dialogical, plurivocal.

This points to a *third gain*—namely, that self-relation is itself defined by relation to others. The self and the other are together in the between; but the self and the other are themselves modes of togetherness; they duplicate the between in themselves; neither constitutes the between from out of itself; this is an impossibility. The community of the between is neither in here nor out there, for it is in here and out there, and yet it is nowhere and everywhere. The self and the other are in the field of communication, and are themselves fields of communication. This is another way of saying that the energy of self-transcendence is just this self-communication that is energized in both the self and the other, and in the space between them. The energy of self-transcendence is the ecstasis of being that communicates itself; but it communicates itself in no void space between atoms inert in themselves; there is no void space, for the between is the ecstasis of the field of communication. In this between both the self and the other are determinately defined as centers of self-communication, whose ecstasis is already a relativity to what is other to itself. Erotic sovereignty holds that ecstasis in the harmonious embrace of a free self-mastery; but it is clear that this ecstasis also embraces and enfolds the ecstasis of the other.

Much of what I have just said already takes us into the metaxological proper. Before turning to this, I must note *dangers* with the community of erotic sovereignty. These dangers turn on, as we might put it, the tension between infinitude and wholeness. For the inward infinitude of sovereign selves is at odds with the notion of an absorbing whole. The dialectical sense of being tends to resolve oppositions by subsuming them into a larger absorbing whole, all the way to the whole of all wholes, which is the absolute absorbing totality. I suggest that the inward infinitude of an erotic sovereign cannot be included without remainder in such an absorbing whole. That is, there is an idiocy to the members of this community that is not the function of a more embracing generality. This idiocy is the dimension of intimacy that opens in the depth of inwardness itself. There is no absorbing of this intimacy into a larger whole. There is indeed a community of intimacy, but there is nothing absorbing about it. Like the metaphorics of organism, the entire language of the absorbing whole will not do to describe any community, wherein this intimacy of being is at play.

Resort to the absorbing whole is typical of a certain logicism for which the particular in itself is nothing in abstraction from the universal or general. This universal is said to be the larger logical community, which binds the particular to others of the same kind, and gives this particular the kind of being that it exemplifies; in itself it is nothing, but is defined in a tissue of general relations. This logicization of wholeness is not adequate to the deeper sense of singularity that is manifested through the dialectical interplay of the community of erotic sovereigns. This deeper sense of singularity can never be made simply the function of a togetherness, precisely because in its idiocy it opens into its own depth dimensions, beyond all finite measuring. When we understand that dialectical self-mediation reveals something of this infinitude in singularity, we have to shed the language of absorbing totality to which classical dialectic is so prone, sometimes with consequences that undermine its own better insights.

This danger is not avoided when the full weight of relation to the other is not understood—that is, when self-relation comes to dominate, even absorb the relation to the other. The result might be called *dialectical totalism*. For a dialectical totalism, this absorption will not happen at the level at which self and other coexist, but relative to the larger whole, which is said to embrace these two. We can say, and I do say, that self-relation and relation to the other coexist in tension. But dialectical totalism risks thinking of this tension as a dualism that is still to be sublated into a higher unity; the higher unity will include within itself these two sides. Indeed these two sides will be seen as simply two sides of the higher unity itself, through which the higher unity is merely mediating with *itself*. This will be the higher community, the whole of subordinate wholes; community will be the self-mediating of the higher unity that sublates within itself the partiality of the lower and subordinate wholes. But notice that the privilege of self-mediation has been preserved and perpetuated; the relation to the other is now just one side of a more inclusive self-relation, which includes also the subordinate self-relation. Instead of a tense doubleness between self-relation and relation to the other, the dialectical community will make these relations into two sides of its own more inclusive *self-mediation*. In the most inclusive of all communities, there will be no real other at all, only the absolute whole mediating with itself in its other, which is only *itself* again in its otherness.

While dialectical totalism looks very exalted, it is untrue to the plurivocal stress of the between and the modes of togetherness. This totalism follows, I believe, from the infiltration of organic metaphors into our understanding of freedom and community. The organic metaphor may be richer than the mechanical, as we saw, but if coupled with a complex logic of dialectical self-mediation, the end result can be a subordination of all otherness to some all-inclusive self-relation. It is not that this all-inclusiveness excludes community, not at all. Quite simply, this all-inclusive self-relation is said to be the universal community of the whole. There is one all-inclusive whole, which is the absorbing community of all finite wholes.

This is essentially the Hegelian view of community, but for all its grandeur, it will not do, and on a number of fronts. First, it will not do relative to the space of transcendence *between the origin and creation*, each of which is for itself and neither of which is merely a subordinate whole relative to the other. For the agapeic origin is not an absorbing god; quite the opposite, the agapeic communication radically releases the creation to be its own whole for itself.

Second, it will not do for the community of being *within creation*, especially vis-à-vis the singularity of the human self who evidences an inward infinity that cannot be subsumed within the world as totalized. I mean what Pascal implied when he said that man is a thinking reed, which a drop of water might destroy, yet as thought he is greater than the universe. The utterance might be unpacked, but one of the points will not be to deny our community with creation, but to deny the meaning of that community in terms of an absorbing totality. We have rather a community of original wholes, none of which is completely exhausted by reduction to the other; nor is this to deny their co-implication, but to define that differently.

Third, it will not do relative to the community *between the human being and the origin*. There is an unmeasured inwardness to the human self, which is its source of infinite value; but this inward infinitude is not the infinitude of the origin; it is the promise of infinity, not its full actuality. Man is not God, man is never identical with God; man and God may be together, but the space of transcendence is never obliterated, even in the most intimate communion of the two. God is more inward to inwardness than inwardness is to itself; and yet this more intimate inwardness, this radical immanence of God, is God's absolute transcendence, since it is immeasurably more unmeasured than the unmeasured infinitude of inwardness itself.

The essential danger of dialectical totalism, we might say, is in giving a wrong priority to the notion of the whole over the excess of the infinite. Or, with Hegel, the whole simply becomes the self-mediation of the infinite, a self-mediation that the infinite effects through its mediation with the finite as *its own other*. Then there is no final otherness; the ultimate community is the self-mediating whole, which can also be called the self-mediation of the infinite with *itself* through the finite creation, as the infinite in *its own otherness*. In other words, Hegel's absolute is *the* erotic sovereign that appropriates within itself all otherness and togetherness; it is the absorbing totality of all modes of community. Marx, Nietzsche, and others merely dedivinize this erotic sovereign; but they divinize the human being, as worker, as creator, as the erotic sovereign, who will take to itself, expropriate, appropriate, all otherness through its will to power. Do I have to repeat how disastrous this will to power has been for all the modes of togetherness, ecological, humanized, religious?

The human being is an intentional infinitude; the creation is an infinite succession of becoming in universal impermanence; the origin is an actual infinitude in excess of all finite creations. There is an excess to each that differently defines its being for itself, and hence its nonsubsumable otherness. This excess is not the death of community, but it does crucially modulate the way in which different togethernesses are defined. None, not even the origin, is an absorbing totality that subsumes the other. Rather, the origin as agapeic gives creation its other-being for itself, for the goodness of creation, and not just mediately for itself as origin. This goodness of being-other for itself reaches its richest ontological expression in creation with the human being as an end of infinite worth.

To conclude: transcendence in community is the very reverse of subsumption, without its being the fracturing of togetherness. There is a community of togetherness between origin, creation, the human being. Because of the excess of infinity effective in each, it cannot be accounted for in terms of any self-mediating totality, and certainly not in terms of any deconstructed versions thereof, of which post-Hegelian philosophy offers us examples in plenty. The community that would do justice to the creative excess of infinity has to be thought outside of, beyond, all absorbing totalities, free of the limitations of both mechanistic and organic metaphors. The community of freedom is the metaxological togetherness of a plurality of sources of transcendence. This mode of togetherness I call the community of agapeic service.

The Community of Agapeic Service

I can recapitulate by using Platonic terms to compare the three communities of distracted desire, erotic sovereignty, agapeic service. The first might be likened to the demos in the Cave, the second to the pride of warriors, the *aristoi* of self-mastery, the third to the community of philosophers who are patient to the sun and who would do its service, beyond self-interest and in service of the good of the others.[5] In terms Plato does not use: in the first, there is heteronomy *less* than autonomy; in the second, there is achieved autonomy, but as sometimes forgetting, sometimes remembering its debt to the other; in the third,

---

5. They serve *dikaiosunē*, moved by *eleos*, pity or compassion (see *Republic*, 516c) for the *dikaiosunē* and *eudaimonia* of others.

there is a heteronomy, relative to the good of others and to the Good itself, *beyond* autonomy. We move from the city of the sword to the city of the spirit, from mastery and slavery to service, from dialectic to dialogue, from war to a willing consent that is beyond rebellion and submission.

We must now speak in more detail of the realization of the pluralized promise of communicative being. First, self-relating sociability entails self-communication, but this is also the broadcasting of selves abroad on the between. Second, this broadcasting can be more than the dissemination that dissipates selves in the community of distraction. Third, the community of erotic sovereignty grants a measure of autonomous, recollected selfhood. Beyond this, selves need not communicate themselves as lacking themselves and seeking themselves. Already they have found themselves in some measure. But they know they may lose themselves, unless they communicate themselves in another mode to that of erotic sovereignty. We are called to the community of agapeic service.

We come to a turning point. For mastery of self in the community of erotic sovereignty can become a self-satisfaction that imprisons the trajectory of transcendence. One is satisfied with self for having sifted the infinite restlessness of equivocal desire; one is content with self as no longer prey to diversion. And yet another restlessness, in excess of erotic sovereignty, insinuates itself. This does not seek self-satisfaction at all; it is a restlessness with self beyond all such satisfactions, a disquiet with self as already a satisfying measure of itself. Restlessness erupts out of this won plenitude, and wonders if self-satisfied plenitude might risk a great betrayal of transcendence, should it settle in its contentment with itself.

What is this new restlessness? It is not contempt for "mediocre contentment," and a haughty disdain for the happiness of the many-too-many, such as one finds in Nietzsche, and his aristocratic overman. It is more than this again. It testifies to a way of being together that is incomprehensible, if our terms are all set by the self-mastery of erotic sovereignty. We meet a kind of creative abdication of this sovereignty. There is a going out of the sovereign self, that goes towards the other, with an aim it does not always know, though certainly it would be there for the other, patiently waiting the occasion of aid, of giving to the other, of self-communication that does not secure from self the license of its broadcast, nor persuade its sovereignty that it is really in its own best interests thus to communicate with the other. There is a consent to the middle as the between of giving, beyond all will to power.

The full richness, complexity, and openness of the between are here called into play. Now the mode of togetherness is just the very giving of freedom to the members in interplay. No embrace closes in; any embrace that does enclose is rather an enfolding that releases the one held. The togetherness itself is the releasing of the participants into their own freedom, supported in the promise of their self-transcendence. Freedom in its promise is let be, and the very letting be is the welcoming of this promise to realize itself in the between, in service of the other, in service to the good.

Since there cannot be any forcing of this service, the letting be always is a hazard. The very openness offered may become the occasion of a violence towards the giver that is gratuitous. Malice is real. The freedom that we are can hate the very call on agapeic service and absolutize its own self-relativity to shut out, shout down, the appeal of the other. And so inevitably the community coming to be in the between is always mixed. Mingled together are aggressive, competitive atoms, creatures of the community of equivocal desire, also selves of erotic sovereignty, as well of selves of agapeic goodwill. Moreover, this particular agapeic self may be willing to go beyond its erotic sovereignty, but there is no guarantee that this other self will. One person will enter the middle in the mode of agapeic service, another in competitive exploitation, another still in search of distraction, another again in search of its own erotic sovereignty. A single individual in community can mingle all of these possibilities.

The self of agapeic service knows this overdetermination of the between. It knows that its own being for the other may well be reduced by some others to the level of their mode of being with. But this is a risk it is willing to take. In fact, such a risking willingness is constitutive of the mode of agapeic service. This is a willingness that not only may be misunderstood, or slandered, or mocked, it may suffer violence at the hands of others. It will take the violence on itself, for in that violence it sees the deformed energy of self-transcending, whose fullest communication is in agapeic service; and the violator will never have intimation of its own promise, if not shown the living of this transcendence as agapeic service. Of course, the one who is served may never see what is there before it. It may just see the mirror of its own violence, even in the goodness of the giver. Or if it does see the promise there, it may hate it, for this promise reflects a show of ugliness to it.

Agapeic service gives one the intimation of one's own fault, not by accusing one, but simply by being what it is. In its simple being with the other, it shows the good, and the good when shown arouses our shame. I do not say the good shames us, or judges us. We shame ourselves. Something in the idiocy of our self-being flares into shame, when it knows its own betrayal of the promise of self-transcendence. We judge ourselves, for we do not even live up to ourselves, much less to the appeal of the other. The good simply gives itself without reckoning. It gives freedom, even to the liberty of evil towards the good.

Thus also the community of agapeic service is a togetherness of compassion. In coming to the help of the other, agapeic service is a devotion of transcendence offered to the good of the other. Compassion is a common patience, a suffering with and for the other. It is not the vague sentimentality, sometimes imputed to a vulgarized romanticism, indistinguishable from a self-serving narcissism, and alas all too widespread today. For in coming to the succor of the other, one may put oneself at the mercy of powerlessness. To offer mercy is to risk being treated without mercy, without even decorum or civility. One might be trampled on. There is a horror in being at the mercy of the malign. Are we capable of a trust that stands fast in the face of this horror? To stand disarmed before the malign, in the hope that one's disarmament will also disarm—such a service is not of the world. It is a transcendent service. It is in the service of a prophetic community.

Why is this community beyond the dialectical togetherness looked at above? I emphasize that dialectic does grant the between, does grant the interplay and togetherness of the self and the other. By contrast, the metaxological understands the pluralism of togetherness in a way that makes any return to the primacy of self-mediation out of the question. It will not do to privilege self-mediation, even on the terms of self-mediation itself. Thus as I have indicated, the erotic sovereign is an open whole, whose self-relation always coexists with relativity to the other, even while the self-relation receives primary emphasis. The openness of the erotic sovereign opens inwardly to infinitude, while it opens to the other as constitutive of its own sense of self-identity; it is doubled within itself, doubled relative to the other.

What follows from this? The inward infinity cannot be exhausted by its own self-mediation; there is always an excess, its own excess, or the excess of the origin beyond its own power to originate from itself. Hence there *cannot be* an absolute erotic sovereignty, entirely self-sufficient or closed on itself. Likewise, the other cannot be exhausted by self-mediation, precisely because there is always the excess of the other too, as it mediates out of its own inward otherness and overdetermined promise. The other not only is beyond its own complete self-mediation, more so it is beyond the self-mediation of other selves. Both these sides are marked by an idiotic excess, something over and above all finite determinacy. This is their freedom as originals unto themselves. This idiotic excess of freedom is also the source out of which the self-communication of self-transcendence emerges.

What happens now if we consider community as shaped by a *plurality of such open self-mediating wholes?* The intermediating between such wholes cannot once more be self-mediation, cannot be a more inclusive self-mediation, of which the original plurality are a manifold of sides or aspects. This intermediation shapes the *inter* such that it can never be closed by either side alone, or even by both sides together, for the very *inter* is kept open just by the openness of the participants in this community. The participants are in excess of self-mediation, the interplay of the participants is in excess of self-mediation, and yet there is a mediation. This is metaxological intermediation. This mode of being together is not that of a more encompassing whole that includes within itself subordinate wholes, let us say self and other, each as a dialectical whole for itself. Metaxological intermediation is not between wholes functioning as parts relative to a larger whole; it is between wholes original for themselves, whose interplay is not another whole that embraces the two. It is a community of originals that in themselves are open wholes that are infinitely self-transcending.

It is not that these open wholes *repulse* each other, thus keeping the *inter* open by opposing a natural drift to closure. Rather the open wholes, by being sources of transcendence, always keep the between open. The closure of the circular whole is actually against the directionality of their transcendence, which is to be ever self-transcending, always a going and a being beyond. The open wholes go out of themselves into the between, and their going out also keeps the between open, though the between is already an opening to freedom that welcomes each participant. Metaxological community is always a being between, supported by the gift of the between, shaped by the self-transcendence of its participants, whose promise it always welcomes, even when blocks stand in their way, or some selves block themselves off. There is no absorbing whole of wholes; there is an open community of self-transcending original wholes.

We might recall again a matter touched on in the last chapter—namely, that agapeic service is beyond self-interest. In a literal sense, being between is an *inter-esse*, where the interest is in the being of the *inter*. All genuine interest is *inter-esse*, and not at all just what we normally call self-interest. The latter bends the *inter-esse* back to the self from the *inter*. True interest is beyond self-interest, for it is truly beyond self and is in the *inter*. Even true self-interest is beyond self-interest, for the self is truly itself beyond itself. We might say: interest is always disinterested. Dis-interest usually means a transcending of self-interest; but *all* interest does this. In that regard, disinterest, normally called, is really a lack of interest, and hence a failure to be between, to be true to the between. True interest is an unmeasurable transcending in the between; self-interest is a short-circuiting of that transcending, hence a narrowing of the between to what the self can appropriate for itself. True interest suggests a limitless expanse of metaxological mindfulness. In that regard, only God is truly interested in being, in community with being. Only God loves all being down to the ontological intimacy of singularity. We humans are not capable of that absolute pitch of interest, of being between.

I am pointing to a movement of transcending that goes forth from beings already integrities for themselves, and that shows forth the work of the good already active in these communicative beings. This movement is agapeic rather than erotic when its self-communication is not for the sake of a return to the self. And though the other *may* return the service or recognize the giver, this is not what moves the movement of transcending. This self-transcendence is willing to be for the other; it puts all the energy of its being at the disposal of the other; it makes itself radically available for the other. It says: Here I am for you; and I am here, because I want nothing.

By contrast, the erotic sovereign wants self, and wins self in a dialectical struggle with otherness. The doing of transcendence is for the self that transcends. In the agapeic movement, there is a going out and towards that asks no return, that reckons no comeback for its outlays, that is beyond calculation and reckoning. It is heedless, in the sense of not counting the cost; but it

is an absolute heeding, since its awakened mindfulness is sleeplessly alert to
the appeal of the other. This agapeic self-transcendence into the between is
not a decentering so much as an *excentering* of self. For the self is still a
center, even when it makes its original energy of being available for the other;
it is centered eccentrically. Even within its own inward centering, it is eccentric, since the inward otherness points beyond the for-self towards an other
origin. The agapeic self is centered beyond itself.

   This is service: it is a giving to the other; and it is not first a giving of
something to the other; it is a giving of oneself to the other. How can one give
oneself? Very difficult, since the self given is still for itself, and hence not
radically given. True giving, service would turn the self inside out. The community of agapeic service asked of us this reversal, that we give ourselves by
giving ourselves up. What does it mean to serve by giving oneself up? There is
no other word for it but *sacrifice*. A sacrifice is a gift that is a giving over and
a giving up. We might say a gift is itself an agapeic movement of transcendence. A giving over is a transmission, or communication, from what one is,
or has, to the other who is to receive. A giving up is a submission to a dimension of height in agapeic self-transcendence. The other to whom one gives is
beyond one, above one. The appeal of the other comes from this beyond.

   One must sacrifice oneself to enact the call of agapeic service; one is
made sacred (*sacer facere*) by this service; it is a divine service. One is made
sacred by one's willingness to give oneself up, radically give oneself over to
the other and its good. The reversal here is like a kind of *death* to erotic
sovereignty. Not incidentally, sacrifice has been frequently associated with
death. Here there is equivocity, since death can range from the violence on
the scapegoat victim, to the willingness to offer one's life in place of another,
or the willingness to offer one's life for the truth or the good. The last sacrifice is that of the martyr. This agapeic service is the testimony of witness.
Giving over, giving up is the agapeic service of transcendence that witnesses,
testifies for the other, on behalf of an order of transcendence that goes beyond the distinction we know between life and death. In that regard, one
might say that agapeic service is a life of transcendence that is beyond life and
death. This is the measure of its generosity beyond measure.

   Let no one think I am talking about some soft, sweet nobility. I am talking about the good of life, but also about suffering, and despair, and the desolation of death. Suppose we compare erotic sovereignty and agapeic service in
terms of the hero and the martyr. Suppose we think of the first in terms of the
statues of the gods, or the warrior, or the athlete in Greek art. We behold the
harmony of the ideal whole. We see the glorification of all that is masterful
about the human being, in its beauty of body, its power of mind and will, the
glory of all that is to be glorified in the world. This is the sovereign beauty of
a bounded whole that is completely there. As a whole for itself such statues
image what an erotic sovereign might be. Yet something eludes, something
more is elusive. Suffering is subordinated to the ideal beauty. There is

inwardness only to the point where inner chaos is conquered. The infinity of inwardness in its otherness and its potential for violent chaos and evil are not shown, though not at all because they are unknown.

Think now of agapeic service in terms of the person of Jesus, in his life, in his death. Suffering is not idealized, even though its very desolation is seen as redemptive. There is the inwardizing of the suffering servant, even unto death, glimpsed in the unbearable agony in the garden of Gethsemane, heard in the shocking cry of abandonment on the cross. This is an idiocy of inwardness when the agapeic origin seems to desert life completely, and the kingdom of death lays waste. The abyss of inwardness itself becomes a horrifying waste—both a desert of meaninglessness, and a waste of being that is crushed by the horror "I am nothing, I count for nothing."

No one hears, no one helps, the I seems absolutely alone, singular in the face of a malign surd of waste. Yet, so it seems, ultimate trust comes in the face of death, trust beyond death. This is the consent to the community of agapeic service. Consent in trust is a giving up, an abandonment for the sake of the community of being and its re-creation. Sacrificial death is the agapeic service of a kingdom that is both within us, and not of this world, a kingdom radically intimate, and radically transcendent.

Transformed Relations and Agapeic Participation

Insofar as the community of agapeic service suggests the light of a different intimacy and transcendence, it transforms our understanding of external and internal relations, as well as the notion of participation. I offer some final remarks on these points.

Concerning external relations, though there is an intimate co-implication of the members of agapeic community, externality nevertheless remains, and not as a mere contiguity without worth, a brute facticity of valueless connection. It remains because agapeic service is respect for the other, even in unmediated otherness. The other can never be reduced to me. We have to do with each other as letting each other be other to each other. This is the rich externality of a tolerance that bears otherness, that bears with otherness.

The point must be put more strongly: this externality asks of us a kind of metaphysical *patience*. Patience here does not mean defeat and humiliation. Being patient to the other means being receptive to what may come to one out of the other's externality. Bearing with otherness means forbearance before the other. Patience before externality is not a dwarfing of self, but a *being in waiting*. What is this waiting? It is a movement of opening that makes ready for the right time to communicate or receive communication. One must wait for the promise of the other to flower according to its own time. This waiting is patience to everything in its season. It is metaphysical consent to creation in universal impermanence, to the good there taking its appropriate and timely shape. Moreover, this patience extends also to the suffering of being, the jagged edges of externality that wound the soul, that bleed its zeal and weary its hope. Patience is an anticipation of the radical amen that is asked of us in the face of the absolute negation of death.

The community of erotic sovereignty does not know this deeper patience but is brusque with obstacles to its own mastery. The patience of agapeic service is a deeper consent to being that would not brush aside or smash down the negative. It awaits the flowering of the good through the negative. Its trust in being is more deeply grounded than that of the erotic sovereign who finally would rely on himself alone. This trust is a metaphysical faith that all will be well.

And so this patience is an obedience of the truth and the good. It is not quietistic, if we mean it does nothing. Not at all, it works tirelessly to prepare for the coming of the good. Its patience is not its defeat, but its willingness never to give up on the promise of the good in the other. We might say: it gives itself up because it never gives up on the promise of good in the other. The vehemence of erotic sovereignty might see only defeat here; but this erotic vehemence makes invisible the great self-overcoming here fructifying, a self-overcoming so radical it no longer needs to insist on itself, call any attention to itself. It is nothing, so that it may be a between of transmission, where the energy of the good may find unhindered passage, and so come to concretion. Patience is self-transcendence that is outside of itself, an ecstasis of self in the between in which it prepares the community for the coming good. Patience is a servant of the good beyond power. It is itself a gift of the power of the good, beyond all will to power.

I come to the second point: the community of agapeic service also transforms internal relations. We move beyond a dualism of internal and external, beyond a dialectic of them. For here internal relations are neither such as to dissolve the singularity of the self into a web of relations, nor are they defined by the internalized other that marks erotic sovereigns. The thrust to interiorize the other by erotic sovereigns meets a *second* check. Recall that the other arrests the external dissipation of equivocal desire, and sends the self back to itself; then the erotic sovereign wins itself in the return to itself; this is the first arrest. The second arrest is when the erotic self realizes, having won itself, that what it seems to have interiorized, it can never master. The other that sends it back to itself is brought home with it, and the excess of its otherness ferments, within the erotic sovereign, a different sleeplessness of transcendence.

The internalized other breaks up any claimed self-mastery, ruptures every effort to close in self-sufficiency the circle of dialectical self-mediation. It works as a reminder of what has been given to it, a gift its self-closure might consign to oblivion, but the oblivion would be a metaphysical betrayal of transcendence and the community of the between. First, the internalized other helps the erotic sovereign master itself, be at home with itself. Now, it reminds the erotic sovereign that mastery is not all; that there is no mastery; that the self is not its own absolute home; that home is a metaxological dwelling with the other, where the erotic sovereign must be willing to be unhoused again before transcendence.

The erotic sovereign is not the I at home. The I at home is not at home; it is at home and not at home; it is double and it is between; it is itself and not itself; it dwells next to the neighbor. Internal relations in the community of agapeic service are relations of neighboring. The other is the neighbor, the other is next to me. Next to me does not mean quantitative proximity, for the nextness, the nearness, is communicated within intimacy. Nextness is neighborliness, but nextness is the intimacy of community that binds us. To be a neighbor is to be a nearby readiness. The intimacy of neighborliness is a relativity, as much in the interiority of the selves, as in the public space where they go about their worldly business. Neighborliness is communal readiness that exceeds inwardness into all worldly business. This drama of readying, of readiness of spirit, is tirelessly at work in inwardness, as well as in the world's work.

So internal relations as metaxological define a community of mindfulness and spirit, of ethical and religious willingness. The self feels the call of agapeic service because the intimacy of the neighbor makes a call on him within interiority itself. It is not possible to retreat into a privacy that is closed off from the other. There is no such privacy. The private is the intimate, but the intimate interiority is always stressed by the doubleness of the metaxological. I cannot escape into myself from the call of the other. I can indeed shut myself off from that call in interiority, but I am shutting the self down as it were, clamping a lid on the thrust of its self-transcendence, brushing aside both the other and my interiority, shutting oneself down in a double betrayal, of the other and of the self.

Another important point follows relative to interiority—namely, that agapeic service is a certain love of singularity. We do not have to see singularity as the opposite of community. Instead love of the singular is the concrete enactment of agapeic community, which is a being together with the goodness of this, this being as being, this being in its being for itself. Put otherwise, the community of agapeic service alone can do justice to the idiocy of selfhood. The latter signals the radical intimacy to singularity that is the infinite worth of the human self. The human being has no price because it is prized, precious beyond all finite measure. The community of agapeic service loves the self for this, not for what it does, or what it might do, but for what it is, its simple elemental being. It does not have to do anything to be loved, for in its being it is a good beyond price.

Does this again mean that nothing is to be done, or that the singular self can purr in self-satisfaction? No. Rather one experiences the exigence of one's being as a task. The other in community with us also knows that idiocy waking, that intimacy of being stirring with unmastered transcendence. The community of agapeic service will wait on, and support, and hope for the full unfolding of this stir, even when the idiotic self follows folly. In other words, agapeic service is in the light of the priority of the goodness of being. This priority likewise distinguishes agapeic service from erotic sovereignty. The latter is in search of a good that it thinks presently does not exist, or that it does not possess. With agapeic service this prior sense of lack gives way to a prior granting of the integrity, plenitude, goodness of being of this self, or this other, or being *simpliciter*. We seek the good because we are already loved by the good. We are because we are already loved.

What I intend is not at all what Nietzsche excoriates in the servility of the slave. The community of agapeic service is beyond the impulse to revenge. Nietzsche did not see far enough beyond erotic sovereignty, which overcomes this slavish servility. He squints when he tries to see a service beyond all servility, and beyond erotic sovereignty, not below it. He is blind when he describes Jesus as a case of delayed or "retarded puberty."[6] Jesus is put *below* the erotic sovereign, one in whom the eros of will to power seems not to have developed. Nietzsche could not comprehend agapeic service *beyond* erotic sovereignty. Not that he lacked an intimation of the momentous issue at stake. Think of his extremely revealing phrase: "Caesar with the soul of Christ!" What do these names together signify but the union of the erotic sovereign's power with the soul of agapeic service. But this is my point: the service of the second, in transcending the power of the first, utterly transfigures the meaning of power, in a manner that can never be mastered by erotic sovereignty or captured under the name of Caesar. Caesar will have to cease to be Caesar, to have even an inkling of the soul of Christ.

Agapeic service is beyond any version of the master and slave dialectic, whether Hegelian or Nietzschean, beyond its historical concretization in the Marxist class war. It is beyond the power and violence of world history. Its inspiration comes from an entirely other dimension. It works vertically to the horror of world history, into which it pierces and seeks to uplift. Agapeic service does not lay the between flat and horizontal. It lives in a space of transcendence between eternity and the meantime of historical time. It tries to enact in the worldly between the generosity of a vertical transcendence. This service is beyond all finite reckoning, beyond every determinate calculation. It lives with pure noninsistence, and yet it is the irrepressible hope "All will be well."

What sustains this community? The trust that at bottom being is an agape. There is suffering, there is evil, there is heart-shattering tragedy. There are losses entirely beyond finite recovery. Least of all is the community of

---

6. *The Anti-Christ*, section 32. See *Zarathustra*, I, 21: "He [Jesus] died too early." As if, with time and maturity, Jesus might have become a Nietzschean sovereign.

agapeic service unmindful of the way we scourge creation and each other. It knows our demonic power to revolt against the goodness of creation and the origin. The horror of evil itself is parasitical on the agape of being, which the horror tries to corrupt. And yet to be the horror it is, it must be let be by the agape of being itself. Evil is, because of the forbearance, the patience of the good. It is not crushed, because the good does not crush, for the good is not a master or an erotic sovereign; it is an agapeic servant.[7]

The creative generosity of being is not confined to human community. We participate in being, which in its goodness is an agape. Let me then conclude with some remarks on this participation. Of course, participation has a long history from Plato onwards. A complex idea, it needs some rethinking. I do not believe we need reduce it to a logic of part and whole. A participant is not a mere part of a more general whole. If this were so, participation would be a relation in which the singularity of the instance is embraced at the more universal level by the general concept or class that constitutes the community of such instances. Were this so, the singularity of the this would be a vanishing reality, devoid of intrinsic being outside of its subsumption within the universal. It would be only what it is in virtue of the general or the universal.

Undoubtedly, we find this kind of approach in many philosophers. The general is said to define the kind of being the singular is; apart from its participation in the general, the singular is not any kind of thing at all, it is nothing. Certainly, dialectic tends to transform this logic into a more dynamic thinking of parts and wholes, in that parts can be wholes in themselves, which nevertheless are subsumable as subordinate parts of more overarching wholes, all the way to the whole of wholes. I want to indicate something other to this understanding. For if participation is thus rendered, the between is not adequately interpreted, nor are singularity, otherness, and transcendence. The vision of community would be the engulfing totality wherein everything is subsumed as but one of the parts of the absolute whole.

Let us not forget that there is a concrete dynamic of participating; participating is not a static structure. Let us take the example of festive being, itself deeply related to agapeic service. What is a festival or a feast? A festival is a happening of a community where the community enacts a certain yes, both to itself and to its joy in creation. It does not just celebrate itself, but in joy renders thanks for the joy of being that is given to it. Festive being is a communal concretion of metaphysical gratitude. When a community dramatizes its rapture, it is carried out of itself. Festive being is a community of transcendence.

---

7. See *Beyond Hegel and Dialectic*, chapter 4, on good and evil beyond world history; also *Perplexity and Ultimacy*, chapter 2, on tragedy and the beloved this.

No doubt, in this there may be some celebration of erotic sovereignty. Some festivals will accentuate this and render equivocal the metaphysical gratitude. But the latter indicates that all genuine festivity has a religious dimension, the vertical dimension in which the community of the human with nature and the divine is enacted and renewed, simply in being enjoyed in this ritualized drama of the festival itself. Without this religious dimension—and it does not have to be named or known as such—a festival that is a celebration of the erotic sovereign degenerates into an idolatrous cult of the community itself, or perhaps its leader.[8]

Or consider the celebration of a birth or a marriage or a death (yes we celebrate a death in the ritual of a wake or a requiem). We are caught up in the community, we participate, and the participation is the energizing of transcendence as something neither I nor you nor anybody could possibly possess. To clasp to oneself one's difference as if it were a possession is a misunderstanding, indeed really a refusal to participate in the festive togetherness. Is this why the festival is often sadly lacking in the individualistic West? To participate is to be oneself in the between, be oneself as beyond oneself, and as together with the others, not insisting on one's singularity, not insisting at all in fact, simply being there in the joy of the community.

And even if the language of "parts" is perhaps impossible to avoid completely,[9] it is not impossible to avoid misunderstanding the meaning. As a relating, participating is not a loss of self in a neutral universal, a loss itself reactive to a self-insistence on particularity that would stubbornly refuse its consent to what is at play in the middle. In fact, there is hubris in this self-insistent particularity that is more reminiscent of erotic sovereignty. Participation is the celebration of a community that gives one the joy of being oneself in the togetherness of the others and oneself.

Participation is often identified with Platonism, but we make a mistake if we mathematicize the relation between the singular and its community. The between is a place of likeness and unlikeness. If we were to say that the interplay of likeness and unlikeness marks a mimetic relation, then, in the *mimēsis* of participating, the likening of the participants does not undercut their unlikeness. Unlikeness is not less primordial than likeness; the pluralism is kept open. Participation must be a creative *mimēsis,* for this likening is again a dynamic doing. It is a becoming like, but this is again the energy of self-transcendence as it gives itself over to the other. In agapeic service, though one might be rich in oneself, one is willing to liken oneself, to become the poverty of the other who is the widow or the orphan. One may liken oneself to the other to the point of becoming nothing for oneself. This is a self-divestment that is entirely creative in its generosity towards the other.

---

8. See *Philosophy and its Others*, 298–303, on festive being.

9. Thus we speak of *being part of, being apart from* a community; this too is the language of participation.

Is all this but to paint a phantom ideal? I do not think so, though a mind of finesse is needed to discern this. Friendship, family, communities of mind and spirit, schools, companionship, religious congregations, societies struggling for justice—all these can show something of metaxological community. Power is not done away with, but its transfiguration gets under way.

Sometimes an intimation of metaxological community with nature is vouchsafed—a covenant of being, not a contract, an espousal. Thus a poet may bespeak our community with the elemental. A poet gives a voice to the silent, elemental things; things ask his gift, offer him themselves in a pact of speaking. Wordsworth had a sense of such a marriage with nature. We find a religious version in the sacral politics of earlier peoples; the king married the land, as in the Irish *Banais Rí*. It is as if relative to the origin, the community of creation intimates a common destiny to all beings in their transcending. All are drawn together by love of the good.

In more explicit religious terms, there is a communion with God that is outside world-history. It is elemental, idiotic, beyond all final determination. Prayer is this community. Moreover, this community respects a difference between a symmetrical and nonsymmetrical relativity. The community with God is asymmetrical; there is no common measure. The community of agapeic service is also beyond measure; it does not demand reciprocity. There is a one-way confidence; a confidence not always univocally returned, but that is still given. And if one is expecting symmetrical communication, one will wonder if something is missing. One will be expecting a return. But that is not the point. Communion here is not like looking without being seen—a temptation of the erotic sovereign when it oversees the other. It is rather allowing oneself to be seen, hence vulnerable, without necessarily seeing; it is allowing oneself to be overlooked, to be open defenselessly. This experience of being seen without being able to see is a vulnerability before the other. It demands absolute trust of the other in this exposure.

But there are many "ordinary" events in which we participate in the generosity of being. Thus if we participate in a game or a race, the stakes are simply our contribution, what we give of ourselves to the game or the race. The togetherness of the communal happening asks of us what we can give. We participate to the extent that we give of ourselves. There is no loss of self in the sense of the abdication of responsibility. Quite the opposite, giving is greatest when it is most responsible, most responsibility. We also participate in intellectual, ethical, and spiritual communities. All such participation is less than genuine if it is not metaxological, responsible to the self's own integrity, to the others in the community, to the truth and the good that gathers the community into the agape of being. This is a participation beyond all the instrumentalities of means and ends. No self is merely a means; it is an end in itself, but not *the* end. Nor is the community a means; it is an end in the sense of a consummation, but it is not *the* end. Participation is the communal togetherness of free integrities, all of whom and the community itself, are in the service of the agape of being. Agapeic service is obedience to the good in which we seek to be true to the good.

CHAPTER TWELVE

BEING TRUE

Truth and Being True

What is truth, what is being true? Pontius Pilate may have mocked, but really this question mocks our own self-satisfaction. It will forever shake our metaphysical perplexity. This is not surprising. The thrust of our self-transcending is an orientation to truth. Our very metaphysical perplexity is called out and thrust forward in quest of the true. That there is truth has, of course, been denied. That this denial itself instances a claim to truth is a performative contradiction, also noted since philosophy's dawn, by Aristotle for instance. The denial of truth cannot twist free of the embrace of truth. There is no escape from the true. The difficult task is interpreting the metaphysical meaning of this necessity.

Even this is not radical enough. Metaphysical perplexity asks that we try to understand the being of truth. Do not object that this is to substantialize truth; the objection is a glib exploitation of a linguistic ambiguity. No reification of truth is intended. We ask: What does it mean to be true? Answer: the truth of being is a being true. This simple saying will be a hard saying to interpret.

This point immediately follows. The question of truth is ontological/metaphysical, not just a matter of epistemological criteria. It is primarily ontological/metaphysical. The truth has been denied in favor of what is true *for us*. There is no truth, there are truths for us. This is true in what it includes, and untrue in what it excludes. If the thrust of self-transcendence is an orientation to truth, this thrust is genuinely self-transcending in its willingness to be for the other. The true is not simply for us, but it may be for us to transcend ourselves to the truth as it is for itself. Self-transcendence is not the master of truth; it may be the servant of the true in its going towards its otherness—that is, in its openness to what is true in and for itself. Being truthful may be an agapeic service of the true.

463

In general, post-Kantian perspectivism is untrue to the "perspective" of this service of the truth. Perspectivism, however, is to the point when what it denies is less truth than that human beings are the lords of absolute truth. Again we must be mindful of the middle and recur to the fact that we are between. We do not possess absolute truth, nor are we devoid of relation to truth. We have neither the bliss of the beast's ignorance nor the blessedness of the god's gnosis. Placed, indeed tensed, between these extremes, the thrust of mindful self-transcendence is subjected to the stress of extremes. We know we do not know the absolute truth, yet we know, and hence are not cut off from, the truth we clearly do not possess. We often are split creatures, torn in two between our dark doubt and a thirst for truth that cannot be slaked. We are other to the truth, yet necessarily related to it in its otherness, and hence the truth as other is intimate to the thrust of our transcending. As Plato clearly saw, we could not search out the true, and recognize it on finding it, were we not from the first implicated with it. Nor is this implication our doing, but is spontaneously manifest in the self-articulation of our transcending.

The opening of self-transcendence would not be possible without an already effective relativity to truth. Our desire for truth anticipates what presently it lacks; but what it anticipates is not just a goal out there; the goal is already at work in the trajectory of self-transcendence towards that goal. Let us say we lack the truth; let us say we desire what we lack and in desire anticipate the truth; but then we must say that this desire itself has to *be truthful* to be the anticipation it is; hence the true is already with it; the truthful desire of truth cannot be a mere lack of truth. If it were, it could not be the desire of truth.

This intermediate condition reflects our habitation of the metaxological milieu. In its own being truthful, mindfulness is always the *promise* of truth. The point is to remain true to the promise, hence become as deeply mindful as possible of that milieu of being. Our already effective relativity with truth means that prior to knowing this or that truth about this or that being, there is an as yet undetermined community of mind with the true, effective in the energy of our self-transcending. We might say that mind is an indeterminate love of truth before it is the assertion of this or that truth. It is this indeterminate love that emerges in the second perplexity of metaphysical thinking. The betrayal of this love is the sin against the light.

In this immediate community of mind and truth, the command is heard: Be true! The energy of minding being is itself simply a being true. Such minding is nothing but a being truthful that is a being true to being. Minding is already articulated in itself as a complex relatedness, a community, a communicating with the other that it is minding. The question then is: Being true to what? To itself? To what is other to itself? To the self in opposition to the other? To the other in subordination of the self? To the self in subordination of the other? To the self and other in metaxological community?

The possible ways of developing the promise of truth are plural. The immediate community has to be mediated, not only because minding is self-transcending, but because what is other to mind participates in the community of the middle out of the mediating energy of its own transcending being. The immediate community is a dynamic, developing, intermediating community. Being true to the promise of the latter demands mindfulness of the pluralism of its mediations, and indeed the betrayals of the promise and the fall from truth into error.

We must say that being true is determined by the plurality of modes of togetherness of mind and being. And so the question of truth concerns the relation of mind to the origin, to creation, to things, to intelligibilities, to selves, to the community between mind and being. Truth is a community between mind and being, most adequately manifested with respect to agapeic mind. In that sense, the origin is the truth, but there is truth in the communities of mind and being in creation, things, intelligibilities, selves, communities. The truth of the latter was implicit in previous chapters. The point now will be to more clearly correlate the plurivocity of truth with the plurivocity of being.

I am not only concerned with cognitive truth—namely, the fidelity of mind to being—but with ontological truth—namely, a being's being true to being. I suggest that this last is twofold: first, truth to self; second, truth to other-being. Being true in the ontological sense comes to mean the exemplification of the community of being in the true being itself. The second dimension opens towards the metaphysical nature of truth. The fourfold sense of being will help us to detail more and more full determinations of the nature of this community. I stress the word community relative to truth: the idea of any merely private truth is not enough, though we must seek an understanding adequate to both the intimacy and the universality of truth. Such a community would be beyond a subjectivism that is false to being in its otherness, hence also untrue to innerness; it would be beyond an objectivism that is reductive of being's otherness, forgetful of the self, and complicit in a wrong neutering of creation and reification of things.

Being true will be as plurivocal as being is. Different beings will be true or untrue, relative to what they are and its possibilities. And in that the plurivocity of being involves reference to the origin, the truth of being relative to the origin must be taken into account, indeed taken into account more than anything else in the final reckoning. We normally consider truth relative to human being, but there is no reason for this restriction to our mindfulness. Rather our mindfulness ought to be as open as possible to the truth of being, and in this respect there is no a priori basis for the restriction. The qualification must come from the truth of being itself, not from a prior contraction of the notion of truth to what is true for us. On its own, this last ultimately corrupts the notion of truth, as we shall see.

The plurivocity of being true for which I will argue, not only stands against a relativism that says "there is no truth," but states that different modes of being true are true in relation to the different senses of being. Thus, for instance, the notion of truth as correctness is more true to ways of being and mindfulness where univocity is a dominant requirement, for instance, practical common sense or empirical science. When the equivocal has to be acknowledged, there are other demands made on being true; indeed the very notion of truth may be contested. As we shall see, the dialectic and metaxological views do not shirk this challenge. Beyond the truth of univocal being, the unavoidable demands of truth to self turn us more towards the truth of the existential, the ethical, the religious, the philosophical. Moreover, the truth to the other is inseparable from the existential and the ethical, indeed from an understanding of philosophy at the limits, and the religious. The unfolding of this chapter will move from this beginning towards such an end.

In a crude way I anticipate by saying we move from, first the truth of things, to second the truth of self, thence to the truth of what is other, finally to some approach to the ground of all these ways of being true. Relative to the first, we find notions like truth as correspondence. In turn, equivocity generates a skepticism concerning univocal truth, out of which dialectically emerges a deeper appreciation of truthfulness to self, whence arises the further metaxological opening in our truthfulness to the other. On this basis arises an understanding of the ground of truth as superior to things, selves, and others. Yet this understanding is only available if we have been transformed. Moreover, there can be a return to things, which now look different in the light of truth, the truth of the origin.

What of being illumined by the most ultimate light of truth? This light is *huper*, comes from beyond us. It is hard to avoid the vertical metaphor: it comes from above, from on high. And yet this light is reflected in the spirit of truth at work in us. Much here depends on the deepening of the truth of self and community in the between; this deepening makes possible the mindfulness of what makes us possible as truth seekers, what makes us possible as mindful of the truth. This is not just our own mind, nor does it belong to our minds. Neither the source of light, nor the light are possessions of the mind. But we are not passive simply; we are patient to this source and this light, though what the source and light give us is dynamic and self-transcending, and hence a source of light from itself, and a light unto itself. When our being truthful is abstracted or isolated from the source and light as other, when it turns in revolt against this other source and light, and asserts itself as the source, we sin against the spirit of truth. This erring is the abjuration of our ultimate patience to truth.

Truth, Correspondence, and Univocity

As already suggested, there is operative, in the dynamism of self-transcending, an immediate community of mind and truth. It is this immediacy that generates the common sense conviction that really there is no question of truth at all. We are so immediately implicated in the embrace of truth that the question of its nature does not arise at all. We live the truth, we live a trust in truth. Nor is this naive faith in truth wrong; rather it is elemental, given, and unsophisticated. Moreover, we never leave entirely this elemental faith. We cannot; for every cognitive quest, even the most radically skeptical, takes place within the indeterminate givenness of this community. As elemental it is lived, and as lived it is more deep and rich than our efforts to articulate reflectively its meaning. Yet because we mindfully inhabit this community, and because mind is dynamic, the immediacy of the elemental will articulate its richness. The desire to say mindfully what is involved in the community of truth will be broached. Inevitably, the immediate givenness of this community will dominate our reflective considerations. Thus relative to reflective accounts, we find perhaps the most ancient and persisting notion of truth— namely, that it consists in a certain *correspondence* between mind and a state of affairs holding in actuality.

The univocal notion of being here influences the thinking of truth. We find versions of it in all ages, Plato and Aristotle in the ancient world, Aquinas in the medieval, Moore and Russell in our time. The univocity of common sense infiltrates this reflective account of truth. Carried in the immediate community of mind and being, common sense claims that the mind simply conforms to the being of things in an immediate, passive receptivity, as a mirror assumes the shape of the object reflected, or a wax tablet becomes imprinted with the contours of the stamp. Between the original being and the imagistic mind there is a determinate one-to-one correspondence. Philosophers will tend to speak of the adequation of intellect and thing, or the correspondence of judgment or proposition to a determinate state of affairs. Much effort has been expended on the specification of the latter view with respect to the determination of truth as a distinctive property marking judgments that correspond to the real.

The correspondence view of truth is not wrong, but it starts too late. There is initially a naïveté about this view, a naïveté that is the overflow of the immediate community of being and mind. But the immediacy, in fact, has already been mediated by a very determinate sense of what being and mind are. Because this view is defined by univocity, being and mind are already understood to be two fixed realms or perhaps substances. The presupposition is that being-other is a reality that is determinately fixed in itself; this determination is the state of affairs to which the correspondence is to hold. Meanwhile, the judgment or proposition that is held to correspond is itself conceived as a determinate proposition, like "the cat is on the mat." Correspondence holds between a mental and an ontological determination. In the best case, these determinations are as univocally precise and clear-cut as possible. Here the immediate community of mind and being is generally determined according to some version of the doctrine of external relations. Mind is "in here," reality is "out there";

truth is a correspondence between the "in here" and the "out there"; truth is an extrinsic relation between two univocally fixed determinacies.

The difficulty is this: correspondence as an extrinsic relation of univocal determinations is already an abstraction from the flow of the immediate community of mind and being. For being in its otherness is not just an aggregate of determinate states of affairs; it is a complex intermediated becoming. Nor is mindfulness the holding of a multiplicity of possible propositions in a receptacle-like container; the dynamism of mindfulness is also complexly intermediated, between innerness and otherness. We see the point if we think of truth as *correctness*. Correctness is tied to the *precision* of a statement with respect to a *precisely* delimited state of affairs. But precision carries the connotation of a cutting, a *praecisio*: a precise statement is a cut from the flow of intermediated mindfulness; a precise state of affairs is a cut from the flow of intermediating becoming. The great difficulty is how to get one cut into correspondence with another cut. There may be no difficulty in the abstract, but when we take into account the openness of becoming, both of being-other and mind, what seems so fixed in its clear determinacy is soon understood to give way to another determination, not precisely like the previous determination.

In ideally abstracted circumstances, the correspondence would hold between a completely determinate original and a fixed facsimile. But in the actuality of the universal impermanence these conditions never fully hold. Hence we need continually to make adjustments and to add qualification after qualification to the theory, until a point when the qualifications become so complex that the initial power of the theory is dissipated or covered over. For the initial power of the view is parasitical upon the immediacy of communication of mind and being; but the refinements of abstraction dissolve this truth of the theory. This happens in versions of the theory in twentieth-century analytic philosophy.

There are determinate truths; this is not in question at all. The question is whether being true has to be understood exclusively in terms of determinate truth, expressed in univocally precise statements. The answer has to be no, since every determinate truth is manifested as such within a context that cannot be itself reduced to another determinate truth, or be univocally expressed in one or a set of univocally precise statements. The context of determinate truth is not itself another determinate truth. Rather the correctness of determinate statements is verified as to their truth within this more inclusive context, and relative to an ensemble of relevant considerations, not all of which can be specified with univocal precision.

A contemporary example of the point arises in analytic philosophy of science relative to the validation of scientific claims. Originally it was thought that the unit of scientific validation was the hypothesis or theory that was to be subjected to experimental verification. It is evident now, however, that much more is at play. There is the role of *ad hoc* hypotheses. There is the role of auxiliary hypotheses, without which the hypothesis being tested would hardly make sense. There is the fact that the result of an experiment can sometimes be equivocal with respect to what it says about the primary and the auxiliary hypotheses. Then there is the specific research program of which this particular community of scientific inquirers are members. Finally, there is the historical community of scientific inquirers whose previous contributions, exploited and as yet unmined in their implications, offers an even wider context relative to the determination of the truth of a scientific hypothesis. The determination of the truth of determinate hypotheses is inseparable from this community of truthseekers. Nor does the disjunction of context of discovery and context of validation allow us to separate absolutely the determination of determinate truth from its communal matrix. Without the latter we would not even know, much less specify, what particular problem we are trying to solve, what specific question we were trying to answer.

The notion of truth as univocal correspondence is tied to the idea of being true to the facts. Positivism provides an example. Truth becomes a property of information. Journalists and positivistic historians will agree. But once again there are ontological presupposition to the view, most especially that all being can be reduced to a collection of possible data. One can say that the verification principle of positivism was untrue to the truth in the name of a version of the correspondence theory. Positivism is a reincarnation of classical empiricism, which is not really a philosophy of experience but a rational abstraction, an abstraction of experience, in which sense impressions were ideally thought of as mirror images, "representations" of original, determinate states of affairs holding outside of the mind. The simplicities of this view have now been deconstructed. There are no data in the sense intended, no givens entirely free of theoretical interpretations.

It is now common to go to the opposite extreme and exult in the demystification of the so-called myth of the given. This is not my view. There are givens, *data* in another sense. The common objectification of data, I believe, was a contraction and abstraction from concrete being. The myth of *that* given is well done away with; but the doing away of givenness per se is nonsense. It generates an infidelity to the immediacy of the trust in truth that is spontaneously operative in the community of being. An enriched intermediated account of the given relates to the metaxological community, as initially given for itself by the agapeic origin; this given is not only immediate but also self-mediating and intermediating. I will say more about this below. This rich matrix of givenness and its truth is not reached, either by the positivistic mythologists or their more recent demythologizers.

The notion of truth as correctness is often developed in connection with mathematical and scientific univocity. The question of the truth of univocal correspondence is reinvented in the debate about what is called scientific realism. In this realism we encounter the presupposition, indeed faith, that the world as a completely determined, literal state of affairs, out there, apart from all relativity to mind. But if truth is a community of mind and being, we cannot escape relativity. Being-other is there, and there are modes of being that are not mind dependent, certainly relative to the human mind. The mind's relativity does not necessitate a subordination of being-other to mind, for there are modes of mind, agapeic mind, that reverse the directionality of such subordinating relativity. The agapeic mind gives itself over to the given. Scientific realism is true as a mode of agapeic mind, but it does not understand this. It misunderstands itself in terms of the ideal of objectivism.

When the ideal of objective validity is offered as the meaning of veridical correctness, the contribution of the knowing self is downplayed. The objectivist ideal is that of a kind of selfless truth in which the neutral thereness of objects or objective happenings alone warrant consideration. Correspondence between the mind and being, in a way, is erased or forgotten, because the validly objective truth is selfless. The self has to be put in parentheses, or even denied relevance to the truth. Of course, on these terms even correspondence is impossible, for one of the terms, the knowing self has been erased. There is left only objective thereness, as if the sweep of self-transcendence were such that the very self in the self-surpassing had rubbed itself out, in its self-overcoming.

I agree that truth does demand a kind of self-forgetfulness, in that there is an orientation of self-transcendence towards being in its otherness as other, and not as merely for the self. But this self-forgetfulness is paradoxical, since the self is not erased, but rather more fully transformed into a more adequate openness to what is there. To understand reflectively what is at play in being true does not sanction an objectivism that simply is oblivious of this transformation of self-surpassing mind into openness to being-other. Objectivism forgets the community between this openness and being in its otherness. In forgetting the sweep of self-transcendence, it also contracts, reifies the richness of being at play in the otherness of thereness. So I am not rejecting the ideal of objective truth; I am rejecting a standard interpretation of objectivism. At its best, objective mind is a mode of agapeic mind that opens to the otherness of finite things and happenings in their otherness. But the terms in which objectivism tends to understand itself make it false to its own truth.

For instance, in its emphasis on univocal determinacy, the correspondence theory tends to narrow the sweep of self-transcending mind to *problems*. A question is not a real question until it has been precisely and determinately formulated. Hence this view cannot account for metaphysical perplexity. It is oblivious that its own determination of truth is a contraction of the original indeterminate love of truth that flowers in the astonished wonder and perplexity that are in excess of every determinate proposition or state of affairs or problem.[1]

---

1. It is all very well for Arthur Fine to talk about what he calls the natural ontological attitude. But there is nothing natural at all about this attitude. It is postpositivistic prescription that we not ask certain philosophical questions about science, especially metaphysical questions. We are told to let science speak for itself; again this sounds fine,

Once again I am not denying the ideal of univocal truth. There is truth at this level. There are determinate answers to determinate problems. There are facts. There are questions like *How do I cross the road?*, or *What time is it?*, which can be given determinate answers that are true. But the truth of this determination does not exhaust the meaning of being true, and is itself embedded in a matrix of indeterminacies that exceed fixation in univocal truths.

Consider. One does not want to know how to cross the road. One does not have a problem. Instead one has lost the way. One is not at home, one is tormented by a deeper doubt, or uncertainty that cannot be specified to this or to that. There is a real and agonizing skepticism about where one is, about where one is going, about what is going on. One is looking to find one's way where there is no way, a way beyond any determinate problem.

With respect to one's geometrical situation, one knows how to find one's way around. But there is something more that nags one. One is agonizing about the truth of the whole situation, in all its determinacy and indeterminacy, the slipping away of time past, the unpredictability of the open future, the issue of one's eternal destiny. One seeks not to be lost anymore, but to be found in a more than geometrical placing. One wants to know one's way, while knowing that one cannot know all the determinate details. What is this true knowing, beyond the determinacies of correct knowing? Is this not an "agreement" with actuality more complex, concrete, manysided, more rich and open than can be captured in any correspondence theory? This knowing would be being true as *being at home*. But to be at home is not a problem; it is a metaphysical enigma.

We might here fruitfully *reconsider* the traditional statement of the correspondence view. This statement speaks of *adaequatio intellectus et rei* and *adaequatio intellectus ad rem*. *First*, the emphasis is on truth to things (*res*), not being true in its full sweep; but being true in its full sweep cannot be confined to the truth of things.[2]

---

but it is really a *diktat*, still governed by scientistic univocity, to ward off philosophical perplexity. The view I espouse is far closer to the natural ontological attitude. It respects the truth of naive common sense, which actually lives the truth of self-transcendence, without always being able to give a reflective account of what it is, or what it is doing.

2. Aristotle will focus on the apophatic truth of determinate judgments and propositions which are either true or false or undetermined (see *Meta*, 1011b26ff.; *Categories*, 4a10–4b19; 14b12–23; *De Interpretatione*, 16a10–19). The view reflects the link of intelligibility with determinate being and the univocity of logic. But if determinate being is the outcome of a process of determination, then apophatic truth will also be the outcome of a process that is both determinately manifest, yet more than any determinate manifestation, a process, so to say, apophatic and kataphatic at one and the same time. This doubleness is emergence in the aesthetic givenness of the immediate community of being, which is not the same as the aggregate of determinate beings in that community.

Second, we must think of *intellectus* in a way that guards against any contracting of the movement of *going towards*; this is the danger of an abstracted intellect. By contrast, concrete intelligence does go towards things, but if we treat this "going towards" as if it were a passive conforming to things, we risk contracting our transcending and the full complexity of mediation. The whole self has to be opened up to the spirit of truth. This is not an abstract intellectual matter; it is being mindful. The mindful self has to purify its participation in the spirit of truth before it can really be true to things. This being truthful is required for it to be truthful to things as things.

Third, the double formulation of *et* and *ad* is important. The *et* may be read to imply a togetherness, while the *ad* implies the going towards. If we put the two together, one might see the *ad*, the movement of going towards, as happening from the two sides, that of being mindful and of being in its otherness. The *ad*, the goings towards, whether of being or of mind, converge in the middle of the *et*, where *and*, *et*, is not an extrinsic connection, a mere conjunction of contiguity, but an ontological community of being.

Fourth, and this point is not in the traditional statement, the true is beyond the truth of *things*. The very movement of transcendence in the *ad*, the going towards, is carried by this excess of truth, and especially the opening of the truth of transcendence from the side of the other. The community of the between points to the truth of being, not just beings, of the origin, and not just creation or things or selves. This is the truth to which there is no adequation; it is truth beyond equation, beyond all equalization, the truth of the Unequal, the truth of the other beyond all thought.

In other words, the power of the correspondence is just in corresponding. A correspondent corresponds. There is a communication to and fro across the difference. The communication is not always simple or unambiguous, but the communication of corresponding is the dynamic relating of a community in effect. Think again here of the question of givenness, relative to the aesthetic presencing of beings. Our sense of the aesthetic harmony of creation arises from a community between the mindful body and the flesh of the world. The human being finds itself in an agreement with being and beings. This is an ontological community such as is known in agapeic mind. Our trust in intelligibility is grounded in the prereflective faith in this agreement, in this ontological community. Being true is defined in this being-with, this *sun-ousia*, this inter-course.

What is this intercourse of creation with the mindful self? Has it anything to do with correspondence? I think it has. Things manifest themselves, communicate themselves to us; they offer us themselves; they radiate towards us. All beings are beings toward, hence self-communicative. This is the vector of self-transcendence. Things are beyond themselves, between their selves and the others. So we might say that consciousness is a knowing with, a *conscientia*. Our epistemic confidence is also communicative. Confidence is a *con-fides*, trust with. Knowing is an ontological trust that being confides.

Self-transcending mind gives itself over to, surrenders to being, opening be-yond guarded self-reserve. The correspondence of being and mind occurs in this communication, this confiding, this confidence.

We might then venture that faith in truth is a witness of communica-tion. There is an obedience of truth. There is an ethical meaning to truth: in trust, I am given over to the goodness of being. Communication is always ethical: the goodness of the other is implied. In being true, one keeps faith with the goodness of being. Moreover, confidence is between self and other; confiding is between; this between of confidence constitutes metaxological community. All betrayal is betrayal of a confidence, a breach of faith; this breach is a shattering of communication. There is a betrayal of truth.

Our reinterpretation of correspondence implies no revocation of the in-telligibility of things as inherent.[3] It demands its reinvocation. This intelligi-bility refers us to the truth of things for themselves. But we go towards, come to the truth of their intelligibility and being. This being and intelligibility is the measure of their truth. Our knowing of their truth is measured by that truth. We are not the measure of the truth of things, except in the sense that we are capable of genuine openness to their otherness. We do not impose on them our measure and call it their measure, and still remain true to them. This means also that what we call "truthfulness to self" does not make the self the measure, but submits it to what is for itself as other to us. Hence truth to self is genuinely self-transcending with respect to the truth of things in their intelligibility and being. The intelligibility is not "created" by us and hence is not our truth—it is their truth.

Another mode of this transcendence of truth is evident, not with respect to the intelligibility of things, but to their very being. *That they are at all*—this is the metaphysical splendor of simply being. This is excessive and occurs in a reference to the origin of being as creation. This excess is also a measure of truth, but a measure that is not our measure, nor indeed a measure that is measured. It is unmeasured, referring us to the excess of the truth of being in an even more ultimate sense than intelligibility as inherent. This is the refer-ence of the truth of being to the creative origin. There is a community with the origin in this reference. This community is ontological truth. The origin is the unmeasured measure of the truth of creation, of things, of intelligibilites, selves, communities, truths. We here see an inadequate adequacy. The second other-ness of simply being at all, with reference to its community with the origin, brings mind to the edge of enigma. This truth we cannot measure. We do not have the measure of it. We are unequal to it. There is a necessary failure, or breakdown on our part. There is a kind of negative knowing, where we know we do not know. Its poverty can be the highest excess of mindfulness.

---

3. See chapter 9 on this, as well as on the basic trust in intelligibility that is also crucial here.

I have run ahead of the theme, so let me make these final remarks on the correspondence theory. Traditionally this view, as it were, *undersells* its own power, by not fully stating or understanding what is thus at work in the communication to and fro between mind and being. Indeed, due to the univocal sense of being, correspondence can be corrupted into its opposite; it sets the two, mind and being, into antithesis; their otherness, properly in communication, becomes an opposition. Then how we bridge this opposition becomes the intractable problem. Indeed, what is in play in the corresponding is not dwelt on at all, nor the fact that corresponding is already a community of corresponding *before* the terms in correspondence are fixed in determinate univocal identity and opposition.

This self-misunderstanding can then lead to an equivocal dissolution of corresponding into two opposite abstractions—namely, the pure mind that only thinks itself, and the pure otherness of being that is in itself mindless, without inherent connection with mind. In the first instance, truth becomes redefined as the self-correspondence of the idealistic mind, mirroring itself endlessly. In the second instance, the objectivism that follows simply makes unintelligible the notion of the true as a community of mind and being. I would say that it makes truth impossible, were it not that the objectivist thesis presents itself as a true theory; though on the terms of the theory, its own truth, as a community of being and mind, is all but impossible to make intelligible.

Historically, we witness the above bifurcation in post-Cartesian theories of representation. The mind "in here" represents to itself the thing "out there"; an idea is an internal representation of an external state of affairs. But if *between* the "in here" and the "out there" there is the stated bifurcation, there can ultimately be no correspondence, no representation, except the representation of the mind to itself.[4] Mental ideas can only correspond with mental ideas, material things with material things. Hence univocal correspondence dissolves into dualism, and can never rescue its own truth on these terms. This dualism would be the despair of truth, were it not for the fact that it presents itself as true, and hence as within the community of truth from which, though it be unacknowledged, there is no escape. But still it makes it impossible to understand that community. It should be the despair of truth, were it to understand itself, but it does not understand itself, nor does it see what is further.

Below I will return to this matter with reference to self-representation, idealism, and the coherence view of truth. We might say here that beyond univocal *foundationalism* the relativity of truth emerges. This relativity is not relativism. It is the interplay and relativity of being and mind, which take

---

4. So also the problem of reference is too often treated at a level of univocal external relation between the "in-here" and the "out-there," or determinate statement and a fixed state of affairs in the world. This will not do. Reference, like correspondence and representation, would have to be rethought.

us beyond simple univocity. The truth of correspondence will have to be rescued at the metaxological level, in terms of a genuine co- (*cum* or *being with*) and responding. Such a genuine correspondence will entail an answering to the self and an answering for the other: a double responsibility of the truth. This is an ethical task, as one would expect with agapeic mind.

Truth, Equivocity, and Skepticism

The psalmist lamented: "truths are decayed from among the children of men" (Ps. 11:1). How can truths decay? The fixity of univocal truth offers no answer. Indeed, the immediate certainty of univocal truth itself cannot stand. It falls apart. On strictly univocal terms, we must fail to make sense of the convergence in the middle that is the correspondence. The true may be given, but it is also withheld and hidden. We must seek what both gives and hides itself. The true is plurivocal: coming into the middle towards us, receding from our possession and eluding our grasp. The univocity of a fixated correspondence generates the despair of truth. Is that all? No. The despair seeks consolation for the decay in renewing the incessant questioning.

What is the true itself to which mind corresponds? We try to fix the truth without qualification, but find in the very fixing that the true is shifting underneath its stabilization. We look for the truth and lose ourselves in bewilderment. We ask: Is the correspondence due to the seeking self, or to being as other? Or to both or to neither? There is no univocal answer, especially if the correspondence is a convergence of the two in the middle. There is even less univocal an answer if our expectation of truth erects a dualism between mind and being, thus entrenching the opposition that truth supposedly overcomes. Our will to shore up an absolute univocity of truth undermines confidence in truth. We fall from immediate certainty into the duplicitous twilight of equivocity. We must further interpret being true in light of this twilight.

I seem to be talking about a loss, but there is a doubleness in question that is much more complex. Not confined to simple univocal truth, we are in a complicated, ambiguous middle where truth and its opposite intermingle. In other words, the true has to be mediated with respect to the untrue. Our self-transcendence towards the truth must find its way in and through the ambiguous middle where being is enigmatic, where actuality is not clear and distinct, where we make mistakes and see being as other than it is. The thrust towards truth has to struggle with mind's own openness, which also means its free indeterminacy, and hence also the possibility of its losing its way, or indeed its closure against what is true. The thrust for truth is articulated in a cleavage between the true and untrue, and this cleavage is not fixable as an external opposition, but enters the heart of the transcending itself. We seekers of the truth are cleft creatures, split between our longing for truth and our fear, even hatred, of the truth.

Even as great a metaphysical univocalist as Parmenides implies as much. In his poem (not exactly the ne plus ultra of univocity), he tells of how the goddess shows two paths to him: that of truth and untruth. And he has to judge according to *logos*; he has to wrestle with the equivocal, the potentially duplicitous double. The experience of the ancient skeptics is also very instructive. Truth's possible equivocity can be evident in the very effort to state the truth univocally. We set forth a truth in a univocal statement, but we find that the opposite statement can equally be set forth, without a univocal way of deciding between the opposite univocities. This is the problem of equipollence, noted by Pyrrho and Sextus Empiricus. There seems to be no way of deciding between two determinate *logoi* or propositions; it seems we must leave undetermined the truth between two claims to determinate truth. Equivocity, so to say, suspends, puts in *epochē*, the claim of determinate truth.[5]

The problem is compounded when even opposite truths seem to *demand each other*. Pascal, for instance, speaks of a reversal pro and con: when we have spoken one truth to the end, then we have to state the opposite truth; and indeed we have to state the opposite truth because of the first truth. The truth, as it were, demands the self-opposition of the truth, certainly the opposition of this truth to that truth. We must hold to the truth even in its self-opposition. Or rather, the truth of truth is also the untruth, the self-opposition of truth itself.[6]

This is not just a logical problem. The equivocity of truth is involved in the saying of the true, and hence the problem also touches on rhetoric. Therefore, the matter is existential, ethical, and political. Plato and Socrates battled the sophists precisely because, so they believed, their rhetoric embodied the equivocity of truth. I do not say that the sophists were in the untruth; this is univocally simplistic; they were in the untruth of being true. The doubleness of the middle allows the duplicity.

---

5. This *epochē* or suspension of judgment is, of course, a key response to the seeming impasse of skeptics like Pyrrho. Or perhaps the truth is not just a property of *logoi*, understood as Aristotelian apophatic propositions. Perhaps it is more related to *logos*— understood relative to the being truthful of our mindfulness.

6. The univocity defining Descartes' claim that clarity and distinctness are the marks of truth was summarized by Pascal in terms of the *esprit de géométrie*. Spinoza will even suggest we treat men like triangles and cubes. This is an implicit monstrousness in this *mathēsis*, though its comedy was seen by Jonathan Swift in his tale of the Flying Island of Laputa. Truth perhaps is a woman, Nietzsche equivocally insinuates. Perhaps. And then he jeers at metaphysicians who lecture on truth. Well, truth is no comfort or consolation in any sentimental sense. There is an obscurity, trepidation in the search of truth, a going out into one knows not where, in answer to a call one does not understand, with no expectation of a certain answer. One needs to be patient with the dark, especially the darkness of the human being. There is a risk, a wager, as Pascal saw, with respect to the equivocal.

And the doubleness itself can be spoken in a double way: in a confused way, or with the intent of seduction, or with the will to illusion, or for purposes of gratifying desire or bolstering vanity, or with plain dishonesty. What is flattery but the equivocity of the truth? Is there a word uttered by human beings that is entirely purged of flattery to ourselves? For instance, the equivocal language of the sophists can be corrupted, even while sophists feel themselves speaking with the purest intention of being true. The speaker may be so at home in the corruption that there is no intention of corrupting truth at all. This is the truth in the untrue, the untruth of being true. A person says confidingly: let me be completely honest with you; and he immediately delivers himself of his first lie.

The semblance of the true can also be *knowing*. Let us be honest. The human being is the lying, deceiving, falsifying animal. There is the equivocity of truth in nature, as we saw with the orchid and the chameleon or the bird that feigns an injured wing to decoy the predators from its chicks. And yet this is not the mindfulness of semblance. But *we* are the lying animal. We do not just experience the loss of true communication; we frustrate the communication of the truth; we exploit the hazard of communicating the truth to communicate a lie. We live a lie. We do not merely fall from truth but are in flight from truth. We hate the truth.

Indeed there is a chilling regard in which lies seem *necessary* and essential for life in human community. One cannot tell the full truth. To tell would be catastrophic for social relations. We need to veil the truth to prosper, indeed survive. This necessary mediation of the truth leads to our necessarily being in the untruth. And this seems *unavoidable*. This equivocity of the truth indicates that truth completely at home with itself is not possible for us. Moreover, the self needs to lie to itself; one cannot be completely honest with oneself; to do so would be a kind of death, while we live. This is the necessary sophistry of being.

Consider Socrates again vis-à-vis his interlocutors. Does he ever tell the truth, the full truth? Tell it directly? Does he not mediate it indirectly in a manner that risks *complicity* with the sophists? Let us assume he is not a sophist, though this is a controversial assumption, as any of his fellow countrymen knew—his countrymen did not have the benefit of later philosophers and classical scholars to reassure them that Socrates was not really a sophist. He has to put himself *below* truth to lead others to truths above them. In a word, he has to lie. He has to *hide* himself, hide his truthfulness; hence his truthfulness risks untruthfulness. He could not teach, hence remain faithful to the truth, without this hiding. The other has to be allowed to see for himself or herself, see the emergence of truthfulness. Just this allowance also always risks the untruth. We may distinguish the noble lie from the lie that poisons. But the noble lie risks perverting truth into the poison of untruth, just as the poisoning of truth sometimes leads to the glaring unmasking of the untruth of the hidden impostor. All is mixture.

Moreover, we weary of the straining for truth; we struggle to ward off our despair of truth. Indeed, we undergo a certain metaphysical helplessness in the equivocity of truth. Nor is there any immediate certainty, immune from the mischievous doubt that whispers: you are duped by the illusion of truth; your transcending is but your serial duping, leading you on via truth from deceit to deceit. Even suppose we stabilize truth relative to the seeming certainties of mathematical univocity, even then the suspicion of the duplicity of truth is hard to allay completely. Remember Descartes and the evil genius. Mathematical truth seems true even in dreams, and hence transcends the normal antithesis of waking and sleeping, actuality and illusion. But the evil genius raises the suspicion of untruth to the ultimate pitch. It implies that our most secure rational truth makes us a dupe of deceit, dupes who cannot even know that we are dupes. The truth of duplicity is so deeply duplicitous that the duped knower cannot detect the dupe.

This is the extreme of the duplicity of truth. It has to be faced with unflinching honesty. It is at the opposite extreme to our being in the immediate community of truth and its basic trust, but this horror of untruth emerges just there, in that community. This extreme produces a liquefaction of all our claims to fix absolute truth. We may risk being crushed metaphysically by this thought. There is no escaping the thought: every seeming liberation might be but our passing from an old to a new prison, which for a span works the illusion that we have escaped the cave of shadows. We grow used to the new darkness, whose newness seemed light, and now we see we are still in bondage to the dark. Darkness and nothing but shades of dark; no light, only the light of dawning horror that there is no light.

Can we be free? How can we be? Is the confidence of self-transcendence broken? Is the truth sought so lost in ambiguity, it cannot even be glimpsed, if every glimpse is only another flicker on the wall of mind's own prison house. Will metaphysical helplessness help?

In being lost, there is a breakdown; we cannot find our way. In this lostness, what then? There is nothing to do but go on, go on into the helplessness. What does this mean? It means that the breakdown of univocity leads to the emergence of radical skepticism. This is a continuation of the breakdown but—and this is the turning point—also the promise of a breakthrough. That is, skepticism may be the not-knowing that spurs renewed transcendence, and hence the knowing of truth beyond naïveté, and perhaps beyond the dissolving of the true in equivocation without mediation. The help does not just come from doubt itself. The help is not just the negation of the negation, which yields an "affirmation." The help comes from the community at work, at work in innerness, in outerness, in otherness. Breakdown and breakthrough are implicated with the shock of elemental community. This is not just reached through the self; it comes to one. Doubt per se does not help until it becomes the willing patience of truth. This patience of truth is a welcome to what comes. In its helplessness it gives up the will to power. The help is beyond will at the limit of will to power: *pathei mathos*.

One might even say that truth has to be adequate to tragic loss. Either tragic loss is the ultimate truth, or ultimate truth passes beyond tragedy, transfigures death. Either death is the truth, or truth is beyond death.

Skepticism, of course, can take many forms. It takes one form in Socratic irony, different forms again in ancient skepticism, a different form again in modern empiricism. Deconstructionist philosophy is a contemporary form of the skeptical impulse, as is clearly evident in its onslaughts against philosophies of identity. Its dissolution of univocity is fueled by an essentially equivocal skepticism. Many forms of skepticism take shape in an epistemic economy where the univocal and equivocal senses dominate reflection on truth.

Recent debates between realists and antirealists in analytic philosophy of science takes place within a similar epistemic economy. Realists champion some more or less sophisticated form of univocity; antirealists are exploiters of the skeptical principle who quickly highlight equivocations in this championing of univocity. Modern scientistic skepticism can, of course, harbor its own dogmatism. We find a division between the purity of univocal truth and the dark outer region of equivocity. The former is inhabited by empirical science and mathematics, the latter by art, religion, ethics, and what used to be called philosophy. Here we find the totalitarian impulse of scientistic univocity whose skepticism about art, religion, philosophy is really its dogmatic rejection of what resists univocity. Its skepticism of the other is the dogmatic self-congratulation of scientism itself. Scientistic intolerance of the obscurity of metaphysics is itself a form of obscurantism. It believes it knows what truth *should be*, and hence is intolerant of forms of possible truth that are other. This is self-serving skepticism and contracts the vector of self-transcendence, in play even when we lose our way to the truth.

Though in skepticism there is a denial of truth, there is nevertheless a deep truth at issue in this denial. Skepticism is nurtured on a sense of the equivocal mingling of truth and untruth, but there may be an affirmative outcome to this. That is, while seeming to deny truth, skepticism is absolutely essential to develop the *inner spirit of truth*. Genuine skepticism is a *servant* of the truth in activating the questioning powers of mind. It serves to purify the powers of self-transcending mind. For doubt comes to doubt mind itself in its naive proclivities; but it may come to fulfil mind more deeply thus.

Mindfulness exercises a violence on itself and its own sense of immediate truth. The violence may be the wrenching of itself out its own proclivity to self-satisfaction, self-certainty. The wound is a wound to the vanity of mind. Mind finds itself wounded with the suggestion that it is vain. Of course, honesty about vanity may destroy the faith of mind in truth, and so lead to the despair of truth. Or it may renew the restlessness of mind for truth, wake it to a metaphysical insomnia that will seek and seek, till it exhaust itself or find.

This violent wrenching is the emergence of an inner otherness within the thrust of self-transcending. This emergence serves the more radical opening up of this self-transcendence to what is other, in a sense different to the inner otherness itself.

The fertility of skepticism thus sharpens the inner truthfulness of mind, even to the point of making mind willing to *find against itself*. It shakes up, loosens up the naive truths of mind, asks for more. It opens up the restless infinity and perplexity of mind to which no merely finite truth seems adequate. If the equivocity of truth produces this restless skepticism, it may induce the inner transformation of the *truthful self*. The truthful self does not possess the truth, yet does not stifle the questions that strike it; as not stifling the hard questions, it is still in quest of the truth it knows not. This kind of skepticism is an honesty in the between: between the truth it seeks and the ignorance it confesses; between the community with being it mindfully seeks and the dissonant perplexity it cannot ignore.

At the same time, such skepticism can lead to a changed perspective on externality. Metaphysical perplexity is double in respondence to the possible duplicity of truth. For it is not only the untruth of self that has to be fought. Perplexity must also struggle with the shifting fluctuations of creation as universal impermanence. The face of the world smiles and snarls, reveals and runs away, floods us with light and shrouds us in thick suffocating night. The two sides of deepening perplexity work together. And so relative to being itself, we may begin to be more deeply attentive to what is there in givenness. The given is not simply univocal, a literal state of affairs to which we correspond without complexity. It is much more ambiguous; appearance is more saturated with possibilities. There is appearance, there is disappearance. There is overtness, there is mystery. The given demands mindful interpretation. Complex appearance calls forth interpretation.

Here we again confront the idea of theory-laden observation. This is sometimes seen as a repudiation of the "foundationalist" truth of univocity, and the thin edge of the wedge of a bad relativism. It may be, but it need not be. It may be the opening up of a more complex sense of realistic truth, where the relativity of mind and being is more deeply complexified. That is, theory-laden observation may be seen as a matter of *mindful attention* to what is there and mindful conception of its intelligibility and truth. Mindfulness is in the looking, because what is looked at demands the respect of the closest and most intimate attention. This is the concentration of mind on the complex givenness of being. Nor is this givenness a once off, once and for all disclosure, but is the dynamic revelation of the real, sometimes more ambiguous, sometimes less, but always asking a demanding vigilance on our part as participant in the community of truth. Being offers itself to us, but we must think hard to be adequate to its offer. The latter *adaequatio* is not naive correspondence, for it is given and won in the equivocity of the true/untrue. Such

mindful vigilance issues from the purgatory of skepticism and inner development of the truthfulness of the self.

Surely, you will say, this is to turn skepticism around and away from
what we know to be its familiar denial of truth. True. And indeed the traditional objection to skepticism that it is caught in self-contradiction is not
without power. The skeptic denies truth, but the denial is asserted as true,
hence the denial is false, hence there is truth. There is force in this reflective
attention to performative contradiction, call it what you will. But the force is
not such as to return us any simple univocity of truth. There is a truth to the
untruth of skepticism that has to be respected and retained. Generally, skepticism is an equivocity of truth that is mired in the equivocity. Even this bad
equivocity allows us to reaffirm truth, since equivocity demands interpretive
mediation, which calls mind back to attend to the mediation of truth, at work
even in the denial of truth. The self-mediation of truth calls attention to the
performative contradiction involved in this brand of skepticism. I admit this
can be a cheap logical trick, if its only purpose is to dismiss the skeptic and to
let us sleep again in mindless univocity. It is *not* a cheap trick, when it is seen
to point to an *inner ananke*, at work even in the free denial of truth. Thus
understood, it opens the energy of self-mediation in the determination of the
community of truth.

This is not all, I think, because the *ananke* is also the necessity of the
otherness of being as involved in the community of truth. Nevertheless, skepticism may also open the respect for, even humility before, the rich otherness
of the givenness of being. So transcendental self-reflection is not enough.
The truth of being is also at stake in the self-dissolution of this equivocal
skepticism. Metaphysical mindfulness of the truth in its otherness to self-
reflection returns skepticism to the thrust of self-transcending and shows it
to be a station on the way to the truth.

In sum, there are negative and positive advances here. Negative: transcendence of fixed univocal truth. Positive: opening up of the mediation of
truth on two sides—that of mindfullness, and that of being-other. Equivocity
introduces division into the immediate community of mind and truth, divides the thrust of transcendence into an articulated sense of the difference of
the true and the untrue, throws self-transcendence into a double, ambiguous
middle where true and untrue promiscuously mix. It puts self-transcending
mind to the ordeal of doubt, of uncertainty. It tempts mind with the untrue,
with its own willingness to give itself over to duplicity and falseness. It tempts
mind with the flight from the true, with the hatred of the true for hiding itself
while it offers itself. It tempts mind to this hatred also because equivocity
shows that we can never absolutely possess truth, that we are never its masters. But it also offers mind the purgatory of a radical perplexity that finds
multiple expressions in skepticism, some of which harbor their own dogmatism, and hence have not radically learned the lesson of perplexity. This lesson

is an unconditional patience to the truth. This is a patience to the plurivocity of truth that shines here and there through the equivocal, a shine that cannot be mastered, but that has to be mindfully mediated in the fluctuating equivocities of being.

Truth, Coherence, and Power

Self-transcending mind is involved in an interplay with the true even in the equivocities of being; hence the true must be mediated. The equivocities bring before us the opposition of true and false, of reality and appearance, of actuality and illusion, and so on. Yet the oppositions are not final in that mind gleans the true from the untrue, the reality from the appearance, the actuality from the illusion. In contrast to the external relation of univocal correspondence, what we must now take into account is a mindfulness of our *internal relativity* to the true. For even in the radical skepticism that seems to separate us totally from the truth, we still cannot sidestep *the exigency of being truthful*.

This internal relativity suggests the importance of the mediating powers of mind itself. Recall the opening up of the inwardness of truthfulness that follows from skepticism. This opening can be unfolded more affirmatively. In the ordeal of skepticism, mind purifies itself and mediates its own inward truthfulness in the face of the untrue. Mindfulness shows itself as the power of truthful self-mediation. It seeks the truth in this self-mediation, which is also a mediation of the equivocity of external appearances.

There are a number of ways this can be developed. The major way concerns the idealistic determination of the true in terms of the self-coherence of thought. Let me illustrate by reference to Kant's response to Hume. Hume's empiricism seems to assume that truth will be a univocal correspondence of representational impression and the thing in itself out there. He cannot find this correspondence, and ends in a skepticism that dissolves both external and internal appearance in a flux of equivocities. With most of the same presuppositions, Kant sought to mediate the truth of the equivocal by placing the primary emphasis on the categorial mediating power of mind itself. The power of mind is different to the flow of external impression; it is active and self-organizing; it is ordering of experience as given. If there is a salvation from equivocity, it will be through this power.

Hence there are no intuitions without concepts, no concepts without intuitions, Kant says. This is his version of theory-laden observation. The point is that truth is not a passive correspondence between a blank internal receptor and an imposing, impressing determinate being or structure in externality. Truth comes to be determined in what the categorially mediating mind brings to bear on the equivocal flux of sense givenness. The locus of truth is internalized; truth is not the property of a thing out there, a passive conformity to a truth out there, already completely determined in itself; it is a happening that comes to determination through the mediating power of mind and its inner (transcendental) truthfulness.

Another way to put this possibility is the following. We may never bridge the dualism of "in-here" and "out-there" in certain correspondence. But on this side of the divide, mind can develop its own self-coherence. Thus we continue but also transcend the representational theory. The true idea represents an object, but now we see that the representing mind primarily knows *itself* in its representing of what is other; representation is self-representation. There are variations on this: we might emphasize the pure logical consistency on the part of mind itself; hence we get purely formal doctrines of truth in terms of systematic self-consistency. Or we might qualify pure logical self-coherence by letting some room for what is given by outerness. This last is what Kant allows, outside of the realm of purely analytical truth. We must let the impressions impress, as well as categorially organizing them into a coherent whole of ordered experience. So Kant will call himself an empirical realist, but a transcendental idealist. The formulation is less a final solution than a more articulate statement of what is involved in the problem. The problem is that if we emphasize internal coherence, then the bond of mind with being-other becomes attenuated or subordinated, and yet we have to retain that bond if an adequate account of truth is to be offered. When we allow being in its otherness to impress us, as we must, as we cannot but do outside of purely analytical truth, the purity of internal coherence is immediately put under pressure.[7]

The full implications of this cannot be contained in idealistic notions of the true, Kant's included. In such notions the self-mediation of mind will be the final judge or determining term that adjudicates the truth of being in its otherness. We so emphasize the transcendental innerness of the truthful mind that we define truth in terms of a self-mediation that does not bow to being as external; for being as other, reduced to equivocality, is suspected of having no real inherent mediations of its own. The truthfulness of self becomes so defined that truth is ultimately an imposition of the self on the known. Hence Kant will praise the revolutionary founders of modern science for learning that "reason has insight only into what it produces after a plan of its own"

---

7. The coherence theory is often tied to the ideal of rational system, stressing the internal relations of the terms within the system. So it often looks to mathematics as a paradigm, and shows the influence of the univocal, as much as the correspondence theory does. Where the coherence theory stresses the analytical, the a priori, the nonempirical, the correspondence theory places primary emphasis on the a posteriori, the synthetic, the empirical. Obviously, there have been philosophers who have sought to do justice to both, for instance, Kant, whose view cannot be reduced to either theory.

(*Critique of Pure Reason*, B xiii). Mind gives its own power the privilege of being the arbitrator, indeed producer, of the truth of being.

Kant opens the door to a more dialectical sense of the internal relativity of the true. Kant's own dialectic is antinomic. So there is a side to his notion of the true that never transcends the equivocities of being; hence the strange character of his philosophizing, as so qualifying every statement he makes that sometimes nothing seems left. Kant vacillates between univocity and equivocity, though this alternation to and fro hints at something momentous beyond the vacillation. Hegelian dialectic claims to redeem this momentous promise; our internal relativity to the true is formulated in the famous phrase "the true is the whole."

Das Wahre ist das Ganze. This is a post-Kantian reformulation of the ancient view that the true and the one are convertible. But the one here is not a univocal unity.[8] The one here is an absolute dialectically self-mediating whole. There is only one such whole, and short of this absolute whole, all truth is conditional. The doctrine of our internal relatedness to the true is here ontologically reformulated in terms of the true as articulated in the internal relations of the absolute whole. Nothing is true outside of this self-coherence. Finite knowing and finite beings are true to the extent that they are self-coherent, in Hegel's language, to the extent that they coincide with their concept. But the self-coincidence of finite knowing and beings cannot be absolute, since self-coincidence is also always self-dissolution. Only in the absolute whole is the self-dissolution completely overcome. Hence the truth of finite wholes is not the truth. Nor is it merely illusory; it is a phase in the self-mediation of the absolute truth at home with itself.

Hegel is more genuinely a dialectician than Kant is that the impact of the other on the knower has to be granted. He has a much more robust sense of the antinomic character of finite being; finite being necessarily will enter into self-contradiction at some point. However, the power of self-mediating thought can overcome such equivocal antinomies and dialectically subordinate the otherness to the whole at home with itself in its own self-mediation. Truth is not at all correspondence with what is external or other; it is the highest coherence, the self-coherence of thought thinking itself in the other that is only itself again. All otherness is subsumed within the truth as this absolute self-coherence.

We might say that idealistic coherence moves from univocal *adequation* to the dialectical *equation* of mind and being: the *ad* or movement of *transcending towards* is elided in final absolute knowing. There is said to be no disproportion or excess; these latter are overcome, mastered. I will contest

---

8. This is linked to the Parmenidean view that to be and to think are one and the same; it is not unrelated to the Aristotelian and Thomist claim of the intentional identity of knower and known.

this in terms of truth beyond totality, truth as the mystery of ultimate transcendence, the truth of the Unequal, the One that is not a principle of equality but of absolute inequality, the One that is more than the one, ultimately
for us imageless, conceptless, unutterable, a dark excess of light. And in a
certain respect, *ad-equation* is truer to transcendence itself, with respect to
its *unequaled* otherness, towards which we must move.

There is an analogous problem with respect to where thinking comes
from. Idealistic coherence seeks to define itself in terms of *presuppositionless*
thought. But one idea presupposes another, and this another, and so on into
the excess of the indeterminate. In our knowing, there is no absolute coherence, no pure thought thinking itself, no closed circle. The equivocal returns.
We are always in the middle, mixing agreement and coherence.

If at the univocal level we have factual and objective truth, if at the
equivocal level we have the skeptical perplexity before putative facts, at this
present dialectical level we are tempted by the ideal of general truth. We
invoke the ideal of universally valid cognition, of truth as tied to validity for
consciousness is general. The true is what holds fast for all, for the whole.
The general truth is the truth of the whole and holds for all. Moreover, the
notion of generality is given a certain twist through the idea of internal
relativity. No finite truth or determinate proposition is true for itself, but
reveals its truthfulness in a network of propositions that offer the context of
its meaning and its relative validity. Thus we find with this general truth a
turning from the particular as particular. The sense of the true as whole can
be such as to produce a result not unlike the self-forgetfulness I noted above
relative to objectivism. That is, the whole is not the singular I as an integrity, mediating in itself the deepening of its own inward truthfulness; rather
the whole is the general rational necessity that has its way, regardless of the
truth of inward singularity.

What I am talking about is the erection of self-coherence into a universal principle that is at work regardless of the singular I. But even if we say that
the whole is a universal community, the latter risks being wrongly conceived
on the model of a total self-mediation, which is at work regardless of the
participation of the singular selves. I am not rejecting the self-mediation at
work in the true. I am now indicating how classical idealism generalizes this
self-mediation as the truth of the whole. The truth of the general is a total
self-mediation. But this general truth makes problematic the truth of the
singular self in its inward truth, and the truth of being in its otherness as
other to all self-mediation.

We see this if we think of Hegel's logic as setting forth the rationale of
idealistic coherence with greatest power and consistency. The turn from the
particular and the necessity of mediation is immediately evident in his discussion of the dialectic of sense-certainty in Hegel's *Phenomenology*. Indeed
the result of that work as a whole is the appropriation to self-knowing of the
knowledge of the other, evident, for instance in the subordination of

consciousness to self-consciousness. Similarly, Hegel's *Logic* purports to give all the logical categories necessary for the intelligibility of the whole; these categories are the dialectical self-mediation of the Hegelian Idea or Absolute. The wounds of untruth inflicted by equivocity are all healed in the absolute embrace of the whole. Error itself turns out to be a moment on the way to the absolutely self-mediating truth.

When the truth of the whole is defined as absolute self-mediation, there is the risk of a *dialectical objectivism*. Paradoxically self-mediation becomes *selfless*, when the singular self is made a moment of the absolute self. Moreover, the truth of what is other to self is subordinated to the truth of the absolute self, for whom there is finally no real otherness as other. The other in its truth is subordinated to the truth of absolutized self-mediation. Both the truth of singularity and of otherness as other will have to be recovered in the metaxological, as also the truth of correspondence, which ruptures the seamless self-coherence of the thought thinking itself.

Again we cannot escape equivocity entirely. For dialectical objectivism is not the only possible outcome of transcendental self-mediation. The truth of self-mediation can be turned in the *exact opposite* direction, from selfless generality towards self-insistent particularity. Skeptical equivocity asks that we mediate the truth of self, but what is self? We answer by turning to the self as *my* self. If we follow this path, we turn against Hegel, and with Nietzsche we say: *the* truth there is not; the truth is *my* truth. In my view, this response is an heir of the self-mediation that comes from Kant and idealism. And there is something to be said for what happens here, especially relative to the untruth of the selfless self of idealistic truth. A passionate protest of honesty will shout: this is not the self at all! The truth of singularity has to be recovered. However, the protester remains within the economy of idealistic self-mediation, even when he protests it. Hence the "existentialism" of Nietzsche is still in thrall to the selfless self, which it seeks to overthrow. But more importantly, the truth of self-mediation is still given a dominance that only ambiguously allows us to recover to the truth of the other, and hence also a different truth to singularity in the community of truth. If we remain within the economy of idealistic self-mediation, the self's power to determine the truth can be still questionably asserted.

Thus the Nietzschean claim: the truth is my truth, where *my* is a strong assertion of aggressive will to stamp my particular view on things. The singular self claims here to be *legislative of the truth*. The self is seen as an active will to power imposing its truth on the being of the world, which has no truth in itself at all. Truth then is a human invention, the invention of the strong legislative selves, those who will that their "truth" be the truth, both for the world in its otherness and the community of less strong selves. This legislation of the truth by the strong self amounts to a dictation of the truth to being. Did Kant fully understand what he might have loosed, when he proclaimed of the understanding: "it is itself the lawgiver of nature" (*Critique of*

Pure Reason, A126)? In a way, Nietzsche's view is only a more rhapsodic version of Kant's: instead of reason determining truth according to a plan of its own (as Kant put it), the will legislates the true and the valuable according to its own power. This is a *willful* rather than *rational* version of self-mediation. Truth is a fiction, something we make, a fiction as much of us, as out of nothing, and with very questionable relations to anything given. Truth is my *fiat*. We seem to imitate the divine origin: Let there be light! But this *fiat* apes the divine light. And even then, the aping cannot explain the source of its own light, when light it is.

Of course, this is an interpretation of truthfulness to self that, in the end, subverts the very notion of the self, and hence also of its truthfulness. The self too becomes a fiction, and its truth the fiction of a fiction. To will that the truth be my truth means there is no truth—if will to power asserts itself in a world that is essentially absurd. We are not returned to an objectivism mirroring univocity, but to a skepticism mirroring equivocity.

I state the point too mildly: not just skepticism but *nihilism* is the unavoidable result, if truth is a projection of will to power. But even here the necessity of truth, in a deeper sense, makes its call in the subversion of "my truth" into "no truth, only fictions." For this subversion of "my truth" into fiction is itself accomplished *within* the truth, otherwise it has no claim on our mindful attentions. It may be a game, but in the long run without the earnestness of truth, even in frivolity, the game is not worth the candle. It becomes inconsequential, we grow bored with it. And it is time again to take the truth seriously.

Only a will to self-deception can sustain belief in "truth" as a fiction, *as if* it were "true." If Nietzsche were consistent, he would have to sustain this will to deception. Instead he play acts with this will. If Nietzsche's claim were true, honesty would dictate nihilism. But here is the crux: honesty may seem to dictate nihilism, but nihilism itself does not, cannot dictate honesty. And Nietzsche, in the end, could not avoid "honesty," a genuine will to genuine truth, honesty *despite* nihilism. Nihilism sanctions nothing, you will say, neither honesty or dishonesty. Perhaps. But there can be no honesty on its terms, hence dishonesty is no stain. Nihilism offers no bar to the sanctioning of shameless dishonesty. But play-acting with the will to deception aside, Nietzsche could not be dishonest, found dishonesty intolerable. The inescapable demand of being true, and of our being truthful, shows itself at work even in nihilism.

The conventionalist theory merits mention here. The theory is usually coupled with a relativism that casts question on any ontological notion of truth. Truth is a social fiction, not the fiction of a strong self. Conventionalism turns to the others as opposed to singular selves; the truth of selves is conditioned by the truth of communities and their conventional agreements. We might say: the social will to power legislates the truth. But this social will to power is open to all the embarrassments of the singular will to power. It too is ultimately self-subverting.

I agree: truth and community are deeply intertwined; truth is a community. The real issue is the nature of that community, and also, of course, whether it supports the truth of singularity in its inwardness. Normally these two are set in antithesis. Dialectic goes beyond that antithesis, and rightly. We also must go beyond that dualism, without the totalism of truth that monistic idealism produces. When conventionalism finally reduces to social will to power, it does not do justice to the thrust to truth in self-transcendence that we find in the metaxological community.

Anticipating somewhat, there is a metaphysical falseness to any instrumental notion of truth, where truth is a means. Many of the post-Hegelian attacks on reason and truth, by Marx, Nietzsche, Heidegger, Adorno, and others, are directed at this instrumentalization.[9] In some cases this attack leads to the repudiation of truth. We have to reject this repudiation. A truer truth saves us. The attack on instrumentalized truth is only sustainable in the name of the truer truth. Truth is not an instrumentality, a means: it is an integrity. It is a condition of being. Being true is a mode of ontological fidelity. Indeed, being true is true being, truly being. The truth of truth cannot be understood apart from the truth of being, apart from truly being.

Instrumental mind gives us an uprooted concept of truth. What are its sources? It follows from lack of ontological fidelity to the truth of the community of being as metaxological. Every conception of truth, univocal, equivocal, dialectical, and their more traditional counterparts like correspondence, correctness, coherence, and so on, share this infidelity in some degree. The instrumentalization of truth comes especially from an accentuation of the truth of self-mediation in a manner that objectifies and flattens the truth of being in its otherness. The latter becomes a mere means for the furthering of the self-development of the former, and its more and more total self-assertion. This is especially evident in modernity following the Cartesian deracination of mind from being, indeed of mind from its own deeper self. Mind here becomes perhaps a hovering voyeur (as in a certain distinterested objectivism), or an aggressive expropriator (as in a self-interested willful subjectivism—itself the complementary opposite of disinterested objectivism). In neither case is the knower a properly mindful participant member of the metaxological community of being. Instrumental objectivism and willful self-assertive subjectivism are forms of mindless mind. They are lacking in metaphysical mindfulness of the community of being, the milieu wherein mind has its being and to which it is to be faithful. They lack fidelity to the *anankē* of the spirit of truth at work in mindful selfhood.

Relative to conventionalism and instrumentalism, what of the pragmatic concept of truth? Truth is said to be what works. Yet the meaning of this all

---

9. See, for instance, *Beyond Hegel and Dialectic*, 83ff. The attack on instrumental reason itself often instrumentalizes reason.

depends on how one understands what truly works, and what true failure is. The sense of community and "work" in the theory of, say, Peirce is much more sophisticated than any standard conventionalism or instrumentalism. It stands against Cartesian subjectivism, affirms truth in terms of its public effect, and what reasonable beings will agree on "in the long run." This is its reference to community. Implicitly, you might say, it testifies to a principle of hope and trust. For the "in the long run" cannot be justified with complete rational certitude. Truth is hence related to trust in a kind of community of honest truthfulness.

In Peirce the relation of truth and practice tends to refer to its bearing on experiment and general experience; practices are the experimental practices of the community of scientific inquirers; these can be repeated for, as it were, consciousness in general. By contrast, William James's pragmatism is more particularistic and stresses the effect of truth relative to a life. There is a concrete being true to life, for instance, in morality and religion. In science truth and repeatable verification may work, but in life? The truth of God— how does this work? Its truth would refer to the benefit and influence on life in the widest sense. James speaks of the "vital benefits" of faith. But even granting that science and religion are "effective," "work" itself is both ambiguous and plurivocal. Work can be a reductive instrumentalizing of being, or a freeing, releasing *energeia*, or being at work beyond instrumentalizing. Think here of the work of art, think of the works of love. Think of the service of truth, not as the truth that works, but as *a working for the truth*. With respect to agapeic mind, this work of truth is not just derivative from my attitude or social background or *Weltanschauung*. Truth is at work; I abandon myself to its effective work; there may a sacrifice for the truth that is at work. This service or work of truth may seem "useless," for it may be beyond the scheme of means/ends.

The pragmatic notion of truth "in the long run" runs into the problem of whether truth is a regulative ideal, and if so, whether there is any respect in which it is also a constitutive actuality. I suggest that if truth is only what will be determined "in the long run," we risk hollowing out the notion of truth. It may be a regulative ideal towards which we move, but how can the ideal be regulative if it is not in some sense operative in our present transcending towards the truth. Truth must now, already be at work, and not just what is established eventually, "in the long run." If our movement *towards* meant that truth were only regulative, this could not be enough. If truth were not already at work, inquirers could not *be truthful*, even when they know that they do not know the truth; this is a *constitutive truthfulness*, this *being truthful* in the between.

I suggest that truth is both a regulative ideal insofar as we never completely possess it, and are always moving towards it, and also a constitutive actuality, with respect to the truth of being, and with respect to truth's already effective being at work in the thrust of self-transcendence. It is the latter in regard to our being truthful, which is the awakening to mindfulness of the truth of being. It is the former to the extent that there is a transcendence to the truth as unconditional and ultimate, towards which we may move and approximate, but with which we are never equal or on a par. This is the transcendence of truth, which calls us towards itself as unconditional, but with which we never are identical.[10]

Truth and power are not unrelated, but there are ambiguities in power that need to be finessed. Normally power is interpreted as the power to overcome and to dominate and to appropriate. This reaches a very sophisticated expression in the dialectical sense of being, the erotic self and the community of erotic sovereigns. This is the power of self-mastery. And there is the possibility of genuine majesty in this self-mastery. Moreover, this majesty is sustained in its health to the extent that it still remains open to what is other to itself. What we need to question, however, is the degeneration of sovereign truth and its majesty into its simulacrum tyrant and its forcing "truth." This sovereignty becomes power as domineering, when it closes itself in on itself and subordinates the other; either when the singular sovereign says, I am the truth of the whole; or when the social sovereign says, we are the whole and thus the truth, and we dictate to all others as to their truth.

When sovereignty does not close in on itself, its power can become releasing rather than domineering. Being true becomes a service in the agapeic community. This is the fulfillment of the original power of being that reaches its richest truth to itself in the service of agapeic being. This is its richest truth to itself, because it is the acme of self-transcending orientation to the truth of being as it is in itself. This is not a neutral objective truth, nor a willful subjective truth; it is beyond their antithesis and the equivocities of a dialectical truth that does not open beyond itself to a nondialectical respect for the truth of otherness. This truth, as the power that releases beyond will to power, is the truth that will make us free.

What this entails is that the power of truth is not constrained by will to power simply. The latter tends towards an erotic conception of truth, which subordinates being to mind or willful selfhood. Instead of will to power the promise of agapeic mind must be affirmed. This also opens beyond the holistic truth of idealism into a new realistic pluralism of truth. In other words, the will to power of erotic truth-seeking has to be transformed into agapeic service of the truth in its transcendence. This is service in the community of

---

10. This point is relevant to the doubleness of the metaxological conception, as we shall see in more detail. My position is neither Kantian nor Hegelian. Kant offers us a regulative ideal—this is an always deferred transcendence, which cannot explain the present work of the unconditioned. Hegel offers us a constitutive ideal—he affirms the immanent work of the unconditioned, but without proper reserve, hence he fails to do justice to the transcendence of truth.

truth beyond any dualism of self and other. It is also beyond dialectical transcendence too, whether the transcending is effected from the side of the self, as in transcendental philosophy, in different idealisms and various subjectivisms, or whether effected from the side of the other, as in different objectivisms, or totalizing holisms, which absorb into the general the particular participation of the singular self.

This service of truth can, in fact, still be discovered in and through dialectical transcending. The power of dialectical truth is that mind can actively mediate the equivocity of appearances. The self-mediation of mind cooperates in articulating the between, as it articulates the thrust of self-transcendence in the between. It contributes to shaping the community of the between, and does so because already in play is the immediacy of our community with the truth. Once more our *trust* in this community is all important. This trust undergirds the self-transcendence of agapeic mind towards the other. It is trust in this community that allows us to see the positive in the negative—namely, the effectiveness of the truth even in the skeptical denial of the truth. Moreover, it is this trust that allows us to discern the ·promise of community even in the antithesis of its participants, indeed even in their mutual estrangement. The community of truth calls back to ontological trust the estranged participants. In a crucial respect, the dialectical sense of truth is simply carried forward by this call.

The call of coherence is also the call of the *peace* of truth, beyond the war of its differently seeking servants. This service transcends the master and slave dialectic of domination and subordination. We are all servants of the truth. In the immediacy of the community of being, we do not always know this, or live up to the ideal promise. But we are in service to truth, and are so, even when we are in hostile opposition to others. Even in the hostile between, the service of the truth is taking place. When we hate the truth, we are servants of the truth.

Dialectic thus offers us some resources for thinking the *ananke* of this service, even when on the surface everything looks exactly the opposite. We spend our season in hell. Hatred of the honest, smiles that are snarls, lies, soft-stroking flattery that secretly assaults uprightness, sordid seduction that does not hesitate to bring down unsuspecting innocence, all vices hold sway in that season. But the light of the infernal is borrowed. The power of hell is held on sufferance. The opposite is tireless, even in this opposition to the true; the call of truth works patiently even in the denial of the truth. Dialectic attunes us to the opposite in the opposite, to the promise of the community of truth in the war of lies that makes darkness visible.

Self and other both have their truth. We must be true to both. A totalizing whole is not true enough. We are pointed to a community of being true, which grounds and preserves the pluralism set forth by the relativity of self and other, mind and being. We must rescue the universal from the abstract general, the particular from the dead fact, rescue the singular from the arbitrariness of existential self-apotheosis. *Always*, whether in the sophistications of a Nietzschean skepticism or otherwise, the presupposed call of truth is at work. This presupposition is the already effective community of mind and truth, at work in mind itself. This work is the silent power of truth, that will speak to mind, if mind stops and listens and does not chatter on ceaselessly about its own marvelous categories, if mind but cease to be conceited about its own clever power. We are in the truth, in this work of truth. The metaxological community reveals the prior conditioning power of truth.

There is no *stepping outside* the truth. There is no pure external standpoint; for this, to have any truth, would then have to be within the truth. Being in the truth transcends the dualism of internal and external, the self and the other. We cannot stand "outside" absolutely, which does not mean that the face of truth is not other, or that it may not turn away from us, be more than all our mediated approaches. Nor is truth simply "inner," because even in inwardness the spirit of truth *exceeds* me, hence calls and judges me. It is more than innerness in inwardness itself, more than externality in the creation that surrounds us. All things and selves and communities have their being in the true. To be is to be true. To be false, to be untrue, is finally to dissolve into nothing. Being in falsity is to be parasitical on being true. This is the ontological conception of truth. Truth is the being true of beings. True to what? True to self? Yes and no. True to the human self? Yes and no. True in their being relative to the origin. Yes. Here being true is the goodness of being. But this being true is also a promise of freedom. Hence also evil and being false are actively correlated.

This allows us to make a final point about the relation of being true and being whole. Traditionally truth was transcendentally correlated with unity. There is truth to this view, but we must certainly move beyond univocity. Being true is not exhausted by being true to one's own self-unity or wholeness. The traditional convertibility of the one and the true has to be reformulated in the light of the agapeic origin, which is the exceeding One that is more than a one. The agapeic origin is the exceeding One beyond the one. Hence in creation truth is plural in the metaxological sense: it is both truth to self and truth to the other. These two are in community; but in that community we come to know the transcendence of the true to every one of our determinations or mediations. The truth of being is hence excess, towards which our self-transcending goes, goes to meet. The truth of being as exceeding is "mystery." This mystery answers to the second indeterminate perplexity of metaphysical thinking. It is first given to us in agapeic astonishment. The mindfulness of this truth is beyond, more than all finite knowing. If it is "known," it is not known in Cartesian clear and distinct concepts, or in logically determinate categories, but in categories that are metaphysical metaphors or hyperboles, like the absolute original.

Truthfulness and the Agapeic Service of Transcendence

Suppose we try to get our bearings. We see that the trajectory of self-transcendence passes into and through the realm of equivocation. There we suffer the ambiguity of truth/falsity, the incompleteness of finite truth, and the inconsolable desire that more is needed to redeem self-transcending. We are turned and twisted in contradiction and uncertainty, out of which no magic dialectic offers a way. We cannot rest with a dialectical unity, or any return to univocal immediacy that has not learned the full lesson of our difference from truth. The true is not identical to *our* truthfulness. In the metaxological community there is constitutive ambiguity, which has to be interpreted. There is no Cartesian certainty, no Hegelian absolute knowledge. Nor is there false contentment with finiteness either.

Even nihilism nihilates itself and still we are left with the question. In the ambiguous between there is the wonder that persists, and the perplexity that deepens. Perplexity deepens as we approach truth beyond measure, beyond our measure, which recedes in its communication. Since there is no absolute overcoming of the ambiguity of the between, we have to confess the possibility that the prison house of equivocity always, in some measure, holds us in its thrall. And yet there are breakthroughs, episodic glimpses of truth that light up the dark interstices. This is why there is also no escape from metaphor. We glean the truth through a glass darkly.

We must now speak of a community of truthfulness.[11] My point, however, is not just an intersubjective ideal of truth. This is not rejected, but it has to be referred to a more ultimate sense of community. I have already alluded to the limitation of a conventionalism that leads to the social apotheosis of will to power. Thus standard intersubjective accounts of truth often risk the dissolution of the singularly honest self in public norms that flatten the unconditional nature of truthful singularity. An honest singular can sometimes be more integrally truthful than a mealy-mouthed community. That truthful singular may be the self in whom the call of the community of truth breaks through. Such a singular is not a precious subjectivist, but prophetic of the true in its unconditional requirement.

We might say that the true community recuperates the truth of correspondence. Beyond univocal facticity, beyond idealistic generality, true adequacy is honest responsibility. The universal is not an aggregate of univocal atoms, not a generality that betrays singularity, but a metaxological community of mind and being. Moreover, the positive contribution of skepticism and

---

11. This is not my present point, but against Enlightenment univocity, traditions as historical communities can be complex carriers of truth; the good of a tradition is its being a truthful community over time.

self-mediation is in awakening us to the unconditional demand of being truthful. There is an honesty of being that is an intermediated condition of being
truthful. We humans do not possess the absolute truth, nor are we deprived
of community with it; we are in the middle between these extremes; the extremes are joined in the unconditional demand of being truthful.

This is an ontological condition with respect to us, but its implications
extend beyond us. Nothing in the between can be the absolute truth. Finite
intermediates are in the community of being, but none is the community or
its ground. Thus the truth of intermediate being is a conditioned truth; ingrained in it is the possibility of its being untrue. All finite things live the
truth of the intermediate community in their distinctive ways. In the human
being the truth of the intermediate becomes mindful of itself. The unconditional call of the truth is awakened in us, though we are not, nor can we ever
be, the unconditional. Always between, we will never be either beasts or gods.
We live the community of being in our being, but we mindfully live this community in the awakening of the middle condition to itself through the unconditional call of truthfulness. This awakening is the call of absolute truth in
our finite being. The call can never be our possession. The call is no drive to
dominion over the truth; it is a call to its agapeic service. It is a call to fidelity
to transcendence.

The call of truth is emergent in dialogue. It comes to pass in a plurivocal
process. There is more than one voice seeking and speaking; the truth pluralizes itself in these many voices. Those who traditionally assert the unity of
truth will disagree, but will misunderstand. It will be said the truth is one and
cannot contradict itself. I suggest that truth entails not just unity but community, and it is within that community of truth that the opposition of contradiction gets its meaning and truth. Contradiction does not put us outside
the truth, but rather gets its truth from its being placed within the work of
the community of truth. Truth pluralizes itself, not because it is the fragmentation of a one into a dispersed many, but because there is transcendence to it
that can never be exhausted by any finite one or determinate unity. If there is
a unity of truth, it must be extraordinarily rich in itself, overdetermined; it
must be a community within itself and hence not adequately described in the
language of unity, which too easily slides back to the unsophisticated ontology of univocal mind.

The truth exceeds every finite determinate truth; it pluralizes itself insofar as the being of all determinate beings reflects it or participates in it. The
service to which we are called is an originative fidelity to this truth. This
pluralized dialogue of truth is the infinitely redoubled catholicity of the
metaxological. The pluralism redoubles itself in the middle. This redoubling
is not the extrinsic relation of a dualism, nor is it reducible to self-coherence,
even of the most exalted form. Thus the truth of the absolute is not *noēsis
noēseōs*, the self-thinking Idea; it is the agapeic origin that is also the good
that creates for the other, offering finite creation its own community of be-

ing, outside the closed circle of thought thinking itself. The agapeic origin is both in itself and beyond itself in giving the between. It is in itself as an excess that retreats into a reserve of transcendence, as we approach it; in itself it is too much for us. And if it is a unity, it is an excessive unity, and hence not a unity, but more than a unity; it is absolute community, or communicative being within itself. Beyond itself in giving the between, it lets the finite community of being be for itself, and hence lets it stand in being with its own truth. This is an orginal truth in the being of the originated. The agapeic origin is in the service of this originality of originated being, and the promise of agapeic service that especially emerges with the ethical and religious transformation of the human being.

We must speak of a double exigence of being truthful in the metaxological mode: there is truth to self; there is being true to being's otherness, truth to the other. The interplay and tension of these two always stress the exigence of truth. The mindful human being is marked by a doubled unconditional demand. This is a more exacting sense of truth than the idealistic one. It is more nuanced than we find in common sense and scientific realism. It is also more perplexed and perplexing than skeptical equivocity. This last is tempted to give up on truth, blithely, like Nietzsche at times, like Rorty all the time. The above realisms do not reflectively appreciate the meaning of the community of mind and being. Idealisms have a sense of this community; but modern idealisms misdescribe it in terms of the privileged truth of the self—the truth of the other is subordinated.

First, the intermediate double of metaxological truth means the unconditional demand of *truth to self*. This may extend to a cruel honesty with self, if necessary. I say, if necessary; it is almost always necessary, since we remain mired in the untruth; all traces of vanity and injustice must be purged in being true to self. But in itself truth to self is not necessarily cruel. Indeed it is an agapeic attitude towards self. There is a consent to the truth of the self even in its otherness, even in its surprises, even in the evil brought painfully to light and confessed. This agapeic consent to the self is truthfulness to self. It is at the opposite extreme to all self-conceit. We are both mercilessly judged by this truth and mercifully accepted, taken back into the consent of the community of being.

I am talking about the love of truth as alive in the self. The being of the self as mindful is a love of the truth. Hence we can die if we live a lie. We continue to exist, but living a lie is death to us over the long run. Truth to self means that we are the promise of living the truth. This entails letting the indeterminate perplexity unfold. There is no bar on any question, though the spirit in which we put questions sometimes is not the spirit of truth. "What is truth?" asked Pilate. But did he ask? Was his question mocking the spirit of truth or in the spirit of truth? Every question, articulated in the spirit of truth, must be allowed its unconditional respect. Even questions mocking the spirit of truth ask our discerning consent, in agapeic allowance of the freedom of their asker. Of course, there are stupid questions. There are malicious questions. Being truthful lives the hope that, given time, we will learn their stupidity, and turn from malice.

What I mean by being truthful is not subjective truth. Perhaps one might give an interpretation of Kierkegaard's "truth is subjectivity" that is not at odds with it. This is not the issue here. Kierkegaard's own sense of subjective truth does not always guard sufficiently against a questionable subjectification of truth. Instead of the community of self and other, he often operates with a dualism of subjective and objective; he protests passionately on behalf of the forgotten truth of the former, in face of the amnesia of Hegel's objectistic totalization of absolute spirit. The metaxological community of truth is not defined by this dualism, and this totalization. Hence we are here talking about the interiorization of truth on the part of the self, but as within the community of truth and within the self's community with the other.

As I have stressed, this interiorization recovers the truth of singularity against the flattening averaging of generality. Thus this interiorization is not the antithesis of community; it is the deepening in inwardness of the realization that the call of unconditional honesty is alive in one; it is the realization that the community of truth, the bond between mind and being, between the self and the origin, or as Augustine might put it, the community of the soul and God, shapes the very articulation of that call of truth in interiority, in mindfulness itself. The community of truth is alive in mindfulness as its inward otherness; and this inward otherness is not the possession of the self, nor is it the voice of one's fellow human beings who have imposed their demands, their conditions on the self; the voice of the self and its fellows are both within the embrace of the community of truth, which is intimately alive in all of them, and beyond all of them. It is a transhuman community at work in human community.

So we must say that *communication* is inseparable from the idea of truth. Mindfulness is an opening to the universal; but the true universal is not an anonymous generality in which singularity is submerged. Truth embodies itself in a readiness for honest communication. It cannot be closed on itself. Truthfulness actualizes itself in the movement of communication itself. It comes to fulfillment in the process of communication. I am reminded of the Kantian *progressus*, the infinite task of the regulative ideal. There is an endless call on self-transformation in communication, *truthfulness*, both singular and communal. This is articulated in the coming to truthfulness by the self and the community; it would not be possible in the majestic solitude of self-thinking thought.

But this is not all, and the qualification now to be added is crucial. There is a sense of truth that is *not constituted by what comes to be* in a process of communication, but that makes possible that process of coming to be of communicative truthfulness. This sense of truth makes possible the constitution of truthfulness, but is not itself constituted by what truthfulness communicates. This is truth that a process of communication *unfolds or reveals*, rather than creates or constitutes. This otherness of truth as for itself is compromised, I think, by the constitutive language of idealism. The same point is applicable to idealism's attitude to metaphysical transcendence, as well as to the possibility of religious truth. The movement of our transcending, even in the communication of truthfulness, communicates with transcendence, as communicating with us out of its own integral otherness. What we do, our becoming truthful, is to be distinguished from what is done to us, our patience to truth. What is done to us does not collapse into what we do. The communication of truth is pluralized.

It should be clear we need *tolerance* relative to the communication of truth. We cannot just insist there is one univocal truth. The truth may be refracted singularly in the specific truthfulness of every singular self. It follows that our mindfulness must be honestly vigilant to the particularities of just that singular refraction. Communication is this vigilance, and this vigilance is respect for the other as other. I use the term refraction, which is not the language of constitutive idealism. Against the latter, our confrontation with breakdown plots the limit of human constitution, and mediately opens a moment of radical receptivity in which we do not communicate the truth, but in which the truth as other is in communication with us. What is communicated is a call that urges us to the truthful obedience of the truth.

We are impelled to turn to *the other side*: not just my truth, not the truth of my fellow others, but the truth, the truth as other. This is the *transcendence* of truth in contrast to its interiorization, in the self, in human fellowship. The unconditional command of the truth as other is even more exacting than the first unconditional demand, if this is possible. The strange thing is that this command is also the *least self-insistent* of all calls on us. It commands and does not command. It is tireless and yet it forces nothing. It will not let us alone and yet it is absolutely patient. It asks everything of us and in another sense demands nothing of us. It seems not to notice us, and yet again and again offers itself and woos us. It sings to our deafness.

A faint air of this music comes through our noise. To listen we must be humble, be patient, forget ourselves, put ourselves in the service of the truth. When we hear at all, what we hear is that we are not the masters of the truth, or our own truth. We are beneficiaries of the truth, given this gift, the gift that, once received, solicits us as servants of the truth. We are beneficiaries of the otherness of truth, participants in the light itself. And even when the truth causes immeasurable spiritual torment, we still are the beneficiaries of an immeasurable gift of the spirit of truth.

Paradoxically, the interiorizing of truth leads to an accentuation of the transcendence of truth as other. Even when we recollect the truth in inwardness, the truth thus recollected recedes beyond recollection. We find ourselves perplexed by the enigma of the truth as excess. It seems always beyond us, and we always in quest of it. And yet the quest is such that already we are intimate with it. We are at home and yet not at home. If you like, the truth imposes on us a kind of forked condition. It is as if in the community of truth, demands were being made on us from all sides at once, and we able to answer only some or few. The voices of the community reach us and we can only listen to one or two, respond to one or two. There is an impossible demand in this, this condition of plural fidelity.

And yet in this impossible asking, being truthful reveals itself as a fealty to the truth. To the degree that we ourselves become agapeic mind, we live self-transcendence as this going of mind towards the truth as other, and for it in its otherness. Put otherwise: agapeic mind is self-transcendence as the service of the truth. We must suggest that science and philosophy are services of the truth in this regard, though the languages they use to describe themselves often disguise or neutralize this service of agapeic mind in the objectivism of the general. The latter fail to express mind's living and intimate relativity to truth as other in the community of being and mind.

If the transcendence of truth as other is not to be described just as objective truth, this does not imply it is our creation. In the community of truth, we cooperate with it creatively. Our being truthful is this original fidelity to the ontological truth of being. And this fidelity confesses that no finite being exhausts the truth of being. None is absolutely true being. Nor is this a betrayal of finitude; quite the opposite, the truth of finitude is just that it is not absolute. We find something suggestive with regard to the truth of equivocity— namely, the truth of finite being is *its untruth*, outside of its relativity to transcendence as other to finitude. The doubleness of finite being points, through its own ambiguous becoming and its being given, to the ground of finite truth in the agapeic origin. The ontological truth of the finite is that truth is an agape of being. But finite being does not exhaust the agape of being. It is a gift of the excess of the agape of the origin.

Truthfulness and the Excess of the Origin

I cannot disguise that this giving of excess is exceedingly perplexing, and its truth excessive from the standpoint of finite truth. The excess means that we will *never* have done with the perplexity it induces in our willingness to be metaphysically honest. The excess recedes beyond our grasp. When it does, we may feel as if thrown on an ash heap of equivocal finitude; the fire of God has gone out, and the gift of thereness no longer flares with the trace of the origin. Moreover, honesty at the retreat of the origin may induce a retreat from the origin on our part. We absolutize our own honesty, truth to self, in a world of neutral, indifferent thereness. What results from this? The nihilistic interim of metaphysical perplexity. Is that all? I have found that obedience to truth cannot betray the community with the origin, even when the origin seems enigmatically to withdraw from community. We remain faithful to the promise of communication, even if we have to wait and prepare ourselves in the interim. The truth demands metaphysical patience.

Can we here think *both* relativity and the unconditional call of the truth? Must we not think both? Is relativity a pointer to ultimate transcendence— truth itself as a transcendence beyond all relativity? Or do we shatter the true into fragments in the equivocities of the relative? Must we not say that the truth is manifest in finite form, but hence is inevitably also hidden in just this manifestness? Yes. The origin retreats beyond creation/finitude, just to let the latter be itself in freedom. The reserve of the "beyond" is manifest as nonmanifest.

Or alternatively, the truth is manifest and yet its reserve as excess still remains beyond—unmastered. Does this manifestation of the nonmanifest make sense? Think of it this way. Consider, for instance, a great work of art, a hero of the ethical, a religious exemplar—these may be singulars, which manifest the truth in finite form, though what is manifest is not a finite deter- mination, and hence is beyond its own manifestation: the manifestation mani- fests the nonmanifest, as nonmanifest in that manifestation itself. We see and we do not see, we hear and we do not hear, we are touched by God and yet there is but the lonely wind.

The closer we get to the truth, the more ambiguous, dangerous, and fragile become our mediations. They may shatter and break down. Or we are made to suffer, as in the *pathei mathos* of tragic knowing. Or else our prox- imity to ultimacy is falsely ascribed to ourselves, by ourselves—and we de- generate into spiritual hubris—a violence to the truth that is very close to the truth. The fall in this self-ascension is all the more disastrous for its prox- imity to being true.

Alternatively again, in this suffering of the true, we may recoil from both the breakdown and the breakthrough. There is our refusal of the suffering, issuing in defection from the true. We defect to the untrue in betrayal of truth, but the defection becomes active hatred of the true. At the extreme there is a revolt against truth, because it puts me in the wrong, and I hate to be in the wrong. I hate the truth for putting me in the wrong, and I want to be in the truth, but on my own terms, which are untrue terms, hence I must destroy the truth for itself, and remake it as the truth for me. But this is to live a lie. It is to use the truth as a means, not loving, respecting it for itself. And yet this hatred and revolt are within the truth that they hate and would destroy. Even this hatred hates to be in the wrong; this hatred of truth still is in the embrace of the love of truth. There is only one answer: a complete reversal of the definition of the truth as simply for me. Rather it is for me to own up to the truth, as it is true to itself and for itself, and thus too for me.

It follows that all finite truth is contested again and again, put in ques- tion again and again, with respect to the sweep of our transcending towards unconditional truth. No finite truth is the truth, and yet we are driven on by the finitude of our truth. At a limit there is a silent struggle for truth, the nonobjectifiable truth that is not subjective but transsubjective, transobjective. It is *huper*, above, across, there, beyond. The image of truth is imageless truth, yet the veiled truth communicates itself. This communication is the openness of truth in its giving; it opens us, opens us to truth of the other; and this opening itself is marked by trust in truth.

Let us say that a metaxological skepticism generates a perplexed astonishment that still will not give up on the quest of truth. This perplexed astonishment is beyond common sense and science and mathematics. When expressed at all, we find it in metaphysics, in art, in religion, in ethics. These become services of the truth in its transcendence, services that do not always know for sure what it is they serve. The very lack of surety is itself essential to this service of the spirit of truth.

For the double exigence of metaxological truth breaks open any seamless self-coherence. The true is not the whole, but comes to appearance in the breakdown of all closed wholes, and in the opening of a community beyond self-coherence. This opening is suffered as the breakdown of the illusion that one has the truth. Self-certainty is split, broken, but not splintered. The break is a breakthrough in the split of opening. The fork of the metaxological doubleness of truth points through the opening to the agapeic origin as the ultimate ontological ground of truth.

Put otherwise, there are interstices in the community of creation and mind's rapport, gaps that rock us back on our own lack of ultimacy. In this *recoil* on our lacking of mastery, there can be effected a more extreme *rebound* of self-transcendence beyond itself. Not having the truth can energize a going out and a going beyond self that is like entrance into darkness. For one does not know univocally what one is looking for, though one does know that to satisfy the ultimate lack, it must itself be ultimate. In this darkness we are the lack of the ultimate, and the unknowing that reaches towards its fullness.

In breakdown the ground opens up. In this opening the ungrounded ground of the absolute origin gives the promise of being truthful to derivative being in the milieu of the metaxological. The being of the finite is true in the measure that the origin is true to it, faithful to it, in continuing community with it. Finite being is true in the measure that it remains true to this prior fealty of the origin. The dynamic transcending of truth as other serves to point us through this opening; just as being truthful serves to activate the transcending mindfulness of the second indeterminate perplexity of metaphysical thinking.

We need to understand the community of being in the light of agapeic mind, in order to get a proper sense of this idea of truth. For there is a *reversal* in the pointing beyond of self-transcending mind: Origin comes to be seen as the ultimate giver of the promise of the truth of being—in creation, in things, in the intelligibility of things, in the interiority of selves, in the togetherness of communities, wherein the promise of agapeic mind is nurtured, sometimes redeemed. Human mindfulness must open towards this first ontological opening of origination, living the double unconditional demand that is set forth in this opening, being true to the community of creation that comes to be in the happening of this primal opening.

What then is this primal opening of the truth of being? Not an opening from the side of "subjectivity" or mind; not from the side of "objectivity" or being; not an opening in the opposition of one side to the other; not an opening in the reduction of one side to the other; not in the dialectical appropriation of one side by the other; not even an opening in the interplay of the two. But the first opening up, creation of the difference in the interplay of the two—that is the very opening of the metaxological community of mind and being, which original opening is the ungrounded ground of that community. And then not even that, since the interplay in plurality points to the giving of the opening by the agapeic origin. The ultimate ontological truth is there, made open there.

The ultimate metaphysical truth is in the agapeic origin that opens up the promise of truth in the difference between itself and creation. The truth of the metaxological community of finite creation is derivative from this ultimate difference, which is given by the ontological generosity of the ultimate other as agapeic source. The self-transcendence of being true is reversed relative to us; for the movement of our self-transcending is carried to itself and its other by the giving of this prior agapeic origin. And yet also the origin withdraws itself in its giving of itself. Hence the truth approaches us, and is hidden from us, at one and the same time. We approach the truth and the truth comes to us, but comes to us in a manner that retreats into its excess, its own transcendence. This retreat is not really a retreat, but the forbearance that allows us to see the truth for ourselves, and not be simply stamped with it, as if self were a wax tablet.

In addition, the comunication of the origin lets free the transcendence of the human being as self-transcending. This is why the promise of being true cannot be forced, even though the *ananke* of the spirit of truth is alive in our freedom. The truth of the origin is a giving of the glorious freedom of the spirit of truth to the self-transcendence of human being. But just that glory as free may turn from the community that supports it; it may set itself in opposition, set itself up as superior to the origin that gives it its free promise of being true. Being false is a fall from the truth of the agapeic origin, a refusal of what, even in refusal, continues to give—indeed a refusal of what makes the continual refusal itself possible. What is suggested here is the infinite patience of the truth as transcendent. This patience keeps opens the metaxological between as the space wherein our community with truth takes shape.

How relate all this to the fourfold sense of being? If transcendent truth is ultimately the truth of the origin as agapeic, and if this generates the between as the milieu of truth defining a community between mind and being, and if we must understand this interplay and emergence as metaxological, then on this milieu are dependent the ideals of univocal correctness and correspondence, the dialectical coherence of truth, and the richness of appearing truth that ambiguously shows us equivocal possibilites. All the latter finally are derivates from the original opening of truth into the metaxological between. The plurivocity of the truth is seen as a realization of the promise of the first opening of ontological truth. Every time we take derivative truths for this first opening of the truth, we fail. Rather we must see the plurality of truth as members of a family, set free into their distinctiveness by the generosity of the origin.

Yet not all are on a par, since there is a greater approximation to ultimacy as we approach the metaxological. One mode of being true can become untrue in the measure that is closes itself off from transcendence as other. For example, a human being true to its own being becomes mired in the untruth, if truth to self is not opened to the truth of the other. Or dialectical truth becomes untrue, if it becomes a closed self-coherence contracting the double mediation between self-integrity and fidelity to the truth of the other. Similarly with respect to univocity and equivocity: Univocal correctness becomes a false fundamentalism or foundationalism when it is untrue to the ambiguities of being. Likewise, equivocity becomes a duplicitous exploitation of ambiguities when it is devoid of the further willingness to sift more truly the truth of the ambiguities. Even the metaxological becomes untrue, if it claims to be a new master category, forgetting that it is a way, or on the way, to think transcendence. This way must really, as it were, forget itself as a way, to make way for the communication of transcendence as other. To be true, it too must be a way of agapeic mindfulness.

I conclude with some final remarks. We seem to have to say that there are two sides to this ontological truth of the origin as other. The first is its open wholeness, the side of its communicative being that is turned towards finite being. The second is the excess of its infinitude, which is really the ground of its unmastered openness, and which remains other and in enigma, "dwelling in inaccessible light which no one has seen or can see" (1 Tim. 6:16). This side is the *reserve of its otherness*, preserved as other, remaining beyond and transcendent. The side turned towards us is in community with finitude, though, as shown, it gives an inkling of what remains in reserve. This hiddenness of the ultimate truth again invokes our need of images and metaphors, themselves both true and untrue, double. We never entirely leave the double. To see the truth without veil is too much for us—it would be our death. Our station of being is still in the middle, even though we now approach the limit in the middle. This reserve is significant because it unequivocally reverses our anticipation that we can reduce the truth of the origin to our truth, be on a par with it in our conceptual mediations.

Nevertheless, this reserve also resonates with a deeper ontological openness within us. Our quest of truth is both surfeited and still hungering. That we do not fully know the truth of this other not only rebounds on our ignorance, but incites more searching self-questioning. In this reversal of self out of the truth of the origin as other, we more truly come to be ourselves. Thus this reversal fosters in us the possibility of agapeic mind. Agapeic mind implies a truthfulness of self that is mindful of the truth of the other, or alternatively, that becomes mindful of what the self is, in its rebound on itself from the excess of the origin as other. But, of course, this is not all. This rebound is not at all the end, but only the beginning of an exodus from self that is not at all for the self. The rebound shakes the self to its foundation, and only after falling to the ground and dying, like the grain of wheat, does it go forth to the other out of the fruitful agape now sprouting in it.

Truth then *claims us*, in the death that gives rise to posthumous mind, that resurrects agapeic astonishment. There is no control of this claim. Again we are never lords of truth; we are servants of the truth. The one who wills to master truth betrays truth; one does not use the truth, rather the truth will set us free. Erotic sovereignty may be tempted to lord it over truth, but beyond this, agapeic service of the truth does not dictate the truth. There is no violent force to the truth. It offers itself. Its command is the call of a welcome, not a coercion. In the exigence that we be truthful, this call of welcome surges up in our being, asking of us the promise of mindfulness. In our community with truth a fidelity is solicited.

It is not by accident that the word truth is the same as *troth*. We are betrothed to truth. There is a marriage of mind and being—not an erotic marriage simply where truth is for us, but an agapeic marriage in which we are for the truth. To be betrothed is to be placed in trust, to place oneself in trust, to offer oneself to the other as a willingness to be from the other, and not just from oneself. Thus we must say that the trust of truth is an ontological and cognitive fidelity. It is loyalty to being. When I give my troth, I offer myself, I give myself, I bestow myself. But again we must reverse this, for we are already by our being in troth, in trust to truth. Truth has been entrusted to us, its responsibility has been entrusted to us, offered to us for our safekeeping, for our faithful stewardship.

Truth, then, involves a gift from the other, before it is for us a responsibility to fidelity. Truth is a bestowing of ontological responsibility from the agapeic other. We are bound to truth, despite our straying and infidelity. Even the betrayals take place within this basic trust of being, this basic ontological bond. Twist and turn as we may, we cannot escape it, not because we cannot escape ourselves, though this is true, but because the offering of the agapeic other is never withdrawn, even though we try to withdraw.

As my giving of troth is a giving of I to the other, so also when I am truthful, I am *doing the truth*. Being truthful is a modality of the truth of being. In other words, there is a performative dimension to truth in being truthful. Thus we can do the truth in an untrue way. The letter of correctness may be observed, but the spirit of truth may be insulted. "Practice the truth in love," the counsel is (Eph. 4:15). What we do, we do in the light of the truth. We are truthful in the light of the truth. And this light is not mine or yours. In fact, this light belongs to no one. This light is no one's property, because it is not a property at all. Thus too the truth of being is not the truth of any being in particular, not because it is the truth of nothing in an indigent sense, but because this light is the agapeic excess of the origin. The light of the truth calls for a de-objectification and de-subjectification of truth. This agapeic excess of light from the origin is what Plato tried to symbolize by the sun: the Good beyond beings. That a metaphysical metaphor is here needed is entirely appropriate. It is not a simple failure of truth, but true to the truth of the origin as beyond our conceptual mastery. Such metaphysical metaphors are imageless images that preserve truth in its intimacy and otherness, its community and transcendence.

CHAPTER THIRTEEN

BEING GOOD

Being True, Transcendence, Being Good

Suppose it were possible to give a completely determinate account of all being. Suppose we could determinately understand its constituents, identify its happenings and processes, lay out its myriad intelligibilities. Would this be enough? Would metaphysical mind rest satisfied? I think not. Why not? There still is the ultimate question that will not let us sleep. This is the elemental question: Is there any good of it all? What is the good of it at all?

The question is not: What is this or that good for? Nor even: What is it all good for? The question is about the good *of* it. We are asking about the onto-logical inherence of good. We often ask: To what point or purpose is it all? We rightly ask this question, but we often wrongly assume that our response must regard some end not yet achieved, that is yet to be achieved. To ask about the good *of* it, however, does not refer us to a future that may never come, but to the very goodness of being itself, regardless of its temporal mode, perhaps regardless of time. There is a certain indeterminacy about the question. It does not regard anything in particular, though it is not unmindful of the good of things in particular. It indeterminately extends to being as such. What is worthy to be ultimately affirmed? Is being worth it? Can we say "It is good"?

In the universal relativity, beings may be for the sake of many things—for themselves, for others of their own kind, for nothing in particular that we seem able to determine. But what is the good of it? This is not the same kind of determinate question about a determinate "for the sake of." I understand this "question," not in terms of a dialectic of the indefinite and the determinate, but in terms of the positive overdetermination of agapeic astonishment and perplexity. Likewise, the "answer" to be explored will have a similar kind of indeterminacy: the good of being is not for the sake of anything in particular; to be is to be good; the good of being is to be, and to be as good; and it is

505

because of this, that good extends to the good of everything in particular, while not being restricted for the sake of anything in particular. The gift of being is itself the first good of being. Our "answer" will bespeak a certain mode of metaphysical gratitude (not unrelated to what elsewhere I spoke of as thought singing its other).[1] The overdetermination of our "answer" will not be, however, a vague indefiniteness. It will be articulated with respect to the metaphysics of the between set forth in this work as a whole.

So we may say the following. Beings are concretions of the original power of being; they are given for themselves in creation where they become themselves and intermediate with other beings in the universal impermanence. Beings become selves in accord with orders of intelligibilities that define their inherent character, as well as the modes of interplay with other beings, with creation and with the origin. Beings become selves in communities shaped by these modes of interplay and togetherness. Beings become true to themselves, to creation and the origin in the milieu of such communities. The truth of being is manifested in this becoming true in the milieu of creation. This becoming true, this truth of being in transcending, is itself nothing but a reference to the good of being. Transcending defines the integral self-becoming of beings. To remain true to this is to remain true to the good of the being. Being true to transcendence is, hence, to be good.

Finite transcending points beyond itself to the absolute origin as the primal giver of the promise of creation, and as the sustaining ground of its metaxological milieu. As giver and sustaining, the origin is immanent in the metaxological milieu. But since its giving and sustaining is agapeic, the milieu is given its promise of being for itself, and hence the absolute origin lets it be free as other. It withdraws from coercive determination of the self-becoming of creation. The absolute origin remains transcendent, as other to the given otherness of the creation as for itself. This being for itself of creation is not a closure into a self-sufficient totality, but an open wholeness that points beyond itself to the excess of the origin that remains other to the creation, even while it enters community with creation.

If creation were the closure of self-sufficient totality, Hegel would be right, and the ultimate would be an absolute dialectically self-mediating whole. There would be no vector of transcending pointing to the origin's excess to the world as a totality. There would be no origin as other. Creation would be the erotic self-creation of the absolute. But since creation is an open whole, it is marked by its own being for itself, and this opens beyond itself, back to its origin, and forward to the passing beyond it of absolute transcendence.

This open wholeness, I think, is unintelligible without reference to the good. The wholeness of beings is just their integral self-becoming in community, whereby they remain true to themselves and to the truth of being. But

---

1. *Philosophy and its Others*, chapter 6.

this is just their being good, in their ontological fidelity to the truth of being. This is their ontological perfection. There can be nothing closed off about this. If we properly understand the communicative exigence of the metaxological, then the openness of a being's wholeness is its becoming perfect—in its unreserved relatedness to otherness beyond itself, as well as in its own integral truth to itself. Thus being good is a double fidelity to being true: integral truth to self, unreserved openness to the truth of the other.

So we find that being true and being good cannot be separated. Nor can either be understood without reference to the complex ontological character of origin, creation, things, intelligibilities, selves, and communities. Hence we must do justice to both the immanence and the otherness of the good. We must not forget, at the beginning, the *immediacy* of otherness with respect to univocity, and, at the end, the *intermediacy* of otherness with respect to the metaxological. The good in its otherness is at work in the beginning, it is at work in the end. We are defined as beings in the middle between these two transcendences.

A metaxological sense of origin, creation, things, intelligibilities, selves, communities, truth is necessary to articulate the meaning of this being between. And if there were no appreciation of the good, not only would our understanding be seriously impoverished, it would be rendered worthless. The worthiness of being is revealed by the truth of being. This we must try to understand, moving from the excess of the good of the beginning, to its excess as the ultimate.

The fourfold understanding of being will light up the pathway we must follow. Relative to *univocity*, we must speak of the goodness of the origin, as well as the ontological goodness of oneness with respect to creation. Relative to *equivocity*, we must face the enigma of evil beyond the first immediacy of the good. Relative to *dialectic*, we must explore the ontological good of wholeness, with stress on the ideal integrity of self-becoming and communal harmony with being-other. Relative to the *metaxological*, we must consider the opening of finite wholeness to the good, in its heteronomy beyond all finite measure.

Ontological Goodness and Nihilism

Ancient tradition identifies the good with the one, and the identification is not without its truth. Being itself is said to be convertible with the true, and this with the one, and this then too with the good. Clearly it is not numerical unity that is at stake. What kind of oneness is in question?

If we think of beings as concretions of the original power of being, if we think of them as intelligibly becoming in the universal impermanence, we can say that they reveal an exigence to be themselves as integral wholes. This *being themselves* is their good; this their unity in process is their good; their being as such is their good. Moreover, this exigence to integral being is immediate. It is not the result of mediated choice; beings simply as being are this exigence to be one. To be one is itself a dynamic process that has to live in the double stress of self-relation and relativity to other-being. In the stress of the middle, beings are immediately an exigence to be at one with themselves. This is the good of their being—good for them, in the primitive sense that they would not *be* as they are without some attainment of such an integrity. They would be falling apart or decaying or dying. The good of their being is inseparable from this ontological integrity.

If we are dealing with univocity here, it is clearly in a sense not reducible to unity without difference. The univocity here at play is the immediacy of the work of oneness. This work will show itself to be complexly mediated, but the mediation itself is an unfolding of a primitive good of oneness itself. To be is to be an integrity of being, which is to be a one. To be at one with being, self-being or other-being, is to be true to being; to be true to being is to be good; hence to be is to be good, in a manner captured by the integrity of existing that every entity is more or less. In that respect, goodness is identical with being integrally true to being. Goodness is the integral truth of being.

There is more at stake here than a simple-minded reiteration of an ancient tradition. Much more is at stake in that ancient tradition itself. Of this "more" many thinkers today have little more than the vaguest of notions. Let us say that the entire issue of *ontological nihilism* is here in question. In modern thought we are accustomed to the standard distinction of fact and value. We think of being as there, just there, a fact or set of facts. We think of values as human constructions that are imposed or projected on the otherwise valueless being. In itself being is worthless. This degrading of the value of being is itself the product of the mind of mathematical and scientistic univocity; it lacks the sense of metaphysical integrity that the univocal can sometimes reveal. This scientistic univocity produces ontological nihilism.

We have lived so long in this nihilism that the shock of the words of nihilism hardly registers: being in itself is worthless; it is neither good nor bad, just a mere valueless thereness. What value it may come to possess will arises from constructions of human beings. Even if all you want to say is that it is an indifferent neutrality, this quickly mutates, under the pressure of human self-transcendence, into something that must be *for us*. Hence the indifference will be aggressively overcome by the human will to power. Still we will claim to superimpose our valuations on the valueless thereness. There seems no ontological basis for resisting the slide from valueless neutrality to ontological aggression on neutral being. For the self-transcending of the human being is still inexorably oriented to the good, any good, if the true good is withheld from it.

Here we have a situation analogous to the one we saw before with intelligibility—namely, being is absurd in itself; it lacks inherent intelligibility; intelligibility is our construction projected into the ontological ooze. What I said about intelligibility, as about truth, also applies here. It is not that I deny any contribution of the human being. Rather the genuine opening of self-transcending towards the other is to be recovered and reaffirmed. This happens especially in agapeic minding. Here the self in its transcending opens beyond itself to the other and for the other as other. Agapeic mind also opens beyond the ontological nihilism that reduces being's otherness to a worthless thereness. Agapeic mind is genuinely self-transcending, because it is a love of being. What it reveals is that being is worthy of affirmation as good in itself.

The dualism of fact and value is only one example of a more pervasive ontological nihilism endemic in modernity. It is one expression of the deracination of the human being from its community with being in its otherness. The dualism is a result of this deracination; it is not the metaphysical primitive it has been held to be. As a metaphysical theory it is, in fact, the expression of a loss of, perhaps hostility towards, our community with being in its otherness. It is a theory trapped in a fall from the elemental goodness of being and our given community with creation.

Even those who managed to diagnose this nihilism, like Nietzsche, often did not realize to what extent their own recommendations for *recovery* were the products of the same degradation of creation's goodness. This goodness will never be recovered through any apotheosis of the human being as the creator of values in a valueless universe. For if the creation is valueless in itself, then the human being as a participant in creation is also ontologically valueless, so likewise his human construction is also ultimately valueless. Every effort to construct values out of himself will be subject to the same deeper, primitive, ultimate valuelessness. Human values collapse ultimately into nothing, if there is not a ground of value in the integrity of being itself. To think otherwise is only metaphysical whistling in the dark. It may seem heroic to be defiant of a worthless, absurd universe. But in truth this whistling is itself as dark as the darkness of the universe. Only subtle self-deception can avoid the collapse of our constructions into the ontological nihilism that is said to affect the whole of being in itself.

If there is no primal regard in which being is good, then no being is good, nor is the human being. The human being is a living nihilism masquerading as ethical, if there is no ontology of the good, if the good is not grounded in being itself, or if being itself is not primally good. I do not underestimate the strangeness of what is being said to us denizens of modernity. The thin gruel of valueless being on which modern enlighteners have supped for centuries has produced an extraordinary emaciation of the spirit. When this emaciation becomes the norm, anything closer to metaphysical health cannot be digested. It is too much to take in, excessive. The feast of being, the agape of being, will seem incredible. The husks and straws of the anorexic spirit will seem more palatable, more assimilable. But the husks and straws will only continue the slow dying, while the agape may restore robustness, maybe even divine intoxication. If we continue to insist that being in itself is worthless and pout about our "creativity," we have declared ourselves for death.

Relative to ontological nihilism, we now face its potentially catastrophic consequences in what we call the ecological crisis. The excision of final causes from the explanatory schemes of modern science confined mindfulness to the fact of being, said to be worthless in itself. Ontological astonishment is deadened, and we end up with a neutering, indeed deadening, of the earth. The ecological crisis is the living sickness of this deadening. Let me relate the ontological good of oneness to what is sometimes called the *integrity of creation*. In the latter a richer suggestion of the unity of the good arises. Against the devaluation of creation through the mechanization of nature, a certain inherent wholeness or community of being is implied, when people speak of this integrity. Nature is not a neutral aggregate of manipulable neutral forces, but a togetherness of beings marked by inherent order and harmony. The harmony of the community of nature points to the integrity of creation, which manifests an inherent worth that is to be respected.

Here we are on the right track. The univocal sense of being is rescued from the ontological nihilism of scientistic univocity. Of course, more must be said. We need to push the question of the good to the extreme. If we want to say that creation has an integrity, we have to grant the following: first, *integrity* itself implies a certain wholeness to nature; second, *creation* suggests the reference of that wholeness to an originative source that grounds and sustains the wholeness of the creation. Moreover, we are made to ponder the basis for asserting that creation itself manifests a prior ontological goodness, itself the basis of the standard sense of value we have—that is, the value we claim to give to things. The question is: Does the value we give to things presuppose a prior sense of the good that marks creation as an integrity for itself, a good in itself before it is good for us?

The answer we give is yes: to be is to be good; being itself is an ontological perfection. Why? Because we think the integrity of creation in light of the origin, as well as of end. The issue of ontological nihilism needs an archeology of the good as well as a teleology. I am not suggesting we totalize nature by means of a kind of hubristic *ratio*. The point is never the mathematization of nature with the view to becoming its masters and possessors, in Descartes' famous words. This scientistic will to power is part of the problem, not the solution. We need a different sense of unity to account for the integrity of creation that preserves the ontological good of being. To my knowledge, contemporary philosophers of science have not done much better than Descartes in addressing the issue of nihilism at the properly ontological level.

Most philosophers seem blissfully unaware of the problem in this form, even when they sing hymns to the brave new world of post-Einsteinian physics. They never ask how the cosmos as described within this physics provides the ontological basis for such ontological hymns. A hymn is a song of praise celebrating the sacred. But such a hymn could only make sense if being itself provides in itself its own worthiness to be praised, its own good, perhaps indeed its own sacredness. But within its own terms, science makes no room for this. The issue is urgent, in some ways more seriously acknowledged in the last century and earlier in this century than now. Loss of urgency marks standard philosophical discourse, loss of the essential resources even to understand the issue.

The human self is in the middle of being, so it is not on a par with the worth of the whole. Creation as a community of being implies reference to a source that, as other, allows for the holding together of the community as an open whole. The origin is in excess of the integral creation, and it is with regard to this excess that we must face the issue of ontological nihilism. Even the self-creativity claimed by the human being involves a reference to an inward otherness, as a source of creation in selving itself. The excess of the origin implies a radical origination by an agapeic source that is bound by nothing finite, and that gives being because being itself is good, because being itself is simply the goodness of its agape.

Whether our account of this is adequate, or whether it takes us beyond determinate reason into the region of metaphysical metaphor, is not now the issue. The fact is that such language carries the charge of the good in a way that is absent in the putatively neutral language of modern cosmology. Not only the being, but the intelligibility and truth and worth of finite creation is articulated with reference to the ultimate source, in excess of all finite determinations and beings. This is why we need metaphysical metaphors, precisely to avoid the objectifying determination of a source that cannot be objectified thus, since it is the source of all objectification, and thus itself beyond all objectification. In the end, there is no such thing as an absolutely neutral metaphysical framework. Neutrality itself is the result of a process of neutering, and so an abstraction from the plenitude of being, rather than the fundamental condition of being it makes claim to be.

Creation is good because to be is to be good. To be thus ontologically good is to be so because one is prized for self. But who prizes the creation for itself? It is not the human being. The answer already suggested is the agapeic origin. And this view does not dispel metaphysical astonishment. It deepens it.

Consider, for instance, Plato's view that no proper accounting of things is really possible outside of some invocation of the absolute good. It need hardly be said that this invocation gives *no determinate explanation of a determinate happening* or event or thing. But that is not its purpose. The point is a sense of being as a whole, not the determinate intelligibility, or indeed the definite worth, of this or that aspect of being or specific entity. The passion of the philosopher to make sense of things remains a futile self-transcendence, outside of some unsurpassable sense of the worth of the whole. The invocation of the absolute good names a kind of positively indeterminate horizon within which we begin to look at things differently. The second indeterminate perplexity of metaphysical thinking turns into marveling before the good of being.

Since we have invoked the origin, it might prove illuminating to turn from Plato to *Genesis*, and God's astonishing saying on beholding creation: it is good, it is very good. God does not say: I am good. God does not say: It is good for this purpose or that purpose. Nor again does God says: It is good for this being or that being—say, the human being—who indeed is offered dominion by God. There is this prior original yes: It is good. It is not good for human beings; *It* is good, good for itself. The giving of being is itself the gift of being as good. There is no other reason for it, beyond the fact that creation as being is good. The fact that there is no other reason is itself the ultimate reason for its being. There is no reason more primal or more ultimate. The valuations we humans may make subsequently follow in the train of this first absolute amen. The meaning of this amen is all but beyond human ken.

The "It is good," does not mean we deny the pragmatic fact that human beings as finite entities often exist in hostile relations to other things, which to that extent are not evidently good *for us*—for instance, rats that carry the bubonic plague. The point is this. The good for us presupposes a more primordial sense of the goodness of being, which it is for us to acknowledge, and to take into account in the ethical mediations with the otherness of beings that we devise. It is for us to respond ethically to being, as not needing the justification of our evaluation for it to be good. If we take to heart this prior "It is good," then the derived good that is for us, or will be for us, will receive a significantly different interpretation than would be possible without the prior "It is good"—certainly one impossible on an ontologically neutral basis.

The reality of *evil* must be faced and to it I return. The good for us, even understood in relation to the prior "It is good," does not preclude suffering and tragic loss, nor iniquity, horror, monstrousness, outrage, ruin, and malevolence. Quite the opposite. The disjunction, hence potential hostility between the "for us," and the "It is good," offers the space of freedom, where the human being "for itself" asserts its "for itself" in enmity to the prior "It is good." This space of freedom, given by the good as agapeic, offers to the self as for itself the sinister opening of evil. Fidelity to the prior "It is good" offers the basis for a goodwill, a different benevolence to being, in our determination of the good for us. This would be a metaphysical goodwill to being, grounded on the origin as agapeic.

We can venture the claim that every being maintains itself in being by a kind of living ontological affirmation of the goodness of being in the goodness of its own being. To be is to be a center of self-affirmation, but to be thus is to be a concretion of the vector of transcendence towards the good at work in all being. The self-affirmation affirms the self of the being, but it is the *being* of the self that is affirmed. Most deeply, and most often not known as such, it is being as such that is affirmed as ultimately and originally good, in the self-affirmation of this being.

Beings are values for themselves—values because good, good because creations. Once given to be, beings maintain their integrity and strive to perpetuate themselves. The self-love of the being is its particularized, lived affirmation of the value of being, determined and finitized by the particularity of its own self-being. Thus each being, as self-affirming, is a determinate affirmation of the love of being, being *simpliciter*. This ontological affirmation does not mean a self-conscious saying; rather the very continuing *to be* is the ontological affirmation. A being is a yes to being, by simply being. It is not mindful of this, or only rarely so, as with the human being.

Even self-interest is a self-affirmation, hence a valuing of the worth of this being. Self-interested being values its own being, in realizing and perpetuating this worth. Continuing existence is continuing worthiness to be, value inherent in being as being. This is not imposed by us, just as intelligibility, which itself has value relative to the harmony of being, is not simply imposed by us. Every entity is a more or less intelligible harmony of the original energy of being, and as such it is a good. This is not to deny that *we do the good*; we must also make ourselves good, just as we erect intelligibility and order. I will come to this below. But this our mediation of the good would not be possible without the first immediacy of the "It is good." The for-self of the finite entity is its affirmation of its own being as good, and hence mediately of all being. This affirmation of the being of the entity comes to it as the particular love of the primal "It is good."

The argument against the ontological nihilism of scientistic univocity is not only a rejection of the classical dichotomy of primary and secondary qualities, where so-called primary qualities are entirely devoid of any charge of value whatever. There is nothing primary about primary qualities, beyond the resolution of scientistic univocity to privilege a particular abstraction of being that is found powerful for a certain system of calculations. The primary, properly speaking, is ontologically prior to this abstraction; hence the "primary quality" is secondary, in being derivative from a mediation produced by scientistic univocity and abstraction. The priority of "to be is to be good" is beyond the antithesis of primary and secondary qualities. For this dichotomy results in the subjectivizing of value in the self, in opposition to the worthlessness of "primary qualities." The so-called primary qualities are univocally calculable happenings, while the secondary qualities are equivocal subjective impressions and constructions. I want to say that the prior "It is good" means a different understanding of *aesthetic value*. Aesthetic value means the worth of the thereness, as given in its sensuous manifestness. In this ontological meaning, aesthetic value is the show of the worth of being.

We here need, and against scientistic univocity, the language of what one might call a sacramental aesthetics. One does not want to silence the voices of the earth. Just so the integrity of creation calls to mind a metaphor of the world itself as a kind of ontological work of art. The wholeness of this work is not a totalism. For a great work of art is a show of significance that is a plenitude in itself and that resists exhaustion in terms of a completely univocal analysis. Such a work creates a world unto itself, yet it mediates the suggestion of the source as transcendent to its own wholeness. Such a world is not a closed whole. The very "unity" of the work communicates relatedness to its source, which as other is not enclosed in the created work itself. The work is the gift of the generosity of being. Its own created plenitude points back to its agapeic source. This show of the generosity of being is the aesthetic value of creation—value that is ontological, relative to the goodness of creation itself; value that is metaphysical, relative to its suggestion of the origin's transcendence.

Precisely because this matter is beyond scientistic univocity, we cannot *prove* aesthetic value. There is no determinate proof. There are images, aesthetic, religious, ethical. There are metaphysical metaphors that articulate our astonishment or perplexity. The creative work is the aesthetic concretion of an intrinsic good. That it is good for itself never closes it off from the good of what is other to itself. The creation opens a space of free value, given for mindfulness in our creative interplay with its rich givenness.

The aesthetic value of creation arouses delight and marveling akin to that aroused by great art. Nor is this delight devoid of troubling thought. Perplexity is not eradicated but shadows the delight. It is deepened by delight into further thought. As an aesthetic work of the original power of being, creation is appreciated. We prize it for itself. Our own agapeic mindfulness is released towards the goodness of its otherness. This mindfulness breaks down the barriers between the aesthetic, the ethical, the religious, and the metaphysical. Admiration of the goodness of being beyond all objectification runs through them all.[2]

Evil and the Equivocity of the Good

I do not say that the aesthetic show of the good is always properly appreciated, in the richest sense of the word appreciate. Appreciation refers us to what is prized for itself, what indeed is inherently precious.[3] But it also im-

---

2. We are mindful of creation as a cosmos in a manner reminiscent of the Pythagorean sense: a well-ordered whole, a beautiful creation unto itself. When the Stoics spoke of *sumpatheia ton holon*, some such admiration was also at issue. I am not enjoining Pythagoreanism or Stoicism, since the agapeic origin invokes a stronger sense of transcendence, without any diminution of creation's goodness. But all these are truer to the aesthetic value of being, deeper than any clockwork world or cybernetic mind can comprehend.

3. *Appretiare* is also related to *pretium*, price, also related to the word *praise*. Appreciation discerns what is worthy to be praised for itself; it sings it.

plies a zone of ambiguity and freedom relative to the good. The aesthetic value of being is overdetermined; it is too much. We might say that the good of being appears in the overwhelming beauty and glory of creation. Beauty is the aesthetic concretion of the good; glory is the intimation of the fullness of the origin in the excessive splendor of creation. There is an openness to the gift of creation in the ontological freedom of the creature to be for itself. The openness of this freedom is both a gift and a promise to be realized. The good of being is proportionate to the original power of this being, that being; its excellence is its realized power of being; its fulfilled actuality is the realized promise that is its goodness. Different beings have different promises, and in finite creation, so far as we know, the greatest promise arises with the free original power of the human being.

If the aesthetic good of the world is overwhelming in its beauty, why is there death, violence, savagery, blood, malformation, malignancy? How does this square with the primal "It is good"? As perplexing as is the being of the good, so also is evil. Where the good calls for astonishment, evil evokes metaphysical horror. Both raise questions that will never be dispelled with a univocal determinate answer, since each is an essential perplexity to which we must recur again and again.

Here are some remarks. If creation is good, it is also a space of freedom, of promise of the good to be realized for themselves by the beings of creation. This follows from the otherness between the origin and creation. This promise, given and let be in its otherness, is realized through the affirmation of being of each entity within the community of creation. There is *equivocity* in this self-affirmation. At its most deep, ontological self-affirmation is an affirmation of being in the being of this particular thing. But because it is in and through the being of this thing that being is affirmed, the affirmation of this being in its *particularity for itself* easily assumes dominance. There is an insistence of being that marks the existence of every being. This is the metaphysical stress of its unique particularity. This means that the particular can stress itself as the good, stress its own good as the good. It can turn its self-insistence into an exclusion of the good of the being of what is other to itself.

The promise of beings is double: first, the promise of its own self-mediation—namely, the perfection of the power of being, singularly concretized in this unique being; second, the promise of a relatedness to other-being, promise of a harmony of being with being beyond itself—this is the promise of integral participation in the metaxological community of being. The self-affirmation of the good of its own being is expressed in the first; the affirmation of being *simpliciter* is suggested by the second. Properly, the first mediation and affirmation are less ultimate than the second intermediation and love of being. But the way this doubleness is stressed in each entity means that the first can crowd out the second, stifle its actualizing in the self. Complete stifling would be actually the death of the first affirmation. Hence no complete stifling is possible, if the being is simply to continue to be.

In that sense, evil is parasitical on the power of being; for the evil has its power from the original power of being which it tries to bend away from the unconditional consent to being, the primal "It is good" that is at work in every being. In the space of openness a cleft can come to be between the "I am" and the "It is good." The "I am," as the self-insistence of existence, is genuinely an "I am good"; for it says "to be is to be good"; but in the cleft of equivocity, "I am good" slides ambiguously towards "I am the good." In this slide begins the usurpation of the good.

Put otherwise, the openness of the promise of the good takes us beyond the immediacy of value. Creation is a pluralism, hence difference, diversity, and potential opposition come to be. The source of potential opposition is in the double mediation of being. The open between is marked by tension between "I am good" and the "It is good." Freedom means that "I am good" can be asserted to mean "I am the good." The singular good usurps the good of the metaxological community of being, and indeed the good of the origin. The doubleness is so inherently ambiguous as to be always a danger and a hazard. There is an unconditionality emergent in the self-insistence of beings, in their "I am"; for their being is self-insistence. Yet each being is tugged by the undertow of its own nothingness, pulling it down into death. It recoils from this, fights it with the energy of self-insistence. It may hate its own nothingness, wanting to secure itself completely, will itself to be the absolute. In finite being, the love of being is in tension with the constitutive nothing. The love of being may cause it to refuse to consent to the latter, to thus fight against finitude, and to rage against its own doubled being. The refusal of consent here, emergent out of the affirmation of being by the singular being, is the withdrawal of affirmation from being-other. It is metaphysical rebellion against being, rather than gratitude for its gift.

The promise of freedom unfolds in the widening of the affirmation of being in the "I am," beyond all closed self-insistence, to the universal community of being. The promise is supported by the good as already at work in the affirmation of being *simpliciter*, which is more ultimate ontologically than the particularized affirmation of self-being. But this promise too is ambiguous, and can be asserted as the widening of *self-insistence*, rather than the transcendence of self-insistence to the good of the others. Then this particular being does not truly come to know the other as other. It may remain, for instance, in a kind of narcissistic innocence. Or, the ambiguous promise of transcending can be willfully bent, and the self-insistence wills itself to be the absolute. It affirms itself as absolute, elevates itself to the status of the origin and the ultimate.

Here may emerge the willfulness of untrammelled self-aggrandizing. Anciently this was seen as the real slide into the equivocity of the good— namely, evil. This self-apotheosis is the sin of *hubris* or *superbia*. It is the equivocity of the good, since it is the particular good trying to mask itself as the absolute good, trying to duplicate the absolute good by saying it is absolutely *mine*. This claim of absolute mineness is the perversion of the "I am," of the "I am good;" for it is the refusal of the metaxological community of being as good, and hence refusal of the primal "It is good." It is in truth even the refusal of itself as good, since its absolutization of its own "I am good" betrays its own true good.

This is the perversion. No one owns the good. The good is the possession of no one. It is not a possession at all. Quite to the contrary, it is a letting being be for itself. It never possesses but always frees. The perversion is the belief that in owning the good one has it. In fact, the good is made one's own only when one refuses to own it and wills to communicate it, give it away, infinitely. One makes the good one's own by giving oneself away—that is to say, by creating away from self towards the other, in an agapeic movement of generosity without expectation. This broadcasting of the good is the being of the origin. Hubris is the finite being claiming the good by refusing to broadcast it. There is an inversion and retraction of the creative power of being. And if there is any broadcast—and there will be—it is because of the secret generosity of the good that lets be, lets the evil be; and this, even though what is broadcast simply mires the world deeper in the duplicitous equivocation.

Moreover, the equivocity of the good becomes most stressed, hence most dangerous, where the power of freedom is most extensive. This arises with the human being. The equivocality above might be applicable to the emergence of disorder in nature; there is no denying the terrors of nature, the chanciness of accident, the merciless crushing of things that nature's awesome might can impose. Some of these disorders are disorders relative to us, or relative to particular beings or kinds of beings. Is it disorder relative to the community of being as a whole? Not always. Order and disorder are defined in the universal relativity, and what seems disorder here, elsewhere may be the phase of a larger order. Likewise, what seems a secure order here is the sleeping quiescence of a larger chaos. The flood that drowns may also cleanse. A carrier of disease may show a beautiful order of being within its own borders, but relative to its victim, this order is fatal. Conversely, a satisfying order for us may harbor disaster for others beyond our complacent horizon.

The human being is the most dangerous being. It is the most singularly stressed being because the promise of freedom in its doubleness is most energized here, most capable of becoming mindful of itself. It is also capable of mindfully coming to terms with the equivocality of its own doubleness and transcending the duplicity of self-insistence. It is most capable of an agapeic transcendence, and most capable of defection from this transcendence.

It is not incidental that a strong propensity in moral reflection in modernity has tended to emphasize our self-insistence, and define our desire in terms of its calculation of self-preservation and self-perpetuation. There is nothing wrong with this per se, except that it is woefully incomplete, and most interpretations of it woefully misguided. When the ancients said that desire seeks the good because it is the good, they were superior to the moderns who said that the good is the good because desire seeks it. The vector of transcendence of desire is ethical love of the good. And as Aristotle says: all things desire the good. The vector of transcendence is at work in all. Hence the energy of the primal "It is good" is not stifled. It is choked to the extent that human desire becomes the *only* source of worth. Then there is no primal "It is good," only an ontologically neutral cosmos that is really hostile to the fragile human self. This modern view is really a systematization of the equivocity of the good, but a systematization not really capable of disentangling the equivocation.

There is a rightness in insisting on our self-insistence. With the human being we find the most intensive self-insistence. Yet we also find the most expansive openness to being beyond self, the greatest promise of the agape of being relative to the other. We must look more deeply into the duplicity of the human self: not take the first as primitive, and from it try to derive the second; not fail to explore a more primal "It is good" from which these two issue. We will never get to the second from the first without some reference to this more primal "It is good." This "It is good" moderates the self-absolutizing of the first, as it also stands against any totalizing of the second that would extirpate the first. The harmony of these two is metaxological, because both are created forms of the primal love of the "It is good," both turned towards the agape of the origin.

The human being is a tangle of anomaly and a sweeping flourish of transcendence. We may say that our good is tied to self-preservation and self-perpetuation in the manner of other beings. This is true to a point, but human desire is not univocal. It is not unidirectionally riveted to a determinable set of biological objectives like food, shelter, procreation. It is pluridirectional, and just so, because it is activated to be itself in the metaxological community of being. The sweep of its transcendence breaks out of the set circle of biological determination; it is lifted above the monolinear teleology of other living things. It often does not know what it wants at all to perfect itself. So much so that it has been said to be infinitely malleable. I would say, it is an infinite restlessness seeking a good commensurate with the call of absoluteness that emerges in its own self-mediation. It is a love of the good, but the good is an excess, as too much for it. Inevitably human desire, in its own self-mediation, feels itself falling away into equivocality. It has lost the immediate certainty of animal instinct. It is thrust into the open promise of freedom; it is asked to choose; but it does not know what to choose. It is often lost, hence miserable, just in the greatness of its self-transcendence.

Then the seeking of our desire becomes equivocal in itself, a succession of appetitive forays that briefly satisfy, only to betray the promise of perfection, and to force desire again in further search. And desire seems unable to find that one thing necessary that will give it the peace beyond measure it seeks. It is lost, it gives up on the search for the good as other. It retracts into the excitement of its own energy of searching. It is the chase that becomes ultimate for it, not the quarry. Desire excites itself, excites itself endlessly. It turns away from the truth of the good as other and seeks its pleasure in the inner tangle and otherness of its own self-activating energy. In its desiring of its own desire, it swoons away into the equivocality of its own inner abyss, sweetly falling into itself, like snowflakes gently dropping into a black lake. The sweetness of its own self has not yet been devoured by the demons of its own deep.

There is more to be said about the falling away into the equivocality of the good. Once more recall the astonishing and perplexing claim made with respect to the "It is good." We approach a good that is excessive; its excellence is exceeding. The closer we approach this good, the more we finite singulars undergo *both* marvel and terror. The beginning of beauty is terror, Rilke rightly said. The excess here is terrifying in its being too much. The beautiful may even appear ugly to us in its terror; we choose the ugly as more proportioned to ourselves. This, if you like, is the ambiguity of the primal good, its mystery: it evokes terror and admiration at once. It is the *mysterium tremendum et fascinans*.

We are doubled again: pulled towards it in attraction, dragging our feet at its exceeding transcendence. Our promise is the between, drawn into community with the ultimate good, terrified about the possible death of our self-insistence that may be asked by this transcendence. We are aghast at the good. We wince at its madness. We retract our transcendence to the good, when we shun the dangerous welcome of the primal "It is good." We would define the good on our terms. But this is a falling from the good, though we assert ourselves as the masters of our fate in this falling away.

The more we fall away, the more horrifying becomes pure beauty and pure goodness, when we are offered some glimpse of it. We cannot endure the good, nor indeed will we ever be able to endure it, if self-insistence is elevated into an unsurpassable absolute. The promise of the freedom of existence is the agapeic movement of transcendence beyond closed self-insistence. This is the welcome of the good; but to closed self-insistence the welcome is a kind of death. The self-insistence is right; it is a death; but this death is the portal that opens to life. Agapeic self-transcendence says yes, even in this death; it discovers in this yes that it is already beyond this death. But to the self that clings to itself, this yes seems like a yawning grave, bleak, abominable, revolting. So it revolts.

And even then a vague sense of the sinister haunts our retraction from the primal "It is good." We retract, fall away from it, and the shadow of a sinister guilt springs up. Of course it does, since there has been a betrayal here. We hate this guilty sense of the sinister, because it is almost nothing, certainly nothing we can master, and yet it unsettles us and robs us of peace. Guilt is the unease of the promise of transcendence that has not been true to itself. The betrayal, revolting against its loss of peace, erects itself into the absolute truth for itself. The betrayal that absolutizes the self-insistence is actually a sundering of the self from its own truth; it is actually as much a betrayal of the self's promise, as of the good as other to the self. Far from elevating the self, the absolutization of self-insistence wounds self in the deepest intimacy of its being. The self-absolutizing self is a duplicitous being, a split being—and this not in the promising sense of stressed between its own good and the good of transcendence as other, but as a split being in itself, untrue to transcendence and ill at ease with itself. This split self has defected, for the exigence of self-transcendence has been turned back on itself into an energy of self-absolutizing.

What I am calling the equivocality of the good is amenable to different *interpretations*, precisely because of its overdetermination. It can serve to articulate the meaning of both good and evil, beyond the vague guilt of the sinister. Thus the sense of opposition between the good and the evil can be erected into a dualism of poles. Thus also it can be *externalized*, though its home is in the inwardness of ethical selfhood. In this case, evil will be given a primal status alongside the good, and both will be seen as ultimate principles at war with each other in the cosmos, and most intensively in the human being as the battle site of the two powers, the dark and the bright. Consider Empedocles' cosmic doubleness of love and strife. Zoroastrianism is perhaps the ancient form of this equivocality of the good, resurrected in Manichaeanism. Such interpretations are destined to be resurrected in some form or other, since they are parasitical on the equivocality of the good. For instance, various left and right wing ideologies crystalize the equivocity of the good into a modern Manichaean dualism of opposites, sometimes with murderous consequences, since the dark principle, whether capitalist or communist, must be destroyed.

I am not subscribing to any of these views, as I indicate in the very phrase "evil is the equivocality of the good." This implies that evil would be nothing in itself apart from its parasitical power on the original power of being as good. The appeal of Zoroastrianism, or any dualism of evil and good, is the often massive sense we have that dark forces are abroad, too massive and uncontrolled for us to have any influence and to be called guilty. We encounter evil that is beyond human mediation. The opposite of the excessive "It is good," this also is too much, excessive. We cry out in helplessness at the darkness that flies loose, pitiless to humans. Evil seems so pervasive that we naturally think of it as, so to say, a *negative absolute*. The power of evil is beyond our power. We lie down desolate and weep. Bereft, we lament our bereavement.

We absolutize ourselves, and the evil in inwardness imposes a terrifying necessity on the course of human affairs. Instead of being the masters of our fate, an evil willfulness in the course of things crushes us. The parasite consumes the life of the host, or the betrayal of the host betrays itself. The hollow splendor of evil's power reveals its mighty impotence. The inverse of the aweful welcome of the good—namely, the leering compulsion of the evil—was once

imaged as the maw of Hell that drags to perdition all who dally with it. Heaven
and Hell symbolize the extremities of the equivocality of the good. There is a
chastening horror here too, since over Hell is also written, so Dante chill-
ingly says: eternal love made this too.

All this is incomprehensible to post-Enlightenment thinking, but there
is a deep truth here that needs thought. The damned damn themselves. Damnation is an ultimate in freedom, the ultimate freedom of refusal. Damnation
is parasitical on the good, the good of freedom, and on the agape that will not
force the consent promised to free humans. We die howling—howling our
refusal. This howl is an imprecation on the good.[4]

All consent and howling point us to an unmeasured depth of inwardness
in selfhood itself. Even Manichaeanism privileges the battle that takes place
in the human soul. Here the equivocality of the good is related to the opposition of the human will to itself. The will doubles itself, is a double will, as in
Augustine's famous discussion. The equivocality of the good is not simply
cosmological; it is existential; it is rooted in the deepest intimacy of being of
the human self. Human inwardness is itself the theater of the equivocality of
the good. This does not exclude reference to the community, but the community of the good cannot be understood in abstraction from this intimacy of
being of the good, this idiocy, as I term it. This intimacy and community are
beyond objectifiable measure.

If the human being is the theater of the equivocality of the good, there is
something almost naive about the sufferings of nature, compared to the tangled
web of malice and vice we can weave. Likewise, the aesthetic good of creation
is innocent compared to the demand of the good on human beings. With
humans the opposition of good and evil is, as it were, invisible; it is the heart's
good, the evil of mindfulness and spirit, the benevolence and malevolence of
will, that are at stake. This good of inwardness is not aesthetically manifest
always. It may retreat from appearing; it may work secretly, hiddenly. It may
be hidden even from the self-consciousness of the agent. The evil retreats
before the light; the good is modest to reveal itself, lest it presume wrongly to
be the good. Who can divine the human heart, who has penetrated the labyrinth of the will? None. By its fruits it will be known. But the root is idiotic,
hidden. And who can say that the sour fruits this season speak a withered
stem, or that a season may yet come when the root has returned to life, bearing sweet and pleasing fruit? Or indeed that the sweet fruits, now so delec-
table, are poisoned pleasures? None. There is no univocity of the human heart.
It is an equivocal abyss. Monsters thrive there. So do saints.

The equivocality inwardizes the sense of the good, the sense of the evil. It
doubles the self in its inwardness, making it potentially a monster of self-will,

---

4. For remarks on radical evil, see *Beyond Hegel and Dialectic*, chapter 4; *Philosophy
and its Others*, 201–205.

or a saint of sacrificial love. This doubleness is our misery and our greatness. It inwardizes the paradox of the good. The inwardizing prepares the way for a possible love of the good that has become mindful of the evil, indeed that has passed through a purgatorial ordeal, not only in the cauldron of externality, but within the pit of its own loathsomeness. The paradox of double inwardness is the cleft and conjunction of two wills in the self, two wills that are also shoots of one willing that is the deeper being of the self: the will of self-insistence; the will of love of being as being, being as other. The will of self-insistence is the flowering of self-being in its singular existence as seeking to perfect itself; the will of love of the other is the flowering of the opening of agapeic goodwill towards the goodness of the being of the other, goodness that is not a mere function of, or means back to, the good of self-will.

The will as double is at war with itself, in opposition to itself, is wounded in itself, is violent towards itself, even in its own self-affirmation. It tears itself apart, even as it insists on itself. It grieves for itself, even as it lacerates itself, or laughs at the world. Indeed there is a self-insistence that is intimately known in inwardness as the violence of the self on itself. There is a disorder of self that is perverse; there is disorder that is divine. There is order that is killing; there is order that gives creation peace. There is a self-love that is really a hatred of the self; there is a hatred of self that is really a love of what is other, and a consent to being. There is a sacrifice of self that affirms the other; there is a negation that is also a transfigured affirmation of self. The opposites oppose themselves, and as self-oppositions they turn into each other. We approach this equivocality with trepidation. The heart is fearsome. This too is part of the endowment of the good.

Dialectic and the Good

This war of opposition does not end the matter. The promise of the good makes its call even in the antagonism to the good. The will that is equivocally double, and at war with itself, is still a root will. It puts its root of willingness down into the idiotic depth of self-being. This is the heart. The good is at work in the heart, the call of the primal "It is good." Were the equivocality of the good all there was, we could never really know or do the good. Good and evil would so mingle that no differentiation could be made between them. Sheer equivocity seems to offer pure difference; in fact, it does away with difference, in the sense of proper discrimination between good and evil. The equivocality of the good is a slipping away into a difference from the "It is good," a difference that turns into a hostile opposition when the "I am good" of the self closes in on itself, in refusal of the already constitutive good of being as other.

The dialectic of the good takes us beyond the equivocation because it offers the mediation of sheer difference and a remembering of the deeper good in the good of the "I am." The fall from the good is itself a trace of the good betrayed; thus the betrayal carries the trace of a return to the promise of the good. This is not always clearly evident. Mindfulness is necessary to read the signs of the equivocal heart and will.

What mindfulness shows is that the violence of sheer opposition cannot stand. Even as the opposites oppose each other, indeed seem to turn into each other, so opposition points beyond itself to a renewed condition of harmony. There is a patience to the good that allows the fall into evil. This patience works *incognito* with the evil to turn around what is still promising in the corruption. There is a patience that the good will yet again offer a return to wholeness of being that the fall into equivocality fragments. If the evil is a corruption of the good of being, its energy carries the betrayed power of being. Were this turned around, were the opposition to oppose itself, this power would offer the opportunity of a return to the good. The opportunity of such a return is always offered. This is the absolute patience of the good. Properly speaking, it can be understood only on agapeic terms. For the agapeic origin is the absolutely patient good, willing to wait for the promise of its gift to be renewed again and again, despite its being betrayed again and again.

Good comes out of evil. The dialectic of the good reveals this reemergence of the good even in evil. This does not mean evil is good. Evil is dialectically related to the good; it would be nothing, were it not in some relativity to that which it opposes. Nor does this mean that the good would be nothing, were it not related to the evil. There is an *asymmetry* here, to which dialectical thinking sometimes lacks attention. The evil is opposition as refusal of the good, and hence would be nothing were there no good to refuse or violate. But the good would be good were there no evil, for primally it is not constituted by its opposition to its opposite. This again is suggested by the primal superlative "It is very good." Since *we* live in the middle as ambiguous, we can barely conceive of this good, beyond all opposition and violence. And when we think of the good of the beyond, we tend to import into it our own ambiguous being, making it an erotic rather than agapeic absolute. The good is in excess of the equivocal, and also of dialectic, when dialectic is defined in terms of mutual opposition or even symmetrical mutuality.

What then does the dialectic of the good show? It shows the necessity to mediate the equivocality of good/evil. We are purged in the stress of opposition; we are tested in this struggle; we are subject to a wearying struggle to remain true to the good. We have to endure despair and despondency, lamentation and sorrow, and yet pass through them, still willing to cling to the "It is good." If we give up on the "It is good," we slide back into the equivocal, and ultimately into a whirlpool of despair, the whirlpool that we ourselves are. We are asked to become good, where *becoming* means holding true to the good, despite every lure away, despite the stray impulses that express our wrath and defection from the worthy. In falling into equivocality, we deem the good unworthy of us; but now we are asked to make ourselves worthy of the good again. The good does not have to prove itself; we have to prove ourselves as capable of fidelity to it. In effect, the dialectic is the struggle wherein a new goodwill is forged. This is a renewal of the root willing that forked into the doubled will. This root willingness is the prior fealty we need to declare in our lives to show ourselves worthy of the good. Our mindfulness and life mediate the good at work in the root willing. They do not mediate this source entirely; for this source is in the deepest intimacy of the self, the idiocy of its own self-origin.

So we must say that the dialectic of the good is a work of faith and hope, despite all horror that stands against the elemental yes. The good works through the opposition; it takes the evil back into itself, in order to bring it back to what is still good in it. This tireless work of the good is in the interest of a condition of being of more inclusive harmony. And if there is no return to unknowing innocence, there may be a struggling advance to a renewal of our harmony with being. Of course, this struggle is always troubled by the possibility of failure. It is troubled by the failure that finally gives into failure and that gives up on the struggle to renew being. The patience of the good makes an excessive demand on our trust, that we not give up the work of perfecting being, even when faced with the extremity of defecting. We are called to a trust and a hope, not a certain cognition, that the good will triumph. There is no certainty here, since we are in the realm of spiritual freedom where, in a sense, everything is permitted, including the ruin of creation and the miracle of being. The agape of being permits everything, which is not to say everything permitted is good. For the essence of the good is freedom, and the patience that lets the free being come of itself to the welcome and embrace of the good.

As I understand it, this dialectic of the good does not exhibit the *historicist necessity* beloved of dialectical philosophers, like Hegel and Marx. There is no necessary knowledge of the certain triumph of the good. Rather there is the work of willing beings that point beyond themselves in their lives to the restoration of harmony of being, both with respect to other selves and communities, and with respect to the whole of creation.

The dialectic of the good is sometimes aligned with a kind of *theodicy* of the whole. From the standpoint of the whole, it is said that the darkness of the various parts are all essential contributors to the beauty of the whole. This view has also been called the aesthetic theodicy. The Marxist turns it into a theodicy of history, albeit in a secularized, politicized form. The iron laws of historical progress are such that the war of the classes is not evil from the standpoint of the communist perfection at the end of history. The seeming evil of war is dialectically exonerated with reference to the teleology of the historical whole. This is *not* at all what I mean by the dialectic of the good.

Nor do I mean Hegel's richer version, which equivocally blurs the difference between world-historical progress and divine providence.[5] Trust and hope are always solicited; and the hazard and uncertainty going with them will never be overcome. We can never be absolutely sure what the outcome will be. We will always continue to seek in the ambiguity of the between. Trust in the good must take its sights from the hazardous signs of perfection at work in the brokenness of being there.

It is not that I reject the aesthetic sense of the good. I have already indicated that the aesthetic show of the good, even when we metaphorically think of creation as a work of art, is double. Creation is not the absolute totality defining its own completion through its own dialectical self-mediation. Rather the aesthetics of creation involves a double mediation: its own self-mediation as a world unto itself, and hence an integrity of being; but since this integrity is an open wholeness that points beyond itself to the origin as other, there is a metaxological intermediation with transcendence as other, which in its excess always remains other. The openness of creation's wholeness, and the excessive otherness of the transcendent origin, mean that we cannot ever have a total aesthetic theodicy of the whole. The ontological aesthetics of the good is more pluralized and more ambiguous. We always dwell in this between of pluralized ambiguity. The dialectic always remains open to what is other to dialectic, to what may surprise and subvert it, to what may shatter the security of every claim to certainty about the good. The dialectic of the good lives with the hazard of evil, always renewing its struggle against an opposite that looks like an infinite hydra, forever sprouting a new leering face once one old head has been axed.

What the dialectic of the good does help forge is the autonomy of the ethical self. In the equivocality of the between, we return to the good through a turn to responsibility for ourselves and the good of being. We are answerable. The self-mediation that dialectic stresses here receives its ethical articulation. Being responsible is not a univocal given, but a self-appropriation of the gift of freedom itself. The self-appropriation means that the character of selfhood must be answerable for itself. This answerability is responsibility for the good. We are called to perfection of selfhood—perfection as the dynamic activation of the promise of the original power of being that unfolds in the self-transcending of the I. This thrust towards mediated wholeness of selfhood is accompanied by a demand that we also see being-other in the light of wholeness. We must try to see things whole, in order to be able to work mindfully for the making whole of creation.

And, of course, this means seeing beyond the fragmentary to the relations holding the many together into a complex community. The self as an open whole is also for the other. Its own wholeness is shaped in its interplay

---

5. See *Beyond Hegel and Dialectic*, chapter 1.

with what is rightfully of the integrity of the other. An intense discipline is demanded by the will to see things whole. The latter phrase may have the ring of cliché, but the actuality of what it signifies is exceedingly rare. Those selves who approximate wholeness in themselves, those who embody the vision of other-being that sees beyond partiality and fragmentation, are not common. The ethical integrity needed borders on a heroism of the good.

I stress that this heroism is an autonomy that is not for itself, in the usual partial, self-serving, self-interested manner. Rather the self as integral tries to lift itself up, in order to transcend itself towards the good as making a universal claim. In its own singularity it tries to embody the life of the ethical universal. Kant's categorical imperative is a very abstract statement of this exigence, in that the moral agent is only moral sofaras he can put his proposed action on a par with a universal ethical requirement. This moral autonomy is often presented as other to moral heteronomy, but I think this is a misinterpretation. To put oneself on the level of the moral universal is to transcend autonomy and make oneself an ethical willingness open to the good of all others. One is only ethical to the extent that all others have been included in the ethical integrity of the self.

In addition, dialectic has the virtue of reminding us of the *education of the singular ethical agent* up to the level of its universal responsibility. In the education the opposition of the equivocal is turned around into an appreciation of the relatedness that goes with the community of being. The will is evil if it is willful, that is, full of itself alone, shut in itself in opposition to the good of the community of being. It renews itself and its integrity when it reopens itself to the good of the community of being. This renewal is the release of a new willingness, or the rejuvenation of an old willingness that in principle is open to the good of the whole. Such a renewal is inseparable from the education of the self's willingness to the level of the ethical universal.

We never have mastery over this universal. Rather we creatively cooperate with it. Nor is it merely a regulative ideal that we project into some future completion. It is already at work, at work from the origin. In it we hear an echo of the primal yes, the "It is good." This is a universal yes; for it excludes nothing; all being as being is good. The good at work in the intimacy of the willing self is the echo of this yes, echoed even in the self-will that insists on its own being as good, its own being alone. We might say that this universal is *original*, as effective in our being from the beginning; it is *ideal*, as a demanding end to which we are insistently directed; and it is *actual* in the middle, for the between is the process of actualizing its promise. In the between it comes to us from the extremes and will not let us sleep, will not turn away from us, even as we turn away from it. It is unbidden, but it tirelessly, soundlessly, bids us to be true to the good, for being is good. And what remains open to perfecting, we must work to perfect, beyond even our best efforts. The patience of the good works behind our backs, stirring up the roots of willingness in the idiotic self, bending the violence of time towards a creative becoming, surprising us fragile agents with an unexpected outcome that, in its new perfection, sometimes astounds and refreshes even the most weary soul.

Beyond the Dialectic of the Good

Again this is no end of the matter. The dialectical emphasis on self-mediation, on autonomy and self-determination, on the thrust for restored wholeness, are to the point. But they become untrue to the good if we forget the doubleness of mediation in our transcendence towards the good. This forgetfulness will also distort the primary agapeic character of the good.

In restoring the self to a sense of its own responsibility for the good, dialectic radicalizes a turn to inwardness that is decisive. The question then is whether this innerness of the goodwill can be mediated in a completely determinate way. I suggest that it cannot. The inwardizing of willingness for the good points to an abyss of receptivity in the self itself. I think such a receptivity is in tension with predominant dialectical ways of describing the self in terms of its own active and autonomous self-determination. We find something other in play in the idiocy of the ethical. This is not only the intimacy of the self's own innerness. It is the unmastered intimacy of the good itself that resounds in the hearing of innerness itself.

It is important here to refer to the claim that the human being is of intrinsic value. This sense of value is mediated by a dialectical sense of the good. Despite all the squalors of existence, despite all the disfigurement we inflict upon fair creation, we still are beings of intrinsic worth, indeed marked by a certain infinite value. This infinity of worth is the image of the good in the human soul in its intimate innerness, in its idiocy. But just this inward infinity is other to complete self-mediation, of the sort dialectic often privileges. There is an otherness to this inward infinitude that is never mastered by any mediation whatever. Something beyond and excessive and transcendent remains. This is the infinite root of the self-transcendence of the human being. Even in the criminal of radical evil, the drama that plays in the intimacy of this abyssal depth cannot be known in any manner that excludes trepidation and uncertainty.

Relative to our mastery of self, relative to the autonomy of self-determination that claims complete control over its being and action, we have to voice a crucial caveat. The claim to that kind of autonomy is a lie. Rather autonomy is made possible by this infinite otherness at work in the innerness of the self. Every claim to autonomy is secondary to a more primal heteronomy. Perhaps heteronomy is not the best word, since what I am referring to is not a law of the other, but *a freeing by the other*. The freedom of the autonomous self is given to it by this other, which frees it to be itself and for itself. This heteroarchic good is never dialectically mastered; nor is the self in the intimacy of its innerness as in community, or in revolt against this heteroarchic good. Dialectic reaches a limit relative to the depth of innerness. This inner infinity breaks up every pretension to total completion. Even the wholeness of the good itself is grounded on a more ultimate sense of its infinity, its excess to every bounded and mediated perfection.

This means that beyond dialectic we have to rethink the *fractures* of being, as not always moments in the reconstitution of restored wholes. There may be wounds of spirit that signify losses that no dialectical mediation will ever redeem. The monstrous idiocy of evil comes to mind again. This is its recalcitrance to the logic of dialectical self-mediation. We must acknowledge that there is a willful refusal that is on the *other* side of every effort at mediation, for it is the very revolt against all mediation, persuasive or coercing or forgiving, in terms of the self-absolutizing of the will for itself alone. In the face of this malevolence we find the patience of the good. But neither the patience nor the malevolence is encapsulated by any dialectical self-mediation. There is an otherness to the will in malevolent revolt: the malevolent revolt is just this absolutely refusing otherness that stands outside all mediations, and insists on itself as not being incorporated into any mediated whole; it wills its own fracturing, its own violent fragmentation, its own proud satisfaction with its being, as completely outside every reconciling community of being. It wills that the evil be its good.

Of course, this is a contradiction, since its hatred is still caught in the exigence of the good. But its willing is still a willful inversion of the good, which swipes at the good to deface its beauty. It thrills just in its defacement and debasement. It hurls again its imprecation at the good. For there are *idiocies of evil* that are beyond dialectic. They will to stand in the outer darkness rejecting every mediation. There is the evil will that loves the dark. Dialectic may have faith that no such love can withstand the unfolding of the good, but this is wrong. There is a love of the dark that spits in the face of all dialectics. Nor can we downplay it as merely contingent or accidental, only a minor triviality in the march of dialectic towards the future whole. Something is lost that dialectic cannot restore. Something is killed that dialectic cannot bring back to life. Something is darkened, and the light of dialectic cannot see this murk beyond all its light. This is the excess of evil to complete determination. This is the mystery of iniquity that humbles every effort at final dialectical determination.[6]

Moreover, there are demands of the good that are not completely within the power of autonomous self-determination to effect. We are called to be perfect, but the truth is that none is equal to the call. Every effort at the perfecting of being is dogged by necessary imperfection. Dialectical autonomy necessarily fails, not only with reference to origins and the abyss of infinite inwardness, but with respect to teleology, the goal of perfecting the promise

---

6. See *Beyond Hegel and Dialectic*, chapter 4.

of creation. Consider what is called *weakness of will*, to which many ethical failures have been attributed. Of course, the moral failure itself has been differently interpreted. Rationalistic and idealistic philosophies will often attribute the failure to ignorance, lack of knowledge. If we were marked by rational enlightenment we would not know ethical failure. Knowledge would put the good within our power. Socrates' identification of knowing and virtue is an example.

This does not appear satisfactory. It is not always that the will is blind, because the reason is ignorant. We are mindful of the good, and yet refuse to will it. We see and turn away. Brilliance of intellect goes with viciousness of will. We cannot overcome the defect of will through knowing or through willing. The will must be made new. The mediations of dialectic cannot create the good will anew. One might, like Kant, order the weak agent: Act rationally! But reason can itself turn out to be infected with ethical equivocity. Nor does reason always put its roots into the idiocy of self, the core contact with the good. The heteroarchic source of the ethical self does not then nourish reason. Unless reason is itself rooted deeply in the heteroarchic source, it becomes a deracinated mind, merely instrumental and functional. It does not carry the full thrust of transcendence, or rather instrumentally short-circuits it.

Reason itself has to be enlivened by contact with its own source, but this too demands a making anew of the self. Self-determining will and reason prove not to be absolutely autonomous. They are the daylight sides of a more basic, pervasive willingness of the integral self, which includes reference to aesthetic passion also. Weakness of will has its source beyond will itself in the character of this willingness. Of course, this willingness is shaped by a lifetime of habit, which forms a character, for good or for ill. This character too may claim autonomy, but this claimed autonomy may be but another form of bondage to a will that is defective, lacking integrity. It is the entire willingness of the self that has to be reoriented, reconstituted with the view to a different integrity. Mindfulness and self-determining will have themselves to become rerooted in the good, for the new self to be re-created. As claiming autonomy, will and reason cannot effect what they clearly need.

One might suggest here that there is a peculiar respect in which autonomous self-determination may be a form of *despair* of the good. One becomes uprooted from the primal good, but one cannot reground oneself in it merely through one's own will; instead one wills to be the good, purely out of oneself. Outwardly, we behold the high nobility of the moral ideal; inwardly, we detect the pride of ethical despair. "I am the good" is not uttered in a howl of refusal; it suavely purrs with all the cultured sophistication of a person who claims to be his or her own sovereign destiny, and the world to be within his or her palm.

In this asserted ethical sovereignty there may be a paradoxical *atrophy* of the good. Sometimes there may be a hollowing out from within. The shell may hold together through will power alone. Holding together—to all appearances the mark of sovereign autonomy—may be the pride of despair itself. It will not confess its need of another, its implication with others, its very being as a gift that it has not earned. For what it hates is to be in debt to any other. It is an intolerable offense to its dignity that it was given being, that it did not choose itself from the beginning. For instance, I find in Sartre traces of this ontologically insulted dignity of proud despair. We are condemned to be and to be free, he may say. The insult is that the origin gives us being, for no reason at all beyond the good of the giving, and the good of the being that is given to itself. This is an extremely complex and twisted form of spiritual pride, in which the human being finds its own gift of finitude intolerable, as if any gift made one beholden to the giver. Of course, in this case there is nothing exacted by the giver. But the very misunderstanding of this is a reflection of the despairing illusion of autonomy.

Of course, there is the seeming opposite extreme, where we find breakdowns so complete that the self has hit rock bottom, and not the primal good. The ethical breakdown seems beyond all repair, beyond all human resource to mend. The aid of a source of succor beyond humankind can only do it. The uplift of a new willingness from beyond the self is needed, but it is not produced by the self. It is a gift. It is gratuitous. It has no why that we can determine. The broken self undergoes a renewal, in the dawning sense that it is accepted, beyond its failure. The "I am good" springs from a ground that says "You are good," "It is good." I, miserable jack, am accepted into this "It is good."

Once again what is needed is a receptivity beyond dialectical autonomy. The failure cannot be healed by the self alone. It is not that the broken self has to be put together. More radically, the self has to be reborn, re-created closer to the primal saying of the "It is good." What is at stake is not just a mediation of the old self, it is the gift of an original beginning, repeatedly given again and again, in the face of *radical failure*.[7] There is an extremity to this. For it names a complete transfiguration of failure. Nietzsche may dismiss this as compounding the initial failure with failure to take responsibility for oneself. One cries out for help; one cannot help oneself; one cannot go on; one appeals to the other for succor; one throws oneself open to the other. Nietzsche will say: one throws oneself away. But there can be something entirely affirming in this throwing of oneself away. One gives up the dignified pride of despair. One confesses one's simple, elemental creaturehood. One asks forgiveness. The humanist will see evasion. And of course despair of oneself in the sense at issue is very odd to the humanist. But this oddity reveals the blindness of the humanist. It reveals the pride of despair that has not yet come to the extreme.

Transformations take place. They witness to the fact that the face of failure is an enigma. Even the most abject wrecks are the promise of something

---

7. On failure, see *Philosophy and its Others*, 242–258.

more than failure. Our ethical expectations are chastened and made less diffident about judging. Shocking renewals burst forth. A flower sings on a refuse pile.

Good beyond Good and Evil

I want to call attention to another ambiguity that mixes the demand of self-responsibility with the *irreversibility* of deeds. I transgress the good; I am responsible; the guilt is mine; my deed is irreversible; what I have done, I cannot undo. If I make amends, I may not be able to mitigate completely the evil consequence of my deed. And still the original deed stands in its guilt. I am completely responsible, and now my responsibility stands *against* me. The pride of self-determination is mocked by the irrevocable.

We might be destroyed by this mockery—one's guilt eats away one's being over a lifetime. We have the stock stories of deathbed confession where the irrevocable is finally confessed. The confession purges and redeems. Redemption comes in the asking for forgiveness. Why are the stories stock? Only because we humans have an ineradicable stake in the possibility of forgiveness.

All of this is beyond dialectical self-mediation, for it is an opening up to the other, in the plea that its goodness be given to one in a gesture of acceptance. Indeed, the plea for forgiveness asks for a forgiveness beyond morality, a *transmoral* forgiveness. For I cannot will the redemption of the irrevocable failure and guilt. Nor can the injured party completely; for even if I were to forgive myself and the injured party were to extend forgiveness, the deed would still stand as irrevocable. *Beyond self and other,* one turns for forgiveness in a more ultimate sense. One asks that the irrevocable evil be set at nought— that is, redeemed. Human being cannot redeem absolutely. There is needed a radical yes, beyond any yes of which humans are capable. It is the primal yes of the agapeic origin that is needed. The being of the self passes beyond what it does, whether these be good or evil in the moral sense; the being of self as passing beyond is its ontological goodness of being; but this has been stained; as we cannot give the primal goodness, so we cannot give this renewal of ontological goodness; only a God can save us. Beyond the good and evil we do, we are *more* that even our irreversible failure, in the ultimacy of the agapeic origin.

Perhaps even the notorious atheist Nietzsche points this way *beyond good and evil*. This transmorality of the good may look amoral. Some moralists will think it is immoral. This washing away of the offense will seem to them like a trivialization of its seriousness. The pride of their moral dignity will not see the divine comedy in it, the healing yes of festive laughter than affirms and says "It is nothing." This is the festive agape of the good, beyond good and evil. This is the renewal of trust. We have to continue, try again and again. Some selves are the spontaneous overflow of this trust, nothing seems to dishearten them. For most of us failure and experience dim the trust. Hearing again the "It is good" allows us to draw close to the source. It reverberates again through the entirety of self. We rise again. Our rising again renews our pledge of trust in the worth of being.

Of course, there is also a dialectical approach, most powerfully articulated in Hegel's philosophy of history, that will displace the issue towards the universal considered in terms of world history. The dialectical self-mediation of spirit in history points forwards to completion in the final restoration of spirit to itself in an unsurpassable success. All failure will be *aufgehoben* into the unity of the absolute at home with itself at the end of history. The Marxist philosophy of world history provides a refashioning of this secular providence of dialectic: the communist paradise will be the restored "It is very good," beyond the war of opposition of the class struggle; human beings will have reclaimed for themselves the creative power previously projected and alienated into God.

Neither of these dialectics does justice to the following: the agape of the origin as the source of the primal good; the idiocy of the inward self in its infinite worth as beyond all mediation. So they show a questionable displacement of the issue from the singular I towards the more neutral and public universal of world history. They do injustice to the metaxological community of being also, for this cannot be preserved without the intimacy of inwardness that marks the absolute singularity of the I. They do not do justice to the goodness of being as it now is. Present evils are not to be justified instrumentally as means to future perfection. Dialectic here risks being a perverse form of a certain logic of perfection: the good of being as given is instrumentalized in favor of being as reconstructed through the power of the human being; this reconstruction will be the putative "perfection" that will justify the instrumentalization.[8]

Moreover, there are losses and gains in the middle that evidence the gleam of ultimacy and that are misdescribed if treated as episodes in the story of world history. They spring up from a different dimension, and point to a sense of the good that is vertical to the horizontal dialectic of world historical progress. Put otherwise, world historical dialectic projects a false clarification of the equivocality of the good in time itself. We have no basis for believing that the equivocality of the good will be finally resolved in time itself. The "end" of time cannot be horizontalized, dialectically immanentized. The "end" is suspended from the vertical, from the height of transcendence itself, that is not at the "end" of history, but is above history.

It is interesting that this dialectical instrumentalization can produce its own variation on ontological nihilism. Marx and Nietzsche both ride on the

---

8. See *Beyond Hegel and Dialectic*, chapters 1 and 4.

claimed power of self-mediation to determine the good. We find the social self-mediation of humanity in Marx, the self-mediation of the superman in Nietzsche, and in a manner that turns against the rational self-mediation of classical idealism in favor of the voluntaristic self-mediation of the heroic, solo will. In both cases, there is an absolutization of self-mediation in its self-assertion of human power over any other that claims to curb its freedom. In either case, the good is the production of human power.

Both Marx and Nietzsche are imbued with the presuppositions of modernity, even when they are critics of modernity. The instrumentalizion of being is a very prison house of presupposition. First, being is neutralized of any intrinsic value; then it is made a means to an end—namely, to serve human desire, flattened into something that can only be *for us*; the ontological yes of the "It is good" is silenced. The metaphysical poverty of this instrumentalization is now evident. Even then, we often still want to devise a new, more effective, instrumentalizing. Henceforth, we animals of calculating power will devise new techniques of control to circumvent the worst consequences of the previous instrumentalizing. We create a new instrumentalizing to hold in check our old instrumentalizing. Yet everything remains instrumentalized, a means to an end. And it is we who are supposed to be the end. Another prison house has been fashioned.

Nietzsche and Marx hated any hint of a metaphysical or theological resonance. Yet Nietzsche has the penetration and honesty to see what was at stake. If nothing really matters in any ultimate sense, even the pragmatic values necessary to survive, to prosper, have no ultimate ground. Nietzsche tried to reground value in the transformed will to power of the human being. He accepted the banishment of inherent worth vis-à-vis being as a whole; there is no ontologically constitutive value to being as such. But his further response to nihilism proceeds to produce a new nihilism. If the overall, indeed integral, character of being is devoid of any inherent value, then to say that human beings (even the coming supermen) are the only source of value, ultimately also leads to the same nihilism. We protect ourselves against nihilism by saying that at least the human being is the source of value. But as soon as we remember that human beings and activity, albeit originative, are themselves participant in the larger process, hence also devoid of any inherent value, the house of cards collapses.

This is my argument: if we are participant in the whole as inherently valueless, we humans are ourselves ultimately a valueless part of the valueless whole. Our creations are engulfed by the valueless, purposeless whole. They too are self-serving, self-deceiving ruses that claim to give value to being. In a word, if being itself has no value, we can give it no value, for our own being itself ultimately has no value. When Nietzsche wanted a transvaluation of values, he wanted to recharge the world with some sense of deeper worth. But the human being cannot do this, if the world itself is not marked by or inherently hospitable to value as an ontological constituent of being in itself.

The integrity of creation must itself provide the basis of this transformed evaluation.

We cannot even say that the human being is the only end in itself, if there is not a deeper sense of intrinsic value on which the human being is grounded. All such efforts to preserve our special place within the valueless whole ultimately fail. We may laugh at any invocation of God. But if nihilism is true (but of course there is supposed to be no truth), we should jeer at the claim that the human being is an end in itself. Kant, for example, sweated with anxiety lest God be introduced as a deus ex machina. He should have sweated when he introduced humankind as an end in itself. (Secretly he did sweat.) From the standpoint of the "whole," this *humanus ex machina* is a joke. I repeat: if the whole is valueless, then the human being as part of the whole partakes of this basic ontological valuelessness; and every assertion of our special place carries no ultimate weight. The human being becomes a this-worldly deus ex machina. The value of being, and indirectly the value of the human being, has to be thought in relation to an other, the creative power of the origin.

In this regard, Hegel is closer to the mindfulness necessary to recover a different sense of creation, for he makes reference to the dialectical self-mediation of the absolute. To think at Hegel's level is extraordinarily difficult; to think metaxologically beyond him even more; but this is necessary. And yet Hegel's dialectic, in its equivocality about otherness as irreducibly other, offers a contributory signature to the remote death warrant of transcendence, which Marx and Nietzsche proceed to execute in different ways. But there is a patience of the good beyond world history. Nor will it do to return behind the equivocality of the good to the innocence of becoming. In all fairness to Nietzsche, one tries to see in his innocence of becoming something of his effort to sing the primal "It is good," beyond good and evil, as defined by the false moralism of self-congratulating enlightenment autonomy.

The patience beyond world history is the waiting of the agapeic origin beyond the impatient aggression on being of will to power. The difference between the erotic and the agapeic absolute is again relevant. The dialectical absolute is an erotic self-becoming that begins as lack and that determines itself in its dialectical self-mediation; its historical dialectical self-mediation is its self-completion in time; and this self-completion is presented as the good—the good as the absolute totality. By contrast, I suggest that this understanding of the erotic absolute is one source of the *idolization* of the immanence of world history, and the redefinition of the good in terms of the progress towards completion at the end of history. But there can be no primal "It is good" here; it is always later. It is always the end that will supply the lack of the beginning. This end that is always later is always too late. We might say: And then "It *will* be good"; but, of course, we never get there; the "It is good" is always postponed to a completion that, in fact, never comes. Meanwhile in the present every equivocality of the good receives its exculpating justification from the "It will be good" that never comes. Not surprisingly, willful humans get impatient, and themselves claim to be erotic absolutes who will complete themselves by subordinating all others. The impatience of a certain progressivism speaks loudly for the good, but in truth it is an erotic flight from the good. It is a contraction of the freedom of agapeic transcendence.

Die Weltgeschichte ist das Weltgericht, Hegel famously said. World history is itself the tribunal of the last judgment, when, we are told, all with be well. On exclusively dialectical grounds, this must prove a lie. I do not propose we stifle the trust expressed in the words "All will be well." But the dialectic of the erotic absolute cannot ground the ontological trust. The agapeic original does, insofar as there is here a movement towards creation and history out of an original plenitude, the transcendent excess of the good, whose excess is its self-diffusion and communication to creation and history. This communication is the primal "It is good." Creation and history do not receive their deepest justification from what will come in the end. They are already and always a gift of the good, and good as given, given simply because to be is to be good.

Creation requires no justification beyond itself. This is not to say that there is nothing to do; for there is a promise to creation that we must work to perfect. A pluralization of perfection is allowed by the agapeic original. There is not just one whole incorporating all other entities as partial realizations of itself. There is a community of wholes, each the promise of its own perfection. Without the primal "It is good," there is no basis for the ontological trust in being that "All will be well."

The Agape of the Good

The metaxological understanding of the good affirms the openness of community beyond any closed whole, affirms that this openness is the sustaining matrix of freedom, wherein resides the promise of perfecting being. Good here is the good of community, but this is the community of agapeic service rather than that of equivocal desire or erotic sovereignty. The stressed paradox of the good is most accentuated in this community. We come across the greatest tension between the immanence and transcendence of the good.

The immanence of the good concerns its working in the intimacy of being itself. This intimacy refers both to the idiocy of the self, and to the community between ethical selves that sustain each other with respect for their inherent worth. The good is at work in this intimacy as the call of conscience in which one's responsibility for the other's good is as important as the call to self-perfection. The double overture is: that we become as whole within ourselves as possible; that we take care for the good of the other and its promise of immanent wholeness, take care for it, even to the point of sacrificing the self-insistence that marks the existence of the "I am." To perfect self as an open whole demands sacrificial discipline. One wills to give up the evil will, plows the soul to let the seed of new wholeness take root. The chaff of self-being must be winnowed. Self-insistence must be coaxed from its tendency to shut itself up, shut itself off. There may follow the freeing up of a more sweeping self-transcendence, released towards the other as other.

Then there is the agapeic sacrifice for the other. One goes towards the other out of an overflow of open wholeness. One does not go simply from a lack that would appropriate the other and make the other serve as a means for self-fulfillment. One goes towards the other, for what one elementally has to give is the self itself in its goodness and integrity. Self and other in the good are not bound to each other in the collusion of deformed wills that marks, say, the dialectic of sadism and masochism. The good at work in them has already been heard. And their hearing of each other is under the sign of another goodness that neither possesses, but in which both participate. Both are under the sign of the primal "It is good." This is a sign of the original plenitude of the origin, in its being pleased with being as inherently worthy of love.

This primal "it is good" makes way for a trust in both the self and other. It opens the middle itself as the space of sacrificial trust—that is, consent to being beyond the horror of evil, consent to being beyond death itself. This middle of trust is the between as the milieu of agapeic service in which the living live self-transcendence for its own goodness, a goodness that no death can finally diminish. Even my own death, which will come, will take nothing from the elemental and primal goodness of being itself. True, we find it almost impossible to say this, for in the face of death an immediate contraction of affirmation takes place, contraction to the affirmation of my being. We are tugged in this tension between the expansion of self-transcendence towards the community of being in its otherness, and our contraction in the face of death, which retracts transcending back to a self-hugging affirmation of the "I am."

The metaxological sense of the good asks the "I am" to give itself up to the other, just as it asks the same sacrifice of the other. The convergence of a plurality of such agapeic selves in the middle creates the community of trust in the good beyond death itself. We give ourselves up because we are most fully the affirmation of what is more than us, the good in the excess of its otherness. The giving up is a finding of this more excessive good. This exceeding good is never spent by being spent, never used up in using itself up, never exhausted in pouring itself out recklessly for the other. To give ourselves up means that we consent to the fact that our being and all of being is a gift. The gift is first a giving over by the agapeic origin. And when we give ourselves up, we liken ourselves to the origin in its ontological generosity. To give ourselves up means that we live the primal "It is good" in the most universal transcendence possible for finite beings. We extend the yes of our own being as "I am" to all of being as other. "It is," affirms its being other; "It is good," affirms the goodness of this being.

We can say that this immanence of the good recalls us to the metaphysical depths of selving, and to their promise of wholeness, now seen to be beyond dialectical self-mediation. In immanent wholeness there is the call of responsibility for the good of the metaxological community. The integrity of the self is marked by a *plurality* of voices *within* itself. Its integrity consists in attending not only to its own voice but to all the voices of the others that speak within the integral self. There is a plurivocity of calls within the call of integral wholeness. So integral wholeness is always tensed between itself and these others, called within itself to be more than itself. And then prior to all this is the voice of the absolute other. This may not always be heard above the calls of the others, but it calls again and again, waiting in forbearance for the opportunity of silence, when this voice from beyond will sound through in immanence itself. There is an indeterminacy to this that is beyond all our mastering, hence beyond the autonomy of absolute self-determination. This indeterminacy is the excess of transcendence sounding in the intimacy of selfhood and the community of agapeic others. It is beyond dialectic, precisely because this transcendence always escapes beyond determination, whether external determination or self-determination.

Relative to this transcendence, there is a heteronomy of the good, but the heteronomy is not an external determination. Heteronomy is normally modeled on an authoritarian sovereign or master who imposes his will on his subjects. Such a model concerns external determination by a source of law that comes from the outside and simply superimposes itself on the subject as other. This is not at all the heteronomy of the good I mean. For this heteronomy is not imposing or dominating; primordially it is giving; it is the giving of the free promise of the finite creation as good for itself. Nor does it simply impose its law and make demands of what it has given; it lets the promise of what is given come to itself out of itself. It is not an other that imposes an external determination but an other that gives the promise of self-determination. And in the realization of that self-determination it again does not impose itself, but it does companion the efforts at self-perfection of the creature. As companion alongside, it is an other that is with the freedom of the creature, even as this freedom strays from its own integral perfection, and turns against the origin as primal giver. Its lets the freedom go, gives up its power over the finite other, to the point of letting that freedom give itself over to evil and refusal. It retracts its power to impose itself; it constrains its own possible sovereignty; for it is an agapeic servant and not an erotic sovereign.

This *heteros* is the compassionate companion that travels *incognito* the way of transcendence. The patience of the good even extends to traveling with the one in evil. It is the companion with the self in evil, with the community in evil. Its generosity lets freedom travel its own way of destruction, to the end of the road of evil. But it too travels that road and waits patiently for the free finite being to turn again to the path of agapeic generosity. It stays with the evil even unto death. Even in the face of death, the reserve of its generosity is never spent. All judgment is withheld. There is no vengeance. The good, like the sun, shines on the ugly and the beautiful alike. For the generosity of the good is beyond good and evil.

Thus this heteronomous good is *beyond* the ordinary oppositions of in-here/out-there, immanent/transcendent, subjective/objective, good/evil, such as mark our being in the middle. The metaxological understanding offers us the best way to think it. The univocal way risks dissolving the oppositions into an absorbing god; the equivocal way is inclined to distort the oppositions into a promiscuous melange, and to compromise the unconditional call to the ultimate good; the dialectical way tends to unify the oppositions in a *coincidentia oppositorum*, which finally falls short of the richness of the middle as beyond self-mediation. By contrast, the metaxological view preserves the richness of unity, remains honest about the constitutive ambiguity of the between, does not renege on the search for mediation of the dialectical. Yet it remains true to both the stress of being in the middle and the will to reconciled peace with being. Its peace does not betray the stress, but rather indirectly through the stress of opposition points further than the middle, not to a coincidence of opposites, but to something entirely other to the finite middle. The doubleness is not the immanent doubleness of the middle itself. It is the otherness between the middle and its transcendent origin. The transcendence of the agapeic origin to the middle will never be completely mediated from the side of the middle itself. Something other comes to the middle, if there is to be any such intermediation. And even if the ultimate other as beyond is beyond the finite opposites, the "unity" of such opposites retreats into the reserve of a mystery that no dialectical logic will ever articulate; the root in itself remains in its inaccessible mystery.

When I speak of the good as beyond good and evil, I am trying to name something of this mystery. I name a *huperagathon*, a *heteroagathon* that is beyond us and our differentiation of the good and the evil. The truth of the agape of being as good is beyond in this regard. The astonishing gift of being comes to us from this beyond. Moreover, the enigma is doubled when we confront the enigma of evil in creation. The evil is let be. Our understanding of good and evil may even be affronted by the tolerance of the origin to evil. Even when we are responsible for the evil, we may still be horrified by the patience of the good. It may look to us like a cruelty and indifference, not a waiting and a forbearance, a turning of the face of God away from creation. How respond to this mystery?

We might reject the idea out of hand and assert some view of the universe as amoral, devoid of any worth. We might even assert this view rhapsodically, as in Nietzsche's innocence of becoming, beyond good and evil. I do not think this is enough. It does not take its stand on a par with the metaphysical depth of the perplexity itself. The human heart in its immediate agony is already on a par, regardless of what philosophers will tell us we should think. I am a human being in agony. I shake my fist at the empty sky and shout why. If becoming is innocent in Nietzsche's sense, there is no proper meaning we can give to this gesture of appeal and defiance. There is an immediacy of the good ingrained in the human being as self-transcending; and when our expectation of the good is thwarted or betrayed, we inevitably ask of the good itself why it seems to have deserted us, when we have most need of its help or consolation. We can give no determinate answer to such perplexities. For we are always in the middle, hence entrapped to some degree in the equivocality of the good, hence also never on a par with the transcendence of the good in itself.

Even if one travels the path to evil, the vector of self-transcendence is still energized, and transcendence always tugs in the opposite direction toward the heteronomous good. This is the transcendent good of creation, things, selves, communities. The transcendence of the good is its excess of creative being. Suppose we think of Plato's Good beyond beings. Such an excessive transcendence is not nothing, though it seems to be nothing, when we take our sense of being solely from determinate entities. There is no determinate univocity to the transcendent Good. If there were, it would be a static eternity and hence uncreative, and hence incapable of exceeding itself in the direction of giving creation its being, hence also incapable of being related to what it brings into being. Thus it would be impotent good. But an impotent good could not be a good at all, for it could not do any good. It would literally do no good at all.

I am talking about the exceeeding good that does good, and in its difference makes a difference. Given the character of metaxological being, this excess of the good cannot be engulfing like the absorbing god, nor dialectically self-appropriate like Hegel's self-returning absolute. The excessive good seeks no return for its goodness. There is no justification for its goodness. Its goodness is its own justification. No return justifies it. Rather its justice is the excess of generosity that gives out of itself and that is not reduced in giving out of itself. The giving of the good is never the diminishment of the good. The doing of the good never diminishes the good. Nor does doing the good increase its excess in any sense that could be determined. The good is not a determinable quality, but the communication of the generosity of being.

The excessive good is not engulfing, it is freeing. There is nothing it frees that is intrinsically worthless. But the freeing lets open the possibility of refusal and hatred and revolt. The gift is freed away from the giver. And since the gift is free for itself, it is turned away from its source. Its otherness may accentuate the turn away, especially insofar as the vector of transcendence may not understand, or refuse to accept, its own relativity to the transcendent good. In other words, the good absolves the creation from its relation, even when remaining in relation. This is a free relation that frees, even while remaining in relation. This is an agapeic relation.

The freedom of this relation extends to the freedom to try and destroy this relation. This is where the evil comes, but this coming of the evil is also let be in its freedom. For this relation of freedom is simply the gift of the good itself, and the good would betray the good were it to retract, or to squash its gift of freedom. It never gives the gift on the insistence of its own terms. Or rather its own terms are absolutely self-transcending, for these terms are the care of the receiver. The gift is absolutely for those who receive it. The terms of the gift are those of the other; they are for the good of the other. This is agapeic giving. This necessity of freedom is the very nature of agapeic giving.

When the evil comes, there seems to be a silence. Is the silence the forbearance of the good? Is it the patience of the agape? We try to trust that this is so, but we cannot claim to know it for certain. Yet the trust is not a blind trust, in the sense of a whistling in the dark, a mere lurch of desperation in a world of indifference and despair. The trust is a metaphysical trust, born of an endeavor to understand what is in play in being, an endeavor articulated in terms of the metaxological community of being. This understanding tries to be honestly true to what is at play in this world. It does the best it can, which is not the absolute best. It is all one can do now, and yet we will be asked to do more than we can do. The trust is most buoyed up by the signs of the good that come to manifestation in the unremitting honesty of the truthful self, and in the ethical heroism that witnesses to the community of agapeic service.

Service of the Good Beyond Nihilism

Those who live the service of the truth, and those who seek to do the good in agapeic service, are witnesses of the good as transcendent. These witnesses are middles that are double: embodiments of the openness of immanent wholeness, that serve to point to the otherness of transcendence. They are doubled middles, at once integral and self-transcending. And yet we know that all transcending in the middle still does not exhaust transcendence. Our best efforts fall short, paltry in the face of the welcome of transcendence itself.

One wills to be good, be the good, in the doing of it. The patience of agapeic service is the doing of the good. This service is beyond any *dualism* of being and the good. The community of agapeic service in being good is the being of the good. Here the ontological nihilism that counterposes fact and value, being and the good, makes no sense. To be is to be good, and the good itself is being, the being of agapeic self-transcendence. This does not entail that the good as transcendent is a being, in the sense of a finitely determined entity. It is not in the same genus as finite being. It is beyond being in that sense. It is *huperbeing*. Its being *huper* traditionally nurtured the claim that the proper manner to speak of it was through the way of eminence.

This is related to what I called the way of proper hyperbole (chapter 5, above). In other words, everything perfect in the middle is to be *heightened* with respect to the saying of this "more" of the good. It is more than the more, excessive with respect to the most excessive excess, other than the most other otherness, beyond the most inaccessible beyond. This hyperbole of the Unequal is echoed in the hyperbole of our self-transcending, the excess of our infinite desire that will not reach an end. For no end will ever match its reaching, except an infinite end; but an infinite end is beyond all determinate ends; precisely as infinite, it is beyond all determination, and hence, in another sense, it is something that we finite middles can never completely reach. We live in the light, or the shadow, of this never-to-be-dispelled enigma. Even were one to die and see God, one would not see God. One would still be blinded by the more, though there would be joy in this sightless seeing.

The divine darkness solicits us be true to the good, that we actualize the self-transcending of agapeic service. This is nothing but the radical freedom that is for the good of the other. My good is for the other; and that is my good, to be for the other. This entails a breakdown of any closure of the "I am good," and the breakthrough of the universal "It is good" in the "I am," such that the being of the I is reversed, turned inside out, driven out beyond its own erotic sovereignty, willing to ask for nothing in return for what it is asked to give for the other. The patience of the agape of being replaces the impatience of erotic sovereignty, which cannot wait long enough for the other as other to fully come into its own. The I willing to be good for the good of the other undergoes an inversion as well as reversal: it is turned upside down. Its transcending is given wings by a vertical gravity that draws it up. Our ramparts of closure are being washed away, slowly, surely, all but unnoticeably. And the agape of the good is absolute tact and nuance and finesse. It loves the singularity of the singular down to the hairs on its head, which are numbered in the singularity of their singularity. By comparison most of our loves are crude and coarse.

What more can we say of the patience of the good? It consents to the common destiny of the weak and strong, the young and old, the infirm and the healthy, the good and the evil. It is beyond good and evil. Its being beyond good and evil is its living of the forbearance of the good. There is consent to the finite, and patience with the imperfect. This patience is not undifferentiated acquiescence. It is the highest discrimination in its love of the singular as singular. For the human being there is a point where one will give up all. One has nothing more to lose for one has given up all, relinquished possession, let go, released and been released. There is nothing to possess. Being good is transcendence beyond all possession. This is why it calls for the patience of the agapeic servant, not the impatience of the erotic sovereign. Beyond the dialectic of possession and self-possession, there is a divestment of the power of mastery in a different energy of pure giving.

There is the following paradox in regard to the love of the singular. In my radical singularity, I cannot be replaced; nor can you be replaced, in your radical singularity. Yet in the agapeic community between us, I place myself in your place, at your service, absolutely available. I place myself before you as replaceable, though in my absolute singularity I am not. My service says: You are absolutely irreplaceable; I am willing to replace myself for you, I am willing to stand for you; I no longer stand; I abandon myself to you, give myself over and away; I am available for you. But if I place myself at your disposal, if I am in your place, it seems that one must take *responsibility for what is not one's responsibility*. One assumes the burden of the other, even the suffering and evil of the other. One may suffer for the other, expiate for the other. But this is a responsibility beyond responsibility. It is generous and gratuitous. I have no responsibility for you, for you are responsible for yourself; yet I am responsible for you beyond all calculating, beyond all measuring.

I know this will seem strange. It is strange. Are we humans really capable of putting ourselves radically in the place of the other, the other as radically irreplaceable? Perhaps only God could be thus absolutely for the other. Through the sacrifice of agape, the immeasurable asking of the excessive good enters into human community.

And yet there are human reminders. Though I am not quite talking about the kingdom of ends, I find a trace of this service in Kant's notion of disinterested respect. Kant's view is a rationalized, diminished version of the community of agapeic service. He also forgets the community of human selves with nature and creation in his moralizing of the good. The notion of the good beyond good and evil would be incomprehensible to him. He could not rationalize this willingness beyond reason that is agapeic service. Nor could his rationalized autonomy accept the heteronomy of agapeic service, nor its heteroarchic reference to the origin. Moreover, his moral agent is too atomized in the putatively neutral context of a homogeneous abstract rationality. Instead of this neutral and disinterested universality, we need concrete ethical mindfulness in the goodness of creation. Nevertheless, Kant is closer to the community of agapeic service than is the utilitarian. The latter cannot get beyond the affirmation of the good in the self-insistence of the "I am"— albeit pluralized in a group of self-seekers. Kant at least produces a rationalistic reconstruction of transcendence to the good, albeit in abstraction from the fullness of the between.

When the metaxological community is defined by agapeic service of the good, the "It is good" is reaffirmed, redoubled. It is given again, given without end, resurrected and re-created, again and again. We finite entities wear away in the interim of our lot in the universal impermanence, but the generosity of the good gives the middle its being as good, again and again. When we do the good in the middle, we redouble the "It is good," and seek to restore what the betrayal of the good has itself undone. We live obedience to the good, but this obedience is pure freedom in which nothing is demanded of us. Nothing is given for purposes of coercion; everything is given because it is good. In the absolute heteronomy of the good, there is no master. There is the father of all who, as Plato said, was exceedingly hard to find, and even harder to tell, were one to find him. The finding is in the service of the truth and the agapeic service of the good. These services themselves are the tellings we have. They alone are telling. No abstract words will tell what they tell.

And what they tell, they tell without dissembling the tragedies of life and the blood of history. Service of the truth tries not to wince before the monstrous and its malign idiocy. This is excess again, but excess from the side hostile to the good. I think there will never be a determinate univocal answer to the misnamed "problem" of evil. For evil is not a problem, it is a metaphysical enigma. There will be no univocal answer to the mystery of iniquity. The only answer is in fidelity to the spirit of truth and unflinching honesty in one's own truthfulness. One will be sacrificed for the truth, and if need be, let oneself be found in the wrong. Likewise, one's service of the good is the answer, service in its living struggle to renew, redouble the primal amen to being. While we are in the middle, the struggle to sing "It is good" in the face of the mystery of iniquity will never be finished.

One is at home in the middle/ one can never be completely at home in the middle. One is insignificant, and counts for nothing/ one is absolutely significant, and counts for something beyond every finite measure. One is perplexed in the middle/ yet the primal consent and astonishment does return, and one sees again that it is good. One can be in the middle, remain in the middle, while yet one's self-transcendence has interiorized the call of the ultimate, and the extremities of being that most stress, distress, and transfigure us. Briefly, suddenly, the good breaks through the darkness. There is a fulfilled perplexity that does not dispel perplexity, but deepens its metaphysical unrest. In the unrest of perplexity, one is also at peace.

I am suggesting that the metaphysical transcending of human perplexity can be gifted with *episodic breakthrough* of the ultimate. Perplexity turns to marveling in this breakthrough. It is not we who break through; the light breaks through; we indeed are fractured by this breakthrough; we suffer it as the breakdown of all our busy mediations. There is a glimpse, abrupt, unexpected, uncontrollable, fleeting, momentous. The significance of the breakthrough remains enigmatic. It is of moment for all, though how so, one cannot say completely. One might dedicate one's life to becoming mindful of its meaning, with trying ethically to enact the task it communicated. It is beyond method, beyond guarantee, beyond self-certainty. It retreats into transcendence and will not be mastered, but its disclosure has renewed the energy of free release. It has also renewed metaphysical perplexity, not as empty and lacking and seeking to overcome a lack, but as stunned into thought by an excess that is too much for its present frail and finite mindfulness.

This end, which is a renewal of the beginning, cannot be described in terms of science. Religious and poetic saying capture something of it. Its gift is rather a metaphysical faith, which is not anything other than the original love of being as good, ingrained on the energy of transcending itself. Our being *is* this metaphysical faith, though we renege on it. The breakthrough is a renewing reminder. We are to be mindful of its meaning to the utmost extent possible. We are to live up to, not only what we ask of ourselves, but what is asked of us. This metaphysical faith cannot finally rest with ontological nihilism. It is itself a perennial struggle with such nihilism, for in the middle we are the possibility of both extremes. Sometimes it is harder to say yes than to say no, and harder still once we have known the crucifixion of the no. But still we struggle to say yes.

Agapeic being is traditionally identified with the so-called *condescending* love of God. For some, it is as if God were the self-satisfied smile of the Chesire cat, infinitely satisfied with itself, infinitely withdrawn beyond the smug smirk. But this is not at all what condescension might mean. There is a *descending*, a way down, a going down that, if you like, reverses the directionality of erotic sovereignty that ascends into its own self-mastery. This descent is a divestment of the self-satisfied power of erotic mastery. The agapeic good comes down to meet finitude in its middle, in its seeking, in the burden of the mystery. The majesty of the agapeic good is beyond erotic sovereignty; it is a kenosis of overpowering superiority. Agapeic majesty is the power that forces nothing. It is embrace of the powerless, companion to the deprived, consent to those broken in the middle. The descent of the agape speaks the word of community in the middle, a word that is its *being with* those broken by the middle. It is community even with the evil in the middle, and consent even to the goodness given and promised in their being, beyond every human measure of the good.

What finally perplexes and astonishes us is this good beyond all finite teleology, beyond every teleology that human purposiveness conceives concerning the middle. God lets the sun shine equally on the wicked and the good. And relative to human teleology, there is an otherness to this agape that is terrifying. God, unlike us, does not hate the hateful. Nothing is hateful. The hateful is loved, the evil is loved. To us this agape may even seem monstrous—this agape that lets even the mostrous be monstrous. The lost are loved, the damned are loved. This exceeds the measure of our justice. Some will feel it even as an insult to our justice. It is beyond every human self-mediating morality such as Kant's, an affront to its rational autonomy. It is a monstrous heteronomy. It is a reminder that the ultimate agape is not to be counted univocally as on the side of what we claim as our good, our morality, our teleology. Its monstrous goodness is beyond our good and evil.

Since all of this giving is for nothing, it may seem very close to a certain *nihilism*. It is giving for nothing, beyond the good of the other as finite. By comparison, in our human giving we almost always secretly expect a return. We cast our bread upon the water, and we think that the good comes in the return, in getting back from one's giving. But the giving of the agape demands nothing back. It casts its bread upon the waters, but goodness flows away from it, with no requirement of return. The purpose of this goodness is without purpose. It is beyond every finite determinate teleology. The purpose of absolute giving is simply the good of the being given, and this is a purposiveness beyond every definite purpose we can determine. This purposiveness is beyond every purpose; this *telos* is beyond every teleology; this end is beyond every end. It is close to the absurd, but in the excessive sense in which a mystery is a surd beyond every finite determination.

Inevitably this proximity of the mystery and the surd entails that a fine line differentiates the agape of being from nihilism. But that difference makes all the difference. One cannot deny that we sometimes undergo the experience of being abandoned by the agape of being. We are crushed by evil and loss and sorrow, and the generosity of being seems to retract, leaving us face to face with malign hopelessness. We are exposed to being shattered, to going under, to becoming nothing. At moments the "It is nothing, it comes to nothing" drowns the "It is good," and we seem unable to make our way back to light. A cry of despair goes out from the depths into the encircling emptiness; the agape has turned its face away, or its coming into the middle seems to have dried up. But this outcry is an appeal. In the extremity of dry abandonment my appeal is again for the agape of the other. In the desert of ontological despair, my power cannot produce the oasis that would water renewal, alleviate thirst in the scorched emptiness. This appeal, in the outcry of despair, is prayer without expectation, that nevertheless hopes beyond all finite hope. It is prayer to the good, beyond good and evil—prayer that is power of the powerless, and that forces nothing, frees only. Indeed there are moments when creation itself seems to arise like a kind of prayer, daily sending up a ceaseless praise and appeal.

Nihilism has been described thus: If God does not exist, everything is permitted. Why reject this view? Not just to reject nihilism, but to reject the imputed nature of God—as if God were the master who would keep subjects in line with the moral order, subjects who would rebel and follow their own sweet will, once the master is gone, or has been gotten rid of, or murdered. But God is not this master; God is the agapeic servant of the good; God is the agapeic good. Is this to be given a platitudinous palliative? No, it is to be brought to the verge of something terrifying: It is *because* God exists, that everything is permitted, even radical evil. This does not mean evil is loved. Freedom is loved, freedom to be the good, freedom as the good. Absolutely nothing is asked of us, yet absolutely everything is being asked of us. The hyperbolic asking in the face of the terror of divine permission resides in the fact that freedom of spirit alone can restore the freedom of being.

The restoration is a re-creation of the goodness of being through agapeic service. In this service we inhabit the metaxological between in a double, redoubling way. The between points us back to the elemental "It is good" and points beyond to an ultimate "It will be good." At a certain extremity we have nothing but metaphysical faith, nurtured by the faint echo in us of the first "It is good," hoping beyond hope in the second "All will be well." This first and last are both beyond the beginning and end of world history, insofar as this is defined by the struggle for erotic sovereignty. They call for a different service of the good in time, in light of transcendence as vertical to the time of the middle.

If transcendence as other is vertical to time, cutting into it, cutting across it, we are asked to be ready for renewal in the interruptions of immanence. This is true of communities and the hiddenness of their good to the struggle of erotic sovereignty. This is true of the idiotic drama of the inward spirit. This is true of the prodigal beauty of creation in its glory. The mystery is always there, seldom named, never dispelled. In ethical, religious, and philosophical service, beyond all determinate cognition, we live from agapeic astonishment, live in metaphysical perplexity before this mystery. In a mindfulness beyond determinate knowing, the Unequal comes towards us, offering over and over again, the unearned gift of the agape of being, singing to our deafness the unbearable music of the ultimate amen.

INDEX

Abel, 433

absolute original, 200, 214, 215, 235, 258, 277, 378, 407, 410, 492, 506

absorbing god, 63, 262, 263, 276, 447, 538, 539

Adorno, T., 488

aesthetic, 9, 20, 43, 47, 66, 68, 69, 73; and univocity, 55–57, 65, 125; and equivocity, 86, 89, 91–95, 97–103; and orchid, 103–105; and human body, 106, 107–110; and desire, 112; and comic, 116; and Kierkegaard, 120–121; and aesthetic self, 113, 152, 220, 386–389, 391, 393, 395, 396, 405; and self-transcendence, 152, 153; and body, 159, 168, 169, 172; and mediation, 220; and elemental, 274, 275–279; and presencing, 303, 307–312, 315, 321, 322, 324, 324; and selving, 384, 385, 386–393, 395, 396, 398, 401, 405, 410–412, 415; spread of being, 419, 420, 422–425; and value, good of being, 437, 513–515, 521, 524, 525

agapeic being, 211, 221, 253, 260, 261, 289, 292, 338, 372, 375, 409, 415, 490, 544

agapeic origin, 43, 71, 166, 167, 169, 193, 207, 208, 211, 214; and q1uestion of radical beginning, 251, 254, 256, 258, 259, 261, 263–265; and creation, 268; and elemental, 277, 278; and monism, 288, 289; and time, 295; and singular things, 330; and creative possibility, 337–339; and principle of sufficient reason, 355, 356; and ontological trust, 359; and creative indeterminacy, 363; and human self, 378, 395, 414, 415; and community, 418, 447, 454; and givenness, 469; and truth, 492, 494, 495, 498, 500, 501; and the good, 511, 514, 523, 531, 534, 536, 538

agapeic self, 64, 115, 252, 392, 396, 401, 404, 406–415, 417, 450, 453, 519, 540

analogy, 16, 45, 68, 211–216. See hyperbole, metaphor, symbol

Anaxagoras, 280

Anaximander, 259, 271

Aquinas, St. Thomas, 17, 18, 214, 242, 260, 336, 467

Arcadia, 276

Aristotle, 8, 9, 16–19, 34, 41, 52, 53, 57, 61, 66, 71, 113, 117, 133–135, 137–140, 149, 165, 170, 172, 212, 214, 216, 233, 247, 271, 272, 293, 314, 316, 334, 337, 346, 352, 365, 370, 463, 467, 471, 518

artist, and equivocity, 94–95, 118; and inexhaustibility, 256; and elemental, 278; and tragic *nihil*, 296; and seeing things, 309–311; and creation, 321, 341; and intelligibility, 348; and selving, 399, 400

astonishment, and metaphysical thinking, xiii, sv, svii, chapter 1, *passim*; and univocity, 50, 52, 58–62, 67, 70, 71; and equivocity, 91, 93, 94, 105, 117, 123; and dialectic, 138, 155, 156, 159, 166, 167, 169, 172–174; and metaxological, 179, 181, 188, 192, 193, 195, 201–206, 209, 214, 219–221; and origin, 225, 226, 227, 228, 235, 236, 243, 263; and creation, 292, 294, 297; and intelligibilities, 333, 339, 349; and selves, 406; and truth, 492, 500, 503; and the good, 505, 510, 511, 514, 515, 543, 546

atomism, 187, 198, 271, 360

Augustine, St., 415, 496, 521

autonomy, 26, 28, 32, 40, 160, 165, 328, 373, 375, 404, 405, 437, 439, 440, 442, 448, 449, 525–530, 534, 537, 542

Bacon, F., 40, 105, 424

beauty, 20, 27, 42, 87, 97, 103, 159, 201, 206, 235, 264, 275, 284, 324, 388, 410, 412, 413, 453, 515, 519, 524, 528, 546

becoming and metaphysics, 5, 27; and

547

CPSIA information can be obtained at www.ICGtesting.com
Printed in the USA
BVOW05s2320061115

425443BV00010BA/1/P

9 780791 422724